P9-AGV-167

Wilde´s WWW

Springer
Berlin
Heidelberg
New York
Barcelona
Hong Kong
London
Milan
Paris
Singapore
Tokyo

Erik Wilde

Wilde's
WWW

Technical Foundations of the World Wide Web

With 78 Figures and 12 Tables

 Springer

Erik Wilde
International Computer Science Institute
1947 Center Street, Suite 600
Berkeley, CA 94704-1198
USA

ISBN 3-540-64285-4 Springer-Verlag Berlin Heidelberg New York

Cataloging-in-Publication Data applied for

© Springer-Verlag Berlin Heidelberg 1999
Printed in Germany

Cover Design: Künkel + Lopka, Heidelberg
Conversion of author´s data: Mercedesdruck, Berlin
Binding: Lüderitz & Bauer, Berlin
Printed on acid-free paper   SPIN 10674568   33/3142   5 4 3 2 1 0

Foreword

What is the difference between a URL and a URI? How does HTTP fulfill its task? Why do we need XML? What is it, and will it eventually replace HTML? This book gives answers to these questions and a chore of others that may be asked by attentive inhabitants of cyberspace. The book is, of course, not just a glossary of abbreviations and frequently used terms. It is rather a comprehensive and still succinct presentation of the technology used in the World Wide Web. It is surprising to note that, even though hundreds of books have been published that discuss the Web, there have been none, so far, to thoroughly explain the inner workings of this popular Internet application, which is so simple to use and yet so complex when it comes to really understand what is going on inside.

The target audience of this book is perhaps best described by how it was first used by the author himself: A draft version was chosen as the supporting text for a class of practitioners, who attended a continuing education course on WWW technology. These were people who knew what the Web is, and how it may be used for business, but needed to know how the technology works. During the planning for this course, the author found that no suitable book was on the market, and decided to write one himself. Needless to say that already the draft version fulfilled its task of providing a reference to all aspects of Web technology. As Erik Wilde points out in his preface, the most obvious handicap of a book that presents a snapshot of such a fast-moving technology is that it could be considered obsolete at the very moment when the manuscript left the author's desk (or, to be more precise, his computer). It will be a challenge to keep the title abreast of the technological development, and to provide its readers with updates in due course. I wonder whether Wilde's WWW '99 will be published on the Web. . .

September 1998   *Prof. Bernhard Plattner, ETH Zürich*

Preface

The idea for this book emerged when I was looking for a publication not only covering one aspect of the web, but all areas which are of importance for today's web infrastructure. There are literally hundreds of books about HTML and Java, a large number of books on CGI and HTTP server configuration and maintenance, and CSS and XML books are quickly appearing as these technologies are maturing. However, when browsing the various impressive computer book stores of the bay area, I did not find a single book which dealt with all these issues.

This book, therefore, is an attempt in providing a source of information which encompasses all relevant areas of web technology as of today. This statement, however, also describes the biggest dilemma of this book, since the phrase "as of today" only refers to a very short time span when speaking of the web. New technologies are announced and promoted almost every week, and it is hard to assess which ones will survive and which ones will be forgotten after a few months. Consequently, this work covers the areas in depth which are certainly of relevance for the web in the coming years. These areas are URI, HTTP, SGML, HTML, CSS, and XML. Although Java evidently is one of the main spin-offs of the web, it is not covered in detail, since I feel that a detailed description of a programming language would not fit into the rest of the book, which is more focused on the description of architectural concepts. The same restriction applies to scripting languages, which are increasingly integrated into the web environment, but too complicated to be explained exhaustively in a book dealing with many other topics.

Many other web-related concepts and technologies are also described in a less detailed way, sometimes because of their secondary importance, sometimes because of their questionable longevity. In a second edition of this book, a number of things will most likely disappear from the glossary and index without a trace, and some other things will have to be added, but this is the way things go in the days of "the net". I am very curious to see for how long this book can serve as a reference for the technical foundations of web technologies.

Finally, I would like to thank the International Computer Science Institute (ICSI) in Berkeley for the opportunity to write this book. It took much more time than I originally thought, and I hope that the result will be useful for many people searching for a thorough technical overview of the web. If the book is used as a text-book for technically oriented lectures about the web, as an introduction to web technology for people who have a minimal background in computer communications, and is also being used by people who want to have a comprehensive reference of web-related topics, then it has become the book I wanted to write.

Berkeley, September 1998   *Erik Wilde*

Overview

Contents

List of Figures

List of Tables

Introduction

The *World Wide Web (WWW)*, in this book simply called "the web", is a set of technologies implementing a distributed hypermedia document model based on the Internet. The web made the Internet as popular as it is today. This book describes all basic concepts of web technology as well as many additional and new concepts.

One of the goals of this book is that each chapter about the different concepts of web technology can be read individually, without having to read through all other chapters. In many cases there will be some cross references between chapters, but they have been made as explicit as possible. An elaborate glossary and an index are provided to quickly find information contained in the book, thus also making it a reference which can be used for looking up the most relevant terms of web technology.

Presenting a large number of concepts which are connected in many ways in a sequential medium as a book is a challenge. It is hard to decide which order of presentation is best suited to meet the requirements of readers who want to read the book sequentially. The sequence of chapters which eventually has been chosen represents the level to which a concept can be considered as being basic for the web. Consequently, the book is divided into three parts, each containing a number of chapters. Preceding the first part, a short discussion of the underlying infrastructure is given.

Very often the web is thoroughly confused with the Internet. Technically speaking, the web simply is a set of applications running on top of the infrastructure provided by the Internet. The fundamentals presented in chapter 1 are an attempt to shortly review the most basic concepts of the Internet (it is no real introduction to the Internet itself, this is left to other books), and to place the web into perspective as an application on top of the Internet. For a reader who has no idea what the Internet really is and how it works, this chapter will probably be too condensed. It is more intended to be a review of concepts which form the technological foundation for the concepts being the topic of this book.

- *Part I – Basics*

  In the first part, the most basic concepts of the web's architecture are presented. The most characteristic property of the web (and the one which gave it its name) is the fact that all available documents form one large interconnected web of information resources. This is achieved by using links between documents, which point from one document to another and can be followed by simply pressing a mouse button. Consequently, the model of web links is described in chapter 2, preceding all other basic concepts.

  The fact that documents on the web not only are connected by links, but also distributed over the entire Internet, residing on servers all over the world, make it necessary to have a means to access remote documents. Each time a link is followed, the document to which the link points must be retrieved from the server on which it resides. This is done using a communications protocol, called *Hypertext Transfer Protocol (HTTP)* and explained in chapter 3.

  Although not being part of the first web versions, the *Standard Generalized Markup Language (SGML)* presented in chapter 4 strongly influenced the design of the web's content language (HTML), and also is the foundation of a new language which will will probably become very important in the future (XML). Another reason for considering SGML as a basic web concept is its separation of content and presentation, an idea which is essential for understanding many other web concepts. Consequently, basic knowledge of SGML is a very good foundation for understanding other web concepts.

  The concepts of documents linked by using URIs and transferred by using HTTP is accompanied by a third concept, describing the format of documents used on the web. The language for this purpose is the *Hypertext Markup Language (HTML)* and is described in chapter 5. HTML is based on SGML, and it is a good idea to first look at the concepts of and ideas behind SGML (although they may seem a bit abstract at first sight) before taking a closer look at HTML.

- *Part II – Advanced*

  The second part of the book deals with more advanced concepts, which are or will be part of the web's infrastructure, but which are not essential to understand the basic working of the web. Before reading any of these chapters, the reader should be familiar with the concepts presented in the first part, often providing the glue being necessary to see how a concept fits into the greater scheme of things.

  In chapter 6, *Cascading Style Sheets (CSS)* are described, which are used to define the presentation of web pages. Since the beginning of the web, it has been seen that the design of web pages in terms of layout and presentation becomes increasingly important, making many web pages a mixture of content and presentation specific information. Since one of the basic concepts of HTML as the language of web pages is to separate content and presentation, CSS has been invented for describing the presentation of web pages. The two main advantages of CSS are more advanced layout features than HTML has, and the clean separation of content and presentation, which makes web documents more accessible for people (such as blind people) or programs (such as search engines) searching only for content.

While HTML continuously evolved from its rather simple beginnings into a document format which now has a large number of powerful features, its application still is limited by the fixed set of elements and attributes and the semantics assigned to them. For much greater flexibility, a mechanism allowing the definition of custom document formats (HTML is an example of such a format) is required. SGML is such a mechanism, but it has some drawbacks which led to the development of the *Extensible Markup Language (XML)*, which essentially is a subset of SGML. XML can be used to define custom document types, to exchange these formats and documents using them, and it furthermore has associated linking and style sheet mechanisms. It is described in chapter 7.

Although HTML has become much more powerful from version to version, and CSS adds even more features to the presentation possibilities of web documents, there still are many limitations and basically only static documents can be designed. To add dynamic features and thus be able to create documents which can be used interactively, scripting and programming has been defined which can be embedded within documents. These features are described in chapter 8. Also included in this chapter is a brief overview of web-related architectures for distributed programming.

Normally, a web server is a remote program being contacted via HTTP when requesting a document from it. Basically, a web server receives a request, performs the requested action, and sends a response indicating the result. There are a number of issues which are common for all web servers, which are described in chapter 9. Furthermore, one specific server program is presented as an example how a web server can be configured. The Apache server, a free product and the the most popular web server, is this example server program. As a last server-related topic, a standard for data exchange between a web server and other programs running on the same computer is described.

In addition to the main components of web technology as described in chapters 2 to 9, there are many other models and concepts which are less popular or simply so new that it is hard to make any assumption about their future significance. In chapter 10, a number of these miscellaneous topics are discussed. This is the chapter which is most likely to change completely in the near future. The selection of topics in this chapter is far from being complete, although the most important topics (such as popular content types and new architectural components) have been included.

Chapter 10 describes a number of concepts which have been specifically designed for the web. There are also a number of technologies which are, judged by their origin, not part of the web infrastructure, but which have been integrated into the web infrastructure as it is today. For example, usually browsers contain support for reading Usenet news and for sending and receiving electronic mail. A short overview of some of the technologies which are used by today's web tools is given in chapter 11.

- *Part III – Appendices*
  In addition to the concepts presented in the first two parts, a number of appendices contain listings and definitions. Furthermore, bibliographic references, a glossary, and an index are provided.

  Some of the formal definitions of HTTP have been omitted from chapter 3 since they would have made it harder to read through the text. However, some of these definitions for HTTP are very important and also useful as a reference, either when trying to understand HTTP messages, or when interpreting HTTP status or warn codes. In appendix A, these definitions are listed.

  Although some of the formal definitions of HTML elements are given in chapter 5, others have been omitted because they are too complex to read through them while reading text. The most interesting formal definitions, tables and forms, are included in appendix B. Furthermore, this appendix contains the SGML declaration of HTML, defining the syntactical basics for HTML, and the entities (SGML shortcuts) which are used in the formal definitions of HTML elements in chapter 5.

  XML is still under development, but one of the most basic definitions of XML, the SGML declaration defining the syntactical basics for XML, will probably remain stable and is listed in appendix C. As an example for a document type defined with XML, the XML definition of the *Synchronized Multimedia Integration Language (SMIL)* is also included in the appendix. The last three appendices are the bibliographic references, the glossary, and the index. Although this books contains some URIs in the glossary, all bibliographic references are paper documents. With relatively little experience and the utilization of the multitude of search engines available on the web, many of these documents can be located online. However, online locations (ie, URIs) often change quickly, while references to paper documents have a very long lifespan. For this reason, the number of URIs in this book has been kept as small as possible (although there are a number of good starting points among the URIs listed in the glossary).

Although it may seem a little odd to publish a book about a medium which is often credited for making paper-based media dispensable in the long run, a book still cannot be entirely replaced by web-based publication. Whether it is just the fact that people in general are much more used to reading books than they are to using web content, or whether the physical reality of a book really makes it easier to cope with it rather than with an abstract web of information resources, is not quite clear (and still is a topic which is discussed among scientists dealing with this issue). However, clearly a book has some limitations which can not be avoided, the two most important ones being the sequential presentation of information, and the delay between the writing of a book and its actual appearance in book stores.

The sequential presentation has been facilitated with cross-references, a glossary, and an index, making the book more useful when searching for information and for connections between concepts and technologies. The delay between writing and publication will be as small as possible, and it is planned to continuously update the book's content in order to publish a second edition in about a year's time. In order for this to be most effective, it would be nice to get as much feedback from the readers as possible. This feedback can have many different forms, for example corrections, updates, reports of outdated or upcoming concepts, remarks about the book's structure and level of abstraction, as well as proposals for glossary or index additions. Please send all this and more to `dret@tik.ee.ethz.ch`, every submission is greatly appreciated, and this way the next edition will include a large number of improvements.

1. Fundamentals

Although this book is not intended as an introduction for readers without some background as web users or without some knowledge of the basics of computer networks and the Internet, we give a very short introduction into the concepts which form the foundation of web technology. We also take a short look at the web's history, where it all came from, and how it started. For a non-technical and very informative overview of the Internet and its history, the excellent book by Comer [48] is a good starting-point.

Even though this book focuses on the technical foundations of the web, in this first chapter we give a short explanation of the original goal of the web's design. The actual motivation behind the invention of the web was to build a globally distributed hypermedia system. The concepts which have been combined to create such a system are shortly described in section 1.1. A brief history of the web is given in section 1.2, showing the development of the web from its beginnings in 1990 until today.

After a short introduction to the most basic terminology of the web in section 1.3, we move on to the technology which forms the base on which the web builds, which is the Internet and the services it provides. Although we assume that the reader is familiar with some basics of the Internet, in particular with its services, we review these concepts in section 1.4. While this section will not be sufficient as an introduction for someone who never heard of these concepts before, it can be used to refresh the memory, and serves as a reference for the Internet concepts which are used by the different components of the web.

1.1 Document models

The basic concepts underlying the web are not very new. Starting in 1960, the *Xanadu* System described by Nelson [195] already contained all concepts which made the success of the web possible. However, neither Xanadu nor other systems providing similar features succeeded on a large scale. The most popular explanation for this is that these early systems could not be used through a comfortable and intuitive interface, which became available for the web on a number of platforms with the *Mosaic* browser (the first fully graphical user interface for accessing the web).

The main concepts behind the web's way of structuring documents are multimedia, hyperdocuments, and distributed documents. *Multimedia*, described in section 1.1.1, is the integration of different media types into one document model. *Hyperdocuments*, described in section 1.1.2, are documents which are linked through mechanisms being part of the document model. *Distributed documents* are documents containing parts or links to documents on other computers, and are explained in section 1.1.3. With the integration of these three concepts the web can be said to implement a *distributed hypermedia document model*. Although this is a simplification, it is a good characterization of the web on a very abstract level.

1.1.1 Multimedia

The first computer-based document processing systems were purely text-oriented. They supported only one media type (text), and provided functions specific to this media type. Consequently, the document model used by these document processing systems (which in many cases was only defined by the file format) only allowed text as document content. Other media types, such as photos or illustrations, had to be inserted manually, for example by leaving white space in the document and then pasting them in.

It soon became clear, though, that computer-based document processing systems should at least support a document format containing the same media types used for paper-based publishing. These media types are text, graphics[1] and images[2]. However, a document model not only determines the possible media types, it also determines how they can be used inside a document. For example, although most text-processing software today supports the media types commonly used in magazines (text, graphics, and images), most programs will not be able to create the same layout. The reason is that the complex arrangement of text, graphics, and images, probably including overlapping and semi-transparent content, usually cannot be expressed within the document model.

Consequently, a document model has two important aspects, the first one being the media types which are supported, the second one being the possi-

---

[1] Graphics consist of a collection of simple graphic elements, such as lines and circles. The advantages of this representation in comparison to bitmaps (also known as raster images) are better scaling capabilities, and an easier way to manipulate a given picture, due to its accessible composition.

[2] Images consist of a number of picture elements (often called pixels), which are used to describe a picture as a two-dimensional array. A typical application for this format are scanned (digitized) photos.

ble ways how these media types can be arranged. So far, we have only discussed time-invariant media types, namely text, graphics, and images. However, there are also time-variant media types, which can only be properly presented with a time-line in mind. The most popular time-variant media types are audio and video. Document models supporting time-variant media types are still in their infancy, because the different nature of time-invariant and time-variant media types makes it difficult to define meaningful arrangements which go beyond the simple button that can be clicked to hear an audio clip or see a piece of video.

There are approaches to integrate time-invariant and time-variant media types by defining synchronization types for events of time-variant media types (so-called *temporal relationships*) which can be seen as the analogy to two-dimensional spatial relationships defined for time-invariant media types for the layout for paper-based presentation. One such approach is the *Synchronized Multimedia Integration Language (SMIL)* described in section 10.5.6.

When speaking of multimedia, mostly only time-invariant media types are referred to. This is legitimate, because the term multimedia only refers to different media types, and not necessarily to media types which use entirely different dimensions for presentation (time-invariant vs. time-variant).

1.1.2 Hypermedia

While multimedia aims at using multiple media types within one document, the target of another development in the history of document models is to generalize the arrangement of information. A book and most other traditional media is a strict sequence of content. To some extent, this sequence may be extenuated by cross-references, but still the main sequence of the content is given by the presentation of content in consecutive chapters on consecutive pages. The concept to overcome this limitation was first called *hypertext*, then *hypermedia* (to express the combination of multimedia and hypertext), and it models documents as interconnected pieces of information.

On a very basic level, the idea behind hypertext is to eliminate the strictly sequential ordering of content which is common to most traditional media. Instead of seeing a document as a linear sequence of pieces of information, a document can be seen as a set of pieces of information which do not have any order, but which are connected by links from one piece to another (this model resembles a card box, where each card represents one piece of information). Each piece of information (eg, each card), can contain references to many other pieces, and can be referenced from many other pieces. Consequently, a hyperdocument has no fixed presentation, instead it is traversed by a reader, who navigates from one piece of information to another one, using the connecting references.

In addition to this basic shift from a sequential to a freely linked arrangement of pieces of information, many documents have relationships to other documents, the most traditional examples being bibliographic references, which essentially are pointers from within one document to external documents. However, when reading bibliographic references, it is up to the reader to actually locate these documents, using a library or whatever seems appropriate. In case of textual bibliographic references (such as the references section of this book), the document model normally does not support the creation of actual links to external documents, it merely treats bibliographic references as a sequence of characters. However, any given document model can be extended to include the concept of external documents, in which case two issues have to be addressed:

- *Embedding of links to external documents*
  If the document model supports the concept of external documents, it must provide a way to reference them. It must also define what a reference to an external document means and how it has to be processed. Two possible ways for processing links to external documents are to automatically include the external document at the position of the link, or to create some kind of pointer, which can be selected during presentation to initiate some kind of action (such as retrieving the external document and displaying it).

- *Link semantics*
  If the document model supports the concept of external documents, it must include a defined way of how these links can be interpreted. In order to perform some kind of automated action involving these links, it must be clearly defined how such a link has to be interpreted and what has to be done to retrieve a document referenced by such a link.

If these two issues are resolved, it is possible to create a document model which supports the interconnection of documents using so-called *hyperlinks*. Whether these links are only able to point to complete documents, or if it is also possible to point to specific parts within a document[3], is only a slight variation of the basic concept. It is not necessarily part of the document model what to do with hyperlinks during presentation. The most important aspect is that a document now has clearly defined links to other documents and can be referenced from within other documents.

Although the first systems using this kind of document model used only text as media type, representing hypertext systems, it is now common to

---

[3] Considering textual bibliographic references, this difference can be seen as whether only entire documents can be referenced or if it is also possible to use references to chapters or page ranges of documents.

combine hypertext and multimedia to form hypermedia document models. One of the first hypermedia document models which was in use on a large scale was Apple's *HyperCard* system, which implemented a document model of interconnected small documents, so-called cards. However, HyperCard was severely limited in its level of distribution of information pieces, which will be explained in the subsequent section.

1.1.3 Distribution

Now that the concepts of multimedia and hypermedia have been introduced, the last interesting aspect is the question of the distribution of the information pieces, or to introduce a more general term, *information resources*. The problem with the notion of a hypermedia document is that intuitively every author creating an information resource regards it as a separate document. However, from the global point of view, the entirety of interlinked information resources form one hypermedia document, and each information resource is only a tiny part of this document. Therefore, it is more appropriate to speak of information resources (or only resources) when speaking of hypermedia.

Although hypermedia includes the concept of external documents, which can be referenced using links, it says nothing about the level of distribution. For example, the HyperCard system was limited to a very small level of distribution, since only cards in the same document (ie, in the same HyperCard file) could be referenced. In general, three levels of distribution can be differentiated.

- *Inside a file*
  This is the most limited level of distribution. This means that a document is constituted by all information contained in one single file. It can still be presented as a hypermedia document, using different media types and non-sequential presentation.
  The advantage of this approach is that the document model can be kept closed, it does not have to take into account any specific properties of the environment in which it is used, since it is entirely isolated from this environment. Hyperlinks inside the document can be designed easily, since a program processing the document always has access to the complete document and can therefore easily check the validity and uniqueness of links.
  The biggest drawback of this approach is that the document is very centralized, only the person having access to the file can change it, and it is not possible to change parts of the document independently from other parts, because usually the level of access on a computer is the file.

- *Inside a file system or computer*
  If the hyperlinks are no longer restricted to be used inside one file, they are usually designed to use path or file names on computers, realizing the next level of distribution. In this case, a document can be created by using many different files on a computer, which may be created, maintained, or deleted by different persons. This makes the document model more prone to invalid links, a case which is easily avoidable using a one-file document model.
  This vulnerability to invalid links is unavoidable in a setting in which the document is not under the sole control of one person, and therefore the document model has to take into account that links may be invalid. Another drawback is the limitation to one computer or file system, which makes it impossible to create documents which span multiple computers. In comparison to the one-file document model, the file system document model allows much more complex documents, which can be distributed over a file system. This makes it easy to create documents which are maintained by many authors. A rather elaborate authoring environment for many authors can be created without much effort, exploiting the access control features of a file system.

- *Inside a network*
  The largest level of distribution which can be achieved is the distribution over a network. In this case, a document can be distributed over multiple networked computers, and access to information resources usually requires the transfer of these resources over the network. This makes it necessary to have a standardized way to refer to information resources on remote systems, and to request and retrieve documents from there.
  This approach allows for the most general way to create documents. Since documents can now span over the boundaries of computer systems, it is possible that all information resources of such a system are somehow linked to each other, creating one single document which contains all resources.

Based on the most general level of distribution, the web's design goal was to create a global hypermedia system, where information resources can be located on a computer anywhere in the world, as long as the computer is networked and understands the standard for accessing information resources.

1.2 Web history

The history of the web is an amazing success story. Although the underlying concepts (distributed hypermedia and the Internet) are much older, the first idea for the web was developed as recently as 1989. We take a short look at the history of the web from two perspectives. The first perspective is the organizational history, which shows how the web developed from a research project to the generally known global system it is today. This perspective is described in section 1.2.1. The second perspective is the technical one, given in section 1.2.2. In this section, we describe how the technical evolution of the web led from the very simple model of the beginnings to the multitude of different concepts and technologies which are in use or promoted today.

1.2.1 Organizational history

The original motivation for inventing a globally distributed hypermedia system was the need for better information exchange among researchers at the *European Laboratory for Particle Physics (CERN)*, where Tim Berners-Lee was working at that time. The first paper outlining a system which was then called *Mesh* was circulated by Berners-Lee in March 1989. In 1990, the paper was recirculated and the development of a prototype (based on NeXT machines) was approved. The project was officially named *World Wide Web*. By the end of 1990, a working prototype was completed, including a line-mode as well as a graphical user interface.

In 1991, the sources of the prototype were made available to the public (by posting them to newsgroups and making them available on the Internet), mailing lists were started, and a first poster presentation and demonstration on a conference (Hypertext '91 in San Antonio, Texas) was given. Also in 1991, the software was generally released on CERN machines, using the web as a new infrastructure for providing and accessing information. Furthermore, a work plan for the first US server at *Stanford Linear Accelerator Laboratory (SLAC)* was produced.

By November 1992, 26 reasonably reliable web servers were available world-wide, including locations all over the world, such as France, Germany, the Netherlands, and the US. More conference presentations during the year made the web much more popular, and first browsers for widely used platforms (such as the X window system) were made available.

An increase in the number of web servers from 50 to well over 200 was seen in 1993, and for the first time web traffic consumed a mentionable fraction of the overall Internet traffic, about 1% of NSF backbone traffic in September 1993. One of the most important developments that led to the success of the web on a large scale was the release of a comfortable and powerful browser, which also happened in 1993. In February, Marc Andresseen (who later founded Netscape) released an alpha version of NCSA's *Mosaic for X*, followed in September by working releases for all major platforms (X,

Windows, and Macintosh). For the first time, the web was recognized by the general public, with articles appearing in the *New York Times* and the *Economist*.

In the beginning of 1994, *Mosaic Communications Corp.* was founded (later becoming Netscape) by Marc Andresseen and colleagues. The first WWW conference took place at CERN in Geneva, receiving very much attention. By mid-year, over 1500 servers were registered world-wide. In the second half of 1994, the *World Wide Web Consortium (W3C)* was founded by NCSA and CERN, in order to create an international association for the evolution of the web. In October, the second WWW conference was held in Chicago. Because of budget limits, CERN decided not to continue WWW development and turned over the responsibility to the *French National Institute for Research in Computer Science and Control (INRIA)*.

W3C is based in part at the *Laboratory of Computer Science (LCS)* at the *Massachusetts Institute of Technology (MIT)* in Cambridge, Massachusetts, and in part at INRIA. W3C started to work on the key areas for developing the web's architecture, which at that time were HTML, HTTP, and style sheets. Meanwhile, Netscape invented new HTML tags, in the process producing de-facto standards which were followed by other HTML applications.

In 1995, Microsoft released its *Internet Explorer* version 1.0 in August and version 2.0 in November. This marked the beginning of the so-called "browser war", where the two main contenders Microsoft and Netscape each invented new features in every version of their browser (either new HTML elements or new components such as *ActiveX* or *Java*), in an attempt to gain a competitive edge over the competitor. Although both opponents now participate in W3C working groups, working on common standards, there is still a lot of competition going on, partly in terms of new browser functionality[4], partly in tactics about browser distribution.

1.2.2 Technical history

Although the web has greatly evolved from its beginnings in 1990 until today, the core architecture has remained stable and still builds on the same fundamentals as the first proposal. The main idea of the web's architecture, which makes it different from most other hyperdocument systems, is to use network-wide links instead of links restricted to one document or one machine (as discussed in section 1.1.3). The key concepts of the first proposal,

---

[4] It has now become essential which company first can claim to implement new standards. Currently, both browsers (both in their version 4.0) do not implement the full HTML or CSS standards, but at least Microsoft is closer to doing so than Netscape.

together with their names and the short phrases explaining them as used in early presentations about the web, are the following three components.

- *URL – How to name a document*
  The key concept of a hyperdocument is to replace an inherently sequential presentation with a mechanism to use *links* for information arrangement. Therefore, a convention how to identify (and subsequently locate) information is required. The model defined for web identifiers is the *Uniform Resource Locator (URL)* as described in chapter 2.

- *HTTP – How to get a document*
  Once information can be named and subsequently located, it is also necessary to have a mechanism to retrieve it. This is especially important since the most important feature of the web is its world-wide *distribution*, requiring a mechanism which can be used for world-wide retrieval. The *Hypertext Transfer Protocol (HTTP)* as described in chapter 3 is used as the web's communication protocol.

- *HTML – The document format for hypertext*
  Finally, after retrieving information it is necessary to know what to do with it, which means that there must be a convention for the document format. This format must provide support for *multimedia* as well as for *hypermedia*. The web's concept in this case is the *Hypertext Markup Language (HTML)* as described in chapter 5.

Over the years, these basic concepts have evolved into much more powerful and complex versions. The individual developments are described in the respective chapters. However, the key concepts as described in the list are still the same.

In addition to the developments of the core standards, many additional components of the overall architecture have been announced and standardized. With the increase of commercial interests in business on the web and by selling web technology, it is often not possible to see whether an announcement introduces something which will gain some relevance. Currently, it seems to be clear that style sheets for web documents as implemented by *Cascading Style Sheets (CSS)* and described in chapter 6 will become a basic part of web technology. However, since support for style sheets is only beginning, it is hard to predict where this development is going.

Another trend which is hotly debated is the *Extensible Markup Language (XML)* as described in chapter 7. XML is intended to provide a platform for defining user-specific document types, in contrast to the fixed document model presented by HTML. However, since the development of this language and all related technologies (such as a style language to specify the presentation of XML documents) is still in a very early phase, the significance of XML in the web's architecture is not completely clear.

Generally, it can be observed that the simplicity which was one of the most intriguing aspects of the web is slowly but continuously disappearing. It is increasingly giving way to a much more complex infrastructure, still being based on the same basic building blocks. But the basic building blocks have become more complex and there also is a large number of additional building blocks, with sometimes complex and irritating interdependencies. However, this development is inevitable, since many problems which seemed to be minor during the initial design of the web are surfacing with its increased usage[5]. Issues like the availability of meta data, the ability to follow hyperlinks in both directions, and an increased level of abstraction in the naming of resources are being addressed in a number of ways.

Whereas in the first years of the web most technical developments concentrated on improving the basic building blocks (by inventing new HTML features or new HTTP functionality), now many developments are building blocks of their own. However, because of increasing commercial interests in contrast to the research spirit which fueled the start of the web, many new developments are rather marketed than seriously announced, and in many cases it is advisable to take a close look at announcements[6]. To summarize, keeping track of the technological progress of the web, and not spending too much time on keeping track of dead ends, can be very time-consuming and complicated. However, it makes it easier to see general trends and also to see which of the solutions being promoted look plausible.

1.3 Terminology

Although we use a consistent terminology throughout the book, there are many abbreviations, slightly overlapping concepts, and multiply named entities. Whenever in doubt about a web-related technical term, the first attempt should be to look it up in the glossary or the index, one of which hopefully leads to a definition of it. There are, however, four central terms for the web which are used very frequently, and which therefore are explained here.

---

[5] Although the initial design of the web was sufficient to make it as successful as it is today, there were and still are some architectural problems, which are mainly caused by the very minimalistic approach. Pam [203] gives a good overview of a number of these areas. Many of the problems discussed is this paper are solved now or are being solved using additional architectural concepts or enhanced versions of existing standards. However, some problems still remain.

[6] A good example for this is Microsoft's *Channel Definition Format (CDF)*, which claims to be an XML application, but which is specified in a way different from what is required for an XML application.

- *User*

  The user is a human being which interacts with the web through some kind of program. The usual scenario is a user sitting in front of the computer on which a browser such as Netscape Navigator or Microsoft Internet Explorer is running.

- *Browser*

  A browser is a program which is used to access web servers and which displays documents retrieved from these servers. The two most popular browsers are Netscape Navigator and Microsoft Internet Explorer. In the well-known client/server-scenario, a browser is a client of a web server.

  Another term often used as a synonym for browser in technical documentation is *user agent*, which refers to the program (ie, the agent) through which a user interacts with the web. However, sometimes the term user agent refers to a more general view than the term browser. While a browser is usually regarded as a visually oriented program implementing a *Graphical User Interface (GUI)*, user agents can be designed for other media, such as voice or braille. However, this distinction is not well-defined, and usually it is appropriate to see the term user agent as a synonym for browser.

- *Client*

  A client in the web is more general than a browser. While every browser is a client (ie, it is used for accessing web servers), not every client is a browser. Other clients (ie, programs contacting web servers and retrieving documents) are search engines, programs which automatically retrieve documents for the purpose of index generation. Generally speaking, a client simply is a program which accesses web servers.

- *Server*

  A web server is a server which can be contacted by clients (such as browsers or search engines) to retrieve documents from it. A web server is not necessarily a dedicated computer (ie, a server in the physical sense that it is a machine only used for this purpose). The term server in a web-related context refers to a process on a machine which implements the functionality to reply to requests from clients. Technically, every computer which has a network connection can run a web server. Chapter 9 gives an overview over server issues as well as an example of one specific product.

In addition to these basic terms, the web (as almost all areas in computer science or maybe science in general) uses a large number of acronyms and very specific terms. Furthermore, with the increased commercialization of the web, it also becomes common practice for many companies to create their own terminology. Sometimes it is very hard to find out what some newly invented word really means (ie, seen from a technical perspective). We tried to collect the most important terms and to include them in the book. However, inevitably some words will be missing, in which case the web itself usually is the best resource (using indices or search engines) to find more information about a specific term or abbreviation.

1.4 The Internet

In this section we will not give an introduction to all concepts of the Internet. We assume that the reader has a basic understanding of computer communications in general and the Internet in particular. However, in order to make a clear distinction between the two sometimes wrongly interchangeably used terms "Internet" and "World Wide Web", we give the following very short definition.

> The *Internet* is the entirety of all computers which are networked (using various networking technologies) and employ the Internet protocol suite on top of their networking systems. The Internet protocol suite implements a wide-area packet-switched network which is able to interconnect networks using different network protocols and very different connection characteristics.
>
> The *World Wide Web* is a distributed hypermedia system which is built on top of some of the services provided by the Internet, the most important being the naming service provided by the *Domain Name System (DNS)*, and the reliable connection-oriented transport service provided by the *Transmission Control Protocol (TCP)*.

Although these definitions are very short (and obviously lack some precision), they draws a clear line between the Internet as a transport infrastructure which offers a number of services, and the web as an application architecture built on top of this infrastructure.

There are various documents which can be consulted for information about the Internet. Internet informational RFC 2235 [280][7] gives a timeline of the Internet, including numbers of hosts, domains, and web servers. It is a very good introduction and helps to get a feeling for the development of the Internet. For answers to the most frequently asked questions, a good Internet documentation for starters is RFC 1594 [168], which also contains a lot of useful pointers to more detailed documentation.

---

[7] The most recent version of this document can always be retrieved by using the web server of the *Internet Society (ISOC)* and requesting the document http://info.isoc.org/guest/zakon/Internet/History/HIT.html.

For general standards about the requirements for Internet host software, Internet standards RFC 1122 and 1123 [29, 30] should be consulted. These standards describe what a host must implement in order to become an Internet host.

The web uses only some services of the Internet infrastructure, which are briefly explained in the following sections. In section 1.4.1, it is explained how a computer is connected to the Internet, and how it gets an address and a name (which is important for creating hyperlinks). In section 1.4.2, the data transfer on the Internet is briefly explained. Because it is possible to transfer different types of data (eg, web pages or audio files), it is crucial that these data types can be differentiated. The mechanism which is used for this purpose is described in section 1.4.3.

1.4.1 The Internet environment

In this section, we will shortly discuss the Internet environment. Two issues are important, the first one is how to get connected to the Internet, which is important for web servers needing a permanent connection, and for users, most of the time using dial-up connections. These possibilities are discussed in section 1.4.1.1. The second step after getting connected to the Internet is to assign an address and maybe a name to a computer[8]. These issues are explained in section 1.4.1.2.

1.4.1.1 Connecting to the Internet

Connecting to the Internet can be done in two principally different ways. There is a large number of technical solutions for both ways, but these two general alternatives can be differentiated by their connection characteristics.

Dial-up connections

If a computer has only client functionality, it is not important that it is constantly connected to the Internet. It is sufficient that the connection is established only if some server on the Internet (such as a mail server or a web server) needs to be contacted. The most common solution for this approach is to have a modem connection[9] between the local computer and a remote

---

[8] Actually, a name and an address must be assigned to a computer before it is connected to the Internet. But it makes more sense to first discuss how to get connected before explaining how the connection can be used.

[9] A modem connection is a phone line which uses modems on both ends. A *modem* is able to transmit digital data over a phone line by converting it into noise for transmitting it over the phone line, and converting received noise back to digital

computer which is activated whenever Internet connectivity is required. The remote computer acts as the access point to the Internet, accepting the call from the local computer's modem, and acting as a relay between the local computer and the Internet.

After the modem connection is established (ie, the local and the remote computer can exchange data), there are two popular methods to transfer Internet data over the modem connection. The older variant is the *Serial Line Internet Protocol (SLIP)*, the newer method is the *Point to Point Protocol (PPP)*, providing some additional features (such as configuration negotiation and standardized authentication procedures).

Permanent connections

If the computer to be connected to the Internet provides server functionality, it is important that it is permanently connected to the Internet. Due to the fact that it is usually not possible to predict when a server will be accessed, and therefore it is in most cases not practical to have a server which is not permanently connected.

Theoretically, it would be possible to use the approach described in the previous section (using modems and a phone line) also for permanently connecting a computer to the Internet. However, the costs for a permanent phone line in most cases are too high. Instead, dedicated lines are being used. The principle is very similar to the phone line approach, the local computer is connected to a remote system acting as a relay between the local computer and the Internet. The costs for these permanent lines differ greatly according to a variety of parameters, such as the bandwidth (the amount of data that can be transferred in a given period of time), the distance between the local computer and the remote system, and the support in case of connectivity problems.

1.4.1.2 Names and addresses

In order to get Internet connectivity, it is not only necessary to have a connection (as described in the previous section) which transports Internet data, it is also necessary to have an address. Addresses on the Internet are so-called *IP addresses* as described in section 1.4.2.2. An IP address is a 32-bit number which is used for globally unique identification of a computer. However, in the context of the web, names for computers (such as `www.w3.org`) are much

---

data. Technically speaking, this is the *modulation* respectively *demodulation* of signals in the frequency range of speech, coding respectively extracting the information to be transmitted. The term "modem" has been derived from the first syllables of these words.

more common than IP addresses. Names on the Internet are so-called *DNS names*. The *Domain Name System (DNS)* as defined by Internet standards RFC 1034 and 1035 [177, 178][10] is a global naming service which maps DNS names to IP addresses.

On an abstract level, DNS can be seen as being similar to a phone book, which also has the function of mapping names onto addresses (in this case, the addresses are phone numbers). Although a phone book is ordered alphabetically, a world-wide search of a name first has to locate the appropriate phone book. Similar to the geographical organization of phone books, DNS also implements a structure of its name space. DNS names are organized into so-called domains, which are hierarchically ordered.

There are two major advantages of DNS. The first one is the easier readability of names. It is much easier to remember the DNS name www.w3.org than to remember the corresponding IP address 18.23.0.22. The second and more technical advantage is the increased level of abstraction. It is possible that the network of W3C is reorganized, changing all IP numbers, or that the web server is being moved to another machine. In these cases, the DNS name remains the same, the only thing that has to be changed is the DNS entry, which then has to map www.w3.org to the new IP address of the web server.

The domains on the first level of the hierarchy are called *top-level domain (TLD)*, and each TLD is either a *country-code top-level domain (ccTLD)*, represented by two letter country-codes from ISO 3166 [128], or a *generic top-level domain (gTLD)*. Domain names are arranged from right to left, so the topmost level stands far right. Consequently, the domain name www.ethz.ch names a host in the ccTLD .ch, which according to ISO 3166 is Switzerland. The second-level domain is ethz, which is the Swiss Federal Institute of Technology in Zürich. The leftmost name identifies a computer, in this case it is named www, which is a common convention for a computer which runs the web server for a domain. DNS defines an architecture where it is possible to send a query for the address of the computer named www.ethz.ch to any DNS server, and the query will be forwarded to the server actually holding the required information, which is the IP address of the www.ethz.ch computer. Queries can easily be forwarded because of the hierarchical structure of the name space.

While the organization of domains below the top-level is left to the authorities administering the respective TLD, the TLDs themselves are organized into ccTLDs and gTLDs, and nothing else. The ccTLDs are organized by country and usually an authority inside the country organizes the domain

---

[10] For an easily understandable description of DNS and its concepts, the reader is referred to Albitz and Liu [5].

structure below the top-level. The following descriptions of the individual gTLDs are taken from Internet informational RFC 1591 [213]:

- edu

  This domain was originally intended for all educational institutions. Many universities, colleges, schools, educational service organizations, and educational consortia have registered here. More recently a decision has been taken to limit further registrations to 4 year colleges and universities. Schools and 2-year colleges will be registered in the country domains.

- com

  This domain is intended for commercial entities, that is companies. This domain has grown very large and there is concern about the administrative load and system performance if the current growth pattern is continued. Consideration is being taken to subdivide the domain and only allow future commercial registrations in the subdomains.

- net

  This domain is intended to hold only the computers of network providers, administrative computers, and network node computers. The customers of network providers have domain names of their own.

- org

  This domain is intended as the miscellaneous TLD for organizations that didn't fit anywhere else. Some non-government organizations such as W3C and other standardization bodies fit here.

- gov

  This domain was originally intended for any kind of government office or agency. More recently a decision was taken to register only agencies of the US Federal government in this domain. State and local agencies are registered in the country domains.

- mil

  This domain is used by the US military.

- int

  This domain is for organizations established by international treaties, or international databases.

These gTLDs have been in use since the introduction of DNS in 1984, and until the mid-90s, there was no problem because the number of registered domain names was not too large. However, with the huge success of the web, many companies want to have their own domain names, and because many companies prefer the .com domain to their ccTLD, or because they are not located in only one country, this domain is getting too large.

Therefore, it has been decided that new gTLDs will be created which can be used to register new domain names. The *Generic Top Level Domain Memorandum of Understanding (gTLD-MoU)* is an international framework in which policies for the administration of the new gTLDs are defined. The new top level domains which will be created are

- `firm` for businesses, or firms,
- `shop` or businesses offering goods to purchase,
- `web` for entities emphasizing activities related to the web,
- `arts` for entities emphasizing cultural and entertainment activities,
- `rec` for entities emphasizing recreation/entertainment activities,
- `info` for entities providing information services, and
- `nom` or those wishing individual or personal nomenclature.

The technical aspects of the domain name system are irrelevant for the purpose of this book. The only important thing to know is that part of the setup of an Internet host is to specify the address of a DNS server[11]. This server accepts DNS queries, forwarding them if it does not have the required information locally, and replies with an answer, which usually is the IP address of the DNS name which was specified in the query. Thus, most web pages are retrieved by a two step process, which is shown in figure 1.1.

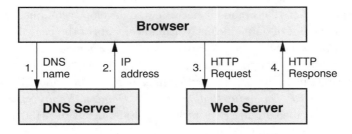

Fig. 1.1 DNS as part of web page retrieval

In order to retrieve a web page from a server, the browser first has to find out the IP address of the server. It therefore extracts the DNS name from the URL (details of URL syntax are given in chapter 2) and sends a query with that DNS name to the DNS server. As a response, the browser receives the

---

[11] The most popular software for DNS servers is the *Berkeley Internet Name Domain (BIND)*, developed and maintained by the *Internet Software Consortium (ISC)*.

IP address of the web server, and can use this address to open a connection to the server for retrieving the web page.

Although in almost every case a URL contains a DNS name, it is more generally defined, in the sense that it has to be a *Fully-Qualified Host Name (FQHN)*. An FQHN is a name which can be interpreted independently from context and uniquely identifies an IP host. Basically, an FQHN can have two forms.

- *Fully-Qualified Domain Name (FQDN)*
  An FQDN is a domain name that includes all higher level domains relevant to the entity named. For a host, an FQDN includes the string that identifies the particular host, plus all domains of which the host is a part, up to and including the top-level domain.

- *IP address*
  An IP address simply is a 32-bit number. The most usual way of writing IP addresses is *dotted decimal*, describing a notation of the form `A.B.C.D`, where each letter represents, in decimal, one byte of the four byte IP address.

The basic service and design of DNS is rather simple. DNS defines a hierarchy of servers forwarding queries for which they do not have a local entry, but the technical reality is much more complex. Especially the growth of the number of DNS names since the invention of the web (the number of registered DNS names increased from under 100'000 to over 30 million from 1989 to the beginning of 1998) made it necessary to develop techniques which can handle this amount of data efficiently. Enhancements of the basic DNS model are the *Mechanism for Prompt Notification of Zone Changes (DNS NOTIFY)* described in Internet proposed standard RFC 1996 [268], DNS security extensions described in Internet proposed standards RFC 2065 and 2137 [70, 71], the mechanism for *Dynamic Updates in the Domain Name System (DNS UPDATE)* described in Internet proposed standard RFC 2136 [269], and concepts like the *Naming Authority Pointer (NAPTR)* described in Internet experimental RFC 2168, and the *Negative Caching of DNS Queries (DNS NCACHE)* described in Internet proposed standard RFC 2308 [10].

1.4.2 Transferring data

One of the fundamental principles of computer communications is the layering of communication architectures. Layering not only makes it easier to reduce the complexity of computer communication systems to a manageable measure, it also promotes the encapsulation of functionality, thereby making layers exchangeable. The layering of a communication architecture can be seen as increasing in abstraction from bottom to the top. The bottom layer deals with the most basic questions, such as physical connections (plugs, cables, voltage levels used), whereas the top layer usually represents an application which uses the services of the communication architecture. In general, each layer uses the services of the layer directly below it, and provides services which are used by the layer directly above it.

There are many different ways how layering can be done. A very simple picture (but sufficient for our discussion of the topic) is shown in figure 1.2, giving a first impression of how the Internet can be seen in a layering model. The most important aspect of the Internet is that it can be based on any networking technology, and that it supports a wide number of applications.

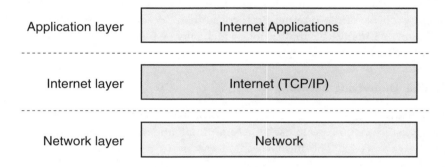

Fig. 1.2 Layering of communication protocols

One of the key aspects which lead to the success of the Internet protocol suite is its robustness. In contrast to many other network technologies, which only work under perfect or near-perfect conditions, the Internet is designed to be robust and to tolerate as much errors as possible. The following quote describes this design principle and the motivation behind it.

> "At every layer of the protocols, there is a general rule whose application can lead to enormous benefits in robustness and interoperability: 'Be liberal in what you accept, and conservative in what you send.' Software should be written to deal with every conceivable error, no matter how unlikely; sooner or later a packet will come in with that particular combination of errors and attributes, and unless the software is prepared, chaos can ensue. In general, it is best to assume that the network is filled with malevolent entities that will send in packets designed to have the worst possible effect. This assumption will lead to suitable protective design, although the most serious problems in the Internet have been caused by unenvisaged mechanisms triggered

by low-probability events; mere human malice would never have taken so devious a course! The second part of the principle is almost as important: software on other hosts may contain deficiencies that make it unwise to exploit legal but obscure protocol features. It is unwise to stray far from the obvious and simple, lest untoward effects result elsewhere. A corollary of this is 'watch out for misbehaving hosts'; host software should be prepared, not just to survive other misbehaving hosts, but also to cooperate to limit the amount of disruption such hosts can cause to the shared communication facility."   *Braden [31]*

For our discussion of the Internet, it is sufficient to see four different layers. The first layer is the network layer, which is the networking technology on which the Internet is built. This layer is described in section 1.4.2.1. The two main protocols of the Internet protocol suite are described in sections 1.4.2.2 and 1.4.2.3. Finally, the applications which may be built on top of the Internet are described in section 1.4.2.4.

1.4.2.1 Underlying networks

As already mentioned, the Internet can be based on any networking technology, since it makes almost no assumptions about the services offered by the network layer. The most common case is to use the Internet protocol suite on top of a *Local Area Network (LAN)*. Popular LANs are *Ethernet* and *Token ring*. However, the Internet protocol suite can also be placed on top of networks which also provide wide-area networking. The possibility to use different underlying protocols is shown in figure 1.3.

1.4.2.2 Internet Protocol (IP)

The two main protocols of the Internet protocol suite are the *Internet Protocol (IP)*, and the *Transmission Control Protocol (TCP)*, which is described in the next section. The layering of these two protocols on top of the underlying services is shown in figure 1.3.

IP is a connection-less, best-effort packet switching protocol. It provides packet routing, fragmentation and re-assembly. IP is defined by Internet standard RFC 791 [209]. IP itself is rather old, and has some limitations which became apparent during the last few years. The biggest concern was the shortage of addresses, mainly caused by the rapid growth of the Internet since the beginning of the nineties. However, there are more areas which also suggest that a new version of IP should be used in the not so far future. Some of them are listed below:

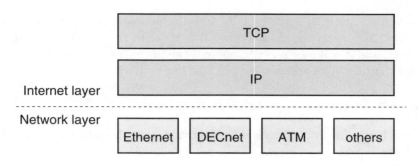

Fig. 1.3 Layering of communication protocols – TCP/IP

- *Shortage of addresses*
  Even though the current 32-bit IP address structure can enumerate over 4 billion hosts on as many as 16.7 million networks, the actual address assignment efficiency is far less than that, even on a theoretical basis as shown by Huitema [107]. This inefficiency is exacerbated by the granularity of assignments using class A, B, and C addresses[12].

- *No resource reservation*
  Although IP works fine for data transmission on a best effort basis, data types with time constraints (such as audio and video) cannot be transferred with performance guarantees. For these data types, it would be much better to have the possibility to reserve resources. This means to have the network either reject a connection request (if there are not enough resources available) or accept the request and guarantee that the resources will be available for that connection.

- *Lack of support for mobile hosts*
  A growing number of computer systems are not permanently connected to the Internet. The best example for this type of computer is a laptop, which can be connected to the Internet from many different locations. Currently, IP does not support this type of connectivity, which will become more and more popular with the increasing miniaturization of personal computer systems.

The solution to these and other problems of the current Internet architecture is *IP next generation (IPng)*, which is a name for a number of new protocols, in particular *IP version 6 (IPv6)*[13], which is specified in Internet

---

[12] The different classes of IP addresses are used to group IP addresses into *networks*. This makes routing in the Internet much easier, but also wastes addresses if not all addresses of a network are actually assigned to machines.

[13] The current version of IP is IPv4.

proposed standard RFC 1883 [61][14]. An introduction to this area is given by
Thomas [262]. However, since we intend to describe the current state of the
Internet, and it will take a long time until the Internet is dominated by IPv6
rather than IPv4, we will not investigate IPng or IPv6 any further.

1.4.2.3 Transmission Control Protocol (TCP)

Although IP provides end-to-end connectivity across boundaries of different
networks, it lacks the support to address individual processes on computers,
and also implements a very simple datagram service. IP datagrams may get
lost, may be duplicated, or may arrive in another order than they have been
sent.

Since most applications require a reliable, flow-controlled communication
service, the *Transmission Control Protocol (TCP)* has been designed, which
in the standard Internet protocol suite is layered on top of IP. TCP assumes
that it can obtain a simple, potentially unreliable, datagram service from
the lower level protocol (in almost all cases this is IP). TCP adds reliable
communication, flow-control, multiplexing and connection-oriented communication. It provides full-duplex, process-to-process connections. In terms of
addressing, TCP adds a *port* number to the IP address, which extends the
addressing scheme from a machine (identified by an IP address) to a process
(identified by the port the process is bound to).

TCP is defined in Internet standard RFC 793 [210]. Although in many
cases the additional features of TCP, in particular reliability and connection-
oriented communication, are useful, there are some application scenarios
where a simpler protocol would be sufficient. In these cases, the *User Datagram Protocol (UDP)* as defined in Internet standard RFC 768 [208] can be
used, which only adds a checksum and process-to-process addressing capabilities to IP.

1.4.2.4 Application protocols

In the preceding sections, the TCP/IP protocol suite is shortly explained.
It can be seen that this protocol suite provides reliable, flow-controlled and
connection-oriented communication capabilities. In addition to these data
transport capabilities, an Internet host also provides access to other Internet services, one example being DNS. In figure 1.4 it is shown that various
application-level protocols use the Internet protocol suite for communications.

---

[14] A detailed discussion of the selection criteria for and the properties of IPv6 can
be found in Internet proposed standard RFC 1752 [33].

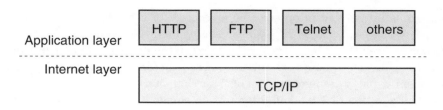

Fig. 1.4 Layering of communication protocols – Application protocols

In addition to the data transport capabilities provided by TCP/IP, these applications also use DNS to resolve host names. DNS normally can be used through calls to a system library, which in turn uses UDP or TCP to send and receive data to and from a DNS server[15]. Most web servers today implement a number of application level protocols. HTTP as the web's own protocol for transferring information is implemented by all browsers, but in many cases the *File Transfer Protocol (FTP)*, and protocols for reading and sending email (described in section 11.1), and accessing Usenet news (described in section 11.3) are also integrated into the browser.

Application protocols based on top of TCP/IP could be based on top of another reliable, flow-controlled and connection-oriented protocol. However, in most cases these applications use other services of the Internet protocol suite (such as DNS) in addition to TCP's data transport service, so that they could not easily be used in a different environment.

1.4.3 Data types

On the application level, it is often important to have some kind of identification for different data types. Although many applications define their own data format and only accept data using this format, an open architecture makes it possible to support data types which are unknown to the application at time of implementation. In section 1.4.3.1 it is discussed how such an architecture can be designed. Originally designed for email messages, an architecture for different content types has been defined for the Internet. Because the web uses the same data types, this architecture is shortly described in section 1.4.3.2.

1.4.3.1 Identification of data types

In most application scenarios where data is received or processed (such as incoming mail in email programs, or browsing web documents), the data

---

[15] While TCP can be used for any DNS activity, UDP is preferred for queries due to its lower overhead and better performance.

has to be interpreted in order to be presented. In case of text-based email, this is very easy, because the mail can simply be displayed in a text window. However, even this is only true for 7-bit text. If the text uses 8-bit characters, including accented characters, this may already become a problem if the email program wrongly assumes the use of 7-bit characters.

The question of 7-bit and 8-bit text in emails is only a very simple example of the problems that arise with processing email containing different content types. In the general case, it is perfectly reasonable to think of email containing multimedia objects, such as images.

In case of the web, the issue of content types is very similar. Although most documents on the web are coded in HTML which is understood by all browsers, there also exist a number of other content types, in particular formats for images, audio, and video. Although many browsers today support most of these formats, it is still very common to find some data on the net which a given browser cannot handle.

In both cases, a solution to the dilemma that there is a large and constantly growing number of content types is the invention of an architecture for content type classification. If all information being sent contains an identification of its content type, the processing application can easily decide if it is able to handle this content type or not. Using simple extension mechanisms (such as configuration files), it is possible to configure the email or web application to accept new content types and forward them to external applications, based on their content type identification.

1.4.3.2 Multipurpose Internet Mail Extensions (MIME)

The original standard for Internet email messages, RFC 822 [53], defines a message representation protocol specifying considerable detail about ASCII message headers, and leaves the message content, or message body, as flat ASCII text. The *Multipurpose Internet Mail Extensions (MIME)*, as defined by a series of RFCs redefine the format of messages to allow for

- textual message bodies in character sets other than US-ASCII,
- an extensible set of different formats for non-textual message bodies,
- multi-part message bodies, and
- textual header information in character sets other than US-ASCII.

The first document, RFC 2045 [80], specifies the various headers used to describe the structure of MIME messages. The second document, RFC 2046 [81], defines the general structure of the MIME media typing system as well as an initial set of content types. The third document, RFC 2047 [183], describes extensions to RFC 822 to allow non-ASCII text data in Internet mail header fields. The fourth document, RFC 2048 [82], specifies various *Internet Assigned Numbers Authority (IANA)* registration procedures for MIME-related facilities. The fifth and final document, RFC 2049 [79], describes MIME conformance criteria and provides some illustrative examples of MIME message formats, acknowledgments, and the bibliography. Generally, MIME provides the following:

- A `MIME-Version` header field, which uses a version number to declare a message to be conformant with a particular version of the MIME specification.

- A `Content-Type` header field which can be used to specify the type and subtype of data in the body of a message and to fully specify the native representation (encoding) of such data. Content types have been defined for text, multipart documents, application specific (including binary) data, messages, still images, video, audio and SGML-encoded structured documents.

- A `Content-Transfer-Encoding` header field, which can be used to specify an auxiliary encoding that was applied to the data in order to allow it to pass through mail transport mechanisms which may have data or character set limitations.

- Two additional header fields that can be used to further describe the data in a message body, the `Content-ID` and `Content-Description` header fields.

In the context of this book, the most relevant issue is the `Content-Type` header field and its content, the so-called *MIME type*. A MIME type defines a specific content type by giving media type and subtype identifiers. In general, the media type is used to declare the general type of data, while the subtype specifies a specific format for that type of data. Media types as well as subtype identifiers are maintained by the *Internet Assigned Numbers Authority (IANA)*. One example for a MIME type is `image/gif`, identifying the content as being an image (the media type) which is encoded using the *Graphics Interchange Format (GIF)*.

Applications can base their action either on the media type (common types are `image`, `audio`, `text`, and `video` for content specific formats, as well as `application` for application-specific formats) or on the subtype identifiers. For example, an email application can forward all `image` data to another application, which is an image viewer. The email application does not have to know which image subtypes can be handled by the image viewer. The image viewer application uses the subtype identifier to determine whether it can interpret an image.

Since MIME makes it possible to dynamically add new content types to existing software by adding new MIME types, it must also be possible to specify how to handle the new content types. Although some software uses proprietary formats, in Internet informational RFC 1524 [24] a mechanism for user agent configuration based on a file format is described. Basically, a file format is defined which specifies mappings from MIME types to program names. Using this mechanism, a user agent can be configured to use a specific program for handling a MIME type it does not support internally.

Part I

Basics

2. Universal Resource Identifier (URI)

The basic design of the web, as introduced in chapter 1, is that of a distributed hypermedia system. The two main architectural constructs at this level are the individual pieces of information or *information resources* (which in most cases are web pages), and the *links* between them, connecting these individual pieces of information to form an interconnected web of information resources. While we discuss the actual pieces of information in later chapters of the book, we first take a closer look on what these links are and how they work.

Although the usual term to refer to pointers to web resources is "links", this is not exactly what this chapter is about. A link is a mechanism which identifies a resource within some kind of framework, for example a link on a web page. The identification itself can be seen separately from the link, and even if no link points to some resource, it still has an identifier. For this reason, it is important to differentiate between *identifiers* for the identification of resources, and *links* which use identifiers to establish connections between resources.

Section 2.1 contains a general discussion of why identifiers are such an important issue for the web. This is done from a user perspective, describing from the user's view where identifiers come into play and why it is necessary to have them. Another perspective is shown from the designer's point of view, giving a more theoretical description of what the design issues were when identifiers were invented as part of the web's core architecture. After this motivation of why identifiers are needed, section 2.2 describes the syntax of web identifiers, that is their formal structure (which is extremely simple). The semantics of web identifiers, that is their meaning and how they can be used, are described in section 2.3. Finally, section 2.4 gives a short discussion about future trends of web identifiers.

2.1 The need for resource identification

One of the main aspects of the web is its world wide distribution and its ability to include a multitude of different information resources, not only web specific ones. This basically means that it must be possible to somehow point to these resources, and the way this is done should be as powerful, yet as simple as possible. The way it is done in the web is via identifiers, which are normally used inside information resources to point to other information resources. However, it should also be possible to use these identifiers externally, thereby making it possible to exchange them in written form or even in conversations (eg, over the phone).

Web identifiers can be seen from two different perspectives. The first perspective, which is the one everyone who ever used the web is familiar with, is the user perspective. We give a description of this perspective in section 2.1.1, which can be seen as a short review of how web identifiers are encountered when using the web. However, there is a more technical and systematic way of looking at web identifiers, and this is the designer's perspective. In section 2.1.2, we discuss the design goals of web identifiers and what has been done to make sure that these goals were met.

2.1.1 Web identifiers from a user perspective

When browsing the web, most links (HTML constructs containing identifiers) can be visually recognized as specially formatted text (colored and/or underlined, depending on the browser and the user's preferences) within the normal flow of text, and selecting such a link with a pointing device usually instructs the browser to load the piece of information pointed to by the link's identifier. Another way a link may be visible is as an image (which normally should contain some visual hint, such as text or graphic symbols like arrows or signs, that is it not only an image but also a link), and these links work the same way as textual ones, in that their selection with a pointing device instructs the browser to follow the link. In both cases (links represented by text or images), most browsers will notify the user about a link by changing the cursor shape when moving over it (additionally, most browsers also display the link's identifier in some form of status line, so that users can actually see what they will do when selecting the link).

In most cases, users do not need to be concerned with how links look and where they point to, all they have to do is click on some text or other visual representation of a link, and the browser will perform whatever is necessary to open this link. It is believed to be one of the main reasons for the huge success of the web that the user normally does not have deal explicitly with identifiers of information resources, but can use simple and intuitive links to use them. Even when not using a link from a currently loaded web page but an identifier of an information resource which has been visited before, often it is not necessary to type in or remember the identifier to this information resource, instead it can be used from what is usually called a *bookmarks folder*.

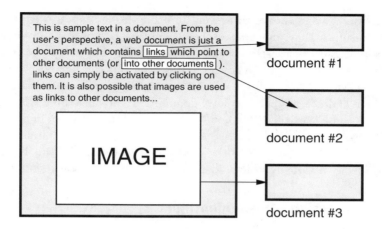

This is sample text in a document. From the user's perspective, a web document is just a document which contains │links│ which point to other documents (or │into other documents│). links can simply be activated by clicking on them. It is also possible that images are used as links to other documents...

IMAGE

document #1

document #2

document #3

Fig. 2.1   User perspective of web links

A bookmarks folder is nothing more than a collection of identifiers, typically associated with the date when they were last visited, the date when the bookmark has been created, and the name of the information resource the identifier is pointing to (in case of web pages this usually is the title of the web page as specified by the page's <TITLE> element, which is normally displayed in the browser window's title bar when reading this page). The exact information and structure of a bookmarks folder depends on the type of browser, but the principle is always the same[1].

When using the web, there must be a start (the first information resource a browser loads when being started). Normally, this is either the home page of the browser's maker, the home page of the service provider, or the home page of the institution where the browser is running (such as the company's home page). However, all browsers can be configured to load any page on being started. This setup makes it very easy for users to browse the web without ever being forced to manually enter (ie, type in) identifiers.

The only time when it is really necessary to type in an identifier explicitly (in contrast to clicking on a link on a web page or choosing a bookmark from the bookmarks folder) is when visiting a new information resource, like a search engine which has not been used before. Even there, most browsers make it very easy to enter the identifier. For example, to visit the HotBot search engine, the correct identifier to type in (using the "open page" command or some similar function of the browser) would be

---

[1] A more powerful model of bookmark management, including categorization and bookmark sharing, has been proposed by Keller et al. [147], but this system is still in a research stage.

`http://www.hotbot.com/`[2]. However, for example Netscape's Navigator implicitly assumes that any address being entered is a web address (unless explicitly stated otherwise by using another prefix than `http`), so it would be sufficient to enter `www.hotbot.com`. But even this can be abbreviated, by exploiting Navigator's assumption that most web servers have `www` as their host name and `com` as their top-level domain[3], so the only thing which actually needs to be typed in is `hotbot` (and because Internet domain names are case insensitive, it is not even necessary to remember any capitalization of the name)[4]. Seeing that this works everywhere on the world, this is an easy way to specify a globally unique identifier for an information resource.

2.1.2 The design of web identifiers

However, up to here this has been a pragmatic description of web identifiers and how they can be used, and although in most cases this is all users need to know when browsing the web, it is interesting to have a closer look at the concepts behind them. Basically, when coming up with the concept of the web, it was necessary to define a means of naming (and thus identifying) information resources. It is important to notice that information resources should not be limited to information available over the web. Any information available on the Internet should be able to be referenced with these identifiers. This not only includes information services which are older than the web, such as file servers running the *File Transfer Protocol (FTP)*, and should be accessible using web identifiers, but also new information services, which will be invented in the future.

The official name for the identifiers being used inside the web is the term *Universal Resource Identifier (URI)*, indicating that a identifier usually points to some kind of information resource, thereby identifying it in a universally unique way. For the rest of this chapter, we will use the term URI rather than the more ambiguous term "identifier". So far, we have seen what URIs can be used for. However, there are some more general requirements which have been taken into account when inventing the URI definition. The three main design goals of URIs have been as follows:

---

[2] We take a closer look at the syntax and the meaning of this identifier in sections 2.2 and 2.3.

[3] See section 1.4.1.2 for a detailed discussion of the concepts of Internet host names and domains.

[4] Microsoft's Internet Explorer goes even a step further by searching a number of potential top-level domains (specifically, `com`, `edu`, and `org`) if no top-level domain is given for a DNS name.

- *Extensibility*
  The goal of extensibility states that it should always be possible to add new schemes for the identification of information resources. This is necessary to make sure that the definition of URIs has a long lifespan, even if new identification schemes are invented.

- *Completeness*
  Completeness is a goal which is required to make sure that every new scheme for the identification of information resources can be used with URIs.

- *Printability*
  Because URIs are not necessarily exchanged in electronic form only, it must be possible to write down any URI using pen and ink and a rather restricted set of characters (ASCII).

Although these goals may sound rather ambitious and general, it has actually been fairly easy to achieve them. The goal of extensibility is met by splitting the URI definition in two halves, one for the identification scheme and one for the identifier, which is interpreted according to the identification scheme. This way, new identification schemes can easily be added by using a new name in the first half of the URI and defining an interpretation (which is specific for this new identification scheme) of the second half.

The second design requirement, completeness, is met by defining a way how non-printable or, in general, binary strings which have to be used in the second half of URIs, are encoded using a mapping to printable characters. This way, any bit string can be expressed, thus allowing any scheme to be used with URIs.

Defining a safe set of characters and a way to escape unsafe characters is the solution to the printability requirement (the % sign has been chosen to be the escape character, more on this in section 2.2).

After the general design goals have been stated and it is also clear how they can be met, it is interesting to see how URIs are eventually defined. Mainly, there are two questions concerning this definition, and we discuss these questions in the following two sections. These questions are

- what is the *syntax* of URIs (ie, what sequence of characters forms a valid URI and what sequence does not, and what kind of syntactical structure is required for the interpretation of a URI), and

- what are the *semantics* of a valid URI, that is once a URI has been verified to be syntactically valid, where does it point to (in other words, once a URI is selected by a user, what should a browser do to find the identified resource)?

In section 2.2, we give a description of the rather simple syntax of URIs. By definition, a URI is either a *Uniform Resource Name (URN)*, or a *Uniform Resource Locator (URL)*, which is shown in figure 2.2. The semantics of a URI are defined by definitions of URN and URL semantics. According to a common definition first given by Shoch [242], "the name of a resource indicates what we seek and an address indicates where it is". In general, this is true for most resources on the Internet. However, the distinction is not always very clear, because in most cases names already contain some kind of information on where an object can be found, for example by using structured name spaces like the Internet's domain name system described in section 1.4.1.2. However, a certain amount of abstraction should always be used when designing name spaces, in order to be independent from the underlying technology. In many cases, the usage of names involves some kind of naming service, which maps names onto addresses (in the same way as the Internet's domain name system maps Internet host names to IP addresses). Using Shoch's definition, URNs are used to specify the names of information resources, while URLs are used to specify their addresses.

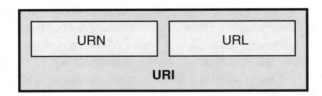

Fig. 2.2   The relationship of URIs, URNs, and URLs

Before we go into the technical details of URNs and URLs in section 2.3, we will give a short motivation of why URLs are not sufficient in the long run. One good example is the URL of a personal home page, which usually points to the web server of the company the home page owner is currently with. There is no other way to do this, because the URL contains (as we will see in section 2.3.2) the name of the server which has to be used for retrieving the page. However, if there was one more indirection, defining the personal home page as a name (ie, a URN), not giving any company specific details in the name, a name service similar to the Internet's domain name service could be used to map this company independent URN to the company specific URL, whenever the home page is accessed.

"A *name* is a symbol – usually a human-readable string – identifying some resource, or set of resources. [...] To be useful, however, there will probably be some mechanism available to the user that will map names into addresses. The name (what we seek) need not be bound to the address (where it is) until this mapping takes place; the address (or addresses) associated with a particular name may change over time."

Shoch [242]

Thus, the home page's URN could remain the same, even when changing the company (or the Internet service provider in case of private home pages), the only entry which needs to be updated would be the mapping in the URN naming service[5]. This scenario is shown in figure 2.3, where a *URN naming service (UNS)* is used for mapping URNs to URLs. How the address of this UNS could be found will be discussed in more detail in section 2.4.

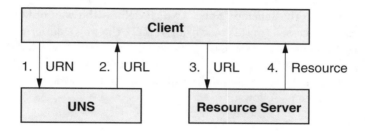

Fig. 2.3   Using a URN naming service (UNS)

There has been and unfortunately still is a lot of confusion about the relation of URIs and URLs. While many specifications contain the term URL (eg, the HTML 3.2 specification [217]), some others contain the term URI (eg, the HTML 4.0 specification [219]), and it is not quite clear whether this difference is intentional in all cases. One solution to this dilemma is to avoid the term URI altogether and to use the term URL everywhere. However, this would eliminate the distinction which has been made between URLs and URNs. The other solution therefore is to use the term URI where it is appropriate (which is the case in almost all places where URL is now being used). The drawback of this approach is that the public knows the term URL, but has no real idea why it should be called URI instead. Up to now, there is no consensus on how to proceed with this problem. Taking the formal definitions, we therefore describe the situation how it is today, giving an overview of URNs in section 2.3.1 and an overview of URLs in section 2.3.2.

---

[5] Internet informational RFC 1900 [42] contains a good description of why naming services should be used. This document is specifically addressing the issue of using IP numbers vs. DNS names, which can be seen as being analogous to the issue of using URLs vs. URNs.

2.2 URI syntax

Internet informational RFC 1630 [17] describes a notation of URIs on a syntactical level, defining which characters have to be used in what way to form a valid URI. The syntax is very simple, with the basic idea being a separation of the URI into two parts, one part coding the identification scheme being used, the other part being the actual identification of the referenced object in a scheme-dependent way. This way it is ensured that URIs can be used with an arbitrary number of schemes.

```
uri = scheme ":" scheme-specific-part
```

Taking the example from above, the URI `http://www.hotbot.com/` can be separated into the scheme "`http`", which defines the way objects in this scheme can be accessed (in this case using HTTP, the web's data transfer protocol), and the scheme specific part "`//www.hotbot.com/`", which defines the actual object being referenced, in this case the root document on the server `www.hotbot.com`. A more general description of the two basic components of URIs can be given as follows:

- *Scheme*
  The scheme of a URI identifies the naming scheme which is used for this particular URI. This part of the URI is separated from the rest of the URI by a colon. Currently, a number of schemes are well defined, and the *Internet Assigned Numbers Authority (IANA)* maintains a list of these schemes and references to their definitions.

- *Scheme specific part*
  The scheme specific part of a URI contains the actual identification of the particular object in a scheme specific way. The interpretation of this part of the URI depends entirely on the scheme being used.

Although the actual syntax of the scheme specific part entirely depends on the scheme of the URI, there are some general rules which have been defined and which have to be followed by all scheme syntaxes.

- *Percent sign*
  The percent sign '%' is used as an escape character in the encoding of URIs and is only used for this purpose. If a percent sign has to be used as a character itself (ie, not as an escape character), it is necessary to use the escaped form of it, which is the character sequence %25 (because the percent sign has the hexadecimal value of 25 in the ASCII character set [8]).

- *Hierarchical forms*

  Because in many cases URIs are used to identify objects which are some-how organized hierarchically, a special character has been reserved (the slash character '/') which can be used to delimit hierarchical substrings of the object's identification. The hierarchy is defined from left to right, meaning the more to the left a substring is, the nearer is the object iden-tified by that substring to the root of the hierarchical structure[6].

  If a slash has to be used as part of a URI, thus not indicating any hier-archical structure, its escaped version (%2F) has to be taken instead of a literal slash.

- *Hash sign*

  The hash sign '#' is used to delimit an object reference from a *fragment identifier*. While the object reference points to a complete object in a given identification scheme, the fragment identifier (if present) points into that object, identifying a specific point inside that object. A common use for this is the identification of different topics or chapters in a longer web page[7].

  If a hash sign has to be used as part of a URI, thus not indicating any fragment identifier pointing into the object, its escaped version (%23) has to be taken instead of a literal hash sign.

- *Query strings*

  Because objects may be queryable (that is, it is possible to submit a query to that object and to get results depending on that query), it is possible to define query strings in URIs. The question mark '?' is used to delimit the boundary between the identification of the object (its URI), and a query on that object.

  The usage of such a URI results in an object which is the result of the query being applied to the object which is identified by the URI part before the '?' character.

  Because queries may often contain spaces (such as strings to be searched for in a database) within the query string, the plus sign '+' is defined as a shorthand notation for a space character. Actual plus signs in the query string must be encoded by using the standard escape mechanism (%2B).

---

[6] This may sound complicated, but it is exactly the same idea as with a file system from an operating system, with the syntax taken from a Unix file system (Win-dows uses backslashes instead). However, it is important to notice that URIs are not file names, only their syntax and structure is similar.

[7] The actual interpretation of the fragment identifier depends on the object's data type. For HTML documents, the fragment identifier identifies an element through its ID attribute as described in section 5.2.2. For XML documents, the fragment identifier has to be an *XPointer* as described in section 7.4.

If a question mark has to be used as part of a URI, thus not indicating any query string for an object, its escaped version (%3F) has to be taken instead of a question mark.

This list of special characters ends the definition of the URI syntax. It can be seen that there is no way of syntactically distinguishing URNs from URLs, this can only be done by interpreting the scheme part of the URI and then deciding whether it is a URN or a URL scheme. It would have been a better approach to make the distinction clear on a syntactical level, from a designer's point of view, but unfortunately this has not been done[8].

Everything we have discussed in this section is used for defining a complete URI, consisting of a scheme and a scheme specific part. However, Internet informational RFC 1630 [17] also describes a partial or relative form of URIs, which can be used inside objects whose URI is well defined. The details of how relative URIs are defined can be found in the RFC, the basic idea is to skip components of the URI which are already defined by the object in which the relative URI is used. These components may be the scheme itself and segments of the scheme specific part.

2.3 URI semantics

As already mentioned in the previous section, the semantics of URIs are defined by the semantics of URNs and URLs. Since it is not possible to differentiate URNs and URLs syntactically, it is always necessary to interpret the scheme part of any given URI in order to decide whether it is a URN or a URL. Currently, URNs are still under development, there is no infrastructure supporting the usage of URNs[9], and therefore the only scheme which is relevant for URNs is the urn scheme, which has been reserved in Internet informational RFC 1630.

2.3.1 Uniform Resource Name (URN)

In Internet informational RFC 1737 [246], the functional requirements for URNs are specified. On a very general level, it is stated that the purpose of a

---

[8] The urn scheme has been reserved for the usage of URNs, but it is possible that other schemes may represent URNs as well, so it is not possible to make the distinction between URNs and URLs without interpreting the URI's scheme part.

[9] A naming service as shown in figure 2.3 (page 41) is necessary if URNs should be used. Such a naming service does not exist at the time of writing and it will, even if there is a technical solution, take a while to establish the infrastructure which is necessary to provide a reliable naming service for URNs on a world-wide scale.

URN is to provide a globally unique, persistent identifier for a resource. This identifier should be usable for recognition, access to characteristics of the resource, or for access to the resource itself. More specifically, the following functional capabilities are listed:

- *Global scope*
  A URN should not imply a location, and it should have the same meaning everywhere.

- *Global uniqueness*
  It must be made sure that the same URN will never be assigned to two different resources.

- *Persistence*
  A URN is intended to be persistent, so the only reason for it to cease to exist should be its explicit deletion. Neither the deletion of the resource, nor its relocation should affect its URN. Furthermore, the lifetime of a URN should also not depend on the lifetime of a naming authority involved in its creation.

- *Scalability*
  URNs can be assigned to any resource which is available on the net, and they might be available for a very long time.

- *Legacy support*
  There are already a number of naming systems in use, such as ISBN numbers, ISO public identifiers, or UPC product codes. URNs must be able to support these naming systems by embedding them into the syntactic requirements of URNs.

- *Extensibility*
  Since new applications for URNs will emerge after a scheme has been defined, any scheme must allow future extensions.

- *Independence*
  Naming authorities should be independent from each other, which means that it should be solely the responsibility of a name issuing authority to determine the conditions under which it will issue a name.

- *Resolution*
  Since URNs specify names, there must be a resolution mechanism mapping these names onto addresses.

The conclusions from these functional requirements are that there must exist a concept of hierarchical naming authorities, and that there should be support for hierarchical naming, although this is not absolutely necessary.

As a first step towards a general concept of URNs, Internet proposed standard RFC 2141 [176] defines a URN syntax. This syntax takes into account the implications of Internet informational RFC 1630 [17] (defining the more general URI syntax), and Internet informational RFC 1737 [246] (defining the functional requirements for URNs).

```
<URN> ::= "urn:" <NID> ":" <NSS>
```

This convention for URNs uses urn as the URI scheme, and defines the scheme specific part (as defined in the URI syntax) to be specified by a *Namespace Identifier (NID)* and a *Namespace Specific String (NSS)*, separated by a colon. Based on this syntactic framework, Internet informational RFC 2276 [245] defines a two step process of URN resolution, using a *Resolver Discovery Service (RDS)*. Based on this model, getting to the resource identified by a URN involves two major steps, which are shown in figure 2.4 (this figure can be seen as a more detailed view of the model shown in figure 2.3).

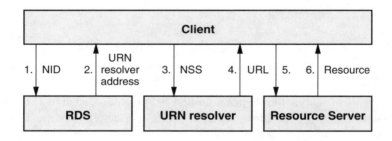

Fig. 2.4   Using RDS and a URN resolver service

- *Contacting the RDS*
  In order to resolve a URN, RDS must be contacted to learn about the resolver service for a particular NID.

- *Contacting the URN resolver*
  Contacting the URN resolver service for the NID specified in the URN, it is possible to perform the resolution of the URN's NSS part.

This process is reflected in the URN syntax. The first part of the syntax defines a URI to be a URN (specifying the urn scheme), which means that RDS must be used to find the URN resolver service for this specific URN scheme. The second part of the URN, the NID, identifies the URN name space, and RDS provides the URN resolution process with a service access point of the URN resolver service for this name space. This URN resolver service can be used to resolve the NSS. The final result of this process is the address of the resource associated with the URN.

Currently, Internet experimental RFC 2168 [60] describes a RDS model based on DNS. It is implemented by adding a new DNS resource record, *Naming Authority Pointer (NAPTR)*, that provides rules for mapping parts of URIs to be mapped onto host addresses which should be contacted to resolve a URI. The possible resolution protocols specified in RFC 2168 are

- *Information Retrieval (Z39.50)* as standardized by ANSI [9],

- *Trivial HTTP (THTTP)* as described in Internet experimental RFC 2169 [59],

- the *Resource Cataloging and Distribution System (RCDS)* as described by Moore et al. [184], and

- the *Handle Resolution Protocol* as specified for the *Handle System* [258].

However, the infrastructure for resolving (and therefore using) URNs is in a very early stage, and it is not quite clear what infrastructure will be used (or created) in the long run. However, it is clear that there is a requirement to have such an infrastructure which can be used to use URNs instead of URLs.

2.3.2 Uniform Resource Locator (URL)

In Internet proposed standards RFC 1738 and 1808 [21, 77], the syntax and semantics of URLs and relative URLs are defined. In general, a URL (being a special form of a URI) consists of a *scheme* and a *scheme specific part*, and the URL definition defines a specific syntax for the scheme specific part, as well as a number of possible values for the scheme. The scheme specific part is defined to have the following syntax.

```
"//" [ user [ ":" password ] "@" ] host [ ":" port ] "/" url-path
```

In this definition, a number of components are present, which (based on the actual scheme being used for a URL) have the following semantics.

- user
  The user part of the URL can be omitted. For some Internet schemes, it does not make sense, in other cases it may not be advisable to include this information inside a URL.

- password
  Because the password is even more sensitive information than a user name, this part can also be omitted, even if a user name is given. It is also possible

to specify an empty password, in which case the colon behind the user name is directly followed by the at-sign preceding the host name.

- host
  The host name can either be given as a fully qualified domain name, or as an IP address in its decimal form. Fully qualified domain names have to be specified as defined in Internet standards RFC 1034 [177] and RFC 1123 [29].

- port
  This part is also optional, because most Internet schemes have a default port number to connect to. Thus, port numbers are only necessary for Internet schemes with no default ports and for hosts which run standard services on non-standard ports (which generally is not advisable).

- url-path
  The rest of the URL, known as the URL path, consists of data specific to the scheme. It specifies how the resource can be accessed on the specified host.

In addition to the syntax and interpretation of the scheme specific part, it is defined how different components of the scheme specific part are interpreted for a number of schemes. Currently, a number of schemes are well defined, and the *Internet Assigned Numbers Authority (IANA)* maintains a list of these schemes and references to their definitions. Some of the schemes included in RFC 1738 are described in the following list:

- ftp
  This scheme is used to reference files which are accessible using the Internet *File Transfer Protocol (FTP)* as specified in Internet standard RFC 959 [207]. A user name and a password may be supplied in the URL, they are used when connecting to the FTP server. If no user name is given, the conventions for anonymous FTP should be used[10]. If no port is specified, the default port number of 21 is used.

- http
  References to this scheme are used for accessing information which is available using the *Hypertext Transfer Protocol (HTTP)* which is described in detail in chapter 3. The user name and the password part of the general scheme are not applicable in case of HTTP URLs, so it is only possible to specify a host, a port number, and a URL path. If the port number is omitted, its default of 80 is used.

---

[10] The conventions for anonymous FTP sessions are to use a user name of "anonymous" and the user's Internet email address as the password.

- `https`
  In case of this scheme, *HTTP over SSL* is used for the transmission of data. This is the standard HTTP protocol used over a secure transport infrastructure (using data encryption techniques, more information can be found in section 3.3.1). Since the transport protocol remains the same (HTTP), the semantics of this type of URL is the same as for ordinary HTTP URLs, except for the secure infrastructure being used. If no port is specified, it defaults to 443.

- `news`
  The news URL scheme refers to newsgroups or to individual articles of Usenet news as defined in Internet RFC 1036 [99]. Because a newsgroup or a news article do not have a location, the news URL scheme does not specify a host. The only things which are part of the news scheme is either the name of the newsgroup, or the message identification of an individual news article.

- `nntp`
  There is a way to specifically refer to an news article on a particular server, and this is the `nntp` URL scheme. The *Network News Transfer Protocol (NNTP)* as defined in Internet proposed standard RFC 977 [146] is the protocol which is used for the exchange of Usenet news between servers. It can therefore be used to access individual articles on a particular server. The host part of the location is mandatory, the port specification can be omitted and defaults to 119. The URL path identifies the name of the newsgroup and the number of the article.

- `mailto`
  This scheme is used to specify the Internet mailing address of an individual or a service. The email address has to be specified according to Internet standard RFC 822 [53]. Because this does not really designate an object, there is no need for a location to be specified. Any program encountering a URL of this scheme should prompt the user for the message content and parameters and then send it to the Internet mailing address, using either the *Simple Mail Transfer Protocol (SMTP)* as defined in Internet standard RFC 821 [211], or the *Extended Simple Mail Transfer Protocol (ESMTP)* as defined in Internet standard RFC 1869 [149].

- `telnet`
  The `telnet` URL scheme is used to refer to interactive services that may be accessed by the Telnet protocol as defined in Internet standard RFC 854 [212]. Since most Telnet services require identification and passwords, the user name and the password part of the URL scheme can be used to specify information for access to a particular service. The host part of

the address is mandatory, while the port specification can be omitted and
defaults to 23.

- ldap
  This scheme defines a method to query an directory server[11] using the
  Lightweight Directory Access Protocol (LDAP) as defined in Internet proposed standard RFC 1959 [102] (it is described in section 11.2.2). The host
  part of the address is optional, if there is no host part, any LDAP server
  may be contacted, otherwise the LDAP server specified in the host part
  has to be contacted. The port specification can be omitted and defaults
  to 389.

Using this definition of URL semantics, it is rather simple to interpret a
given URL. However, it is always necessary to know the specific scheme in
order to correctly interpret the scheme specific part. The list of known and
widely used schemes is constantly growing, and implementations supporting
the use of URLs should make sure that the most popular URLs are supported
or at least understood.

2.4 The future of URI

As described in section 2.3.1, an infrastructure is under construction which
should finally provide a productive service for URN resolution. To accomplish
this, Internet experimental RFC 2168 [60] describes a *Resolver Discovery Service (RDS)* for which recently a proposal has been published by Mealling [172]
defining a part of the look-up algorithm. RDS is a resolution service which is
used to locate URN resolution services. One possible URN resolution services,
based on *Trivial HTTP (THTTP)*, is described in Internet experimental RFC
2169 [59]. However, this area of work is still under construction, and is not
yet clear which will be the final solution for URN resolution.

Internet draft documents by Daigle et al. [58] and Mealling [172] show a
possible path to establishing an infrastructure for URN resolution. However,
there are some systems which are already implementing working solutions
such as the *Handle System* or the *Persistent URL (PURL)* approach, but it
remains an open question how they can be integrated into a uniform URI
scheme.

Although the discussion in this chapter focuses on URIs, URNs, and
URLs, it should not remain unmentioned that the design of a URN resolution service also involves the concept of *Uniform Resource Characteristics*

---

[11] It is not required that the directory server contacted with LDAP is actually an
X.500 server, it can also be a stand-alone server or a server running a different
directory system.

(URC). When resolving a URN, the client can either request the address (ie, URL) of the resource, or it can request information about the resource, such as its owner, copyright information, information about potential usage fees, and more meta data of the resource. All this meta data of the resource is contained in the URC. However, URCs are still under construction, and there is currently no standard for them. But as the work on web meta data goes on, for example with the *Resource Description Framework (RDF)* described in section 10.5.3, it is likely that URCs will receive more attention in the near future.

3. Hypertext Transfer Protocol (HTTP)

Basically, the World Wide Web is a distributed hypermedia system, with information stored in the form of web pages, which are linked to each other using web links (better known by their official names URI or URL). This property of the web makes it necessary to have a means of accessing remote information from any system retrieving information from the web's database (which is formed by all web pages which are available world wide). This method of accessing remote information is the *Hypertext Transfer Protocol (HTTP)*, which is one of the key components of the web. The underlying model of the protocol is that of a client/server architecture, where the client wants to retrieve some information from the web and contacts a web server to do so.

Although a normal web user never directly gets in touch with HTTP, it frequently shows up even for users, such as when a request for some resource results in a 404 (not found) status code (probably the best known part of HTTP for most users), which in fact is a status code of the response which has been sent by the server which could not find the requested resource. Next to HTML, HTTP is the component of the web architecture which is closest to the user. Many interactions with a browser, such as setting communication preferences or simply clicking on an anchor in a document, have direct impact on the HTTP messages a browser generates.

Besides being of interest to anyone who wants to know how the web works internally (ie, what information is and can be transferred between a client and a server), knowledge of HTTP is important for web server administrators as well as for programmers of *Common Gateway Interface (CGI)* It is also important for content providers to know the functionality of HTTP in order to be able to asses which kind of services can be implemented using HTTP.

This chapter describes many aspects of HTTP, beginning with a brief history in section 3.1. In section 3.2, the latest version of HTTP (called HTTP/1.1) is discussed in detail. Although not being an integral part of HTTP itself, there are two issues which are tightly coupled with HTTP. The first one is a discussion of approaches and current practices to add security features to HTTP, which is given in section 3.3. The other issue is the mechanism of so-called *cookies*, described in section 3.4, which is used to compensate for the stateless nature of HTTP.

Because a theoretical discussion of a communications protocol is rather static and abstract, compared to the dynamic way in which it is used for transferring data, section 3.5 gives a short overview over some typical figures for HTTP usage on the web. Furthermore, some non-standard extensions are in wide use, although they are not part of any HTTP standard. These extensions are described in section 3.6.

As almost all components making up the web's infrastructure, HTTP is under constant development, although HTTP/1.1 is supposed to have a longer lifespan that it predecessor, HTTP/1.0. We review a few of the approaches to future directions of HTTP and the environment in which it will be used in section 3.7.

3.1 History

The initial design of HTTP (which was one of the three basic components of the web architecture, consisting of URL, HTML, and HTTP specifications) focused on a protocol which was easy to implement and enabled the retrieval of simple, text-based documents from a server. The two major design goals can be given as follows.

- *Light protocol*
  The protocol should be light in a sense that it can easily be implemented in servers and clients, and that its processing does not consume large amounts of resources on a server or a client.

- *Fast protocol*
  Since the web's model of data distribution results in a large number of documents being spread out over a large number of servers, the protocol should be as fast as possible to facilitate quick retrieval of information.

These goals have remained the same until today. However, because of the web's growth and the amount of information which is transferred using HTTP, now also efficiency and management issues are of great concern. In the following sections, we shortly describe the HTTP versions and their features and disadvantages. Section 3.1.1 describes the very first version of HTTP, which, although being extremely simple, laid the foundations for today's success of the web. The next version, HTTP/1.0, is described in section 3.1.2, this version looks very similar to the HTTP version of today, but it still had some severe drawbacks. Finally, section 3.1.3 describes the HTTP version of today, which is HTTP/1.1.

3.1.1 HTTP/0.9

The first protocol version was simply called HTTP (without a version number) and the specification of the whole protocol, although never formally approved by (or even submitted to) any organization, consisted only of a few pages. This version now is often referred to as HTTP/0.9. It only supported the GET method, and a client would simply open a connection to the server and send a line consisting of the keyword GET and the document name (separated by a space character). The server responded with the document itself and closed the connection to signal the end of the document.

However, after the web rapidly became more widespread and it became apparent that it would be a truly large-scale application, the shortcomings of HTTP/0.9 were rather obvious. The most severe limitations were the inability to transmit anything but text documents (HTTP/0.9 did not include the concept of media types), and the inability for a client to transmit data to a server. In HTTP/0.9, the server simply responded with the requested document, so there was no way to transmit any information about the request (such as error codes) or about the document.

3.1.2 HTTP/1.0

In an effort to overcome the limitations of HTTP/0.9, HTTP/1.0 was developed, starting in 1992. However, a final version of it was never released until May 1996, and even then HTTP/1.0, published as Internet informational RFC 1945 [20], was not intended to be a standard document, it was only an informational document. It just documented what had been implemented by the major client and server programmers in addition to the basic HTTP/0.9 specification. RFC 1945 specified both HTTP/0.9 and HTTP/1.0, but it was clear that it should soon be replaced with a newer version of the protocol.

However, HTTP/1.0 was a big improvement over HTTP/0.9. It included the concept of media types (it adopted the *Multipurpose Internet Mail Extensions (MIME)*, which already described a framework for the identification and the exchange of information using different media types), and enabled the server to respond with more than only the entity, including information about the entity (such as its media type). HTTP/1.0 in general defined a versatile message format, consisting of an initial line and a variable number of lines consisting header fields. These header fields could be used to pass information between the client and the server and back.

Another improvement was, among other new methods in addition to the GET method which was the only one defined in HTTP/0.9, the POST method, which enabled clients to transmit information to servers. Furthermore, with the new structured response format, the server could include status codes in its response and therefore could include helpful information if a request failed.

HTTP/1.0 also introduced the concept of user authentication, which is the idea of restricted access to resources and a mechanism how users could authenticate themselves in order to make authorization checks possible. The mechanism defined in HTTP/1.0 was basic authentication, which is still part of the HTTP standard.

On the network side, however, HTTP/1.0 did not change much, it was still based on the model of a single request/response interaction per connection and required the server to close the connection after sending the request. This model resulted in serious performance problems described by Spero [249], mainly caused by the slow start mechanism of TCP[1]. It became clear that the next version of HTTP would have to include improvements of this model of request/response interactions.

It also became a problem that initially never had been thought of, that HTTP/1.0 did not support non IP-based virtual hosts (the concept of virtual hosts is described in detail in section 9.2.2), because the server had no way to find out for which of the virtual hosts a particular request was sent. This resulted in the necessity to use IP-based virtual hosts, which for large hosts meant a large number of IP numbers which had to be assigned to one computer or network interface. This not only increased the problem of the shortage of available IP numbers, but also led to problems with some routers.

Other areas where weaknesses of HTTP/1.0 became apparent were the primitive caching model, the lack of support for partial transfer of entities, and the very insecure basic authentication mechanism.

3.1.3 HTTP/1.1

One of the areas where an improvement of HTTP/1.0 was absolutely necessary was the model of request/response interactions, which was too simple and led to inefficient usage of resources. Several ways to approach this problem and to achieve better efficiency were discussed during the creation of the next version of HTTP, a few of them are described in a paper by Heidemann et al. [95]. The two major contenders for the future model of request/response interactions were *Persistent HTTP (P-HTTP)* and *HTTP over Transaction TCP (T/TCP)*.

---

[1] The TCP slow start mechanism is intended to avoid the flooding of network resources when a new TCP connection is opened. It is described in an early paper by Jacobson and Karels [143] and a recent Internet document by Stevens [257].

- *Persistent HTTP (P-HTTP)*
  The basic idea of P-HTTP is to keep an connection open after a request/response interaction and to wait whether other requests have to be sent to the same server. This effectively reduces the number of times a TCP connection has to be closed and opened again.

- *HTTP over Transaction TCP (T/TCP)*
  In this approach, the trasnport connection is still closed after a single request/response interaction, but the usage of *Transaction TCP (T/TCP)* as described by Braden [31, 32] rather than raw TCP reduces much of the inefficiency of making several connections in a row to the same server[2].

Finally, the model of persistent connections was chosen and incorporated into the new version of HTTP, which was released in January 1997 as HTTP/1.1 in the document Internet proposed standard RFC 2068 [75]. HTTP/1.1 improves HTTP/1.0 in many ways and is expected to be in use much longer use than its predecessor. The major changes of HTTP/1.1 are given in the following list.

- *Supporting the* Host *header field*
  A new header field has been introduced which is necessary for the support of non IP-based virtual hosts. The Host header field is used by a client to specify for which host a request is being sent.

- *Reporting an error if the* Host *header field is missing*
  The new Host header field only makes sense if its use is mandatory. Otherwise servers using a non IP-based virtual hosts configuration have no way to find out for which host a particular request has been sent. Therefore a request without a Host header field gets an error response.

- *Accepting absolute URIs in requests*
  In HTTP/1.0, it was only legal to use absolute URIs in requests if the request was sent to a proxy. Now absolute URIs can also be used in requests to servers and can be used to identify the host name on a server using virtual hosts.

- *New request methods*
  A number of new request methods are defined, which greatly increase the functionality of HTTP/1.1. The new request methods defined in HTTP/1.1 are DELETE, OPTIONS, PUT, and TRACE[3].

---

[2] For a general description of transaction processing applications and their special requirements, see Internet RFC 955 [28] for a detailed discussion of the concepts.

[3] The DELETE and PUT methods are already mentioned in the HTTP/1.0 specification, but they are not part of it, they are only listed for informational purposes because they were implemented in some systems using HTTP/1.0.

- *Supporting the transfer of partial entities*
  Clients can now request parts of entities by explicitly specifying byte
  ranges of a resource they want to receive. This is particularly useful if the
  transfer of a large resource has been interrupted, and the client wants to
  request the remaining part of it.

- *Content negotiation*
  Content negotiation is an which is used to make a selection between different representations for a resource. Different representations can be characterized by language, quality, encoding, or other parameters which do
  not affect the content of a resource.

- *Introduction of chunked encoding*
  With the introduction of persistent connections, the length of a resource
  can no longer be implicitly signaled by closing the connection. However,
  for the majority of resources, the length is known in advance. For all other
  resources (such as dynamically created content), chunked encoding can be
  used.

- *More sophisticated support for caching*
  Caching in HTTP/1.0 was much to simple to be used on a large scale.
  HTTP/1.1 introduces a sophisticated caching model, which allows servers
  and proxies detailed control over how caching should be performed for
  particular resources.

- *More secure authentication scheme*
  In addition to the very insecure basic authentication method of HTTP/1.0,
  a digest access authentication method is defined, which eliminates the
  clear text transmission of the user name and password.

In November 1997, a first revision of the specification of HTTP/1.1 was
published. In March 1998, the latest revision has been published, which can
be referred to as HTTP/1.1 revision 03 [76]. Since newer versions of HTTP
are likely to be based on the revised version of HTTP/1.1, we took this latest
version of HTTP/1.1 as the reference for our description of HTTP/1.1 in the
following section.

3.2 Hypertext Transfer Protocol 1.1 (HTTP/1.1)

HTTP is a rather simple request/response protocol, based on a reliable,
connection-oriented transport service. As such, it uses the roles of *clients*
(sending requests) and *servers* (sending responses). Figure 3.1 shows the
most basic HTTP operation, where a client sends a request directly to a
server, which replies with a response.

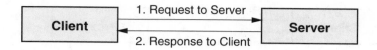

Fig. 3.1 Basic HTTP operation

In addition to these two basic roles, intermediaries may be present in the request/response chain. HTTP defines *proxies*, *gateways*, and *tunnels* to be common forms of intermediaries. However, it is important to notice that these roles are not static and not exclusive, which means that any program may switch roles, and any program may have more than one of these roles at a time. These roles are only static for a single HTTP request/response interaction.

- *Client*
  A client is a program that establishes connections for the purpose of sending requests. Typically, a client will be a WWW browser, but it may also be a search engine (an automated client which searches the web for information without user interaction, for more information see section 10.3) or some other sort of program.

- *Server*
  Any program accepting connections in order to service requests by sending back responses is a server. A server has to interpret and understand the contents of a request.

- *Proxy*
  A proxy is an intermediary program which acts as both a server and a client, receiving a request and then acting as a client and making requests on behalf of other clients. However, requests to a proxy can also be serviced internally, for example if the proxy uses its cache (see section 3.2.9 for a detailed discussion of caching) instead of sending a request to the origin server[4]. Figure 3.2 shows how a proxy is used in an HTTP operation. It is worth noticing that the client's request is explicitly addressed to the proxy, which then sends a request to the origin server.

- *Gateway*
  A gateway is a program which also acts as an intermediary for some other server, therefore it is similar to a proxy. However, a client sending a request to a gateway does not know that it is not communicating with the origin server, while a client communicating with a proxy does so explicitly.

---

[4] An *origin server* is a server on which a given resource resides or is to be created, depending on the nature of the request.

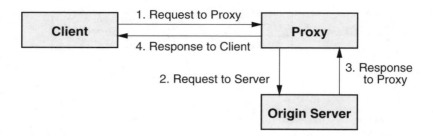

Fig. 3.2   HTTP operation involving a proxy

- *Tunnel*
  Unlike a proxy or a gateway, a tunnel is a program which acts as a blind intermediary program for HTTP communication, which means that it does not interpret or understand (and therefore also not modify) passing messages. In figure 3.3 it can be seen that the tunnel only forwards the request sent by the client and the response sent by the server.

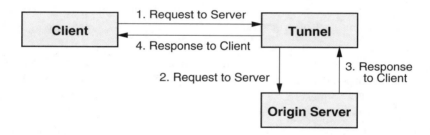

Fig. 3.3   HTTP operation involving a tunnel

Although being simple in principle, HTTP has evolved to a state where it is not so easy to understand the protocol with all its options and many ways to use it. The basic interaction of HTTP is sending a message, which can either be a request or a response. We describe the general format of HTTP messages in section 3.2.1 and the parts of messages which are common to requests and responses (general and entity headers) in section 3.2.2. Requests with their methods and specific header fields are described in section 3.2.3. Responses with their status codes and specific header fields are described in section 3.2.4

Since many of the concepts of HTTP can not be explained only from the point of view of messages, we describe the most important concepts of HTTP in individual sections. Readers who are not concerned with the exact details of how HTTP works, but are looking for an overview of the important concepts behind the actual message formats, should consider reading these sections first and only refer to the more detailed message format section when necessary.

In section 3.2.5, content negotiation is explained. This is the procedure which is used to agree on a particular resource, if a request could be answered with different resources (such as different language version of a page). Authentication, the method to grant access only to authorized users after their successful identification, is explained in section 3.2.6. Section 3.2.7 describes how connections between a client and a server are handled. The introduction of persistent messages made it necessary to define a new type of transfer encoding for resources of which the length is not known in advance. This transfer encoding is called chunked encoding and described in section 3.2.8. Finally, caching is described in section 3.2.9, which is a technique for improving the efficiency of the web.

3.2.1 Messages

HTTP has a very simple interaction scheme between the client and the server, it consists of a *request*, which is sent from the client to a server, and a *response*, which is sent by the server to the client. The format of both message types is also very simple, they are messages according to RFC 822 [53] (which defines the way text messages are sent on the Internet), consisting of a `start-line`, zero or more `message-header` fields (which can also be called *headers*), an empty line, and an optional `message-body` (which, if present, contains the so-called *entity* of the message). According to the standard, any HTTP message therefore looks like this:

```
generic-message =
  start-line
  *message-header
  CRLF
  [ message-body ]

start-line =
  request-line | status-line
```

The start line of a message is either a `request-line` (if the HTTP message is a *request*, described in detail in section 3.2.3), or a `status-line` (if the HTTP message is a *response*, described in detail in section 3.2.4). Following the start line, HTTP messages also contain zero or more message header fields, which can be grouped into four different message header field types:

- *General headers*
  General headers apply to both request and response messages, and they do not apply to the entity being transferred.

- *Entity headers*
  If the entity being transferred by a request or response needs to be described by some meta information[5], this can be done by using entity headers in the message being sent. If no message body (ie, no entity) is present, the information given in the entity headers describes the resource identified by the request.

- *Request headers*
  The purpose of request headers is to allow the client to pass information about the request, and about the client itself, to the server. They do not contain any information about the message body (ie, the entity of the message).

- *Response headers*
  Response headers are used by the server to pass any information which can not be given in the status line (discussed in detail in section 3.2.4). They do not contain any information about the message body (ie, the entity of the message).

In table 3.1, all header fields currently defined in HTTP/1.1[6] are listed together with their type (general, request, response, or entity) and a reference to the page where they are described in detail. In the following sections, we have grouped the headers according to their type. General and entity headers are described in section 3.2.2, request headers in section 3.2.3.2, and response headers in section 3.2.4.2.

3.2.2 General and entity headers

General and entity headers can be used in request and in response messages. While general headers, described in section 3.2.2.1, do not apply to an entity being transferred inside a message, entity headers, described in section 3.2.2.2, are used for information about the entity being transferred or the resource being identified by the request.

3.2.2.1 General headers

General headers apply only to the message being transmitted and have general applicability for both request and response messages. They do not apply to the entity being transferred.

---

[5] The term meta information refers to information about the entity, such as its encoding or length, and not its actual content.

[6] The `Alternates`, `Content-Version`, `Derived-From`, `Link`, `URI`, `Public`, and `Content-Base` header fields were part of the first version of the HTTP/1.1 specification, but have been removed from the latest revisions of the specification.

Table 3.1 Overview of HTTP/1.1 header fields

Header field name	Header field type	Page
Accept	request	74
Accept-Charset	request	75
Accept-Encoding	request	75
Accept-Language	request	75
Accept-Ranges	response	82
Age	response	83
Allow	entity	66
Authorization	request	76
Cache-Control	general	64
Connection	general	64
Content-Base	entity	66
Content-Encoding	entity	66
Content-Language	entity	67
Content-Length	entity	67
Content-Location	entity	67
Content-MD5	entity	67
Content-Range	entity	68
Content-Type	entity	68
Date	general	64
ETag	entity	68
Expect	request	76
Expires	entity	68
From	request	76
Host	request	76
If-Match	request	77
If-Modified-Since	request	76
If-None-Match	request	77
If-Range	request	78
If-Unmodified-Since	request	78
Last-Modified	entity	68
Location	response	83
MIME-Version	general	64
Max-Forwards	request	78
Pragma	general	64
Proxy-Authenticate	response	83
Proxy-Authorization	request	78
Range	request	79
Referer	request	79
Retry-After	response	84
Server	response	84
TE	request	79
Trailer	general	65
Transfer-Encoding	general	65
Upgrade	general	65
User-Agent	request	80
Vary	response	84
Via	general	65
Warning	response	84
WWW-Authenticate	response	85

- Cache-Control

  The Cache-Control header field is used for specifying directives which must be obeyed by all caching systems sending a message including these fields. The purpose of the caching information is to instruct all caching systems what to do with a particular message. Since caching is a complex issue in HTTP/1.1, we have dedicated an entire section to it, which explains the general idea of caching and how it is used in HTTP. Consequently, details about this header field can be found in section 3.2.9

- Connection

  This header field allows the sender (either client or server) to specify options which should be applied to a particular connection, which means that it must not be communicated by proxies over further connections. Each proxy must therefore parse the Connection header field and, for each token in this field, remove any header fields from the message with the same name as the token. In addition to the tokens referring to particular header fields, HTTP/1.1 defines the close connection option, which indicates that the sender wants to close the connection after the response in completed. Clients or servers that do not support persistent connections (as described in section 3.2.7) must include the close connection option in every message.

- Date

  This field is used to indicate when the message originated, that is when the entity which is included in the message has been generated. The Date header field is required to be included in responses except in very few cases where the server can not generate a reliable date field. Clients should only send a Date header field in a request including an entity, and even then it is optional.

- MIME-Version

  Strictly speaking, HTTP is not a MIME-compliant protocol (MIME is described in section 1.4.3.2). However, it is possible for the creator of an HTTP message to indicate what version of MIME was used to create the message. Use of this header field indicates that the HTTP message is in full compliance with the MIME protocol version specified in the MIME-Version header field.

- Pragma

  This header field is used to specify implementation-specific directives that may apply to any recipient along the request/response chain. For backwards compatibility with HTTP/1.0, the no-cache directive is defined, which is identical to an HTTP/1.1 Cache-Control: no-cache header. No new Pragma directives will be defined in HTTP.

- Trailer

  The `Trailer` header field is used to indicate that the specified header fields are present in the trailer of a message encoded with chunked transfer coding. It is defined as a sequence of field names. The purpose of this is to allow the recipient to know which header fields to expect in the trailer.

- Transfer-Encoding

  Since a message body can be encoded before transferring it over an HTTP connection, this can be indicated using the `Transfer-Encoding` header field. Popular uses of this field are the `chunked` directive, indicating that a message body is sent as a series of chunks, and the `gzip` directive, indicating that the message body is encoded according to the *gzip file format* as specified in Internet informational RFC 1952 [63]. The *Internet Assigned Numbers Authority (IANA)* acts as a registry for possible values for the `Transfer-Encoding` header field[7].

- Upgrade

  This header field can be used by a client to indicate what additional communication protocols it supports and would like to use if the server also supports these protocols and wants to switch protocols. The server has to use this header field in a `101 (switching protocols)` response, indicating which protocols are being switched. A possible future use of this header field is a client using it with the `HTTP/2.0` directive within an HTTP/1.1 request, indicating that the client is willing to switch to a newer version of HTTP, if it is supported by the server.

- Via

  Gateways and proxies must use this header field to indicate the intermediate protocols and recipients of a message. The purpose of this header field is to allow the tracking of messages (including protocol capabilities). This can be used to avoid loops and to have an easy way to find out what happens with a particular request or response. Each intermediary adds one `Via` header field, so that the recipient of a message can easily reconstruct the message's way through different systems.

General header fields can only extended reliably with a change in the protocol version, because unrecognized header field names by default are treated as entity headers. However, if all parties in a closed environment agree on a new general header field, it can be used without a change in the protocol version.

---

[7] These encoding types are also used for the `Content-Encoding` entity header described in section 3.2.2.2 and the `Accept-Encoding` request header described in section 3.2.3.2.

3.2.2.2 Entity headers

Entity header fields define information about the entity body (contained in
the message) or, if no body is present, about the resource which is identified
by the request (the most common example for this is the response to a HEAD
request, which will only contain the information about the entity, but not the
entity itself).

- Allow

  The Allow header field is used to transmit to the recipient a list of methods (such as GET or HEAD as described in detail in section 3.2.3.1) which
  is supported for a particular resource. A server must use this field if it
  returns a 405 (method not allowed) response. A client can not be prevented from trying other methods, although it is specified that it should
  not do so.

- Content-Base

  Since entities may contain relative URIs, the recipient of an entity must
  have a well-defined way of resolving these URIs. The Content-Base
  header field is used to specify the base URI for resolving relative URIs
  within the entity. If no Content-Base header field is present, the base URI
  is defined either by its Content-Location (which is another entity header
  field) or the URI used to initiate the request. It is also important to notice
  that the base URI of an entity may also be redefined within that entity,
  in case of HTML with a <BASE> element as described in section 5.2.3.1.

- Content-Encoding

  The Content-Encoding header field indicates what type of encoding has
  been applied to the message body. It is therefore necessary to apply the
  corresponding decoding mechanism in order to obtain the media type
  referenced in the Content-Type header field described below. The *Internet
  Assigned Numbers Authority (IANA)* acts as a registry for possible values
  for the Content-Encoding header field[8]. Usually, a content encoding is
  used for an entity for storage on the server, for example in order to save
  storage space[9]. If multiple codings have been applied to an entity, they
  must be listed in the order in which they have been applied.

---

[8] These encoding types are also used for the Transfer-Encoding general header
described in section 3.2.2.1 and the Accept-Encoding request header described
in section 3.2.3.2.

[9] This distinguishes the Content-Encoding of an entity from the
Transfer-Encoding described in section 3.2.2.1, which usually is only applied for the transfer of an entity.

- Content-Language

  For entities which contain any language (in most cases written or spoken), this header field indicates the natural language(s) of the intended audience. This does not necessarily include all languages used within the entity. Languages are specified by language tags as defined in Internet proposed standard RFC 1766 [7], consisting of primary tags and optional subtags. Any two letter primary tag is a language abbreviation according to ISO 639 [112], and any two-letter initial subtag is a country code according to ISO 3166 [128][10].

- Content-Length

  The Content-Length header field is used to specify the size of the message body in decimal number of octets, or in case of a response to a request using the HEAD method as described in section 3.2.3.1, the size of the message body that would have been sent had the request been a GET. If persistent connection as described in section 3.2.7 should be used, it is absolutely necessary that both client and server specify the length of any entity sent.

- Content-Location

  If the entity returned by a server is accessible from a location separate from the requested resource's URI, the server should identify this location within a Content-Location header field. This is useful in cases where a resource has multiple entities associated with it (such as different language variants of a web page), and the server chooses one of these entities depending on the request. If no Content-Base header field is present, the Content-Location also defines the base URI for the entity. The Content-Location does not specify a replacement for a particular URI, but it can be used in future requests if the client wants to access this particular entity rather than the resource associated with the original URI.

- Content-MD5

  The Content-MD5 header field, as defined by Internet draft standard RFC 1864 [186], contains a MD5 digest of the entity body. This makes it possible to perform an end-to-end integrity check of the entity, making sure that it has not been altered on its way from the origin server to the client. This is useful in detecting accidental modifications of the message body, but can not be seen as a security feature[11].

---

[10] Language tags are also used in the Accept-Language request header described in section 3.2.3.2.

[11] A malicious attack could easily be performed by altering the entity body and inserting the MD5 digest of the altered body in the Content-MD5 header field.

- Content-Range
  Since HTTP/1.1 allows the transfer of partial entities, there has to be a
  way to indicate where a partial entity body has to be inserted in the full
  entity body. Basically, there are two possibilities. If the returned partial
  entity body consists of one byte range, the position and the length of the
  partial entity body is specified by the Content-Range header field. If the
  returned partial entity body consists of multiple ranges, the MIME type
  multipart/byteranges has to be used, and each of the multiple byte
  ranges in this format contains its own Content-Range field[12].

- Content-Type
  The Content-Type header field identifies the media type of the enclosed
  entity. In case of a response to a request using the HEAD method as described in section 3.2.3.1, it contains the media type of the message body
  that would have been sent had the request been a GET. It is important to
  remember that the actual encoding of the entity may be different than indicated by the Content-Type header field because of additional encodings
  which have been applied to the entity body[13].

- ETag
  If the entity is associated with a validator (as described in section 3.2.9.3),
  the ETag header field contains the tag which is used as a validator. The
  entity tag may be used for comparison with other entities from the same
  resource. It is also used in the If-Match, If-None-Match, and If-Range
  request header fields described in section 3.2.3.2.

- Expires
  The Expires header field is used to specify the date and time after which
  an entity should be considered stale. After this time, any cache should not
  return a copy of the entity but validate it first. A complete description of
  this procedure can be found in section 3.2.9.3, which describes the validation model of HTTP. The Expires header field should always contain
  an absolute date and time specified according to the format specified in
  Internet standard RFC 1123 [29]. If a Cache-Control header field using a
  max-age directive (as described in detail in section 3.2.9.4) is also present
  in a response, it overrides the Expires header field.

- Last-Modified
  This is a header field which should be included in a response whenever
  possible. The Last-Modified header field indicates the date and time at

---

[12] And possibly other fields, such as identification of the media type with a
Content-Type field.
[13] The two possibilities for such an encoding are a Transfer-Encoding as described
in section 3.2.2.1 and a Content-Encoding as described in this section.

which the origin server believes the entity was last modified. Depending on the type of the entity (or the type of storage on the origin server), this may be a modification date from a file system, a time stamp from a data base, or the current date and time, if the entity is dynamically generated from data which changes constantly. If the entity is combined from other entities with different modification dates, the `Last-Modified` header field should contain the most recent of these modification dates.

- `extension-header`
  The `extension-header` mechanism allows additional entity header fields to be defined without changing the protocol, but these fields cannot be assumed to be recognizable by the recipient. Any header field with a name which is not standardized can be interpreted as an extension header field, and therefore is an entity header field. Unrecognized header fields should be ignored by the recipient and must be forwarded by proxies.

Since the extension header mechanism defines every header which is not standardized to be an entity header, the list of entity header fields can be extended without changing the protocol version.

3.2.3 Request

A request message always is the first message in an HTTP interaction, it is sent from the client to the server after the successful establishment of the connection and specifies the clients request. According to the generic message format, the format of a request message is rather simple.

```
request =
  request-line
  *( general-header | request-header | entity-header)
  CRLF
  [ message-body ]

request-line =
  method SP request-URI SP HTTP-version CRLF
```

In case of an request message, the generic `start-line` of the generic message format is a `request-line`, which contains the most important information of the request. Following the `request-line` there are zero or more headers, which can be general headers, request headers, or entity headers. Separated by a blank line, an optional `message-body` can be part of the request message. The `request-line` contains three fields separated by space characters.

- method
  The method field specifies the method to be performed by the server on the resource identified by the request-URI. There are, however, methods which do not apply to a particular resource.

- request-URI
  The request-URI is a URI as described in chapter 2 and identifies the resource upon which to apply the request. If the request does not apply to a particular resource, the request-URI field should contain an asterisk character '*'. The absolute form (containing the host name) must be used when sending a request to a proxy. If the request is sent directly to the origin server, the path form can be used, which uniquely identifies the resource on the server[14].

- HTTP-version
  The HTTP-version field indicates the version of an HTTP message[15]. Any application sending a request message as defined by the HTTP/1.1 specification must include a string indicating a HTTP-version of HTTP/1.1.

The two functionally most important elements of a request are the request method, which determines the action that the client requests from the server, and the header fields, which are used to pass additional information from the client to the server. The request methods are described in section 3.2.3.1. The header fields of a request can be general or entity headers, which are described in a previous section, or request headers, which are described in section 3.2.3.2.

3.2.3.1 Request methods

The request methods of HTTP define the action to be performed by a server. The most basic request method (and the only one defined in the very first HTTP version) is the GET method, which requests a resource from a server. Since HTTP now supports more methods, they have been characterized according to two properties. Implementors of HTTP should be aware that these properties are observed by their implementations.

- *Safe methods*
  Safe methods should never have the significance of taking an action other than retrieval. This allows clients do distinguish between methods which do not have any unexpected significance to themselves or others, and methods which may have that.

---

[14] The path form gets its name from being only the url-path part of a URL (with a leading slash character '/') as defined in section 2.3.2.

[15] Internet informational RFC 2145 [182] gives guidelines for the use and interpretation of HTTP version numbers.

- *Idempotent methods*
  For idempotent methods, it can be said that the side-effects of more than one identical request are the same as for a single request[16]. Consequently, every method which is safe also is idempotent.

Using these definitions, the methods defined in HTTP/1.1 can be classified. The result of this classification is shown in table 3.2[17]. It should be noticed that the CONNECT method is not part of the original HTTP/1.1 specification, but has been added to the first revision of it, on which our description of HTTP/1.1 is based. However, it is only a reserved method name as far as the HTTP/1.1 specification is concerned, and will probably be added to future revisions or versions of the specification.

Table 3.2   Overview of HTTP/1.1 request methods

Request method name	Safe	Idempotent	Page
CONNECT			71
DELETE		•	71
GET	•	•	72
HEAD	•	•	72
OPTIONS		•	73
POST			73
PUT		•	73
TRACE		•	74

- CONNECT
  The CONNECT method is only reserved in the HTTP/1.1 specification, its usage is described in an Internet draft by Luotonen [163]. The method is used for *SSL proxying* as described in section 9.2.4.2. Basically, it is used to initiate a transparent path between a client and an origin server for SSL communications, where proxies simply pass data back and forth.

- DELETE
  A client can request to delete a resource from an origin server with a request containing the DELETE method. However, even if the server responds

---

[16] However, it is possible that a sequence of several idempotent requests is non-idempotent. This may happen if the result of the entire sequence of requests depends on a value that is altered within that sequence.

[17] The PATCH, LINK, and UNLINK methods were part of the first version of the HTTP/1.1 specification, but have been removed from the latest revisions of the specification.

indicates success, the client can not be sure that the resource has actually been deleted, the server only indicates that it intends to do so.

The server can indicate success in different ways. If the response includes an entity describing the status, the response should have a 200 (ok) status code. If the server has not yet enacted the action, it should send a response having a 202 (accepted) status code. If the response is OK, but the response does not contain an entity, the response should have a 204 (no content) status code.

A DELETE request passing through a cache should be interpreted by the cache and the cache should mark cache entries which are identified by the same URI as stale.

- GET

  The GET method is used by a client to retrieve whatever information (in the form of an entity) is identified by the request-URI. Normally, this would be a document or any other static data (such as an image or an audio file) stored on the server. However, the request-URI in the request line might also refer to a resource which generates the data which is to be sent back to the client. HTTP/1.1 makes no assumptions about any distinction between an URI referring to static data and a URI referring to a data-producing process[18].

  If any of the If-Match, If-Modified-Since, If-None-Match, If-Range, or If-Unmodified-Since header fields is present, the GET method changes its semantics to a "conditional GET". These semantics specify that the entity the GET refers to should be transferred only under the circumstances described by the conditional header fields which are present in the request. If the Range header field is present, the GET method changes its semantics to a "partial GET". These semantics specify that the entity the GET refers to should only be transferred partially as specified in the request.

- HEAD

  The HEAD method is very similar to the GET method, the only difference is that the server must not return a message body in the response. This method is often used for testing URIs for validity, accessibility, and recent modification. If the response to a HEAD request indicates that a resource has changed (for example if one of the Content-Length, Content-MD5, ETag, or Last-Modified header fields has changed), a cache through which this response is passing must mark the cache entry (if the resource has been cached) as stale.

---

[18] Two possible scenarios where the data requested with a GET method is not static is accessing a *Common Gateway Interface (CGI)* script as described in section 9.4, or requesting a document containing *Server-Side Includes (SSI)* as described in section 9.3.2.5.

- OPTIONS

  This method can be used by a client to get information about the communication options available on the request/response chain for a particular resource. It is also possible to specify no resource (using the asterisk character '*' as the request-URI on the request line), the client will be informed about the general communication options for the request/response chain to the server, and not for a particular resource.

  A response to an OPTIONS request should include any header fields which indicate optional features implemented by the server. For example, an Allow header field may be used to list the methods which are supported for the resource or by the server in general (depending on whether the request-URI has been set to the asterisk character '*' or a URI). Other headers which may be used in a response to an OPTIONS request include Accept, Accept-Charset, Accept-Encoding, Accept-Language, and Accept-Ranges.

- POST

  If a client wants to submit information to an entity identified by an URI, it can do so by using the POST method. In contrast to the PUT method, where a new entity is being created, the POST method is used to specify an existing entity and the data which should be transferred to it. The most popular application of the POST method is the submission of form data to CGI applications, as described in detail in section 9.4.2.

  If the data has successfully been transmitted and the request resulted in an entity being sent back, the server should reply with a 200 (ok) status code. If the data has successfully been transmitted and the request did not result in an entity being sent back, the server should reply with a 204 (no content) status code. If the data has successfully been transmitted and the request resulted in a new resource being created, the server should reply with a 201 (created) status code.

- PUT

  The PUT method can be used by a client to store an entity on a server under a particular URI. The request specifies the request-URI, which is the URI under which the entity should be stored, and it also contains an entity, which should be stored on the server. If a new entity is created, the server should reply with a 201 (created) status code. If an existing entity is updated (such as replacing a document with a newer version), the server should reply with a 200 (ok) or 204 (no content) status code, depending on whether the response also contains an entity.

- TRACE

  For diagnostic reasons, it may be interesting for a client to know how a
  message sent to an origin server[19] actually is received, assuming that the
  request/response chain may contain one or more proxies which may act as
  caches and may also modify or add header fields. The client simply sends
  a request with a TRACE method, to which the recipient responds with a
  200 (ok) status code and an entity body which contains the request as
  received by the recipient. The most interesting header field in the request
  as received by the recipient will most often be the Via header field, which
  contains a trace of the request chain.

The HTTP/1.1 specification makes all methods but GET and HEAD optional, which means that every server has to implement at least these two
methods. If a requested method is not implemented on a server, it should send
a 501 (not implemented) response. If a method is known by the server, but
not allowed for the resource specified in the request, the server should send
a 405 (method not allowed) response.

3.2.3.2 Request headers

Request header fields are used by a client to pass additional information
about the request and about the client itself to the server. As such, the
request header fields act as request modifiers. While some of them only pass
additional parameters to the server which it may use or may ignore (such
as the software being used on the client side), others effectively change the
semantics of the request and must be properly interpreted by the server (such
as making conditional or partial requests for resources).

- Accept

  The Accept header field can be used to specify media types which are acceptable for the response. The specification of the media type can be very
  basic, such as specifying that only an HTML document will be accepted
  for the response, or rather complex. One example for a more complex
  Accept header field specification would be a request for a text document,
  which should be sent as HTML, if available, otherwise as plain text. Using
  this header field, clients can be very specific about media type capabilities (which media types they can interpret) and media type preferences
  (which media types they would like to get, if available).

---

[19] It is also possible to limit the number of hops a TRACE request makes by using the
Max-Forwards header field. This way any intermediate in the request/response
chain can be addressed as recipient of a TRACE request.

- Accept-Charset

  Using the `Accept-Charset` header field, clients can indicate which character sets they are willing to accept in a response. Clients with the ability to understand more comprehensive or special-purpose character sets can therefore signal to the server that they are capable of understanding these sets. The ISO 8859-1 [111] character set can be assumed to be acceptable to all clients. If a server is not capable of satisfying a requested character set specification, it can either send a 406 (`not acceptable`) response or reply with an unacceptable response (eg, using the ISO 8859-1 character set).

- Accept-Encoding

  The `Accept-Encoding` header field can be used to specify the content encodings of a response which are acceptable for a client. The absence of the `Accept-Encoding` header field signifies to the server that the client will accept any content encoding. The *Internet Assigned Numbers Authority (IANA)* acts as a registry for possible values for the `Accept-Encoding` header field[20]. If a server is not capable of satisfying a requested content encoding, it should send a 406 (`not acceptable`) response.

- Accept-Language

  This header field is similar to other accept header field in that it allows clients to specify language preferences for responses. Consequently, in some cases this field can be ignored by the server (when the response is an image which is not language specific), while in other cases (such as HTML pages containing text) it should be observed. Languages are specified by language tags as defined in Internet proposed standard RFC 1766 [7], consisting of primary tags and optional subtags. Any two letter primary tag is a language abbreviation according to ISO 639 [112], and any two-letter initial subtag is a country code according to ISO 3166 [128][21]. Language tags are matched exactly and as a function of the prefix, therefore allowing perfect and best effort matches. The client should make the choice of language preferences available to the user, but if it is not available, the client should not use an `Accept-Language` header field in its requests.

---

[20] These encoding types are also used for the `Transfer-Encoding` entity header described in section 3.2.2.1 and the `Content-Encoding` general header described in section 3.2.2.2.

[21] Language tags are also used in the `Content-Language` entity header described in section 3.2.2.2.

- Authorization

  The Authorization header field is used by clients to authenticate itself
  with a server[22]. Depending on the authentication method the client is
  using, the Authorization header field contains credentials for basic or
  digest access authorization. Because HTTP authentication is a rather
  complex issue, we describe it in a separate section, so for details about
  authentication see section 3.2.6.

- Expect

  If a client expects a certain behavior from a server, it can indicate its
  expectations using an Expect header field. A server which is not able
  to meet a clients expectations should respond with a 417 (expectation
  failed) status. Since the Expect header field is defined to have an extensible syntax for future extensions, it is possible that a server receives
  an Expect header field with extensions that it does not support. In this
  case the server must respond with a 417 (expectation failed) status.

- From

  The From header field is used to specify the Internet email address for the
  human user who is controlling the requesting client. The address should be
  given according to the formats defined in Internet standard RFC 822 [53]
  (as updated by Internet standard RFC 1123 [29]). Clients should not
  send the user's email address without his approval. For automated clients
  (such as search engines as described in section 10.3), the From header field
  should be included in requests and contain a contact address which can
  be used in case the automated client is causing problems for a server.

- Host

  This is the only header field which is required in every request which
  is sent to an HTTP/1.1 server. A server receiving a request without a
  Host header field must respond with a 400 (bad request) status code.
  The Host header field specifies the Internet host and port number of
  the resource being requested, as obtained from the original URL given
  by the user or the referring resource. This allows the origin server to
  differentiate between requests which are received on a single IP address
  which is associated with multiple host names.

- If-Modified-Since

  The If-Modified-Since header field is used to make a GET request conditional. There are three different cases what can happen after a server
  received a request including an If-Modified-Since header field.

---

[22] Usually, but not necessarily after receiving a 401 (unauthorized) response.

- If the resource specified in the request has not been modified since the date specified in the If-Modified-Since header field, the server sends a 304 (not modified) response.
- If the resource has been modified, the response is exactly the same as in case of a normal (unconditional) GET method.
- If the request is invalid or the request results in a response other than a 200 (ok), the error response is exactly the same as in case of a normal (unconditional) GET method.

This header field allows the efficient use of caching, if a cached entity is still valid, a client can verify this easily and only a minimal amount of data is transferred (the 304 (not modified) response). On the other hand, if a cached entity has been modified, the response contains the updated version and there is no need for a second request/response interaction. It is important to notice that the Range request header field modifies the meaning of the If-Modified-Since header field.

- If-Match
  The If-Match header field is used to make a request conditional by specifying one or more entity tags. This header field can be used for any method. If a request contains an If-Match header field, the server compares the entity tag which is associated with the resource specified in the request with all entity tags specified in the If-Match header field. If there is a match, the server performs the method as requested. If there is no match, the server should send a 412 (precondition failed) response. Only strong validators (as described in section 3.2.9.3) should be used for the comparison of entity tags. A common example for using the If-Match header field is a PUT request which should only update an entity if it has not changed since the client last retrieved it.

- If-None-Match
  This header field serves the same purpose as the If-Match header field, in that it makes a request conditional by specifying one or more entity tags. However, in case of the If-None-Match header field, the operation is only performed if none of the resources identified by the entity tags in the If-None-Match header field is current. If any of the entity tags match the entity tag that would have been returned in the response to a similar GET request (without the If-None-Match header field), the server should not perform the requested method. In case of GET and HEAD methods, it should send a 304 (not modified) response. In all other cases, the server should send a 412 (precondition failed) response. An example where this feature could be used is to prevent races between PUT operations.

- If-Range

  If a client has a partial copy of an entity in its cache and wants to get the entire entity, it could request the rest of the entity using a conditional GET and a Range request header field. However, if the conditional GET failed, the client would have to make a second request for the entire (modified) entity. To avoid this second request, the client could use an If-Range header field, which can be used with a date (giving the semantics of the If-Unmodified-Since header field), or an entity tag (giving the semantics of the If-Match header field). An If-Range header field must always be used together with a Range request header field. If the entity has not changed, the server should send a 206 (partial response), if it did change, a 200 (ok) response containing the entire entity should be sent.

- If-Unmodified-Since

  The If-Unmodified-Since header field can be used to make a request conditional. If a request contains an If-Unmodified-Since header field, the server should perform the method only if the requested resource has not been modified since the time specified in this field. If the requested resource has been modified, the server should not perform the requested method and replay with a 412 (precondition failed) response.

- Max-Forwards

  The Max-Forwards header field can only be used together with the TRACE and OPTION methods. It is used to limit the number of times that a request can be forwarded by proxies or gateways. Each proxy or gateway receiving a TRACE or OPTION request containing a Max-Forwards header field must decrement its value by one before forwarding the request. If the received value is zero, however, the proxy or gateway must not forward the request, instead it must respond as the final recipient. The purpose of this header field is to make it easier for a client to trace requests which appears to be failing or looping in mid-chain.

- Proxy-Authorization

  In contrast to the Authorization request header field, used by a client to authenticate itself with an origin server, the Proxy-Authorization header field is used by a client to authenticate itself with the nearest proxy which requires authentication. This header field only applies to the nearest proxy that demanded authentication using the Proxy-Authenticate response header field (as described in section 3.2.4.2). The proxy which requested the authentication (by using a 407 (proxy authentication required) response containing a Proxy-Authenticate response header field) can either consume this header field (ie, not forward it) or forward it to the next proxy, if this is the method how proxies cooperatively authenticate a given request. The details and various methods of HTTP authentication are described in section 3.2.6.

- Range

  The Range header field is used by clients to specify range requests, that is to specify a number of byte ranges of an entity. Byte ranges can be given in a number of different specifications, basically it is possible to specify absolute (from the beginning) and relative (from the end) ranges, and to combine multiple ranges into one single range request. In case of multiple ranges, the client must be able to handle multipart/byteranges responses, since this is the mechanism which is used for sending a response containing multiple ranges. Range requests may be unconditional or conditional. If a range request is successful, the server replies with a 206 (partial response) containing the requested ranges. If the range request can not be satisfied because the entity does not contain the specified ranges, the server should send a 416 (requested range not satisfiable) response. If a conditional range request fails because the conditional is false, the server should respond with a 304 (not modified) response. If a proxy sends a range request and receives an entire entity, it should cache the entire entity and return only the requested ranges to its client[23].

- Referer

  This header field can be used by a client to inform the server about the address (URI) of the resource from which the URI of the request was obtained. The server can use this information for interest, logging, optimized caching or other purposes[24]. If the request URI was obtained from a source that does not have its own URI (such as a bookmark or input from the user's keyboard), the Referer header field must not be used. If the Referer header field contains a relative URI, it should be interpreted relative to the request URI.

- TE

  The TE header field is similar to the Accept-Encoding request header field, but restricts the transfer encodings that are acceptable in the response. The TE header field only applies to the immediate connection, therefore its token must be supplied in a Connection general header field

---

[23] This can happen because the HTTP specification states that clients as well as servers do not need to support range operations, thus ignoring range specifications in requests and replying with an entire entity instead of the requested range only.

[24] If the URI identifies a *Common Gateway Interface (CGI)* application, the Referer header field is used to set the HTTP_REFERER environment variable which can be examined by the CGI application.

whenever it is present in a message. If a server can not send a response which is acceptable according to the TE header field of a request, it should reply with a 406 (not acceptable) response.

- User-Agent
  The User-Agent header field contains information about the client originating the request. Typically, this is the type and version of a browser. This information can be used by the server[25] for statistical purposes and for recognizing user agents which might require a tailored response because of limitations or special abilities of these user agents. The User-Agent header field can hold multiple product tokens, eg identifying a particular user agent and the type of library which has been used for the implementation of the user agent.

Request header fields can only extended reliably with a change in the protocol version, because unrecognized header field names by default are treated as entity headers. However, if all parties in a closed environment agree on a new request header field, it can be used without a change in the protocol version.

3.2.4 Response

A response message always is the second message in an HTTP interaction, it is sent from the server to the client after the server has received and processed the client's request and contains the result of the server's request processing. According to the generic message format, the format of a response message is rather simple.

```
response =
  status-line
  *( general-header | response-header | entity-header)
  CRLF
  [ message-body ]

status-line =
  HTTP-version SP status-code SP reason-phrase CRLF
```

In case of an response message, the generic start-line of the generic message format is a status-line, which contains the most important information of the response. Following the status-line there are zero or more headers, which can be general headers, response headers, or entity headers.

---

[25] In addition, if the URI identifies a *Common Gateway Interface (CGI)* application, the User-Agent header field is used to set the HTTP_USER_AGENT environment variable which can then be examined by the CGI application.

Separated by a blank line, an optional `message-body` can be part of the response message. The `response-line` contains three fields separated by space characters.

- `HTTP-version`
  The `HTTP-version` field indicates the version of an HTTP message. Any application sending a response message as defined by the HTTP/1.1 specification must include a string indicating a `HTTP-version` of `HTTP/1.1`.

- `status-code`
  The `status-code` element is a 3-digit integer result code of the attempt to understand and satisfy the request. These codes are fully defined in section. The status code is intended for use by programs.

- `reason-phrase`
  The `reason-phrase` is intended to give a short textual description of the status code, it is intended for the human user. The client is not required to examine or display the `reason-phrase`. The reason phrases are only recommended, they may be replaced by local equivalents without affecting the protocol.

The two functionally most important elements of a response are the status code, which specifies the result of the request as indicated by the server, and the header fields, which are used to pass additional information from the server to the client. The status codes are described in section 3.2.4.1. The header fields of a request can be general or entity headers, which are described in a previous section, or response headers, which are described in section 3.2.4.2.

3.2.4.1 Status code definitions

The status code, which is present in every HTTP response message, is a three digit number which specifies the result of the server's attempt to understand and satisfy the request. A complete listing of all status codes currently defined in HTTP/1.1 can be found in appendix A.2. The first digit of the status code defines the class of response. The last two digits do not have any categorization role. Currently, there are five values for the first digit.

- `Informational (1xx)`
  This class of status codes indicates that the request has been successfully received by the HTTP server, and that the server is processing the request. Thus, a response with a status code of this class is only provisional.

- `Successful (2xx)`
  After the server has received, understood, and accepted the request, it sends back a response with a status code of this class.

- `Redirection (3xx)`
  If a response is received which carries a status code of this class, the client must take further action to complete the request, for example it must send a request to another server, which is specified in the response.

- `Client error (4xx)`
  If the HTTP request can not be processed because the client has made an error in its request (such as syntactical errors or sending unauthorized requests), the server responds with a status code of this class.

- `Server error (5xx)`
  In many cases, the client's request may have been correct, but the server is incapable of performing the request. It then responds with a status code of this class. The server should specify whether the error situation is a temporary or permanent condition.

In addition to the numerical values (which carry the semantics of the status codes), each status code also is associated with a reason phrase. While the status code is intended for use by programs, the reason phrase is intended for the human user and may be replaced by local equivalents without affecting the protocol. A client is not required to examine or display the reason phrase.

Although a number of status codes are defined in the HTTP/1.1 specification, this list is not final, which means that status code are extensible. HTTP applications are not required to understand the meaning of all registered status codes. However, applications must understand the class of any status code, as indicated by the first digit, and treat any unrecognized response as being equivalent to the x00 status code of that class.

3.2.4.2 Response headers

Response header fields are used by a server to pass additional information about the response which cannot be placed in the status line, the first line of the response. These header fields give information about the server and about further access to the resource identified by the `request-URI` of the client's request.

- `Accept-Ranges`
  This header field can be used by a server to indicate its acceptance of range requests for a resource. Generally, the `Accept-Ranges` header field specifies range units which may be used in range requests. In HTTP/1.1, only a `bytes` and a `none` range unit have been defined. This header field can be ignored by clients or may not be sent at all by servers which do accept range requests. It can be used, however, to reduce the number of request/response interactions between a client and a server. Whenever a

server receives an OPTIONS request, it should include a Accept-Ranges header field in its response.

- Age

  The Age header field is used to convey the estimated age of a response message when obtained from a cache. Servers including caches must use this header field for every response they generate from their own cache. The Age header field is the cache's estimate of the amount of time since the response was generated or revalidated by the origin server. The presence of an Age header field in a response therefore implies that a response is not first-hand[26]. A detailed description of caching and how age calculations are performed by caches and used for caching purposes is given in section 3.2.9.

- Location

  If a client requested the creation of a resource, the server replies with a 201 (created) response (if there was no error) and reports the URI of the newly created resource with the Location header field. If the response has any 3xx (redirection) status code, the Location header field is used to redirect the recipient to the new location of the resource. This is useful if a web page moved to a new URI, in which case the Location header can be used to automatically redirect clients using the old URI to the new one[27].

- Proxy-Authenticate

  The Proxy-Authenticate header field must be included in a response with a 407 (proxy authentication required) status code, and may be included in a response with a 401 (unauthorized) status code, if this response has been generated by a proxy asking for authentication. The Proxy-Authenticate header field includes at least one challenge which indicates the authentication scheme and parameters applicable to the request URI of the request. The client is expected to use the information provided in the Proxy-Authenticate header field to create a request which contains authentication information in the Proxy-Authorization request header field.

---

[26] The opposite is not true, since a cache using HTTP/1.0 will not implement the Age header field.

[27] However, this method only works if the administrator of the web server configures the server to reply with the Location header and a 3xx (redirection) status code to any request for the old URI. A method which can be used without any server configuration is described in section 3.6.1, although it should be noted that it is based on a non-standard mechanism.

- Retry-After
  If the server responds with a 503 (service unavailable) status code, the Retry-After header field can be used to indicate how long the service in expected to be unavailable. Another possible use of this header field is to indicate the minimum time a user agent should wait before trying a redirected request (which has been indicated by any 3xx (redirection) status code).

- Server
  The Server header field contains information about the server sending the response. Typically, this is the type and version of some kind of server software. This information can be used by the client for statistical purposes. The Server header field can hold multiple product tokens, for example identifying a particular type of server software and also the type of library which has been used for the implementation of the server. Because revealing the software type and version of a server may allow the server machine to become more vulnerable to attacks against known security holes, it is recommended that the Server header field should be a configurable option of the server software.

- Vary
  The Vary field contains information about the dimensions over which a response which has been generated as a result of server-driven negotiation (which is described in detail in section 3.2.5.1) is varying. It contains a list field names which specify the criteria that were used to select a particular representation. A field value consisting of the asterisk character '*' signals that parameters not limited to the request headers play a role in the selection of the response representation.

- Warning
  The Warning header field can be used to carry additional information for a response which can not be carried by the status code. This header is typically used by caches to inform a client about a possible lack of semantic transparency from a caching operation, but it may also be used for other purposes. The Warning header field contains one or more warn codes (with a syntax similar to status codes) which may be associated with a time stamp. A complete listing of all warn codes currently defined in HTTP/1.1 can be found in section 3.2.9.4. The first digit of the three digit warn code indicates whether the warning must or must not be deleted from a stored cache entry after a successful revalidation.

  - 1xx warnings
    These warning describe the freshness or revalidation status of the response and therefore must be deleted after a successful revalidation.

  − 2xx warnings
  These warnings describe something which is not rectified by a revalidation and therefore must not be deleted after a successful revalidation.

Any server or cache may add Warning headers to a response. New Warning headers should be added after any existing Warning headers. A cache must not delete any Warning headers that it received with a response. However, if a cache performs a successful revalidation, the Warning headers which applied to the invalidated entry should be deleted from the entry, and the Warning headers received in the validating response should be added to the entry.

- WWW-Authenticate
  The WWW-Authenticate header field must be included in a response with a 401 (unauthorized) status code. The WWW-Authenticate header field includes at least one challenge which indicates the authentication scheme and parameters applicable to the request URI of the request. The client is expected to use the information provided in the WWW-Authenticate header field to create a request which contains authentication information in the Authorization request header field.

Response header fields can only extended reliably with a change in the protocol version, because unrecognized header field names by default are treated as entity headers. However, if all parties in a closed environment agree on a new response header field, it can be used without a change in the protocol version.

3.2.5 Content negotiation

In many cases, it is possible that a requested resource on a server exists in different variants. Normally, any reference (URI) pointing to this resource would point to all variants, and depending on the request, it is necessary to decide which of the variants should be used (ie, presented to the user). There are different reasons while it may be advantageous to have different variants of a resource, the most popular ones are listed below.

- *Language specific variants*
  A resource containing language specific material (such as written text in a text document, written text in an image, or spoken language in audio or video clips) may be stored in different languages, so that users speaking different languages can use it.

- *Quality specific variants*
  Depending on the capacity of the network connection a user has, the tolerable amounts of data to be transmitted are very different. While

a user connected with a slow modem might be best served with a low resolution or grayscale version of an image, other users who can afford it would like to see a high resolution and color variant.

- *Encoding specific variants*
  Depending on the varying capabilities of different clients, it can be useful to have different encodings of a resource, which can be used depending on a client's capabilities. A possible example is the encoding of images, where the encoding type (popular image encodings are GIF and JPEG, as described in section 5.2.5) determines the quality and the compression of images.

The common property of all these variants is that they all contain the same resource (from an abstract point of view which is based on content and not language or encoding), although in different representations. HTTP/1.1 defines *content negotiation* procedures which can be used between a client and a server to determine which representation of a resource should be used for a particular request of a resource.

There are two orthogonal types of content negotiation, the first one is *server-driven content negotiation*, which defines the server to be responsible for the selection of a particular representation of a resource, it is described in section 3.2.5.1. The second type of content negotiation is *agent-driven content negotiation*, here the responsibility of selecting a particular representation of a resource is shifted to the client side, this type of negotiation is described in section 3.2.5.2. Since these two types of content negotiation are orthogonal, it is possible to combine them. One possible scenario for such a combination is the situation where a cache uses the agent-driven negotiation information provided by the origin server in order to provide server-driven negotiation for subsequent requests. This method is called *transparent content negotiation* and is described in section 3.2.5.3.

3.2.5.1 Server-driven negotiation

If the selection of a particular representation for a resource is made by an algorithm located at the server, the content negotiation is called server-driven. This method of content negotiation places the selection as close as possible to the resource. In server-driven content negotiation, the server can make its selection according to different sources of information.

- *Available representations*
  Since the server knows all representations which are available for a particular resource, it knows the dimensions over which these representations can vary, such as language, quality, or encoding types.

- *Request header fields*

  A client may include special headers in its request which are used to specify which kind of representation would fit best. These request header fields are `Accept`, `Accept-Charset`, `Accept-Encoding`, and the `Accept-Language` header as described in section 3.2.3.2. A server can, however, use other fields (such as the `User-Agent` request header field) as a source of information for content negotiation.

- *Other information*

  A server might also use any other information that is available to it to perform content negotiation. An example for this kind of information is the network address of the client.

Using these sources of information, a server makes its selection of a particular representation of a resource for an incoming request. The basic procedure is depicted in figure 3.4, which, between the client and the server, shows the HTTP request/response interaction, and on the server side illustrates how a particular representation of a resource is chosen and sent back in the HTTP response.

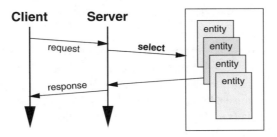

Fig. 3.4 Server-driven content negotiation

Depending on whether the response generated by the server is cacheable or not[28], the standard specifies that the server either should (for cacheable responses) or may (for non-cacheable responses) include a `Vary` header field to inform the client (and, in case of cacheable responses, intermediate caches, if present) about the criteria which were used to select the representation included in the response.

---

[28] Responses to `GET` and `HEAD` requests are cacheable, if the request did not contain an `Authorization` header. All other responses are non-cacheable. However, the responses to `GET` and `HEAD` requests are only cacheable if they do not contain a status code or header field which makes them non-cacheable.

Server-driven content negotiation is advantageous when the selection of a representation is difficult to describe to the user agent or based entirely on internal server issues. There are, however, a number of drawbacks associated with server-driven content negotiation.

- *The server's limited knowledge*
  Depending on the dimensions over which the different representations of a resource are varying, it is sometimes very difficult for a server to make the right selection among all representations. Theoretically, the optimal selection would require the server to have complete knowledge of the user agent's capabilities and the user's intended use, which is impossible.

- *Inefficiency*
  Since usually most resources on a server will only have one representation, it is inefficient to have the client send its capabilities and requirements in all requests. In most cases it will be sufficient to simply request a resource, because only one representation is available at the server.

- *Complicated server implementation*
  Server-driven content negotiation complicates the server implementation and also requires some processing power on the server. If the server is a heavily loaded system, this additional load can be intolerable.

- *Caching*
  Since the response is determined according to an algorithm inside the server, the response will in many cases not be cached, either because the cache noticed some headers which indicate multiple representations of a resource, or because the server explicitly marks the response as not or only private cacheable (see section 3.2.9.4 for more details on cache control and different levels of cacheability).

Because of these limitations of server-driven content negotiation, HTTP defines a second mechanism of content negotiation, the agent-driven content negotiation. This mechanism should be used if any of the points in the list above seems to make the application of server-driven content negotiation unsuitable.

3.2.5.2 Agent-driven negotiation

In case of agent-driven content negotiation, the origin server responds with a list of all available representations, and the client (or the user) selects one of these representations which is finally requested from the origin server. The basic procedure is depicted in figure 3.5. It should be noted that the first request only identifies a set of representations, while the second request specifically selects one representation out of this set, which is sent back in the response.

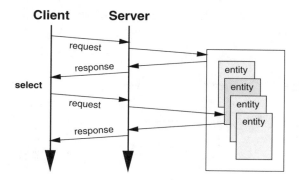

Fig. 3.5   Agent-driven content negotiation

Currently, there is no way to perform an automatic selection at the client side, because the current version of HTTP does not specify a format of the set of representations which is returned to the client. However, the specification reserves the field name `Alternates` which will be defined in a future specification. Therefore, currently the only way to perform agent-driven content negotiation is for the origin server to reply with an entity containing a list of all representations together with their URIs. This response must have a 300 (`multiple choices`) status code. Because the specification does not define a format for this list, it is not possible to process this list automatically (with the client using its own selection algorithm based on its capabilities and user preferences). The only way to perform agent-driven content negotiation on the client side therefore is to present this list to the user, who can make a selection from it.

If the server has a preferred selection among the list of representations, it should specify this representation in the `Location` response header field as described in section 3.2.4.2. In this case, the client may either still present the list of representations to the user, or perform an automatic redirect and request the preferred representation without user interaction.

3.2.5.3 Transparent negotiation

Transparent content negotiation is the combination of server-driven and agent-driven content negotiation. The basic idea of transparent content negotiation is depicted in figure 3.6. A client sends a request for a resource through a proxy, which forwards the request to the origin server. The server acts as in agent-driven content negotiation and returns a list of available representations to the proxy. The proxy selects one of the representations and requests it from the origin server without interacting with the client. The response from the origin server, which contains the selected representation, is sent to the client. Therefore, the proxy provides a server-driven content negotiation to the client.

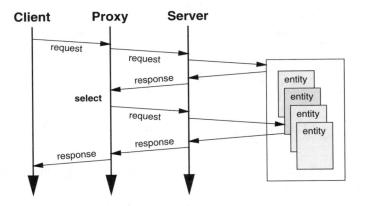

Fig. 3.6   Transparent content negotiation

There are two main advantages of this approach. The first one is the load sharing between the different agents. The second advantage is that the client does not have to make a second request, because the proxy takes the role of the agent in the agent-driven content negotiation. This reduces network delays and network traffic. However, since the current HTTP/1.1 specification does not define a specific way for agent-driven content negotiation (in particular for the list of available representations which is returned by the origin server), it is not possible to implement a generally working mechanism for transparent content negotiation.

3.2.6 Authentication

In most cases, the web is used anonymously, which means that the client requests the information it wants to have from a server without identification or authorization. Even more important, in case of POST or PUT operations, the client submits data to the client without any identification or authorization. However, when discussing security issues, it is necessary for some information to be made available only to users which are authorized to get it (or, in case of POST or PUT operations, to allow only authorized users to submit data to the server)[29]. Before going into the details, there are a few terms which should be used with a well-defined meaning.

- *Identification*

  Basically, security with regard to authorization requires some kind of identification, which makes it possible to assign some set of access privileges to an identity. Whenever this identification is used, it is assumed that the user associated with this identity is using it and therefore the associated access privileges (such as reading or modifying a resource) are granted. In terms of operating systems, the identification of a user is the user name.

- *Authentication*

  Although identification is necessary when trying to realize authorization, it is not sufficient. There must also be a mechanism which prevents attackers from falsely claiming an identity which is not theirs. This is assured by authentication methods, which are used to make sure that an identity can only be used by the user associated with it. In terms of operating systems, the authentication of a user is the user's password.

- *Authorization*

  If a user is identified and authenticated, it is known (within the given frame of reference) that the user really is who he claims to be. It is therefore possible to grant the user access to any information which is registered as being accessible to the user. Authorization is realized by associating an identity with certain access rights for information resources, such as the right to read or modify a certain file. In terms of operating systems, authorization in most cases is based on file ownerships (users and user groups) and file permissions (based on identity and group membership).

In case of the web, authentication and authorization must be handled in a stateless way, because the model of HTTP is based of stateless request/response messages. Whenever a client requests a resource which is protected by the server (ie, the server will not grant access to this resource without successful authorization of a client), the server responds with a 401 (`unauthorized`) status code. The server also includes a `WWW-Authenticate` response header as described in section 3.2.4.2. The client is expected to repeat the request including an `Authorization` header field which contains the information which is necessary to authenticate itself with the server.

A very similar authentication scheme is available for a client's authentication with proxies. Like an origin server, a proxy may require authorization before processing a client's request. A proxy can indicate its need

---

[29] It should be noted that in this section, only security with respect to authentication is discussed. Privacy issues are discussed in section 3.3.

for client authentication by sending a response with a 401 (unauthorized) or 407 (proxy authentication required) status code, which contains a Proxy-Authenticate response header field. The client is expected to repeat the request including a Proxy-Authorization header field which contains the information which is necessary to authenticate itself with the proxy.

The WWW-Authenticate header specifies the authentication scheme the server wants to use and, if present, parameters of the authentication scheme. Currently, HTTP defines two authentication schemes, which are described in the following sections. A very simple (and rather insecure) method of authentication, which has already been specified in HTTP/1.0, is basic authentication, as described in section 3.2.6.1. Since basic authentication has a lot of weaknesses (the most severe being that the password is sent in clear text), HTTP/1.1 includes a new authentication scheme, digest access authentication, which is described in section 3.2.6.2.

3.2.6.1 Basic authentication

Basic authentication is a very simple authentication scheme, which has been introduced very early in HTTP. If a server wants to use basic authentication, it responds with a 401 (unauthorized) status code and a WWW-Authenticate response header containing the identification of the basic authentication scheme and a realm value. The realm value specifies the protection space of the server which has been affected by the client's request. The client should display the realm value when prompting the user for a user name and a password. The basic authentication scheme has no other parameters.

The client repeats its request and includes a Authorization request header with it. This header contains the requests credentials, in case of basic authentication these credentials contain the user's identification and the user's password in *Base64* encoding as specified in Internet draft standard RFC 2045 [80][30].

This simplicity of basic authentication is its greatest weakness, because it results in the user's identification and the user's password to be sent in clear text over the network. This is a serious problem, because an attacker can easily gain access to this information. Consequently, basic authentication should never be used to protect sensitive or valuable information. Therefore, a common use of basic authentication is for pure identification purposes which may be used in collecting usage information for a set of resources. However,

---

[30] It is important to notice that Base64 encoding is not a cryptographic method, because it can easily be decoded without the need for a key or any other security mechanism. Therefore, the Base64 encoding of the user name and the password does not provide any security.

it should be noted that this procedure is only recommended if the server issues both a user name and a password to the users and does not allow the users to change the password. Otherwise, many users will choose a password which they already are using on other systems (which may contain sensitive or valuable information), because users generally try to minimize the number of passwords they have to remember. This password could easily be captured by an attacker and used to gain access to other accounts of the user which have the same password.

To overcome the weaknesses of basic authentication, HTTP/1.1 introduces a new authentication scheme, which does not send the user's password in clear text over the network. Every server with sensitive or valuable information therefore should use the new method instead of basic authentication.

3.2.6.2 Digest access authentication

Digest access authentication is an authentication scheme which is used to avoid sending the user's password in clear text over the network. Although it is part of HTTP/1.1, it is described in a different document, which is Internet proposed standard RFC 2069 [78]. The basic idea of digest access authentication relies on the existence of functions which make it virtually impossible to compute the input even though the output is known. One such function is the MD5 message digest algorithm as specified in Internet informational RFC 1321 [227]. Rather than exchanging the password in clear text, its MD5 encoded version (also called a *fingerprint*) is transmitted, which makes it almost impossible for an attacker to get the password through eavesdropping.

However, if only the MD5 encoded password would be transmitted, an attacker could capture this encrypted password and use it (without knowing the clear text password) in an attempt to gain access to the server. To avoid this type of attack, RFC 2069 specifies that the password must be MD5 encoded together with other information of the request, thus making it virtually impossible for an attacker to reuse the MD5 message digest for another request. The following information is MD5 encoded in a request using digest access authentication.

- *Username*
  The user name as known by the server. This is important for identification purposes, because the server must know the identity of the requesting user in order to check the authorization of the request.

- *Realm*
  This realm string has been originally included in the WWW-Authenticate header field of the server's 401 (unauthorized) response. The string

should be displayed to the user and be explanatory enough so that users know which user name and password to use.

- *Password*
  The ultimate goal of digest access authentication is the authentication of the requesting user, and the password is used to check the authenticity of the requesting user.

- *Nonce*
  The nonce is a server-specified data string (given in the `WWW-Authenticate` header field of the server's `401 (unauthorized)` response) which is used by the server to prevent replay attacks. A carefully chosen nonce value should contain at least the client's IP address, a time stamp, and a private server key.

- *HTTP method*
  This is simply the HTTP method used in the client's request, so it is just a copy from the first line of the client's request (which always contains the HTTP method).

- *Requested URI*
  This is simply the requested URI specified in the client's request, so it is just a copy from the first line of the client's request (which always contains the requested URI). According to the definition in RFC 2068, this can either be a star character (meaning that the request does not apply to a particular resource), an absolute URI, or an absolute path.

On receipt of the request containing the MD5 encoded information, the server assembles a string which also contains all the information listed above (everything but the password is included in the request, the password itself is stored in the server's user database), and computes the MD5 fingerprint of it. If the computed MD5 fingerprint equals the one in the request, the server can conclude that the password used by the client has been correct, hence the authentication can be considered successful and the server subsequently checks the user's authorization. If the two MD5 fingerprints differ, the authentication fails and there is no need to check the user's authorization.

Another feature of digest access authentication is the possibility to include an *entity digest*[31] in the transaction. Although an entity digest can not provide any privacy of the transmitted entity (the entity is still transferred in clear text or some kind of transfer encoding), it can be used to assure the integrity of the entity, which for some applications may be sufficient.

---

[31] An entity digest simply is the MD5 fingerprint of the entity and almost all information which is also present in the response digest (except the requested URI), in particular the password, which is only known to the client and the server.

It is important to notice, however, that although digest access authentication does not require the password to be sent in clear text for the purpose of authentication, it does not specify a secure way of transmitting the password initially (either from the server to the client if the password has been generated by the server, or from the client to the server is the user can set a password). Only if this initial transmission of the password is performed in a secure way, a substantial security improvement over basic authentication can be achieved.

Although digest access authentication can be seen as a significant improvement of the weak basic authentication scheme, it is still not suited for secure HTTP transaction. In particular, digest access authentication does not support the encryption of content, the resource which is transmitted from the server to the authenticated and authorized client is transferred in clear text. Applications which require the encryption of content must use additional security mechanisms which are discussed in detail in section 3.3.

3.2.7 Persistent connections

One of the big drawbacks of HTTP/1.0, briefly mentioned in section 3.1, was the limitation to one request/response interaction per client/server connection. This quickly lead to the development of clients which routinely used a large number of parallel HTTP connections, speeding up the data transmission, but also causing a number of other problems, such as a huge overhead of many TCP open and close operations, the usage of many operating system resources for maintaining a large number of parallel connections[32], and unfair behavior compared to other Internet protocols (such as FTP) which use only one connection per client.

To overcome all these problems, HTTP/1.1 introduces the concept of *persistent connections* and specifies that a single-user client should not have more than two simultaneous connections to one server or proxy. A good motivation of why persistent connections are desirable is given by Mogul [180]. Persistent connections are defined by sending multiple request/response interactions between the client and the server over one connection. Figure 3.7 shows the general idea of persistent connections, where the client uses one connection to send three requests over one HTTP connection (shown on the right side of the figure), while in the case of prior HTTP versions (specifically HTTP/1.0) it would have been necessary to individually open and close a connection for each request/response interaction (shown on the left side of the figure).

---

[32] Especially the problem that the TCP specification requires to retain the control blocks of a connection for some time (120 seconds is the default value) after it has been closed.

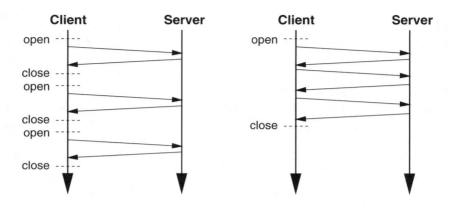

Fig. 3.7   Persistent HTTP connections

Since both the client and the server need to know when a message is finished (ie, when the next HTTP message starts in the stream of bytes they are receiving over the TCP connection), it is necessary that each message containing an entity includes a `Content-Length` header field as described in section 3.2.2.2. If this field is not present, there is no way for the receiver of the message to find out where the entity ends and where the next HTTP message starts. In non-persistent HTTP, this was clearly indicated by closing the connection.

If, for some reason, a client or a server does not want keep a connection open after a request/response interaction, it can use the `Connection` general header field with the `close` option to indicate that the connection will be closed after the completion of the response. HTTP/1.1 applications which do not support persistent connections must include this indication in every message.

A survey by Nielsen et al. [196] shows that the performance enhancements achieved by using HTTP/1.1 persistent connections are significant in comparison to the model used in HTTP/1.0. There are, however, cases where HTTP/1.1 persistent connections may perform considerably worse than HTTP/1.0, an investigation of one such case has been given by Heidemann [94]. However, these problems are caused by specific optimizations of TCP implementations and do not indicate a general design problem of HTTP/1.1 persistent connections. We are pointing out this fact because it is important to know about these possible problems when using HTTP/1.1, which is more sensitive on how implementations close connections that HTTP/1.0.

The usage of persistent connections has a number of advantages, which can be summarized as follows:

- *Operating system resources*
  There are two operating system resources which are affected most by avoiding the large number of TCP connections which are necessary for HTTP without persistent connections. The first resource is CPU time, which is saved because less connection setup and tear-down are necessary. The second resource is TCP control blocks, which are necessary for each TCP connection (and are kept for some time even after the connection has been closed).

- *Pipelining*
  If it is possible to send multiple requests on one connection, it is also possible to send these requests without waiting for the first response before sending the second request. This mechanism is called *pipelining* and is discussed at the end of the current section.

- *Fewer packets*
  Since there are less connection setup and tear-down phases, fewer packets are sent over the network, which is therefore less loaded. Since TCP connection setup and tear-down are rather complicated procedures (using a three-way handshake mechanism), the reduction in the number of packets being sent between a client and a server can be very dramatic in case of a large number of interactions with the same server[33].

- *Greater tolerance to HTTP version inconsistencies*
  Since multiple requests can be sent on one connection, clients can try new features of future HTTP versions without running the risk that the connection is closed. If the server does not implement that feature or an older HTTP version, it responds with an error message and the client can send another request (using older semantics) using the same connection.

In this list of advantages, the possibility to use pipelining with persistent connections has been mentioned. The idea of pipelining is rather simple. When using persistent connections, it is not only to possible to send multiple requests over one connection, but it would also be possible to send multiple requests without waiting for responses. Figure 3.8 depicts how pipelining can be used to optimize the transfer between a client and a server. Since the client does not wait for each response to arrive before sending the next request, there is a better utilization of the connection. In particular, the number of times the client has to wait for a complete round trip time is reduced to zero, it just sends all its requests and then waits for the responses to arrive.

Since pipelining of requests enables the server to process more than one request concurrently, it could send back the responses in the order in which

---

[33] Which is a realistic scenario, because many web pages contain a large number of small images which have to be fetched from the same server.

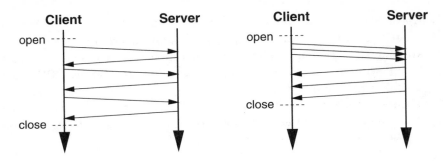

Fig. 3.8   Pipelining of HTTP requests

their processing has been completed (this would lead to the most efficient transmission, since wait times would be minimized). There is, however, no identification method in HTTP which would allow to associate requests with responses (rather than implicitly by the sequence in which they are being sent or received), so the HTTP/1.1 specification states that the server must send responses to pipelined requests in the same order that the requests were received.

3.2.8 Chunked encoding

Prior to HTTP/1.1, the connection model of HTTP was exactly one request/response interaction per connection and therefore the end of a resource was implicitly defined by the end of the data transmission from the server to the client. However, with the introduction of persistent connections, this can no longer be done. For most resources, the server knows its length in advance and can specify the length in the `Content-Length` header field of the response. However, there are some cases when the length of a resource is not known in advance, for example when the resource is generated by a *Common Gateway Interface (CGI)* script. For these purposes, HTTP/1.1 defines a *chunked transfer coding*, which can be specified in the `Transfer-Encoding` general header field of a message. This type of encoding is depicted in figure 3.9 (the figure shows how a message body, that is an entity in chunked transfer coding, is coded).

chunk size	chunk data	chunk size	chunk data	0 size	trailer

Fig. 3.9   Chunked transfer coding

The entity in simply split into chunks of known length, and the server or the CGI application can generate these chunks in any size it feels is appropriate for the particular application. If there is no more data to transfer, a zero chunk size field is transmitted, followed by an optional trailer. The trailer contains entity headers. One example for an entity header which might be useful and which has to be transmitted after the entity is the `Content-MD5` header field, which contains a fingerprint of the entity and can only be computed if the entire entity has been generated.

3.2.9 Caching

In general, HTTP is a protocol which is used for the transfer of information in distributed information systems, in particular the World Wide Web. Since many of the connections which are used to transfer information are inherently slow (such as dial-up connections) or almost permanently overloaded (such as a number of trans-atlantic connections), it is a good idea to think about possible optimizations of information transfer.

The general idea of reducing the amount of network traffic generated by an application is to implement smarter communication peers, which use some kind of intelligence to reduce the amount of generated traffic. One common idea is to use compression techniques, which can reduce the amount of data dramatically (but which also depend heavily on the data being compressed)[34]. An idea which goes even further is the application of caching techniques. A *cache* is a storage which is used for temporarily storing responses. It is a third component in a typical client/server scenario, located between the client and the server (as shown in figure 3.2, where the proxy can also act as a cache). In general, however, a cache is nothing more than a storage which has faster response times than the original storage. Consequently, in the HTTP scenario, three different kinds of caches are possible, which are shown in figure 3.10.

1. *Client side cache*

   A client side cache is located inside the client and caches responses this client has received. A popular application of this kind of cache is the history mechanism, which is existent in virtually all browsers. The browser simply saves the most recent pages a user has visited, and if the user hits the back button, the browser displays the cached copy rather than requesting the document from the server again.

---

[34] A good introduction to compression techniques for HTTP and some experimental results is given by Mogul et al. [181].

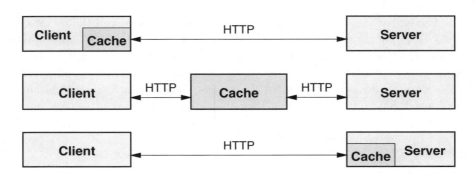

Fig. 3.10 Possible cache locations

2. *Cache as an intermediate in the request/response chain*
   This type of cache is a separate component, which is localized somewhere in the request/response chain between the client and the server[35]. A client must specifically be configured to use this kind of cache, because requests for resources must be sent to the cache rather than directly to the origin server. The cache decides what to do with the request. If the cache has a local copy of the requested resource, the request cab be served from the cache's storage, otherwise the cache has to forward the request to the origin server. It could, however, also forward the request to another cache, thus creating a hierarchy of caches.

3. *Server side cache*
   A server side cache is located inside the server and caches responses the server has given. This kind of cache is useful if the server has to serve a large number of requests. Resources which are requested frequently could be stored in main memory, while other resources are stored in the file system[36]. Markatos [169] describes how a rather small amount of main memory used as cache storage inside a server can increase its performance dramatically.

In the remainder of this section, we only discuss the second kind of caching, regarding a cache as an intermediate in the request/response chain. The other two kinds of caching are implementation issues of clients respectively servers and are therefore outside the scope of our subject, which is the

---

[35] Although it is a logically separate component, this type of cache can be located at the same machine as the client or server.

[36] Accessing a document stored in main memory is significantly faster than accessing a document which is stored in the file system on a hard disk.

communication protocol between different distributed components of the web architecture[37].

The most common example for the application of caching techniques is a company network, which has only one (rather slow and maybe expensive) link to the Internet. If this link (ie, the system connecting the company network and the outside line) includes a cache and is intelligent enough to interpret HTTP requests, it could in many cases eliminate the need for requests from the company network to be sent to the Internet. A web page which has already been requested by some user inside the company could have been stored by the cache, and the second request to that web page (from an entirely different user who has no idea that another user inside the company has already accessed this page) could be served by the cache, thus totally eliminating the need to send the request to the Internet, reducing the amount of traffic on the Internet, resulting in lower communication costs for the company, and giving faster response times for the users.

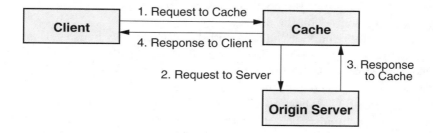

Fig. 3.11 HTTP cache operation and a cache miss

This general idea is depicted in figures 3.11 and 3.12. The first figure shows a cache which experiences a *cache miss*, which means that the resource which is requested is not cached and must therefore be requested from the origin server (which is the server which stores the resource), using a normal HTTP request and response interaction where the cache acts as client. In the second figure, showing a so-called *cache hit*, the cache can service the request from its internal storage and therefore does not have to send a request to the origin server.

So, if caching is such a good thing and only has benefits for all sides being involved, why is it not used from the very beginning and why is there such a big difference in caching in HTTP/1.0 and HTTP/1.1? The answer is, because caching is a simple idea, but implementing fast, efficient, and reliable caching

---

[37] However, it is possible to use HTTP's caching mechanisms for controlling client or server side caches.

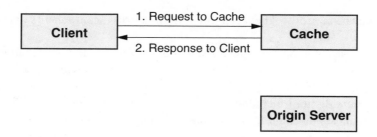

Fig. 3.12   HTTP cache operation and a cache hit

is not easy. In the example above, if the web page, which had been cached after
the first request, was modified by the page's owner between the first and the
second request to the cache, the second user requesting it would have received
an old version from the cache. Consequently, the implementation of caching
strategies also needs a number of mechanisms to implement cache control (or
cache consistency, how the goal to keep the cache's content consistent with
the original resources on the origin servers is called).

As a general remark, it could be said that caching heavily depends on the
existence of a common time base among all parties involved. Otherwise, the
use of time stamps for expiration dates or validation checks will not have the
intended results. Therefore, the HTTP specification recommends that every
host that uses HTTP, but especially origin servers and caches, should use a
protocol to synchronize their clocks to a globally accurate time standard. One
such protocol is the *Network Time Protocol (NTP)* as specified in Internet
draft standard RFC 1305 [175].

While caching was already defined in HTTP/1.0, it was very simple and
had a lot of drawbacks and limitations. Consequently, many people decided
to ignore it (or to explicitly work around it whenever possible) rather than
using it. As a result of this, caching has been greatly improved in HTTP/1.1.
The rest of this section describes HTTP/1.1 caching in detail. Section 3.2.9.1
describes the improvements of HTTP/1.1 caching compared to HTTP/1.0.
Sections 3.2.9.2 and 3.2.9.3 describe the expiration respectively the validation
model of HTTP/1.1. Section 3.2.9.4 gives a more practical explanation of
caching with a description of how HTTP/1.1 supports the control of caches
using a special header field. Finally, section 3.2.9.5 shortly describes how
caching can be implemented using the mechanisms described in the preceding
sections.

3.2.9.1 History of HTTP caching

As mentioned earlier, caching has already been defined in HTTP/1.0, but the mechanisms defined there were so simple that it was not possible to effectively support efficient and transparent caching. This is one of the crucial points of caching. Caching should provide as much *semantic transparency* as possible. A cache is said to behave semantically transparent, if the use of the cache does nothing but to improve performance when a request for an entity which is stored by the cache is served by the cache rather than the origin server. An interesting study of potentials and limitations of HTTP intermediaries which act as caches has been published by Abrams et al. [1].

Caching in HTTP/1.0

The basic mechanisms of HTTP/1.0 supporting caching were three header fields. The Expires header field could be used by a server to specify the date and time after which an entity should be considered stale. The If-Modified-Since header field could be used to make a GET request conditional, only requesting an entity if it had been modified after the specified date. The last header was the Pragma field, which could be used with the no-cache directive to instruct the client that an entity should not be cached.

This rudimentary support of caching caused many implementors not to support caching at all, and many server administrator decided to routinely generate Pragma: no-cache headers to prevent caches from storing responses (a technique called *cache-busting*). As a result, it became clear that caching would be an important are of improvement for the next version of HTTP.

Caching improvements in HTTP/1.1

The main goal of caching in HTTP/1.1 is to achieve *semantic transparency*. A cache behaves semantically transparent when its use affects neither the requesting client nor the origin server, except to improve performance. When a cache is semantically transparent, the client receives exactly the same response that it would have received had its request been handled directly by the origin server. The design principle of the protocol is that semantic transparency is only relaxed if explicitly requested by a client or an origin server, or only with an explicit warning to the end user. And whenever semantic transparency is relaxed, this should be notified, so that the user can decide what to do.

- *Detailed cache control*
  The cache control provided in HTTP/1.1 allows a number of cache directives to be specified in requests and responses. These directives are

interpreted by caches and can be used to control the behavior of caches and the way requests and responses are processed.

- *Minimum requirements for cache behavior*
  HTTP/1.1 defines a number of minimum requirements for caches which must be fulfilled by every cache implementation. This makes it possible to define some cache directives which are guaranteed to be observed by caches.

- *Warn codes*
  Although HTTP/1.1 is designed to provide semantic transparency, in some situations (requested by the client or dictated by the environment, for example the loss of connectivity) this can not be achieved. A number of warn codes are used to inform the user about a lack of semantic transparency. In these cases, it is up to the user whether the response is accepted or ignored.

In the following sections, we describe some of the key aspects of caching in HTTP/1.1, which are the expiration model and the validation model. Subsequently, the protocol mechanisms provided by HTTP/1.1 to control the caching behavior are explained.

3.2.9.2 Expiration model

Much of HTTP caching is based on the expiration of responses. This model assumes that responses have a certain lifetime. Before this lifetime has expired, a response is said to be *fresh*, if its lifetime has expired, it is *stale*[38]. The basic idea of HTTP caching is that caches should store fresh responses and should also keep track of a response's lifetime (ie, monitoring its *freshness*). If a response becomes stale, it should not be used for answering requests (with the exception of situations where the client explicitly accepts stale responses or when it is impossible to contact the origin server to obtain a fresh copy of the stale response). HTTP has two basic models how the lifetime of a response may be determined.

- *Server-specified expiration*
  A server may specify the expiration time for a response. This may be done using the `Expires` header field or by using the `Cache-Control` header field specifying the `max-age` directive[39]. In doing so, the server sets the lifetime of the response. The expiration time specified by a server is the time

---

[38] If a response has a unlimited lifetime, it will never become stale, and if it has a lifetime of zero seconds, it will never be fresh.

[39] If both ways are used, the `max-age` directive overrides the `Expires` header field.

during which a response is supposed to not change in a semantically significant way. A cache treats a response with a server-specified expiration time as stale as soon as this time has expired, before that it is assumed to be fresh.

In some cases (for example, for dynamically generated pages which have permanently changing content, such as up-to-date statistics), a server may want to explicitly specify a response as not being cached as a fresh response at all. In this case, there are two scenarios what a server can use.

- *Requests should be revalidated*
  If a server specifies an expiration time in the past, the response is considered stale immediately and has to be revalidated if it is requested from the cache. However, if the request specifies that stale responses are acceptable, or if the cache can not contact the origin server, the cache may return the stale response, including a 110 (`response is stale`) warn code.

- *Requests must be revalidated*
  If a server decides that a response must be revalidated, it can use the `Cache-Control` header field specifying the `must-revalidate` directive as described in section 3.2.9.4. In this case, the cache must revalidate the response if it is requested from the cache. If the cache can not contact the origin server for revalidation, it must send a response with a 504 (`gateway time-out`) status code.

A server therefore has the possibility to decide whether a response has an expiration time at all, and also how a cache should handle a stale response.

- *Heuristic expiration*
  HTTP does not require origin servers to set expiration times, so caches will probably receive many responses with no expiration time set. In this case, it is up to the cache to employ heuristic algorithms to assign expiration times to these responses. A possible source for such an heuristic may be the `Last-Modified` header field, assuming that a page which has not been changed in a long time will also not change in the next time.

  However, since caches using heuristic expiration times may compromise semantic transparency, it is advisable to use them with caution and to be more pessimistic than optimistic in the assumptions about the expiration times. HTTP also encourages origin servers to use server-specified expiration times in order to avoid the usage of heuristic expiration times whenever possible. If a cache heuristically assigns a freshness lifetime greater than 24 hours to a response and the response's age is greater than 24 hours, it must include a 113 (`heuristic expiration`) warn code whenever it uses this response without prior validation.

Once the expiration time of a response is known, either because it has been specified by the origin server, or because it has been assigned based on a heuristic, a cache need to make calculations involving the response's status. Because a cache bases its calculations on the local time as well as time specifications which have been set by other hosts, caches should use the *Network Time Protocol (NTP)* or some other means to synchronize their clocks to a globally accurate time standard.

- *Age calculations*
  A cache has to set the `Age` header field in every response it sends. This header field specifies the time the response has been resident in each of the cache along the path from the origin server (if multiple caches are involved), plus the amount of time it has been in transit. There are two different ways to calculate the age of a response, one is based on the `Date` header field of the response (which should be included in the response from the origin server), the other one is based on the `Age` header field of the response (if there is one). The HTTP specification defines a conservative algorithm to calculate the age of a response, which should then be sent in the `Age` header field.

- *Expiration calculations*
  The second important calculation which is done by a cache is the expiration calculation, which determines whether a response is fresh or stale. This calculation is done by comparing the freshness lifetime of the response to its age. The freshness lifetime can be calculated in three different ways.

  1. If a `Cache-Control` header field using a `max-age` directive is present in a response, the freshness lifetime of the response is equal to the time specified with the `max-age` directive.
  2. If an `Expires` header field is present in a response (but no `max-age` directive), the freshness lifetime of the response is equal to the value of the `Expires` header field minus the value of the `Date` header field. Since both the `Expires` header field and the `Date` header field are specified by the origin server, this method is not vulnerable to clock differences.
  3. If neither a `Expires` header field nor a `max-age` directive is present in the response, the cache may compute a freshness lifetime using a heuristic.

Based on the age and the freshness lifetime of a response, a cache can then simply decide whether a response is fresh. A response is fresh if the freshness lifetime is greater than its age.

These two aspects (specification of expiration times and calculations of age and expiration) are the core of HTTP's expiration model. Caches base most of their actions on the freshness of a response. If a response is fresh, it may be taken from the cache (rather than being requested from the origin server). However, it is still open what a cache does if it receives a request for a stale response. It could simply request a fresh response from the origin server, but HTTP defines a more elaborate model which enables caches to *validate* stale responses. Validation can be used to determine whether a stale cache entry is still usable and may therefore be used by the cache instead of requesting a new copy from the origin server.

3.2.9.3 Validation model

The basic idea of validation is that a stale response in many cases is still valid (ie, the resource on the origin server did not change), so that it would be a waste of bandwidth to retransmit the resource from the origin server to the cache. Consequently, if a cache has a stale entry it would like to use as a response to a client's request, it checks with the origin server to see if the cached response is still usable. This is shown in figure 3.13[40].

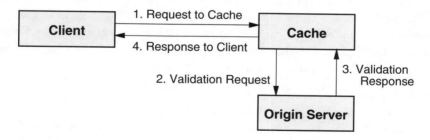

Fig. 3.13 HTTP validation of cached entities

The key idea behind this validation model is the use of *validators*, which are associated with resources. When an origin server sends a response, it sends a validator with it, identifying the resource which is included in the response. This validator is stored with the response in all caches receiving

---

[40] The difference to the cache miss scenario as shown in figure 3.11 is that the validation response will usually be much smaller if the cached response is still usable, because the resource itself is not transmitted again.

the response and in the user agent. If a client (user agent or cache) makes a validation request for this response, it simply sends the response's validator. The origin server associates the validator with the resource and can decide whether the response which has included the validator is still usable.

If the response is still usable, the origin server sends a response with a 304 (not modified) status code and no entity body. If the response is no longer usable (because the associated resource has changed on the origin server), the origin server returns a full response. This way, in both cases only one round-trip between the validating client and the origin server is necessary. The procedure depends on the existence of validators, of which two types can be used with HTTP:

- Last-Modified header field
  In this case, the date of the last modification of a resource is used as a validator. Consequently, a cache entry is considered to be valid if the associated resource has not been modified since the value of the Last-Modified header field.

- ETag header field
  In addition to the modification date, a server may also generate an entity tag for a resource, serving as a validator. An entity tag may either be *strong* or *weak*, as described in the following text.

It is possible to think of scenarios where a resource on an origin server has changed, but it would make sense to still treat cached responses of this resource as usable. The main motivation here is HTTP's general goal of semantic transparency for caching. In order to support origin servers which want to implement a caching strategy which is based on the semantics of resources, HTTP supports two types of validators:

- *Strong validator*
  A strong validator is a validator which changes whenever the entity it represents changes. Thus, a strong validator can be seen as a validator which identifies a single entity, or a single version of an entity, if an entity is modified a couple of times.

- *Weak validator*
  A weak validator is a validator which changes whenever there is a semantically significant modification to the entity is represents. Thus, a weak validator can be seen as a validator which identifies a set of semantically equivalent entities. For example, if spelling errors are corrected on a web

page, a weak validator probably would not change, because the corrected spelling does not change the semantics of the web page[41].

While strong validators can be used in any context, weak validators can only be used in certain contexts. For example, if a client makes a range request (using the Range or If-Range header fields), it is necessary that the server uses the exact same entity (ie, using strong semantics) as the client, otherwise the client may get a corrupted entity when combining the local entity and the requested range. Consequently, HTTP defines two comparison functions, one for contexts where strong validators are required, and another one for contexts where strong as well as weak validators are usable.

- *Strong comparison*
  In order to satisfy the strong comparison function on validators, both validators must be strong, and they must be identical in every way.

- *Weak comparison*
  For the weak comparison function on validators, both validators must be identical in every way, but either or both of them may be weak.

Based on these rules about expiration times, validator types, and validator comparison functions, HTTP clients, caches, and origin servers can implement a caching model which in many cases will help to greatly improve HTTP efficiency by avoiding entity transfers. It can also be seen that HTTP caching heavily relies on cooperating clients, caches, and origin servers. After the basic model of expiration and validation has been explained, the next issue is how caches, and origin servers can communicate with each other in an effort to use caching most efficiently. This issue is discussed in the following section.

3.2.9.4 Cache control

The most important header field for caching is the Cache-Control general header field, which is used to specify directives that must be obeyed by all caching mechanisms along the request/response chain. If a request or response is passed on by a proxy or gateway that does not implement caching functionality, it must pass through the cache directives, since the directives may apply to a recipient behind it.

---

[41] However, there is no clearly definable border between semantically insignificant and semantically significant modifications. It is up to the origin server to define this border and to assign weak validators according to this definition.

   Since the syntax of the `Cache-Control` general header field is much more
complex than the syntax of most other header fields, it is given below[42] to
give an overview over the cache directives which may be specified.

```
Cache-Control   = "Cache-Control" ":" +cache-directive

cache-directive = cache-request-directive
                | cache-response-directive

cache-request-directive =
                "no-cache"    [ "=" <"> +field-name <"> ]
              | "no-store"
              | "max-age"       "=" delta-seconds
              | "max-stale" [ "=" delta-seconds ]
              | "min-fresh"     "=" delta-seconds
              | "only-if-cached"

cache-response-directive =
                "public"
              | "private"    [ "=" <"> +field-name <"> ]
              | "no-cache"   [ "=" <"> +field-name <"> ]
              | "no-store"
              | "no-transform"
              | "must-revalidate"
              | "proxy-revalidate"
              | "max-age"       "=" delta-seconds
```

   It can be seen that the cache directives are divided into two major groups,
directives used for requests and directives used for responses. However, some
directives can be used for requests and responses. Cache directives specified
with the `Cache-Control` general header field can be divided into several
groups, which are described in the following list:

- *Restrictions on what is cacheable*
  There are default rules which define when a response is cacheable. These
  rules take the request method, the request header fields, and the response
  status into account. However, an origin server may override these defaults
  by using special `Cache-Control` response directives which specify the
  cacheability of a response.

  − `public`
    This value indicates that a response is cacheable by any cache, even
    if it would normally (ie, without overriding the default rules) be

---

[42] The plus sign '+' in front of a term means that one or more occurrences of the
term are allowed in that position. Vertical bars '|' represent alternatives, and
brackets '[ ]' optional parts of the syntax. Normally, double quotes '"' are used
as delimiters for strings, but if double quotes themselves appear inside a string,
angle brackets '< >' are used to delimit the string.

non-cacheable or cacheable only within a non-shared cache (which is for example the default for responses to requests which contain an `Authorization` request header field).

— `private`
This value indicates that a response is not cacheable by a shared cache, but can be cached by a private cache[43], even if it would normally (ie, without overriding the default rules) be non-cacheable or cacheable within a shared cache. A typical example for this kind of response is a response which has been generated specifically for one user and is not a valid response for another user.

— `no-cache`
There are two ways to use the `no-cache` directive for cache control. The two ways are differentiated by the presence or absence of any field names which are specified for the `no-cache` directive.

- *No field names*
  If no field name is specified in the `no-cache` directive, caches are instructed to not use the response to satisfy a subsequent request without successful revalidation with the origin server. This way even caches which have been configured to return stale responses to client requests can be forced to use revalidation.

- *Field names*
  If there are any field names specified in the `no-cache` directive, this instructs caches to not use the specified fields in a response which is taken from the cache. Other restrictions to the cacheability of the response may also apply, but the `no-cache` directive in this case only excludes specific header fields from being cached.

- *Restrictions on what may be stored by a cache*
  In case of sensitive information being sent over the net, it may not be sufficient for a client or server to specify that the information in the HTTP message should not be cached. Consequently, either in a request or in a response a cache directive can be used which prevents caches from storing a message.

  — `no-store`
  If the `no-store` directive is set, the cache should not store any part of the message in non-volatile storage (such as a hard disk), and should make a best-effort attempt to remove the message from volatile storage as promptly as possible after forwarding it.

---

[43] It is important to notice that this only controls where the response may be cached, but does not ensure the privacy of the response.

However, even if this directive is used, the user may still save the response outside of the caching system, and the user agent may store the response as part of the normal history buffer.

- *Modifications of the basic expiration mechanism*
  The basic expiration mechanism used by a cache normally takes the expiration time of a response (which can be defined explicitly or heuristically as described in section 3.2.9.2) for determining its operation. However, it is possible to control the cache's expiration mechanism using a number of directives.

  - `max-age`
    This directive indicates that the client is willing to accept a response whose age is no greater than the specified time in seconds. The `max-age` directive may also be sent in a response to indicate the expiration time for a response. If a response includes a `Cache-Control` field with the `max-age` directive, that directive overrides the `Expires` header field.

  - `min-fresh`
    A client can request a response which will remain fresh for a given amount of time. Thus, the cache has to verify that the response will still be fresh at the time which is determined by adding the current age and the time requested with the `min-fresh` directive.

  - `max-stale`
    This indicates that the client is willing to accept a stale response (ie, a response which is past its expiration time). This directive is set by a user agent and may be used to increase the chances of a cache hit. If no value is given, the client is willing to accept a stale response of any age, a value indicates that the client is willing to accept a response that has exceeded its expiration time by no more than the specified number of seconds. If a cache returns a stale response, it must attach a `Warning` header to the response, indicating a 110 (`response is stale`) warning.

- *Controls over cache revalidation and reload*
  In addition to the scenarios where control over the basic expiration mechanism is required, it is also possible that the behavior of caches with regard to validation (as described in section 3.2.9.3) should be modified. There are a number directives which can be used to control the validation and reload of cached responses.

  - `no-cache`
    This directive, when present in a request and having no field names associated with it, always causes a reload from the origin server.

– `must-revalidate`

The `must-revalidate` directive can only be used in responses. It instructs caches that the response may be cached, but that it must be revalidated after it becomes stale. In all circumstances (even if the client used a request with a `max-stale` directive) a cache must obey the `must-revalidate` directive. If the cache can not reach the origin server for revalidation, it must send a `504` (`gateway time-out`) status code instead of the stale response.

– `proxy-revalidate`

This directive is very similar in nature to the `must-revalidate` directive. The only difference is that it allows non-shared user agent caches to use a stale response. All caches along the request/response chain have to follow the same rules as for the `must-revalidate` directive.

– `only-if-cached`

In some cases, such as times of extremely poor network connectivity, a client may want a cache to return only those responses that it currently has stored, and not to reload or revalidate with the origin server. The `only-if-cached` directive can be used in a request to specify that the cache should not reload or revalidate a response. A cache should either respond using a cached entry or with a `504` (`gateway time-out`) status code.

- *Control over transformation of entities*

  In some cases, caches may want to transform entities, such as using different image compression algorithms to minimize storage space of cache entries. However, there may be application scenarios where such a transformation is undesirable.

  – `no-transform`

  If a request contains the `no-transform` directive, the cache must not change the entity. Therefore, applications which rely on end-to-end identical entities should use the `no-transform` directive in requests. User agents can determine whether an intermediate cache applied a transformation by checking for a `214` (`transformation applied`) warn code.

In addition to these cache directives which can be used to control caching in a number of ways, a number of warn codes have been defined which are used in addition to the standard HTTP status codes as described in section 3.2.4.1. The `Warning` response header field is used to communicate different types of warnings, but in the current version of HTTP it is only used for warnings regarding caching. The first digit of the three digit warn code indicates whether the warning must (`1xx` warn codes) or must not (`2xx` warn codes) be deleted from a stored cache entry after a successful revalidation. The following warn codes are defined in the HTTP specification:

- **110 (response is stale)**
  This warning must be included whenever a response is stale. A cache may add this warning to a response, but it may never be removed from a response unless the cache knows that the response is fresh.

- **111 (revalidation failed)**
  This warning must be returned by a cache whose attempt to revalidate a response failed. This revalidation failure occurs if the cache can not contact the origin server of the response.

- **112 (disconnected operation)**
  If a cache is intentionally disconnected from the rest of the network for a period of time (eg, a company's cache may keep running but the network connection to the Internet may be down due to maintenance reasons), this warning should be included in the responses given by the cache.

- **113 (heuristic expiration)**
  This warning must be included in a response from a cache if the cache heuristically chose a freshness lifetime greater than 24 hours and the response's age is greater than 24 hours.

- **214 (transformation applied)**
  This warning must be added by a cache if it applies any transformation changing the content-coding (as specified in the `Content-Encoding` header) or media-type (as specified in the `Content-Type` header) of the response.

Using the `Cache-Control` and `Warning` header fields, user agents, caches, and origin servers can implement a powerful caching system. It should be noted, however, that HTTP only defines mechanisms how information about caching can be exchanged, the caching policies of user agents, caches, and origin servers are not defined. There are only a few cases in which cases the HTTP specification is very rigid, but these are cases in which it is important to prevent caches from storing responses too long or without revalidation.

Generally, this model of cooperating caches, where every cache implements its own caching strategy, reflects the Internet design philosophy, by defining only the minimal standard which must be met to assure that the overall system is working properly.

3.2.9.5 Implementation of caching

As already mentioned in the previous section, the HTTP specification only defines general rules how information about resources, expirations times, response validation and warnings may be exchanged. However, it is up to a cache's implementation what to do with this information, as long as it conforms to the requirements defined by the HTTP specification. To give an impression of possible implementation variants, the following examples are possible (but not necessarily useful) ways to implement an HTTP cache.

- *No caching*
  Since the HTTP specification is only concerned with preventing a cache from storing responses too long or without revalidation, a cache which does not store responses at all is a valid HTTP cache implementation. However, such an implementation does not make sense because such a cache would always delay requests by adding the processing delay inside the cache.

- *Active caches*
  Although the most popular cache implementation is a reactive cache, which only becomes active in response to an incoming message, it is also possible to design a cache which for example automatically validates cache entries when they become stale. This introduces the risk of performing unnecessary validations, but it also has the benefit that the cache entries are more likely to be fresh when the cache receives a request. The cache could also implement some kind of strategy (for example, how often a response has been requested) to decide whether it should automatically revalidate a stale response or wait for requests before performing a revalidation.

- *Proprietary inter-cache protocols*
  Although a cache in the model defined by HTTP is a system which uses only HTTP for the exchange of messages with other caches, it is also possible to think of a system of cooperating caches which use other means of communications than HTTP. This way, it would be possible to exchange more information about cache contents than can be done with HTTP. All the cooperating caches would also accept and generate HTTP messages, but a more sophisticated caching system could be built if a proprietary inter-cache protocol would be used.

These examples are only very simple, but they should be sufficient to demonstrate that the HTTP specification is only a framework within which cache implementors have a lot of freedom to choose strategies which best fit their needs. Papers by Dingle and Partl [66], Wooster and Abrams [276], and Scheuermann et al. [236] describe different aspects of cache implementation. Many more papers exist which focus on different aspects of cache design.

3.3 Security

So far, we have discussed security aspects of HTTP only with regard to authenticity, describing the authentication methods of HTTP in section 3.2.6. Although authenticity may be sufficient for a number of applications, very often there also is a need for privacy, that is for mechanisms which can guarantee that any information which is transmitted between the client and the server can only be interpreted by these two peers. Generally, it is not possible to physically protect the network from attackers. The Internet is based on an architecture which gives only little control over how data is transferred between two communication peers, so it is necessary to use mechanisms which make any data which can be captured through eavesdropping or other methods useless to attackers. This is achieved by using cryptographic methods.

There are, however, different kinds of attacks, and depending on the techniques being used in order to achieve secure communications, it is important to know which kinds of attack are technically possible and are to be expected. A simple method called eavesdropping is an easy way of attacking a connection on the Internet. It consists of a third party listening to all data being sent between the two communication peers. A more complicated and more powerful attack is the middleperson attack, where the attacker is located in between the two communication peers and can modify data before forwarding it to the other side. While some techniques for secure communications can be used to protect oneself against eavesdropping and middleperson attacks, other techniques can only guarantee safety against eavesdropping and will be useless in the case of middleperson attacks.

From the application point of view, there are two ways how secure communications between a client and a server can be achieved, depending on whether security should be implemented inside the transport infrastructure, or inside the application[44].

- *Using a secure transport infrastructure*
  In this scenario, the application protocol is not changed. It is assumed that the transport infrastructure itself provides the security, so the only issue remaining to be solved is the question of how it is decided whether the normal (insecure) or the secure transport infrastructure should be used and how a connection using the secure transport infrastructure can

---

[44] This also raises the question whether a user trusts the local transport infrastructure (which is typically part of the operating system), trusts the local application (which typically made by a different company than the operating system), or none of both. However, this kind of question is outside the scope of this book, although an important issue when thinking about secure communication architectures.

be established. This type of security can be used by all applications which are aware of the secure transport infrastructure.

- *Using a secure application-level protocol*
  In the second case, it is assumed that the transport infrastructure is insecure, and therefore the application protocol itself is modified to incorporate security features. In this approach, the requirements regarding the transport infrastructure are much lower, but the work to be done inside the application (adding security features to the application-level protocol) is much harder. Furthermore, the security features can only be used for one particular application.

Deciding which of these approaches should be taken is a complex issue. While the first approach has its advantages regarding modularity and also in providing a secure transport infrastructure which may also be used by other applications, the second approach gives more control to the application protocol designer and requires less trust in the secure transport infrastructure. Rather than being a purely technical question which could be answered in only one way which is right for all possible scenarios, it is more a philosophical question.

With regard to HTTP, both approaches have been taken. In section 3.3.1, *HTTP over SSL (HTTPS)* is discussed, which is a solution using normal HTTP over a secure transport infrastructure (the *Secure Sockets Layer (SSL)*. The other approach, *Secure HTTP (S-HTTP)*, is described in section 3.3.2 and defines a new application protocol. Currently, HTTPS is the common solution for web applications with the need for secure transactions, while S-HTTP seems to have disappeared almost completely. However, because both approaches to security for HTTP are interesting, we also include a short description of S-HTTP in this section.

3.3.1 HTTP over SSL (HTTPS)

When looking for a way to provide secure transactions on the web, Netscape decided to implement its own solution, which now is known as *HTTP over SSL (HTTPS)* [222][45]. The approach taken in HTTPS is that of a secure transport infrastructure, which is an additional layer between the normally used TCP/IP layer and HTTP as the application protocol. This architecture is depicted in figure 3.14, which also shows that the approach taken

---

[45] This Internet draft is actually called "HTTP over TLS", using the IETF version of SSL which is called *Transport Layer Security (TLS)* (currently under development and documented in another Internet draft entitled "The TLS Protocol Version 1.0" [64]). Since TLS is very similar to and compatible with SSL, this draft is the most accurate description of the current practice which is available.

with HTTPS can easily be used to add more security to other applications normally sitting on top of TCP/IP.

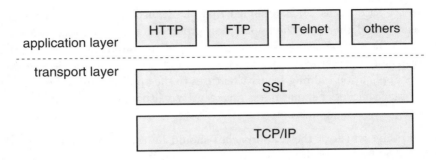

Fig. 3.14   Layering of communication protocols with SSL

Although SSL is intended to be used on top of any reliable transport infrastructure and can be used by any application which normally uses an insecure reliable transport infrastructure to achieve secure communications, its primary purpose and most widespread usage is on top of TCP/IP and as secure transport infrastructure for HTTP. However, because SSL and HTTPS are two independent concepts, in section 3.3.1.1 we first shortly describe how SSL works. Section 3.3.1.2 describes how HTTP and SSL are used together to create HTTPS.

3.3.1.1 Secure Sockets Layer (SSL)

SSL borrows its name from the most common programming interface to TCP/IP, which is the sockets library which originally has been implemented in early versions of the Unix operating system. While TCP/IP is a well-defined protocol for computer communications, it does not define how the services realized by it can be accessed within a programming environment. Unix sockets as described by Stevens [256] have become a de-facto standard for network programming. SSL, however, does not specify a programming interface, it only specifies a protocol, thus different SSL implementations have different programming interfaces and are not interchangeable without modifications of the software using them[46].

---

[46] In some cases, it may be possible to write *wrappers* for particular SSL implementations which make it possible to use one SSL implementation (together with the wrapper) in the same way as another SSL implementation. However, in general applications using SSL must be ported to use another SSL implementation.

With the goal of secure communications over an insecure medium in mind, SSL specifies a protocol which provides connection security that has three basic properties.

- *Connection privacy*
  Encryption is used after an initial handshake to define a secret key. Symmetric cryptography is used for data encryption.

- *Optional authentication*
  The peer's identity can be authenticated using asymmetric (ie, public key) cryptography.

- *Connection reliability*
  The connection is reliable. Message transport includes a message integrity check using a keyed *Message Authentication Code (MAC)*. Secure hash functions are used for MAC computations.

In the order of their importance, the goals of the SSL protocol are as follows.

- *Cryptographic security*
  SSL should be used to establish a secure connection between two parties.

- *Interoperability*
  Independent programmers should be able to develop applications utilizing SSL that will be able to successfully exchange cryptographic parameters without knowledge of one another's code[47].

- *Extensibility*
  SSL seeks to provide a framework into which new public key and bulk encryption methods can be incorporated as necessary. This will also accomplish two sub-goals: to prevent the need to create a new protocol (and risking the introduction of possible new weaknesses) and to avoid the need to implement an entire new security library.

- *Relative efficiency*
  Cryptographic operations tend to be highly CPU intensive, particularly public key operations. For this reason, the SSL protocol has incorporated an optional session caching scheme to reduce the number of connections that need to be established from scratch. Additionally, care has been taken to reduce network activity.

---

[47] It is not the case that all instances of SSL (even in the same application domain) will be able to successfully connect. For instance, if the server supports a particular hardware token, and the client does not have access to such a token, the connection will not succeed.

In general, SSL can be used to create three different types of connections between a client and a server, depending on the authentication which takes place. Authentication is a process which requires a certificate which has been issued by an acceptable certificate authority[48].

- *Anonymity*
  In this scenario, neither the client nor the server are authenticated.

- *Server authentication*
  Server authentication requires the server to present a certificate which is accepted by the client. Although the server does not know the client's identity, the client can be sure about the server's identity.

- *Authentication of both parties*
  In this scenario, both the client and the server are authenticated through certificates, so both parties know the other side's identity.

It should be noted that the anonymous scenario only provides protection against eavesdropping, while middleperson attacks are still possible. If SSL is used in an environment where this type of attack is a concern, at least server authentication should be used to achieve protection against middleperson attacks.

SSL consists of two phases, first a handshake phase, which is used to determine the capabilities of both sides, optionally perform authentication, and select an encryption method to use for the SSL session. SSL is based on the session concept, powerful encryption methods are used to securely exchange a session key, which is used to encrypt the data which is exchanged between the client and the server. This session key uses a weaker (but more efficient) encryption method than the key exchange, which is tolerable since the key is only used for the lifetime of a session[49]. SSL defines a number of different algorithms for key exchange and a number of different algorithms for session keys. Part of the handshake phase is to find the strongest key exchange and session key algorithms which are supported by both parties.

3.3.1.2 Combining HTTP and SSL

Although the application-level protocol between a client and a server using HTTPS is normal HTTP, it is necessary for the client to know that it must

---

[48] It is up to the user to decide which certificate authorities are acceptable.

[49] SSL also includes a session caching concept, which caches the session key at both the server and the client side. If both parties agree to use the cached session key in a new session, the key exchange phase can be skipped. If either party suspects that the session key may have been compromised, a full handshake including the generation of a new session key is initiated.

open an SSL connection to the server instead of a normal (insecure) TCP connection. This is achieved by using a new URL naming scheme for HTTPS, defining the "https" prefix for URLs (more on URL naming schemes can be found in section 2.3.2).

In an Internet draft by Rescorla [222] it is described how HTTP over SSL (or TLS) should be used. With regard to an actual implementation of HTTPS, two different scenarios as shown in figure 3.15 are possible.

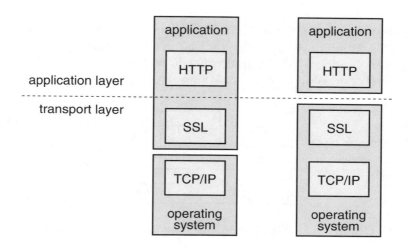

Fig. 3.15 Possible locations of SSL and TCP implementation

Although SSL (or TLS) is designed to be a transport layer protocol which is not specifically designed for a single application-level protocol, it is currently not part of a standard transport protocol layer as provided by most operating systems. Therefore, it is necessary for an application (such as a browser or a server supporting HTTPS) to include an SSL implementation, which is shown in the left diagram of figure 3.15. In the right diagram, the ideal situation is depicted, where SSL is provided by the operating system, and the application only needs to implement HTTP, using the operating system's SSL implementation.

However, it will take a long time until SSL will be a standard part of operating systems, and until then, HTTPS applications need to include SSL implementations, which eliminates some of the architectural advantages of HTTPS over S-HTTP. For example, if two different browsers supporting HTTPS are used on one computer, both will include their own SSL implementations, although it would be more efficient in terms of application size if they could share one SSL implementation provided by the operating system.

Also of interest is the question how HTTPS should be handled when the connection between client and server is going through a proxy. The two basic approaches are to transparently forward all data by the proxy, an approach which is called *SSL proxying*, or to have the proxy "understand" the data, which is called *HTTPS proxying*. These two approaches are described in more detail in section 9.2.4.2.

3.3.2 Secure HTTP (S-HTTP)

The alternative to HTTPS is S-HTTP as described by Rescorla and Schiffman [223]. Although the protocol is similar in its cryptographic capabilities, it is not very widespread. The principal architecture of how S-HTTP fits into the picture of other application-level protocols is shown in figure 3.16.

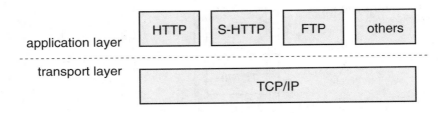

Fig. 3.16   Layering of communication protocols with S-HTTP

S-HTTP defines a message format which uses HTTP as the base. It adds security features to HTTP which make it possible to use authentication, secure data transfer, and negotiation of options between clients and servers. The basic idea of S-HTTP is to encapsulate HTTP messages in a secure way. This makes S-HTTP independent from a specific HTTP version, since the encapsulation of HTTP messages does not depend on the exact syntax of HTTP.

S-HTTP supports two ways to cryptographic message format standards, one is the format according to *MIME Object Security Services (MOSS)*, and the other one is the format defined by the *Cryptographic Message Syntax (CMS)*. However, S-HTTP is not limited to these formats and it is easily possible to incorporate new cryptographic message format standards into S-HTTP.

3.4 Cookies

One of the main characteristics of HTTP is that it is a stateless protocol. This means that the exchange of HTTP messages is not embedded into a larger framework (such as sessions, consisting of multiple request/response interactions), instead each request/response interaction between a client and a server is not influenced by former interactions and will not influence later interactions. However, in many application scenarios, this would be a big advantage, such as in virtual shopping malls, where a customer should be able to use some kind of "shopping cart", which is used to collect all items he wants to buy, and finally used for placing the order.

Initially, Netscape created a solution which, for no apparent reason, has been called *cookies*. Basically, a cookie is a piece of information which is exchanged between a client and a server and is used to maintain the state information which is not part of HTTP. Consequently, the Internet proposed standard RFC 2109 [152][50] which has evolved from Netscape's initial specification is called "HTTP State Management Mechanism". The latest version of the Internet document defines a cookie mechanism which very similar to and compatible with the one proposed by Netscape.

The basic idea of the cookie mechanism is to pass back and forth state information between the client and the server, thereby creating a logical session which does not refer to some physical equivalent such as a persistent network connection. A server can send a cookie to a client using a new response header Set-Cookie, which is stored by the client. When sending a request to this server, the client includes the cookie using the new request header Cookie, which makes it possible for the server to identify the session through analyzing the cookie's content.

This process is shown in figure 3.17, which assumes that the cookie processing on the server is done by a separate application (ie, not directly by the HTTP server), and that information between the HTTP server and the application handling the cookies is exchanged using the *Common Gateway Interface (CGI)* as described in section 9.4. In this figure, it can be seen that by sending a cookie to the client in its first response, the server can treat both request/response interactions as one logical session by recognizing the cookie which is sent back by the client in its second request.

In order to make this scheme work, the client must know which cookie it has to send to which server, since it would be impractical and also a violation of privacy issues for a client to send to each server it sends requests to all cookies it currently stores. The mechanism used for doing this is really straight-forward, it is a simple match of server names (ie, Internet host names, which can be domain names or IP addresses as described in section 1.4.1.2). If a client sends a request to a server for which (based on the comparison of the host name) it currently stores a cookie, it includes the cookie in the

---

[50] A new Internet draft [153] is being prepared during the time of writing, which will eventually replace RFC 2109.

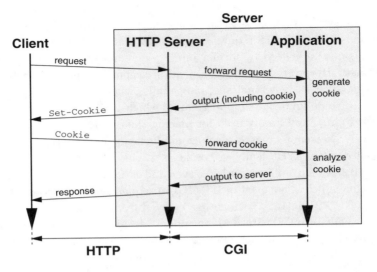

Fig. 3.17   HTTP state management using cookies

request using the Cookie header field, otherwise the request will not contain a cookie.

- Set-Cookie

    The Set-Cookie response header is used by a server to set a cookie on the client, that is to send a cookie to a client which the client is supposed to store (if the client supports cookies, otherwise it will simply ignore the Set-Cookie header field). The header field contains one or more cookies which are defined by a name and a number of attribute/value pairs, which are explained below.

- Cookie

    A client sends cookies to a server using the Cookie request header. The client's decision on whether a particular cookie should be sent to a server is based on the server's name, the request URI, and the cookie's age. If all these criteria match, the client includes one or more cookies in the request using the Cookie header field.

Until now, nothing has been said about the actual information which is carried by a cookie. It is important to notice that the concept of a cookie is more like that of a way to identify actual state information on the origin server (ie, the server which generated the cookie), than actually carrying this information. Therefore, unless the implementor of a cookie server violates this principle, it is very unlikely that a cookie will contain any information that may require privacy[51]. However, apart from the actual state information which is stored on the cookie's origin server, a cookie is identified by a name and a value, both of which are chosen by the origin server, and a number of attribute/value pairs, most of which are optional.

- Comment
  This optional attribute contains information which the server can use to document its intended use of the cookie. The user can inspect this information to decide whether he wants to actually use this cookie.

- Domain
  Using this optional attribute, the server can specify the domain for which a cookie is valid. This way it is possible to create cookies which are not only valid for a single server as identified by the server's name, but for a set of servers which are identified by the DNS domain they are part of.

- Max-Age
  Since many applications of cookies are based towards more short-lived interactions, servers can use the optional Max-Age attribute to specify the lifetime of a cookie in seconds. Clients should discard cookies after their lifetime has elapsed.

- Path
  Since a cookie might not apply to all URIs on a server, an optional Path attribute can be used by the server to specify a subset of URIs to which a cookie applies.

- Secure
  This optional attribute directs the client to only use secure means to contact the origin server whenever it sends back the cookie. However, it is unspecified which means of communication are to be considered secure[52] by the client. Therefore, this attribute can be seen as the server giving the client the advice to protect the cookie contents.

- Version
  This is the only mandatory attribute which identifies the version of the state management specification the cookie is conforming to.

Although there has been some controversy about cookies in general and also a rather negative attitude towards the usage of cookies, seeing it as a potential hazard to privacy and security issues, this mechanism is not powerful

---

[51] On the other hand, a cookie is a reference to information which in most cases will require a certain degree of privacy, so unless a server is well protected against an unauthorized client using another user's cookie, it still is a security issue how well cookies are protected.

[52] Some possible methods for secure communications using HTTP are discussed in section 3.3.

enough to present a severe danger to users. Furthermore, since the mechanism entirely depends on the cooperation of the client, it can very easily be switched off by configuring the client in a way where it does not accept or send any cookies[53]. However, in this case all web sites which base their interaction with users on the cookie mechanism can not be used any more, which may greatly reduce the number of commercial web sites which can be used.

3.5 Usage of HTTP

Although HTTP itself is a pretty simple protocol, it is sometimes not so easy to figure out how it is actually being used. One of the reasons for this is that a normal user never actually sees HTTP messages. In most cases, this is exactly what the average user wants to have, but sometimes it would be interesting to know how HTTP is used, that is which headers are generated by a browser and which headers are sent back by a server.

Table 3.3   Header count of HTTP responses

	Header count	Count	Percent
1.	5	10844	41.73%
2.	6	6615	24.45%
3.	8	4008	15.42%
4.	3	2444	9.40%
5.	4	1047	4.03%
6.	7	909	3.50%
7.	9	50	0.19%
8.	2	46	0.18%
9.	0	20	0.08%
10.	1	4	0.02%
11.	10	1	0.00%

A study of web servers in the UK carried out by Beck [15] gives some numbers which can be seen as representative for the web in general, although only web servers in the UK were used to collect the data. The way the data was collected is quite simple, all UK domains were searched for hosts named

---

[53] The most popular browsers can also be configured in a way which makes them prompt before cookies are being accepted or sent. This is a good way to figure out which sites are using cookies, and decisions can be made based on the individual case.

www, and if such a host was present, an HTTP request was sent to the host's standard HTTP port (80)[54].

This way, only the home pages of the servers were accessed, which may have caused some statistical distortions, since web servers hosting a large number of web pages have the same weight as servers only hosting a few pages. However, the data is still interesting and can be used for some observations. Using the methodology describes above, 25988 home pages were retrieved from UK web servers, and the HTTP responses (in particular, the header fields, which are of interest for us) were analyzed. Table 3.3 gives a summary of how many header fields were present in the responses. For 67% of the responses, the response message contained five or six header fields, so this can be seen as the most usual case. The most frequent header fields are summarized in table 3.4, which lists the absolute number of occurrences, and the percentage (in relation to the total of 25988 responses). Only the header fields which have been present in at least one percent of the responses are listed in the table.

Table 3.4   Frequency of HTTP response headers

	Header field name	Frequency	Percent	Page
1.	Content-Type	25960	99.89%	68
2.	Server	25951	99.86%	84
3.	Date	25679	98.81%	64
4.	Last-Modified	22353	86.01%	68
5.	Content-Length	20945	80.59%	67
6.	Accept-Ranges	9666	37.19%	82
7.	Connection	4780	18.39%	64
8.	ETag	4033	15.52%	68
9.	Expires	1493	5.74%	68
10.	MIME-Version	1358	5.23%	64
11.	Set-Cookie	1115	4.29%	124

It can be seen that there is a set of very popular five header fields, Content-Type, Server, Date, Last-Modified, and Content-Length, which are present in most responses. The first three of these fields are present in virtually every response. Without a Content-Type header field, a response is almost useless for a client, since it does not know how to interpret the entity

---

[54] Although the description of the survey is taken from the original paper, the survey's figures presented here are from a newer survey (carried out in August 1997) which is available at http://www.hensa.ac.uk/uksites/survey/.

in the response[55]. The `Server` header field is very easy to add for the server, since it is static for a server instance and can be included in every response by default. Furthermore, the `Date` header field can also very easily be created, since it contains the date when the message has been sent by the server. The `Last-Modified` and `Content-Length` header fields are less ubiquitous than the first three headers, but since they also contain important information about the entity (the date when the entity was last modified and the entity's size), they are also used very frequently by servers.

3.6 Non-standard HTTP extensions

Although HTTP/1.1 greatly increased the number of standardized header fields in comparison to HTTP/1.0, there still are some headers which are not part of the HTTP/1.1 standard, even though they are widely used and supported. While some of these header fields have been included in the first drafts of HTTP/1.1 and have then been removed to be included in later versions (this happened to the `Refresh` header field described in section 3.6.1), other header fields are entirely proprietary and will probably never be standardized (such as Microsoft's page transition headers described in section 3.6.2).

3.6.1 Refreshing web pages

The most popular non-standard header field is the `Refresh` header field, which usually is used within web pages to automatically refresh (ie, reload) them after a given time[56]. Although it is mostly used directly in the HTML document within the <META> element as described in section 5.2.3.1, formally it is an HTTP header, since it is used in the <META> element's HTTP-EQUIV attribute. However, the advantage of using the `Refresh` header field inside a web page rather than as an HTTP header field generated in the server's response is the possibility for a page author to use it without any changes to the web server's configuration.

Basically, there are two major uses of the `Refresh` header field, the first one being the possibility to periodically reload a page (for example, to reflect periodical changes which are made to the web page on the server). The value of the `Refresh` header field is specified in the <META> element's CONTENT attribute.

---

[55] Theoretically, the client could make an educated guess based on the entity's URI, which in most cases will carry some information about the entity's media type (such as file names ending in `.html`, `.gif`, or `.jpeg`), but this is strongly discouraged, since by definition URIs should not carry these semantics.

[56] It is also possible to load another web page instead of reloading the same page.

```
<META HTTP-EQUIV="Refresh" CONTENT="300">
```

If this HTML code is included in a web page's document header, the browser will reload the current document every 300 seconds (provided it supports the Refresh header field). Depending on whether the reloaded page also contains a Refresh header field, this will either continue until the user leaves the page (if the reloaded page contains a Refresh header field), or the automatic reloading will stop (if the reloaded page does not include a Refresh header field, for example because there will be no more updates of the page on the web server).

```
<META HTTP-EQUIV="Refresh" CONTENT="0; URL=http://www.w3.org/">
```

In many cases, it is necessary not to reload the same document, but to instruct the browser to load a new document. In this case (which is mainly used if a document has been moved to a new URI and the old URI should remain usable for some transitional period), the document contains a Refresh header field specifying a delay of 0 seconds and the new URI (although for historic reasons the syntax requires to specify the URL keyword). Upon recognizing such a Refresh header field, the browser instantly is redirected to the new URI. Typically, if a document has been moved, the old URI contains a minimal HTML document consisting only of the required HTML elements to include a <META> element, which redirects the browser to the new URI. However, since it is not guaranteed that a browser will support the Refresh header field, it is a good idea to also include some very minimal HTML code (such as text and a hypertext link) for non-refresh browsers.

```
<HTML><HEAD>
<META HTTP-EQUIV="Refresh" CONTENT="10; URL=http://www.w3.org/">
</HEAD><BODY>
<P>This page has been <A HREF="http://www.w3.org/">moved</A>.
</BODY></HTML>
```

Since in some cases it may be necessary to inform users that the page has been moved, the delayed refresh and redirection features of the Refresh header field can be combined. In this example, the message will be displayed for 10 seconds, before the new page is automatically loaded. If the browser does not support the Refresh header field, the user can select the link to get to the new location.

3.6.2 Interpage transitions

A more proprietary mechanism has been introduced by Microsoft to specify transitions between pages. The transitions are purely visually oriented with a number of predefined effects. It is possible to specify the duration of an effect and the effect itself. Four possible transitions has been defined, which are (similar to the `Refresh` header field described in the previous section) specified using the <META> element's HTTP-EQUIV and CONTENT attributes. The transitions are `Page-Enter`, `Page-Exit`, `Site-Enter`, and `Site-Exit`. They are used for determining the transition being used when a user enters or leaves a page, respectively when a user enters or leaves a site.

3.7 The future of HTTP

Although HTTP is not as visible for the web user as is HTML, the description language for web documents, the design and performance of HTTP is noticeable for users through the time it takes to retrieve documents from web servers. Because HTTP has become a major factor of bandwidth usage on almost all parts of the Internet, a lot of work is going on which tries to improve HTTP. At the moment, a number of areas can be identified where there is potential to improve HTTP/1.1.

- *Caching*
  Although caching was greatly improved from HTTP/1.0 to HTTP/1.1, there still is some more work to do. One paper discussing these issues is a publication about the improvement of caching algorithms, which is proposed by Scheuermann et al. [236].

- *Hit count reporting*
  Currently, an origin server has no reliable way of determining the usage data for a document, because it may be cached in a proxy. In an Internet draft by Mogul and Leach [179], a new HTTP header field, the `Meter` header field, has been proposed to send hit reports from proxies to origin servers. A newer approach described by Pitkow [205] is based on *sampling* taken from mathematical statistics. It is not clear which of these approaches will be used in the future, but it is agreed that HTTP must support hit count reporting across proxies.
  Currently, there is no way for origin servers to get reliable usage data about their pages. A commonly used technique is *cache-busting*, which is done by using cache-specific HTTP headers to defeat all caching attempts (possible header fields which can be used for this purpose are `Cache-Control` and `Expires`). This technique is very resource consuming, and it also is not reliable, because it depends on cooperating caches. For these reasons, there is a strong requirement to integrate reliable and efficient hit count reporting into HTTP.

- *Compression*
  Currently, although some optimization has been integrated into HTTP with regard to caching of data (ie, to reduce the network load by reducing the number of necessary data transfers), there is no data compression specified in HTTP. Mogul et al. [181] describe two areas where data compression in HTTP would be beneficial.

  - *Data compression*
    This is the most obvious area of improvement, which assumes that HTTP includes standardized compression algorithms, which can be applied to any message. The efficiency of these algorithms is highly influenced by the data being compressed, while GIF images will not compress very well (because they are already compressed), a typical HTML document can be reduced in size by an average of almost 70%, as the paper suggests, using a standard compression algorithm and a large sample of HTTP messages.

  - *Delta encoding*
    A second way of data compression is the usage of delta encoding for cache updates. Instead of sending the new document from an origin server to a cache, it would be sufficient to send only the changes between the new version and the cache's version. A proposed `Delta` header could be used by a client or proxy to specify the set of supported delta-encoding algorithms.

  The potential for data compression in HTTP is quite obvious, and it is likely that future versions of HTTP will include support for data compression. However, the problem may arise which compression algorithm to use, and it is possible that, although a future HTTP version supports data compression, incompatible compression algorithms of clients and servers will sometimes make data compression impossible.

- *Distributed Authoring and Versioning of web documents*
  Although HTTP defines a `PUT` method, the support for authoring and versioning is very minimal. Consequently, these features are not widely used. *WWW Distributed Authoring and Versioning (WebDAV)* is an approach to define extensions for HTML to properly support distributed web authoring tools. A first version of the protocol extensions proposed by WebDAV is expected in late 1998.

- *Transparent content negotiation*
  In the current specification of HTTP, different content negotiation mechanisms are described. However, especially the transparent content negotiation as described in section 3.2.5.3 currently suffers from a lack of semantics in the list of available representations which is returned by the origin

server. Additional work is necessary to define a transparent content negotiation mechanism which can be used by automated mechanisms. Internet
experimental RFCs 2295 and 2296 [97, 98] describe a representation for
the list of available representations as well as a *Remote Variant Selection
Algorithm (RVSA)* defining how such a list should be processed.

- *HTTP protocol extensibility*
  Although the functionality of HTTP in terms of methods, header fields,
  and status codes has been greatly improved from HTTP/1.0 to HTTP/1.1,
  it still is a limited and fixed set. Seeing that it might be useful to have
  a more open concept, allowing protocol extensions to be defined dynamically without the need to define a new protocol version, an extension
  mechanism for HTTP would be desirable. Several approaches targeting
  different levels of extensibility are possible. One approach is described in
  section 3.7.1.

- *Multiplexing of HTTP streams*
  HTTP/1.1 persistent connections and pipelining reduce network traffic
  and the amount of TCP overhead caused by opening and closing TCP connections. However, the serialized behavior of HTTP/1.1 pipelining does
  not adequately support simultaneous rendering of inline objects which is
  part of most web pages today. It would therefore be advantageous to be
  able to multiplex several data transfers. A possible approach for this is
  the *Multiplexing Protocol (SMUX)* as described in section 3.7.3.

Although these are a number of points which could be improved in future
versions of HTTP, it is not clear when such a version will be produced.
HTTP/1.1 now seems to be a stable protocol which will be in use for some
time.

There are different approaches how a future version of HTTP could be
designed. The first approach is to design HTTP/1.2, which would be very similar in nature to HTTP/1.1, only incorporating new methods, header fields,
and status codes. A more open approach, which is described in section 3.7.1,
is the definition of an extension mechanism which could be used to dynamically add features to HTTP without the need for constant updates of the
basic HTTP specifications. A more revolutionary approach entirely replaces
the simple, text-based approach of HTTP by a completely re-designed, binary protocol. This approach is described in section 3.7.2. In section 3.7.3,
it is described how an underlying multiplexing mechanism could be used to
use the old HTTP protocol as well as the new, binary one concurrently over
one transport connection.

3.7.1 Protocol Extension Protocol (PEP)

Experience with HTTP has shown that protocol extensions are often deployed dynamically. An implementor of an HTTP application may choose to extend HTTP by introducing new header fields. The *Protocol Extension Protocol (PEP)* as described in Internet draft [84] is designed to dynamically extend HTTP. The main motivation of PEP is that three key areas of HTTP are currently limited by the specification:

- *Methods*
  Currently, HTTP defines a small number of methods as described in section 3.2.3.1. If a server receives a request with a method it does not support, it sends a 405 (method not allowed) response.

- *Status codes*
  An HTTP status code as described in sections 3.2.4.1 and A.2 is a 3-digit integer result code of the attempt to understand and satisfy a request. Status codes are like method tokens in that there can only be a single status code in a response. However, status codes are somewhat easier to extend, as unknown status codes must be treated as the x00 code of that class.

- *Headers*
  Header fields can be used to pass information about any of the parties involved in the transaction, the transaction itself, or the resource identified by the Request-URI. The advantage of headers is that the header space is relatively open compared to that of methods and status codes. New headers can be introduced and must be ignored if the recipient does not recognize the header without affecting the outcome of the transaction The non-standard HTTP extensions described in section 3.6 are an example for header fields which are quite common, but not standardized in HTTP.

In order to achieve the desired flexibility, PEP is designed to use the header space for describing extensions and not directly HTTP methods or status codes. Instead, PEP introduces a placeholder in the method space and status code space respectively guaranteeing that all interactions with existing HTTP applications perform according to the PEP specification. The two placeholders are

- a special PEP method and a PEP- method prefix which indicates that a request contains one or more PEP extensions that must be adhered to or the transaction aborted, and

- a special status code 420 (policy not fulfilled) that indicates that the policy for accessing the resource was not met and that further information can be found in the response for diagnosing the problem.

These two placeholders allow for multiple PEP extensions to be deployed simultaneously without overloading the method space or the status code space. PEP is intended to be used as follows:

- Some party designs and specifies an extension; the party assigns the extension an identifier, which is a URI, and makes one or more representations of the extension available at that address.

- A party using a PEP compliant agent with an implementation of the extension wishes to use it; the agent declares the use of the extension by referencing its URI in a PEP extension declaration.

- Information about extensions can be passed between agents including information of where they can be used and under what conditions.

If an extension becomes ubiquitous, it may be incorporated into a new version of the base protocol, hence transitioning from dynamic extension to static specification. In this case, applications can refer to the new version of the base protocol instead of the PEP extension.

3.7.2 HTTP next generation (HTTP-ng)

In contrast to an evolution of HTTP versions (such as the step from HTTP/1.0 to HTTP/1.1), which leaves the overall design principles of HTTP untouched, the *HTTP next generation (HTTP-ng)* initiative attempts to design a version of HTTP which is very different from HTTP/1.1. Although the application area is the same, the protocol itself does not have much to do with HTTP/1.1. A first working draft [144] has been published. However, currently the HTTP-ng initiative is in a fairly early stage, and it is yet unclear whether the results produced will be used to define a new version of HTTP which should replace the current design of HTTP.

Part of the HTTP-ng initiative is the *Multiplexing Protocol (SMUX)* as described in section 3.7.3, which could be used to multiplex multiple HTTP-ng connections (or also HTTP-ng and HTTP connections simultaneously) over a single transport connection.

3.7.3 Multiplexing Protocol (SMUX)

Although HTTP/1.1 includes many performance improvements over the previous version HTTP/1.0, such as persistent connections and pipelining, it still has a number of restrictions. The most noticeable one is that requests and responses must still be serialized on the TCP connection, and that it therefore is not possible to transfer requests or responses in parallel over a single HTTP connection. This serialization could be avoided if HTTP would be based on a multiplexing mechanism which allowed the parallel transfer of multiple requests and responses. The *Multiplexing Protocol (SMUX)* as described in [86] is such a protocol that is designed as a layer between the transport layer (TCP) and the application layer (HTTP). The basic idea of SMUX is to multiplex a number of HTTP transfers over a single transport connection.

4. Standard Generalized Markup Language (SGML)

In 1986, some years before the web was invented, a language called *Standard Generalized Markup Language (SGML)* was defined and standardized in ISO international standard 8879 [110][1]. In order to better understand HTML and XML, it is advantageous to know SGML, and to know a little bit about its concepts. DeRose [62] answers many of the questions which may arise when taking a closer look at SGML.

The most popular web standard certainly is the *Hypertext Markup Language (HTML)* as described in chapter 5, which is the language used to write web pages. Although it is possible to learn HTML without learning anything else of the standards related to the web, it is very useful to take a look at the ideas underlying HTML, and it helps in creating better web pages.

The *Extensible Markup Language (XML)* as described in chapter 7 is getting more important as a more variable way of creating documents. Although XML is still in an early phase, it is already clear that it will gain more importance in the future. Since XML is very closely related to SGML, and HTML is based on SGML, basic knowledge of SGML becomes more important than it has been before.

We limit our explanation of SGML to the concepts and constructs which are relevant for HTML (and XML), and sometimes just mention some of the more advanced features of SGML which are not used for HTML or XML. In section 4.1, the basic concepts of SGML are described, this is the section which is fundamental to the understanding of HTML and its design, as well as the motivation to create XML. More specific, section 4.2 discusses how these concepts are realized in SGML, that is which mechanisms are used in SGML to apply these concepts to a data processing environment. Section 4.3 discusses how SGML is being used today and how SGML software for the

---

[1] An annotated version of the standard, giving many useful explanations, and written by one of the creators of SGML, is available as a book, published by Goldfarb [88]. More recently, a book by Bryan [39] explains SGML and HTML, and the relationship between them (unfortunately, it is based on HTML 3.2 rather than HTML 4.0, but the basic concepts did not change between these two versions).

web differs from SGML software in other environments. Finally, we give a very short description of the future of SGML (in relation to the web) in section 4.4.

4.1 SGML concepts

The basic idea of SGML is the separation of content and presentation. SGML only deals with content and the structure of content, and leaves the presentation of this structured content to other mechanisms. Travis and Waldt [263] give a good introduction into the principles of SGML and its application as a language for information structuring.

Although SGML has been used in many areas, especially in the publishing world, as well as the aerospace, automotive, semiconductor, defense and other industries, it never was known on a truly large scale outside these industries. This changed after HTML became the language for publishing on the web[2], and today HTML (and therefore SGML as its basis) can be said to be the most popular and most widespread way to structure information[3].

SGML's separation of information into logically structured content and presentation specific information is described in section 4.1.1. Understanding this concept is essential for understanding HTML and why HTML can be used in good and not so good ways. SGML defines a framework for how content can be structured, and it also defines an abstract syntax, so-called *markup*, described in section 4.1.2.

The understanding of document content and the way how it is structured and marked up also leads to another concept of SGML, the notion of document classes, which are explained in section 4.1.3. Although this concept is not very important for HTML (because HTML defines exactly one class of documents and therefore is defined by a single SGML document class), it is of increasing importance for the web because of the advent of the *Extensible Markup Language (XML)*, which is a language for describing different document classes.

Finally, there is the question of how the structured content can be presented, provided there is a well-defined way of exchanging it. Although this question lies outside the scope of SGML, we shortly discuss it in section 4.1.4.

---

[2] In the first specification, HTML looked like an SGML application (borrowing the syntax and some structuring rules from it) without being one. This changed with HTML 2.0, being the first version of HTML which was a true SGML application, based on a formal SGML definition.

[3] It has been noticed, however, that HTML as one specific SGML document type is not sufficient for all requirements to structure information. This is the reason for the invention of a new concept, the *Extensible Markup Language (XML)*, described in detail in chapter 7.

It is particularly relevant when looking at the application of SGML concepts to the web, where mechanisms like *Cascading Style Sheets (CSS)* and the *Extensible Style Language (XSL)* have been specifically designed for this task.

4.1.1 Content and presentation

The key idea of SGML is the separation between the *content* of a document and its *presentation*. In the standards world, the *Document Style Semantics and Specification Language (DSSSL)* [127] has been defined to specify the presentation aspects of SGML documents, and although DSSSL is not used directly for web applications, the latest development in the area of style sheets (which is the web's mechanism to define the presentation aspects of documents), the *Extensible Style Language (XSL)* as described in section 7.5, is using parts of the DSSSL standard. Furthermore, the also relatively new mechanism of *Cascading Style Sheets (CSS)*, described in chapter 6, uses concepts and mechanisms similar to DSSSL (although it is much less powerful than DSSSL).

To understand SGML's idea of a separation of document content and presentation, it is useful to think of a document (like this book) as a number of logical elements, such as chapters, sections (which are parts of chapters), subsections (which in turn are parts of sections) lists, paragraphs, tables, figures, and others, which are defined by their content. The structural organization of these elements is hierarchical. That means for each of these elements, that it is possible to say which other elements are part of the element, and of which other elements it is a part of. For example, this paragraph is a part of the chapter about SGML, and it is also part of the section about content and presentation. This structure can be depicted in a tree-like representation, therefore called a *document tree*, as shown in figure 4.1:

The important thing to notice about structured content is that it is entirely independent from the presentation. Whether the contents of this book are displayed on a computer screen or formatted to be printed, and how this formatting looks like, has nothing to do with the content of the book itself. This is what makes SGML so attractive for the publishing industry. An author just provides the content of a book, and depending on the publisher's layout guidelines, a chapter can be formatted to start with some blank space, on a new page, or on a right-hand new page. Formatting aspects can be changed without the need to change the contents of the book. The separation of content and presentation therefore reflects the separation of two different stages in the publication process. In general, the following observations can be made regarding document content and presentation:

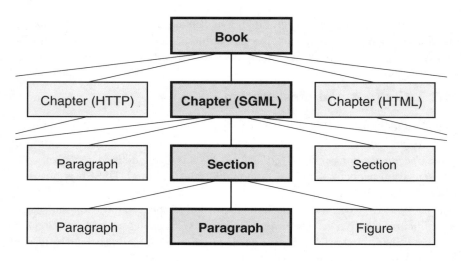

Fig. 4.1   Example for structured content

- *Document content*

  Document content consists of the logical structure of a document, and of the actual content of the structural elements (for example, a chapter heading is the structural element, and the actual content of this structural element is the text of a chapter heading). The logical structure is application dependent, for a usual type of document it consists of different levels of sectioning, structured text such as lists and tables, special ways to emphasize text (such as quotes and technical terms), and special text elements (such as footnotes, index entries, or glossary entries).

- *Document presentation*

  Document presentation is a way to physically present a document, on pages, on the screen, or in any other conceivable way. Normally, there are rules of how content has to be presented. These rules are independent from the content and different sets of rules can be used to produce different presentations of the same content (ie, document). Some possible variations of presentation rules are given below:

  - *Section numbering*

    Section headings can be numbered automatically. There are different schemes how to handle section numbers and also different schemes down to what level headings should be numbered. Furthermore, section headings can be compiled into a table of contents, which can be added to the document as a section of its own, automatically added during presentation.

– *Section formatting*
  Sections can be formatted differently. For paper based presentation, it is mostly the question of whether sections should start on new (maybe only odd) pages, and which spacing should be used between sections. When creating web documents, it is possible to change the section level which should be used to create separate web pages, if a document is formatted into more than one web page[4].

– *Location of footnotes*
  The most usual presentation style for footnotes on paper is to print them at the bottom of the page on which they appear. However, there are presentation styles which print the footnotes at the end of a chapter or at the end of the entire document (sometimes this type of notes is called endnotes). For the presentation of documents on the web, in most cases one of these endnote approaches (or putting footnotes on a separate page) is used, since the concept of the bottom of a page as with presentation on paper does not exist.

A web-specific example for document presentation is the way a web page is displayed by different browsers. Even if a web page does not contain any browser-specific HTML constructs, it looks differently when viewed with different browsers. The reason for this is that each browser implements a different set of rules of how to present web pages (although the basic formatting is always the same, it is very unlikely that an HTML page looks absolutely identical when viewed with different browsers).

In addition to being independent from presentation issues, the structured content also allows the automated processing of the document, for example the creation of a table of contents, a list of figures, or a list of tables, which can be added to the presentation of the book without any modification of the book's content.

4.1.2 Using markup for structuring

Using the idea of separation of content and presentation, there is still the quesion of how the structured content of a document can be represented, that is how the content and the content structure can be coded in a way which allows humans (such as a book's author) and software (such as a publisher's formatting program) to interpret a document unambiguously.

---

[4] A good example for the many different ways to present a document is the multitude of options of the *LaTeX2HTML* tool originally implemented by Drakos [67], which converts LATEX documents to HTML. A more detailed discussion of publishing with HTML is given in section 5.3.

The general idea of mixing content and information about content in one document is that of using *markup*. Markup generally is information about a document's content which is embedded in the content and can somehow be identified during the interpretation of the document. This is usually achieved by some kind of special character or character sequence which is used to designate markup. A program interpreting the document can simply look for this special character (or sequence of characters) and distinguish content from markup.

Markup can be used to carry any kind of information, and in early document processing systems, most of the markup was used for presentation information, such as indicating page breaks, font size changes, or controlling the spacing between two elements of the document. However, with the separation of content and presentation, markup can also be used for identifying structuring information, such as chapters, sections, and paragraphs. The program interpreting such a document has to know how to format a chapter and can, for example, insert a page break whenever it encounters markup for a new chapter.

Markup itself is very easily defined. Structural information is defined in terms of *elements*, which have unique element names, such as `chapter` or `heading`. However, to identify these names as element names rather than document content (such as the heading's text), the element names are placed within *markup delimiters*, which mark the start and end of the markup for an element. Each occurrence of an element name within markup delimiters is called a *tag*.

To illustrate the concept of markup, the following fragment shows how the document from figure 4.1 could be coded using markup. The markup shown in this example is identified by beginning with a '<' character and ending with a '>' character, which are the markup delimiters[5].

```
<book><author>Erik Wilde</author>
<heading>Wilde's WWW</heading>
<chapter>...
<chapter><heading>Standard Generalized Markup Language</heading>
<paragraph>...
<section><heading>Content and presentation</heading>
<paragraph>...
<paragraph>The key idea of SGML is the separation...</paragraph>
<figure>...
</section>
<section>...
</section>
```

---

[5] A '<' character which should appear in the text (ie, which should not be recognized as markup delimiter but as part of the document's content) would be entered using an entity as described in section 4.2.2.6.

```
<chapter>...
</chapter>
</book>
```

Some things about this example are interesting to note. The markup contains easy to recognize information about what structural component of the document is following. For example, the `<chapter>` tag indicates the beginning of a new chapter. Furthermore, two types of markup can be identified, markup beginning with a '<' character and markup beginning with a '</' character sequence. While the first type of markup indicates the start of a structural element (for example the beginning of the heading of a section), the second type of markup indicates the end of a structural element (for example the end of the heading of a section).

Since both the start and the beginning of an element is marked up by an element tag, these tags are called *start tag* (using '<' and '>' as markup delimiters) and *end tag* (using '</' and '>' as markup delimiters). Since SGML defines a structure as a strictly hierarchical topology, tags must be neatly nested, for example it is necessary to end a paragraph before a chapter can be ended (if a paragraph was the last start tag which has been used inside a chapter).

However, as can be seen in the example above, some of the end tags have been omitted. Depending on the way SGML is used, this may be allowed (it is allowed in HTML, but it is not allowed in XML), but only as long as the context makes it clear where an end tag can be expected. For example, if the definition of a document type (as explained in detail in the following section) makes it clear that a paragraph is not allowed inside a section's heading, the heading's end tag can be omitted, because the following paragraph start tag implicitly ends the heading element.

It is also important to note the different structure of the elements. While some elements contain other elements (for example, the `book` element contains the `author` element), a second type of structural relationship is a sequence of elements (for example, the `author` element is followed by a `chapter` element). These two types of relationships correspond to vertical or horizontal ordering in figure 4.1. It can also be seen as a different level of abstraction, seeing that each book has an author, so each `book` element contains an `author` element, and each book has an author as well as chapters, so each book contains an `author` element followed by one or more `chapter` elements.

Since it is often necessary to include additional information inside an element (which is not the element's content, but information about the element), SGML defines an attribute concept which makes it possible to include this additional information in the start tag of an element. An example how this might be used is shown in the following text, which also demonstrates the omitted end tags of the heading element.

```
<chapter id="sgml"><heading>Standard Generalized Markup Language
<paragraph>...
<section id="content"><heading>Content and presentation
<paragraph>...
```

Now the `chapter` and `section` elements contain additional information, in this case an identification which may be used for future references inside the book. For example, the processing software may replace references to the `ids` with section number or page numbers or it may do both, as demonstrated by the following piece of SGML:

```
...in section <reference type="section" id="content"></reference>
on page <reference type="page" id="content">...
```

In this example, a second attribute `type` has been introduced which determines the type of reference to be generated, either a `section` (generating the section number) or a `page` (generating the page number). Depending on the type of formatting, this may have different effects (since, for example, page numbers are a non-existing concept for the presentation on web pages or other scrolled media). Since the reference itself has no content (other than the `type` and the `id`, which are included in the attributes), the element is empty, which is why the start tag is immediately followed by the end tag in the first occurrence of the element. However, since it is clear that the `reference` element is always empty, the end tag can also be omitted, as shown in the second occurrence of the element.

4.1.3 Document classes

In the examples in the previous section this book served as a potential SGML document. However, since SGML should be able to specify the structure of a number of documents, it is useful to think of this book as only one instance of a number of structurally similar documents which are all books. SGML defines a way to specify this class of documents as a so-called *Document Type Definition (DTD)*. Using this definition of a document class, authors and publishers can exchange books as long as they conform to the book DTD which has been defined. The following example shows how a fragment of a very simple book DTD may look like:

```
<!ELEMENT  book       (author,heading,chapter+) >
<!ELEMENT  chapter    (heading,(paragraph|figure)*,section*) >
<!ELEMENT  section    (heading,(paragraph|figure)*) >
<!ELEMENT  author     (#PCDATA) >
```

```
<!ELEMENT  heading    (#PCDATA) >
<!ELEMENT  paragraph  ((#PCDATA|reference)*) >
<!ELEMENT  reference  EMPTY >
```

The exact syntax of this example is explained in section 4.2.2. This short example of a DTD contains a lot of structural information in form of definitions how a book may be composed using different elements. According to this definition a book contains an author, a heading (the book's title), and a number of chapters (the '+' indicating that there has to be at least one chapter).

A chapter contains a heading and may contain a sequence of paragraphs and figures (the '*' indicating zero or more occurrences of a choice of a paragraph or a figure), and a number of sections. A section also contains a heading and may contain a sequence of paragraphs and figures, as already defined for the chapter element. Up to now, the DTD only defines the structuring of elements (for example, a chapter has to contain a heading), but it is not clear where actual content (as opposed to content structure) can be used.

The author and heading elements contain only characters, as described by the keyword #PCDATA, so this is a place where actual content (the author's name or the text of a heading) can be used. A paragraph contains a mixture of characters and references, so a paragraph may contain text including references as shown in the previous section. Finally, the reference element itself does not have any content, as specified by the keyword EMPTY.

Using this example of a simple DTD and the example of a book which is first shown in figure 4.1, we can also depict the document tree as a tree of SGML elements as shown in figure 4.2. Basically, a DTD defines how this tree can be constructed (in terms of usable elements and possible combinations of them), and a document is one particular instance (ie, one tree) out of this set of possible trees.

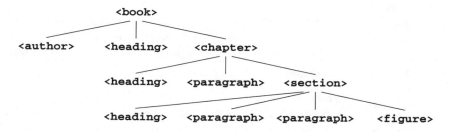

Fig. 4.2 Hierarchical structure of an SGML document

In conclusion, the *element declarations* (as they are called in SGML) define the possible structures of documents, that is the possible ways in which the elements defined by the DTD may be used to create a document. A document (in case of this example, a particular book) is an instance of this document type, which means it is one possible way to use the DTD for books for the creation of an actual book.

Since the attributes are also part of the document type, they must be defined in the DTD. Again, the exact syntax of the following example is explained in section 4.2.2.

```
<!ATTLIST  (chapter|section)
    id         CDATA           #IMPLIED >
<!ATTLIST  reference
    id         CDATA           #REQUIRED
    type       (section|page)  section >
```

The first definition defines the list of attributes for `chapter` and `section` elements, which share the same definition. It defines a single attribute with the name `id`, which takes as values character data (defined by the keyword `CDATA`). This attribute is optional, indicated by the keyword `#IMPLIED`, because a chapter or section does not necessarily need an identification[6].

Since a reference without a referenced element does not make any sense, the `id` attribute of the `reference` element is mandatory, which is specified by the keyword `#REQUIRED`. The `reference` element has a second attribute specifying whether a reference should generate a section number or a page number, consequently this attribute is defined to have the two possible values `section` and `page`, with `section` being the default which is assumed if the author does not explicitly specify the attribute.

Again, the *attribute declarations* (as they are called in SGML) define the attributes of elements, their possible values and the way in which they can be used (making them for example optional or mandatory). As with the element declarations of a DTD, the attribute declarations define possible ways in which attributes may be used.

Using element and attribute declarations, the possible structures of a document are well-defined. It is therefore possible to use these definitions as the base for document processing software. Basically, there are two ways how a DTD and a document may be used by an application:

- *Document generation*
  Using the DTD, a document processor can guide a user when generating a document, for example prompting for a chapter heading when a new

---

[6] Naturally, it is up to the DTD designer to make that decision, it would also be justifiable to make the `id` attribute mandatory and consequently to force authors to make each chapter and section identifiable.

chapter is created, or displaying the possible values of attributes when elements using these attributes are created. This way, a user can be very well supported by the authoring system, which knows the structure of the document to be created.

A second advantage of this method is that a document created this way is always a valid document because the document processor simply does not allow to create documents which do not conform to the DTD.

- *Document validation*

  While document creation, when done with a document processor which knows and follows the DTD, always results in a document which is conforming to the DTD, there is no guarantee that all documents which are, for example, submitted to a publisher, were actually generated with such a tool. Therefore, it is important to be able to check a document's validity. Using a program interpreting the DTD and a given document, the validity of this document can easily be checked by testing whether the document actually is an instance of the DTD. This decision can be used to either reject the document as not conforming to the DTD, or to process the document, for example to produce a printed version of it.

Consequently, a document class as defined by an SGML DTD can be seen as the link between different processing steps in an SGML environment, making it possible for all participants in the environment to use the same definition of a document class. If at some point in time a new document class is being defined, maybe because the publisher decides that some optional elements should be made mandatory or vice versa, the only thing to do is to distribute the new DTD as defined by the publisher. After DTD distribution, all SGML based applications of the processing environment (in particular, the author's document processor and the publisher's document validation and formatting tools) are able to process documents conforming to the new DTD.

4.1.4 The presentation of content

So far, we have discussed the general concept of content structures in section 4.1.1, the way to use markup for its coding in section 4.1.2, and the idea of document classes defining possible ways to use content structures in the previous section. There is, however, still the question how, continuing the example of the previous section, a publisher should be able to actually process a document to produce a formatted book.

In a very simple system, a formatting tool could, after verifying that a document conforms to a given DTD, simply replace each element with formatting instructions (such as font type or size changes or spacing). For example, the start of a `heading` element could be formatted to insert two blank lines and switch to a bold font, while the end of a `heading` element could be formatted to insert one blank line and switch back to a normal font. This is the simplest way of formatting SGML documents and is also the way most word processors do it. There are two additional aspects which can be used to define more advanced document formatting.

- *Element context*

  In many cases, elements should be formatted differently according to the context in which they appear. Using the example of the heading, it is likely that a chapter heading is formatted differently than a section heading, using different font sizes and spacing. Even though the formatting may be different, it is still possible to use the same `heading` element for chapter and section headings, because an SGML formatting tool can base its formatting on the context in which the `heading` element occurs.

  Most word processors do not support this context specific formatting, and it not only makes document creation easier (because there is just one `heading` element to remember rather than an individual `heading` element for each sectioning level), it also enforces the creation of neatly structured documents. In a normal word processor, it is possible to use a third-level section directly after a first-level section, without using a second-level section. This is possible because the word processor does not take the context into account. An SGML processing environment, on the other hand, could make sure that a third-level section can only be used inside a second-level section, thereby avoiding the creation of ill-formed documents[7].

- *Additional processing instructions*

  In addition to simply substitute element start or end tags with formatting instructions, additional processing instructions could be used for elements. For example, in case of headings, a document processor could insert the heading not only into the running text, but also write it to a separate section which, after processing all headings, is used as a table of contents, and it could also automatically add section numbers.

```
<!ELEMENT  book      (author,heading,contents*,chapter+) >
<!ELEMENT  contents  (#PCDATA) >
<!ATTLIST  contents
   level   NUMBER    1 >
```

Using this new definition of a book, optional `contents` elements can be used to indicate that (maybe multiple) tables of contents should be in-

---

[7] This, of course, only works if the DTD is designed in a way which only allows the usage of third-level sections inside second-level sections.

serted before the actual chapters, with the content of the `contents` element containing the title of the contents section. A `level` attribute (which defaults to one) is used to specify the level of sectioning down to which the table of contents should be compiled.

```
<book><author>Erik Wilde</author>
<heading>Wilde's WWW</heading>
<contents level="2">Overview</contents>
<contents level="4">Contents</contents>
<chapter>...
```

Using this new definition of a book, the way in which the contents are presented in this book could easily be specified in two lines of SGML code, which is processed by the publisher's formatting software.

Until now the presentation of a document is something which is defined inside the publisher's document formatting tool and can not be exchanged with other document formatting tools (unless they use the same format of formatting specification, probably a format which is proprietary to the software being used). However, there are applications were it is required to exchange formatting instructions independently from a specific software product. The most relevant application in the context of this book is the exchange of formatting instructions for HTML documents, and the exchange of formatting instructions for XML documents.

- *Presentation of HTML documents*
  In the first version of HTML, formatting was part of the HTML document itself, and this still can be seen in the current version of HTML (this is discussed in detail in section 5.2.1). However, the invention of *Cascading Style Sheets (CSS)* as described in chapter 6 now makes it possible to define a document's content in an HTML document, and to specify its presentation in a CSS style sheet. Since both HTML and CSS are standardized, content and presentation information can be exchanged in a platform-independent way.

- *Presentation of XML documents*
  Because HTML is limited to a single document type, XML has been introduced to allow the exchange of arbitrary document types and documents. Since for a custom document type it is unclear how it should be formatted, the *Extensible Style Language (XSL)* as described in section 7.5 has been introduced as part of the XML activities. XSL makes it possible for users to define the way documents of a specific XML document class should be formatted and to exchange this information in a platform-independent way.

SGML as a language for defining document classes which can be used to process documents in a document processing environment also needs a way to specify how documents should be formatted. Whether this information should be exchangeable in a platform-independent way or can be specified in a way which is limited to one specific processing platform entirely depends on the application. The ISO international standard for specifying exchangeable formatting information is the *Document Style Semantics and Specification Language (DSSSL)* [127]. Both CSS2 (the next version of Cascading Style Sheets, briefly introduced in section 6.6.2) and XSL are partly based on DSSSL, but DSSSL itself is not used within the web.

4.2 The SGML standard

In the previous section, the concepts underlying SGML have been explained. However, to ensure the exchangeability of SGML DTDs and SGML documents, there must be well-defined syntax and semantics for all components of an SGML document processing environment. Since SGML is a very complex standard, we give a short introduction to the features which are most important and most relevant for the application of SGML to the web. For a more detailed explanation of SGML, the standard itself or the books mentioned in this chapter's introduction (for SGML itself the book by Goldfarb [88], for SGML and its relationship with HTML the book by Bryan [39]) should be consulted.

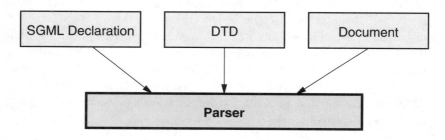

Fig. 4.3   A general SGML parser

A very general view of an SGML processing system (or an *SGML parser*, as the part doing the actual analysis of the document structure is often called) is shown in figure 4.3. In addition to the two components which have already been introduced (the DTD and a document), a third component, the *SGML declaration*, appears in this figure. We now give a more formal definition of these components:

- *SGML declaration*

  Since SGML only describes the abstract syntax of a markup language, there has to be a way to specify how this abstract syntax (defining abstract markup delimiters) is mapped onto concrete characters (like the '<' and '>' characters used so far). Furthermore, SGML defines a number of options which can be used in different ways. Also, the character sets being used and some capacity definitions (declaring processing limits such as the maximal length of element names) have to be defined. All these things must be specified prior to defining an actual DTD, and this is done in the SGML declaration, which is described in section 4.2.1.

- *Document Type Definition (DTD)*

  While the SGML declaration defines a concrete syntax to be used for the exchange of DTDs and documents, the DTD defines the rules according to which a document has to be structured. It does so by defining the elements (which identify the structural components of a document), their attributes, and the way in which the elements can be used. A detailed explanation of SGML DTDs is given in section 4.2.2.

- *Document*

  The third and most specific component which goes into the parser is an actual document, which uses the syntax defined in the SGML declaration and the elements defined in a DTD. Possible examples for SGML documents are given in chapter 5, where HTML documents using the HTML SGML declaration and the HTML DTD are explained in detail, and in chapter 7, which describes the ways in which XML makes use of user-defined DTDs to enable the exchange of documents of arbitrary DTDs over the web. A short overview about SGML documents is given in section 4.2.3.

Figure 4.3 shows the most general SGML parser which can be used for any SGML declaration and DTD and therefore can be used in a very flexible way. However, there are two other possible ways how an SGML parser may be implemented. In figure 4.4, it is shown how an SGML parser may be used which has a built-in SGML declaration, but accepts both a DTD and a document as input. Such a parser would implement a fixed concrete syntax including all other SGML features which are defined in the SGML declaration. It would, however, allow users to specify their own DTDs and to parse documents using them. An example for this type of parser is an XML parser, which has the XML SGML declaration built into it and accepts XML DTDs and XML documents as input.

A third possible way to built an SGML parser is depicted in figure 4.5. In this figure, it is shown that a parser could also have the SGML declaration

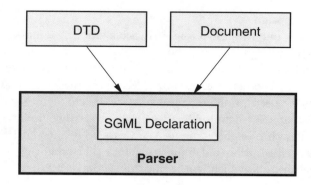

Fig. 4.4   A specialized SGML parser (eg, for XML)

and the DTD built into it and only accept documents which use them. This type of parser is the least general way to built an SGML parser, since only documents of a predefined DTD can be used and every time the DTD changes, the parser itself has to be modified to incorporate the new DTD.

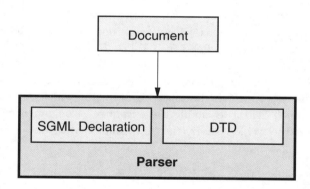

Fig. 4.5   A specialized SGML parser (eg, for HTML)

An example for this type of parser is an HTML parser (which is one component of a browser, analyzing a web page before it is being formatted), which has both the HTML SGML declaration and the HTML DTD built into it. Every time the HTML DTD is changed (for example from HTML 3.2 to HTML 4.0), the parser needs to be changed to incorporate the new DTD and, thus, to accept documents based on the new DTD.

4.2.1 SGML declaration

The SGML declaration is the most basic component of an SGML based document processing environment. It is used by the parser to define a number of parameters which are necessary for parsing both the DTD and the document itself. Examples for SGML declarations are the HTML SGML declaration listed in appendix B.1, and the XML SGML declaration listed in appendix C.1.

The SGML declaration consists of a number of sections, which in SGML terminology are called *clauses*. Each of these clauses defines a certain aspect for the processing of SGML DTDs and documents. As before, we limit our description of SGML declaration clauses to those clauses being most interesting for the SGML declarations used on the web.

In section 4.2.1.1, the syntax clause is discussed, which assigns actual characters to the abstract syntactic elements described in SGML. Section 4.2.1.2 describes the way in which character sets are defined in an SGML declaration. The processing capacities of an SGML implementation are defined in a capacity clause, described in section 4.2.1.3. Finally, SGML defines a number of optional features, which are enabled or disabled in the features clause described in section 4.2.1.4.

4.2.1.1 Defining a concrete syntax

Although in the examples so far we have used specific characters as syntactic delimiters of SGML constructs (such as the '<' and '>' characters for delimiting element markup), SGML uses abstract concepts to define its syntax. This leads to two syntaxes used in the context of SGML:

- *Abstract syntax*
  An abstract syntax defines syntactic elements of a language in terms of their function, such as delimiters for markup. In SGML abstract syntax notation, the delimiters for the start tags of elements are the *start-tag open* delimiter (STAGO) and the *tag close* delimiter (TAGC).

- *Concrete syntax*
  A concrete syntax assigns actual characters to the syntactic elements defined in the abstract syntax. For the *reference concrete syntax*[8], there is a mapping which defines the abstract *start-tag open* delimiter (STAGO) to be represented by the '<' character, and the abstract *tag close* delimiter (TAGC) construct to be represented by the '>' character.

---

[8] The *reference concrete syntax* is one particular concrete syntax which is defined by the SGML standard. It is the default concrete syntax being used if no other concrete syntax is specified.

The SGML declaration's SYNTAX clause defines these and other aspects of the concrete syntax to be used for a set of documents. In particular, the SGML declaration's SYNTAX clause contains a number of sub-clauses:

- SHUNCHAR

  This sub-clause defines the character codes which the SGML processing program has to ignore because they are control characters (or *shunned characters*).

- BASESET and DESCSET

  The *base character set* defines the character set to be used as the concrete syntax character set, while the *described character set* defines how these characters are to be used to define the concrete syntax.

- FUNCTION

  A number of special *function characters* can be defined in the FUNCTION sub-clause.

- NAMING

  The *naming rules* define which characters can be used in the different syntactic elements which are defined by SGML. For example, the NAMING sub-clause defines which characters can be used for element names, and whether element names should be case-sensitive or case-insensitive.

- DELIM

  The markup *delimiters* to be used in a document (such as the characters for the *start-tag open* and *tag close* abstract syntax constructs described above) are defined by the DELIM sub-clause of the SYNTAX clause.

- NAMES

  The NAMES sub-clause defines the *reserved names* for SGML constructs used in a DTD, such as ELEMENT and ATTLIST.

- QUANTITY

  The *quantity set* defines a number of quantities which are defined for the document set, such as the maximum length of element names, maximum nesting levels in different contexts, maximum number of open elements, and a number of other quantities.

For these sub-clauses, it is always possible to define specific values, or to refer to the definitions of the reference concrete syntax using the keyword SGMLREF. It is also possible to refer to the reference concrete syntax and afterwards to modify selected settings from it, one example for this is the QUANTITY sub-clause of the HTML SGML declaration listed in appendix B.1.

4.2.1.2 Used character sets

The BASESET and DESCSET sub-clauses of the SYNTAX clause (as described in the previous section) define the character set to be used for the document syntax. The BASESET and DESCSET sub-clauses of the CHARSET clause, on the other hand, define the *character set description*, which is the character set to be used for the document.

4.2.1.3 Processing capacities

The CAPACITY clause is used to define the *reference capacity set*, which defines a number of capacity restrictions for documents. It should be noted that the values of the reference concrete syntax for the CAPACITY clause are very conservative (in other words, too restrictive), since they are mainly based on the processing capabilities of computer systems of the time when SGML was standardized (1986). It is therefore common to use larger values for the CAPACITY clause than the values defined by the reference concrete syntax.

4.2.1.4 Features

Since SGML is a very versatile standard with a lot of optional features, the FEATURES clause of the SGML declaration is used to specify the optional features which are enabled for a set of documents. We only discuss the features of SGML which are of importance to HTML and XML, for a complete overview the SGML standard [110] should be consulted.

The most important feature of SGML is *markup minimization*, which has already been introduced in examples earlier in this chapter. The idea behind markup minimization is that in many cases full SGML syntax is not necessary to unambiguously interpret a document. For example, end tags can often be omitted if the context makes it clear that an end tag is required.

Basically, markup minimization was designed with the human author in mind who should be allowed to create less markup as long as it is still unambiguously interpretable. This consideration applies to SGML authors who write their document using general purpose text editors, manually entering SGML markup. However, for the automated processing of SGML documents, markup minimization is not really necessary, since a program can easily be designed to create full markup. On the other hand, it is considerably harder to write a program interpreting a document using markup minimization than to write a program which only accepts full markup.

HTML (created in 1990) allows markup minimization, and in the beginning, the only way to create HTML documents was to use a general purpose text editor, since no HTML editors were available. Even today, many people still create HTML this way, and since markup minimization as well as

the error tolerance of HTML browsers make it very easy to create acceptable HTML pages, in many cases this way is a viable alternative. However,
the increasing availability of HTML editors makes HTML pages created "by
hand" less and less popular. More information about this issue can be found
in section 4.3.3.

XML (created in 1996) does not allow markup minimization. It is assumed
that basically all processing of XML documents will be done using XML
software. For this software, it is much easier if documents are always using
full markup. Furthermore, only if markup minimization is disallowed, it is
possible to process documents without knowledge of their DTD, for more
information about this issue, refer to section 7.2.

The two most important markup minimization features of SGML (and the
only features which are used in either HTML or XML) are the two features
described in the following list:

- OMITTAG

  If *tag omission* is used, different mechanisms can be used to minimize
  markup. *Start-tag omission* makes it possible to omit a start tag (if the
  context makes it clear that there should be a start tag). *End-tag omission*
  makes it possible to omit an end tag (if the context makes it clear that
  there should be an end tag).

  ```
  <book>Erik Wilde
  <heading>Wilde's WWW
  <contents level="2">Overview
  <contents level="4">Contents
  <chapter>...
  ```

  In this short example, the start- as well as the end-tags of the author
  element have been omitted. This is possible, since the simple DTD shown
  on page 148 makes it clear that a book element must include an author
  element (therefore, the start-tag can be omitted), and that the heading
  element ends the author element (therefore, the end-tag can be omitted).

- SHORTTAG

  The *short tags* feature makes it possible to use *empty tags*, *unclosed tags*,
  null end-tags, and *attribute name omission*. Of all these features, only
  attribute name omission is widely implemented in HTML browsers[9]. Attribute name omission has two variants:

---

[9] This is one of the areas where it becomes clear that almost no HTML browser
is a true SGML implementation. Usually, HTML browsers only implement the
features which are commonly used in HTML, and not the features which would
be required by the SGML standard.

- *Omitting attribute value delimiters*
  If the value of an attribute only consists of name characters (according to the naming rules sub-clause of the SYNTAX clause), the literal delimiters of the attribute value can be omitted. In case of HTML this means that the *start or end of literal string* delimiter (LIT) normally represented by quotes '"' around an attribute value can be omitted.
- *Omitting attribute names*
  If the attribute value has been declared as a member of a set of valid attribute values, the attribute name as well as the following *value indicator* delimiter (VI) (usually '=') can be omitted.

These two rules for attribute name omission make it possible to minimize the markup of the small example shown on page 144:

```
...in section <reference section id=content></reference>
on page <reference page id=content>.
```

Since the section and page attribute values are predefined in the DTD, it is possible to omit both the literal delimiters and the attribute name. The id attribute, however, is defined as character data, so the attribute name must still be present, but the literal delimiters can be omitted (because the attribute value only uses name characters).

The FEATURES clause has a number of other sub-clauses and uses which are not discussed in this section. The most interesting point for this clause is the difference for the OMITTAG feature between the HTML and the XML SGML declaration (as listed in appendices B.1 and C.1). While HTML specifies OMITTAG as enabled, XML disables it. Both HTML and XML enable the SHORTTAG feature[10].

4.2.2 Document Type Definition (DTD)

A *Document Type Definition (DTD)*, as introduced in section 4.1.3, defines a class of documents which are all of the same type. A DTD mainly defines two aspects:

- *The elements of a document class*
  A document as seen by SGML is a collection of element instances, with each of these instances being of a certain element type. The DTD defines all elements for a document type, and also the attributes which are defined for these elements.

---

[10] Although its support in HTML is very poor, and its use in XML is restricted to one particular application area, so-called *null end-tags*.

- *The rules for combining these elements*

  Since SGML sees a document as a structured collection of element instances (they are always arranged in a tree-shaped hierarchy), it is also
  necessary to define how elements may be arranged. Therefore, the DTD
  specifies a *content model* for each element, which defines the allowed content for an element.

The formal definition of an SGML DTD consists of a number of different constructs which are described in the following sections. Section 4.2.2.1
describes how elements are defined in general. There are some other aspects
to the definition of elements, such as the definition of allowed content, which
is done using so-called *model groups* which are explained in section 4.2.2.2.
A special kind of elements may contain text (and not only other elements).
These elements are called *text elements* and are described in section 4.2.2.3.
Since the allowed content of elements can be defined by model groups as well
as by inclusion or exclusion, the SGML mechanism for inclusion or exclusion,
the so-called *exceptions*, is explained in section 4.2.2.4.

In addition to the basic model of elements, SGML uses the concept of
element attributes. The formal definition of attribute definitions is given in
section 4.2.2.5. As a last aspect of DTDs, *entities* (references to characters
and sequences of characters) are described in section 4.2.2.6.

4.2.2.1 Elements

An *element declaration* consists of the *markup declaration open* delimiter
(MDO), usually represented by '<!', and the reserved name ELEMENT[11], followed
by the element's name. The element's name is followed by the so-called *model*,
which specifies the allowed content for the element. The element declaration
is closed by a *markup declaration close* delimiter (MDC), usually represented
by '>'.

```
<!ELEMENT author    (#PCDATA) >
```

It is also possible for a number of elements to share the same element
declaration, in which case the element names are grouped using brackets and
separated by an *OR* connector (described in section 4.2.2.2). Using this kind
of short notation[12], the example on page 144 could be specified more concise
to read:

```
<!ELEMENT (author|heading) (#PCDATA) >
```

---

[11] This name can be changed by using the NAMES sub-clause of the SYNTAX clause
of the SGML declaration.

[12] In XML, this kind of short notation is not allowed. All elements must have their
own separate declaration.

Depending on the `OMITTAG` entry in the `FEATURES` clause of the SGML declaration, *tag omission* may be enabled (which for HTML is true as can be seen in the HTML 4.0 SGML declaration listed in appendix B.1). In this case every element declaration within a DTD must contain two characters between the element name and the model to specify whether start or end tags of the elements may be omitted.

```
<!ELEMENT author    O O (#PCDATA) >
```

The characters are either the letter 'O', indicating that the start- or end-tag may be omitted, or a hyphen character '-', specifying that the tag may not be omitted[13].

4.2.2.2 Model groups

Following the element name (or the `OMITTAG` specifications if the SGML declaration enables this feature) the *model group* specifies the allowed content for the element. A model group consists of one or more connected element names. Because model groups specify the possible ways in which elements may occur inside another elements, different types of *connectors* exist for different kinds of element occurrences. These connectors are shown in table 4.1.

Table 4.1 SGML connectors

Default character	Delimiter name	Meaning
,	*SEQ*	all must occur, in the order specified
&	*AND*	all must occur, in any order
|	*OR*	one (and only one) must occur

The *sequence* connector is used to specify elements which must occur in a sequence. In the following example, the `book` element must contain a sequence of an `author` element, a `body` element, and a `trailer` element[14]:

```
<!ELEMENT book    (front,body,trailer) >
```

If the elements in the model group may occur in any order (but all of them must occur), the *AND* connector can be used[15]. The following definition

---

[13] Since tag omission is not allowed in XML, element declarations in XML never specify tag omission.

[14] In order to make the examples as simple as possible, we assumed for the following examples that tag omission is not being used.

[15] The *AND* connector is not allowed in XML.

specifies the `front` element to contain the `author`, `title`, and `date` elements in any order:

```
<!ELEMENT front      (author & title & date) >
```

If only one element out of a set of elements is allowed to occur, the *OR* connector is used. The following example defines an `author` element to contain either an `editor` or a `writer` element:

```
<!ELEMENT author     (editor|writer) >
```

In addition to the connectors it is possible to further qualify an element's occurrence using an *occurrence indicator*. The occurrence indicators which can be used with SGML are shown in table 4.2.

Table 4.2   SGML occurrence indicators

Default character	Delimiter name	Meaning
+	*PLUS*	repeatable, must occur at least once
*	*REP*	optional, may be repeated
?	*OPT*	optional, can occur at most once

The *required and repeatable* occurrence indicator (PLUS) is used to specify that an element must occur at least once, but may be repeated. The following example defines a `body` element to contain at least one `chapter` element:

```
<!ELEMENT body      (chapter+) >
```

If an element can be repeated, but does not have to appear at least once (as with the *PLUS* occurrence indicator), the *optional and repeatable* occurrence indicator (REP) can be used. If an element may occur at most once (ie, it is optional), the *optional* occurrence indicator (OPT) can be used. The following definition specifies that the `trailer` element contains a sequence of zero or more `appendix` elements, an optional `glossary` element, and a mandatory `index` element:

```
<!ELEMENT trailer   (appendix*,glossary?,index) >
```

As shown in this last example, connectors and occurrence indicators can be combined to yield more complex model groups[16]. A very good and realistic example for the use of nested connectors and occurrence indicators is the HTML <TABLE> element as described in section 5.2.4.3.

---

[16] This nesting may be used up to a level specified in the *quantity set* defined by the `QUANTITY` sub-clause of the `SYNTAX` clause of the SGML declaration.

4.2.2.3 Text elements

So far, we have only discussed how model groups may be specified which define the occurrence of elements inside elements. At some point in the definition of elements, it is usually necessary that it is also possible to use character data inside an element. This character data is the actual document content, in contrast to the document structure, which is specified using nested instances of different elements.

```
<!ELEMENT chapter   (heading,(paragraph|table)*) >
<!ELEMENT heading   (#PCDATA) >
<!ELEMENT paragraph (#PCDATA|emphasis)+ >
<!ELEMENT emphasis  (#PCDATA) >
```

In this example, the heading, paragraph, and emphasis elements can contain character data, as specified by the reserved name #PCDATA. In the model group of the paragraph element it is specified that character data may be mixed with emphasis element instances, which means that a paragraph consists of text which may be marked up using a special emphasis element.

4.2.2.4 Exceptions

Although in most cases the model groups for elements as described in the previous two sections are sufficient, SGML defines additional mechanisms for specifying element content. These mechanisms can be used to include or exclude elements (XML generally prohibits the use of these inclusions and exclusions):

- *Inclusions*
  If inclusions are used within an element's definition, this means that the included elements can be used at any point in the model group (ie, within the current element or within any element embedded in it).

- *Exclusions*
  Exclusions, on the other hand, identify elements that can not be used in the context of the current element.

SGML defines that inclusions and exclusions are specified between the model group and the closing delimiter of the element declaration. Furthermore, any exclusions must be specified before inclusions. Inclusions are specified using a bracketed list of element preceded by a plus sign '+', exclusions are specified using a bracketed list of element preceded by a minus sign '--'.

```
<!ELEMENT chapter   (heading,(paragraph|table)*) +(emphasis) >
<!ELEMENT paragraph (#PCDATA) >
<!ELEMENT emphasis  (#PCDATA) -(emphasis) >
```

If the `emphasis` element is defined by inclusion to the `chapter` element (which means that the `emphasis` element may be used anywhere in the context of the `chapter` element), it is normally appropriate to exclude the `emphasis` element from its own content model (in which it is included because of the inclusion for the `chapter` element), because otherwise nested `emphasis` elements would be allowed.

Inclusions and exclusions make DTDs harder to read, because it becomes less explicit which elements actually can appear inside other elements (in the example above, in the definition of the `paragraph` element there is no indication that the `emphasis` element is allowed). Inclusions and exclusions in some cases are very useful constructs, but they should be applied restrainedly, using regular model groups whenever possible.

4.2.2.5 Attributes

An *attribute definition list declaration* consists of the *markup declaration open* delimiter (`MDO`), which usually is '`<!`', and the reserved name `ATTLIST`[17], followed by the name of the element for which attributes are to be defined. The name of the element is followed by one or more *attribute definitions*. The element declaration is closed by a *markup declaration close* delimiter (`MDC`), usually represented by '`>`'. An example of such an attribute definition list declaration is the `reference` element's attribute declaration that first appeared on page 146:

```
<!ATTLIST  reference
   id        CDATA          #REQUIRED
   type      (section|page)  section >
```

An attribute definition consists of an *attribute name*, a *declared value*, and a *default value*, each separated by *parameter separators* (usually spaces, line breaks, or tabs). Attribute names must start with a certain kind of character (a valid *name start character*), are limited to a restricted set of characters (the valid *name characters*) and a certain length defined in the SGML declaration. With the default SGML declaration, this means that attribute names must consist of no more than eight alphanumeric characters, full stops, or hyphens, starting with a letter. The HTML 4.0 SGML declaration, however, increases the maximum length of names to 65536 characters, so there is no real limit to the length of attribute names in HTML.

The declared value of an attribute is either a bracketed list of *attribute values* or a *reserved name* indicating the type of value which is allowed for this attribute:

---

[17] This name can be changed by using the `NAMES` sub-clause of the `SYNTAX` clause of the SGML declaration.

```
type    (section|page)   section
```

The declared value of this attribute is (section|page), which means that the attribute type can have one of the two values section and page. If no value is specified in an element instance, the default value section will be assumed.

```
id      CDATA            #REQUIRED
```

In case of the id attribute, taken from the same example attribute definition list declaration, the declared value of the attribute uses the reserved name CDATA, indicating that character data can be used as attribute value. The default value is specified by the reserved name #REQUIRED, which makes this attribute mandatory (ie, each element instance of the reference element must specify a value for the id attribute).

In general, reserved names for declared values are used to specify value types for attributes. The following list shows all reserved values which are used for HTML[18]:

- CDATA
  This attribute type indicates that character data can be used as attribute value, containing any valid SGML characters, in particular SGML delimiters.

- ID
  This attribute type indicates that a unique identifier is given to the element, which means that the particular instance of the element is uniquely identified within the scope of the document.

- IDREF
  Using the unique identifier from the ID attribute type, the IDREF attribute type references an element within the document through its unique identifier.

- IDREFS
  This type is the same as the IDREF type, except that it specifies a list of IDREF values instead of just one.

- NAME
  In this case, the attribute value must be a valid *SGML name*, which means that the restrictions concerning characters and lengths as specified by the SGML declaration must be observed.

---

[18] In addition to these reserved names, SGML also defines ENTITY, ENTITIES, NAMES, NMTOKEN, NMTOKENS, NOTATION, NUMBERS, NUTOKEN, and NUTOKENS as reserved names for attribute declared values.

- NUMBER
  This reserved name specifies that the attribute value must be a number. It is not possible to specify any restrictions for numbers (such as allowed number ranges).

In addition to these reserved names for declared values, SGML also defines some reserved names for attribute default values, which are described in the following list[19]:

- #IMPLIED
  If no parameter value is supplied in the document, the program interpreting the document may imply a value.

- #REQUIRED
  This attribute value must be entered within the start tag of the element, it is required for the processing of the document.

- #FIXED
  This attribute type is used if an attribute is defined for an element, but should always be set to the same value without the possibility to change it in a document.

Using these reserved values for declared values and default values, it is possible to define attributes in many different ways. However, for many application scenarios (such as HTML and possibly many XML applications), the possible definitions of attributes are semantically too weak. In this case, it is common practice to use SGML comments (which are enclosed with the *start or end of comment* delimiter (COM), usually represented by double hyphens '--') behind the attribute declaration to write down, in plain text, additional requirements. This method, extensively used in the HTML DTD, requires more specialized parsing than a pure SGML parser, since the additional requirements can not be checked by an SGML parser. An additional processing step is required to make sure that the attribute values actually conform to the additional requirements as given by the SGML comments. This is the reason why an HTML page, although valid SGML and conforming to the HTML DTD, may be an invalid HTML document. An HTML parser implements an SGML parser and furthermore implements checks for the restrictions of HTML which are not formally part of the HTML DTD.

4.2.2.6 Entities

The concept of using markup for specifying the document structure and mixing markup and document content makes it possible to define special char-

---

[19] In addition to these reserved default values, SGML also defines #CURRENT and #CONREF as reserved names for attribute default values.

acters as markup delimiters[20], but usually these are characters which should also be usable as document text. For example, to use the '<' character in an HTML document, it is necessary to use '<', which references the '<' character without actually using it. In addition to the characters which are occupied by special roles for representing markup, there also is a large number of characters which are not available on keyboards, but which also should be usable in SGML documents. For example, the greek upper case letter sigma 'Σ' (as well as a multitude of other foreign letters and special symbols) can be used in HTML using 'Σ'.

The concept of an *entity* in SGML is generally defined as "a collection of characters that can be referenced as a unit". SGML's concept of entities differentiates *entity references* and *entity declarations*. The example given above is an entity reference, which is a reference to an entity declaration (the lt entity) specified in the HTML DTD. Two types of entity references can be distinguished:

- *General entity references*
  General entity references are used to refer to entity declarations which are part of the DTD or the document[21]. Such an entity declaration simply defines an entity by defining its name and the *replacement text* which should be generated whenever the entity is used inside a document. General entity references are used by specifying the *entity reference open* delimiter (ERO), which normally is the ampersand character '&', directly followed by the *entity name* and the *entity reference close* delimiter (REFC), which normally is the semicolon character ';'.

- *Character entity references*
  Character entity references can be used to directly specify characters from a character set, usually characters which are not available using a keyboard[22]. Character entity references are used by specifying the *character reference open* delimiter (CRO), which normally is the character sequence '&#', directly followed by the decimal value of the required character within the character set, and the *entity reference close* delimiter (REFC), which normally is the semicolon character ';'.

---

[20] Such as the '<' and '>' characters in case of the reference concrete syntax. However, the markup delimiters can be freely defined using the delimiters sub-clause of the SYNTAX clause.

[21] It should be noted that virtually all browsers do not support entity declarations inside documents, so that only general entity references to entity declarations from the HTML DTD are possible.

[22] Since character entity references directly reference characters from the document's character set, there is no such thing as a "character entity declaration".

An *entity declaration* consists of the *markup declaration open* delimiter (MDO), usually represented by '`<!`', and the reserved name ENTITY[23], followed by the entity's name. The entity name is followed by an optional CDATA keyword[24] and the entity's *replacement text*. The entity declaration is closed by a *markup declaration close* delimiter (MDC), usually represented by '`>`'.

```
<!ENTITY  Sigma  CDATA  "&#931;" >
```

This general entity declaration (taken from the HTML DTD) declares the Sigma entity to be replaced by the character entity reference '`&#931;`', which references the greek upper case letter sigma within the ISO 10646 character set. Thus, this example uses an entity reference inside an entity declaration, which is possible in SGML.

4.2.3 SGML documents

In theory, the exchange of an SGML document always includes the exchange of the associated SGML declaration and the DTD. Since HTML and XML have fixed SGML declarations, it is not necessary to exchange the SGML declaration. HTML also has a fixed DTD, so it furthermore is not necessary to exchange the DTD. However, because different versions of HTML exist, it is necessary to refer to the version of HTML which is used for a specific HTML page. This is done using a *document type declaration*, which is specified before the actual document instance (starting with the <HTML> element):

```
<!DOCTYPE HTML PUBLIC "-//W3C//DTD HTML 4.0//EN"
          "http://www.w3.org/TR/REC-html40/strict.dtd">
```

This is the document type declaration to be used for an HTML document using the strict HTML 4.0 DTD as described in section 5.2.1. Although many HTML documents do not contain a document type declaration, this part should always be specified, because this is the only way to recognize the specific version of HTML which is used for a web page.

Since XML documents do not use a common DTD as HTML does, but can be based on any user-defined XML DTD, XML documents need a more complex way of pointing to the DTD.

- *Internal DTD*
  In this case, the DTD is part of the document, which means that the actual text of the DTD, containing element and attribute definitions, is inside

---

[23] This name can be changed by using the NAMES sub-clause of the SYNTAX clause of the SGML declaration.

[24] This keyword defines the entity's replacement text to be treated as character data, causing any markup inside the replacement text to be ignored.

the document. Such a document can be processed by an XML processor without the need to refer to any external resources.

- *External DTD*
  Similar to the approach described for HTML, it is possible to refer to an external DTD. The difference in this case is that the XML processor actually has to retrieve the DTD, while an HTML processor usually has the HTML DTD (at least one version of it) built-in.

- *No DTD*
  It is also possible to specify no DTD, in which case the XML processor can only process the document as a well-formed document, but is not able to validate it against a DTD. For more information about this issue, refer to section 7.2 and its discussion of *valid* and *well-formed* XML documents.

After this document type declaration (which may be omitted in case of XML), the actual document instance starts, which is the hierarchically structured set of elements according to the rules defined by the SGML declaration and the DTD.

4.3 Usage of SGML

In the following two sections we describe the ways in which SGML is used for the specific requirements of web applications. Section 4.3.1 explains *SGML profiles*, defining a functional subset of the full SGML functionality (XML is an SGML profile). In section 4.3.2, *SGML applications* are explained, which are a way to use SGML for one specific application area (ie, one specific DTD). To give an impression how SGML is actually used, in section 4.3.3 about SGML validation we give some examples of how correctly SGML (in the form of HTML) is applied on the web.

4.3.1 SGML profiles

SGML is a complex standard which has been designed while it was still common practice to edit SGML documents by hand, using general purpose text editors. In the meantime, specialized software for processing SGML documents (in particular, SGML editors) is widespread, and the number of working environments supporting SGML documents is growing. Seeing this development, the numerous and complex markup minimization features (only a fraction of SGML's markup minimization features have been described in the previous sections) are no longer absolutely necessary. In fact, program-based interpretation of SGML documents using full markup is much simpler than processing documents making heavy use of markup minimization.

When it became apparent that HTML would not be sufficient as the only content language on the web, SGML as the base of HTML was a good candidate to design a language which could be used to define custom document types. However, SGML seemed too complex and loaded with unnecessary features, so it was finally decided to choose a functional subset, or *profile*, of SGML for the definition of a new language for custom document type definition.

The *Extensible Markup Language (XML)* as described in chapter 7 is a functional subset of SGML. The goal of XML was to create a "variant" of SGML which is best suited for applications on the web. A comparison of SGML and XML carried out by Clark [46] provides a complete and detailed list of all differences between these two standards. XML imposes many limitations on DTDs and documents which are not necessary for SGML conformance, so in essence every XML document is an SGML document, although there are many SGML documents which are not valid XML. However, many of the differences between SGML and XML could be automatically resolved in an attempt to convert SGML documents to XML. There are, however, a few differences where conversion from SGML to XML would be hard or even impossible (this depends on the SGML declaration and the DTD).

The main objective of most of the limitations of XML is to enable XML applications to process XML documents without a DTD. For the interpretation of SGML documents, the DTD is always necessary, because markup minimization may have been used to omit start as well as end tags of elements, in which case their existence is only ascertainable by interpreting the DTD. XML's requirement to use full markup makes it possible to process a document without using its DTD (for more information about this issue, refer to section 7.2 and its discussion of *valid* and *well-formed* XML documents).

One of the most obvious differences between SGML and XML is the fact that XML is based on a particular SGML declaration (which is listed in appendix C.1), while SGML leaves it to the application to provide its own SGML declaration.

4.3.2 SGML applications

An SGML profile as described in the previous section is a functional subset of SGML, having less features than SGML, but serving the same purpose (the definition of document types). However, the ultimate goal of SGML (and XML as an SGML profile) is the definition of actual document types. Every document type (in conjunction with an SGML declaration) is called an SGML *application*. The most popular SGML application is the *Hypertext Markup Language (HTML)* as described in chapter 5.

Although HTML and XML are the most visible representations of SGML on the web, it should be noted that HTML can not be seen as an XML application. This is caused by the HTML SGML declaration, which enabled features (such as *tag omission* and *attribute name omission*) which are not allowed in XML. It would be fairly simple to write a program converting HTML documents to XML documents. However, to achieve this, the HTML DTD would have to be converted to an XML DTD, because XML does not allow a number features which can be used in SGML DTDs (and which are used in the HTML DTD). More information about this issue can be found in section 7.6.1.

4.3.3 SGML validation

The theory of SGML defining DTDs and documents conforming to these DTDs is one side, but the practice on the web is a different issue. Since most of the HTML pages on the web are created by hand (rather than using software which knows the HTML DTD)[25], the typical web page contains errors which, strictly speaking, make it an invalid HTML document.

A very simple way to validate web pages has been used in an early survey by Bray [34], carried out in 1996, where web pages were grouped into three categories, based on whether they did not contain a <TITLE> element (which is mandatory), contained a <TITLE> but no document type declaration (which also is mandatory in an SGML document), or a <TITLE> element and an HTML document type declaration. However, no actual validation was performed, so the figures are rather optimistic. According to these categories, 12.6% of the pages did not even include a <TITLE> element, 82.5% contained a <TITLE> but no document type declaration, and only 4.9% actually contained a document type declaration.

Another study of web pages went a step further by using an SGML parser to actually validate the documents (ie, check them for syntactic correctness according to the syntactic and structural rules defined by HTML). This study was a little bit more relaxed on the documents in the first place, because if a document did not contain a document type declaration, a standard DTD was used (HTML 3.2, which was the latest HTML version at the time the study took place). Using this methodology, the results listed in table 4.3 were found.

These results are taken from a study of web servers in the UK carried out by Beck [15]. It gives numbers which can be seen as representative for

---

[25] With the increasing complexity of HTML, new mechanisms like *Cascading Style Sheets (CSS)* as described in chapter 6, and the increasing availability of software tools for creating web pages, this will change. For the near future, however, there will be many pages on the web which have been created manually.

Table 4.3   Validation of HTML pages

	HTML validation result	Count	Percent
1.	validation failed with default DTD	15766	60.67%
2.	validation failed	8730	33.59%
3.	validation succeeded with default DTD	1013	3.90%
4.	validation succeeded	335	1.29%
5.	no DTD found	144	0.55%

the web in general, although only web servers in the UK were used to collect the data. The way the data was collected is quite simple, all UK domains were searched for hosts named www, and if such a host was present, an HTTP request was sent to the host's standard HTTP port (80)[26].

However, despite the fact that most HTML documents on the web are invalid when looking at them from a rigid point of view, it is important for browsers to be tolerant in these cases. A user browsing the web would be very disappointed if for more than 90% of the web pages the browser would simply display an error message stating that the page does not contain valid HTML.

It is also worth mentioning that validating an HTML document with a general purpose SGML parser is not sufficient to make sure that an HTML document is valid. The validation with a general purpose SGML parser can check all syntactic and structural rules which are formally specified in the HTML SGML declaration and DTD, but it can not check for other things. One example are attributes which are defined as CDATA values, and thus can (from the point of view of an SGML parser) contain letters, but which are (only by comments in the HTML DTD, which the parser does not understand) required to contain numbers, for example for length specifications. Consequently, only a specialized HTML parser which rigidly checks for SGML conformance and also understands all non-formal aspects of the HTML DTD is able to really validate an HTML document.

All HTML browsers implement SGML parsers trying to be as error tolerant as possible. In the majority of cases, these browsers display web pages even though they might (and in most cases do) contain errors. Since the interpretation of invalid SGML documents is not defined by the standard (a normal SGML parser would simply reject such a document), it is not well-defined how an erroneous document is displayed.

---

[26] Although the description of the survey is taken from the original paper, the survey's figures presented here are from a newer survey (carried out in August 1997) which is available at http://www.hensa.ac.uk/uksites/survey/.

4.4 The future of SGML

Prior to the success of the web, SGML was a standard which, in contrast to many other standards in information processing, was very widely accepted and used in many application areas. With the increasing momentum of the *Extensible Markup Language (XML)*, SGML will gain significantly more importance, since the conversion between SGML and XML is very simple. Companies relying on SGML infrastructures can easily add applications for information distribution on the web, and as soon as the first full XML browsers become available, web publishing for an unlimited number of users will be very simple and powerful, using custom document types and formatting instructions (however, it may take some time until XML with all its accompanying standards, in particular the *Extensible Style Language (XSL)*, will be a stable and widely implemented set of standards).

The current SGML standard is rather old, and some aspects of it are not very well suited for SGML's application for web technologies. For example, the features which can be switched on or off in the SGML declaration's FEATURES clause have been designed with the human author in mind who manually enters SGML markup. To adapt SGML to its new application areas, *WebSGML* has been defined, which is an integral part of the revised SGML standard.

A number of additional parameters for the SGML declaration have been defined. One popular example is the SHORTTAG entry in the FEATURES clause of the SGML declaration, which in SGML does not allow the separate specification of the *empty tags, unclosed tags, null end-tags*, and *attribute name omission* features. WebSGML defines a way to separately specify these features, so that the common practice of many web browsers to only support attribute name omission and ignore all other features can now be reflected in the HTML SGML declaration (if it is rewritten to conform to WebSGML).

It can be expected that future versions of HTML, XML, or other SGML-based web technology will be based on WebSGML rather than normal SGML. Furthermore, the increasing importance of the HyTime standard, which also is an SGML application, will make SGML more important in the future.

5. Hypertext Markup Language (HTML)

The most visible part of web technology for users is the *Hypertext Markup Language (HTML)*, the language which is used to design web pages. Normally, a web page is displayed in a formatted style, which means that the browser interprets the HTML page to generate a formatted presentation. However, since HTML has a limited number of constructs, pages may look similar because they use the same HTML constructs. Since its invention in 1990, HTML has undergone many revisions and extensions, and the current version (4.0) is far more powerful than the first one. The design goals of HTML, as stated in early publications about the web, can be summarized as follows:

- *Richness*
  HTML should be rich (ie, powerful) enough to support a large number of possible applications. In order to achieve this goal, HTML must be general enough to be used for many different application areas.

- *Simplicity*
  On the other hand, HTML should be simple to use so that the application of HTML is easy and many authors are encouraged to use it. For an average user (ie, no computer scientist), it should be easy to understand the concepts of HTML and to create HTML pages.

- *Accessibility and platform-independence*
  HTML should be a language focusing on content rather than presentation. Using a content-oriented approach, information on HTML pages is accessible to a large audience, regardless of the presentation form (popular examples are visual and aural presentation). Furthermore, with the focus on content, HTML will also be platform-independent.

HTML is based on the *Standard Generalized Markup Language (SGML)* as described in chapter 4. SGML was chosen because it can be used to define arbitrary document types, can easily be used without specialized processing software (because typically, SGML documents are entirely text-based and can be processed using general-purpose text-processing software), and has a long and successful history of being a base for platform-independent exchange of content-oriented documents.

In figure 4.5 (on page 152), it is shown how a specialized SGML parser includes an SGML declaration and DTD. The application of SGML for HTML
(ie, seeing HTML as an *SGML application* as described in section 4.3.2) leads
to the configuration shown in figure 5.1, with an HTML parser being a program which has a built-in HTML SGML declaration and HTML DTD. An
HTML parser is part of every piece of HTML processing software, so each
browser contains an HTML parser.

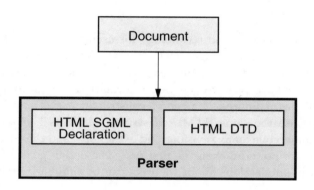

Fig. 5.1 An HTML parser

In the following sections, we give an overview of HTML and an introduction to its usage as well as a description of most elements. In section 5.1,
a very short history of HTML is given, showing the evolution from its very
simple beginnings to the rather complex version which is in use today. In the
largest section of this chapter, section 5.2, the most recent version of HTML
is described in detail.

In section 5.3, the process of web publishing with HTML is described.
Web publishing is the usage of custom document formats for the generation
of content which is accessible via the net. To give an idea about the actual
usage of HTML, in section 5.4 statistics about HTML documents on the
web are presented. Finally, section 5.5 gives a short outlook to the future of
HTML.

5.1 History

It has always been a rule for HTML implementations (such as browsers) to
simply ignore elements and attributes they do not understand. The various
versions of HTML exploit this rule by defining new features (ie, elements
and attributes) in a way which does not interfere with proper interpretation

of the web page if the new features are unknown to an implementation and therefore ignored. A good example for this kind of design is the <OBJECT> element as described in section 5.2.8.2, or the <OPTGROUP> element, which is used in forms and described in section 5.2.7.2.

The very early versions of HTML, which were used for the first implementations, are described in section 5.1.1. With the rapid growth of the web, it took a while for standardization to catch up with HTML implementations. The first official version to be published was HTML 2.0 as described in section 5.1.2. Even this version was outdated pretty soon and replaced by HTML 3.2, which is explained in section 5.1.3. The latest version of HTML is HTML 4.0 as described in section 5.1.4. However, this section only describes the historical aspects of this version. The HTML 4.0 standard itself is explained in detail in section 5.2.

5.1.1 Early versions

In May 1989, a first project proposal for a distributed hypermedia system is written and circulated for comment at *European Laboratory for Particle Physics (CERN)*. HTML as the language for transmitting hypermedia documents was one central part of this concept. The development of a first prototype (including a server and a browser), based on NeXT workstations, starts in September 1990. By the end of the year, a first version of the prototype is finished. This prototype already includes a line-mode and a graphical browser, so that the ability of HTML to be used for different platforms can be demonstrated.

The first conference paper about the web is presented in May 1992 by Tim Berners-Lee [16], after a poster presentation and demonstration on another conference in December 1991. These presentations already describe all basic concepts of the web, which are URLs, HTTP, and HTML. In comparison to the most recent standard, the early versions of HTML were rather simple in functionality. They included elements for text headings of different levels, paragraphs, as well as for ordered, unordered and definition lists. Naturally, the most important aspect of HTML, the <A> element for specifying hypertext links, was also part of HTML from the very beginning.

5.1.2 HTML 2.0

After the first prototypes of web software were built based on the very first version of HTML, in late 1991 an improved version called HTML+ was designed by Dave Raggett (who also is one of the authors of HTML 4.0). This version of HTML was implemented in the *Arena* browser (which in the following years was used as W3C's testbed for new HTML versions and style sheets). However, HTML+ never reached any formal status. However, while Arena was being developed in 1993, NCSA was also working on a web browser, called *Mosaic*. Mosaic included a number of additions to the first version of HTML, and naturally these were different from Arena's HTML+.

After it became clear that the web would continue to grow fast, and that the new features added by Mosaic, Arena, and other browsers should somehow be combined into a single version of HTML, a new version of HTML was released in July 1994. HTML 2.0 [18] also was the first version of HTML which was a proper SGML application, because it was defined by an SGML DTD. However, very soon after HTML 2.0 was released, in late 1994, Netscape was formed and began inventing new elements. Although these elements were crucial for Netscape's success and also helped to accelerate the evolution of HTML, they almost immediately obsoleted the new version.

5.1.3 HTML 3.2

One of the first major recommendations produced by the *World Wide Web Consortium (W3C)*, which had been founded in late 1994, was a draft version of HTML 3.0. It was published as an Internet draft, but it was never ratified. During the process of ratification, browsers were released which implemented extensions of HTML 3.0 (while not fully supporting HTML 3.0 itself), so in the end, this version of HTML was outdated even before it reached any official status.

While new features of HTML appeared in new browser versions or implementations (features such as tables, frames, and scripting), the only official version of HTML still was HTML 2.0. This was not changed until January 1997, when HTML 3.2 [217] was released. This version included tables, applets, text flow around images, subscripts and superscripts, and other features which were already quite common at the time it was released. However, frames were not part of HTML 3.2, although a first proposal for frames had been submitted by Netscape as early as September 1995.

5.1.4 HTML 4.0

With HTML 3.2 already being behind the state of the art when it was published, it became clear that a new version would soon have to follow. This time, it took less than a year for the next version to appear, and in December 1997 a first version of the HTML 4.0 recommendation [219][1] was published. As before, W3C first implemented the suggested HTML features

---

[1] The latest revision of the HTML 4.0 recommendation from W3C has been published in April 1998.

in their testbed browser, which at this time is *Amaya* (the Arena browser development stopped with HTML 3.0).

The new features of HTML 4.0 in comparison to HTML 3.2 include internationalization as described in Internet proposed standard RFC 2070 [279], support for style sheets, frames, a greatly improved table model, support for the general inclusion of multimedia objects, and richer forms.

In addition to the document produced by W3C, HTML 4.0 now is also standardized by ISO, currently it is a draft version of ISO 15445 [135]. The ISO version of HTML 4.0 (also called *ISO-HTML*) is a subset of the W3C specification[2]. It is more strict in enforcing good HTML practice by explicitly forbidding HTML constructs which should no longer be used (because they are outdated or because style sheets should be used for their functionality).

5.2 Hypertext Markup Language 4.0 (HTML 4.0)

The latest version of the Hypertext Markup Language, HTML 4.0 [219], has been specified by W3C in December 1997. The recommendation has been revised since then and the most recent version, on which this section is based, has been published in April 1998. Although the HTML 4.0 recommendation is easy to read in comparison to other standards and recommendation, it may be hard to understand as an introduction[3]. A description of HTML 4.0 published by Raggett et al. [220] (one of the authors of the HTML 4.0 recommendation) is a good introduction to HTML.

Although HTML 4.0 is one version of HTML, three DTDs have been defined in the recommendation to serve different purposes. These three DTDs and the motivation for their definition are described in section 5.2.1. Since a number of attributes are used for a large number of elements, these attributes are described in section 5.2.2, before the actual description of HTML elements. The basic structure of an HTML document and the elements which are used to define this structure are described in section 5.2.3.

As actual document content, that is the part of the document which is actually displayed in a browser, text in different structures as described in section 5.2.4 can be used. Images as well as image maps (clickable images) are detailed in section 5.2.5. The usage of hyperlinks in HTML documents is described in section 5.2.6. The most complex ways to create HTML documents, using frames or forms, are discussed in detail in section 5.2.7. Finally,

---

[2] This means that every document which conforms to ISO-HTML also conforms to W3C's HTML 4.0.

[3] A very good online reference of HTML 4.0 (and more readable and useful than W3C's HTML 4.0 specification) is available on the *Web Design Group's (WDG)* web site at http://www.htmlhelp.com/. It is also possible to download the reference and install it locally.

the techniques to define dynamic documents, using scripts and multimedia objects, are described in section 5.2.8.

5.2.1 HTML 4.0 DTDs

Since the web is constantly evolving, it does not make sense to revolutionary introduce a new version of HTML and thereby make all older web pages invalid. HTML 4.0 solves this problem rather elegantly by introducing the concept of *deprecated* language constructs. The idea is that HTML 4.0 implementations should be able to understand these constructs, but they should never use them when generating HTML 4.0 content.

In order to support this concept, HTML 4.0 defines three SGML document type definitions (DTDs), which can be used for the interpretation and generation of HTML documents.

- *Transitional DTD*
  This is the DTD which should only be used for interpreting HTML 4.0 documents, not for generating them. It contains a number of elements and attributes which should not be used, but which are still valid HTML (they will probably not be part of the next version of HTML, though).
  The <BASEFONT>, <CENTER>, <FONT>, <S>, <STRIKE>, and <U> elements are only part of the transitional DTD. They are used for specifying formatting, which should now be done using CSS style sheets as introduced in chapter 6.
  There are also some elements in the transitional DTD which should be replaced by other elements which should take their place in the future. These are <APPLET> which should be replaced by <OBJECT>, <DIR> and <MENU> which should be replaced by <UL>, and <ISINDEX> which should be replaced by an <INPUT> element used in a <FORM>.
  In addition to these elements, the transitional DTD also contains a number of attributes which should not be used any more. Most of these attributes are related to formatting, which should now be done using CSS style sheets as introduced in chapter 6.

- *Strict DTD*
  Since a number of elements and attributes in the transitional DTD should not be used anymore, a strict DTD has been defined which does not include these constructs. Therefore, the strict DTD should be used when generating HTML 4.0, for example in HTML editors.

- *Frameset DTD*
  If frames are being used (which have been introduced in HTML 4.0), the content of a page (as seen in the browser's window) is actually defined in

different HTML documents, one specifying the structure of the frames of the window (called the frameset), and a number of others containing the actual HTML code of the frames (a more in-depth discussion of this is given in section 5.2.7.1). HTML 4.0 therefore specifies a third DTD, which is used for the document containing the specification of the frameset.

Ideally, web pages should conform to the strict DTD rather than the transitional DTD. This could be done by using a converter which reads an HTML 4.0 document conforming to the transitional DTD and produces as output an HTML document conforming to the strict DTD and perhaps an associated style sheet (if there was some formatting information in the document which should be preserved). This process is shown in figure 5.2.

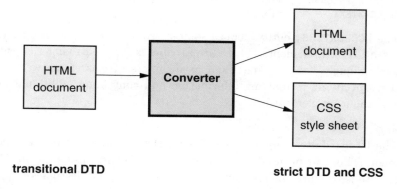

transitional DTD   **strict DTD and CSS**

Fig. 5.2   Converting from transitional to strict HTML 4.0

However, although this process can be performed automatically in many cases (for example when mapping formatting information from HTML elements and attributes to a CSS style sheet), there will always be cases where it is necessary that additional information has to be supplied to make the conversion possible. Furthermore, in many cases web pages do not exist as separate entities, but are produced dynamically either offline or online, and in these cases the converter would have to be integrated into the environment.

5.2.2 Common attributes

In the descriptions of the HTML elements in the following sections, in many cases we have included the element and attribute specifications from the HTML 4.0 strict DTD[4]. The syntax and semantics of these specifications is

---

[4] However, for a number of elements we have not included their formal DTD specification. Therefore, this book does not provide a complete formal reference

described in section 4.2.2. However, the HTML 4.0 DTD also uses a number
of entities for the definition of attributes, serving as short cuts for individual
attribute definitions. The advantage of this method is a more concise DTD
and the possibility to reuse attribute definitions, which avoids inconsistencies.
All entities used in the element and attribute specifications are listed in table B.1 in appendix B.2, where also most of the entities are shortly explained.
However, there are a few entities (specifying some standard attributes being
defined for many elements) which are used very often, and we describe these
in the following paragraphs.

```
<!ENTITY % COREATTRS
   "ID    ID           #IMPLIED
    CLASS CDATA         #IMPLIED
    STYLE %STYLESHEET;  #IMPLIED
    TITLE %TEXT;        #IMPLIED" >
```

The %COREATTRS; entity defines some attributes which are essential for
almost all HTML elements. These are attributes for identifying element instances uniquely, for marking them as members of classes, as well as attributes specifying formatting information and containing additional information about an element instance.

- ID
  The ID attribute uniquely identifies an element instance inside a document. This can be used for two purposes. The first usage of an ID attribute is to mark the element instance as a potential destination anchor
  as described in section 5.2.6.2[5]. The second purpose of the ID attribute
  is to mark an element instance for being referenced from within a style
  sheet as described in section 6.3.2.2.

- CLASS
  The CLASS attribute identifies an element instance as belonging to a certain class of elements. Unlike the ID attribute, the CLASS attribute allows
  more than one element instance to have the same class name assigned, and
  it also allows the sharing of class names among different element types.
  The main purpose of classes is to identify elements for the usage of style
  sheets as described in section 6.3.2.2. It is also important to notice that
  an element may be assigned multiple classes, in which case the CLASS
  attribute is specified as a space separated list of class names.

---

of HTML 4.0, but it contains all information which is necessary in almost all
cases of HTML usage. For the rare occasions where a complete HTML 4.0 DTD
is really necessary, the reader is referred to the HTML 4.0 standard.

[5] It should, however, be noticed, that most browsers today do not support this type
of destination anchor, although it is part of the HTML 4.0 standard. Instead, an
<A> element using the NAME attribute must be used.

- STYLE

  Also the suggested method for specifying formatting information is the usage of style sheets, it is also possible to directly specify the formatting of an element instance using the STYLE attribute as described in section 6.3.2.2.

- TITLE

  The TITLE attribute is used to provide additional information about an element instance which should not be displayed in the normal flow of text. Most browsers supporting the TITLE attribute implement this by using its content as "tool-tip", which is displayed if the pointer is moved over the element instance. The TITLE attribute is most useful for the <A>, <LINK>, <IMG>, and <OBJECT> elements. It is also useful to specify the long form of an abbreviation specified with <ABBR> or <ACRONYM>.

These attributes make up the core attributes and are defined for almost all HTML 4.0 elements. If any new elements are introduced in later versions of HTML, they will also be defined to include these attributes.

```
<!ENTITY % I18N
  "LANG %LANGUAGECODE; #IMPLIED
   DIR   (LTR|RTL)     #IMPLIED" >
```

One important new feature of HTML 4.0 is its support for the internationalization[6] of web pages. It has first been described in Internet proposed standard RFC 2070 [279] (which is based on HTML 2.0), but now it is an integral part of the HTML 4.0 standard. In order to support internationalization, it must be possible to identify the language of content, and to specify the directionality[7] which has to be used for the rendering of the content.

- LANG

  Language information specified using the LANG attribute may be used by a user agent to control rendering in a variety of ways. Its possible values are defined by the %LANGUAGECODE; entity. There are a number of situations where author-supplied language information may be helpful.

  - Assisting search engines
  - Assisting speech synthesizers
  - Helping a user agent select glyph variants for high quality typography
  - Helping a user agent choose a set of quotation marks

---

[6] The length of the word "internationalization" is the source of the entity's name %I18N;, meaning the letter 'i' followed by 18 letters followed by the letter 'n'.

[7] The *directionality* of a text specifies the direction of its flow of characters, for western languages it is left to right, other languages sometimes use other directions (Hebrew is written from right to left).

- Helping a user agent make decisions about hyphenation, ligatures, and spacing
- Assisting spell checkers and grammar checkers

Languages are specified by language tags as defined in Internet proposed standard RFC 1766 [7], consisting of primary tags and optional subtags. Any two letter primary tag is a language abbreviation according to ISO 639 [112], and any two-letter initial subtag is a country code according to ISO 3166 [128].

- DIR

  The DIR attribute specifies the directionality of text as well as that of tables. However, in most cases it is not necessary to specify this attribute, because the directionality of an element can be deduced from the characters being used. Only when different texts with different directionality are nested (for example Hebrew quotes in english text), it may be necessary to explicitly specify the directionality of text.

In addition to the core attributes and the attributes supporting internationalization, there is also a number of attributes which provide support for client side scripting. These attributes are the hooks which can be used to link scripts to a number of events. Therefore, these attributes are essential for using *Dynamic HTML (DHTML)*[8].

```
<!ENTITY % EVENTS
  "ONCLICK      %SCRIPT; #IMPLIED
   ONDBLCLICK   %SCRIPT; #IMPLIED
   ONMOUSEDOWN  %SCRIPT; #IMPLIED
   ONMOUSEUP    %SCRIPT; #IMPLIED
   ONMOUSEOVER  %SCRIPT; #IMPLIED
   ONMOUSEMOVE  %SCRIPT; #IMPLIED
   ONMOUSEOUT   %SCRIPT; #IMPLIED
   ONKEYPRESS   %SCRIPT; #IMPLIED
   ONKEYDOWN    %SCRIPT; #IMPLIED
   ONKEYUP      %SCRIPT; #IMPLIED" >
```

Although HTML is aimed at being a content language rather than specifying a document's presentation, scripting support somehow violates this scheme. Scripting support is focused on graphical user interfaces using a pointing device. This is reflected in the names and the definitions of the scripting attributes. Each attribute may contain a script (in many cases this

---

[8] In addition to scripting support in HTML, the components of DHTML are *Cascading Style Sheets (CSS)* as described in chapter 6, a scripting language like ECMAScript described in section 8.1.1, and the *Document Object Model (DOM)* as described in section 10.5.5.

script is just a function call to a script function defined elsewhere within the document, typically in the <SCRIPT> element in the document head).

- ONCLICK

  This attribute specifies a script which is executed when the corresponding element is clicked, which means the mouse pointer has been moved over the element and the mouse button has been pressed and released.

- ONDBLCLICK

  The ONDBLCLICK attribute specifies a script which is executed when the corresponding element is double-clicked, which means the mouse pointer has been moved over the element and the mouse button has been pressed and released twice.

- ONMOUSEDOWN

  It is also possible to specify a script which is called when the mouse button is pressed over the element. This script is called before the mouse button is released.

- ONMOUSEUP

  As a companion to the ONMOUSEDOWN attribute, the ONMOUSEUP attribute specifies a script which is called when the mouse button is released.

- ONMOUSEOVER

  It is also possible to define scripts for events which do not require any buttons being pressed. The ONMOUSEOVER attribute is a script which is called if the mouse pointer is moved over the element.

- ONMOUSEMOVE

  This attribute specifies a script which is called if the mouse is moved while the pointer is over the element.

- ONMOUSEOUT

  The third possibility of mouse pointer movements is that the mouse pointer is moved away from the element. The ONMOUSEOUT specifies a script which is called in this case.

- ONKEYPRESS

  This attribute defines a script which is called if a key is pressed and released while the mouse pointer is over the element.

- ONKEYDOWN

  The ONKEYDOWN attribute defines a script which is called if a key is pressed while the mouse pointer is over the element.

- ONKEYUP

  As a companion to the ONKEYDOWN attribute, the ONKEYUP attribute specifies a script which is called when the key is released.

When using these attributes, it should be kept in mind that the associated scripts may be called very frequently (this is especially true for the script associated with the ONMOUSEMOVE attribute), so care should be taken not to specify too complex scripts.

```
<!ENTITY % ATTRS
  "%COREATTRS; %I18N; %EVENTS;" >
```

The %ATTRS; entity simply groups together the three entities described above. Since all three entities describe rather basic attributes of HTML elements, many elements are using the %ATTRS; entity in their attribute definition.

5.2.3 Basic structure of an HTML document

When writing HTML documents, the first thing to do is to indicate which version of HTML is being used. As explained in chapter 4, this has to be done with a *document type declaration*, the first thing to appear in any SGML document, which actually is a pointer to a *Document Type Definition (DTD)* as described in section 4.3.2.

```
<!DOCTYPE HTML PUBLIC "-//W3C//DTD HTML 4.0//EN"
          "http://www.w3.org/TR/REC-html40/strict.dtd" >
```

As described in section 5.2.1, there are three DTDs defined in the HTML 4.0 standard, the transitional DTD, the strict DTD, and the frameset DTD. Since the transitional DTD should not be used for authoring documents but only for interpretation, and the frameset DTD is only used for framesets as described in section 5.2.7.1, the strict DTD is what is used in most cases for writing or generating HTML documents.

As shown in figure 5.3, an HTML document contains two parts, the document head and the document body. The document head contains information about the document, which is not actual document content, but information describing it. The document content is defined in the document body. This is the part of the document which is actually displayed, if the document is viewed with a visual user agent.

As already shown in figure 4.2, each SGML document can be regarded as a document tree representing the hierarchical relationships between the individual element instances of a particular document. Because HTML is an

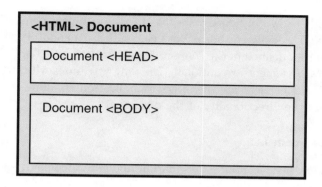

Fig. 5.3   Basic structure of an HTML document

SGML application, each HTML document can also be regarded as a document tree consisting of a number of HTML element instances which are structured according to the rules defined by the HTML DTD. A very small example for such a tree (using only very few HTML elements) is shown in figure 5.4.

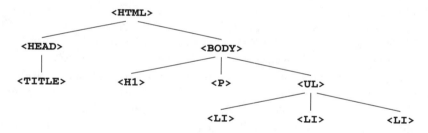

Fig. 5.4   Hierarchical structure of an HTML document

It should be kept in mind that the tree representation is only possible for documents, while document types can not be described by simple trees. Document types have to be described by a language which makes it possible to describe a set of potential trees. This is done by specifying rules how to assemble a particular tree (SGML's way of doing this are content models as described in section 4.2.2.1). The excerpts from the HTML DTD which are used throughout this chapter are nothing more than this, they describe how HTML elements must be used to form a valid HTML document.

```
<!ELEMENT HTML O O (HEAD, BODY) >
<!ATTLIST HTML
  %I18N; >
```

As already shown in figure 5.3, each HTML document consist of a document head and a document body. Both elements are mandatory and must be used in the order defined in the content model. Both the start and the end tag of the <HTML> element are optional. The only attributes which can be used for the <HTML> element are the internationalization attributes, defining the language and the directionality of the document.

5.2.3.1 Document head

The document head contains information about a document, such as such as its title, keywords, description, style sheet, and other information. The document head is particularly important to specify information which can be used for processing by automated clients such as search engines.

```
<!ELEMENT HEAD O O (TITLE & BASE?) +(%HEAD.MISC;) >
<!ATTLIST HEAD
  %I18N;
  PROFILE %URI;    #IMPLIED >
```

The document head is specified using the <HEAD> element, its start and end tags are both optional. The <HEAD> element contains a mandatory <TITLE> element and an optional <BASE> element[9]. The <HEAD> element also includes the %HEAD.MISC; entity, which allows zero or more inclusions of the <SCRIPT>, <STYLE>, <META>, <LINK>, and <OBJECT> elements.

In addition to the internationalization attributes, the <HEAD> element also defines a PROFILE attribute. This attribute specifies the location of one or more meta data profiles, separated by white space. These profiles allow authors to assign richer machine-readable information about HTML documents and other network-accessible resources. The profile itself is based on the *Resource Description Framework (RDF)* as described in section 10.5.3. Currently, RDF is still under development.

Changing the base URI

HTML documents may contain relative URIs, in which case it is necessary to know the base URI which should be used for these URIs. By default, this is the URI of the HTML document itself. However, this can be changed using either

---

[9] In the transitional DTD, the <ISINDEX> element is also allowed as optional content of the <HEAD> element. The <ISINDEX> element was used to mark an HTML document as a searchable index, allowing the user to input one line of text which was sent to the server. It should be noticed, however, that the <ISINDEX> element is deprecated. Documents which require user input should now be created using the forms mechanism as described in section 5.2.7.2.

the HTTP `Content-Base` entity header[10] as described in section 3.2.2.2, or using the `<BASE>` element. If both a `<BASE>` element and a `Content-Base` entity header are present, the `<BASE>` element's value overrides the value specified by the `Content-Base` entity header field.

```
<!ELEMENT BASE - O EMPTY >
<!ATTLIST BASE
   HREF    %URI;          #REQUIRED
   TARGET  %FRAMETARGET;  #IMPLIED >
```

The `<BASE>` element is empty, its start tag must be specified (since it carries the information which is important for that element), and the end tag may be omitted. The required attribute defined for the `<BASE>` element is the HREF attribute which specifies an absolute URI that acts as the base URI for resolving relative URIs. When the document is used with framesets and frames as described in section 5.2.7.1, the TARGET attribute can be used to specify which frame should be the target frame for all links inside the document, that is into which frame the document pointed to by any element containing a reference to an external resource (unless explicitly changed inside the individual element instances) should be loaded. The possible values of the TARGET attribute are described by the `%FRAMETARGET;` entity.

Links to other documents

One aspect of HTML document which will be of increasing importance in the future is the linking between documents. Currently, documents are only linked to each other through traditional hypertext links using the `<A>` element. However, such a link does not carry any additional semantics, and this is where the `<LINK>` element provides additional functionality.

Instead of linking content inside one document to a resource, the `<LINK>` element links complete documents to other documents. The biggest advantage of these links is that they carry semantics, because they have a type. The `<LINK>` element also allows the use of forward and backward links.

```
<!ELEMENT LINK - O EMPTY >
<!ATTLIST LINK
   %ATTRS;
   CHARSET   %CHARSET;       #IMPLIED
   HREF      %URI;           #IMPLIED
   HREFLANG  %LANGUAGECODE;  #IMPLIED
   TYPE      %CONTENTTYPE;   #IMPLIED
   REL       %LINKTYPES;     #IMPLIED
   REV       %LINKTYPES;     #IMPLIED
```

---

[10] In this case, the `Content-Base` information has to be provided at the time the document is transferred using HTTP.

```
MEDIA    %MEDIADESC;    #IMPLIED
TARGET   %FRAMETARGET;  #IMPLIED >
```

Because all information for the link is specified in the attributes of the <LINK> element, the element is defined to be empty. As for all empty elements, the start tag is required and the end tag is optional. In addition to the standard attributes defined by the %ATTRS; entity, the <LINK> element defines a number of attributes.

- CHARSET

  This attribute is used to specify the character set which is used in the resource the link points to. Its possible values are defined by the %CHARSET; entity.

- HREF

  The HREF attribute points to the resource, which means it specifies the URI of the link. Basically, this is the most important attribute of the <LINK> element because it specifies the link itself. However, it can not be used in a meaningful way if not at least the link's type is specified using the TYPE attribute.

- HREFLANG

  As a companion to the CHARSET attribute, the HREFLANG attribute can be used to specify the language of the resource the link points to. Its possible values are defined by the %LANGUAGECODE; entity. Languages are specified by language tags as defined in Internet proposed standard RFC 1766 [7], consisting of primary tags and optional subtags. Any two letter primary tag is a language abbreviation according to ISO 639 [112] (for example "en" for english), and any two-letter initial subtag is a country code according to ISO 3166 [128] (for example "US" for the USA, resulting in "en-US" for american english).

- TYPE

  This attribute specifies the content type of the resource the link points to. Its possible values are defined by the %CONTENTTYPE; entity. When the <LINK> element links an external style sheet to a document, the TYPE attribute specifies the style sheet language and the MEDIA attribute specifies the intended rendering medium or media. User agents may save time by retrieving from the network only those style sheets that apply to the current device, and only those style sheets that use a language they understand.

- REL

  The REL attribute specifies the relationship between the document containing the <LINK> element and the document to which the link points.

One possible application of the REL attribute is to specify that another document is the index for the document containing the <LINK> element. The possible attribute values are defined by the %LINKTYPES; entity. It is possible to specify more than one link type, using a space separated list of link types.

- REV

  Whereas the REL attribute specifies links in the forward direction, the counterpart of it is the REV attribute, specifying backward (or reverse, hence the name) links. For example, this attribute could be used to specify that the document containing the <LINK> element is the table of contents of the document to which the link points. Consequently, the possible attribute values are the same as for the REL attribute, defined by the %LINKTYPES; entity. It is possible to specify more than one link type, using a space separated list of link types.

- MEDIA

  The MEDIA attribute allows the specification of the media type for which a certain style sheet has been designed. Using this attribute, it is therefore possible to automatically use different style sheets depending on the media being used, for example a style for the presentation on a normal computer screen, and a more compact presentation style for hand-held devices. The available media types are defined by the %MEDIADESC; entity (they are listed in appendix B.2).

- TARGET

  When used with framesets and frames as described in section 5.2.7.1, the TARGET attribute can be used to specify which frame should be the target frame if the link is selected, that is into which frame the document pointed to by the HREF attribute should be loaded. The possible values of the TARGET attribute are described by the %FRAMETARGET; entity.

Although the <LINK> element has many potential uses, currently it is almost exclusively being used for specifying links to style sheets such as *Cascading Style Sheets (CSS)* as described in section 6 (a detailed description of how to link HTML documents to CSS style sheets is given in section 6.3.5.1).

However, the set of possible link types can be used to express semantic relationships between HTML documents. An example of a set of HTML documents using links of various types is shown in figure 5.5. There are already a large number of documents on the web which are structured in this way, but today these documents are using untyped links, where in most cases the type of the link is specified in the text inside the <A> element.

The disadvantage of using untyped links are that the relations between the different HTML pages are not usable by automated clients, and that the

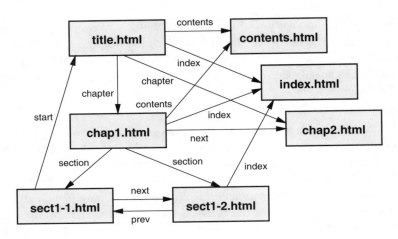

Fig. 5.5 Document relationships expressed with <LINK>

design of the navigation between the different HTML pages is entirely document specific. However, using typed links, it is possible to make these relations
between pages accessible for automated clients[11], and it is furthermore possible for a browser to generate navigation aids, such as buttons for accessing
the table of contents or the index. These buttons are browser specific, being
the same for all documents.

The REL attribute of the <LINK> element could also be used for prefetching as described in section 10.2.2. For example, a user agent may choose to
prefetch the table of contents of a document, but not its individual chapters.
It is also possible for a user agent to offer configurable prefetching, where a
user can specify which types of links should be used for prefetching.

Document meta data

The <META> element can be used to specify document meta data. Document
meta data can be regarded as information about a document in contrast to
information which is part of the document. In general, all elements which are
part of the document head contain meta data. However, all other elements
of the document head are used for a specific kind of meta data (determined
by the element type), while the <META> element is a general mechanism to
specify name/value pairs of document meta data.

```
<!ELEMENT META - O EMPTY >
```

---

[11] For example, a search engine can use this information to create an index of
complete documents rather than individual HTML pages, or it can decide to
direct all links which identify search terms inside a document's HTML page to
the title page rather than the original HTML page.

```
<!ATTLIST META
  %I18N;
  HTTP-EQUIV   NAME    #IMPLIED
  NAME         NAME    #IMPLIED
  CONTENT      CDATA   #REQUIRED
  SCHEME       CDATA   #IMPLIED >
```

The <META> element does not contain any content, all the information is specified using attributes. As for all empty elements, the start tag is required and the end tag is optional. In addition to the internationalization attributes defined by the %I18N; entity, the <META> element defines a number of attributes.

- HTTP-EQUIV

  This attribute is used to specify an HTTP header field name. A user agent receiving a document with an <META> element using the HTTP-EQUIV attribute is supposed to act as if the HTTP response which contained the document also contained the header field specified in the <META> element. The value of the HTTP header field is specified in the <META> element's CONTENT attribute.

- NAME

  The NAME attribute specifies the name of a name/value pair which is specified in a <META> element. HTML 4.0 does not specify any specific values for the NAME attribute.

- CONTENT

  The value of the name/value pairs which are usually specified using the <META> element is contained in the CONTENT attribute. The legal values of this attribute depend on the NAME attribute, which defines the type of the CONTENT attribute.

- SCHEME

  In some cases, it may be useful to provide additional information to a name/value pair, such as when different types of attribute values are allowed for an attribute name. In this case, the SCHEME attribute can be used to correctly interpret the value of the CONTENT attribute.

Although the HTML standard defines no values for the NAME attribute, there are some values which are common practice for helping search engines to index a web page. These values are described in section 10.3

Sharing data among frames

Normally, an <OBJECT> element is part of the document body and not part of the document head. There are, however, cases, in which it may be useful to include an <OBJECT> element in the document head. If an object is used more than once inside a document, it may be useful to specify the object's implementation only once, while all actual appearances of the object are just instantiations of the implementation declared in the document head. The <OBJECT> element itself is explained in detail in section 5.2.8.2.

A second possibility for using an <OBJECT> element in the document head is the sharing of data across multiple frames in a frameset document (described in section 5.2.7.1). In this case, the object implementation is declared in the document head of the frameset document. This implementation can be used in all frames of the frameset document, thus making it possible to share the implementation of an object across multiple documents.

Scripts

The <SCRIPT> element is used to define scripts for an HTML page which can be used within the document body. Scripting itself is explained in section 8.1. When writing as web page, care should be taken to make sure that the web page can also be used if it is viewed with a browser which does not support scripting or has scripting switched off. One way of doing this is using the <NOSCRIPT> element. More remarks on using scripts for web pages can be found in section 5.2.8.1.

The <SCRIPT> element can be used in the document head and in the document body, although it is common practice to use it in the document head. The element can either be used to embed a script in the document (ie, to include the actual script in the document), or to refer to an external entity which contains the script.

```
<!ELEMENT SCRIPT - - %SCRIPT; >
<!ATTLIST SCRIPT
   CHARSET    %CHARSET;       #IMPLIED
   TYPE       %CONTENTTYPE;   #REQUIRED
   LANGUAGE   CDATA           #IMPLIED
   SRC        %URI;           #IMPLIED
   DEFER      (DEFER)         #IMPLIED
   EVENT      CDATA           #IMPLIED
   FOR        %URI;           #IMPLIED >
```

Basically, there are two ways of using the <SCRIPT> element. If it is used to embed a script in the document, the content of the <SCRIPT> element is the script, as specified by the %SCRIPT; entity. If the SRC attribute is used to specify the URI of an external script, the user agent should ignore the element's content and retrieve the script using the URI. Both the start and the end tag of the <SCRIPT> element are mandatory.

- CHARSET

  This attribute designated the character set of the script, if it is an external script referred to by the SRC attribute. The CHARSET attribute does not apply to embedded scripts, which use the document's character set. The possible value of this attribute are defined by the %CHARSET; entity.

- TYPE

  The TYPE attribute is used to specify the type of the script. The possible values of this attribute are defined by the %CONTENTTYPE; entity. However, the HTML standard recommends to use a default script type declaration (using the <META> element with the HTTP-EQUIV attribute set to Content-Script-Type[12]) instead of type declarations for individual <SCRIPT> elements.

- LANGUAGE

  Before the TYPE attribute was introduced, the LANGUAGE attribute was used to specify the scripting language. It should be noticed, however, that the LANGUAGE attribute now is deprecated, the TYPE attribute should be used instead.

- SRC

  The SRC attribute is used to refer to a URI which contains an external script. If this attribute is present, the content of the <SCRIPT> element will be ignored.

- DEFER

  The DEFER attribute indicates that the browser may wait to parse or execute the script until the rest of the document has been rendered. Scripts that use DEFER must not generate any document content, and should not be required to respond to user events (eg, form submission) that may occur while the document is loading. The DEFER attribute can be useful for delaying scripts that pre-load images.

A common practice for using scripts is to define a number of script functions in a <SCRIPT> element, typically in the document header. Calls to these functions are placed in the event attributes of elements, where they are executed whenever the corresponding event occurs. This way, the functions are nicely grouped together, and the HTML body contains only function calls rather than complete scripts.

It is also a good idea to use external scripts rather than embedded scripts, at least if the amount of script data is not very small. This way, clients which are not interested in a script (like search engines or user agents which do

---

[12] The Content-Script-Type header field is not defined by HTTP/1.1. However, since it is specified in the HTML 4.0 standard, it should be used for setting the default script type of a document.

not support the script's language), can choose to ignore the script data. If the script data is embedded in the document, all clients have to transfer it, regardless of whether they need it or not.

Style sheets

Style sheets in general are discussed in section 6. Style sheets are a way of specifying presentation preferences for documents. One of the mechanisms how a style sheet can be specified for a document is to embed it in its head. This is done using the <STYLE> element. A general discussion of the different ways to link style sheets to documents is given in section 6.1.

```
<!ELEMENT STYLE - - %STYLESHEET; >
<!ATTLIST STYLE
   %I18N;
   TYPE    %CONTENTTYPE;  #REQUIRED
   MEDIA   %MEDIADESC;    #IMPLIED
   TITLE   %TEXT;         #IMPLIED >
```

The content of the <STYLE> element is the style sheet, as specified by the %STYLESHEET; entity. Both the start and the end tag of the <STYLE> element are mandatory. In addition to the internationalization attributes defined by the %I18N; entity, the <STYLE> element defines a number of attributes.

- TYPE
  This attribute specifies the content type (ie, the scripting language) of the <SCRIPT> element. Its possible values are defined by the %CONTENTTYPE; entity. It is a required attribute which has to be specified with each instance of the <SCRIPT> element.

- MEDIA
  The MEDIA attribute is used to define a style sheet for a certain media type. Its possible values are defined by the %MEDIADESC; entity. The MEDIA attribute allows authors to restrict a style sheet to certain output devices, such as printers or aural browsers.

- TITLE
  The optional TITLE attribute gives a title for the style sheet. Without a TITLE attribute, the style sheet is always applied when style sheets are enabled. With a TITLE attribute, the style sheet is automatically applied, but the user may choose to disable the style sheet while keeping or enabling other style sheets. Style sheets with the same title are considered to be the same style sheet.

Although in some cases it may be appropriate to embed a style sheet in a document using the <STYLE> element, in most cases it is better to use an external style sheet which is linked to the document using the <LINK> element. This way, clients which are not interested in the style sheet (like search engines or user agents which do not support the style sheet language), can choose to ignore the style sheet. If the style sheet is embedded in the document, all clients have to transfer it, regardless of whether they need it or not.

Document title

The <TITLE> element specifies the document title. This title is not part of the document content (ie, it does not appear in the document window), instead it is the title of the document. User agents normally display the document title in the window's title bar, and also use it in history lists, for bookmarks or similar mechanisms.

```
<!ELEMENT TITLE - - (#PCDATA) -(%HEAD.MISC;) >
<!ATTLIST TITLE
  %I18N >
```

The <TITLE> element is the only mandatory element in the document head. It contains character text, and the elements which have been included in the <HEAD> element using the %HEAD.MISC; entity are excluded for the <TITLE> element, so that only character text is allowed as content. Both the start and the end tag of the <TITLE> element are mandatory. The only attributes defined for the <TITLE> are the internationalization attributes defined by the %I18N; entity.

5.2.3.2 Document body

The actual document content is part of the document body. In general, HTML groups content elements into two categories, which are *block-level elements* and *inline elements*. The HTML standard makes the following distinctions between these two types of elements:

- *Content model*
  Generally, block-level elements may contain inline elements and other block-level elements. Inline elements may contain only data and other inline elements. Inherent in this structural distinction is the idea that block elements create "larger" structures than inline elements.

- *Formatting*
  By default, block-level elements are formatted differently than inline elements. Generally, block-level elements begin on new lines, inline elements do not. Also, inline elements can be broken across lines (such as text in

a paragraph is broken across lines), while block-level elements are not subject to line breaking.

- *Directionality*
  For technical reasons involving Unicode's bidirectional text algorithm, block-level and inline elements differ in how they inherit directionality information[13].

Both categories of elements are defined by entities which specify which elements are block-level elements and which elements are inline elements.

```
<!ENTITY % BLOCK
   "P | %HEADING; | %LIST; | %PREFORMATTED; | DL | DIV | NOSCRIPT |
   BLOCKQUOTE | FORM | HR | TABLE | FIELDSET | ADDRESS" >
```

In general, the elements which are part of the %BLOCK; entity are elements which are formatted as blocks inside the document. In contrast, the %INLINE; entity specifies elements which can appear inside text, being placed on the same line as the content before them.

```
<!ENTITY % INLINE
   "#PCDATA | %FONTSTYLE; | %PHRASE; | %SPECIAL; | %FORMCTRL;" >
```

Although the distinction between block-level and inline elements in HTML is reflected in the standard and the DTDs, the formatting of the elements is not as static as it may seem. A style sheet language mechanism can be used to change the classification of an HTML document in terms of formatting, hence making it possible to format block-level elements as inline elements and vice versa.

```
<!ELEMENT BODY O O (%BLOCK;|SCRIPT)+ +(INS|DEL) >
<!ATTLIST BODY
   %ATTRS;
   ONLOAD   %SCRIPT; #IMPLIED
   ONUNLOAD %SCRIPT; #IMPLIED >
```

The content of the <BODY> element can be any block-level element as specified by the %BLOCK; entity as well as scripts[14]. Furthermore, the <BODY> element includes the <INS> and <DEL> elements, which are used for marking

---

[13] An exact explanation of the concept of directionality and the inheritance of directionality information can be found in the HTML specification (generally spoken, block-level elements inherit the directionality information of the surrounding element while inline elements do not). The directionality of text can be changed using the <BDO> element or the DIR attribute described in section 5.2.2.

[14] In the transitional DTD, the <BODY> element's content model is specified to be (%FLOW;)*, which allows inline elements directly inside the <BODY> element. However, this usage of the <BODY> element is deprecated, it should only contain block-level elements, which in turn can contain inline elements.

document changes. The start and the end tag of the <BODY> element are optional.

In addition to the standard attributes defined by the %ATTRS; entity, the <BODY> element defines two attributes[15] for additional event types which only apply to the <BODY> (and the <FRAMESET>) element.

- ONLOAD

  The ONLOAD attribute specifies a script which is called when the document is loaded into the browser.

- ONUNLOAD

  As a complement to the ONLOAD attribute, the ONUNLOAD attribute specifies a script which is called when the document is removed from the browser's window.

A document which specifies a frameset rather than a normal document has a <FRAMESET> element instead of a <BODY> element (a detailed description of framesets can be found in section 5.2.7.1).

5.2.4 Simple and structured text

Although HTML is a language which allows multimedia content, there are still many documents which are mainly or exclusively text-based. HTML provides extensive support for text structuring and formatting. First of all, simple text can be marked up in many different ways, which are described in section 5.2.4.1. For more advanced structuring, HTML defines three varieties of lists, which are explained in section 5.2.4.2. Finally, the most advanced way of structuring text is to use a table. HTML's table model has been improved very much in comparison to earlier version of the language. It is described in section 5.2.4.3.

5.2.4.1 Text

The most basic way of writing text on an HTML page is to put it in paragraphs. Paragraphs are logical pieces of text which are visually separated through formatting, for example by vertical spacing or indentation of the first line.

---

[15] In the transitional DTD, the <BODY> element also has the attributes BACKGROUND, BGCOLOR, TEXT, LINK, VLINK, and ALINK. These attributes were used to set the document's background and different colors. However, these attributes are deprecated and backgrounds and colors should be handled through style sheets. Style sheet properties which handle backgrounds and colors are described in section 6.3.4.4.

```
<!ELEMENT P - O (%INLINE;)* >
<!ATTLIST P
  %ATTRS; >
```

The <P> element has as content any inline element as defined by the %INLINE; entity. The start tag of the <P> element is mandatory, while the end tag can be omitted. The only attributes defined for the <P> element are the standard attributes defined by the %ATTRS; entity[16].

If it is necessary to specify line breaks within paragraphs, this can be done using the <BR> element. Normally, a browser automatically reduces the number of spaces, tabs, and newlines (collectively called *white-space characters*) to achieve a formatting which is independent from the formatting of the HTML file. Exceptions are line breaks specified with the <BR> element[17].

Headings

Most documents are structured into chapters, which are structured into subchapters (or sections) and so forth. HTML defines six levels of headings for marking up these different levels of structuring. However, HTML does not require the different heading levels to be neatly nested, so it is possible that a document contains only level one and level four headings.

```
<!ELEMENT (%HEADING;) - - (%INLINE;)* >
<!ATTLIST (%HEADING;)
  %ATTRS; >
```

The heading elements <H1> through <H6> as defined by the %HEADING; entity (and in the future collectively referred to as <H1-H6>) have as content any inline element as defined by the %INLINE; entity. Their start and end tags both are required. The only attributes defined for the <H1-H6> elements are the standard attributes defined by the %ATTRS; entity[18].

---

[16] In the transitional DTD, the <P> element also has an ALIGN attribute which is declared inside the %ALIGN; entity. This attribute is used to specify the text alignment of a paragraph. It should be noticed, however, that the ALIGN attribute is deprecated and paragraph alignment should be specified using style sheets.

[17] It is also possible to change this default formatting of paragraphs using style sheets as described in section 6.3.4.5.

[18] In the transitional DTD, the <H1-H6> elements also have an ALIGN attribute which is declared inside the %ALIGN; entity. This attribute is used to specify the text alignment of a heading. It should be noticed, however, that the ALIGN attribute is deprecated and heading alignment should be specified using style sheets.

Text styles

In addition to normal text, HTML also defines a number of additional text styles which can be assigned to pieces of text. These text styles usually are used to identify text which has a special meaning or should be emphasized for some reason.

```
<!ELEMENT (%FONTSTYLE;|%PHRASE;) - - (%INLINE;)* >
<!ATTLIST (%FONTSTYLE;|%PHRASE;)
  %ATTRS; >
```

HTML supports two types of how text can be marked up to be formatted differently than normal text. The elements defined by the %FONTSTYLE; entity are based on formatting style only. Although not all of these elements are deprecated, their use is discouraged in favor of style sheets.

- <TT>
  Renders as teletype or mono-spaced text.

- <I>
  Renders as italic text style.

- <B>
  Renders as bold text style.

- <BIG>
  Renders text in a "large" font.

- <SMALL>
  Renders text in a "small" font.

- <STRIKE> and <S>
  Render strike-through style text.

- <U>
  Renders underlined text.

It should be noticed that the <STRIKE>, <S> and <U> elements are deprecated. Style sheets should be used to specify strike-through or underlined text styles. This can be done using style sheet font properties described in section 6.3.4.1. However, the same is true for the other elements of the above lists, although they are not deprecated. To support HTML's model of the separation of content and presentation, the above elements should not be used.

The more logical way to mark up special phrases is to base the markup on content rather than on presentation. The %PHRASE; entity defines a number of elements which can be used to mark up words or phrases and bases this markup on their semantics.

- <EM>
  This indicates that a piece of text should be emphasized.

- <STRONG>
  This indicates that a piece of text should be strongly emphasized.

- <DFN>
  This element indicates that its content is the defining instance of the enclosed term.

- <CODE>
  Designates a fragment of computer code.

- <SAMP>
  Designates sample output from programs, scripts, etc.

- <KBD>
  Indicates text to be entered by the user.

- <VAR>
  Indicates an instance of a variable or program argument.

- <CITE>
  Contains a citation or a reference to other sources.

- <ABBR>
  Indicates an abbreviated form (WWW, HTTP, URI, Mass., etc.).

- <ACRONYM>
  Indicates an acronym (sonar, radar, etc.).

The content of the ABBR and ACRONYM elements specifies the abbreviated expression itself, as it would normally appear in running text. The TITLE attribute of these elements may be used to provide the full or expanded form of the expression. A browser supporting the TITLE attribute could display the full form of the abbreviated expression as "tool-tip", which is displayed if the pointer is moved over the element instance.

The text style elements have as content any inline element as defined by the %INLINE; entity. Their start and end tags both are required. The only attributes defined for the text style elements are the standard attributes defined by the %ATTRS; entity.

Finally, it is also possible to create superscript or subscript text, using the <SUP> and <SUB> elements. Both elements accept inline elements as defined by the %INLINE; entity as their content and should be used instead of font size changes or other visually oriented techniques whenever super- or subscripts are required. The only attributes defined for super- or subscripts are the standard attributes defined by the %ATTRS; entity.

Contact information

For many web pages, it is very useful to have some contact information about the page's author or for the page's content. HTML defines a special element for this contact information. It is not exactly defined what kind of contact information should be specified inside the <ADDRESS> element, it can be just an email address, a postal address, or some other kind of contact information, such as links to the page author's web page.

```
<!ELEMENT ADDRESS - - (%INLINE;)* >
<!ATTLIST ADDRESS
  %ATTRS; >
```

The <ADDRESS> element has as content any inline element as defined by the %INLINE; entity[19]. The start and the end tag both are required. The only attributes defined for the <ADDRESS> element are the standard attributes defined by the %ATTRS; entity.

Fonts

Introduced in HTML 3.2, there are two elements which can be used to change the font for the presentation of a document. The elements are <BASEFONT> and <FONT>. <BASEFONT> sets the base font for a document or a part of a document, which can be changed using the <FONT> element. Both elements have attributes which can be used to set the SIZE, COLOR, or FACE of a font. It should be noticed, however, that the <BASEFONT> and <FONT> elements are deprecated and font changes should be handled through style sheets. Style sheet properties handling fonts are described in section 6.3.4.1.

Quotations

A common type of text especially in scientific documents are quotations from other documents. HTML defines two elements for quotations, one for block-level elements, whenever the quote should be treated as block-level and contains block-level elements, and the other for inline quotations. Both elements can also specify the origin of the quotation via a URI.

```
<!ELEMENT BLOCKQUOTE - - (%BLOCK;|SCRIPT)+ >
<!ATTLIST BLOCKQUOTE
  %ATTRS;
  CITE    %URI; #IMPLIED >
```

---

[19] In the transitional DTD, the <ADDRESS> element's content model is ((%INLINE;)|P)*, also allowing paragraphs inside the <ADDRESS> element.

The content of the <BLOCKQUOTE> element can be any block-level element as specified by the %BLOCK; entity as well as scripts. Both the start and the end tag of the <BLOCKQUOTE> element are mandatory. In addition to the standard attributes defined by the %ATTRS; entity, the <BLOCKQUOTE> element defines a CITE attribute which can be used to specify a URI which points to the origin of the quote.

```
<!ELEMENT Q - - (%INLINE;)* >
<!ATTLIST Q
  %ATTRS;
  CITE    %URI; #IMPLIED >
```

The <Q> element has as content any inline element as defined by the %INLINE; entity. Both the start and the end tag of the <Q> element are mandatory. In addition to the standard attributes defined by the %ATTRS; entity, the <Q> element defines a CITE attribute which can be used to specify a URI which points to the origin of the quote.

Preformatted text

Preformatted text can be specified using the <PRE> element[20]. Usually, visual user agents will leave white space intact (ie, not reduce multiple white spaces to one space, and also not remove or insert line breaks), observe the line breaking of the input, use a fixed width character font, and switch off automatic word wrap. This can be used to display text which is formatted in a distinctive way, two common examples are poetry and computer programs. However, it should be noticed that these effects are purely visual, so a non-visual user agents will not be able to render the content of the <PRE> element according to the user's specification (if there are any semantics associated with the formatting, which will normally be the case).

Text changes

In some cases, it may be useful to have the possibility to mark document changes. HTML provides support for this type of information with the <INS> and <DEL> elements. The <INS> element is used to mark up document content which has been inserted since the last version of a document, the <DEL> element contains content which has been deleted. A usual way to render this for visual user agent would be to underline the contents of <INS> elements and to strike-through the contents of <DEL> elements. It would also be possible for a user agent to make the rendering of <DEL> content configurable, showing it either as strike-through content, or not displaying it at all, resulting in a more compact presentation of the document.

---

[20] In early versions of HTML, this element was named <PLAINTEXT>.

```
<!ELEMENT (INS|DEL) - - (%FLOW;)* >
<!ATTLIST (INS|DEL)
   %ATTRS;
   CITE      %URI;       #IMPLIED
   DATETIME  %DATETIME;  #IMPLIED >
```

Both elements can act as block-level element or as inline element, depending on their context. If they are used as block-level elements, they may contain block-level elements. If they are used as inline elements, they may also only contain inline elements. Consequently, the DTD's content model, which allows block-level and inline content using the %FLOW; entity, is more permissive than the HTML standard specifies[21]. In addition to the standard attributes defined by the %ATTRS; entity, the <INS> and <DEL> elements define a CITE attribute which is intended to point to information explaining why a document was changed. Furthermore, the DATETIME attribute specifies the date and time when the change was made.

It should be noticed, however, that HTML does not specify a mechanism or framework for a document revision control system. However, the <INS> and <DEL> elements can be used to display the information which is generated by such a system. The information which can be maintained inside a document revision control system usually is much richer than the simple model of HTML, including identification of authors, different revision levels, branches of document revisions, and features for locking and unlocking specific revisions.

Horizontal rules

It is possible to specify horizontal rules for visual user agents using the <HR> element. Non-visual user agents can interpret this element as some kind of structural divider between different sections, but this is not specified in the HTML standard. The <HR> element is defined to be empty. As for all empty elements, the start tag is required and the end tag is optional. The attributes defined for the <HR> element are the core attributes defined by the %COREATTRS; entity and the event attributes defined by the %EVENTS; entity[22].

---

[21] This is a good example for what is described in section 4.3.3 about HTML validation. The HTML DTD allows, on the SGML level, the generation of documents which are not valid HTML, because of restrictions of HTML which are not reflected in the DTD.

[22] In the transitional DTD, the <HR> element also has the ALIGN, NOSHADE, SIZE, and WIDTH attributes. These attributes, however, are deprecated and should not be used.

5.2.4.2 Lists

HTML defines three types of lists, which are unordered lists (lists without any particular ordering of the list items), ordered lists (lists where there is an ordering of the items which is reflected in a numbering scheme for the items), and definition lists, which are defined by list items composed out of a definition term and a definition description.

Unordered lists

The simplest list type of HTML is the unordered list. An unordered list consists of a set of list items which do not have any inherent order and which are displayed in a way which does not reflect any particular sequence of the list items[23].

```
<!ELEMENT UL - - (LI)+ >
<!ATTLIST UL
  %ATTRS; >
<!ELEMENT LI - O (%FLOW;)* >
<!ATTLIST LI
  %ATTRS; >
```

The <UL> element simply is a sequence of one or more list items represented by the <LI> element. Both the start and the end tag of the <UL> element are mandatory. The <LI> element uses the %FLOW; entity as its content model, allowing both block-level and inline content. The start tag of the <LI> element is mandatory. Because the end of a list item can be deduced from the context (either by the start of the next list item or by the end of the list), the end tag of the <LI> element is optional. The only attributes defined for the <UL> and <LI> elements are the standard attributes defined by the %ATTRS; entity[24].

---

[23] Two other elements, <DIR> and <MENU>, share the same formal definition with <UL>, which means they are used in exactly the same way (with regard to their content, one or more <LI> elements). However, their formatting is different, <DIR> is used for creating multicolumn directory lists, and <MENU> is used for single column menu lists. Both elements are deprecated, not implemented very widely and should therefore not be used. The HTML standard recommends to use <UL> instead.

[24] The transitional DTD also defines deprecated TYPE and COMPACT attributes for the <UL> element. These are used for setting the itemization type and for requesting a more compact formatting of the list. These aspects should be handled through style sheets (as described in section 6.3.4.5). Furthermore, the transitional DTD defines deprecated TYPE and VALUE attributes for the <LI> element. These are used for setting the itemization type and for setting a sequence number. These aspects should also be handled through style sheets.

Ordered lists

In many cases, it is necessary to use lists where the individual list items are numbered. HTML provides this type of list through ordered lists, which can be used with different numbering schemes (selected using style sheet mechanisms). Apart from the usage of a numbering scheme for items rather than constant symbols, the ordered lists of HTML are used in the same way as unordered lists.

```
<!ELEMENT OL - - (LI)+ >
<!ATTLIST OL
  %ATTRS; >
```

The <OL> element simply is a sequence of one or more list items represented by the <LI> element. Both the start and the end tag of the <OL> element are mandatory. The <LI> element is explained in the previous section about unordered lists. The only attributes defined for the <OL> element are the standard attributes defined by the %ATTRS; entity[25]

Definition lists

The third type of list available in HTML is a definition list. A definition list does not use generated labels for the items (such as hyphens in unordered lists and numbers in ordered lists), but allows the list author to specify the item labels. A popular application of this kind of list the a list of terms which has to be defined, putting the term inside the label and the explanation of it into the item text, hence the name definition list.

```
<!ELEMENT DL - - (DT|DD)+ >
<!ATTLIST DL
  %ATTRS; >
```

The <DL> element simply is a sequence of one or more list items, each one represented by a sequence of a <DT> element representing the definition term, and a <DD> element representing the definition description. Both the start and the end tag of the <DL> element are mandatory. The only attributes defined for the <DL> element are the standard attributes defined by the %ATTRS; entity[26].

---

[25] In the transitional DTD, TYPE, COMPACT, and START attributes are defined for the <OL> element. These deprecated attributes are used for setting the numbering type, for requesting a more compact formatting of the list, and for setting a start value for the sequence numbers. These aspects should be handled through style sheets (as described in section 6.3.4.5).

[26] The transitional DTD also defines the deprecated COMPACT attribute for the <DL> element. It is used for requesting a more compact formatting of the list. This aspect should be handled through style sheets (as described in section 6.3.4.5).

```
<!ELEMENT DT - O (%INLINE;)* >
<!ELEMENT DD - O (%FLOW;)* >
<!ATTLIST (DT|DD)
  %ATTRS; >
```

The <DT> element defines the definition term and can have inline elements as content which are defined by the %INLINE; entity. The <DD> element defines the definition description and uses the %FLOW; entity as its content model, allowing both block-level and inline content. The start tags for both elements are mandatory, but both elements' end tags are optional, for the <DT> element because its end can be deduced from the start of a <DD> element, and for the <DD> element because its end can be deduced from the start of a <DT> element or the end of the <DL> element. The <DT> and <DD> elements share the same attribute definition, the only attributes defined for these elements are the standard attributes defined by the %ATTRS; entity.

5.2.4.3 Tables

Tables first appeared in HTML 3.2, using a fairly simple model. A more powerful model was first published in IETF experimental RFC 1942 [216]. Basically, this model was included in HTML 4.0, it introduced support for incremental rendering of tables, for breaking tables across pages, and for making tables more accessible for non-visual use. Although the new table model introduced a number of new elements, it is designed in a way which is compatible with HTML 3.2, so that old tables can still be used.

In the current version of HTML, tables have a special position because they are the only set of elements which still have a lot of formatting attributes associated with them which are not deprecated. The reason for this is that the style sheet language at which HTML is targeted, *Cascading Style Sheets (CSS)*, in its current version (CSS1 as described in section 6.3) does not support tables. However, the next version of CSS (*CSS2* as described in section 6.6.2) includes support for tables. Therefore it is very likely that in the next version of HTML, when it is assumed that CSS2 will be used as style sheet language, the formatting attribute of all table elements will also be deprecated.

```
<!ELEMENT TABLE    - - (CAPTION?, (COL*|COLGROUP*),
                       THEAD?, TFOOT?, TBODY+) >
<!ELEMENT TBODY    O O (TR)+ >
<!ELEMENT TR       - O (TH|TD)+ >
<!ELEMENT (TH|TD)  - O (%FLOW;)* >
```

This is a list of elements which are mandatory inside a table. It should be noticed, however, that the <TBODY> does not have to appear at all, because its start and end tags are optional. According to the definition above, a minimal HTML table consists of a table body, which is a sequence of one or more rows, which in turn are sequences of table header or data cells. The start and end tags of the <TABLE> element are mandatory.

Basically, a table consists of an optional caption represented by the <CAPTION> element, and the table specification itself. The caption is followed by optional <COL> and <COLGROUP> elements which specify column widths and groupings. Also optional are <THEAD> and <TFOOT> elements, which contain header and footer rows. The only mandatory part of the <TABLE> element is the <TBODY> element, which constitutes the table body. It is possible to use multiple table bodies in one table.

Basic structuring of tables

HTML has a table model which is row-oriented, meaning that a table's rows are the basic way of structuring a table. This is due to the fact that the basic flow of content in a document is from top to bottom, and then, looking at each line, from left to right (at least, this is true for western languages, which are the basis for HTML). Similarly, the flow of table cells in HTML tables is specified in rows, going from top to bottom, and then, in each row, going from left to right from cell to cell.

The <TBODY> element therefore is defined as a sequence of table rows represented by the <TR> element. Because the start and the end of the <TBODY> element can be identified by the context, both the start and the end tag of the <TBODY> element are optional. A table row is a sequence of table header or data cells, represented by <TH> and <TD> elements. The <TBODY>, <TH>, and <TD> elements all have mandatory start and optional end tags, because their end can be identified by the context.

- *Table body*
  The <TBODY> element is used to mark up the body of a table, which is constituted by the table's rows which are not part of special table sections (which are the table head and the table foot, as described in the subsequent section). A table body is a set of table rows which are related to each other by their content. If there are multiple sets of table rows which are related to each other by their content, it is possible to use multiple <TBODY> elements inside a table. In addition to the standard attributes defined by the %ATTRS; entity, the <TBODY> element defines attributes for specifying the horizontal and vertical alignment of table cells, these attributes are defined by the %CELLHALIGN; and %CELLVALIGN; entities.

- *Rows*

  The basic structuring of tables is a structure of rows, which are represented by the <TR> element. A table row simply is a sequence of table
  cells, whereas HTML differentiates two types of table cells, table header
  cells represented by the <TH> element, and table data cells represented
  by the <TD> element. In addition to the standard attributes defined by
  the %ATTRS; entity, the <TR> element defines attributes for specifying
  the horizontal and vertical alignment of table cells, these attributes are
  defined by the %CELLHALIGN; and %CELLVALIGN; entities. The horizontal and vertical alignment of table cells specified in the <TR> element
  overrides the alignment set in the <TBODY> element[27].

- *Table cells*

  Table header cells are formatted a little bit different than table data
  cells, they are specified using the <TH> element. Apart from the slightly
  different formatting[28] and the different semantics of header cells and data
  cells (which is important for non-visual presentation), header cells and
  data cells are very similar.

	using <th colspan="2">	
<th> for row 1	cell 1	second <td> cell
<th> for second row	another cell	the last cell

Fig. 5.6 Formatting of <TH> and the COLSPAN attribute

Most table data is contained in table data cells, which are specified using
the <TD> element. Table cells may contain block-level and inline content
as specified by the %FLOW; entity. In addition to the standard attributes
defined by the %ATTRS; entity, the <TH> and <TD> elements define attributes for specifying the horizontal and vertical alignment of table cells,
these attributes are defined by the %CELLHALIGN; and %CELLVALIGN; entities. The horizontal and vertical alignment of table cells specified in the
<TH> or <TD> elements overrides the alignment set in the <TR> element.

---

[27] The same is true for overriding the cell alignment attributes of the<THEAD> and
<TFOOT> elements, if the <TR> element is used inside these.

[28] Most user agents display table header cells in bold face and centered, while table
data cells are formatted using a normal font and are left-aligned. However, this
entirely depends on the browser, which may choose any style of formatting it
finds most useful.

Furthermore, the <TD> element also specifies a number of attributes for logically grouping together table cells. The ROWSPAN and COLSPAN attributes can be used to define table cells which span multiple rows or columns. This is especially useful when creating table headers.

These are the elements which are used for simple tables. In general, tables are the most complex structures which can be used in HTML, and all table elements have a considerable number of attributes, some for structuring the content, and some for specifying the presentation. For the table elements, we have omitted a detailed description of all attributes, which are, however, listed as a reference in appendix B.3.

Advanced structuring of tables

In addition to the basic structures presented in the previous section, tables can contain a number of additional elements which specify additional information about a table and also allow more advanced formatting and structuring of table information.

```
<!ELEMENT CAPTION  - - (%INLINE;)* >
<!ELEMENT THEAD    - O (TR)+ >
<!ELEMENT TFOOT    - O (TR)+ >
<!ELEMENT COLGROUP - O (COL)* >
<!ELEMENT COL      - O EMPTY >
```

- *Caption*
  The <CAPTION> element can be used to specify a table caption, which may contain any inline content as specified by the %INLINE; entity. The only attributes defined for the <CAPTION> element are the standard attributes defined by the %ATTRS; entity.

- *Head section*
  The head section of a table can be specified using the <THEAD> element. It must be specified before the optional foot section and before the table body. A table head marks a section of the table which should be treated specially for formatting. For example, it should be displayed constantly at the top of the window when scrolling through a large table, or it should be put on top of every page for paged media and a table spanning multiple pages. In addition to the standard attributes defined by the %ATTRS; entity, the <THEAD> element defines attributes for specifying the horizontal and vertical alignment of table cells, these attributes are defined by the %CELLHALIGN; and %CELLVALIGN; entities.

- *Foot section*
  The foot section of a table is marked up after the head section (and before the body section) using the <TFOOT> element. Although it may

seem odd that the foot section is specified before the body section, it makes sense because HTML tables are designed to be displayed in only one pass[29]. If displayed on a paged media (such as being printed on paper), the foot section may be required before the body section is complete, to display the table footer on the first page (this happens if the table spans multiple pages). In addition to the standard attributes defined by the %ATTRS; entity, the <TFOOT> element defines attributes for specifying the horizontal and vertical alignment of table cells, these attributes are defined by the %CELLHALIGN; and %CELLVALIGN; entities.

- *Column groups*

  The <COLGROUP> element allows the grouping of columns into column groups. Column groups serve two purposes. User agents may use column groups to base their presentation on this information, visual user agents for example can separate column groups differently than columns inside a column group. The second purpose of column groups is to specify the layout for a number of columns using only one element. A <COLGROUP> element is either empty, or it contains <COL> elements, which may be used to specify the layout for columns inside a column group.

  In addition to the standard attributes defined by the %ATTRS; entity, the <COLHEAD> element defines attributes for specifying the horizontal and vertical alignment of table cells, these attributes are defined by the %CELLHALIGN; and %CELLVALIGN; entities. The <COLGROUP> element defines a SPAN attribute, specifying the number of columns a column group has, and a WIDTH attribute, which is used to specify the width of the column group's columns.

- *Grouping attributes for column specification*

  The <COL> element is used to specify the layout for a column. Because it does not define an actual table cell, it is defined to be empty. The <COL> element may either be used within a <COLGROUP> element, in which case it is used to specify the layout for a column inside a column group, or without a <COLGROUP> element, in which case it specifies the layout for a column without an associated column group.

  In addition to the standard attributes defined by the %ATTRS; entity, the <COL> element defines attributes for specifying the horizontal and vertical alignment of table cells, these attributes are defined by the %CELLHALIGN; and %CELLVALIGN; entities. Furthermore, the <COL> element defines a SPAN attribute, which defines the number of columns a <COL> definition

---

[29] This means that a browser or any other client processing HTML should be able to display a table incrementally while receiving its data, without the need to wait for the whole data of the table.

spans, and a WIDTH attribute, which is used to specify the width of the columns associated with the <COL> element.

It should be noted that both the <COLHEAD> and the <COL> element do not contain actual table content. In the content model of the SGML definition of the <TABLE> element it can be seen that both elements appear outside the table's content, which is contained in the table's head, foot, and body section. <COLHEAD> and <COL> are only used for specifying presentation attributes which should be used for an entire column, and to logically group columns. The actual content still is specified in table cells as represented by the <TH> and <TD> elements.

Formatting options

As mentioned above, table formatting is not part of the CSS1 standard and is therefore still specified using HTML. Basically, the formatting of tables is concerned with borders between table cells, and the placement of content within table cells. HTML defines a large number of attributes for various table elements which are concerned with borders and alignment. Also defined is a model of inheritance and precedence, which defines which attributes can be inherited from parent elements (for example, the cell alignment is inherited from table rows to table cells), and how multiply defined formatting attributes are interpreted (for example, the cell alignment specified in a table cell element overrides the cell alignment specified in a table row).

However, because of the multitude of different attributes, and because this way of formatting tables will disappear as soon as CSS2 with its support for specifying table layout is being used, we do not discuss table formatting in detail. The HTML standard itself contains a good description of table formatting, another good source of information is the book by Raggett et al. [220].

5.2.5 Images and image maps

The most widely used multimedia element of HTML is the image, which can be integrated into web pages in different ways. HTML 4.0 defines am <IMG> and an <OBJECT> element, which can both be used to integrate images into HTML documents. It is intended that the <IMG> element in the long run will be replaced by the <OBJECT> element (as described in section 5.2.8.2), which is more general than <IMG>. However, currently <OBJECT> is not very widely supported, and therefore the <IMG> element will remain in use for some time[30].

---

[30] The most acceptable way would be to use an <IMG> element inside an <OBJECT> element. This way, a browser knowing the <OBJECT> element would use it,

Webster [272] describes the data formats of images which are most widely used on the web. He also describes a number of tools which can be used to work with these formats. Baumgardt [14] goes a step further by also describing a number of design issues which are important for well-designed web pages.

It is important to notice that HTML itself does not specify any format for image data, nor does it define any formats which should be supported by HTML browsers. HTML simply regards images as external data, which has to be handled by a browser, but which may be coded in any way[31]. However, because there are so many image formats which are used for various reasons, applications, and platforms, a de-facto standard has been established which is implemented by all major browsers.

- *GIF*

  The *Graphics Interchange Format (GIF)* is one of the most widely used formats for simple graphics. Its most obvious limitations are the ability to handle only 256 different colors in an image, and its usage of a patented compression algorithm. GIF exists in two versions, GIF87 [49] and GIF89a [50], but many of the features of the newer version are nor widely implemented. GIF is mostly used for graphics (because of its limitations of 256 colors it is not well suited for photographic images) and is supported by almost all browsers.

- *JPEG*

  For photographic images, the format defined by the *Joint Photographic Experts Group (JPEG)* is the most popular way of coding. Strictly speaking, JPEG is only the algorithm, which is standardized in ISO 10918 [121, 123, 130]. The most popular file format is the *JPEG File Interchange Format (JFIF)* as described by Hamilton [93][32]. This is the second image format which is supported by almost all browsers.

- *PNG*

  The *Portable Network Graphics (PNG)* [26, 27] format as described in section 10.4.3 is designed to be a replacement for GIF. It has almost all features of GIF and also supports truecolor up to 32bit, an 8bit alpha

---

ignoring its content (as described in section 5.2.8.2), and older browsers would ignore the unknown <OBJECT> element and simply interpret the <IMG> element.

[31] This is the reason why the <IMG> element should be replaced by the more general <OBJECT> element. For HTML, it is not important what kind of external data is defined by an element such as <IMG> or <OBJECT>, it therefore makes sense to have only one type of element which generally is used for external data.

[32] The *Still Picture Interchange File Format (SPIFF)* is the official JPEG file format defined by ISO 10918 [131]. However, it is not widely used, because JFIF was available much earlier and is very popular today.

channel and some other features. It is expected that support for PNG will be widespread in the near future. However, animations are not supported by PNG, which will therefore not be able to completely replace GIF.

Basically, images can be used in two ways in HTML. They can either be used as images which are just displayed and do not have any additional functionality. This type of images is described in section 5.2.5.1. It is also possible to use images as image maps, thereby making it possible to define regions inside an image being associated with actions which are executed when the user clicks on them. This way to use images (called image maps or clickable images) is described in section 5.2.5.2.

5.2.5.1 Images

As mentioned already, for HTML an image is external information which has to be displayed in the document. The information which is absolutely necessary therefore is a pointer to the external information (the image data), and the size of the image (this is necessary for formatting). However, since the image data formats used on the web contain the size of the image, the browser can get the size information from the image data and consequently only needs the pointer to it.

```
<!ELEMENT IMG - O EMPTY >
<!ATTLIST IMG
   %ATTRS;
   SRC        %URI;        #REQUIRED
   ALT        %TEXT;       #REQUIRED
   LONGDESC   %URI;        #IMPLIED
   HEIGHT     %LENGTH;     #IMPLIED
   WIDTH      %LENGTH;     #IMPLIED
   ISMAP      (ISMAP)      #IMPLIED
   USEMAP     %URI;        #IMPLIED >
```

Because all information for the image is specified in the attributes of the <IMG> element, the element is defined to be empty. As for all empty elements, the start tag is required and the end tag is optional. In addition to the standard attributes defined by the %ATTRS; entity, the <IMG> element defines a number of attributes.

- SRC[33]

  The SRC attribute specifies a URI which points to the image data, it is a required attribute.

- ALT

  Although most browsers today support the display of images, there are several reasons why images may not be displayed. A user might want to save bandwidth by not transferring all images on a web page, the image format of a specific image may not be supported by a browser, or the web page may be used by a visually impaired user. In all these cases, it would be very useful to have a short description of the image's content. This description is given in the ALT attribute, and because it is necessary in a variety of scenarios, it is also specified as being mandatory.

- LONGDESC

  In some cases, there may be a longer description of an image, which exists on a separate web page. In this case, the URI of this web page can be specified in the image's LONGDESC attribute.

- HEIGHT and WIDTH

  These attributes give user agents an idea of the size of an image so that they may reserve space for it and continue rendering the document while waiting for the image data. So in most cases, these attributes contain the actual size of the image. However, it is also possible to specify the desired size of an image using these attributes, and the user agent should scale the image to the specified size. Both attributes accept values as specified for the %LENGTH; entity.

As can be seen, it is very easy to incorporate images into web pages, it only takes the <IMG> element and the two mandatory attributes SRC and ALT. However, it should be made a general habit to also specify the HEIGHT and WIDTH attributes, because this makes rendering for browsers much easier, and they don't have to reformat the document after receiving the image data.

5.2.5.2 Image maps

In the definition of the <IMG> element in the previous section, two attributes have not been explained. These attributes are used for specifying images as image maps, and they are therefore explained here. An image map (sometimes

---

[33] Most browsers also support a LOWSRC attribute, which points to a smaller version of the image (usually the same size, but black and white) which can be displayed while the full-resolution version pointed to by the SRC attribute is loaded. However, it should be noted that the LOWSRC attribute is not specified in any HTML standard.

also called a clickable image) is an image which has a map defined for it which consists of sensitive areas. When the user clicks in one of these areas, the action associated with this area is executed.

- ISMAP

  The **ISMAP** attribute identifies, when set, an image as using a server-side image map. The URI identifying the server is not part of the <IMG> element, but specified in the surrounding <A> element.

- USEMAP

  This attribute associates an image map with the image. The image map is defined by a <MAP> element. The value of the **USEMAP** attribute must match the value of the **NAME** attribute of the associated <MAP> element.

Client-side image maps are preferred over server-side image maps for at least two reasons: they are accessible to people browsing with non-graphical user agents (because the map is known to the browser, it can be presented in an alternative way), and they offer immediate feedback as to whether or not the pointer is over an active region (this depends on the browser, but if the areas are also associated with events calling scripts, a much more powerful user interface can be defined than by using server-side image maps).

Server-side image maps

A server-side image map is defined by an <IMG> element with the **ISMAP** attribute set, where the <IMG> element is used inside an <A> element. The <A> element defines the URI for the server-side mechanism which handles the coordinates. The basic procedure of how server-side image maps are handled by the client and the server is shown in figure 5.7.

1. The user clicks on a point inside the image, which has been identified as an image map. The browser recognizes the coordinates of the pointer.

2. The browser uses the coordinates by appending them to the URI which has been specified in the map's link (ie, the link specified in the <A> element containing the <IMG> element). Specifically, the browser appends a question mark and the two coordinates, separated by a comma, to the URI, and then the link is followed using the new URI.

3. The server receives the request and either passes the coordinates on to some external program which analyzes them (for example, using a CGI script as described in section 9.4). The other possibility (the one shown

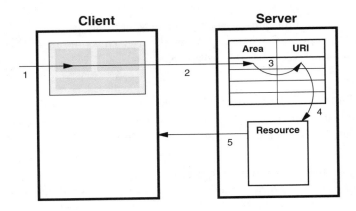

Fig. 5.7   Server-side image map

in the figure) is that the server itself interprets the coordinates through some built-in mechanism for server-side image map support[34].

4. The server (or the external program) locates the resource associated with the area. Depending on the URI associated with the area, the server either takes the resource (if the resource is located on the server, which is shown in the figure), or the server composes a redirection response with a `Location` header field containing the URI.

5. The server sends a response to the browser, which contains either the resource itself, or a reference to it in the `Location` header field. In the second case, the browser has to initiate another request with the URI it received in the redirection response.

The basic process of server-side image map handling is rather simple. It keeps most of the complexity on the server side, the only thing the client has to do is to locate the pointer inside the image and to append its coordinates to the link specified in the `<A>` element. There are two main disadvantages to this approach.

- *Server load*
  Since the server handles the actual processing of coordinates, most of the work load of image map handling is on the server side. Even if the server does not store the resource which is associated with a map area, it still has to handle the client's request and compose a redirection response. For servers handling a large number of requests, the amount of processing

---

[34] Almost all server implementations provide server-side image map support, although the specific mechanism and data format used for the definition of image maps vary between different server implementations.

required for image map requests can become a significant performance problem.

- *Limited functionality*
It is possible to think of additional functionality for image maps, such as highlighting certain areas, when the user moves over a part of the image, or triggering an event (executing a script associated with it) instead of creating an HTTP request when a certain area is clicked. This type of functionality is not possible with server-side image maps, because the map is only known to the server.

In response to these limitations of server-side image maps, a new mechanism, called client-side image maps, was introduced in HTML. This new type of image maps does not suffer from the limitations of server-side image maps, but requires more functionality to be included on the client side.

Client-side image maps

Client-side image maps have first been described by Internet informational RFC 1980 [240], which has now been fully integrated into the HTML standard. A client-side image map is created using an <IMG> element with the USEMAP attribute pointing to an image map[35]. This image map is located and interpreted by the browser, which locally handles the mapping from clicks inside the image to associated actions. The procedure how client-side image maps are processed the client and the server is shown in figure 5.8.

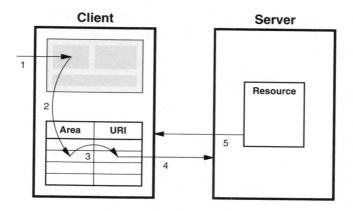

Fig. 5.8 Client-side image map

---

[35] Although the USEMAP attribute can be used to specify a complete URI, today's browsers mostly support only image maps inside the same document as the image itself, effectively limiting the USEMAP value to a fragment identifier.

1. The user clicks on a point inside the image, which has been identified as an image map (by setting its **USEMAP** attribute). The browser recognizes the coordinates of the pointer.

2. The browser uses the coordinates to find an area in the list of areas which have been defined as clickable areas for this image map. If there is no area which includes the coordinates where the click occurred, and if there is no default area defined, nothing happens.

3. The browser finds the URI which is associated with the area where the click occurred. However, it is not necessary for an area to be associated with a URI, it is also possible that an area only defines events which are used to execute scripts. In this case, there is no need for a client-server interaction, and the browser simply executes the script associated with the area's event.

4. The browser retrieves the resource associated with the URI by requesting it from the appropriate server just as it would have requested this resource if its URI had been specified in a normal link on the web page.

5. The server sends a response which contains the resource associated with the URI. Depending on the type of the resource, the browser uses it to display a new page (if the resource was an HTML page) or perform some other action.

The procedure described above makes it necessary to have a clearly defined standard for the specification of image maps (in case of server-side image maps, this is not necessary, because the image map is never exchanged, it always remains on the server which handles the image map). HTML defines an image map to be a number of areas, which are used to assign links (using URIs) or events to them.

```
<!ELEMENT MAP - - ((%BLOCK;)+ | AREA+) >
   %ATTRS;
   NAME          CDATA           #REQUIRED >
<!ELEMENT AREA - O EMPTY >
   %ATTRS;
   SHAPE         %SHAPE;         RECT
   COORDS        %COORDS;        #IMPLIED
   HREF          %URI;           #IMPLIED
   TARGET        %FRAMETARGET;   #IMPLIED
   NOHREF        (NOHREF)        #IMPLIED
   ALT           %TEXT;          #REQUIRED
   TABINDEX      NUMBER          #IMPLIED
   ACCESSKEY     %CHARACTER;     #IMPLIED
   ONFOCUS       %SCRIPT;        #IMPLIED
   ONBLUR        %SCRIPT;        #IMPLIED >
```

The <MAP> element defines a client-side image map. Its content model allows block-level content as specified by the %BLOCK; entity, which may be used to provide an text-oriented alternative to the image map. This type of <MAP> content is used in conjunction with the <OBJECT> element as described in section 5.2.8.2. As an alternative to the block-level content, the <MAP> element may contain one or more areas represented by the <AREA> element. The start and the end tag of the <MAP> element are mandatory. In addition to the standard attributes defined by the %ATTRS; entity, the <MAP> element defines a NAME attribute which is required. This attribute assigns a name to the image map and is the name by which it is referred to in the <IMG> element's USEMAP attribute.

An area in an image map is represented by the <AREA> element. The element is defined to be empty, its start tag must be specified (since it carries the information which is important for that element), and the end tag may be omitted. The attributes defined for the <AREA> element are the standard attributes defined by the %ATTRS; entity, and a number of additional attributes, which are used to specify information associated with the area.

- SHAPE

  The SHAPE attribute defines the shape of the area according to the possible shapes defined by the %SHAPE; entity.

- COORDS

  For all area shapes except the default value (which defines the default area for an image), it is necessary to define the coordinates for the region to be specified. The format of the COORDS attribute depends on the value of of the SHAPE attribute, it is defined by the %COORDS; entity.

- HREF

  In many cases, there will be a URI associated with an area, which has to be followed if the user clicks on it. This link is specified using the HREF attribute.

- TARGET

  When used with framesets and frames as described in section 5.2.7.1, the TARGET attribute can be used to specify which frame should be the target frame if the area is selected, that is into which frame the document pointed to by the HREF attribute should be loaded. The possible values of the TARGET attribute are described by the %FRAMETARGET; entity.

- NOHREF

  However, it is also possible that no URI is associated with an area, in which case the NOHREF attribute should be set to indicate that the area has no link. However, it is still possible to specify scripts which are asso-

ciated with an area's events (such as ONMOUSEOVER, which is triggered
if the user moves the mouse pointer over the area).

- **ALT**
  Although most browsers today support image maps, there are several
  reasons why images maps may not be useful for all users. A user might
  want to save bandwidth by not transferring all images on a web page, the
  image format of a specific image may not be supported by a browser, or
  the web page may be used by a visually impaired user. In all these cases, it
  would be very useful to have a short description of the area's function (eg,
  where its link specified in the HREF attribute points to). This description
  is given in the ALT attribute, and because it is necessary in a variety of
  scenarios, it is specified as being mandatory.

- **TABINDEX**
  The TABINDEX attribute is defined to assign a tabbing order to areas of a
  map. Areas are visited in the sequence of their tabbing order values (which
  are positive numbers). Selecting areas by using the tab key rather than
  pointing and clicking with a mouse may be used for interfaces without
  pointing devices.

- **ACCESSKEY**
  It is also possible to define one-key short cuts for areas using the AC-
  CESSKEY attribute. The value of the ACCESSKEY attribute can be a
  single Unicode character as specified by the %CHARACTER; entity.

- **ONFOCUS**
  This attribute specifies a script which is executed when the corresponding
  region receives focus.

- **ONBLUR**
  As a companion to the ONFOCUS attribute, the ONBLUR attribute specifies a script which is called when the region loses focus.

One of the main advantages of client-side image maps over server-side
image maps is that they also allow to associate events with areas. For a server-
side image map, it is always clear that by clicking inside an area, an HTTP
interaction with the server will be initiated, sending the coordinates to the
server and waiting for the reply. With a client-side image map, on the other
hand, it is possible that no link is associated with an area (using the NOHREF
attribute), but several events can be defined for it. These events trigger the
execution of scripts, which in turn can do anything which is possible with
DHTML. Client-side image maps in conjunction with a scripting language
can therefore be used to create highly dynamic web pages, which do not
require much server interaction.

5.2.6 Links

Links are connections between pieces of information which can be used for different purposes. One example is the <LINK> element as described in section 5.2.3.1, which makes it possible to link style sheets to documents or to define relationships (such as "table of contents") between documents. However, the most popular way how links are used in the web is a link from one document to another document, which can be followed by simply clicking on it. Image maps, as described in the previous section, are also specifying links, although in a more complex way. The easiest way to create a link in a document is by using an anchor, as defined by the <A> element.

```
<!ELEMENT A - - (%INLINE;)* -(A) >
<!ATTLIST A
  %ATTRS;
  CHARSET      %CHARSET;       #IMPLIED
  TYPE         %CONTENTTYPE;   #IMPLIED
  NAME         CDATA           #IMPLIED
  HREF         %URI;           #IMPLIED
  HREFLANG     %LANGUAGECODE;  #IMPLIED
  TARGET       %FRAMETARGET;   #IMPLIED
  REL          %LINKTYPES;     #IMPLIED
  REV          %LINKTYPES;     #IMPLIED
  TABINDEX     NUMBER          #IMPLIED
  ACCESSKEY    %CHARACTER;     #IMPLIED
  SHAPE        %SHAPE;         RECT
  COORDS       %COORDS;        #IMPLIED
  ONFOCUS      %SCRIPT;        #IMPLIED
  ONBLUR       %SCRIPT;        #IMPLIED >
```

The <A> element has as content any inline element as defined by the %INLINE; entity. The <A> element is excluded from the content model to avoid nested anchors. Both the start and the end tag of the <A> element are mandatory. In addition to the standard attributes defined by the %ATTRS; entity, the <A> element defines a number of attributes.

- CHARSET
  This attribute is used to specify the character set which is used in the resource the link points to. Its possible values are defined by the %CHARSET; entity.

- TYPE
  This attribute specifies the content type of the resource the anchor points to. Its possible values are defined by the %CONTENTTYPE; entity.

- NAME

  This attribute assigns a name to the anchor so that it may be used as
  destination by another anchor. This name must be unique in the document.

- HREF

  The HREF attribute defines the location of a resource using a URI as
  defined by the %URI; entity. Using the HREF attribute creates a source
  anchor, which points to a destination.

- HREFLANG

  As a companion to the CHARSET attribute, the HREFLANG attribute
  can be used to specify the language of the resource the link points to. Its
  possible values are defined by the %LANGUAGECODE; entity. Languages are
  specified by language tags as defined in Internet proposed standard RFC
  1766 [7], consisting of primary tags and optional subtags. Any two letter
  primary tag is a language abbreviation according to ISO 639 [112], and
  any two-letter initial subtag is a country code according to ISO 3166 [128].

- TARGET

  When used with framesets and frames as described in section 5.2.7.1,
  the TARGET attribute can be used to specify which frame should be the
  target frame if the link is selected, that is into which frame the document
  pointed to by the HREF attribute should be loaded. The possible values
  of the TARGET attribute are described by the %FRAMETARGET; entity.

- REL

  The REL attribute specifies the relationship between the document containing the <A> element and the document to which the anchor points.
  The possible attribute values are defined by the %LINKTYPES; entity. It is
  possible to specify more than one link type, using a space separated list
  of link types.

- REV

  Whereas the REL attribute specifies links in the forward direction, the
  counterpart of it is the REV attribute, specifying backward (or reverse,
  hence the name) links. Consequently, the possible attribute values are the
  same as for the REL attribute, defined by the %LINKTYPES; entity. It is
  possible to specify more than one link type, using a space separated list
  of link types.

- TABINDEX

  The TABINDEX attribute is defined to assign a tabbing order to anchors.
  Anchors are visited in the sequence of their tabbing order values (which
  are positive numbers). Selecting anchors by using the tab key rather than

pointing and clicking with a mouse may be used for interfaces without pointing devices.

- ACCESSKEY
  It is also possible to define one-key short cuts for anchors using the AC-CESSKEY attribute. The value of the ACCESSKEY attribute can be a single Unicode character as specified by the %CHARACTER; entity.

- SHAPE and COORDS
  These attributes are only used if the <A> element is used inside a <MAP> element. This is only the case if the <MAP> element is used inside an <OBJECT> element to specify a client-side image map as described in section 5.2.8.2.

- ONFOCUS
  This attribute specifies a script which is executed when the anchor receives the input focus either by the pointing device or by tabbing navigation.

- ONBLUR
  As a companion to the ONFOCUS attribute, the ONBLUR attribute specifies a script which is called when the anchor loses the input focus either by the pointing device or by tabbing navigation.

An anchor can either specify the source or the destination of a link, depending on which attributes are used. In section 5.2.6.1, it is described how source anchors are specified. In section 5.2.6.2, destination anchors are described.

5.2.6.1 Source anchors

A source anchor is the origin of a link. A source anchor can be followed to its destination. The destination of a source anchor is specified by the HREF attribute. In addition to this attribute, it is possible to specify additional information about the destination, using the REL, REV, CHARSET, TYPE, and HREFLANG attributes.

```
... the <A HREF="index.html">index</A> can be found ...
```

In this example, the anchor points to a document called index.html, which resides on the same server. Most browsers will render the text inside the <A> element in a special way, such as using a different color or underlining it.

5.2.6.2 Destination anchors

If a document is addressed as a whole, there is no need for an explicit destination anchor, since the document's URI serves as the anchor. However, a

URI also can contain a *fragment identifier* as described in section 2.2. In this case the URI points into an object, and HTML defines two ways to specify fragment identifiers.

- NAME

  The <A> element can also be used to create a destination anchor by using its NAME attribute. The content of the NAME attribute defines the fragment identifier which can be used to point to the <A> element inside the document.

  ```
  <P><A NAME="copyright"></A>The copyright of the...
  ```

  This example marks a paragraph in a document as a destination anchor by inserting an empty <A> element at its start.

- ID

  As a new way of specifying destination anchors is to use the ID attribute, which is part of the %COREATTRS; entity described in section 5.2.2 (and therefore defined for almost all elements). This way, it is not necessary to insert an extra element into the document as it is with the <A> element. However, because this attribute is new to HTML 4.0, its use as destination anchor not very widely supported.

  ```
  <P ID="copyright">The copyright of the...
  ```

  The same effect as in the previous example can be achieved by using the <P> element's ID attribute.

Both examples can be used to refer to the paragraph from within the document or from the outside. If the source anchor is defined in the same document, only the fragment identifier has to be used.

```
... the <A HREF="#copyright">copyright notice</A> contains ...
```

Although the method of using the ID attribute is more elegant, it may cause problems if the document is accessed with older browsers. This should be kept in mind when defining destination anchors.

5.2.7 Frames and forms

Besides the structuring of text, the integration of images, and the utilization of links, HTML also offers other possibilities of designing a document. A way to create documents which are actually collections of other documents are framesets, which are described in section 5.2.7.1. The inclusion of interactive elements into a document, which allow the user of a document to enter data and transmit it to a server for processing, is achieved by using HTML forms, described in section 5.2.7.2.

5.2.7.1 Frames

Although using frames quickly became popular after Netscape invented the elements, officially frames have only been integrated in HTML 4.0. The main advantage of frames is that it is fairly easy to create web pages which actually are collections of web pages, integrating multiple documents into one window. This is often used to achieve page designs which have a lot in common with designs of user interfaces of computer programs. One popular usage of frames is to have a document displaying a table of contents in one frame, and to have the actual content displayed in another frame. The HTML structure necessary to create such a design is shown in figure 5.9.

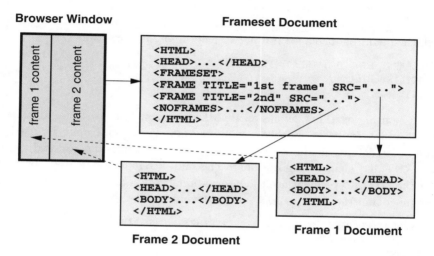

Fig. 5.9 The structure of an HTML page using frames

Using frames, the content displayed in the browser window is taken from more than one document. There is one document which defines the structure of the frames, this is the so-called *frameset document*. This frame does not contain any content[36], it only defines the layout of the window and contains links to the documents to be displayed in the different frames. Because of that special structure of the frameset document, it uses a DTD which is different from the normal HTML 4.0 DTD (more about HTML 4.0 DTDs can be found in section 5.2.1).

```
<!DOCTYPE HTML PUBLIC "-//W3C//DTD HTML 4.0 Frameset//EN"
         "http://www.w3.org/TR/REC-html40/frameset.dtd" >
```

---

[36] Although it may contain content for browsers not supporting frames using the <NOFRAMES> element, as described later.

The *frame documents* are normal HTML documents, they do not contain any special elements or attributes. The only way frames may interact (for example, how the table of contents document of the example above can load a new chapter into its neighboring window) is by the frame's name, which is defined using the NAME attribute of the <FRAME> element inside the frameset document.

Frameset

A frameset document (ie, a document using the frameset DTD) contains a normal HTML document head and specifies the structure of a frameset. It defines the layout of the window, the contents of the different frames of the window (which may change while a frameset is being viewed), and the content which should be displayed if a browser does not support frames.

```
<!ELEMENT HTML O O (HEAD, FRAMESET) >
<!ATTLIST HTML
  %I18N; >
```

The frameset DTD defines an HTML document to consist of a document head and a frameset. Both elements are mandatory and must be used in the order defined in the content model. Both the start and the end tag of the <HTML> element are optional. The only attributes which can be used for the <HTML> element are the internationalization attributes, defining the language and the directionality of the document.

```
<!ELEMENT FRAMESET - - ((FRAMESET|FRAME)+ & NOFRAMES?) >
<!ATTLIST FRAMESET
  %COREATTRS;
  ROWS          %MULTILENGTHS; #IMPLIED
  COLS          %MULTILENGTHS; #IMPLIED
  ONLOAD        %SCRIPT;       #IMPLIED
  ONUNLOAD      %SCRIPT;       #IMPLIED >
```

The <FRAMESET> element may contain <FRAMESET> elements (allowing nested framesets for defining complex frame arrangement, as shown in figure 5.10) or <FRAME> elements. <FRAMESET> elements represent another level of nesting, where the layout of a frameset may be specified, while <FRAME> elements refer to HTML documents, specifying the actual content of a frame. In addition to these two elements, the <NOFRAMES> element can appear within the <FRAMESET> element, specifying content for non-frame browsers. Both the start and the end tag of the <FRAMESET> element are mandatory. In addition to the core attributes defined by the %COREATTRS; entity, the <FRAMESET> element defines a number of attributes.

- ROWS and COLS

  These attributes are used to define the dimensions for each frame in the frameset. The values specified for the ROWS attribute give the height of each row, from top to bottom. The COLS attribute gives the width of each column from left to right. If ROWS or COLS is omitted, the implied value for the attribute is 100%. If both attributes are specified, a grid is defined and filled left-to-right and then top-to-bottom. Each attribute takes a comma-separated list of lengths as defined by the %MULTILENGTHS; entity, specified in pixels, as a percentage, or as a relative length.

  – *Pixel*

    A pixel length specifies the total amount of space required for a frame in pixels. This should only be used for images or other fixed width documents, because it does not scale if the window is resized. A pixel length is specified by simply using a number.

  – *Percentage*

    A percentage specifies the desired size of a frame as a percentage of the available space. A percentage is specified by using a number and a percent sign.

  – *Relative*

    Relative lengths make it possible to assign space to frames relative to each other. They are specified using a number followed by an asterisk character. The specification "3*,*" would assign three times as much space to the first frame than to the second.

If the ROWS and COLS attributes are used in the same <FRAMESET> element, this results in a complete grid of frames. In most cases, it is required to have a layout which has a different number of columns in different rows or vice versa, as shown in figure 5.10.

This type of layout can be achieved by nesting <FRAMESET> elements, each frameset specifying a column or a row and defining the sizes for the frames in that column or row.

```
<FRAMESET ROWS="50,70%,*">
  <FRAME TITLE="Title" SRC="document 1">
  <FRAMESET COLS="100,*">
    <FRAME TITLE="Navigation bar" SRC="document 2">
    <FRAME TITLE="Content" SRC="document 3">
  </FRAMESET>
  <FRAME TITLE="Bottom" SRC="document 4">
</FRAMESET>
```

Normally, it is advisable to use percentages or relative lengths, which allow the frames to be scaled if the window is resized. However, if the top row contains an image of fixed size, it is useful to set this row to a fixed size,

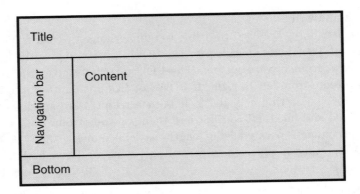

Fig. 5.10   An example layout using nested <FRAMESET> elements

to assign 70% of the vertical window size to the middle row, and to assign the rest (using a relative length without a number) to the bottom row. Because the navigation bar (for example containing a table of contents) also is designed to have a fixed width, its column size is set to a fixed size, the rest of the middle rows is assigned to the content frame, which shows the actual content which has been selected using the navigation bar.

- ONLOAD
  The ONLOAD attribute specifies a script which is called when the document is loaded into the browser.

- ONUNLOAD
  As a complement to the ONLOAD attribute, the ONUNLOAD attribute specifies a script which is called when the document is removed from the browser's window.

As described in section 5.2.3.1, it is possible to share an object across multiple frames by making it part of the document head of the frameset document and setting its DECLARE attribute. The usage of the <OBJECT> element is described in section 5.2.8.2. This, of course, requires the individual HTML pages which make up the frames of the frameset to be designed in a way which depends on the frameset document to provide the object's implementation.

```
<!ELEMENT NOFRAMES - - (BODY) -(NOFRAMES) >
<!ATTLIST NOFRAMES
    %ATTRS; >
```

Most browsers today support frames, but frameset documents should always be designed in a way which also makes it possible to use them with a non-frame browser. The <NOFRAMES> element should therefore always be used within frameset documents. If the browser does not understand frames, it will ignore all <FRAMESET> and <FRAME> elements, also ignore the <NOFRAMES> element, and finally recognize the <BODY> element, which is the only element of the <NOFRAMES> element's content model. The content of the <NOFRAMES> element should at least contain a short message which informs users that the page is designed to be used with frames. Even better, the <NOFRAMES> element should contain a list of links which contain all (or at least the most important) pages which are accessible using the frames version of the page. Both the start and the end tag of the <NOFRAMES> element are mandatory. The only attributes defined for the <NOFRAMES> element are the standard attributes defined by the %ATTRS; entity.

Frame

The <FRAME> element defines a frame, an area within a frameset document. Each frame must be included in a <FRAMESET> element, which defines the dimensions of the frame. The frame element serves as a placeholder, defining a number of properties for the frame as well as providing a pointer to the content of the frame. Therefore, the actual content of a frame is not defined inside the <FRAME> element, which only specifies a link to the content, which usually is a normal HTML document.

```
<!ELEMENT FRAME - O EMPTY >
<!ATTLIST FRAME
  %COREATTRS;
  LONGDESC      %URI;          #IMPLIED
  NAME          CDATA          #IMPLIED
  SRC           %URI;          #IMPLIED
  FRAMEBORDER   (1|0)          1
  MARGINWIDTH   %PIXELS;       #IMPLIED
  MARGINHEIGHT  %PIXELS;       #IMPLIED
  NORESIZE      (NORESIZE)     #IMPLIED
  SCROLLING     (YES|NO|AUTO)  AUTO >
```

Because all information for a frame is specified in the attributes of the <FRAME> element, the element is defined to be empty. As for all empty elements, the start tag is required and the end tag is optional. In addition to the core attributes defined by the %COREATTRS; entity, the <FRAME> element defines a number of attributes.

- LONGDESC
  The LONGDESC attribute specifies a reference to a page which contains a long description of the frame. This description should supplement the short description provided using the TITLE attribute (which is part of the %COREATTRS; entity), and may be particularly useful for non-visual user agents.

- NAME
  This attribute gives a name to the frame which may be used in the TARGET attribute of an <A>, <AREA>, <BASE>, <FORM>, or <LINK> element.

- SRC
  This attribute specifies the location of the initial contents to be contained in the frame. If the frame's content is an image, video, or similar object, and if the object cannot be described adequately using the TITLE, authors should use the LONGDESC attribute to provide the URI of a full HTML description of the object.

- FRAMEBORDER
  The FRAMEBORDER attribute specifies whether the browser should draw a border around a frame. The default value of 1 instructs the browser to draw a border, while a value of 0 will create a frame without a border. However, it should be noticed that in order to have no border drawn between two frames, both frames must have their FRAMEBORDER attributes set to 0.

- MARGINWIDTH and MARGINHEIGHT
  It is possible to specify the amount of space which should be left between a frame's content and its border. The MARGINWIDTH attribute specifies the amount of space to the left and right of the frame's content. The MARGINHEIGHT attribute specifies the amount of space for the top and bottom margins. Both values are specified in pixels as specified by the %PIXELS; entity.

- NORESIZE
  This attribute prevents the user from resizing a frame. If set for all frames, the layout specified in the <FRAMESET> element(s) will be fixed, otherwise it just specifies the initial layout, which may be altered by the user. In most cases, the NORESIZE should not be set, because users may want to change the layout of the frameset.

- SCROLLING
  The SCROLLING attribute can take one of three values. The value YES creates scroll bars for the frame all the time, even if all of the contents of the frame document fit into the frame. The default value AUTO generates scroll bars only if necessary, that is if the frame document does not fit into the frame. Otherwise, no scrollbars are displayed. The value NO never creates scrollbars, even if the document does not fit into the frame. This makes parts of the frame content inaccessible for users and should be used with care.

Using the <FRAME> element, it is possible to specify the initial content of a frame. However, one of the powerful features of frameset is that the content of individual frames can be changed, for example displaying a frame on the left which shows a table of contents of a document and which always remains the same, and a frame to the right which displays the chapter of the document which has been selected by clicking on it in the table of contents (a possible layout for this is shown in figure 5.10). In the following section, it is described how this can be implemented using framesets and frame's names.

How frames interact

One of the most interesting features of framesets is their ability to dynamically change the contents of individual frames. The initial content of the frames of a frameset is specified using <FRAME> elements, but this content may change while the user is interacting with the frameset, for example by selecting links. In general, the procedure how a frameset which changes its frame contents is designed, involves the following steps.

1. In the <FRAME> elements of the frameset document, the frames are assigned names using the NAME attribute. These names should reflect the intended use of the frames, for example the content frame in figure 5.10 should use the name CONTENT[37]

2. For any element which contains a link which specifies a link to a resource (using the SRC attribute), the TARGET attribute can be used to specify the name of the frame into which the new document should be loaded. The elements which can be used in this way are <A>, <AREA>, <BASE>, <FORM>, and <LINK>.

   ```
   <LI><A SRC="chapter2.html" TARGET="CONTENT">Chapter 3: HTTP</A>
   ```

   This list item in a list in the table of contents would cause the browser to load the document chapter2.html into the frame with the NAME attribute set to CONTENT. As an side-effect, the table of contents remains loaded in its own frame.

3. Although the individual documents loaded into different frames are normal HTML documents, for a complex frameset it is always necessary that the documents are specifically designed for the frameset, using special target names (such as _parent or _top) and knowing the names of the other documents of the frameset.

---

[37] Although this frame might initially contain the first chapter of a document, the frame should not be called CHAPTER1, because this is only the initial content and may change if the user selects another chapter from the table of contents.

Using these steps, it is possible to create very complex designs of frameset web pages, which dynamically change the number of frames inside the window and are highly configurable by the user. However, when designing frameset web pages, it is especially important to keep in mind that they (or parts of them) should also be accessible to non-frame or even non-visual browsers.

Inline frame

There also is a way how a frame can be inserted directly into a document by using an inline frame. An inline frame, specified with the <IFRAME> element, is an object inside an HTML page, like an image or a table, but contains a complete HTML document. It is also possible to include HTML documents into documents using the <OBJECT> element as described in section 5.2.8.2. This method should be preferred over using the <IFRAME> element, because the <IFRAME> element is not widely implemented, and because the <OBJECT> element should become the only way to embed objects of any kind into documents.

```
<!ELEMENT IFRAME - - (%FLOW;)* >
<!ATTLIST IFRAME
  %COREATTRS;
  LONGDESC     %URI;           #IMPLIED
  NAME         CDATA           #IMPLIED
  SRC          %URI;           #IMPLIED
  FRAMEBORDER  (1|0)           1
  MARGINWIDTH  %PIXELS;        #IMPLIED
  MARGINHEIGHT %PIXELS;        #IMPLIED
  SCROLLING    (YES|NO|AUTO)   AUTO
  ALIGN        %IALIGN;        #IMPLIED
  HEIGHT       %LENGTH;        #IMPLIED
  WIDTH        %LENGTH;        #IMPLIED >
```

Similar to other elements referring to external information, the <IFRAME> element is defined to allow content which should only be rendered if the HTML document pointed to by the SRC attribute can not be displayed. The <IFRAME> element uses the %FLOW; entity as its content model, allowing both block-level and inline content. The start as well as the end tag of the <IFRAME> element are mandatory. In addition to the core attributes defined by the %COREATTRS; entity, the <IFRAME> element defines a number of attributes.

- LONGDESC

  The LONGDESC attribute specifies a reference to a page which contains a long description of the inline frame. This description should supplement the short description provided using the TITLE attribute (which is part of the %COREATTRS; entity), and may be particularly useful for non-visual user agents.

- NAME

  This attribute gives a name to the inline frame which may be used in the TARGET attribute of an <A>, <AREA>, <BASE>, <FORM>, or <LINK> element.

- SRC

  This attribute specifies the location of the initial contents to be contained in the inline frame. If the inline frame's content is an image, video, or similar object, and if the object cannot be described adequately using the TITLE, authors should use the LONGDESC attribute to provide the URI of a full HTML description of the object.

- FRAMEBORDER

  The FRAMEBORDER attribute specifies whether the browser should draw a border around an inline frame. The default value of 1 instructs the browser to draw a border, while a value of 0 will create an inline frame without a border.

- MARGINWIDTH and MARGINHEIGHT

  It is possible to specify the amount of space which should be left between an inline frame's content and its border. The MARGINWIDTH attribute specifies the amount of space to the left and right of the inline frame's content, The MARGINWIDTH attribute the a mount of space for the top and bottom margins. Both values are specified in pixels as specified by the %PIXELS; entity.

- SCROLLING

  The SCROLLING attribute can take one of three values. The value YES creates scroll bars for the inline frame all the time, even if all of the contents of the document fit into the inline frame. The default value AUTO generates scroll bars only if necessary, ie if the document does not fit into the inline frame. Otherwise, no scrollbars are displayed. The value NO never creates scrollbars, even if the document does not fit into the inline frame. This may parts of the inline frame content inaccessible for users and should be used with care.

- ALIGN

  The ALIGN attribute specifies the horizontal alignment the inline frame with respect to the surrounding context. Its possible values are defined by the %IALIGN; entity.

- HEIGHT and WIDTH

  The attributes specify the height and the width of the inline frame. Both attributes accept values as specified for the %LENGTH; entity.

It should also be noted that the <IFRAME> element is only part of the transitional DTD (as described in section 5.2.1, so any page which should conform to the strict DTD should not include inline frames created with the <IFRAME> element.

5.2.7.2 Forms

Although in the first versions, HTML was almost only used for reading documents, it soon became clear that it would be very useful to have a mechanism for submitting data to a client. The first element invented for this purpose, <ISINDEX> (which is now deprecated), allowed a very simple way of submitting keywords to a server. Soon after that, forms were invented, defining a number of elements for data entry, which can be grouped inside a form. The values entered by the user can be submitted to a server. HTML 4.0 adds a lot of new features to forms, although HTML forms still are much simpler than graphical user interfaces of normal computer programs[38]. The proper design of forms (using tables and other HTML elements to create a good layout) is rather difficult, as in general is the design of user interfaces. However, we do not this discuss this aspect of forms.

In addition to the basic client-side scripting attributes defined by the %EVENTS; entity as described in section 5.2.2, many of the form-specific HTML elements described in this section accept two more events, which are controlling an element's scripts for getting or losing the input focus. The following events are defined for the <INPUT>, <BUTTON>, <SELECT>, <TEXTAREA>, and <LABEL> elements. For most of the form elements, we have omitted a detailed description of all attributes, which are, however, as a reference listed in appendix B.4.

- ONFOCUS

  This attribute specifies a script which is executed when the corresponding element receives the input focus either by the pointing device or by tabbing navigation.

- ONBLUR

  As a companion to the ONFOCUS attribute, the ONBLUR attribute specifies a script which is called when the element loses the input focus either by the pointing device or by tabbing navigation.

---

[38] A much richer variant of HTML forms is described by Girgensohn and Lee [87]. This paper gives a good overview about features which could be added to HTML forms to make them more comfortable and powerful.

The <INPUT>, <BUTTON>, <SELECT>, <TEXTAREA>, and <LABEL> elements are also included in the %FORMCTRL; entity, which allows these elements to appear outside of a form, at any place where inline elements are allowed[39]. The purpose of this may be to associate events with these elements, but not making them part of an actual form.

The <FORM> element

The <FORM> element acts as a container for content defining a form. HTML forms are constructed using normal HTML elements together with special elements, called *controls*, which accept data entry. A typical form consists of a number of controls used for data entry, combined with normal HTML elements, such as text or paragraphs for control labels, and lists or tables for the layout of the form.

A <FORM> element defines what to do with the form data specified by the controls (such as marked check-boxes or text being entered into a text field). It does so by defining where the data should be sent, and how it should be sent. Data submission is triggered by special controls, but the two most important issues, where and how to send the data, are defined by the <FORM> element itself.

```
<!ELEMENT FORM    - - (%BLOCK;|SCRIPT)+ -(FORM) >
<!ATTLIST FORM
  %ATTRS;
  ACTION          %URI;          #REQUIRED
  METHOD          (GET|POST)     GET
  ENCTYPE         %CONTENTTYPE;  "application/x-www-form-urlencoded"
  ONSUBMIT        %SCRIPT;       #IMPLIED
  ONRESET         %SCRIPT;       #IMPLIED
  TARGET          %FRAMETARGET;  #IMPLIED
  ACCEPT-CHARSET  %CHARSETS;     #IMPLIED >
```

The <FORM> element accepts normal block-level content as specified by the %BLOCK; entity as well as scripts, defined by the <SCRIPT> element. The <FORM> element itself is excluded from the content model, in order to prohibit nested forms. The start and the end tags of the <FORM> element are mandatory. In addition to the standard attributes defined by the %ATTRS; entity, the <FORM> element defines a number of attributes.

- ACTION
  This attribute specifies the form processing agent. In most cases, this attribute contains an HTTP URI which points to some kind of process on

---

[39] This is possible because the DTD defines the %FORMCTRL; entity to be part of the %INLINE; entity.

a server handling the form data (section 9.4.2 describes a usual way of how form data is processed on the server using a CGI script). However, the ACTION attribute could also specify a URI containing an email address, in which case the form data would be submitted as an email message.

- METHOD
  If the ACTION attribute is an HTTP URI, the METHOD attribute specifies the HTTP method to use for sending the form contents to the server specified in the ACTION attribute's URI. A general description of HTTP's methods is given in section 3.2.3.1. In case of the METHOD attribute, it is possible to specify two different methods for submitting the form content to the server in an HTTP request.

  - GET
    This attribute value specifies that the form content should be submitted using the HTTP GET method. Using this method, the form data is appended to the URI specified in the ACTION attribute (using the query string URI notation).

  - POST
    The second alternative is to use the HTTP POST method, which includes the form data in the body of the request. This value is better suited for bigger forms and forms possibly containing non-ASCII characters.

  Normally, the GET method is used for small forms (as a general guideline, up to 100 characters of form data), while the POST method is used for bigger forms. However, it should be noticed that for security reasons, it is better to use the POST method, since the GET method puts all attributes into the request URI, which is often logged at intermediates or on the origin server and therefore is more likely to be seen by unauthorized people than the message body inside which the POST method is transferring the form attributes. Consequently, if a form contains sensitive data, it is highly recommended to use the POST method for submitting the form data.

- ENCTYPE
  If the form is submitted using the HTTP POST method (specified in the METHOD attribute), the ENCTYPE attribute is used to specify the encoding of the request. The possible values are defined by the %CONTENTTYPE; entity. Normally, the form data is coded in a single sequence of characters, using so-called URL encoding. If, however, the form contains an <INPUT> element with the TYPE attribute set to FILE, it is necessary to use the multipart/form-data type as specified in Internet experimental RFC 1867 [194].

- ONSUBMIT and ONRESET

  In addition to the core events, the <INPUT> element defines two more events, which can be used to assign scripts if the form data is submitted or if the form is reset.

- TARGET

  When used with framesets and frames as described in section 5.2.7.1, the TARGET attribute can be used to specify which frame should be the target frame if the form is submitted, that is into which frame the document which is result of the form submission should be loaded. The possible values of the TARGET attribute are described by the %FRAMETARGET; entity.

- ACCEPT-CHARSET

  This attribute describes the character sets which can be processed by the server handling the form data. It is defined by the %CHARSETS; entity.

The <FORM> element serves as a container for form controls, defining the most basic properties of a form, such as what to do with the form data if the form is submitted, and how to encode this data. In the following sections, we describe the individual HTML elements which can be used to specify controls.

The <INPUT> element

The <INPUT> element is the most general of all HTML for controls, in that it offers many different types of controls. The type of control an <INPUT> element generates is determined by an attribute, as well as many other properties of the control.

```
<!ELEMENT INPUT - O EMPTY >
<!ATTLIST INPUT
  %ATTRS;
  TYPE       %INPUTTYPE;    TEXT
  NAME       CDATA          #IMPLIED
  VALUE      CDATA          #IMPLIED
  CHECKED    (CHECKED)      #IMPLIED
  DISABLED   (DISABLED)     #IMPLIED
  READONLY   (READONLY)     #IMPLIED
  SIZE       CDATA          #IMPLIED
  MAXLENGTH  NUMBER         #IMPLIED
  SRC        %URI;          #IMPLIED
  ALT        CDATA          #IMPLIED
  USEMAP     %URI;          #IMPLIED
  TABINDEX   NUMBER         #IMPLIED
  ACCESSKEY  %CHARACTER;    #IMPLIED
  ONFOCUS    %SCRIPT;       #IMPLIED
  ONBLUR     %SCRIPT;       #IMPLIED
  ONSELECT   %SCRIPT;       #IMPLIED
```

```
ONCHANGE    %SCRIPT;       #IMPLIED
ACCEPT      %CONTENTTYPES; #IMPLIED >
```

The <INPUT> element has no content, because all the information for the controls is specified by attributes. As for all empty elements, the start tag is required and the end tag is optional. In addition to the standard attributes defined by the %ATTRS; entity, the <INPUT> element defines a number of attributes. The most important is the TYPE attribute, which specifies of type of control generated by an <INPUT> element. The possible values of the TYPE attribute are defined by the %INPUTTYPE; entity.

```
<!ENTITY % INPUTTYPE
 "( TEXT | PASSWORD | CHECKBOX | RADIO | SUBMIT |
  RESET | FILE | HIDDEN | IMAGE | BUTTON )" >
```

Each of these values defines another type of control, the following list describes all the different types of controls which can be created using the <INPUT> element for the corresponding TYPE attribute value.

- TEXT

  This value defines a control for text input. It is the default value of the TYPE attribute. The initial value of the text field is defined by the VALUE attribute, its size (in visible characters) by the SIZE attribute, and its maximal length by the MAXLENGTH attribute[40].

- PASSWORD

  This type of control is almost identical to the TEXT type, but the characters on the screen are masked, usually as asterisks. However, the value itself is transmitted in clear text when submitting the form, so using the PASSWORD control only provides very limited security.

- CHECKBOX and RADIO

  This type of control creates a check-box or a radio box. The only difference between these two is that from a group of controls (identified by the same NAME attribute of the <INPUT> element), any number of check-boxes can be selected, while only radio button can be selected at any time. If the CHECKED attribute is set, it indicates that the check-box or radio box is checked initially. The VALUE attribute of CHECKBOX and RADIO controls must be set, it gives the value of the control when it is set.

```
<P><INPUT TYPE=RADIO NAME="CARD" VALUE="Visa" CHECKED> Visa
<P><INPUT TYPE=RADIO NAME="CARD" VALUE="MC"> MasterCard
<P><INPUT TYPE=RADIO NAME="CARD" VALUE="AmEx"> Amercian Express
```

---

[40] The text field specified by the <INPUT> element always creates one-line text fields. In order to create text fields with more than one line, the <TEXTAREA> element can be used.

In this short example, three radio buttons are created (logically grouped by using the same NAME attribute value). Initially, the first radio button is selected. If the form is submitted without changing the initial setting, these three controls will cause the form data CARD=Visa to be submitted.

- SUBMIT

    Using the SUBMIT value, it is possible to create a submit button. Each form must have at least one submit button associated with it, otherwise it can not be submitted by the user. The VALUE attribute can be used to override the browser's default text for the button. If the NAME attribute is set, the browser generates a name/value pair for the submit button which has been used for submitting the form. If a form contains more than one submit button, this is necessary so that the program processing the form data knows which submit button has been used.

- RESET

    This type of control creates a reset button, which resets a form to its initial values. The VALUE attribute can be used to override the browser's default text for the button.

- FILE

    It is also possible to specify a file which should be uploaded to the server. This is done using the FILE control. A file selection window (which looks differently depending on the type of browser and the operating system the browser is running on) is displayed which can be used to select a file. The ACCEPT attribute can be used to specify a list of allowed file types as specified by the %CONTENTTYPES; entity. However, this feature currently is not very widely supported.

    When using this type of form control, it is necessary to use a form which submits its data using the POST method, and which has <FORM> element's ENCTYPE attribute set to use the multipart/form-data encoding type as specified in Internet experimental RFC 1867 [194].

- HIDDEN

    This type of input control is not displayed by the browser. It is generally used to include information in HTML pages which should be carried from one page to another without being visible to users, such as forms which span multiple pages. This type of control usually has the NAME and VALUE attributes set.

- IMAGE

    An image input control defines an image to act as a submit button. In addition to submitting a form, an image submit button also submits the coordinates where the user clicked on the image. The NAME attribute identifies the image input control, and if user clicks on the image, the browser creates two name/value pairs of the form `name.x=x-coord` and `name.y=y-coord`, which specify the x- and y-coordinates of where the user clicked[41].

- BUTTON
  The BUTTON value makes it possible to create a *push button*. A push button does not cause any data to be submitted, but can be used to associate scripts with events for this button. The VALUE attribute is used to specify the button's text.

For all the controls, it is also possible to set the READONLY and DIS-ABLED attributes. Both attributes make it impossible for the user to modify the control. However, if the READONLY attribute is used, the control's data is still submitted with all the form data. If the DISABLED attribute is used, the data is not included in the form data on submission. Both attributes can be changed dynamically using a script, which makes it possible to create forms with conditional controls.

In addition to the core events, two more events are defined for the <INPUT> element, ONSELECT and ONCHANGE. The ONSELECT event is triggered whenever text inside a control is selected. The ONCHANGE event is triggered if a control loses focus and its value has been modified since gaining focus. As with all events, these attributes accept scripts as specified by the %SCRIPT; entity.

The <BUTTON> element

In addition to the buttons which can be created using the <INPUT> element, HTML 4.0 defines a <BUTTON> element which allows more general buttons than the <INPUT> element. The only way how buttons can be designed using the <INPUT> element is changing their default text using the <INPUT> element's VALUE attribute, or placing images on them. The <BUTTON> element makes it possible to create buttons which may contain almost all HTML elements.

```
<!ELEMENT BUTTON - - (%FLOW;)* -(A|%FORMCTRL;|FORM|FIELDSET) >
```

The <BUTTON> element uses the %FLOW; entity as its content model, allowing both block-level and inline content. It excludes a number of elements from this general content model to avoid nested forms or form elements as well as anchors appearing inside a <BUTTON> element. Both the start and

---

[41] It is also possible to define a client-side image map, using the USEMAP attribute of the <INPUT> element. In this case, the URI refers to a client-side image map as described in section 5.2.5.2. However, this feature is currently not widely supported.

the end tag of the <BUTTON> element are mandatory. The most important attribute of the <BUTTON> element is the TYPE attribute, which specifies the type of button to be created.

- SUBMIT

  This is the default value of the TYPE attribute. It defines a submit button, which can be used to submit a form. A form can have more than one submit button. The program handling the form data can find out which submit button has been used by searching for a name/value pair where the name is specified for the NAME attribute for a submit button (either using the <BUTTON> or the <INPUT> element), and the value is set to submit.

- RESET

  Using this value, the <BUTTON> element can be used to create a reset button, which resets a form to its initial values.

- BUTTON

  This value creates a *push button*. A push button does not cause any pre-defined action to occur, it just defines a general button which normally will have scripts associated with some of its events.

The <BUTTON> element is new to HTML and currently not very widely implemented. It is therefore safer to use the buttons created by the <INPUT> element, although they do not provide the flexibility of the <BUTTON> element.

The <SELECT>, <OPTGROUP>, and <OPTION> elements

A very frequent requirement for designing forms is to present choices. The radio and check-box controls created with the <INPUT> element may be used to do that, but if a large number of choices is available, in most cases they are not well-suited. What is much better in such a case is a mechanism which allows the creation of pop-up menus, which are only displayed if the user selects them. Originally, HTML form provided this functionality with the <SELECT> and <OPTION> elements, HTML 4.0 added the <OPTGROUP> element for creating sub-menus.

```
<!ELEMENT SELECT   - - (OPTGROUP|OPTION)+ >
<!ELEMENT OPTGROUP - - (OPTION)+ >
<!ELEMENT OPTION   - O (#PCDATA) >
```

A <SELECT> element specifies a selection of options. These options can be either grouped into option groups (represented by the <OPTGROUP> element), or they can appear directly inside the <SELECT> element. The start tag as well as the end tag of the <SELECT> element are mandatory.

An option group is specified using the <OPTGROUP> element and simply is a sequence of one or more options (represented by the <OPTION> element). It should be noted that <OPTGROUP> elements can not be nested, so it is not possible to create sub-sub-menus. The text to be displayed in the menu is specified using the LABEL attribute. The start tag as well as the end tag of the <OPTGROUP> element are mandatory.

An option is represented by the <OPTION> element. It contains character data, which is shown as the menu item's text, if the <OPTION> element contains no LABEL attribute. Otherwise, the LABEL attribute's content should be used as the menu item's text. The start tag of the <OPTION> element is mandatory, while the end tag may be omitted.

The design of the new <OPTGROUP> element and the LABEL attribute has been done in a way to make sure that both browsers not fully implementing HTML 4.0 (called HTML 3.2 browsers in the following list), and full HTML 4.0 implementations can display the <SELECT> element's content without any loss of information.

- *HTML 3.2 browsers*
  These browsers will not recognize the <OPTGROUP> element, completely ignoring it, and also the LABEL attribute of the <OPTION> element, also ignoring it. They will take the content of the <OPTION> element and display it in the menu.

- *HTML 4.0 browsers*
  Browsers implementing HTML 4.0 recognize the <OPTGROUP> element as well as the <OPTION> elements' LABEL attribute values. They will display the <OPTGROUP> elements' LABEL attribute values inside the main menu, and the <OPTION> elements' LABEL attribute values in the sub-menus. The content of the <OPTION> elements will be ignored by these browsers.

As can be seen, the new <OPTGROUP> element can be used in HTML documents without sacrificing compatibility with older HTML implementations. It is therefore a good design choice to group options inside <SELECT> elements whenever it is possible, and it is especially important for <SELECT> elements containing a large number of options.

The <TEXTAREA> element

One-line text input controls can be created using the <INPUT> element. However, there are many scenarios where is is important to have text input controls with multiple lines. In this case, the <TEXTAREA> element can be used to create a text input control of arbitrary size.

```
<!ELEMENT TEXTAREA - - (#PCDATA) >
```

The <TEXTAREA> element accepts character data as content, which should be used as the initial content of the text input control. Both the start and the end tag of the <TEXTAREA> element are mandatory. The two most important attributes of the <TEXTAREA> element are the ROWS and COLS attributes. These attributes accept numbers and specify the size of the text input control to be created.

In addition to the core events, two more events are defined for the <TEXTAREA> element, ONSELECT and ONCHANGE. The ONSELECT event is triggered whenever text inside a control is selected. The ONCHANGE event is triggered if a control loses focus and its value has been modified since gaining focus. As with all events, these attributes accept scripts as specified by the %SCRIPT; entity.

The <LABEL> element

Although some form controls have labels associated with them (buttons and the text or content which is displayed on the button), most form controls do not have labels. Before HTML 4.0, the association between a label and a form control was only defined by the layout, which usually displays some text or other kind of label between a form control. However, this method makes it very difficult for non-visual browsers to handle forms, because it is not clearly defined which text is associated with which form control. HTML 4.0 changes that by introducing a <LABEL> element, which can be used to associate a label with a form control.

```
<!ELEMENT LABEL - - (%INLINE;)* -(LABEL) >
```

The <LABEL> element specifies as content any inline elements as defined by the %INLINE; entity. In order to prohibit nested labels, the <LABEL> element itself is excluded from the content model. Both the start and the end tag of the <LABEL> element are mandatory. Labels can be associated with form controls in two different ways.

- *Implicit labeling*
  In this case, the form control is part of the content of the <LABEL> element. The <LABEL> element has to contain exactly one form control.

- *Explicit labeling*
  In some cases it is impossible to include the form control in the <LABEL> element's content. One example is the layout of a form using a table, where the label and the form control are in different cells of the table. In this case, the FOR attribute of the <LABEL> element must be the same as the value of the ID attribute of the associated form control element

The <LABEL> element's ACCESSKEY attribute can be used to assign a one-key short cut to a label and the associated form control. The value of the ACCESSKEY attribute can be a single Unicode character as specified by the %CHARACTER; entity. The rendering of access keys depends on the browser. A usual way of doing it is to underline the first occurrence of the character in the label's text.

As many other new features of HTML 4.0, the <LABEL> element currently is not widely supported. However, it is also designed in a way that it can be used without compromising the compatibility of a document with older browsers. Browsers not implementing the <LABEL> element will simply ignore it, and the form will be rendered as usual. It is therefore advisable to include <LABEL> elements when creating forms.

Structuring forms

If a form contains a large number of form controls, it can be made more accessible for user by structuring the form controls into groups. HTML 4.0 introduces a <FIELDSET> element which can be used to group form controls. Grouped form controls especially make a form more accessible for non-visual browsers.

```
<!ELEMENT FIELDSET - - (#PCDATA,LEGEND,(%FLOW;)*) >
<!ELEMENT LEGEND   - - (%INLINE;)* >
```

A <FIELDSET> element contains a legend of the form control group, as specified by the <LEGEND> element, and block-level and inline content using the %FLOW; entity. This content contains all markup which is necessary for the form control group, which are the form controls themselves as well as any other elements which are used to structure them (eg, lists or tables). Both the start and the end tag of the <FIELDSET> element are mandatory. The <LEGEND> element contains the legend of the form control group. It can have inline elements as content which are defined by the %INLINE; entity. Both the start and the end tag of the <LEGEND> element are mandatory.

Because the <FIELDSET>and <LEGEND> elements are new to HTML, currently they are not widely supported. However, it is safe to use these elements for forms, because a browser not knowing them will simply ignore them. When designing a form, it must be made sure that the content of the <LEGEND> element will create an acceptable layout, whether it is interpreted as a <LEGEND> element by a browser implementing it, or whether it is displayed as normal content, because a browser ignored the <FIELDSET>and <LEGEND> elements.

5.2.8 Dynamic documents

Web design has become a very important issue. The web is used for many commercial applications, and creating eye-catching web pages has become important for many companies. The easiest way to do create web pages which contain dynamic content is still the usage of animated GIFs, simply including them using the <IMG> element. However, this kind of content is not interactive, and for many professionally designed web pages, this is a necessity.

The most important technique to create a dynamic and interactive web page is by using scripts, as described in section 5.2.8.1. HTML 4.0 also introduces a new element, called <OBJECT>, which is used to include multimedia objects, it is explained in section 5.2.8.2.

5.2.8.1 Scripts

Client side scripting is one of the most important components of creating dynamic web pages. It is the most important component of *Dynamic HTML (DHTML)*. From HTML's point of view, scripting is not limited to any particular scripting language, there are different scripting languages as described in section 8.1. The most important issue is the connection between scripts and documents, and this is specified in the *Document Object Model (DOM)* as described in section 10.5.5. This model describes the ways in which scripts may access and modify documents. In addition to the general specification of how documents may be accessed and modified, DOM also defines *language bindings* for different languages.

In general, scripts in HTML pages are executed at different times, depending on where they are specified.

- *Scripts executed upon loading a document*
  Every script specified within a <SCRIPT> element is executed upon loading a document. In many cases, this behavior is used to declare a number of functions which can be called later, from scripts associated with events.

- *Scripts executed upon event occurrences*
  Unlike the scripts specified within a <SCRIPT> element, scripts associated with events are executed when this event occurs. The most widely used events are defined by the %EVENTS; entity as described in section 5.2.2. However, a number of additional events are defined by some HTML elements, all sharing the convention that the name of the attribute which defines the script starts with ON.

Using these two categories of scripts, it is possible to create web pages which, when being loaded, declare a number of possibly complex script functions, which are called with simple function calls upon occurrences of certain events.

Since it is not guaranteed that a browser will execute scripts contained in an HTML page[42], the <NOSCRIPT> element can be used to specify alternate content which should only be rendered by the browser if a script which occurred earlier could no be executed. The <NOSCRIPT> element is part of the %BLOCK; entity and can therefore be used in all places where block-level elements are allowed. Generally, a <NOSCRIPT> element should occur directly after a <SCRIPT> element. However, because scripts often implement dynamic and possibly interactive behavior, in most cases it is difficult or impossible to specify a useful HTML replacement for a script.

5.2.8.2 Objects

Apart from the possibility to add scripts to web pages (which make it possible to access and modify the content of the page), it is also possible to embed objects in an HTML page. In earlier and proprietary versions of HTML, special elements were invented to insert different types of objects, the <IMG> element for embedding images, or special elements for including Java applets (described in section 8.2.1) in pages. The <APPLET> element of HTML 3.2[43], the <DYNSRC> element by Microsoft, and the <EMBED> element (accompanied by the <NOEMBED> element) by Netscape were all designed to embed programs into web pages[44]. With HTML 4.0, it has been recognized that it makes more sense to have one element which acts as a general container for external content. Although the <IMG> element remains part of HTML and will be in use for some more time, it is intended that in the long run, the only element to be used for external content will be the <OBJECT> element.

Because the <OBJECT> element is designed to be a general container for including external content (which may be a program to be executed or just data such as an image or a video sequence), there are different types of data which may be required for an object.

- *Implementation*
  If the object is a program (such as a Java applet), it is necessary for the browser to locate the program code (ie, the implementation). The CLASSID attribute is used to point to the implementation of an object.

---

[42] A browser may not execute scripts because it does not implement scripting at all, because the script contained in the page uses a scripting language not supported by the browser, or because the user has switched off client-side scripting.

[43] The <APPLET> element is still part of the transitional DTD of HTML 4.0, but it is deprecated and the <OBJECT> element should be used instead.

[44] Microsoft's proprietary <BGSOUND> element also is used to embed objects in HTML pages, in this case a sound which is played when the page is displayed.

The optional CODETYPE attribute specifies the type of program code, thus enabling browsers to avoid downloading program code that they can not execute (because the language is either not supported or the browser is configured not to execute programs using that language).

If however, the object contains data which can be interpreted by the browser (for example an image in a format supported by the browser), there is no need to point to an implementation, and the CLASSID attribute is not used.

- *Data to be rendered*

  The DATA attribute specifies data to be rendered. In case of images or other multimedia objects (such as a video sequence or a sound file), this is the attribute containing the reference to the data (thus being the equivalent of the <IMG> element's SRC attribute). Depending on whether the data is displayed by the browser (such as an image), or used as input for an external program, the DATA attribute is used without or with the CLASSID attribute. The optional TYPE attribute specifies the type of data, thus enabling browsers to avoid downloading data that they can not process (such as an image format which is not supported by the browser). It is possible that a program (specified by the CLASSID attribute) is self-contained in the sense that it does not need any data as input. In this case, the DATA attribute is not used.

- *Additional parameters*

  In addition to the implementation and data to be rendered, an object may also contain <PARAM> elements to provide run-time initialization data. These parameters are used when the object is rendered, their names and values depend entirely on the object being rendered.

These three types of data which may be used for an <OBJECT> element instance can be used in any combination, depending on the type of object and the support of the browser. For example, while some browsers may have built-in support for some media types (such as a special image format or video sequences) and do not require an external implementation to render them, others may not support these format, thus making it necessary to provide an external implementation[45].

```
<!ELEMENT OBJECT - - (PARAM | %FLOW;)* >
<!ATTLIST OBJECT
   %ATTRS;
```

---

[45] In case of external implementations for the rendering of media types, it would be possible to specify an object which contains a Java applet (located with the CLASSID attribute) which displays the data of the media type (located with the DATA attribute) which is not supported by the browser.

```
   DECLARE   (DECLARE)            #IMPLIED
   CLASSID   %URI;                #IMPLIED
   CODEBASE  %URI;                #IMPLIED
   DATA      %URI;                #IMPLIED
   TYPE      %CONTENTTYPE;        #IMPLIED
   CODETYPE  %CONTENTTYPE;        #IMPLIED
   ARCHIVE   %URI;                #IMPLIED
   STANDBY   %TEXT;               #IMPLIED
   HEIGHT    %LENGTH;             #IMPLIED
   WIDTH     %LENGTH;             #IMPLIED
   USEMAP    %URI;                #IMPLIED
   NAME      CDATA                #IMPLIED
   TABINDEX  NUMBER               #IMPLIED >
<!ELEMENT PARAM - O EMPTY >
<!ATTLIST PARAM
   ID        ID                   #IMPLIED
   NAME      CDATA                #REQUIRED
   VALUE     CDATA                #IMPLIED
   VALUETYPE (DATA|REF|OBJECT)    DATA
   TYPE      %CONTENTTYPE;        #IMPLIED   >
```

The <OBJECT> element may contain <PARAM> elements, used for run-time initialization data for the object itself, and block-level and inline content as specified by the %FLOW; entity. Both the start and the end tag of the <OBJECT> element are mandatory. The attributes defined for the <OBJECT> element are the standard attributes defined by the %ATTRS; entity, and a number of additional attributes, which are used to specify information about the object.

- DECLARE

  The DECLARE attribute can be used to declare an object, which means that the object is not instantiated at that occurrence of the <OBJECT> element instance containing the DECLARE attribute. This is often done for objects inside the document header, where it is possible to share objects among frames, if the document is a frameset document. The declared object can be instantiated by activating a link pointing to it, which can be an anchor using the <A> element.

- CLASSID

  This attribute points to the implementation of the object, if present. Depending on the type of object, the CLASSID attribute points to an implementation such as a Java applet, or is not present at all, if the object is an image which can be interpreted by the browser. The optional CODETYPE attribute specifies the type of implementation.

- CODEBASE

  The **CODEBASE** attribute specifies a URI which will, if present, be taken as the base URI for the **CLASSID**, **DATA**, and **ARCHIVE** attributes. If the **CODEBASE** attribute is not present, the base URI of the document will be taken as the base for relative URIs.

- DATA

  This attribute points to the object's data, if present. Depending on the type of object, the **DATA** attribute points to the object's data such as an image, or is not present at all, if the object is a Java applet and does not require any additional data. The optional **TYPE** attribute specifies the type of data.

- TYPE

  This attribute specifies the content type of the resource specified by the **DATA** attribute (if this attribute is used). Its possible values are defined by the %CONTENTTYPE; entity. This attribute is optional but recommended when **DATA** is specified, since it allows the user agent to avoid loading information for unsupported content types.

- CODETYPE

  This attribute specifies the content type of the implementation specified by the **CLASSID** attribute (if this attribute is used). Its possible values are defined by the %CONTENTTYPE; entity. This attribute is optional but recommended when **CLASSID** is specified, since it allows the user agent to avoid loading implementations for unsupported languages.

- ARCHIVE

  It is possible to specify a space-separated list of archives which contain resources which are relevant to the object. This may include resources specified with the **CLASSID** or **DATA** attributes. Archives specified as relative URIs should be interpreted relative to the **CODEBASE** attribute. The standard format for Java archives is the *Java Archive (JAR)* format. Preloading archives will generally result in reduced load times for objects.

- STANDBY

  This attribute can be used to specify a short message which is displayed while the object is loading. The allowed content of the **STANDBY** attribute is specified by the %TEXT; entity.

- HEIGHT and WIDTH

  These attributes specify the size of an object. The size instructs the browser how much space it has to reserve for displaying the object. Both attributes accept values as specified for the %LENGTH; entity.

- USEMAP

  This attribute associates an image map with an object. The image map is defined by a <MAP> element. The value of the USEMAP attribute must match the value of the NAME attribute of the associated <MAP> element. The presence of the USEMAP attribute for an object implies that the object being included is an image.

- NAME

  If the object is part of a form and its value should be part of the form submission, the object's NAME attribute must be set.

- TABINDEX

  The TABINDEX attribute is defined to assign a tabbing order to objects. Objects are visited in the sequence of their tabbing order values (which are positive numbers).

If the object contains a program which needs parameters for run-time initialization, these can be specified using the <PARAM> element. Any number of <PARAM> elements can be used inside an <OBJECT> element, but they must be placed at the start of the content of the enclosing <OBJECT> element. Each <PARAM> element represents one parameter as a name/value pair, and the syntax of names and values is assumed to be understood by the object's implementation. Because all information for a parameter is specified in the attributes of the <PARAM> element, the element is defined to be empty. As for all empty elements, the start tag is required and the end tag is optional.

- ID

  The ID attribute uniquely identifies an element instance inside a document. Since the <PARAM> element does not include the usual core attributes, the ID attribute is explicitly specified.

- NAME

  This attribute specifies a parameter's name. Since parameter names are specific to object implementations, the possible parameter names entirely depend on the object implementation. Parameter names which are unknown to an object implementation should be ignored.

- VALUE

  The VALUE attribute specifies the value of a parameter. Possible parameter values are determined by the parameter name are assumed to be understood by the object's implementation. The interpretation of a parameter value also depend on the <PARAM> element's VALUETYPE attribute.

- VALUETYPE

  This attribute determines how the VALUE attribute has to be interpreted. There are three different ways how a parameter value may be specified.

  - DATA

    In this case, the parameter value itself is specified in the VALUE attribute. This attribute contains a string of characters, so the DATA value type restricts parameters to strings.

  - REF

    In this case, the VALUE attribute contains a URI that designates a resource where run-time values are stored.

  - OBJECT

    It is also possible to specify an object in the same document as the source for a parameter value. If the VALUETYPE attribute is set to OBJECT, the VALUE attribute specifies an identifier (ie, the value of the ID attribute) of a separate <OBJECT> element instance in the document.

  Using these values, run-time parameters can be specified in a number of different ways. The default for the VALUETYPE attribute is the DATA value.

- TYPE

  If the VALUETYPE attribute is set to REF, the TYPE attribute specifies the media type of the values that will be found at the URI designated by the VALUE attribute. The possible values of this attribute are defined by the %CONTENTTYPE; entity.

Unfortunately, the support for the <OBJECT> element currently is rather weak, mostly because it is an entirely new element. Consequently, currently most page authors will prefer the <IMG> element for images and the <APPLET> element for Java applets. However, it is very likely that the next generation of browsers will support the <OBJECT> element more completely, and since this is the element which will be supported in future versions of HTML, authors should use it whenever possible.

Client-side image maps

Since the <OBJECT> element should replace the <IMG> element, it is necessary that all the <OBJECT> element supports all possible uses of the <IMG> element. A very popular and useful way for using images on web pages is the creation of image maps as described in section 5.2.5.2. However, since server-side image maps are not as popular as client-side image maps (and client-side image maps have a number of advantages over server-side image maps), it is only possible to create client-side image maps using the <OBJECT> element.

The basic mechanism of client-side image maps using the <OBJECT> element is similar to the <IMG> element. The image map is defined by a <MAP> element. The value of the <OBJECT> element's USEMAP attribute must match the value of the NAME attribute of the associated <MAP> element. However, the <MAP> element may contain block-level content, including <A> elements using the SHAPE and COORDS attributes. These attributes are used in the same way they are used with the <AREA> element. If the <MAP> element is specified as part of the <OBJECT> element's content, it is possible to create client-side image maps which can also be used for text-only browsers.

```
<OBJECT DATA="menu.gif" TYPE="image/gif" USEMAP="#map1">
  <MAP NAME="map1">
    <P>Possible choices:
    <A HREF="guide.html" SHAPE=RECT COORDS="0,0,100,80">Guide</A> |
    <A HREF="search.html" SHAPE=CIRCLE COORDS="200,200,60">Search</A>
  </MAP>
</OBJECT>
```

In this example, the <OBJECT> element specifies an image using the DATA attribute and an client-side image map using the USEMAP attribute. The map itself is part of the <OBJECT> element's content. If the browser support client-side image maps using the <OBJECT> element, it uses the image and the shape and coordinate attributes of the <A> elements to render the image map. If the browser does not support client-side image maps using the <OBJECT> element, it renders the content of the <OBJECT> element, which is a simple, text-oriented menu of the image map links. Using this technique, it is possible to create client-side image maps which are also accessible to users with browsers not supporting the display of images.

Nested objects

As stated already and also demonstrated using the client-side image map example, the <OBJECT> element's specification defines that a browser not able to render an object should instead render the <OBJECT> element's content. This can be exploited to create web pages which use different representations for the same object, and to hopefully include a representation which can be displayed by the user's browser.

```
<OBJECT CLASSID="TheEarth.py" CODETYPE="application/python">
  <OBJECT DATA="TheEarth.mpeg" TYPE="application/mpeg">
    <OBJECT DATA="TheEarth.gif" TYPE="image/gif">
      <P>The <STRONG>Earth</STRONG> as seen from space.
    </OBJECT>
```

```
  </OBJECT>
</OBJECT>
```

In this example, the first <OBJECT> element specifies an implementation using the *Python* language. If the browser does not support this language, it will instead render the <OBJECT> element's content, which is another <OBJECT> element, this time specifying a video sequence using the *MPEG* format. If the browser does not support this format, it will again render the element's content, which is yet another <OBJECT> element. This third object element specifies an image using the *GIF* format, which is supported by most browsers. However, if the browser also does not support this format (or can not render it because it is a non-visual browser), it will display a simple text line.

However, this HTML code would only display the image if the browser supports the <OBJECT> element, which currently is not generally the case. An alternate version of the example could therefore use the following HTML code.

```
<OBJECT CLASSID="TheEarth.py" CODETYPE="application/python">
  <OBJECT DATA="TheEarth.mpeg" TYPE="application/mpeg">
    <OBJECT DATA="TheEarth.gif" TYPE="image/gif">
      <IMG SRC="TheEarth.gif" ALT="The Earth as seen from space.">
    </OBJECT>
  </OBJECT>
</OBJECT>
```

In this example, the innermost content is an <IMG> element, which can be used by the browser if it does not support or even know the <OBJECT> element.

Another possible usage of nested <OBJECT> elements is the inclusion of new data formats. While the most basic data formats for images, JPEG and GIF, are supported by almost all browsers, it is not always clear that a newer format is supported by a user's browser. It is therefore a good idea to use fall-back solutions if new data formats are used on web pages.

```
<OBJECT DATA="earth.png" TYPE="image/png">
  <OBJECT CLASSID="png.cls" CODETYPE="application/java"
          DATA="earth.png">
    <OBJECT DATA="TheEarth.gif" TYPE="image/gif">
      <IMG SRC="TheEarth.gif" ALT="The Earth as seen from space.">
    </OBJECT>
  </OBJECT>
</OBJECT>
```

In this example, the first <OBJECT> element instance specifies an image which is coded in the *Portable Network Graphics (PNG)* format, which is not yet supported by all browsers. If the browser does not support PNG, a Java applet is specified in the second object. This Java applet implements a PNG viewer and takes as input the same PNG data as the first object. If the browser does not support Java, the third object specified a GIF image, which is a format supported by almost all browsers. If the browser does not support the <OBJECT> element (thus ignoring the three <OBJECT> element instances), the innermost <IMG> element will most likely be recognized by the browser.

As these examples demonstrate, the <OBJECT> element can be used to design web pages which are suitable for different browsers, and a carefully designed web page using nested <OBJECT> elements will be acceptable for a much larger audience.

5.3 Publishing with HTML

In many cases, HTML will not be the primary language of the documents being published on the web, but it will be used as the publishing language, using the web as the media for presentation. In this case, a two stage process of document processing can be observed, which is shown in figure 5.11.In this figure, it is shown that first some kind of converter is being used to convert some document format to HTML. This conversion is based on the knowledge of the document's structure (as defined by some kind of document type definition) and the actual instance of the document. This first step takes the document from some custom environment to the environment of the web. It is important to notice that since the structural definition of the HTML is fixed, the conversion process from the custom environment to the web environment can only use the structural elements as defined by HTML.

The second step, which is located entirely in the web's environment, is the transmission of HTML pages to clients, where they are presented by some kind of browser. It is important to notice that this is not necessarily a browser which displays the page on a screen, it can also be a browser for blind people[46] or some program which automatically collects web pages for compiling a searchable index.

It is also not necessarily the case that the source of the process is a document or something similar (which is the case shown in the figure), it can be any source of information (like a database or dynamically gathered information) which is used to create an HTML page. However, in all these cases we

---

[46] Raman [221] describes a technique which could be used to tailor an aural browser's presentation according to user preferences using *Cascaded Speech Style Sheets*. This technique heavily depends on the assumption that the document is marked up according to the content structure as defined by HTML.

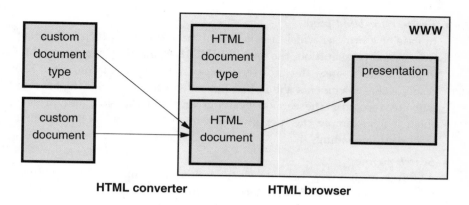

Fig. 5.11 Publishing with HTML

assume that the source of the publishing process is structured information, and that the knowledge of this structure is used for transforming the actual document information to HTML.

There are many ways how information with a given structure can be transformed to HTML. For example, if the source of the publishing process is a document with different levels of headings (which is quite common for normal documents such as reports or books), HTML's <H1-H6> elements can be used to represent the heading. However, the designer of the transformation process could also decide that he does not like the standard formatting of these elements and rather use the <FONT> element to increase the font size of headings (although he could achieve the same effect using style sheet assignments for the headings, as described in chapter 6) which are marked up with ordinary <P> elements.

For the average user working with a visually oriented browser, the effect of using one these two methods may be similar, even identical, if the assignment of styles (or the formatting using HTML elements such as <B>, <I>, or <FONT>) is done carefully. However, it is very important to notice that in the second case (using the HTML formatting elements), important structural information is lost, because the client does not know that the text parts marked up with the HTML formatting elements represent section headings. While this may have the same visual effect on the average browser, the effect for other clients (such as a browser using the *Cascaded Speech Style Sheets* mentioned before) can be quite dramatic.

- *Browser for blind people*[47]

  In case of a browser which uses a presentation method which is different
  from visual presentation, the usage of HTML formatting elements will be
  almost useless, since the browser is based on non-visual concepts. The
  result is that documents will not be presented properly, since the browser
  will not recognize the section headings and will therefore not present
  them if for example the user gives a command to read to him all first
  level section headings.

- *Search engine*

  A search engine may base its classification of documents on structural
  information extracted from a document, for example it may give a higher
  weight to a document being matched by a certain search phrase if this
  phrase is used in a section heading. If there is no structural information in the document because the section heading were marked up using
  HTML formatting elements, the document will not be indexed correctly,
  if the notion of correct indexing is based on the intended structure of the
  document.

The baseline of these discussions (and it would be easy to give a large
number of similar examples) is that by definition, a content provider publishing on the web has no way to predict the usage of a document. Although
most people will look at the documents using a visually oriented browser,
this is not the only possible usage and it would be against the concept of
HTML to rely a document's markup on this assumption. A document should
contain as much content structure as possible, and every conversion process
to HTML should have this as the primary goal in mind.

The evolution of the web (its conversion from an infrastructure for the distribution of scientific information to a commercially dominated marketplace)
resulted in many developments which were not exactly following the spirit of
HTML. Many of the HTML formatting elements were introduced by browsers
and later integrated into HTML standards because of their widespread use.
This happened because more and more, graphic designers were producing web
pages, who were not very worried about structural information, but were interested in as much control over visual effects as possible. The new solution
to this problem is the usage of *Cascading Style Sheets (CSS)* (described in
chapter 6), which are used to separate layout from content[48]. However, since

---

[47] The term *blind people* in this case encompasses *functionally blind people* as defined by Raman [221], referring to people which are for various reasons not able
to use a visual browser. These reasons may be the user's environment (if the user
is unable to use a visual browser) or a user's physical visual impairment.

[48] In figures 6.1 and 6.2 it is shown how CSS style sheets are can be used to extend
the HTML publishing process as shown in figure 5.11.

CSS style sheets are very new to the web, it is still common practice to use HTML for visual formatting.

However, even if the conversion form a custom document type to HTML is designed very carefully and with the primary goal in mind to preserve as much structural information as possible, there are limits which are set by the definition of the HTML document type. Two examples (many more can easily be thought of) are given below.

- *Footnotes*

  Although a footnote is a quite common construct in conventional documents, there is no such thing in HTML. Therefore, when converting footnotes inside a custom document to HTML, it is necessary to use some HTML constructs which seem to be most appropriate to represent footnotes.

  - *Footnotes in parentheses*

    Footnotes could easily be embedded into the text by placing them in parentheses. However, this makes them indistinguishable from an authors text placed in parentheses, which may cause a problem if an author uses parentheses and footnotes to carry different semantics.

    Furthermore, if footnotes contain large amounts of text (which is quite common in some fields of publishing), placing them in parentheses may severely distract a reader by stretching out single sentences over many lines by inserting large amount of parenthesized text.

  - *Footnotes as hyperlinks*

    Footnotes could also be converted to hyperlinks, pointing to the note's text on the bottom of the same HTML page or to an individual footnote page. However, this is more what something usually called endnotes (notes which appear at the end of a chapter or the publication) should be used for, and it also is more distracting than a real footnote in a printed publication, which can be read without turning over a page.

  It becomes clear that the conversion of footnotes is a question which should be decided not only based on general principles, but also on the actual usage of footnotes in the documents to be converted. The source of this problem is the absence of an appropriate structural concept in HTML.

- *Mathematical formulas*

  While in case of footnotes it is possible to think of alternatives to represent footnotes, in case of mathematical formulas it is simply impossible to represent them using HTML. The most common way to deal with HTML's lack of support for mathematical formulas is to generate small images which are inserted into the document. Obviously, this method is crude and has some disadvantages.

- *Large number of images*
  If a document contains a large number of mathematical formulas, its HTML version will contain a large number of images, which is very inefficient in terms of transmission (for each image, an HTTP interaction is required), storage, and management, since the single document is represented by an HTML page and a large number of small images.
- *Loss of information*
  Since mathematical formulas are essentially converted to bitmaps, almost all information which is contained in the original formula (such as variable names and the structural relationships of mathematical elements) is lost. And, like already mentioned above, a non-visually oriented browser has no way of presenting a formula, since the HTML document only contains a visual representation of mathematical formulas but not their original content (which could be rendered to speech or other kinds of representation).

As can be seen, in case of mathematical formulas the absence of appropriate structural concepts becomes obvious and a problem when documents containing mathematical formulas should be published on the web. Since mathematical formulas are a common type of document content in some areas, this is a well-known problem, and a solution to this (the *Mathematical Markup Language (MathML)*) is described in section 10.4.2.

There is no real solution to the dilemma exemplified by these examples. For some time now, HTML tried to encompass as much structural information as possible, but is simply impossible to design one document type which will be sufficient to represent all information which will be published on the web. The most popular constructs of documents, such as sectioning, lists, and tables, are now integrated into HTML with a sufficient degree of generality, and it is not very plausible that structurally new concepts will be integrated into HTML in the near future.

In fact, it has now been accepted that HTML is not sufficient for all information to be published on the web, and a new mechanism has been defined which can be used to define a publisher's own structural definition of some information. This mechanism is the *Extensible Markup Language (XML)* described in chapter 7, which is a standardized way to define the structure of documents on the web, ie to define custom document types which are interchangeable between XML-enabled applications.

5.4 Usage of HTML

A study of web servers in the UK carried out by Beck [15] gives some numbers which can be seen as representative for the web in general, although only web servers in the UK were used to collect the data. The way the data was collected is quite simple, all UK domains were searched for hosts named www, and if such a host was present, an HTTP request was sent to the host's standard HTTP port (80)[49]. Consequently, table 5.1 contains statistics only for the web servers with a host name www and also only for the root documents of these servers. We have only included elements which appear with an average of at least one time per document.

Table 5.1   Frequency of HTML elements per page

	HTML element	Count	Count per page
1.	\<A\>	200396	7.71
2.	\<TD\>	190547	7.33
3.	\<P\>	180676	6.95
4.	\<BR\>	176625	6.80
5.	\<IMG\>	160143	6.16
6.	\<FONT\>	137192	5.28
7.	\<TR\>	86217	3.32
8.	\<B\>	48648	1.87
9.	\<CENTER\>	48258	1.86
10.	\<TABLE\>	25252	1.74
11.	\<META\>	32713	1.26
12.	\<OPTION\>	30364	1.17
13.	\<HEAD\>	26254	1.01
14.	\<HTML\>	25988	1.00
15.	\<BODY\>	25982	1.00
16.	\<TITLE\>	25967	1.00

As can be seen in this table, the most popular element is the element for creating hyperlinks, which is used an average of almost eight times per page. Seeing that many pages are rather simple texts containing a number of links to other pages, this result is no surprise. However, it must be said that the result of such a survey very much depends on the nature of the sites which are used to collect the data.

---

[49] Although the description of the survey is taken from the original paper, the survey's figures presented here are from a newer survey (carried out in August 1997) which is available at http://www.hensa.ac.uk/uksites/survey/.

- *Information-oriented sites*
  For these sites, the results most probably very much look like the statistics shown in table 5.1. These sites tend to be more text based (maybe using text structuring with lists or tables), and usually contain a number of links.

- *Commercially oriented sites*
  Commercially oriented sites, on the other hand, will usually contain more elements which are used to create visually appealing pages, such as a large number of images, font changes, and information structured with tables or frames.

However, it is very hard to make general statements about the usage of HTML on the web. It can, however, be stated, that the amount of layout-oriented web pages (ie, web pages which are focused on presentation rather than content) has greatly increased since the web has been discovered as a new medium for commerce. The near future will show whether the definition of a standardized way to separate content and presentation (*Cascading Style Sheets (CSS)* as described in chapter 6) will be sufficient to revive HTML's original goal of presentation-independent accessibility.

In section 4.3.3 on SGML validation of HTML documents, it has been observed that a large majority of web pages do not contain valid HTML. This can be explained with two major error sources:

- *HTML errors*
  These are errors which are mostly used by violations of SGML rules, such as unclosed tag delimiters, misspelled element names, or missing required start or end tags. Another possible error of this category is the absence of a document type declaration, which makes it impossible to determine which version of HTML has been used to create the page.

- *Proprietary HTML extensions*
  Many pages use non-standards extensions of HTML which technically speaking also make pages invalid (although these pages can be presented without any problems on the browsers which support these non-standards extensions). However, since one goal of HTML is the creation of platform-independent pages, which can be presented on a large variety of platforms, non-standards extensions of HTML should not be used.

In general, it is a good idea to validate web pages before making them public. This can be done with local software utilities or with validation services which are available on the web, such as W3C's "HTML validation service" (available at `http://validator.w3.org/`).

Another detailed analysis of web documents carried out by Woodruff et al. [275] in 1996 used more than 2.6 million web pages as a base for web page statistics. It shows that the average size of an HTML document is 4.4 KB, with a median of 2.0 KB. The most used elements according to this study are <A>, <P>, <BR>, <IMG>, and <HR> (which is very similar to the results found by Beck and shown in table 5.1). Another interesting result from this study is that the large majority of hyperlinks are HTTP hyperlinks, the two following most widely used links being mail addresses (using the "mailto:" prefix) and FTP links. The study also contains statistics about the most popular HTML errors which were found after validating a subset of the entirety of web pages which were used for the study.

5.5 The future of HTML

Although the transition between HTML 3.2 and HTML 4.0 was rather fast (less than a year's time between these specifications), it can be assumed that HTML 4.0 will have a longer lifespan than its predecessor. Most of the really important issues which had challenged HTML 3.2, such as a more sophisticated table model, frames, and the integration of style sheets, have been resolved in HTML 4.0.

With the emergence of the *Extensible Markup Language (XML)* as described in chapter 7 the prospect of using a different approach for further HTML extensions appeared. Until now, each HTML version defines a new and closed set of elements in a DTD. XML makes it possible to define HTML as a variety of *tag sets*. Each tag set defines one functional aspect of HTML. There would be core, table, forms, list, and many other tag sets, each tag set defined by a separate XML DTD and formatting rules. One example for such a tag set which is already a W3C recommendation is the *Mathematical Markup Language (MathML)* described in section 10.4.2.

If the future development of HTML is based on individual XML tag sets, which can be individually included if required in a document, HTML 4.0 will be the last version of HTML which is defined using a monolithic SGML DTD. However, for this to happen, XML must be more widely supported than it is now, and in particular the mechanisms to specify XML style sheets (using the *Extensible Style Language (XSL)* described in section 7.5) must be widely accepted and implemented. Also, a transition path between old HTML documents (using SGML features such as *tag omission* and *attribute name omission*) and new HTML documents based on XML (which does not allow these features) must be defined.

Apart from these future developments of HTML, it can also be observed that HTML 4.0 is being accepted as a true standard for HTML. The recent adoption of HTML by ISO (in April 1998, ISO Commentary Draft 15445 [135] for *ISO-HTML* has been published) shows that HTML 4.0 is a version of HTML which attracts more attention than its predecessors.

Part II

Advanced

6. Cascading Style Sheets (CSS)

In the previous two chapters about SGML and HTML, a lot has been said about the separation of content and presentation, about HTML as a language intended to carry content and not presentation aspects. For this idea to be realistic, there has to be a mechanism for specifying the presentation aspects of an HTML document. This mechanism is called *Cascading Style Sheets (CSS)* and is discussed in this section.

In addition to being an important technology for the separation of content and presentation, CSS is also one component of *Dynamic HTML (DHTML)*[1], which is used very often for carefully designed web pages.

The basic principles of CSS and the link between CSS and HTML are explained in section 6.1. A very short history of CSS (because it has no predecessors) is given in section 6.2. Section 6.3 describes CSS1, the first version of CSS. This is by far the longest section of this chapter. Although being fairly new, there are similar concepts in other areas than the web, we shortly describe these related approaches to style sheet languages in section 6.4. It is an interesting question how the current, HTML-based document systems can be redesigned to support HTML and CSS. This issue is discussed in section 6.5. Finally, a short outlook regarding the future of CSS is given in section 6.6.

6.1 Principles of CSS

Figure 5.11 shows how publishing in general is done using only HTML. Regardless of whether HTML converters are used or whether documents are created directly in HTML, the only input for presentation on the web is an HTML document. This model suffers from all the disadvantages of mixing content and presentation aspects which have been described in the previous two chapters. Theoretically, this approach would be sufficient if all HTML authors would agree not to worry about the presentation of their documents.

---

[1] The other components of DHTML are HTML as described in chapter 5, a scripting language like ECMAScript described in section 8.1.1, and the *Document Object Model (DOM)* as described in section 10.5.5.

In reality, the situation is very different. Layout (or presentation) is an important aspect of web publishing (especially for commercial applications, where visual appearance is an important way to distinguish oneself from similar services or offers), and therefore most HTML documents contain a lot of presentation specific code. Figure 6.1 shows how this can be changed, by introducing a special and separate mechanism for specifying presentation aspects of a document. In this new model, the presentation of a document now is determined by the content coming from the HTML document, as well as by the layout, which is taken from a CSS style sheet. As also shown in this figure, it is even possible to automatically generate these style sheets, based on information about document types and their presentation.

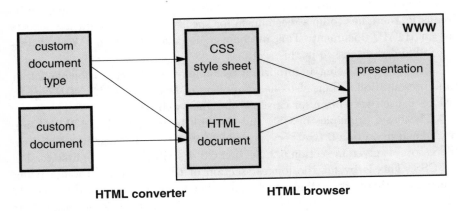

Fig. 6.1   Publishing with CSS

Going one step further, the presentation of a document can be determined by different factors, such as (on the designer's side) the intention of the page designer or general guidelines which the page designer had to follow. On the presentation side, user preferences as well as limitations caused by the presentation device can be important. Seeing these presentation requirements from different sources, it becomes obvious that it is necessary to use multiple style sheets, and that the style sheet mechanism must support the combination of multiple style sheets coming from different sources. This is the origin of the word *cascading* in CSS's name and is shown in figure 6.2.

In this figure, there are two designer style sheets, one generic document type style sheet, which is the same for all documents of a given document type (maybe for all documents of a web site), and one style sheet which has been specifically designed for a single document. For the proper presentation of the document, both style sheets must be used. This configuration can be

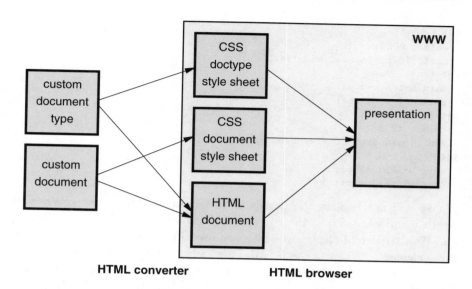

Fig. 6.2 Publishing with CSS using cascading style sheets

seen as the first style sheet defining aspects of the overall appearance, thereby realizing the "corporate identity" layout of all documents, and the second style sheet handling all issues which are specific for a particular document.

After all these more theoretical thoughts about style sheets and their use in the web environment, a short example of what a style sheet actually looks like is probably helpful. The following HTML code is a fragment of W3C's style sheets page.

```
<BODY>
<P>
<A HREF="../"><IMG BORDER="0" SRC="../Icons/WWW/w3c_home.gif"></A>
<H1>Web Style Sheets</H1>
<P CLASS=hide>(This page uses CSS style sheets)
<P ID=p1><A HREF="#new"><SPAN ID=s1>What's new?</SPAN></A>
<P ID=p2><A HREF="#what"><SPAN ID=s2>What are style sheets?</SPAN></A>
<P ID=p3><A HREF="#press"><SPAN ID=s3>Press clippings</SPAN></A>
<P ID=p4><A HREF="#software"><SPAN ID=s4>Styled software</SPAN></A>
<P ID=p5><A HREF="./css"><SPAN ID=s5>CSS</SPAN></A>
<P ID=p6><A HREF="#dsssl"><SPAN ID=s6>DSSSL</SPAN></A>
<P ID=p7><A HREF="XSL"><SPAN ID=s7>XSL</SPAN></A>
```

As mentioned before, the HTML code only contains the document content, the following fragment of the associated style sheet contains the actual formatting information, which in turn produces the presentation shown in figure 6.3.

```
#s1 {
  color: #DDD;
  font: 100px Impact, sans-serif; }
#p1 {
  margin-top: -30px;
  text-align: right; }
#s4 {
  color: #37F;
  font: bold 40px Courier New, monospace; }
#p4 {
  margin-top: -20px;
  text-align: right; }
```

We will not explain the details of this example, but a few things are worth mentioning. First, the content contains special markers (the CLASS and ID attribute of elements) which are used in the style sheet to refer to these elements. Whereas the HTML page only contains the actual text (for example "What's new?"), the style sheet contains the formatting for this text (identified by the p1 and s1 attribute values), changing the color, the font, and the position of the text.

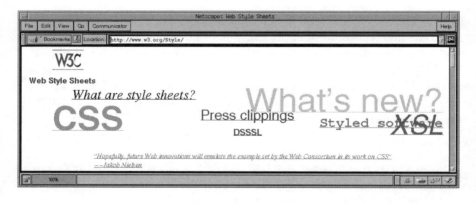

Fig. 6.3   W3C's style sheet web page

After seeing the HTML and the CSS style sheet, there still remains the question how these two are linked together. HTML defines two mechanisms for doing that, the first one being the <STYLE> element, the second one being the <LINK> element. Both elements are part of the HTML document head and are explained in detail in section 5.2.3.1.

- *Using the* <STYLE> *element*
  In this case, the style sheet is embedded in the HTML document. The content of the <STYLE> element is the style sheet itself. Although in this

case the physical separation of content and presentation is not existing (because the style sheet is actually part of the HTML document), there still is a logical separation of the two components. The disadvantage of this approach is that the style sheet can only be used for the document in which it is embedded.

- *Using the* <LINK> *element*
  Using the <LINK> element, the HTML document only contains a reference to the style sheet (using a URL). The main advantage of this approach is that the style sheet can be used by more than one document. If multiple style sheets are being used, the HTML document simply contains multiple <LINK> elements.

- *Combining both methods*
  It is also possible for an HTML document to combine both methods. In such a scenario, the <LINK> element is used to refer to a general style sheet which is used for a set of documents. The second style sheet (which is specific to the document) can be embedded using the <STYLE> element, because it is only used for this document.

As a first general introduction into CSS this short example is sufficient. The details of CSS1 are explained in section 6.3, and it is a good exercise to reread the example above after reading the section on CSS1, and to figure out what the style sheet exactly does.

6.2 History

In the web environment, style sheets itself do not have a long history, because CSS1, which is the style sheet language which is currently supported by existing tools, is the first style sheet language which has been defined for HTML. However, there is a history of how formatting has been done before the appearance of a standardized style sheet language using HTML's limited formatting capabilities.

- *Proprietary HTML extensions*
  One common way was (and unfortunately still is) the utilization of proprietary HTML extensions. Some of these extensions make it into the next version of an HTML standard, others just disappear[2]. However, because

---

[2] For example, the <BLINK> and <MARQUEE> elements, invented by Netscape respectively Microsoft, never made it into an official HTML version. When HTML 3.2 was finalized, both companies agreed to not have their elements being part of the standard. The <SPACER>, <MULTICOL>, <NOBR>, and <WBR> elements introduced by Netscape are other examples for a layout-oriented proprietary HTML extensions which are not generally supported.

proprietary HTML extensions always result in web pages which cannot be viewed with all browsers, their use is problematic, to say the least.

- *Using images instead of text*
  Since many effects with text (such as font size changes and font selection in general) were not possible with standard HTML, a common way was the conversion of text into images. The two major disadvantages of this method are the increased size of web pages, since images are significantly larger than text, and the loss of information. While an automated client (such as a search engine) can download and index web pages containing text, there is no reasonable way to automatically process text which has been converted to an image. In addition to that, there is no possibility to present this content in a non-visual browser.

- *Placing text into tables*
  Since tables have been introduced in HTML 3.2, they were often used for controlling the layout. Putting text into tables allows a number of effects which are otherwise not possible. However, this method creates very complicated HTML documents, and because tables were not designed for formatting text, the results may be not very good in some cases.

Consequently, the demand for advanced formatting capabilities, and the danger that increasingly complex web pages would be created to achieve formatting effects which were not really supported in HTML, led to the creation of a style sheet language. Seeing that HTML was inspired by SGML from the very beginning, this was a natural decision, because SGML's idea of the separation of content and presentation (as described in section 4.1.1) is rather old and has also been proven to be very useful.

CSS1 is the first style sheet language which has been created specifically for HTML, and it is already supported (although mostly only subsets of it) by many tools, ranging from browsers to HTML editors. CSS2 is already on its way, improving CSS1 in many areas where this first version still has some limitations.

6.3 Cascading Style Sheets, level 1 (CSS1)

In this section we give an overview of *Cascading Style Sheets, level 1 (CSS1)* [159], the current standard for style sheets on the web. This overview can not replace the standard itself or a detailed description of it. There is an entire book about CSS1, written by Lie and Bos [160], the authors of CSS1[3]. A book by Graham [90] focuses more on examples and the design aspects

---

[3] A very good online reference of CSS1 (and more readable and useful than W3C's CSS1 specification) is available on the *Web Design Group's (WDG)* web site at

than the technical background of CSS1. As CSS1's acceptance increases, it is foreseeable that the number of books on CSS1 will increase rapidly in the near future (in addition to that, new books on HTML also have to cover CSS1 as well, because only very few people will be interested in pure HTML without knowing how its presentation can be controlled using style sheets).

Basically, a CSS1 style sheet is a set of *rules* which apply to an HTML document. Each rule consists of two parts, a *selector* and a *declaration*. An example for a very simple (although complete) style sheet, which consists of only one rule, could be given as follows.

```
P { color: green }
```

The "P" in this case is the selector, which specifies that this rule applies to all <P> elements in the document. The declaration in this example is "`color: green`", causing all text inside <P> elements to be rendered in green. A CSS1 declaration such as the one above typically assigns a *value* (`green`) to a *property*[4] (`color`). It is also possible to use declarations which specify multiple assignments (ie, which set more than one property), these assignments are separated by semicolons.

In order to understand many concepts of CSS, it is important to understand how properties are inherited through the hierarchy of an HTML document. This is explained in section 6.3.1. CSS1 offers a variety of selectors, which can be used to select the scope of declarations in a number of ways. These selectors are explained in section 6.3.2. A short overview over units used in CSS1 is given in section 6.3.3. The properties which can be used to specify which effect a rule will have are described in detail in section 6.3.4. Furthermore, CSS1 also defines how different style sheets can be combined (or *cascaded*) for one document. This aspect is discussed in section 6.3.5.

6.3.1 Inheritance

One important observation of SGML documents in general is that every document can be seen as a tree structured graph of elements (the *document tree*) as first shown in figure 4.2. Since HTML is an SGML application, the same document structuring is existent within HTML documents, so every HTML document can be represented as a tree, as shown in figure 5.4. This property of HTML documents has been used for a very powerful and useful CSS mechanism called *inheritance*. Inheritance defines how properties of elements

---

`http:/www.htmlhelp.com/`. It is also possible to download the reference and install it locally.

[4] In CSS terminology, a *property* is a quality or characteristic that something possesses. CSS1 defines a large number of properties, which are described in section 6.3.4.

(such as color or margins) are inherited through the hierarchy defined by the document tree. Figure 6.4 shows an example for inheritance.

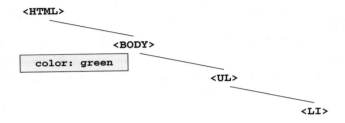

Fig. 6.4 Hierarchical structure of an HTML document and inheritance

Although the style sheet only explicitly assigns a foreground color to the <BODY> element, the property is inherited through the document structure and therefore the <LIST> and the <LI> elements inherit the foreground color of the <BODY> element. For many properties, this behavior makes sense, because it is quite normal to assume that the assignment of a color property to an unordered list sets the color of the list as a whole, including all content of that list[5]. However, for some properties, inheritance is not a very useful concept, therefore CSS also defines a number of properties which do not inherit. One example for such a property is the background property as described in section 6.3.4.4.

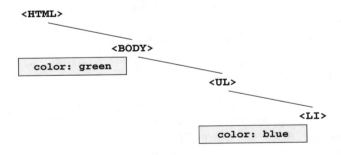

Fig. 6.5 Overriding inheritance

However, although inheritance is a useful concept as a default behavior (instead of making it necessary to specify a property for every element in the

---

[5] Hierarchically, the content of the list is the subtree of elements which descends from the <UL> element, so in this case the concepts of "all content" and hierarchical inheritance are identical.

document tree's hierarchy), it must also be possible to override this mechanism. CSS inheritance can very easily be overridden by explicitly assigning a new value to an inherited property for an element which is lower in the hierarchy than the one where the inherited value has been defined. An example for this is shown in figure 6.5, where the value of the color property is inherited by the <UL> element and then overridden by the color property of the <LI> element.

This idea of inheritance and the overriding of inheritance can be used for rather complex effects. The usual way is to use assignments more up in the hierarchy to define a default value for a property for all elements below this assignment, and to use overriding whenever the default has to be changed somewhere below. A more complex example for using inheritance and overriding is shown in figure 6.6.

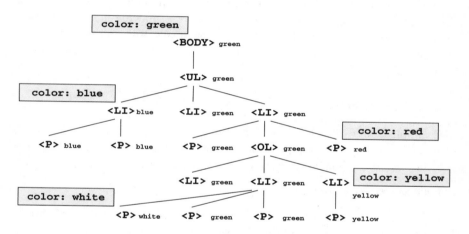

Fig. 6.6 Using inheritance for defaults and exceptions

In this figure, explicit assignments are shown in boxes (as before), while the actual value of the color property for each element is shown in small characters next to the element's name. The first assignment defines the default foreground color of the document to be green, the <UL> element does not override that value and therefore inherits it from the <BODY> element. Inside the list's items (represented by <LI> elements), the first item changes its color to blue, while the other list items do not change the color property's value. Inside the third list item, the last paragraph changes the color to red. The ordered list, which is also part of the third list item of the unordered list, has three list items, of which the last one changes its color to `yellow`. Finally, the first paragraph in the second item of the ordered list changes its `color` to `white`.

Although the example with the `color` property is not of real practical importance (producing a much too colorful document), inheritance and the overriding of inheritance can be very useful for other properties such as spacing and margins as described in section 6.3.4.2. Furthermore, inheritance is a very important mechanism in using multiple style sheets as described in section 6.3.5.

6.3.2 Selectors

Selectors are the CSS mechanism which allows the identification of elements by their type, by attributes, an element's context, or external information about the element. In any case, a selector is used to limit the scope of a declaration (which contains information how to format an element). Consequently, the careful use of the different types of selectors and their usage in style sheets enable CSS authors to achieve a number of effects which can be very complex.

6.3.2.1 Type selectors

The simplest kind of selector is a *type selector*. A type selector selects an element according to its type. Consequently, a rule using a type selector specifies to use the declaration for every element instance of the given type.

```
P { color: green }
```

This type of selector specifies that the declaration "color: green" should be applied to every instance of the <P> element. If a certain declaration should be applied to a number of elements, CSS makes it possible to use a grouping mechanism.

```
H1 { color: blue }
H2 { color: blue }
H3 { color: blue }
```

These three rules specify that content of the elements <H1>, <H2>, and <H3> should be rendered in blue.

```
H1, H2, H3 { color: blue }
```

This short-hand notation can be used to specify the same style sheet in a more concise way. If declarations apply to a number of elements, it is advisable to use this notation, because it is more compact and avoids inconsistencies if the declarations are modified.

6.3.2.2 Attribute selectors

While selecting document content with type selectors may be appropriate for some simple tasks or basic settings, very often more sophisticated mechanisms for selection are required. The most important consideration is to give users the ability to select content based on their own criteria, rather than criteria which are defined by the document model (such as element names).

CSS uses HTML attributes to achieve this, following the SGML concept that attributes describe properties of an instance of an element which apply only to this instance. Document content may be selected based on two attributes, the CLASS and the ID attribute, and a third mechanism (which, strictly speaking, is not a selection mechanism but also uses attributes for assigning style to content) based on the STYLE attribute is also described in this section[6].

The CLASS attribute

The CLASS attribute can be used to assign a "class" to an element (it is also possible to assign multiple classes by specifying a list of class names). A class is a logical construct which should be used to group elements which carry content which shares certain properties, such as belonging to a certain type of information.

```
<P CLASS="IMPORTANT">However, under no circumstances...
```

In this example, the paragraph is assigned the class "IMPORTANT", which identifies it as containing information of special importance. HTML does not define any classes nor does it assign any semantics to classes, so an HTML author is completely free to choose the class names used in a document. However, it is advisable to choose class names which carry some semantics. Furthermore, if style sheets are to be shared by several documents, it is a good idea to first define a number of classes which are used in the documents before the actual document authoring takes place.

It is important to notice that class names can be assigned to any number of elements inside a document, so the normal case for the application of the CLASS attribute is that in a document there is more than one element belonging to any given class.

After assigning classes to HTML elements using the CLASS attribute, there must be a way to select these element instances in a CSS style sheet.

```
.IMPORTANT { color: red }
```

---

[6] As described in section 5.2.2, the CLASS, ID, and STYLE attributes are part of the %COREATTRS; attribute set of HTML 4.0 and are therefore defined in almost all elements.

This rule specifies the formatting of any element labeled with the CLASS attribute specifying the value "IMPORTANT". In this case, the declaration causes all text to be rendered in red. There are two main differences between the CLASS attribute selection mechanism and the type selection mechanism described in section 6.3.2.1

- *Selection of a subset of element instances*
  Since a CLASS attribute selector only selects the element instances with a given CLASS value, it is more specific than a type selector which will always select all instances of an element type.

- *Selection independent of element types*
  A CLASS attribute selector is defined to select all element instances with a given CLASS value, and because the CLASS attribute can be used in almost all HTML elements, it can select element instances of more than one element type.

In summary, the CLASS attribute selection mechanism is designed to enable HTML authors to create their own logical classes of elements, which are not restricted to an element type. The CLASS attribute selection mechanism therefore is a much more general mechanism than the type selection mechanism and is the preferred method of designing style sheets.

It should be kept in mind, however, that the CLASS attribute selection mechanism can only be used with HTML pages which have been written with style sheets in mind, ie, pages which use CLASS attributes. If a style sheet should be applied to an HTML page which has not been designed in this way, there is no way to identify classes of elements using the CLASS attribute selection mechanism, and the only way to use styles in this case is by applying them to elements using the type selection mechanism[7].

The ID attribute

While the CLASS attribute described in the previous section has been introduced for the use of style sheets, the ID attribute, which also can be used as a means to identify an element, has been present in older HTML versions. The important restriction for the ID attribute is that no two element instances in a document may have the same ID attribute value. This has been defined because the ID attribute originally was meant to serve as a target for links, which must be unique.

```
<P ID="COPYRIGHT">The copyright for...
```

---

[7] A more flexible way of designing style sheets for pages without CLASS attributes is possible by using contextual selectors as described in section 6.3.2.3.

This HTML fragment shows a paragraph which may have been marked with an ID attribute to serve as target for links which point to the copyright of a document. In an HTML document, such a link can easily be created using an <A> element.

```
...in the <A HREF="#COPYRIGHT">copyright notes</A> it has been...
```

However, the ID attribute of the paragraph in this example may also be used in a style sheet for selecting the paragraph and define some special formatting for it.

```
#COPYRIGHT { font-size: small }
```

This usage of style sheets is discouraged by the CSS recommendation, because it is not according to the idea of CSS. Style sheets should specify the formatting of classes of elements (although these classes in some cases may only contain one element instance). However, the mechanism can be useful if the HTML document cannot be changed, and the formatting of a certain element identified by an ID attribute should be changed. In all other cases, other selection mechanisms should be used instead.

The STYLE attribute

Strictly speaking, the STYLE attribute does not belong into this section because it is not used as a selector. However, it is best explained in this section because it is a mechanism which can also be used for specifying the formatting of an element and is therefore very similar to the selection mechanisms. In contrast to the CLASS and ID attributes, the STYLE attribute is used to directly declare the formatting of an element.

```
<P STYLE="font-style: italic">This text demonstrates...
```

There are two sides to this approach. On the one hand, it is much better to have style information clearly marked (by using the STYLE attribute) rather than having it created with the aid of other mechanisms (such as using <BLOCKQUOTE> elements for indentation, which is standard practice for HTML pages without CSS). This way, the interpretation of a page can clearly separate between content and presentation.

However, using the STYLE attribute for specifying formatting declarations of elements does not neatly separate content and presentation in a way which would make it easy to exchange the style sheet information. Using external or internal style sheets, it is only necessary to modify an external document or one section inside a document in order to modify the style sheet information. Using STYLE attributes, it is necessary to make changes in all elements using this attribute. It is therefore advisable to use external or internal style sheets rather than using the STYLE attribute.

6.3.2.3 Contextual selectors

Up to now, only so-called *simple selectors* have been discussed. These selectors specify a criterion (an element type for *type selectors* as described in section 6.3.2.1 or an element's attributes for *attribute selectors* as described in section 6.3.2.2) which is defined for a single element instance. A more complex mechanism are *contextual selectors.*

Contextual selectors use simple selectors to specify a contextual relationship. Contextual selectors are specified by concatenating simple selectors separated by a white space. The simplest contextual selector consists of two type selectors.

```
LI P { margin-top: 0mm }
```

This selector selects all <P> elements which occur in the context of an <LI> element, effectively selecting all paragraphs which are inside list items (ie, inside ordered or unordered lists). The selector does not need to specify an immediate hierarchical relationship (ie, a parent-child relationship), the only criterion is that the simple selectors which are on the left side of the contextual selector must be satisfied on a higher level of the hierarchy than the ones on the right side[8].

```
TABLE .SMALL P { font-size: smaller }
```

This contextual selector specifies all paragraphs which are inside an element with a CLASS attribute set to SMALL (as specified by the CLASS attribute selection mechanism), which in turn is part of a table. This may be useful by marking specific rows or cells of a table as being part of a particular class, and then specifying properties for specific elements inside these rows or cells.

The more complex a contextual selection is (using many and different types of simple selectors), the more alternative representations are possible. As a general guideline, one should choose the selector which fits best what one would describe in a verbal explanation of the desired selection.

6.3.2.4 External selectors

In some cases, the selection of content should be made based on external information, which means information not being part of the HTML page. CSS1 defines two types of the external information, which are *pseudo-classes* and *pseudo-elements.*

---

[8] It is possible to think of different kinds of contextual selectors, one kind specifying ancestor relationships (as CSS1 contextual selectors) and another kind specifying parent-child relationships or other kinds of relationships. However, CSS1 only defines contextual selectors using ancestor relationships.

- *Pseudo-classes*

  A pseudo-class is a property of an element which is determined by external information, such as the status (new vs. visited) of a hyperlink. It can be regarded as an attribute (although it is not defined by an actual HTML attribute) which changes its value according to external information. In principle, pseudo-classes are characteristics that cannot be deduced from the document tree.

- *Pseudo-elements*

  A pseudo-element is content which is identified by external information and which is not explicitly marked up as an HTML element, such as the first character of a paragraph. Depending on the type of presentation, the pseudo-element's content may change (for example the first line of a paragraph changes when the width of the browser's window is changed).

Currently, CSS1 defines only one pseudo-class and two pseudo-elements, and the CSS1 specification allows a CSS1 implementation to not implement these external selectors. However, it is very likely that the mechanism of external selectors will become more popular in future versions of CSS[9].

The anchor pseudo-class

Typically, hyperlinks in an HTML document (which are defined using the <A> element) are displayed in some special formatting to make them recognizable as hyperlinks. This is important for showing users that the hyperlink is a piece of content which can be selected and which will direct the browser to jump to the place where the hyperlink is pointing to (this may be a new document or another location in the current document).

For an author of a web page, there is no way to distinguish the different states of a hyperlink, these states are only meaningful if a page is actually viewed and can therefore only be determined by the browser (and not be set by some attribute of the <A> element)[10]. CSS1 defines three states for the <A> element.

- link

  The link pseudo-class is used for a link which has not yet been visited. This indicates that selecting the link will take the user to a location he has not visited before.

---

[9] The CSS2 style sheet language as described in section 6.6.2 includes a number of new pseudo-classes and pseudo-elements.

[10] Before CSS, it was possible to set the colors of links in their different states using the LINK, VLINK, and ALINK attributes of the <BODY> element. These attributes are now deprecated.

- `visited`

  Since a browser normally remembers which links have been visited before, it is possible to display these links differently. The `visited` pseudo-class is used for specifying the formatting of links which have already been visited by the user.

- `active`

  The third pseudo-class is used for displaying an active link, which is a link currently being selected. For a normal user interface with a pointing device the link will be in the `active` pseudo-class as long as the pointing device's button is pressed (normally only a very short period of time).

Using these pseudo-classes, an author can specify the formatting of an anchor depending on the status of the link. The browser will change the formatting of the `<A>` elements depending on the associated declarations.

```
A:LINK    { color: green }
A:ACTIVE  { color: red }
A:VISITED { color: blue }
```

In this example, links are formatted with a different color than usual text (assuming that the default color for text is black). Unvisited links are displayed in `green`, and change their color to `red` while they are active (for example, while the user pushes the mouse button). Once a link has been visited, it changes its color to `blue`.

CSS implementations are allowed to support only a limited number of properties for the pseudo-classes of the `<A>` element. For example, a CSS implementation may choose to ignore any declaration which changes the size of the element's content (such as changing the font size), because changing the size would make it necessary to re-format the document whenever a link changes its state.

Pseudo-elements

While pseudo-classes are defined by external information about existing HTML elements, pseudo-elements are defined by content which is not explicitly marked up by existing HTML elements, but which can be determined by external information (such as the formatting of a paragraph). Currently, CSS1 only defines two pseudo-elements, which are both applicable only for the `<P>` element.

- `first-letter`

  The `first-letter` pseudo-element is defined by the first letter of a paragraph. In typography, it is quite common to typeset the first letter of a paragraph (or of the first paragraph of a chapter) differently than the rest of the text. However, in HTML there is no such construct as the first letter of a paragraph[11], but CSS's `first-letter` pseudo-element makes it possible to specify formatting instructions which apply only to the first letter of a paragraph.

- `first-line`

  Another usual way to typeset paragraphs is to typeset the first line of a paragraph differently than the rest of the text. Since the first line of a paragraph is not known when writing an HTML page (because the width of the display is not known and can even change while viewing the document), it is not possible to use HTML to specify the first line of a paragraph. However, the `first-line` pseudo-element can be used to specify formatting instructions which apply only to the first line of a paragraph.

In most cases, the formatting of the first letter or the first line of a paragraph should not be changed for all paragraphs but only for special paragraphs, such as the first paragraph of a chapter or section. It is therefore a usual application of the `first-letter` and `first-line` pseudo-elements to be used in conjunction with other selection mechanisms, such as attribute selectors[12].

```
P.INITIAL:FIRST-LETTER { font-size: 200%; float: left }
P.INITIAL:FIRST-LINE   { text-transform: uppercase }
```

This example shows how the first paragraph of a chapter or section (which must be marked with a CLASS attribute value of INITIAL) can be formatted in a way which makes the first letter of the paragraph twice as big as the rest of the text. Furthermore, the first letter drops into the paragraph rather than sitting on the same baseline than the rest of the first line. The text in the first line of the paragraph is transformed to upper case characters.

---

[11] In theory, the `first-letter` pseudo-element could be omitted and the first letter of a paragraph could be marked up using a <SPAN> element as described in section 6.3.2.5. However, the `first-letter` pseudo-element solution makes the HTML code more readable and also is a nice companion to the `first-line` pseudo-element, whose effect could not be achieved with any HTML construct.

[12] This is a somewhat awkward solution since it depends on the HTML author to assign the appropriate CLASS attribute value to all these paragraphs. A much better solution is the usage of *adjacent selectors* which are defined in CSS2 (briefly described in section 6.6.2). However, CSS1 offers no such mechanism and therefore there is no alternative to using the CLASS attribute selection mechanism for selecting the first paragraph of a chapter or section.

6.3.2.5 New elements

Using the CLASS attribute selection mechanism, it is possible to define new "element types" in HTML by specifying the formatting for specific element instances. However, so far it is necessary to use the CLASS attribute selection mechanism in conjunction with an HTML element which itself has some formatting semantics. To avoid this, HTML defines two new elements, <DIV> and <SPAN>, which have no other semantics than grouping together HTML content. Because HTML makes a difference between block-level and inline elements (this differentiation is described in section 5.2.3.2, two elements have been defined instead of one.

Block-level element

<DIV> is the block-level element which can be used to mark up block-level content. Used without style sheets, a <DIV> element does not change the formatting of its content. Used with a CLASS or ID attribute, it can be used to specify the formatting of block-level content. The HTML definition of the <DIV> element uses the %FLOW; entity as content model:

```
<!ELEMENT DIV - - (%FLOW;)* >
<!ATTLIST DIV
  %ATTRS; >
```

Although the <DIV> element could easily be used to simulate the visual formatting of existing HTML block-level elements (such as paragraphs using the <P> element or unordered lists using the <UL> element) by defining appropriate style sheets, this is not the intended use of the <DIV> element and should be avoided. The reason for this is that an unordered lists marked up with an <UL> element can easily be identified as an unordered list and always be rendered as such, even for non-visual presentation. On the other hand, content marked up using the <DIV> element does not carry any semantics and therefore may cause problems for presentation on media for which no style has been defined.

Inline element

<SPAN> is the inline element which can be used to mark up inline content (typically a portion of text). As the <DIV> element, used without style sheets, a <SPAN> element does not change the formatting of its content. However, used with a CLASS or ID attribute, it can be used to specify the formatting of inline content. The HTML definition of the <SPAN> element uses the %INLINE; entity as content model:

```
<!ELEMENT SPAN - - (%INLINE;)* >
<!ATTLIST SPAN
  %ATTRS; >
```

For the <SPAN> element, the same remarks apply that have been given for the <DIV> element. The <SPAN> element could easily be used to simulate the visual formatting of existing HTML inline elements (such as emphases using the EM element) by defining appropriate style sheets. However, this is not the intended use of the <SPAN> element and should be avoided for the same reasons that have been given for the <DIV> element.

6.3.2.6 Combining selector types

Up to now, we have discussed different selector types and their usage for selecting element instances inside HTML pages. Although in some of the examples, we already used multiple selection mechanisms[13], we did not explicitly explain the combination of selection mechanisms.

```
P.INITIAL:FIRST-LETTER { font-size: 200%; float: left }
```

It is possible to combine all the selector types described in this section to create very elaborate selection mechanisms. In more complex style sheets, in the majority of cases contextual selectors will be used to limit the effect of declarations to certain contexts.

```
P.INITIAL:FIRST-LETTER { font-size: 200%; float: left }
TABLE P.INITIAL:FIRST-LETTER { font-weight: bold }
```

In this example of combining selector types, it is specified that the first letter of any paragraph of the INITIAL class should be treated specially. However, since text inside tables in most cases is shorter and the available space is more restricted than in ordinary text or lists, it is defined that the first letter of INITIAL paragraphs inside tables should be treated differently. This can easily be achieved by combining CSS1's type, contextual, CLASS attribute, and pseudo-element selection mechanisms.

6.3.3 Units

Since many of the properties described in section 6.3.4 accept units of different kinds, we give a short overview of the units which are commonly used for CSS1 properties. Colors can be used for different properties and are described in section 6.3.3.1. Even more properties accept length specifications providing a number of different ways to specify a length. These are described in section 6.3.3.2.

---

[13] In the sections on contextual selectors and pseudo-elements, we also used the CLASS attribute selection mechanism.

6.3.3.1 Colors

In CSS1, colors can be defined in two different formats. Either as one of the predefined color names, or as a more general specification of a color based on its red, green, and blue components.

CSS1 defines sixteen color names, which have been taken from the Windows palette. These are aqua, black, blue, fuchsia, gray, green, lime, maroon, navy, olive, purple, red, silver, teal, white, and yellow. This is the same set of color names which is defined in the HTML 4.0 standard.

The second way of specifying a color is to use *RGB triplets,* consisting of three values which define the amount of red, green, and blue which should be used for the color. CSS1 (as well as HTML 4.0) defines these triplets to use *standard RGB (sRGB)* [109], an RGB system which has been designed to yield more consistent results than the usual RGB system. Colors can be specified in three different ways, which all give the same results, so choosing one of them is a matter of preference.

- *Percentages*
  In this case, a color is specified as percentages of red, green and blue light, for example rgb(0%,100%,0%), which specifies the predefined color lime.

- *Decimal numbers*
  Another way of specifying a color is to use decimal values between 0 and 255, which also specify the intensity of red, green and blue light to be used for the color. An example for such a specification is rgb(255,255,0), which specifies the predefined color yellow.

- *Hexadecimal numbers*
  As a third alternative, hexadecimal values can be used, ranging from 00 to FF. A color specification of this kind is #FF00FF[14], selecting the predefined color fuchsia.

If in one of the first two methods a number larger than the allowed range is specified (a percentage larger than 100%, or a decimal value larger than 255), the corresponding value will be clipped, meaning that it is reduced to the maximum value allowed.

---

[14] There is a rather crude short cut mechanism which allows the use of three-digit hexadecimal values, meaning the standard six-digit form with each of the three digits doubled. Therefore, this example could also be specified as #F0F. However, this variation of specifying a color is more confusing than useful and should therefore be avoided.

6.3.3.2 Lengths

In many CSS1 properties, lengths are being used. They can be classified into two categories, one containing lengths which are measured in relation to something else, the other one containing lengths which use absolute units.

Relative lengths can be relative to different things in the environment of a CSS browser. The current relative units defined by CSS1 are either relative to the font being used, or relative to the output device. In both cases, it is important to notice that the actual length (in absolute units such as millimeters) which is used for the formatting of the document is not known when the style sheet is created. The actual length is only known after the font has been selected, and the display device is known. Therefore, relative lengths can result in different absolute lengths depending on the presentation of a document.

- *em* – font specific, the width of the capital 'M'
- *ex* – font specific, the height of the letter 'x'
- *px* – display specific, size of one pixel

It is important to notice that in some cases relative lengths are automatically converted to absolute lengths. For example, in case of the `word-spacing` property described in section 6.3.4, a relative unit such as *1em* is converted to an absolute length (such as *10pt* in case that the current font of the element is a 10 point font), and this result is inherited to the element's children as their word spacing. So if the child element changes the font size, it will not get the word spacing set to the relative value, but to the absolute value of *10pt*. Consequently, when using relative lengths, the CSS1 specification should be consulted how these lengths are inherited for the specific property in question.

Absolute lengths can be used to specify fixed lengths which will not change depending on the presentation. In some applications, this may be an advantage, but in most cases this is not very useful, because it limits the scalability of a document. The following absolute units of measure can be used with CSS1.

- *in* – inches ($1 \, \text{in} = 2.54 \, \text{cm}$)
- *cm* – centimeters
- *mm* – millimeters ($1 \, \text{mm} = 0.1 \, \text{cm}$)
- *pt* – points ($1 \, \text{pt} = \frac{1}{72} \, \text{in} \approx 0.35 \, \text{mm}$)
- *pc* – picas ($1 \, \text{pc} = 12 \, \text{pt} = \frac{1}{6} \, \text{in} \approx 4.23 \, \text{mm}$)

Scalability (or, in other words, the independence from particular presentation environments) is an important aspect of HTML in general and CSS1 in particular, and therefore care should be taken when using absolute lengths. In some cases, absolute lengths may be useful, but as a general guideline, they should be avoided and relative lengths should be used instead.

Finally, in many cases specific it is also possible to use a *percentage* rather than a relative or absolute length. This can also be seen as a kind of relative length, but it is different from the relative lengths described above, because it is relative to something inside the document (in most cases, the parent element) rather than to the presentation environment. However, percentages are also very useful in creating scalable documents and should therefore be preferred over absolute lengths.

6.3.4 Declarations

In the last section, we have described what selection mechanisms can be used to select a certain set of element instances inside an HTML page. However, this is only the prerequisite for the real work which needs to be done, which is the specification of formatting instructions (ie, the assignment of values to properties) in the declarations of CSS1 rules. In the examples in section 6.3.2, we already used some declarations for changing the formatting, and now we give a more systematic overview over the formatting capabilities of CSS1.

In section 6.3.4.1, fonts are described and the ways in which fonts and their appearance and size can be selected. Spacing is another important issue of formatting, it is described in section 6.3.4.2. The treatment of images is discussed in section 6.3.4.3. Furthermore, CSS1's model of using colors and backgrounds is described in section 6.3.4.4. Finally, there are some declarations which can be used to change the classification of elements, these are described in section 6.3.4.5.

6.3.4.1 Fonts

One of the most important aspects of style sheets is the specification of type. Since most of the content of a typical web page is text, the selection of a certain type makes a big difference in appearance and formatting. Although in traditional printing, there was a big difference between *type* and *font* (type meaning a family of fonts, encompassing different sizes, weights, and styles), today these words are used interchangeably, and we will follow CSS1's convention to do so.

Before the introduction of the <BASEFONT> and <FONT> elements in HTML 3.2, the choice of a certain font was entirely up to the browser, and authors had no way to specify the font which should be used. HTML 4.0

specifies <BASEFONT> and <FONT> as deprecated elements and therefore practically removes the font selection capabilities from HTML, which are now to be implemented in style sheets. CSS1 introduces a font model and defines a number of font properties specifying which font should be used.

However, up to now this requires all fonts to be installed locally, since there currently is no standard for font interchange (this will be available as soon as *Dynamic Fonts* as described in section 10.5.4 become standardized). It also requires all browsers to classify locally installed fonts according to the categories defined by CSS1. CSS1 defines five different families of fonts, and each font should be assigned to one of these families. Also, a number of parameters are defined for each font (which are *style, variant, weight*, and *size*), and each font must also be classified according to these parameters.

> "Unfortunately, there exists no well-defined and universally accepted taxonomy for classifying fonts, and terms that apply to one font family may not be appropriate for others. [...] Therefore it is not a simple problem to map typical font selection properties to a specific font."
>
> *CSS1 specification [159]*

However, CSS1 attempts to define a common framework for font classification and selection by defining a number of properties which can be used for font selection. Unfortunately, this still does not address the question how existing fonts are classified according to this scheme, at the moment this is completely under the control of CSS1 implementations (ie, browsers and their usage of locally installed fonts).

- `font-family`
  This property is used to specify preferences about font families, either by using a specific family name (such as `Times`), or by using one of the defined generic family names, which are `serif`, `sans-serif`, `monospace`, `cursive`, and `fantasy`. It is possible to use multiple values separated by commas, in which case the values specify font preferences in decreasing order.

  ```
  BODY { font-family: Times, serif }
  ```

  This specification means that the <BODY> element (and its content, because the `font` property is inherited) should use a `Times` font, if available, and otherwise any `serif` font family which is available.

- `font-style`
  For some font families, there are different font styles, which can be selected using the `font-style` property. This property can have the values `normal` (sometimes also referred to as *roman, regular,* or *upright*), `oblique` (also

known as *inclined* or *slanted*), or `italic` (sometimes called *cursive*). If the requested font style is not defined in a font family, it will either be substituted, or the next family in the list of accepted font families will be searched for the requested style[15].

- `font-variant`
  The `font-variant` property accepts the values `normal` and `small-caps` and selects either a normal or a small caps style of the current font family. If there is no small caps style, a browser may choose to simulate this style by using capitals from a smaller font size as the small letters of the simulated font style[16].

- `font-weight`
  Using the `font-weight` property, the weight of the desired font can be specified. Most generally, the `font-weight` property accepts values from 100 to 900, in steps of hundreds, 100 being the lightest and 900 being the heaviest weight of a font. The two common words `normal` and `bold` refer to a 400 respectively a 700 weight of the font. If the desired weight is not available, the browser will use the next closest match. It is also possible to use the words `lighter` or `bolder` to choose a relative weight in comparison to the parent's weight.

  `STRONG { font-weight: bolder }`

  In this example, the style sheets specifies a relative weight for the content of the `<STRONG>` element. If the parent font (used in the `<P>` element containing the `<STRONG>` element instance) is normal (ie, a 400 weight), `<STRONG>` will use a bold weight (eg, a 700 weight). If, however, the parent font is bold, `<STRONG>` will use a bolder weight (eg, a 900 weight) if it is available in the current font family. Using the relative weight, this happens without the need to change the style sheet declaration for the `<STRONG>` element.

- `font-size`
  The `font-size` property sets the desired size of the font. There a number of different ways to specify a font size using this property.

---

[15] Depending on the combination of requested and existing styles, either substitution or the selection of the next family will be chosen.

[16] This is not the proper way to create a small caps style, because in a true small caps style, the small capitals are specifically designed (with regard to their width and the thickness of the lines) and not simply capitals taken from a smaller font size. However, it may be better to have a simulated small caps style than to have none at all.

– *Absolute size*

In this case, the browser maintains a number of fixed font sizes (based on the output device and maybe user preferences). The available sizes are xx-small, x-small, small, medium, large, x-large, and xx-large. The CSS1 specification suggests that each size should be 1.5 times as large as the previous one.

– *Relative size*

Using this way of size specification, it is possible to set the size of a font in relation to the parent element's font size. The two values smaller and larger can be used to specify a relative size, and scale the font one size down or up on the scale of absolute values described above.

– *Length*

It is also possible to specify the font size using an absolute value. The traditional unit for measuring the size of a font is the *point*, but other units (as described in section 6.3.3.2) can be used as well. It should be kept in mind, however, that this way of specifying a font size can easily specify an unavailable size and that it may also be inappropriate for some output media[17].

– *Percentage*

A method similar to the relative size value is the percentage, which specifies the desired font size relative to the parent element's font size. A value of 120% will select a font which is 1.2 times as large as the parent element's font. However, because it is possible to specify any percentage, it is easily possible to specify a font size which is not available.

• font

It is also possible to set all the previous font properties including the line-height property (described in section 6.3.4.2) using the font property. This property can be used to explicitly set all font properties, or it will set the properties to their initial values if no explicit value is given in the font property.

• text-decoration

Although the text-decoration property does not select a font (instead it specifies a certain decoration of a font), it is rather closely related to the font selection properties and is therefore described here. The text-decoration property can either have the value none, meaning no

---

[17] While a smaller font size for notes such as this footnote is good in printed documents, it may lead to hard to read text if it is rendered on a screen and set to an absolute length such as 9 point size.

decoration at all (which is the normal case), or any combination of the following values.

 - `underline`

   This indicates that the characters of the current font should be underlined. This is an effect which is similar to that achieved with the HTML `<U>` element (which is deprecated).

 - `overline`

   This indicates that the characters of the current font should have a line above them.

 - `line-through`

   This text decoration specifies that the characters of the current font should have a horizontal line inserted through the text (which is also known as *strike-through*). This is an effect which is similar to that achieved with HTML's `<STRIKE>` or `<S>` elements (which are deprecated).

 - `blink`

   Using this value, a blinking appearance of the characters is selected, ie, the user agent should alternate the text between visible and invisible.

Using these values, it is possible to change the decoration of a font which has been selected by the font properties. However, it is not sure that all possible text decorations are available for a selected font or even are available at all (the `blink` text decoration is most likely not to be supported by some user agents and will also have no effect when being printed).

- `text-transform`

  Similar to the `text-decoration` property, the `text-transform` also does not select a font, but changes the capitalization of text and is therefore also listed in this section. The `text-transform` property is used to change the case of text and can have different values for controlling this.

 - `capitalize`

   In this case, the browser capitalizes the first letter of each word in the text. This type of text capitalization is common practice in english headings (although some words usually are not capitalized, and the `capitalize` text transformation is not able to make this distinction).

 - `uppercase`

   This value is used to transform all characters to upper case.

 - `lowercase`

   This value does the opposite of the `uppercase` text transformation, it transforms all characters to lower case.

— `none`

If no transformation should be done, a `none` value can be used, which will leave the character's case unchanged.

The exact rules for changing from one case to another depend on the language and on the browser. They may include the removal of accents and other transformations (such as characters which exist only in lower case variants like the german 'ß' character).

When working with CSS1 font properties, it should always be kept in mind that in most cases a style sheet should support scalability. Therefore, whenever possible, relative measures should be used instead of absolute values, which in most cases make it hard to scale a document. Furthermore, a carefully designed style sheet should always specify fall-back solutions[18], for example for the font family. Instead of specifying just one font (which may not be installed on the system where the document is viewed), it is always a good idea to specify alternative fonts, and, as a last resort, one of the generic font family names (such as `serif`).

6.3.4.2 Space

One important aspect of formatting is to choose the right spacing. Spacing comes into play in many different areas of formatting, from the space between letters and words to the margins of the whole document. CSS1 defines a spacing model for block-level elements, which is shown in figure 6.7. It is based on three different belts around the actual content of an element. The element's content is surrounded by padding, which separates the content from the border[19]. The border is surrounded by the element's margin, which separates the border from everything outside the element's box.

Margins can be set individually for each side or using a property which sets all four margins in one step. Values can either be *lengths*, specifying a length in an absolute or relative measure, or *percentages*. Percentages are used to specify lengths in relation to the width of the parent element. Furthermore, the `margin-left` and `margin-right` properties can also be set to `auto`, in which case the browser determines the actual value based on a width calculation defined in the CSS1 specification.

---

[18] Although this is certainly true as a general remark regarding style sheet design, it is even more important for font specification, because a style sheet designer has no control over the fonts which are installed locally where the document is viewed.

[19] The padding is also used extend the background around the element, if it has any background set (the background properties are described in section 6.3.4.4).

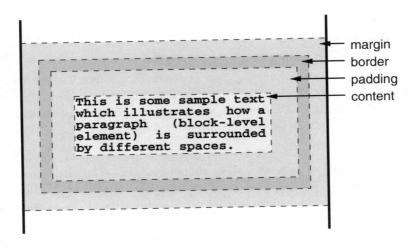

Fig. 6.7   Spacing for block-level elements

- `margin-left`
  This property sets the left margin of an element. It may be set to `auto` to specify width calculation.

- `margin-right`
  The `margin-right` property sets the right margin of an element. It may be set to `auto` to specify width calculation.

- `margin-top`
  Using the `margin-top` property, it is possible to set the top margin of an element.

- `margin-bottom`
  This property sets the bottom margin of an element.

- `margin`
  The `margin` property can be used to specify all four margins in one step. Depending on the number of values specified, the margins are set according to the following rules.

  - *One value*
    If only one value is specified, this values applies to all four sides.

  - *Two values*
    If two values are specified, the missing values are taken from the opposite sides. The first value defines the top and the bottom margins, and the second value defines the left and right margins.

— *Three values*

Similarly, if three values are specified, the missing value is taken from the opposite side. The first value defines the top margin, the second value defines the left and right margins, and the third value defines the bottom margin.

— *Four values*

If four values are specified, all four sides are set in the order top, right, bottom, and left.

Using the `margin` property, it is therefore possible to use more compact specifications of margins.

In addition to the margins, which specify the distance between the outer bounding box of an element and the border, it is also possible to specify the padding for an element, which is the distance between the border of an element and the bounding box of its content.

The padding can be set individually for each side or using a property which sets the padding for all four sides in one step. Values can either be *lengths*, specifying a length in an absolute or relative measure, or *percentages*. Percentages are used to specify lengths in relation to the width of the parent element. Padding will always take on the same appearance as an element's background, while the margins will not, so using padding and margins also makes sense if no border is used at all.

- `padding-left`

  This property sets the padding on the left side of an element.

- `padding-right`

  The `padding-right` property sets the padding on the right side of an element.

- `padding-top`

  Using the `padding-top` property, it is possible to set the padding on top of an element.

- `padding-bottom`

  This property sets the padding on the bottom of an element.

- `padding`

  The `padding` property can be used to specify the padding on all four sides in one step. Depending on the number of values specified, the padding is set according to the following rules.

  — *One value*

  If only one value is specified, this values applies to all four sides.

– *Two values*
If two values are specified, the missing values are taken from the opposite sides. The first value defines the top and the bottom padding, and the second value defines the left and right padding.

– *Three values*
Similarly, if three values are specified, the missing value is taken from the opposite side. The first value defines the top padding, the second value defines the left and right padding, and the third value defines the bottom padding.

– *Four values*
If four values are specified, the padding for all four sides is set in the order top, right, bottom, and left.

Using the `padding` property, it is therefore possible to use more compact specifications of an element's padding.

In addition to the spacing defined with margins and padding, it is also possible to define borders which should be drawn around elements. If a border is requested, it is drawn between the padding and the margin, as shown in figure 6.7. The three properties of borders which can be set are a border's style, its width, and its color. Using a number of different CSS1 properties, these aspects can be set in different ways.

- `border-style`
This property is used to control the style of the border of an element. CSS1 distinguishes no border at all, and two different groups of border styles.

  – `none`
  Using this value, it is specified that an element should have no border.

  – *Line styles*
  The line styles specify border styles which are using only simple lines and are therefore appropriate for display types where the number of colors is limited. The possible line styles are `dotted`, `dashed`, `solid`, and `double`.

  – *3D styles*
  For more appealing visual effects, CSS1 defines a number of 3D border styles. However, because these border styles require shading (to visualize lighter and darker edges of embossed contours), they may not be rendered very well on display devices with limited color palettes. The possible 3D style are `groove` and `ridge` (showing an embossed border), and `inset` and `outset` (embossing the whole box of the element content).

The `border-style` property can be used to set the border style of all four border sides at once, the way this is done is determined by the number of values set for the property.

- *One value*

  In this case, the style of all four borders is set to the given value.

- *Two values*

  In case of two values, the top and bottom borders are set to the first value, and the left and right borders are set to the second value.

- *Three values*

  If three values are present, the top border is set to the first value, the left and right borders are set to the second value, and the bottom border is set to the third value.

- *Four values*

  In this case, the four values are applied in the order top, right, bottom, and left.

When specifying the appearance of an element's border, it should always be kept in mind that the 3D styles may be less appropriate on certain devices, especially when shading can become a problem.

- `border-width`

  In addition to the border's style, it is also possible to specify a border's width. The width itself can be specified in different ways.

  - `none`

    Using the `none` keyword, it is specified that no border should be used at all.

  - *Thickness keywords*

    Three keywords can be used to set a border's width. These keywords are `thin`, `medium` (which is the default for the border width), and `thick`. The actual width used for the border width depends on the browser.

  - *Length*

    Using a length, the border width can be set explicitly set in any unit of measurement known to CSS1.

The `border-width` property can be used to specify all four border widths in one step. Depending on the number of values specified, the widths are set according to the following rules.

- *One value*

  In this case, the width of all four borders is set to the given value.

- *Two values*
  In case of two values, the top and bottom border width is set to the first value, and the left and right width is set to the second value.
- *Three values*
  If three values are present, the top border width is set to the first value, the left and right border width is set to the second value, and the bottom border width is set to the third value.
- *Four values*
  In this case, the four values are applied in the order top, right, bottom, and left.

Using the `border-width` property, it is therefore possible to define compact specifications of border widths[20].

- `border-color`
  In addition to border style and width, it is also possible to set the border's color using the `border-color` property. If no color is specified for the border color, the border takes the color of the element itself. The `border-color` property can be used to specify the color of all four borders in one step. Depending on the number of values specified, the colors are set according to the following rules.

  - *One value*
    In this case, the color of all four borders is set to the given value.
  - *Two values*
    In case of two values, the top and bottom border color is set to the first value, and the left and right border color is set to the second value.
  - *Three values*
    If three values are present, the top border color is set to the first value, the left and right border color is set to the second value, and the bottom border color is set to the third value.
  - *Four values*
    In this case, the four values are applied in the order top, right, bottom, and left.

Using the `border-color` property, it is therefore possible to use compact specifications of border colors.

---

[20] It is also possible to set the four border widths individually using the four properties `border-left-width`, `border-right-width`, `border-top-width`, and `border-bottom-width`.

- `border`

  If all four borders should be set to the same values, it is possible to set the style, the width, and the color in one step using the `border` property. This property accepts the same values as the individual properties for style, width, and color[21].

  The border properties have, to some extent, overlapping functionality. It is therefore possible to achieve the same effects using different combinations of the border properties. Which of these properties are used depends on the application, but in most cases the `border`, `border-left`, `border-right`, `border-top`, and `border-bottom` properties will be used most frequently, because they allow the specification of all border properties (style, width, and color) in one step.

  To end this discussion of margin and padding spaces (and borders) around element content, CSS1's concept of *collapsing margins* has to be mentioned. Whenever a top and a bottom margin touch directly, only the larger margin is used, while the smaller margin is discarded. This is done to make sure that there is not too much space between elements. A similar mechanism is used when more than one element begin or end at the same time[22]. In this case, the margins from all these elements (and maybe a margin from a touching element) are taken, and the maximum value is used for determining the formatting, while all other margins are discarded.

  In addition to the spacing around block-level elements (using margins, padding, and borders), which has been described so far, CSS1 also defines a number of properties which are used to control the spacing inside block-level elements.

- `text-align`

  This property sets the way lines are adjusted horizontally between the left and right margins of the element. It is possible to set this property to four different values.

  - `left`

    This is the most usual way of text alignment in most browsers today. The lines are aligned at the left margin and the right margin is ragged.

---

[21] If it is required to set the borders of an element to different values of style, width, or color, the `border-left`, `border-right`, `border-top`, or `border-bottom` properties can be used. These properties make it possible to set style, width, and color for one border in one step.

[22] This frequently happens in list environments, where at the end of the list, a <P>, a <LI>, and a <UL> element may end simultaneously. It is possible that all these elements have a non-zero bottom margin assigned.

- `right`

  This type of text alignment is the opposite of left alignment, the lines are aligned at the right margin and the left margin is ragged. This type of text alignment is often used for marginal notes on the left side of left aligned or justified text.

- `centered`

  This type of alignment specifies lines which are individually centered between the left and right margin, so the left and right margin of the text will appear ragged.

- `justified`

  This type of text alignment aligns lines on both the left and the right margin by adjusting the spacing between words, so that all lines have the same length. This type of text alignment is typically seen in printed documents such as books and journals.

Although most browsers today by default use left text alignment, the CSS1 standard specifies that the default of this property is specific to a user agent. If text alignment is important, it should therefore always be specified in the style sheet (for example in a rule selecting the <BODY> element, from where it is inherited to all elements of the document).

- `text-indent`

  It is possible to specify the indentation of the first line of a paragraph using the `text-indent` property. Indentations can be either positive or negative, with negative values causing the first line of the paragraph to stick out of the bounding box of the paragraph. The text indentation can be specified using a *length* or a *percentage*, with the latter meaning a percentage of the width of the paragraph.

- `line-height`

  This property specifies how far apart the lines in a paragraph are. However, since lines may contain larger elements than the line height, causing the line to be larger, the `line-height` property actually specifies the minimum distance between the lines of a paragraph. The line height can be specified in three different ways.

  - *Length*

    This specifies the line height as a length, which may be an absolute or (which most cases will be better) a relative value which takes into account the font's size (*em* or *ex* would be used in this case).

  - *Percentage*

    This type of value sets the line height relative to the font size. The resulting line height is computed and inherited by all children of the element. Consequently, if a child uses a smaller font and does not change the line height, the line height remains the same as for the parent, resulting in a line height which is larger in relation to the font size.

- *Number*

  This type of value also sets the line height relative to the font size. However, in contrast to a percentage value, a number value causes the line height to be calculated for each child of an element. As a consequence, if a child uses a smaller font and does not explicitly change the line height, the line height is calculated in relation to the new font size and will therefore be set to a smaller value.

The line height of a text is very important with regard to the visual appearance of a document. Small line height may make a text look too dense, while large line heights often result in reduced readability. Furthermore, the line height of a text also is heavily influenced by the font being used (and not only its size, but also the style and the overall appearance).

- `word-spacing`

  The `word-spacing` property allows the adjustment of the amount of spacing between words. Normally, a font will have a word spacing defined specifically for its appearance, but this spacing can be expanded or shrunk using the `word-spacing` property. The property can either be set to `normal`, leaving the word spacing up to the browser, or to a *length*. In this case, the latter is added to the normal word spacing. It is possible to use negative values, in which case the word spacing will be narrower than the font's default. This may cause words to overlap.

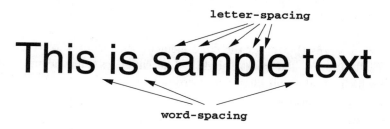

Fig. 6.8 The `word-spacing` and `letter-spacing` properties

- `letter-spacing`

  This property is similar to the `word-spacing` property described above, but rather than setting the spacing between different words, it affects the spacing of the letters of a word. Normally, a font will have a letter spacing defined specifically for its appearance, but this spacing can be expanded or shrunk using the `letter-spacing` property. The property can either be set to `normal`, leaving the letter spacing up to the browser, or a *length*. In case of a length being used, the given value is added to the normal letter spacing. It is also possible to use negative values, in which case the letter spacing will be narrower than the font's default. This may cause letters to overlap.

- `vertical-align`
  Using the `vertical-align` property, it is possible to raise or lower letters or images above or below the baseline of a text. The vertical alignment of an element can be set in a number of ways. For elements without a baseline, such as images, the alignment is based on the bottom of the element whenever the baseline is used for the alignment of text.

  - `baseline`
    This is the default and aligns the baseline of the child element with the baseline of its parent.

  - `sub`
    This puts the child element in the parent's preferred position for subscripts, which normally is determined by the font being used. The alignment is based on the child's baseline.

  - `super`
    This puts the child element in the parent's preferred position for superscripts, which normally is determined by the font being used. The alignment is based on the child's baseline.

  - `top`
    This alignment uses the top of the child element and aligns it with the tallest thing on the line.

  - `text-top`
    This aligns the top of the child element with the top of the parent's tallest letter. This gives a slightly different effect than the `super` value, which usually will align superscripts to stick out over the top of the parent's tallest letter.

  - `middle`
    This alignment aligns the vertical midpoint of the child element with the parent element's baseline plus half the x-height, that is, the middle of the lower case letters.

  - `text-bottom`
    This aligns the bottom of the child element with the bottom of the parent's font. This gives a slightly different effect than the `sub` value.

- bottom

    This alignment uses the bottom of the child element and aligns it with the lowest thing on the line.

- *Percentage*

    Finally, it is also possible to specify a percentage (which may also be a negative value). A percentage value indicates how much the element is to be raised or lowered in comparison to the element's line height.

Setting the vertical alignment of elements is one of the points of fine-tuning the appearance of a text (for example by deciding whether superscripts should be displayed using super or text-top alignment). While for text the vertical alignment will most often not be used, the vertical-alignment property is often used for aligning images with regard to text.

These properties end the description of spacing properties for block-level elements and inside block-level elements, which is one of the most important aspects of formatting. In the next section, the handling of images in CSS1 is discussed, which also has a lot to do with the visual appearance of an HTML page.

6.3.4.3 Images

Although in many cases images will be the most frequently used content besides text, the following discussion of properties applies to all *replaced elements*, which are elements whose content is replaced by an image or an object such as a button. Examples for replaced elements are <IMG>, <OBJECT>, <INPUT>, <SELECT>, and <TEXTAREA>. CSS1 treats all these elements in the same way, assuming that they have a *natural* (or *intrinsic*) size, which is the normal size of the element if it is not explicitly scaled.

- width

    This property sets the width of an element. Although it is possible to set the width of normal block-level elements, it is most frequently done with replaced elements such as images. The width can either be set to auto (which is the default), using a *length* value, or specifying a *percentage*. In case of a percentage being used, the width is set in relation to the width of the parent element.

- height

    This property sets the height of an element. Although it is possible to set the height of normal block-level elements, it is most frequently done with replaced elements such as images. The height can either be set to auto (which is the default), or using a *length* value.

- float

  The `float` property allows to place an element at the left or right edge of the parent element. The element is taken out of the normal flow of text or other non-floating elements and is placed at one of the edges.

  - left

    This value floats the element to the left margin.

  - right

    This value floats the element to the right margin.

  - none

    This is the default and places the element in the flow of text where it appears, which will most likely not be at the left or right edge of the parent element.

  The `float` property in most cases is used for the placement of images (or other large replaced elements) which are part of the text (ie, the text should float around them), but should be aligned with one of the text's borders.

- clear

  This property works with the `float` property. Because elements using the `float` property are placed outside the flow of text (or more general, non-floating content), it is possible that they interfere with the placement of other elements. The `clear` property specifies whether an element allows floating elements at its sides.

  - none

    This is the default and specifies that the element allows floating elements on both of its sides.

  - left

    In this case, the element does not allow floating elements on its left side, but accepts floating elements on its right side.

  - right

    In this case, the element does not allow floating elements on its right side, but accepts floating elements on its left side.

  - both

    This is the most restrictive case and specifies that the element does not allow floating elements on either of its sides.

A common use for this property is to set headings of different levels to different `clear` values, for example setting that <H1> headings have to have `both` sides without floating elements. Lower level headings (such as <H2>) can accept floating elements on their right side (by using the `left` value for the `clear` property). Headings below this level then may accept floating elements on both sides, using the `none` value.

The properties which can be used for replaced elements define the placement of these elements in the flow of text and other elements. Using certain kinds of formatting (such as floating elements), the formatting becomes more complex and may have implications for the formatting of other elements (such as in the example with the heading elements). It is therefore necessary to think about formatting more carefully when using replaced elements inside a document.

Although more unusual than using them for replaced elements, it is also easily possible to use the properties described in this section for non-replaced elements. One example would be a list, which could be taken out of the normal flow of text using the `float` property, with its width set using the `width` property (most likely to some percentage of the parent element's width). In this case, the list would appear formatted separately, and it would be advisable to surround it with a `border`.

6.3.4.4 Colors and backgrounds

In addition to the properties which have been discussed in the previous section and which change the actual formatting of a document, it is also possible to change colors. This does not change the actual layout (in terms of geometry), but color can be a very important factor for the presentation of a document[23]. CSS1 defines a number of properties to define foreground and background colors, and also to define background images, which can be used instead of a background using only one color.

- `color`
  The foreground color of an element can be set using the `color` property. This is the color which is used for text and text decorations. If a border is present and the border color is not explicitly set using the `border-color` or `border` properties discussed in section 6.3.4.2, the foreground color also determines the color of the border. A common use of the `color` property is to set the color of hyperlinks depending on their state, using the anchor pseudo-class as described in section 6.3.2.4

- `background-color`
  Using the `background-color` property, it is possible to set the background color of an element. The background color can be set to be `transparent`

---

[23] The two most important factors for using color are increased readability by using visually pleasing color combinations, and the marking of special sections, such as using red text for warnings or important remarks.

(which is the default) or to any color. In addition to the surface behind the text of the element (which is displayed in the foreground color), the padding (described in section 6.3.4.2) will also have the background color. If the element also uses a background image, this may partially or totally cover the background color.

- background-image
  If an image should be used for the background, the background-image property can be used to specify a URL. This URL points to an image which is used as the background image.

- background-repeat
  This property determines whether and how a background image is repeated in the element[24]. The effect of the background-repeat property is shown in figure 6.9, assuming that the background image has been centered (this position can be changed using the background-position property described below).

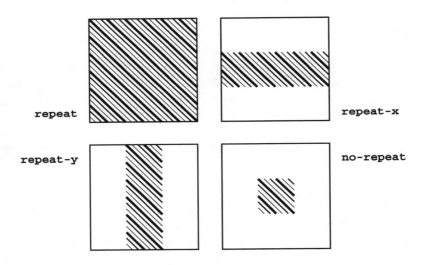

Fig. 6.9 Effects of the background-repeat property

- repeat
  In this case, the image is repeated both vertically and horizontally, so that the entire background is covered by the image. This is the default value.

---

[24] The process of repeating an image so that it fills a given surface is called *tiling*.

- repeat-x

  If the image should only be repeated horizontally, the repeat-x value can be used. If the image is not as high as the element, there will be no background image above and below the single row of repeated background images.

- repeat-y

  If the image should only be repeated vertically, the repeat-y value can be used. If the image is not as wide as the element, there will be no background image to the left and right of the single column of repeated background images.

- no-repeat

  In some cases it may also be desirable to have the background image only once. This effect can be achieved using the no-repeat value.

Using the background-repeat property, it is possible to achieve a large number of effects, depending on the design of the background image, in particular its tiling. Finer control over background design is possible using the background-attachment and background-position properties described below.

- background-attachment

  Normally, the background image is attached to an element, so when the element is scrolled in a browser, the background image scrolls with it. This can be changed using the background-attachment property.

  - scroll

    This is the default, where the background image is attached to the element and scrolls with it.

  - fixed

    If the background should be attached to the window (or *canvas*, as it is called in CSS1), this can be specified using the fixed value.

  The background-attachment property can be used to achieve special effects, such as a logo which always stays in one corner of the window, even if the document content is scrolled back and forth. This effect can be achieved by setting a fixed background attachment for the background of the <BODY> element.

- background-position

  The background position determines where the background image is placed in relation to the surface covered by the element. The default is for the background image to be placed in the upper left corner. This placement can be changed using several methods.

– *Percentages*
Percentages can be used to place the background relative to the size
of the element. The way it is defined in CSS1 is shown in figure 6.10.
The percentages are taken relative to the background image's size
and relative to the element's size and the background image is placed
accordingly. If only one value is given, it is used for the horizontal
placement and the background image is centered vertically (as if the
second value had been given as 50%).

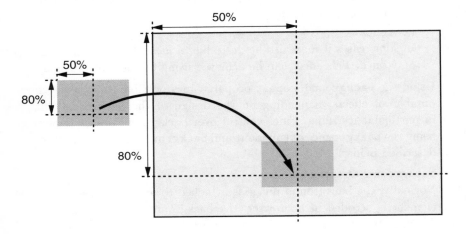

Fig. 6.10   Using percentages for the `background-position` property

– *Lengths*
Using lengths, the upper left corner of the background image is placed
that far away from the upper left corner of the element. If only one
value is given, it is used for horizontal placement and the background
image is centered vertically.

– *Keywords*
It is also possible to use keywords, which serve as short cuts for
percentages. For horizontal placement, the keywords `top`, `center`,
and `bottom` can be used. For vertical placement, the keywords `left`,
`center`, and `right` can be used. These keywords correspond to the
percentages 0%, 50%, and 100%. If only one keyword is specified, the
unspecified dimension is assumed to be `center`.

Although the usage of the `background-position` property might look a
bit complicated, it is a very flexible mechanism for specifying all kinds of
positionings of background images.

- `background`

  The `background` property is a short cut to set all aspects of a background at once. If some of the properties are not set (which is possible by specifying only some of the background properties), they are set to their default values.

Colors and backgrounds are an important aspect of web page design, and therefore CSS offers a number of properties which can be used to set them to a number of different values. When using colors and backgrounds, special care should be taken to ensure the readability of the document, even if it is displayed on devices with only a limited number of colors or even black and white.

6.3.4.5 Classification properties

In addition to the properties described in the previous sections, there also is one property which can be used to change an element's classification according to HTML's differentiation between block-level and inline elements as described in section 5.2.3.2. In addition to that, the treatment of lists and white-space characters in element content can also be changed using CSS1 properties, and because all these properties are changing the way an element is formatted on a very basic level, they are summarized in this last section about CSS1 properties.

- `display`

  HTML differentiates between block-level and inline elements, and the HTML standard specifies for each element whether it is a block-level or an inline element. However, sometimes it may be desirable to change this assignment, and this can be done with the `display` property[25].

  - `block`

    Using this value, the formatting of an element can be set to block-level, so that it is treated like an HTML block-level element. This means that it is started on a new line.

  - `inline`

    It is possible to achieve the opposite effect by using the `inline` value, which sets an element to be formatted like an HTML inline element. Consequently, the content of the element will be displayed on the same line as the previous content.

---

[25] A common application for this may be to change lower level headings (such as <H3> or lower) to inline elements, thus starting the text of the section directly after its heading and not on a new line.

- `list-item`

  If the `display` property of an element is set to `list-item`, it will be displayed as a box with a label. The formatting of the box and appearance of the label can be set using the list style properties described below.

- `none`

  It is also possible to hide an element completely by setting its `display` property to `none`. A browser displays the document as if all the elements with their `display` property set to `none` were not present at all.

Using these values, it is possible to achieve effects which are very different from the usual formatting of HTML, for example by setting `<LI>` elements to `inline`. In this case, list items no longer are displayed on individual lines, but are formatted as running text, which is the most compact way a list can be displayed[26].

- `list-style-type`

  This property only affects elements whose display type is either `list-item` by default (this is true for the `<LI>` element), or whose display type has been set to `list-item` using the `display` property. The `list-style-type` property sets whether there is a label and, if so, its appearance.

  - `disc`

    This value sets the label to a disc ('•'), this is the default value.

  - `circle`

    Another unnumbered list style type can be set using the `circle` value, which uses a circle ('o') as list label.

  - `square`

    The third available unnumbered list style type is the box ('□').

  - `decimal`

    Lists can be numbered using decimal numbers (1, 2, 3, ...). This is often used for first-level numbering.

  - `lower-roman`

    Another possible way of numbering lists is to use lower case roman numerals (i, ii, iii, ...), which can get a bit confusing for larger numbers.

---

[26] Even though this effect could also be achieved by simply entering the list as text inside one paragraph, the `display` property method has two advantages. The formatting can be changed to the usual `list-item` display style without changing the HTML document, and non-visual user agents can still recognize the content as a list rather than a simple sentence including some commas or semicolons.

- upper-roman

  It is also possible to use upper case roman numerals (I, II, III, ...), which may be as confusing as lower case roman numerals for large numbers.

- lower-alpha

  Another possibility is to use lower case alphanumeric numbering (a, b, c, ...). This is often used for second-level numbering, but is limited to the number of characters available.

- upper-alpha

  Upper case alphanumeric numbering (A, B, C, ...) can also be used but has the same limitations as lower case alphanumeric numbering.

- none

  If no label is required at all, the list style type can be set to none and no label will be used.

List style types are already built into browsers, which will normally automatically select different list style types for different levels of nested lists. However, this can easily be changed with contextual selectors.

```
OL       { list-style-type: decimal }
OL OL    { list-style-type: lower-alpha }
OL OL OL { list-style-type: lower-roman }
```

Using this or a similar style sheet, the list style type of lists and nested lists can be changed for a complete document, without the need to modify the HTML code or to individually set the list style types.

- list-style-image

  This property only affects elements whose display type is either list-item by default (this is true for the <LI> element), or whose display type has been set to list-item using the display property. If it is necessary to use a list label different from the symbols described above, the list-style-image property can be used to specify a URL. This URL points to an image which is used as the label. If for some reason the browser is not able to download or display the image, the list-style-type property will be used to determine the label.

- list-style-position

  This property only affects elements whose display type is either list-item by default (this is true for the <LI> element), or whose display type has been set to list-item using the display property. For these elements, the list-style-position property is used to determine where the label of a list item should be displayed.

– `inside`

This value specifies that the label should be placed inside the list item box, aligned with the first line of text. This results in a more compact display, which has the disadvantage that labels are not as easily recognizable as with the `outside` style.

– `outside`

The `outside` value, which is the default, places the label of a list item outside the item's box, aligned with the first line of text inside the box.

Basically, the two variants of the label position are a trade-off between compactness and visibility, so typically style sheets optimized for compact display will use `inside` label placement, while the more usual `outside` will be used in most other cases.

- `list-style`

This property only affects elements whose display type is either `list-item` by default (this is true for the \<LI\> element), or whose display type has been set to `list-item` using the `display` property. The `list-style` property can be used to set the other list style properties together, so it is only a short hand way for setting the values of `list-style-type`, `list-style-image`, and `list-style-position`.

- `white-space`

Usually (with the only exception of the \<PRE\> element described in section 5.2.4), a browser automatically reduces the number of spaces, tabs, and newlines (collectively called *white-space characters*) to achieve a formatting which is independent from the formatting of the HTML file. Normally, this is useful and it is also what is expected. However, for certain elements it may be necessary to retain the formatting of the input file. This can be done using the `white-space` property.

– `normal`

This is the default (for all elements except \<PRE\>) and means that the browser ignores or collapses extra white-space characters and formats the elements according to the rules of the style sheet.

– `pre`

A value of `pre` causes all extra white-space characters to be retained and newlines to cause line breaks. This is the default for the \<PRE\> element.

– `nowrap`

This value will collapse spaces and tabs as `normal`, but it will not automatically break lines that are too long to be displayed. Line breaks only occur when there is a \<BR\> in the text.

Using these special ways for handling white-space characters, it is possible to create style sheets for different kinds of pre-formatted text, such as poetry or computer programs.

Using the properties described in this section, it is possible to achieve formatting effects which are very different from the standard formatting of HTML documents (ie, the default formatting style which is built into a browser). However, there are still many limitations with CSS1. CSS2 as described in section 6.6.2 allows more formatting effects than CSS1 does.

6.3.5 Using multiple style sheets

The basic idea of CSS is the combination of multiple style sheets (which is called *cascading*), and even though in many cases it may look as if there were only one document-specific style sheet involved, this is not true. If there is a document-specific style sheet, a browser already has to combine the internal formatting rules (which are also some kind of style sheet) and this external style sheet for determining the document's formatting. Therefore, even for simple configurations like one document-specific style sheet, it is already necessary to specify how style sheets can be combined. The basic configuration is shown in figure 6.11, which shows multiple style sheets, and the relation of cascading and inheritance.

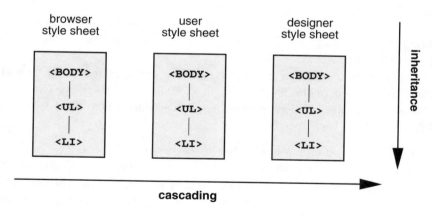

Fig. 6.11   Cascading and inheritance with CSS

Basically, inheritance (as described in section 6.3.1) is based on only one style sheet, with properties being inherited from element instances to their children (ie, to the element instances they contain). On the other hand, cascading always involves multiple style sheets and defines how they can be consistently used together. In section 6.3.5.1, the basic idea of cascading is explained and how it can be specified. Since different style sheets can contain rules for the same element instance, it is possible that conflicts appear[27], a situation which is described in section 6.3.5.2. However, in order to resolve these conflicts, a well-defined process has to be defined which makes it possible to predict the outcome of conflicting rules in cascaded style sheets. CSS1's conflict resolution process is described in section 6.3.5.3.

6.3.5.1 Cascading

As shown in figure 6.11, even the usage of a single document-specific style sheets involves cascading, because this style sheet has to be cascaded with the browser's style sheet. The HTML <LINK> element is used to link a style sheet to a document, it is part of the HTML document's head (which is described in detail in section 5.2.3.1).

```
<LINK REL="stylesheet" HREF="common.css" TYPE="text/css">
```

Using this very simple form of cascading, the browser first loads the HTML document, inspects the document head, discovers the style sheet specification in the <LINK> element and also retrieves the style sheet from the same HTTP server and path from where it retrieved the document. Since the HREF attribute accepts any URL, the style sheet can reside anywhere, it does not have to be stored in the same directory or even on the same server. After retrieving the style sheet, the browser combines its own built-in style sheet and the retrieved style sheet in order to determine the formatting of the HTML document.

However, this situation is simpler than the one depicted in figure 6.11, where in addition to the browser's built-in style sheet, there are two other style sheets involved. There are two possible scenarios how these two style sheets may have been specified.

- *User style sheet and designer style sheet*
  A browser may allow the user to define a style sheet setting the presentation preferences. This style sheet is more important than the browser's built-in style sheet (since it customizes the browser's formatting), but less important than style sheets which are supplied by page designers (since these style sheets are written specifically for a web page and may define important presentation aspects of it).

---

[27] It is also possible that conflicts appear between rules specified in a single style sheet.

- *Multiple designer style sheets*

  The design of an HTML page may involve the usage of multiple style sheets, and for different reasons it may be desirable to keep these style sheets separate rather than merging them into a single style sheet.

  - *Modular organization of style sheets*

    For reasons of complexity, it may be preferable to split the functionality of one rather complex style sheet into several smaller style sheets, which may be easier to maintain and to test than one large style sheet.

  - *Hierarchical organization of style sheets*

    The organization of a web site may involve the definition of a common style sheet, which has to be used for all documents (setting basic parameters such as the font and colors), and page specific style sheets. These style sheets define formatting aspects of specific pages, such as special paragraph classes and their presentation.

  - *Alternate style sheets*

    Another possibility is the provision of multiple style sheets for supporting different presentation styles. In this case, a common style sheet defines the basic appearance of the document, and different alternate style sheets are defined to specify different presentation styles[28].

There are other motivations to use multiple designer style sheets, but in general these three issues are a good classification (and they are also supported by HTML through the use of alternate style sheets which can be specified using the <LINK> element's REL attribute).

Naturally, these scenarios are not limited to two style sheets, they may be extended to three or more style sheets, and they may also be combined. However, in the first case (user and designer style sheets), there is only one style sheet specified in the HTML document, and the user style sheet is only known to the browser (ie, it is not related to any specific HTML document), which combines the three style sheets. This configuration is shown in figure 6.12.

In this scenario, the browser needs a mechanism for defining user style sheets. Most browsers today make it possible for a user to define a number of presentation preferences, but usually in a browser-specific way. Because of this design, a user's presentation preferences are browser specific (ie, they cannot be used for different browsers) and are usually more limited than CSS1. Hopefully, in the near future these browser-specific presentation preferences will be replaced with a mechanism to define the user's presentation preferences in a browser-independent way using CSS style sheets.

---

[28] One possible application for this is the definition of a compact presentation style and a presentation style for clearer presentation.

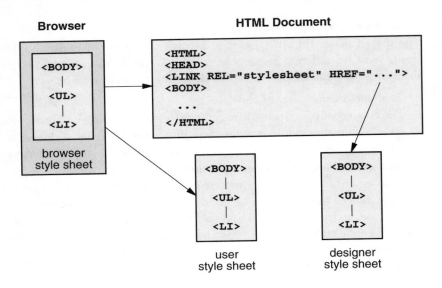

Fig. 6.12 User and designer style sheets in a CSS browser

Another scenario includes the presence of multiple designer style sheets. In this case, the page's designer used multiple style sheets for specifying its presentation, and therefore the page itself contains references to these style sheets. This situation is shown in figure 6.13. Since there are multiple style sheets being referenced from the HTML document, it is necessary to specify them using multiple <LINK> elements in the HTML document.

```
<LINK REL="stylesheet" HREF="special.css" TYPE="text/css">
<LINK REL="stylesheet" HREF="common.css" TYPE="text/css">
```

The HTML standard defines that the order of <LINK> elements in the HTML document is significant. The most specific style sheet is specified first, so in the example the common.css style sheet is the more general one, for example containing presentation preferences which are defined for all documents of the web site. The special.css style sheet contains presentation preferences specific to that page.

Another possible way of combining a common style sheet and style information for a single web page is to include that information directly inside the HTML page rather than storing it in an external style sheet, using the <STYLE> element.

```
<LINK REL="stylesheet" HREF="common.css" TYPE="text/css">
<STYLE TYPE="text/css">
  BODY { font-family: sans-serif }
</STYLE>
```

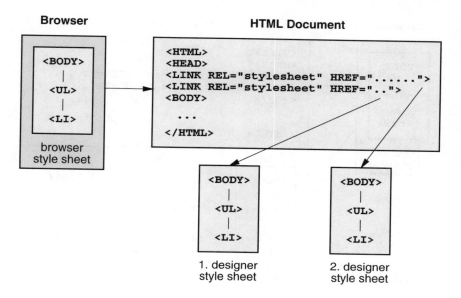

Fig. 6.13 Multiple designer style sheets in a CSS browser

As said before, it is also possible to combine the two main motivations for using multiple style sheets, which are user style sheets and multiple designer style sheets. In this case, there are even more style sheets involved, and the situation can be depicted as shown in figure 6.14.

Furthermore, as mentioned above, it is possible to use alternate style sheets, which make it possible for a designer to create different presentation styles for one web page. In this case, the browser must be informed that there are style sheets to choose from, and this is done using a special keyword for the REL attribute of the <LINK> element.

```
<LINK REL="alternate stylesheet" TITLE="compact"
      HREF="compact.css" TYPE="text/css">
<LINK REL="alternate stylesheet" TITLE="big"
      HREF="big.css" TYPE="text/css">
<LINK REL="stylesheet" HREF="common.css" TYPE="text/css">
```

If a browser encounters this specification, it should offer the user the possibility to choose from the alternate style sheets, and typically this choice will be based on the <LINK> element's TITLE attribute. Currently, there are no standardized values for this attribute (which would make it possible to have a browser choose automatically rather than always asking the user)[29].

---

[29] There are standardized values for media-dependent style sheets, using the <LINK> element's MEDIA attribute. However, media-dependent style sheets is a different

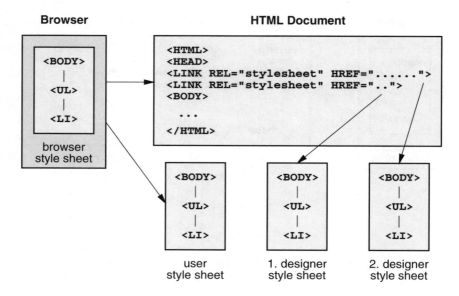

Fig. 6.14 User and multiple designer style sheets in a CSS browser

Although the current versions of browsers do not support all the various uses of style sheets (for example, alternate style sheets are not supported at all), this will change in the future and enable the creation of web pages with many different appearances, depending on media and user preferences.

Whenever a browser is using multiple (in other words cascading) style sheets, for the presentation of each element it searches the cascade of style sheets for rules applying to this element. Only if no rules can be found, the inheritance mechanism will be used to check whether some of the properties which are needed for the presentation are inherited through parent elements.

6.3.5.2 Conflicts

Naturally, the cascading mechanism described in the previous section also leads to conflicts, which may appear for different reasons. In general, conflicts are defined by the existence of different rules setting the same property.

- *Rules inside one style sheet*
  It is possible that there are conflicts inside a single style sheet, since the different ways of selecting elements very often will lead to overlapping selectors. One simple example for this is a type selector for a paragraph

---

mechanism than alternate style sheets, since they normally do not require any user intervention.

(selecting all paragraphs inside a document) and a contextual selector which only selects paragraphs inside other elements (such as lists or tables).

- *User styles and designer styles*
  Since a user style sheet has nothing to do with a specific web page, it can easily be the case that a user style sheet has conflicts with a designer style sheet. The general idea here is that a user style sheet should specify all the presentation preferences which are important for a user, but which may be overridden by a page designer's style sheet.

- *Multiple designer styles*
  If multiple designer style sheets are being used, it is also possible for conflicts to appear. One possible scenario here is the existence of a site wide style sheet, which is used in conjunction with page specific style sheets. It is possible that the designer of a specific page defines rules which conflict with the site wide style sheet.

Theoretically, there are different ways how conflicts could be resolved. One way would be to define a mechanism which tries to find a compromise between conflicting rules, for example taking the average value if there is more than one rule setting a certain length. However, this approach does not work for all types of properties, and it may also often lead to unexpected results, so CSS1 resolves conflicts by selecting one rule which applies and ignoring all other rules. The way how this rule is selected is described in the following section.

6.3.5.3 Conflict resolution

The basic process for resolving conflicts consists of five steps, but this process is ended as soon as the conflicts are eliminated by reducing the choice of rules that apply to the element in question to one. Basically, the process is designed to built a set of rules and to apply certain criteria to this set defining a partial ordering on it, and to repeat this until a single rule is found which ranks highest according to a certain criterion.

1. *Find all the rules that apply*
   The first thing is to find all the rules which apply to the element in question. This is done by taking the selectors as described in section 6.3.2, which clearly define which rules apply to which elements. If no explicit rules apply to the element, inherited rules will be used.

2. *Sort the rules by explicit weight*
   It is possible to mark rules as being important to the style sheet designer by labeling them "!important". These rules are given precedence over

normal rules not having this label. If there is not more than one rule being marked as important (which is considered to be the normal case if this mechanism is used at all), the search ends here.

3. *Sort by origin*
   This step uses the origin of rules for defining an order on them. According to figure 6.11, the highest precedence is given to rules on the right side. Consequently, after this step, only rules from one style sheet are remaining in the set of rules which are taken into consideration.

4. *Sort by specificity*
   The specificity of a rule is determined by the generality of a rule. For example, a rule defined for "P" is more general than a rule defined for "LI P", since it applies to all paragraphs and not only the paragraphs in list items. The formal definition of the specificity of a rule is based on counting the number of ID and CLASS attributes (as described in section 6.3.2.2), and the number of element names in the selector (as described in sections 6.3.2.1 and 6.3.2.3)[30].

5. *Sort by order specified*
   The last step of the conflict resolution process sorts the rules by the order in which they were specified. Rules which are specified later in a style sheet have a higher precedence. Rules in imported style sheets[31] are considered to be before any rules in the style sheet itself.

The last rule ensures that conflict resolution will always be deterministic, because there is a clearly defined order of all the rules inside the style sheet. It should be noted, however, that this order in the style sheet is the last thing which is taken into consideration, so normally, conflict resolution will end at an earlier time and the order of rules inside a style sheet will not be significant.

6.4 Related approaches

CSS is only one possible way for defining style sheets, and although it certainly is the most widely known standard, there are other style sheet languages. HTML itself is not restricted to CSS, using the <LINK> element's TYPE attribute it is possible to define the style sheet language being used.

---

[30] These numbers are concatenated and a comparison is made based on this concatenated number, which means that a difference in the number of ID attributes will always outweigh everything else, and a difference in the number of CLASS attributes (if the number of ID attributes is the same) will always outweigh a difference in the number of element names in the selector.

[31] CSS1 defines a mechanism for the inclusion of style sheets into other style sheets by using the import command inside a style sheet.

Much more important than HTML's support for style sheet languages is the support which can be expected from browsers. At the time of writing, the two most important browsers, Netscape's Navigator and Microsoft's Internet Explorer, both implement subsets of CSS1, and it is very likely that the next versions will provide full support for CSS1 and maybe also limited support for CSS2.

The two other most important style sheet languages in the context of the web are much more complex, which is based on the fact that they are not limited to a certain document type. CSS can be rather simple because it is specifically tailored to HTML and has been optimized for the usage with this document type.

- *Document Style Semantics and Specification Language (DSSSL)* [127]
  This is the style language which has been defined for SGML, and although it is much more powerful than CSS (with every character being an element which has a number of properties which can be manipulated), it is also much more complex. The main reason for the greater complexity is that DSSSL has been designed to specify the formatting of any SGML document type rather than only one specific type (such as HTML).

- *Extensible Style Language (XSL)*
  XSL is the style language which has been defined for XML, it is described in section 7.5. XSL has been derived from DSSSL, and therefore inherits both its power and complexity.

Although there are other style languages, it seems very likely that CSS will be the language being used for HTML style sheets. In the context of the web, XSL will also be used for specifying style sheets for XML documents, but it is unlikely that CSS will be replaced by XSL, because XSL is much more complex and therefore more difficult to use and to implement.

6.5 Converting to CSS

With all the new possibilities which CSS offers, it is also an important question how migration can be done from HTML to HTML/CSS. Because of the limited support for CSS in the current browsers, it may be a little too early or at least not necessary to convert from HTML to HTML/CSS. However, once CSS support is available more widely, the increased formatting capabilities of HTML/CSS and the structural advantages of separating HTML content from CSS presentation information will encourage the use of HTML/CSS rather than simple HTML.

The HTML 4.0 standard already defines two different DTDs, the *transitional* and the *strict* DTD as described in section 5.2.1. While the transitional

DTD contains all the attributes and elements which have been used for specifying formatting before the invention of CSS, the strict DTD does not. As a general rule, the transitional DTD should be used for interpreting documents, while the strict DTD should be used for generating documents. This way it can be ensured that in new HTML documents no features are used which are only there for compatibility reasons with older versions.

If this procedure is taken as a guideline, it is also advisable to not only generate HTML pages, but also to start generating CSS style sheets together with these pages. Since CSS is not very old, the support for CSS in authoring tools and other web software is in an early stage. However, in the near future there will be tools which take existing web pages and try to separate content from presentation, producing HTML and CSS as output. Raggett [218] describes such a tool, called *HTML Tidy*, which currently only cleans up HTML code, but in the future will also be able to convert HTML documents to HTML/CSS.

In the long run, support for CSS will improve, resulting in tools which also support the creation and use of alternate and media dependent style sheets, thus managing a whole web site as a collection of HTML pages, which are linked to possibly multiple style sheets. Since a set of style sheets should be used consistently for a whole collection of web pages, tools for managing and structuring style sheets will soon emerge.

6.6 The future of CSS

The CSS1 standard has been finalized by the end of 1996. Currently, the most popular browsers, Netscape's Navigator 4.0 and Microsoft's Internet Explorer 4.0, both implement CSS1, but only a (although substantial) subset of it. It is foreseeable that CSS1 will not be the style sheet standard for a long time, and in this section we will take a short look at two newer developments, *Cascading Style Sheets Positioning (CSS-P)* described in section 6.6.1, and *Cascading Style Sheets, level 2 (CSS2)* described in section 6.6.2. Another interesting development in the area of style sheet languages is the *Extensible Style Language (XSL)*, but this language is more related to XML and is therefore described in section 7.5.

6.6.1 Cascading Style Sheets Positioning (CSS-P)

Netscape's Navigator 4.0 currently implements a subset of CSS1 and also some additional functionality which has been invented by Netscape. Netscape has issued the specification of this functionality, called *Cascading Style Sheets Positioning (CSS-P)*, as a W3C working draft [255], but it never made its way into a new version of CSS1. However, the ideas of CSS-P were used as input for CSS2 (described in the following section), so they are part of a standard now.

However, because CSS-P appeared as an idea of its own and also is implemented in a very popular browser, we describe it very shortly. The two main ideas of CSS-P are the definition of additional positioning capabilities (in addition to the spacing model defined by CSS1) and the introduction of a third axis, thus facilitating layering.

- *Relative positioning*
  Elements with relative positioning flow into place just like any other HTML, and can be positioned relative to their natural position within the document flow. When these elements are positioned, they keep their naturally rendered shape, including line breaks, and the space originally reserved for them remains. Any following elements do not re-flow.

- *Absolute positioning*
  Elements with absolute positioning are formatted as rectangular overlays, outside the normal flow of the document, into which their contents flow. An absolutely positioned element is laid out independently of both its parent and child elements, without regard for their dimensions or position. For that matter, the layout of each absolutely positioned element is independent of any others.

Since absolute positioning almost unavoidably introduces the overlapping of element content, it is necessary to also think about *layering*. CSS-P therefore introduces a z-axis and also defines the default ordering of elements among this axis and furthermore ways to change that ordering.

6.6.2 Cascading Style Sheets, level 2 (CSS2)

Since the finalization of CSS1, the authors of this standard were working on the next level of CSS, known under the name *Cascading Style Sheets, level 2 (CSS2)* [25]. Working through W3C's normal process of working drafts and proposed recommendation, CSS2 reached the final status as a W3C recommendation in May 1998. CSS2 is much more powerful (and complex) than CSS1, therefore the following list is not exhaustive, but it summarizes all the important improvements of CSS2 over CSS1.

- *Media types*
  In CSS1, there is no concept of media types, the only way how media types are supported is through the use of different style sheets from within the HTML document. CSS2 introduces the concept of media types, allowing

the use of a single style sheet for different media. This may be useful because style sheets for different media may share a number of properties and differ in others, which can be specified in CSS2. Furthermore, CSS2 defines a number of properties (such as volume for aural presentation) which only apply to a limited set of media. In order to make the creation of media-dependent style sheets more effective, CSS2 also introduces the concept of media groups. Media groups make it possible to share some properties among a set (but not all) media defined by CSS2.

- *Paged media*
  Together with the concept of media types, CSS2 also introduces the concept of paged media (which is one media group which contrasts continuous media such as a web browser's scrollable window). Paged media require a number of new properties which make it possible to specify how a document is broken into pages and how these pages should be formatted.

- *Tables*
  In CSS1, tables cannot be formatted using style sheets, because CSS1 does not define special table properties[32]. CSS2 introduces a number of properties for the formatting tables. This allows the separation of content and presentation for tables as well.

- *Positioning*
  CSS2 introduces the concept of *absolute positioning*, where it is possible to determine the position of an element independent from the normal flow of formatting. Also new in CSS2 is the definition of *fixed positioning*, which is a variant of absolute positioning where the position of an element is determined with respect to the viewport[33].

- *Selectors*
  In addition to the selectors of CSS1 (as described in section 6.3.2), CSS2 defines a number of new selectors. *Child selectors* match if an element is the child of some element. *Adjacent selectors* match if two elements have the same parent in the document tree and the first element immediately precedes the second element of the selector. *Attribute selectors* may be used to specify rules that match attributes defined in the source document.

- *Generated content*
  It is easy to think of a number of applications which make it necessary to insert content for a presentation which is not part of the initial

---

[32] However, table content (such as text or images) can be formatted using CSS1, but there is no way to change the appearance of a table itself with CSS1.

[33] User agents for continuous media generally offer users a viewport (a window or other viewing area on the screen) through which users see a document. User agents may change the document's layout when the viewport is resized.

document[34]. CSS2 defines a mechanism (including new *pseudo-elements*) which makes it possible to insert content before or after elements.

- *Automated numbering*
  There are also a number of applications (such as lists or chapter or section headings) where *automated numbering* is very useful. CSS2 defines a mechanism for generating numbers (which can be regarded as a generalization of generated content), making it possible to insert not only fixed content, but to use counters which are incremented according to a style sheet's specifications.

- *Pseudo-classes*
  Interactive user agents sometimes change the rendering in response to user actions. CSS2 provides three new pseudo-classes for common cases, which are a class for an element being pointed to (but not selected) with a pointing device, an element being activated with a pointing device (such as a mouse click), and an element having the input focus (such as a text box which accepts input from the keyboard). Furthermore, CSS2 defines a pseudo-class which can be used to match an element depending on its language (if this information is provided in the document).

Netscape has already announced that the next version of their Navigator browser will fully support CSS1 and also provide partial CSS2 support, and it is likely that the new major versions of Netscape's and Microsoft's browser will offer only limited CSS2 support, in the same way that they now offer only limited CSS1 support. However, in the long run CSS2 will replace CSS1 because of its better functionality. However, the increased functionality also increases implementation times and costs, so it will be a while until full CSS2 support is really available, ranging from browsers to authoring tools and style sheet management systems.

---

[34] A simple example is the requirement to insert the string "Example:" before every paragraph which is of class `example`.

7. Extensible Markup Language (XML)

Seeing that HTML implements only one particular document model, the *Extensible Markup Language (XML)* has been defined, making it possible to use documents of *application-specific document types*, which can be created, distributed, and interpreted in an XML environment.

An additional benefit of XML is its design as a general *data structuring language*, which means that it can be used for structured information other than documents as well. In the following discussion of XML, the main focus is on the application-specific document type aspect of XML, but it should always be kept in mind that XML is not limited to this application area.

Although the *Standard Generalized Markup Language (SGML)* would have served the same purpose as XML. XML is a subset of SGML that was defined to avoid some of the complexity of SGML, and to allow some ways of usage which would not have been possible with full SGML. Thus, the design of XML was motivated by two observations:

- *The inflexibility of HTML*
  Although HTML has evolved into a rich language for structuring documents, it still defines only one particular document type. This document type is appropriate for a large number of applications, but still a considerable number of applications could benefit from a more flexible (ie, application-specific) way of structuring documents.
  Furthermore, a number of web technologies are in need of a general data structuring language, and a language as document-specific as HTML is not usable for these technologies.

- *The complexity of SGML*
  SGML, which is the base of HTML, is a mechanism to specify structuring rules for arbitrary structured data. However, SGML is rather complex and contains a number of features which make SGML processing software hard to implement. By omitting these features (without sacrificing any of SGML's functionality to specify arbitrary data types), an easier to use language can be created which still has all the structural power of SGML.

XML can be used to specify application-specific document types, and one example of such a document types is an XML variant of HTML. Future versions of HTML may very well be based on XML, allowing a modular approach and easy extensibility. Furthermore, some proposals for data structures on the web already use XML as their foundation (one example is the *Resource Description Framework (RDF)* as described in section 10.5.3).

Since mapping existing data structures to XML DTDs in many cases is a rather simple task, the transition between existing systems and XML can in many cases be made easily. However, it will take some time until XML itself and the whole family of XML specifications is in a state where XML is as widely accepted and as widely usable as HTML. Especially the formatting of XML documents is something which still is in a rather early development phase.

Section 7.1 gives an introduction to the basic principles of XML. It gives a practically oriented description of the applications areas which can benefit from using XML. Although the term XML often is used to refer to the whole set of XML standards, technically speaking XML only defines the SGML subset which is described in section 7.2. The other standards which also belong to the set of XML recommendations are described in subsequent sections.

There are two related concepts which together constitute the *Extensible Linking Language (XLL)*. These concepts are the *XML Linking Language (XLink)*, describing how to embed links into XML documents, and the *XML Pointer Language (XPointer)*, describing how to point into XML documents. XLink is described in section 7.3, while section 7.4 gives an overview of XPointer. Both specifications are currently working drafts and are therefore still subject to modifications.

The last important component of the set of XML recommendations is the *Extensible Style Language (XSL)* described in section 7.5, which is a user-extensible and primarily declarative mechanism for adding style information to XML documents. Since XSL currently is the least stable and developed part of the XML framework, the description is mainly an overview about the functionality that XSL is supposed to provide.

Since XML is a new language which can be used to distribute documents on the web, it is important to see it in perspective with the already existing languages HTML and SGML. Such a comparison is given in section 7.6. Finally, some remarks about the future of XML are given in section 7.7.

7.1 Principles of XML

The general idea of XML is to free web publishers from the limitations of the single document type provided by HTML. The basic architecture of HTML-based web publishing is shown in figure 4.5 (on page 152), which shows that both the SGML declaration and the DTD are built into the application program (eg, the publishing tool or the browser). A more general approach is depicted in figure 4.4, where only the SGML declaration is built into the application, and both the DTD and the document are provided as input to the parser. This design is the general idea of XML, as shown in figure 7.1.

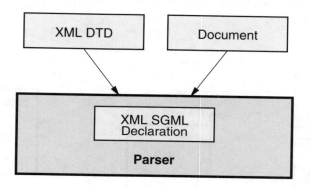

Fig. 7.1 An XML parser

In the following sections it is described how XML can be used in the context of the web. First of all, in section 7.1.1 it is explained why the ability to create custom document types is an advantage and can be beneficial in many application areas.

However, the increased flexibility of XML also results in an increase in complexity of the web infrastructure. While for HTML the set of elements is clearly defined, and the HTML standard also defines formatting rules for these elements, in case of XML no such fixed definition is possible, since elements are defined by users in application-specific DTDs. In section 7.1.2, it is described how this problem can be solved.

XML can be seen as a language for the definition of custom data structures. As such it relates to other data structuring mechanisms (such as document architectures or databases) and, in particular, HTML as the document structuring language of the web. In section 7.1.3, it is described how XML fits into this picture, and how data conversion between XML and other formats can be done.

7.1.1 Creating document types

Before the invention of XML, the most common way of publishing structured content on the web was to use HTML as shown in figure 5.11 (on page 255).

The usual publishing process (if not directly authoring in HTML) in this scenario is to define a mapping between the custom document type and HTML, and to use this mapping to convert documents from the custom format to HTML. The big disadvantage with this approach is the inflexibility of HTML, which is a single fixed document type. For many mainly text-based custom document types, a mapping between such a type and HTML may be easy to define, but in most cases structural information will be lost during the conversion process.

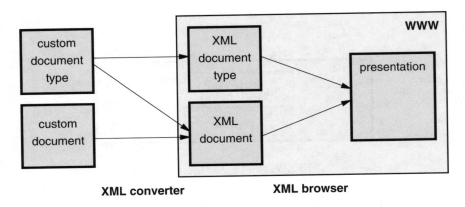

Fig. 7.2   Publishing with XML

For example, if a custom document type contains three different types of paragraphs, these types will usually be mapped to the <P> element which represents paragraphs in HTML. Using XML, it is no longer necessary to lose structural information because of mappings like this. As shown in figure 7.2, it is possible to define a custom document type which contains three different element types for paragraphs. The conversion software converts the custom document type to an XML DTD, and documents to XML documents using this DTD, which can afterwards be processed on XML systems (in particular, viewed with XML browsers). The structural information about three different types of paragraphs is still present in the XML documents, using different XML elements for each of the paragraph types.

This possibility of creating and exchanging custom document types makes publishing on the web more expressive (since the XML DTD can be designed to preserve all of the structure which is expressed in the custom document type) and more flexible.

Apart from being a mechanism for document representation, XML can also be used for other application areas. Technically, an XML DTD is a *grammar*, making it possible to define data structures. In many cases, these data structures will be used for representing documents, but XML itself makes no assumptions about the semantics of the data, so it is possible to represent other types of structured information using XML. Examples for other uses of XML are the *Resource Description Framework (RDF)* as described in section 10.5.3, and one part of the XML infrastructure itself, the *Extensible Style Language (XSL)*.

7.1.2 Formatting of XML documents

Moving away from HTML's fixed document model also means moving away from HTML's fixed rules how to format a document. Although HTML is designed as a language for content rather than presentation, it also associates presentation semantics with all elements. These semantics are not part of the HTML DTD (which only defines the elements and the structuring rules for these elements), instead they are defined in the text of the HTML specification which describes the intended use and presentation for every element.

A browser retrieving an HTML document from a web server has built-in presentation rules which are used to format the document (possibly using a style sheet associated with the document). With the loss of predefined formatting semantics of elements when using XML, the problem arises how to interpret an XML document. An XML browser has no built-in rules, it does not even know the elements of the document until it analyzes the DTD. Basically, there are two approaches to deal with that situation. The first approach is to focus on content, in which case no presentation information is necessary. This approach is described in section 7.1.2.1. The second approach is the definition of a mechanism which associates presentation rules with the elements, this alternative is described in section 7.1.2.2.

7.1.2.1 Focusing on content

The original design goal of the web was the construction of a distributed hypermedia system which could be used for globally accessing information in a platform-independent way. Because of this goal, the separation of content and presentation has always been an important issue in web technology. An XML document with no associated presentation rules is only content and structure, nothing is known about its presentation. However, it is less informative than HTML because the semantics of the elements are not known.

For example, a program which does not implement any presentation for HTML still can be used to search through documents using HTML semantics, for example rating search terms found in headings higher than those found in normal paragraphs. This is not possible for XML documents, since there are no semantics associated with the elements inside a document[1]. However, it is still possible to interpret XML documents as structured information, and in many cases this may be sufficient, even without any semantics or presentation rules. An XML document looks very much like a normal SGML document, but it is started by a *processing instruction* containing the specification of the XML version. XML processing instructions are enclosed between a *processing instruction open* delimiter (PIO) and a *processing instruction close* delimiter (PIC), which are represented by the character sequences '<?' and '?>'[2].

```
<?xml version="1.0"?>
<result>
<item><name>Wilde</name><email>dret@tik.ee.ethz.ch</email></item>
<item><name>Puder</name><email>puder@icsi.berkeley.edu</email></item>
</result>
```

The most obvious observation is that this document uses full markup, which is a general rule of XML (in contrast to HTML's markup minimization). Although not associated with any formal semantics, such an XML document could be interpreted by a human user without many problems. And it could be displayed by an XML browser in a structured way (somehow representing its tree structure as shown in figure 7.3).

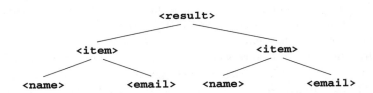

Fig. 7.3 Structure of a small XML document

Since XML allows the DTD to be part of the document, the example given above could also be represented as the following XML document. In this case, it would be possible for the XML application to show which other element types are allowed (but not used) in the document.

```
<?xml version="1.0"?>
<!DOCTYPE result [
  <!ELEMENT result (item*) >
  <!ELEMENT item    (name,phone?,email?)+ >
```

---

[1] Clearly, from the author's point of view, there are semantics associated with the elements inside a document, but XML only provides a platform for exchanging the syntactic structure of the document.

[2] This differs from the SGML reference concrete syntax, where the *processing instruction close* delimiter (PIC) is '>'.

```
<!ELEMENT name   (#PCDATA) >
<!ELEMENT phone  (#PCDATA) >
<!ELEMENT email  (#PCDATA) >
]>
<result>
<item><name>Wilde</name><email>dret@tik.ee.ethz.ch</email></item>
<item><name>Puder</name><email>puder@icsi.berkeley.edu</email></item>
</result>
```

Receiving a document like this, an XML application can not only display the document in a structured way, but the XML software can also create other documents conforming to the DTD. The distinction between the two cases (unknown or known DTD) is important, because XML software has no possibility to infer the DTD from the document alone. For example, the following XML DTD also allows to create the document shown in figure 7.3.

```
<!DOCTYPE result [
  <!ELEMENT result (item+) >
  <!ELEMENT item   (name,(phone|email)*)+ >
  <!ELEMENT name   (#PCDATA) >
  <!ELEMENT phone  (#PCDATA) >
  <!ELEMENT email  (#PCDATA) >
]>
```

However, in all these cases, the only information exchanged is document content (and maybe the rules which have been used for structuring the document content). Although this may be sufficient for some applications, in many cases it is also necessary to provide presentation rules which can be used for formatting the document. These rules must be specified in a form which is understood by XML applications.

7.1.2.2 Using style sheet languages

The approach of style sheet languages has already been described in chapter 6, discussing *Cascading Style Sheets (CSS)*. However, CSS primarily has been designed to tune the fine points of the presentation of HTML documents. With XML, a more general approach is required, because the assumptions which can be made about the basic formatting of HTML elements (such as the basic formatting of lists, where CSS can be used to change the characters in front of list items and other aspects of the list formatting), are not possible for XML documents.

Although CSS may be not powerful enough in some cases (a more general approach, the *Extensible Style Language (XSL)*, is described in section 7.5), it is sufficient to demonstrate the concept of content and presentation in an XML environment. And in cases where presentation similar to HTML documents is sufficient, users may choose to use CSS rather than the more complex

XSL. The general model of the publishing process in an XML environment including a style sheet language (in this case showing XSL as the style sheet language of choice) is shown in figure 7.4.

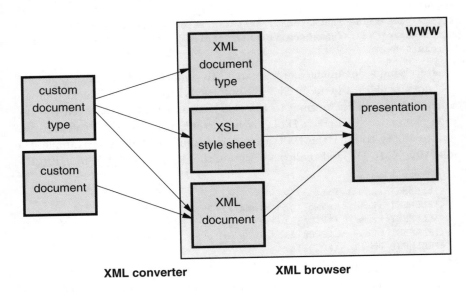

Fig. 7.4 Publishing with XML/XSL

The general idea of a style sheet language for XML is the same as it is for HTML, which is the separation of content and presentation. In XML, however, the situation is a bit different from HTML. The default presentation for HTML documents (ie, for HTML documents which do not contain any formatting attributes or style sheet information) is based on the semantics of HTML elements, displaying lists as sequences of indented list items and tables as rectangular grids of table cells. A default presentation for XML documents, however, is much simpler, because there is no information which could be used for formatting[3].

Consequently, it is very likely that XML documents in many cases are used in conjunction with style sheet information. This may be, in a simple case, a CSS style sheet, which assigns HTML-like formatting properties to XML elements. Although such a document may be displayed exactly like an HTML document (because it uses the same formatting mechanisms and

---

[3] Browsers could, of course, make assumptions about formatting or simply display every element as an individual paragraph. However, since there is no semantics associated with XML elements on which to base assumptions, this method would in many cases be inappropriate.

options as HTML's CSS), it is still richer in content, because the elements can be more descriptive than HTML elements (for example, using the different types of paragraphs mentioned above).

```
item  { display: block; margin-bottom: 5mm }
name  { display: list-item; font-weight: bold }
phone { display: list-item; font-style: italic }
email { display: list-item; text-decoration: underline }
```

A simple CSS style sheet like this could be used to set some basic presentation preferences for the example introduced in the previous section. The processing of such a document could be more specific (although it would be displayed like an HTML unordered list), for example allowing searches only within name elements. Furthermore, if the document has to be converted to another format, maybe into some kind of database, the information associated with the XML elements is invaluable, because a simple HTML list would not contain the information about the content of the individual list items.

7.1.3 Conversion

Seeing XML as yet another language for coding structured information, one of the first questions that come to mind is the question of how XML fits into the existing formats which are in use for the same purposes. First, it is important to notice that XML has a number of features which are not common in all formats, and that there is no format which has all these features.

- *Self-describing documents*
  XML's ability to include DTDs inside the document make it possible to create self-describing documents. This means that a single XML document can contain the rules that were used to compose the document (ie, the DTD) as well as the actual document content.

- *Browseable document structure*
  Since XML does not include the markup minimization features of SGML, XML software can easily analyze an XML document, even if it does not contain a DTD. Consequently, even documents which are not self-describing by including a DTD still can be interpreted and browsed using the descriptive XML syntax.

- *Powerful linking*
  XML together with the *XML Linking Language (XLink)* and *XML Pointer Language (XPointer)* specifications defines a very flexible and powerful model for creating links from and to XML documents as well as other resources available on the Internet.

- *Easy conversion to web data formats*
  Since XML is based on SGML (which is the base of HTML) and will probably be integrated into future versions of browsers, the conversion between in-house data[4] and data to be published on the web will most often be very simple.

- *Platform-independence*
  XML is an open standard and can therefore be implemented by anyone interested in XML applications. The advantage over a product is the independence from a specific platform or a specific vendor. The future development of XML will show how many XML applications will be available.

All these issues are important advantages of XML. However, today many in-house applications are based on other data formats. For some time to come, converting between other data formats and XML will therefore be an issue.

In section 7.1.3.1, the issues which arise when other formats are converted to XML are described. This conversion is the process of importing documents into XML environments and will be the activity which is most important when XML is chosen as the new format in an information processing environment. Conversion from other formats to XML is also important if data from an in-house application has to be published on the web using XML instead of HTML.

Since XML allows the creation of custom document types, there also will be a large number of conversions between XML documents, converting an XML document of one document type to an XML document of another document type. These conversions are described in section 7.1.3.2.

In section 7.1.3.3, the question of converting XML documents to other formats is discussed, which can be seen as exporting documents from an XML environment. Because HTML is by far the most popular SGML document type, in section 7.1.3.4 it is specifically described what is necessary for conversions between HTML and XML.

7.1.3.1 Other formats to XML

The general process of converting other formats to XML is shown in figures 7.2 and 7.4 (depending on whether a style sheet language is being used).

---

[4] The term *in-house data* is used to describe data formats being used in in-house data processing applications. These applications normally use proprietary data formats which can only be processed by a specific product or product range (usually from a single vendor). Another term often used for this kind of systems (in contrast to more open systems using open standard formats) is the term *legacy systems*.

Although these figures are focused on web publishing (ie, converting to XML for the purpose of making documents available on the web), a more general view of converting other formats to XML also includes a conversion of in-house data from some other format to XML.

In both cases, a mapping from the in-house format to XML must be defined, both for the document types (or the database schema, if a more general view is applied), and the individual documents. However, two different strategies are required in both scenarios.

- *Converting for publishing*
  If XML is only chosen as a publishing tool, the mapping between the in-house format and XML has to be designed in a way that all information which should be made available on the web has to be mapped to XML. This means that the XML DTD to be defined should cover all the structural aspects to be published, and that the documents must be converted accordingly. In most cases, this also includes the design of style sheets which are used to control the presentation of XML documents as shown in figure 7.4.

- *Converting for in-house use*
  If the goal is to replace the in-house format with XML, it is important to make sure that no information is lost during the conversion. Therefore, the creation of appropriate and well-designed XML DTDs is essential, and this is the part of the conversion process which should be approached with great care. Once a set of XML DTDs is defined, a mapping between in-house data and XML should be fairly easy[5]. Once the conversion is finished, web publishing becomes an easy XML to XML conversion task as described in section 7.1.3.2.

As can be seen, both application scenarios of a conversion process from an in-house format to XML have different focuses. While converting for publishing focuses on the selection of relevant information and its presentation, the focus of converting for in-house use is the creation of XML DTDs which fully represent the data structures to be captured.

7.1.3.2 XML to XML

If the in-house format already is XML, in many cases conversions from XML are necessary, either to exchange data with other XML-based applications, or to publish XML data on the web. Conversion between different XML DTDs in many cases will include a loss of information. This is either intentional

---

[5] If such a mapping is not easy, this may indicate that the XML DTDs should be redesigned.

(because not all data available in-house should be published) or dictated by the conversion (if the DTD which is used as target is structurally less rich than the origin).

In most cases, XML conversion is a mapping between different DTDs (maybe also involving style sheets), and as long as the conversion is based on a clearly defined mapping between the DTDs, it can be fully automated. However, it is possible that some conversions will require human intervention, for example when the conversion target DTD requires some information which can not be automatically retrieved from the origin.

7.1.3.3 XML to other formats

The conversion of XML to other formats can be seen as the export of data from an XML environment. Usually, this means that a converter has to be used which maps XML DTDs to the structuring mechanisms of the target format. Depending on the target format, the design of such a converter is of varying difficulty.

If the target format is as structurally rich as XML (ie, it allows the same document type structures as XML) or richer, the design of an conversion component is fairly easy. It is mostly a question of mapping the syntax of XML DTDs and XML documents to the target format.

However, if the target format is structurally less rich than XML, it can be hard to automatically convert XML DTDs to the target format. In this case, it may be necessary to manually design the target format data structure, since most likely some structural information will be lost during the conversion, and the decision how this should be done in the most graceful way can be complicated.

7.1.3.4 HTML and XML

Although HTML is, from XML's point of view, an external format (since HTML is not an XML application), it is very close to XML and also will often be the candidate for conversion from and to XML. Therefore, this section is included, specifically dealing with the conversion of HTML and XML. The first issue is the design of an XML variant of HTML, afterwards the conversion process in both directions is discussed.

An XML HTML DTD

In many cases, conversions between HTML and XML will only be necessary to comply to the different syntactic rules of HTML and XML, which imply that a valid XML document is not valid HTML, and that a valid HTML document is not valid XML. The easiest way out of this dilemma is to design an XML DTD for HTML (called XHTML in the following text), which simply is an adoption of the HTML DTD (which is based on SGML) to XML.

Since HTML makes heavy use of some of the features of SGML which are not allowed in XML, it is necessary that these features are eliminated from the original HTML DTD in order to make it XML compliant. A number of steps are necessary to make the current HTML specification (HTML 4.0) XML-compatible, and unfortunately, the resulting DTD will represent a document type which is different from HTML 4.0[6].

Conversion from HTML to XHTML

The conversion from HTML to XML is in most cases a process which will reveal that many documents which are supposed to be HTML are actually only close to HTML. As described in sections 4.3.3 and 5.4, many web pages are not valid HTML and are only displayed correctly because most web browsers are very error-tolerant implementations of HTML parsers. The two principal error sources are SGML errors (failure to comply to SGML syntax), and the usage of non-standard HTML extensions. Since it is likely that a converter used to convert HTML to XHTML also has to deal with technically invalid HTML pages, it should be designed so that it is as error-tolerant as a web browser. It could also implement a superset of HTML, including non-standard but widely used HTML extensions.

The second step after accepting a document as input is the generation of XHTML. This step includes the inclusion of omitted tags, the XML-compliant specification of attribute values, and a number of other syntactic conversions which are necessary for valid XML. Depending on the definition of XHTML, it could also be necessary to change the document structure, maybe omitting non-standard HTML extensions (or replacing them by XML versions of standard HTML elements).

After this conversion process, an XHTML document has been produced. It should be kept in mind that XHTML (at least at the moment) is not a standard, but simply a user-defined XML version of the HTML specification. Two XML designers, when asked to create a DTD which represents HTML in XML will very likely produce two different XHTML DTDs. However, since the user-defined version of XHTML can be distributed which each converted document[7], there is no need for a unique definition.

---

[6] This is the result of XML's restrictions of *occurrence indicators, exceptions,* and *attribute types.* An explanation of these differences can be found in section 7.2.1.

[7] Since DTDs (as XHTML) can be quite large, it is also possible to only include a URI reference to the DTD in the XML document and to make the DTD available at this URI.

Conversion from XHTML to HTML

The conversion process from XHTML to HTML usually will be easier than
the other direction, since XML documents are required to be well-formed (ie,
they do not use tag omission or attribute name omission), so all there is to
do is to remove the XML-specific syntax from the XHTML document (which
basically means to change the document preamble from XML to HTML and
to change the syntax of empty elements).

Depending on the design of the XHTML DTD, it may be necessary to
also perform some structural changes, such as converting some elements of
the XHTML DTD to other elements of the HTML standard. However, if
the XHTML DTD is properly designed, this step should be minimal or even
non-existent.

7.2 Extensible Markup Language 1.0 (XML 1.0)

After the introduction to the general principles of XML, now a more technical description of the language is given, which is formally defined in a W3C
recommendation [36]. As said before, XML is based on SGML [110] as described in chapter 4, and it is assumed that the reader is familiar with the
general principles and the syntax of SGML.

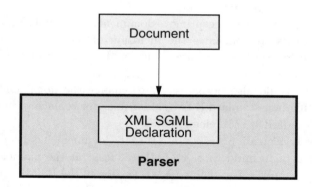

Fig. 7.5 An XML parser for well-formed XML documents

One of the major differences to SGML is that XML always requires full
markup (which means that the OMITTAG and SHORTTAG features which are
known from HTML do not work with XML[8]). The only mechanism of markup

---

[8] The technical reason for this is the XML SGML declaration, which does not
enable these features. Although the SHORTTAG feature is enabled, it is explicitly

minimization defined by SGML allowed in XML is the *null end-tags* feature (SGML's markup minimization features are explained in section 4.2.1.4). However, even this feature is only allowed for empty elements. Using this feature, the closing delimiters of instances of empty elements can be changed to the '/>' character sequence in the following way:

```
...empty elements in XML may marked up using the usual
full SGML markup <br></br> or may be marked up using the
special null end-tags markup <br/>.
```

All features of markup minimization other than that, such as tag omission and attribute name omission, are not allowed in XML documents. There are two major reasons for making the XML standard in this case noticeably different from the known practice on the web:

- *Easier processing*
  SGML's markup minimization features make the parsing of a document much harder than the parsing of a document using full markup. Furthermore, the features do not add any structural advantages over documents using full markup, they simply save some keystrokes, thus making typing SGML documents more efficient and error tolerant from the author's point of view.

- *Self-describing documents*
  One design goal of XML was to make XML documents as accessible as possible. This includes the goal to be able to browse through XML documents even without a DTD, which is only possible if the document is fully marked up. Documents using full markup can be interpreted unambiguously, and a browser can display the document tree (ie, the hierarchical structure of elements) although the rules which were used to create this structure (ie, the DTD) are unknown.

Using this new property of XML documents, XML defines two different types of documents, depending on whether the DTD of a document is available or not:

- *Well-formed documents*
  A well-formed XML document is one that is syntactically correct, whether or not it has been checked against a DTD. In order to be syntactically correct XML, all elements must be neatly nested, and all entities referenced by the document must have been properly declared. Figure 7.5 shows the processing of a well-formed XML document. The XML parser uses

---

stated in the XML specification that this is only done to allow *null end-tags*, all other SHORTTAG features are not allowed.

the XML SGML declaration and parses the document without having a DTD.

However, it should be noted that some information contained in the DTD may be necessary to correctly interpret a well-formed XML document, such as default attribute values, and entities referenced in the document. Therefore, only for a limited number of applications well-formed XML documents will be used.

- *Valid documents*
  A valid XML document is a well-formed XML document that also has been validated against a DTD. It has been processed in the usual parsing process as shown in figure 7.1, where the parser uses the DTD to check whether the document complies to the rules defined by the DTD[9].

Since XML is fairly new, it is not yet clear how XML will be used in the web. However, it is assumed that HTML will remain the standard format for simpler documents for some time, and that only applications depending on a richer document structure will use XML. Therefore, XML will mainly be used for applications which before the invention of XML may have relied on SGML. It is therefore useful to give a comparison between XML and SGML, contained in section 7.2.1.

7.2.1 Differences to SGML

This section is not intended to give a complete list of all differences between XML and SGML. A comparison of SGML and XML carried out by Clark [46] provides a complete and detailed list of all differences between these two standards. Instead, the intention is to provide a short list of the most important differences between these two languages.

- *Connectors*
  Whereas the SGML *seq* connector (SEQ) and the *or* connector (OR), represented by the ',' and '|' characters, are allowed in XML, the *and* connector (AND), usually represented by the '&' character, can not be used. Content models must be designed in a way which only uses the SEQ and OR connectors.

- *Markup minimization*
  Although the XML SGML declaration enables the SHORTTAG feature, all markup minimization which usually is allowed when SHORTTAG is enabled

---

[9] Using this terminology, HTML documents are always valid (or not valid), since the DTD is known to the parser, that can therefore always validate the HTML document against it.

is disallowed, with the exception of the *null end-tag* delimiter (NET). Null end-tags delimiters (represented by the '/>' character sequence) can only be used to close an empty element[10].

- *Processing instruction delimiters*
  In the SGML reference concrete syntax, the *processing instruction close* delimiter (PIC) is represented by the '>' character. In XML, the *processing instruction close* delimiter (PIC) is represented by the '?>' character sequence.

- *Element type declarations*
  In XML it is not possible to use an element type declaration for a group of elements. Consequently, each element type in XML must have its own element type declaration.

- *No exceptions*
  It is not possible to use exceptions (as described in section 4.2.2.4) in element type declarations. It is therefore not possible to use inclusions and exclusions, thus making it necessary to explicitly declare the allowed content of each element type in the model group.

- *Attribute definition list declarations*
  XML does not allow all attribute declared values which are specified in SGML. In particular, the attribute declared values NUTOKEN, NUTOKENS, NUMBER, NUMBERS, NAME, and NAMES are not allowed. In addition, XML does not allow attributes to have a #CURRENT default value.
  Furthermore, it is not possible to use attribute definition list declarations for a group of elements. Consequently, each element type in XML must have its own attribute definition list declaration.

In addition to these major differences, there are also some more small differences between SGML and XML. It should be noted that for a proper definition of XML, the complete specification has to be consulted. It is not sufficient to look at the SGML declaration listed in appendix C.1. This means that an SGML parser using the XML SGML declaration is not a fully validating XML parser, since XML specifies more things than can be expressed through the SGML declaration.

7.3 XML Linking Language (XLink)

XML specifies how a document type's structure can be freely defined using an XML DTD, at the same time making it impossible for XML applications

---

[10] XML differs from the SGML reference concrete syntax, which defines the *null end-tag* delimiter (NET) to be the slash character '/'.

to know the semantics of XML elements and attributes, because these are entirely application-specific[11]. However, in order to use links within XML documents, and to have these links recognized by applications (eg, XML browsers expected to present XML links differently from other elements, and associating actions with links, the actions being either automatic or initiated by the user), it is necessary to have a defined framework which makes it possible for XML applications to recognize and interpret links within XML documents. This framework is defined by the *XML Linking Language (XLink)*, which defines how to insert links into XML documents. Currently, XLink is defined by a W3C draft recommendation [165].

XLink is one part of the *Extensible Linking Language (XLL)*, a term which is frequently used to refer to XLink and the *XML Pointer Language (XPointer)* as described in section 7.4. XPointer defines how to point into XML documents, effectively describing how to use URI fragment identifiers for XML documents.

XLink's linking model is based on HyTime [132], HTML's link mechanisms, and the linking mechanisms defined by the *Text Encoding Initiative Guidelines (TEI P3)* [248].

In section 7.3.1, XLink's linking concepts are explained, which are a generalization of HTML's rather simple linking concept. In section 7.3.2, the information which XLink associates with links is described. XLink defines different types of links, described in section 7.3.3. The actual integration of XLink into XML is done with special attributes, which are explained in section 7.3.4.

7.3.1 Linking concepts

Conceptually, a link between a number of entities (such as a web page containing a link, and another web page to which the link points) does not have to be part of any of these entities. Although HTML's linking concept only supports the usage of links which are part of an entity they are linking[12], it is possible to define more general concepts. In section 7.3.1.1 it is described why and how HTML's concept of the location of links can be extended to a more general model.

Another limitation of HTML links is that only links connecting two resources are allowed, and that these links are always unidirectional, meaning that it is only possible to follow these links in one direction. It is possible

---

[11] In HTML, this is not a problem, because all elements and attributes are specified within the HTML standard and the semantics are clearly defined.

[12] The <LINK> element is part of the document it links to another document, and the <A> element contains the resource (often an image or a small amount of text which is enclosed inside the element) it links to another entity.

to define concepts which are less restrictive, and these generalizations of the link topology are described in section 7.3.1.2.

7.3.1.1 Link location

In HTML, links are always part of the resource they are linking. Links specified with the <LINK> element link the whole document to another resource and are specified in the document head. Links specified with the <A> element represent a link from the element's content (which usually is HTML, with the exception of clickable images) to another resource. In all cases, the link is inextricably inserted into the HTML document. For some applications, this is adequate, but in other application areas this can be a severe limitation. Consequently, XLink defines a link type which is not part of the resource it is linking.

Inline links

This is the simpler type of link, which is comparable to the links provided in HTML. An inline link is part of the resource it is linking (eg, in HTML, a link using the <A> element links the content of the element itself to the resource specified in the element's HREF attribute). Because of this design, simple links can be used very easily (they are integrated into the document) and are suitable for applications where the restrictions of the inline link model are acceptable. The inline link model is very asymmetrical, since it tightly bounds the link to one resource.

Out-of-line links

While inline links are part of the resource they are linking, out-of-line links are specified elsewhere. This difference between inline links and out-of-line links is shown in figure 7.6. It should be noticed that out-of-line links not necessarily are outside of the document for which they define links. However, this is possible and since XLink also includes this generalization, for this discussion we assume that out-of-line links are outside of the documents for which they define links.

The main question which arises when introducing the concept of out-of-line links is how these links can be found, because they are no longer part of the resource they are linking. Since it is practically impossible to search for out-of-line links without prior knowledge, a model including out-of-line links also has to include mechanisms to refer to out-of-line links. This introduces a second level of indirection, since now it is necessary to point to out-of-line links, something which could also be regarded as creating a link to

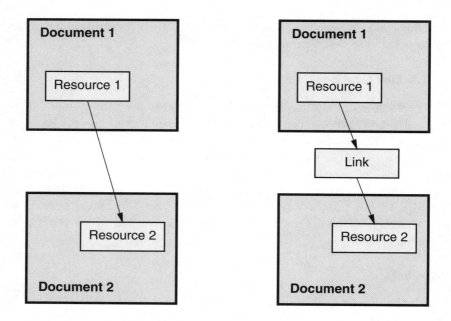

Fig. 7.6 Out-of-line links

links[13]. However, such an increase in complexity is unavoidable if the goal is
to decouple resources and links. The model of out-of-line links leaves it open
whether a document itself contains a pointer to these links, or if the links are
located by another mechanism.

If out-of-line links cause such an increase in complexity of the linking
model, there must be a good motivation to use them. There are application areas which can only be adequately addressed using out-of-line links,
so the increase in complexity is justified by the greater number of possible
applications.

- *Multidirectional links*

  In section 7.3.1.2 it is described that there are link topologies which are
  more general than HTML's linking model, in particular multidirectional
  links. Since it is not practical to assign a multidirectional link to one of
  the resources it is linking (which would be necessary if inline links were
  being used, because the multidirectional link would have to be specified
  as part of one of the resources it is linking), the only way to represent

---

[13] It is important to notice that in the figures shown in this and the subsequent
sections, only the link semantics are depicted by arrows, and not the mechanism
to locate out-of-line links.

multidirectional links in a structurally sound way is to use out-of-line links.

- *Outgoing links for read-only documents*
  Another application area for out-of-line links is the specification of outgoing links for read-only documents. In HTML, it is only possible to create a link from a page (pointing to some resource) if that page can be modified to include the necessary HTML markup. However, it is easy to think of scenarios where it would be useful to create outgoing links within read-only documents (eg, when making annotations to a page that can not be changed). Out-of-line links could be created in a separate document which could be used together with the read-only document.

The concept of out-of-line links greatly enhances the generality of links and allows new ways to use links. From the user's point of view, out-of-line links may be less intuitive in the beginning, because links exist independently from the resources they are linking. Conceptually, however, this is the better way of modeling links, since there is no reason why resources and links to resources should be intermingled.

7.3.1.2 Link topology

Link topology is the most important feature of links. HTML links are very limited in their topology, allowing only unidirectional point-to-point links. Two possible generalizations to HTML links are possible. The first generalization allows to use bidirectional links, and the second generalization makes it possible to link more than two resources.

Directionality

In figure 7.7 it is shown how unidirectional and bidirectional links can be compared. While in the left case it is only possible to follow the link from the first document to the second document, in the right figure it is possible to follow the link from both resources.

HTML with its inline links only allows unidirectional links. The link is embedded in one document, pointing to another resource, and it is only possible to follow the link from the document in which it is embedded to the resource it is pointing to. With inline links, this behavior is almost unavoidable, because in the second document, there is no information about the existence of the first document and the link inside it.

Using out-of-line links makes it possible to define bidirectional links, because they establish a more symmetrical model of linking. Both documents must somehow know about the out-of-line link, but if this is the case, it is simply a question of link semantics whether it is uni- or bidirectional.

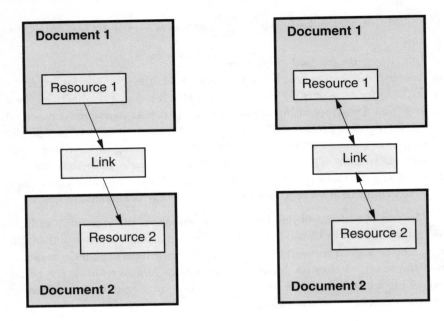

Fig. 7.7 Directionality of links

Bidirectional links can be very useful in extending the semantics of unidirectional links. For example, while unidirectional links only allow to follow a literature reference from the document making the reference to the document being referenced, a bidirectional link used for referencing could be used to locate all documents which make references to a given document.

Number of nodes

After discussing the generalizations of link location and link directionality, the third possible way to define a more general model of links is the number of nodes specified by a link. Although many of the intuitive link types are two-ended, it is easily possible to think of link types which can be used linking more than two resources. In figure 7.8 it is shown how this generalization extends the model of two-ended links.

One example for a multi-ended link is a mailing list, linking the mailing list itself (maybe the resource defining the mailing list is a web page describing the purpose of the list) with all of its participants. Depending on the exact definition of this mailing list link type, links to participants can be links to their home pages, or links to their mail addresses. The important issue is that each participant of the mailing list can use the mailing list link to locate all other participants or the resource defining the mailing list.

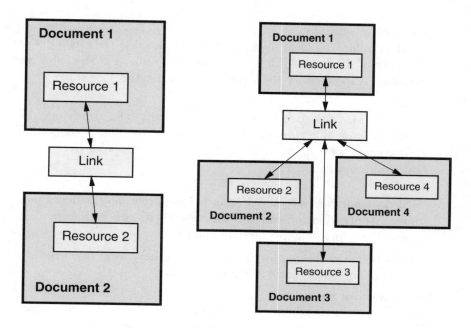

Fig. 7.8 Number of linked resources

With the concept of multi-ended links, the idea of bidirectionality can be extended to multidirectionality. A multidirectional link simply is a multi-ended link which can be used from more than one of the resources it is linking.

7.3.2 Link information

A link as described in the previous section must be able carry different types of information. The following classes of information can be identified as relevant for a linking model as specified by XLink:

- *Locator*
  A locator is information to identify a participating resource. For each remote resource (ie, each resource which is not the content of an inline link), a link must specify a locator. Typically, in a web environment, a locator is a URI.

- *Link semantics*
  Although a link specifies some kind of relationship between resources, the link alone is not sufficient to identify the nature of this relationship. Link semantics are used to further qualify a link, for example identifying a link as connecting a document with (possibly multiple) chapters.

- *Local resource semantics*

  If a link is inline, the local resource semantics describe the semantics of the content of the link (which is called the *local resource*). The following information is specified for the local resource semantics:

  - *Role*

    The role of a link is used to identify different roles which may be applicable for link semantics. For example, if the link is connecting a document with (possibly multiple) chapters, the possible roles are document and chapter.

  - *Title*

    This is additional information which has purely informational purposes. Application software can use a resource's title to inform users about the part a resource plays in a link.

  It should be noted that out-of-line links do not have local resources and therefore do not specify local resource semantics.

- *Remote resource semantics*

  Remote resources are all resources identified by locators. For inline links, all resources but the local one are remote, and for out-of-line links, all participating resources are remote resources. In addition to the role and title information already described for local resource semantics, remote resource semantics describe information what to do when using the link:

  - *Behavior*

    Remote resource behavior tells application software what to do when encountering the link. Remote resource behavior specifies whether the remote resource should be embedded where the link was encountered, replace the resource which was used to follow the link (such as replacing a thumbnail with a full-size image), or create a new context (such as opening a new window). Remote resource behavior furthermore specifies whether this behavior should be initiated automatically or on request.

  Remote resource semantics therefore specify the same information as local resource semantics, as well as additional information how the remote resource should be handled.

In XLink, this information is expressed with XML attributes. Since not all information is necessary for all types of links, different linking element types use different attributes. Section 7.3.3 describes the different linking element types of XLink as well as the information associated with them, while section 7.3.4 describes the actual XML attributes which are used to specify this information.

7.3.3 Link types

In order to provide mechanisms supporting the concepts described in the previous section, XLink defines different element types which can be used to create different link types. The basic idea of XLink is to define attributes which can be used to identify arbitrary XML elements as having XLink semantics (the exact way of how this is done is described in section 7.3.4).

In section 7.3.3.1, XLink *simple links* are described, which are the easiest but also the most restricted way of using XLinks. The biggest restriction of simple links is that they are always unidirectional links. A more general form of XLinks are *extended links* described in section 7.3.3.2.

Out-of-line links introduce the problem of locating links which are associated with a resource. XLink defines *extended link groups* as a mechanism to associate resources that together constitute an interlinked group. Extended link groups are described in section 7.3.3.3.

7.3.3.1 Simple links

A simple link is the most basic type of link that can be defined with XLink. A simple link can be either inline or out-of-line, but it is always unidirectional. Although a simple link is the less complex of the XLink link types, it still is much more powerful than an HTML link as specified with the <A> element, since the XLink simple link specifies additional information such as link and resource semantics.

Although simple links in most cases will be used inline, it is also possible to use out-of-line simple links. However, since a simple link only has one locator (pointing to the remote resource), an out-of-line simple link is "one-ended" and rather uncommon. The *link semantics* associated with a simple link only identify the link as inline or out-of-line.

Furthermore, simple links contain a *locator* to identify the remote resource, and information for *remote resource semantics* and *local resource semantics*.

7.3.3.2 Extended links

An extended link is a more versatile link type, since extended links are not limited to unidirectional links. XLink defines an extended link as having *link semantics* and *local resource semantics* (if the extended link is inline) associated with it.

Locators for extended links are specified as XML elements of their own, which are contained in the XML extended link element. The elements representing XLink locators carry locator information to locate the remote resources, and information about the *remote resource semantics* associated with that particular resource.

Thus, XLink models extended links as two different types of elements, the first element type representing the link itself and defining the information relevant for the link as a whole, and the second element type representing the extended link's remote resources. XLink specifies that XML elements representing XLink locators must be child elements of XML elements representing extended links.

7.3.3.3 Extended link groups

Although conceptually the model of an out-of-line link is sufficient to define multidirectional links, there remains the question how documents and out-of-line links are associated. XLink introduces the concept of *extended link groups*, which are a special kind of extended link. The semantics of extended link groups is defined by the XLink specification as pointing to resources containing extended links. Applications can therefore use extended link groups to locate these resources and interpret the extended links found therein.

An extended link group contains a sequence of *extended link document* elements, being a special case of locator elements which have been described for extended links. The semantics of a resource pointed to by an extended link document are clear, therefore an extended link document only contains locator information.

Since extended link groups have fixed semantics, the XML elements representing extended link groups do not have to specify link semantics. The only information carried by an extended link group element is the number of steps that an application should perform while following links of extended link groups. This is necessary since a document located by an extended link group may also contain an extended link group pointing to other documents, and the steps information limits the process of following these links.

Thus, XLink models extended link groups as two different types of elements, the first element type representing the link group itself, and the second element type representing the extended link documents. XLink specifies that XML elements representing XLink extended link documents must be child elements of XML elements representing extended link groups.

7.3.4 Attributes

Basically, it would be possible to include linking in XML in a number of ways. Possible alternatives include reserving special element names, reserving attribute names, or leaving the specification of linking semantics entirely up to style sheets. XLink uses a number of predefined attribute names to realize linking within XML.

XLink specifies a number of attribute names which have well-defined semantics if used as specified. This way it is possible to create linking elements with any name and additional attributes, as long as they also include the attributes required by XLink. The following attributes are defined by the XLink specification:

- `xml:link`[14]

  This attribute is the most important attribute of an XML element, because it identifies the element as having XLink semantics and also determines the role of the element. According to the link types described in section 7.3.3 and the different XML elements used for these types, the following values can be used for the `xml:link` attribute:

  - `simple`

    This attribute value indicates that the element represents a simple link as described in section 7.3.3.1.

  - `extended`

    If the `extended` value is used, the element represents an extended link as described in section 7.3.3.2. In the XML DTD, the element representing an extended link must specify elements representing locators as children in its content model.

  - `locator`

    Locators are used within extended links for representing remote resources. A locator element must occur as child element of an extended link element.

  - `group`

    This attribute value indicates that the element represents an extended link group as described in section 7.3.3.3. In the XML DTD, the element representing an extended link group must specify elements representing extended link documents as children in its content model.

  - `document`

    Extended link documents are used within extended link groups for representing remote resources containing extended links pertaining to the resource specifying the extended link group. An extended link document element must occur as child element of an extended link group element.

---

[14] Although the current specification defines the attribute name to be `xml:link`, it is planned to change the name of the attribute to `xlink:form` in a future version of XLink. The naming will be completely redesigned as soon as the *XML namespaces* work is completed.

Since each type of XLink element has different additional attributes, table 7.1 can be consulted to find out which additional attributes are allowed for each element type.

Table 7.1   Allowed attributes for XLink element types

| Attribute name | XLink element type | | | | | Page |
	simple	extended	locator	group	document	
role	•	•	•			352
href	•		•		•	352
title	•		•			352
inline	•	•				353
content-role	•	•				353
content-title	•	•				353
show	•		•			353
actuate	•		•			353
behavior	•		•			354
steps				•		354

- role

  This attribute is used to specify the role of a resource or of a link. The role of a resource is part of the resource semantics, and the role attribute is used in simple links and locators to describe the remote resource semantics. In extended links, the attribute is used to describe the link semantics. There are no predefined values for this attribute, its interpretation is entirely application-dependent.

- href

  The href attribute is used as a locator to point to remote resources. It is used in simple links to point to the remote resource of the link. In locators and extended link documents, the href attribute points to the remote resource represented by the respective element.

- title

  This attribute is used to to specify title information about a resource. Title information can be used by applications to inform users about the role a resource plays in a link. The title attribute is used in simple links and locators to specify title information for the remote resource.

  There are no predefined values for this attribute, its interpretation is entirely application-dependent.

- `inline`

  This attribute decides whether a link is inline or out-of-line (these concepts are described in section 7.3.1.1). The `inline` attribute is applicable for simple links and extended links. It can have the values `true` or `false`, indicating that the link is either inline or out-of-line.

- `content-role`

  If a link is inline, it always has a local resource. The role of the local resource is specified using the `content-role` attribute. There are no predefined values for this attribute, its interpretation is entirely application-dependent.

- `content-title`

  If a link is inline, it always has a local resource. The title information for the local resource is specified using the `content-title` attribute. There are no predefined values for this attribute, its interpretation is entirely application-dependent.

- `show`

  The remote resource semantics associated with a simple link or a locator specify two types of predefined behavior. The `show` attribute defines what an application should do when a link to a local resource is traversed:

  - `embed`

    In this case, the remote resource should be embedded, for the purpose of display or processing, at the location where the traversal started.

  - `replace`

    This attribute value specifies that the remote resource should, for the purpose of display or processing, replace the resource where the traversal started.

  - `new`

    The last value indicates that the remote resource should be displayed or processed in a new context, not affecting the context of the resource where the traversal started.

  Although this defines what to do when a link is traversed, it does not specify when a link to a remote resource will be traversed. This is specified in the second attribute specifying predefined behavior for remote resource semantics.

- `actuate`

  The remote resource semantics associated with a simple link or a locator specify two types of predefined behavior. The `actuate` attribute defines when an application should traverse a link to a remote resource:

- `auto`

  In this case, the traversal of the link should be initiated automatically when one of the resources of the link is encountered. The display or processing of a resource is not complete until all of its links with this behavior are traversed and processed according to the behavior specified by the respective `show` attributes.

- `user`

  This attribute value specifies that link traversal should be initiated by the user. Applications are responsible for giving user the opportunity to initiate link traversal.

Combining the `show` and `actuate` attributes makes it possible to define a number of different behaviors of links. All possible combinations of the attribute values for these attributes are meaningful.

- `behavior`

  If the behavior of a link has to be specified in a more specific way than is possible with the `show` and `actuate` attributes, the `behavior` attribute can be used for application-specific data.

- `steps`

  The `steps` attribute is used with extended link groups to specify the maximum number of indirection levels of nested extended link groups an application should follow when processing an extended link group. This is a useful mechanism to limit the amount of extended link group processing that an application has to perform. However, this attribute does not have any normative effect and is specified to serve merely as a hint that authors may give to applications.

The current XLink working draft also defines a `xml:attributes` attribute which can be used to change the names of the attributes. However, when the *XML namespaces* recommendation is completed[15], this mechanism will be obsoleted and probably removed from the XLink specification.

Xlink defines conformance to the specification as purely syntactical. An element conforms to XLink if it has an `xml:link` attribute having one of the predefined values, and if the element and all of its XLink-related attributes are conforming to the syntactic requirements defined by the XLink specification.

7.4 XML Pointer Language (XPointer)

XML describes a language for the definition of user-definable document types, and XLink defines a way how links can be used in such an environment.

---

[15] The XML namespaces specification generally addresses the problem of name clashes when using multiple schemas in one DTD or document.

However, XLink defines pointers to documents rather generally as locators, pointing to resources. In XLink, a locator can either identify an external resource (using a URI), or an internal resource, in which case the located resource is part of the same document as the XLink containing the locator. In this case it is necessary to identify a resource within an XML document (called a *sub-resource*, because the entire XML document is seen as the resource). The *XML Pointer Language (XPointer)*, currently defined in a W3C draft recommendation [166], has been designed to serve that purpose. The XPointer language is one part of the *Extensible Linking Language (XLL)*, a term which is frequently used to refer to XPointer and the *XML Linking Language (XLink)* as described in section 7.3.

Apart from defining links which are local to one XML document, the XPointer language is intended to be generally usable as a fragment identifier (separated from the URI path by the hash sign '#') in URIs as described in section 2.2.

In both cases (XLinks pointing to resources inside the same document, and XLinks specifying URIs), XPointer establishes the concept of the *containing resource*. If a link is relative (ie, does only specify an XPointer and no URI), the containing resource is the document containing the link. In all other cases, the containing resource is the document identified by the URI.

In section 7.4.1 the general concepts of XPointer are described. The basic building block of an XPointer is a *location term*. The different types of location terms are described in section 7.4.2. Although in most cases XPointers locate one element inside a document, it is also possible to define XPointers which locate only parts of elements or multiple elements. The situations where this may occur are described in section 7.4.3. Finally, section 7.4.4 discusses the persistence of XPointers.

7.4.1 Concepts

Generally, XPointer defines a way for addressing into the internal structures of XML documents. This can be done in different ways, which can be combined. The idea is to define *location terms*, which can be used to locate specific parts of an XML document based on different criteria. Basically, an XPointer is a sequence of location terms.

```
XPointer     ::=  AbsTerm '.' OtherTerms | AbsTerm | OtherTerms
OtherTerms   ::=  OtherTerm | OtherTerm '.' OtherTerms
OtherTerm    ::=  RelTerm | SpanTerm | AttrTerm | StringTerm
```

XPointer defines two different groups of location terms, an absolute term, and other terms (which are all terms not being absolute). The definition above shows that an XPointer can either start with an absolute term, or with an other term. All following terms (if there are any) are other terms.

An absolute term is used to define a location inside the containing resource. Absolute terms are described in section 7.4.2.1. In contrast to absolute terms, other terms specify a location in terms of another location, called the *location source*. Other terms are described in sections 7.4.2.2 through 7.4.2.5. If there is no preceding absolute location term, the location source for such a location term is the entire resource, otherwise it is the location specified by the preceding location term.

7.4.2 Location terms

The basic building blocks of XPointers are location terms. Basically, an XPointer is a sequence of location terms, the first one being either absolute or other, and all following location terms being other terms. The following terms are interpreted using the preceding location term as their location source, which makes it possible to look at XPointers as a sequence of constraints, which finally locate a sub-resource inside an XML document.

7.4.2.1 Absolute term

An absolute location term can only occur as the first element of an XPointer. It does not depend on the existence of a location source. Absolute location terms can be used to establish a location source for following location terms, or they can be used as the only location term of an XPointer. There are four different types of absolute location terms:

- `root`
  The `root` absolute location term selects the root element of the containing resource as the location source. This is the default value for XPointers which do not specify an absolute location term. They are implicitly assigned the `root` absolute location term.

- `origin`
  This keyword only makes sense if the XPointer is part of an XML document. In this case, the location source is the sub-resource from which the XPointer was traversed. For example, if the text of an element contains an XLink using an XPointer with the `origin` absolute location term as locator, the location source is that element of the XML document.

- `id`
  Since an attribute using the attribute type ID has special meaning in XML (it is used for the unique identification of elements), it can be addressed

with an XPointer. For example, the XPointer `id(s54)` selects the XML element with an ID attribute set to `s54` as the location source.

- `html`

    Before the ID attribute was defined for almost all HTML elements, another mechanism was used to define HTML fragment identifiers. The `html` location term makes it possible to access these older HTML fragment identifiers. The `html` location term selects the first `<A>` element whose NAME attribute has the value given by the `html` keyword.

    This mechanism supports an old way to define fragment identifiers in HTML documents and should only be used if there is no possibility to use the newer `id` absolute location term.

The empty parentheses which are required after the `root` and `origin` absolute location terms have been defined for syntactical consistency with other keywords, and also because a simple string without parentheses is interpreted as a short form of the `id` absolute location term. This short hand notation makes XPointers compatible with simple HTML fragment identifiers.

7.4.2.2 Relative term

A relative location term is a keyword followed by arguments. The keyword identifies a sequence of elements or other XML node types which is used to choose the resulting location source. The arguments can be seen as a specialization of the keyword, determining which node types from that sequence (and which instances of these types) are chosen.

Keywords

The keywords can be seen as navigational aids for traversing the document tree. They make it possible to make selections based on different types of relations between nodes. If no keyword is given, it is assumed to be the same keyword as the immediately preceding relative location term. Therefore, it is not allowed to omit the keyword of the first relative location term. The following keywords (illustrated in figure 7.9) can be used:

- `child`

    This relative locator identifies direct child nodes (ie, nodes directly below the given node in the document tree) of the location source.

- `descendant`

    The `descendant` relative locator is more general than the `child` locator. It identifies nodes appearing anywhere in the content of the location source. In the document tree, these are nodes anywhere below the given node.

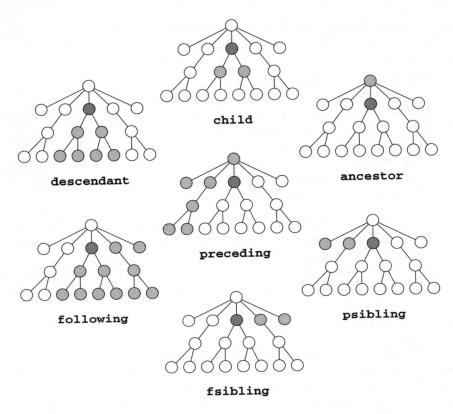

Fig. 7.9 XPointer navigational keywords for the document tree

- `ancestor`
  This relative locator identifies nodes containing (ie, nodes being above the given node) the location source.

- `preceding`
  The `preceding` locator identifies nodes that appear before the location source. In the document tree, these are nodes located on branches left to the given node, and nodes above it.

- `following`
  This relative locator identifies nodes that appear after the location source. In the document tree, these are nodes below the given node, and nodes located on branches to the right.

- `psibling`
  The `psibling` locator identifies sibling nodes (ie, sharing their parent with the location source) that appear before the location source. In the

document tree, these are the nodes having the same parent node as the given node and being on its left side.

- `fsibling`
  The `fsibling` locator identifies sibling nodes (ie, sharing their parent with the location source) that appear after the location source. In the document tree, these are the nodes having the same parent node as the given node and being on its right side.

Using these keywords, selection of parts of the document tree can be done based on various structural criteria. This selection can be further narrowed by using arguments for the keywords.

Arguments

The arguments of a relative location term are used to further qualify the nodes selected by the location term. Placed in parentheses the arguments first of all specify whether all nodes or only one particular instance are to be selected. All instances are selected with the `all` keyword, so `child(all)` selects all child nodes of the current location source.

Specific instances can be selected by a leading plus sign '+' or minus sign '-' (if no sign is specified, the plus sign is taken as the default) and a following number. For the plus sign, element instances are counted from first to last, and for the minus sign, element instances are counted from last to first[16]. For example, `child(2)` selects the second child node of the current location source, and `fsibling(-1)` selects the rightmost sibling of the current location source.

All other arguments to relative location terms are optional. The first possibility is to select a certain node type, which makes it possible to select among the node types of an XML document. The node type is separated by a comma directly following the instance specification. The following node types can be used:

- *Name*
  If no keyword is given as a node type (a keyword is identified by the preceding hash sign '#') but a simple string is used, this string identifies a particular XML element type. Thus, the relative location term `descendant(-1,chapter)` selects the last `chapter` element instance in the location source.

---

[16] The exact way of counting depends on the keyword. For example, for the `sibling` keywords positive numbers always count starting at the current location source. This means that positive numbers count from right to left for the `psibling` keyword.

- #element

  This keyword selects XML elements as node type. It is the default, so if no node type is explicitly specified, a relative location term operates on XML elements. A very simple relative location term therefore is `child(2)`, selecting the second child element of the location source.

- #pi

  In this case, XML processing instructions are selected as node type. Since processing instructions do not contain any structured XML content, only strings (as described in section 7.4.2.5) can be selected with a processing instruction as location source.

- #comment

  In this case, XML comments are selected as node type. Since comments do not contain any structured XML content, only strings (as described in section 7.4.2.5) can be selected with a comment as location source.

- #text

  In this case, text is selected (inside elements or CDATA sections) as node type. Since text does not contain any structured XML content, only strings (as described in section 7.4.2.5) can be selected with text as location source.

- #cdata

  In this case, text is selected (only inside CDATA sections) as node type. Since text does not contain any structured XML content, only strings (as described in section 7.4.2.5) can be selected with text as location source.

- #all

  This keyword selects nodes of all above types. However, since only elements can satisfy attribute constraints, `#all` is equivalent to `#element` if any attribute constraints are specified.

In addition to the node type, optional *attribute constraints* can be specified, which are only applicable to element nodes. Attribute constraints are used to specify constraints for particular attribute name or value specifications and are specified directly after the node selection keyword. For example, the `child(2,#element,author,*)` relative location term selects the second child element for which the `author` attribute has a value. In most cases, a string will be used as attribute value. For example, the `descendant(1,#element,lang,"de")` relative location term selects the first descendant element for which the `lang` attribute has the value `de`.

Using attribute constraints, the `id` and `html` absolute location terms can be seen as shortcuts for `root().descendant(1,#element,ID,"value")` respectively `root().descendant(1,A,NAME,"value")` XPointers, where `value` is the parameter given to `id` and `html`.

7.4.2.3 Spanning term

A spanning location term is identified by the `span` keyword. It contains two XPointers, separated by commas. The spanning location term locates a sub-resource starting at the beginning of the data selected by the first XPointer, and continuing through to the end of the data selected by the second XPointer. Both XPointers are interpreted relative to the location source of the spanning location term.

For example, the `id(Chapter3).span(child(2),child(4))` XPointer locates a sub-resource starting at the beginning of the second child of the element with an ID attribute set to `Chapter3` and continuing to the end of the fourth child.

7.4.2.4 Attribute term

An attribute location term is used to locate specific attribute values inside a document. It is almost always used in conjunction with other location terms, which select the element from which the attribute value should be located. The attribute location term takes an attribute name as the only parameter of the `attr` keyword, and returns the attribute's assignment. Thus, the `descendant(2,chapter).attr(author)` XPointer locates the assignment of the `author` attribute of the second `chapter` element instance inside a document.

7.4.2.5 String term

A string location term is used to select one or more strings or positions between strings in the location source. The `string` keyword can be used to specify occurrences of strings or all strings, and occurrences can be counted right from the start or left from the end of the location source. Any string can be specified to be matched, and an empty string identifies the position immediately preceding each character in the location source. Thus, the string location term `string(5,"")` selects the position before the fifth character of the location source.

Optionally, a position and a length can be specified. The position specifies a character offset from the start of the matched string to the beginning of the desired sub-resource. A positive number counts right from the beginning of the string, a negative number counts left from the end of the string. A position value of `end` selects the position immediately following the last character of the match. The string location term `string(1,"Match",2)` therefore selects the position before the letter 'a' in the first occurrence of the word "Match".

Furthermore, it is possible to select strings by specifying a length, which, if specified, always has to follow a position. The length specifies the number of characters which should be selected. The `string(1,"Match",2,2)` string location term therefore selects the string "at" in the first occurrence of the word "Match".

7.4.3 Spanning locators

It is possible to define XPointers which do not select only nodes arranged in a proper subtree. For example, the XPointer `descendant(all,table)` selects all instances of the `table` element inside a document. If there is more than one table, the XPointer selects a number of node subtrees (which are probably in different branches of the document tree) rather than only one. In XPointer, selections like this are called *spans*. Depending on what the XPointer is used for, spans may be useful, or it may be difficult to interpret them appropriately.

7.4.4 Persistence

XPointers can point into XML documents using different mechanisms. The most popular ways are probably the `id` and `html` absolute location terms, since they are equivalent to the fragment identifiers which are the only way to point into HTML documents. However, this mechanism depends on attributes being used in the document which may or may not be present. Since in many cases XPointers will be created without cooperation of the author of the document into which they are pointing, it can be simply impossible to use `id` and `html` absolute location terms, since the required attributes are not used in the document.

In this case, it is necessary to use the navigational mechanisms of XPointers to identify the required sub-resource inside the document. However, there are many ways how to point to a particular sub-resource. Although many different XPointers can be used to point to a sub-resource, they are differently robust against modifications of the XML document.

One example is the simple document tree shown in figure 7.10. There are many different ways how the second section in the second chapter can be located using an XPointer, some of them are:

- `descendant(8,#element)`
  This XPointer identifies the desired section as the eighth element in the document. This is the most simple form of identification, but the XPointer

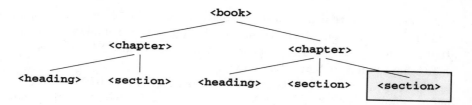

Fig. 7.10 Different XPointers selecting the same sub-resource

will break[17] as soon as any elements are inserted or deleted before the section element instance to be selected.

- child(2,#element).child(3,#element)

  This XPointer is more specific in that it uses a little bit of navigational functionality by selecting element instances based on their hierarchical level in the document tree. Any changes made inside the first chapter will no longer break the XPointer. However, if the document is modified to include a preface (or some other) element before the first chapter, or if any elements are inserted directly under the second chapter element instance and before the second section element instance, the XPointer will still break.

- descendant(2,chapter).descendant(2,section)

  This is the most specific and most robust XPointer which can be defined for the given situation. It clearly defines to select the second chapter element instance of the document, and to subsequently select the second section element instance from this location source. Even if the document structure is modified to include additional levels of hierarchy (such as a part element which is used between the book element and chapter elements to group chapters into parts), this XPointer does not break.

However, it is impossible to define XPointers withstanding all kinds of modifications to the document. The most robust type of locator is the locator based on an id absolute location term. However, if this can not be used, the goal is to find the structurally most precise description of the sub-resource to be selected, such as in the example above.

If there are other elements using ID attributes, but not the element to be selected, both methods should be combined by first selecting the nearest

---

[17] Breaking in this case does not necessarily mean that it is no longer a valid XPointer. For example, if a second section is inserted in the first chapter, the XPointer will still be valid, but it selects the first section of the second chapter. A breaking XPointer therefore is an XPointer which does no longer select the intended sub-resource.

containing element that does have an ID attribute, and then using a navigational locator. For example, if the second chapter of the example uses an ID attribute but the second section does not, the most robust XPointer would be `id(chap2).descendant(2,section)`.

Currently, it is discussed to add a checksum mechanism to XPointer, so that an application following an XPointer could easily detect whether the pointer is still valid or broken. This mechanism could protect users against XPointers which are still pointing to a resource, but where the content has been changed since the creation of the XPointer.

7.5 Extensible Style Language (XSL)

XML, XLink, and XPointer are used for defining document types and links between documents. These are content-oriented issues, and XML also needs a way to specify the presentation of documents. This is done using the *Extensible Style Language (XSL)*, which is currently defined in a W3C working draft [47]. XSL is far more important for XML than *Cascading Style Sheets (CSS)* is for HTML, because HTML specifies semantics and a standard formatting for all elements (which, if necessary, can be modified using CSS), while XML documents do not contain any formatting information, unless specified by a style sheet. Consequently, without any style sheet information, XML documents can only be displayed in a structure-oriented way, for example by graphically representing the document tree[18].

XSL is based on a subset of the full *Document Style Semantics and Specification Language (DSSSL)* (specified in ISO 10179 [127]) called *DSSSL-Online (DSSSL-O)*. DSSSL-O can be seen as a profile (ie, a functional subset) of DSSSL optimized for use in on-line applications in the same way as XML is a profile of SGML.

XSL is far more powerful than CSS, which is a necessity because CSS is mainly designed to slightly modify the predefined formatting semantics of HTML documents, while XSL style sheets are used for XML documents, which do not have any predefined formatting semantics. Therefore, XSL must be able to specify formatting semantics is a more general way. Furthermore, since XML documents can represent application-specific document structures, a greater degree of freedom for formatting is required than it is for HTML documents. In addition to the features of CSS, XSL has the following additional functionality:

---

[18] Another possibility is the structure view implemented by W3C's *Amaya* browser. In this view, the depth of an element in the document tree is represented by the level of indentation in a line-oriented display of all elements.

- *Element reordering*
  XSL style sheets can format elements independent of their order in the source document.

- *Powerful selection mechanism for source elements*
  It is possible to select elements based on ancestry/children, position, and uniqueness.

- *Generated text*
  XSL style sheets can insert text and graphics into the formatted document.

- *Support for ECMAScript*
  User-defined ECMAScript functions can be included in the XSL style sheet to evaluate the formatting characteristics of a document.

- *Extensibility*
  It is possible to extend XSL to support new formatting applications.

Although the general model of XSL is relatively clear, there are still many open issues in the draft recommendation. The basic concepts of how XSL works are described in section 7.5.1. The actual design of XSL style sheets as well as the functionality provided by XSL is not yet finalized. Section 7.5.2 gives a short overview of how XSL style sheets are specified.

7.5.1 Concepts

The basic idea of XSL is based on DSSSL's formatting model. However, since one of the design goals of XSL is to have a common underlying formatting model with CSS, some aspects of formatting have to be changed. A common underlying formatting model of CSS and XSL makes the design of HTML/XML applications (such as future browsers) much easier, since only one formatting engine has to be implemented. This formatting engine takes as input either CSS or XSL information, but in both cases the basic formatting procedures (such as calculating object sizes and breaking text into lines) are the same.

XSL's process has two steps. The first step is called *result tree construction* and structurally transforms an XML document. This process is described in section 7.5.1.1. The result of the transformation is a tree of formatting objects. This tree is used as input for the actual formatting process, which is based on the semantics of the formatting objects and the result tree's structure. This second step of XSL is described in section 7.5.1.2.

7.5.1.1 Tree construction

Every XML document can be represented as a tree, based on the hierarchical structure of elements. This document tree is called the *source tree*. The first step of XSL processing is a transformation of this source tree into another tree, the *result tree*. These two trees are completely separated. To specify this transformation process, a style sheet contains a set of *template rules*. Each template rule has two parts:

- *Pattern*
  A pattern is used to match nodes in the source tree. The pattern of a template rule determines whether a particular rule should be applied to a node. Patterns can match nodes based on element names, attribute values, parent-child relationships, ancestor-descendant relationships, position in the source tree, and a variety of other criteria.

  Functionally, XSL patterns are similar to XPointer location terms as described in section 7.4.2. However, XSL uses another notation and is more powerful than XPointer. It is not yet clear whether XPointer location terms and XSL patterns will be modified to share a common notation.

- *Template*
  A template is a collection of instructions which are instantiated when the pattern of a template rule matches a given node. Templates can contain literal result elements (elements not belonging to the XSL namespace), character data, and instructions for creating fragments of the result tree (these instructions are represented by elements belonging to the XSL namespace).

  Literal result elements can be any XML elements, and in particular *formatting objects*, which are elements having XSL formatting semantics. Literal result elements are part of the result tree.

  Instructions are used to define the transformation process, for example by specifying that the child elements of an element should be processed or ignored. Instructions are used to create the result tree, but they are not part of the result tree.

The transformation process from the source tree to the result tree is based on matching patterns to nodes in the source tree, while the source tree is traversed to create the result tree. If patterns in more than one template rule match a given node, conflict resolution rules are used and only one of the template rules is chosen and the associated template instantiated.

Although primarily designed to be used in conjunction with XSL formatting, XSL tree construction can be used to produce arbitrary result trees (using literal result elements other than formatting objects in templates).

This makes it possible to use XSL as a language for general XML transformations. In figure 7.11 it is shown how XSL tree construction can be used to convert an XML document to HTML.

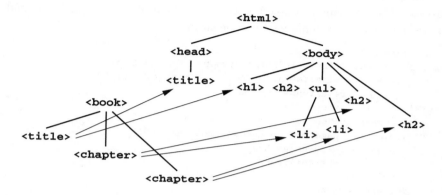

Fig. 7.11   XSL result tree construction (mapping XML to HTML)

In this example, an XML document (represented by the source tree on the left) is converted to an HTML page (represented by the result tree on the right). The title of the book is used as the page's <TITLE> and also as the <H1> heading in the page's <BODY>. Each chapter heading is added to a <UL> list which represents the table of contents as well as to the page's content as an <H2> heading. This conversion is a good example for some of XSL's capabilities which are very useful for transformation purposes, in particular the ability to generate content in different locations of the result tree.

7.5.1.2 Formatting

Formatting is the second step of XSL processing. The input to the formatting process is the result tree created by the transformation process. Generally, a result tree contains a formatting instructions in the form of XSL formatting objects. The current XSL specification defines a number of formatting objects which are used for setting various formatting parameters, such as different layout objects (eg, blocks, lists, or list items) and the formatting of links. However, since the coordination between XSL's formatting model and CSS is in an early stage, this part of the XSL specification is expected to change considerably.

7.5.2 Style sheets

An XSL style sheet is an instance of the XSL style sheet DTD, which defines the elements (ie, instructions) which are used to define the transformation process. The following example is taken from the draft recommendation and shows a simple but complete XSL style sheet:

```
<?xml version='1.0'?>
<xsl:stylesheet xmlns:xsl="http://www.w3.org/TR/WD-xsl"
                xmlns:fo="http://www.w3.org/TR/WD-xsl/FO"
                result-ns="fo">
  <xsl:template match='/'>
    <fo:page-sequence font-family="serif">
      <fo:simple-page-master name='scrolling'/>
      <fo:queue queue-name='body'>
        <xsl:process-children/>
      </fo:queue>
    </fo:page-sequence>
  </xsl:template>
  <xsl:template match="title">
    <fo:block font-weight="bold">
      <xsl:process-children/>
    </fo:block>
  </xsl:template>
  <xsl:template match="p">
    <fo:block>
      <xsl:process-children/>
    </fo:block>
  </xsl:template>
  <xsl:template match="emph">
    <fo:sequence font-style="italic">
      <xsl:process-children/>
    </fo:sequence>
  </xsl:template>
</xsl:stylesheet>
```

This example makes use of the XML namespace mechanism, defining all elements of the XSL DTD to have the `xsl` prefix, and all formatting objects to have the `fo` prefix. The style sheet contains four template rules, each defining a pattern and a template for creating the result tree.

- `<xsl:template match='/'>`
  This template rule matches the document root, and the associated template is instantiated at the beginning of the tree construction process. The formatting objects specify initial parameters for formatting, in this case a page master and a queue, which is used to group flow objects which are to be placed in one flow. The `process-children` instruction is used to process all children of the node.

- `<xsl:template match="title">`
  A `title` element is formatted using a `block` formatting object and its attribute to change the font weight. Any children of the `title` element are processed in the context of the formatting object.

- `<xsl:template match="p">`
  A paragraph is processed very similar to a `title` element, except that it does not have the font weight changed.

- `<xsl:template match="emph">`
  The `emph` pattern defines a template rule which uses a `sequence` formatting object instead of a `block` and sets the font style of this formatting object. A `sequence` formatting object does not start a new formatting block and is used to format emphasized text.

This style sheet can be used with any XML document containing `title`, `p`, and `emph` elements. The tree construction process takes such a document and the style sheet as input. Matching patterns of template rules with element names builds the result tree, which finally consists of different and nested formatting objects as defined by the templates. This result tree is used as input for the formatting process, finally resulting in a formatted document.

Although this is only an example, it shows the basics of an XSL style sheet. Since XSL is expected to change considerably, a complete description of the XSL DTD and formatting objects can not be given. The underlying mechanisms of XSL (tree construction and formatting) most likely will not be changed in future versions of XSL.

7.6 XML and other markup languages

XML as a new markup language for the web offers a flexibility which has not been possible before. However, it also introduces a new level of complexity, defining powerful linking mechanisms and a style sheet language much more complex than HTML's formatting capabilities. A short comparison of XML and older markup languages can help putting XML in the right perspective. In section 7.6.1, XML is compared to HTML. A comparison between XML and SGML is given in section 7.6.2.

7.6.1 Comparison of XML and HTML

HTML as an SGML application is somehow related to XML. However, as described in section 7.1.3.4, HTML is not an XML application, because the HTML DTD is not conformant to XML. Until HTML is completely replaced by XML (including a new XML-based version of HTML), these two languages will coexist. HTML is the language of choice for simple content and for all content which is already published on the web and shall not be converted.

Currently, the future of XML still is a bit unclear. Although very promising, some of the crucial specifications (XLink, XPointer, and XSL) are still in early stages, and it is not yet clear how much the draft versions will change until the final specifications. And only if there are stable specifications it will be possible to implement applications based on these specifications. So it will take some time until XML is widely supported and publishing in XML is a safe way to reach the majority of web users.

Although still in its infancy, it can be seen that XML is a great improvement for publishing documents on the web. Although it will be important for some time to come to publish documents in HTML, XML documents will begin to appear on the web as soon as the first XML implementations are widely available. As a short-term task, XML and its companion specifications should be analyzed to see how XML could be integrated into the publishing process. The mid-term strategy should include a way to publish documents in HTML as well as in XML, simultaneously making users aware of the advantages of XML documents. The long-term strategy is to completely replace HTML with XML, using its advanced linking and formatting features to publish richer content than is possible with HTML.

Publishing with HTML always results in a loss of structural information (unless the information is only trivially structured), because all application-specific document structures have to be mapped to HTML elements and attributes. XML makes it possible to define application-specific document structures for publication on the web, and will therefore be the language of choice whenever the preservation of structural information is important.

7.6.2 Comparison of XML and SGML

Put simply, XML is a subset of SGML. From this point of view, it is very easy to compare these two, because SGML is a superset of XML, including all features of XML. However, the main advantage of XML lies in its acceptance as a standard for web publishing, and in its companion specifications XLink, XPointer, and XSL. This advantage is believed to outweigh the restrictions of XML, which are described in section 7.6.2.1. XML should always be seen in the light of ubiquitous XML-enabled software (although this may take some time to become true), in contrast to SGML, which still has a very limited distribution.

Although not known as widely as the web, SGML has a large user group, and a lot of SGML-based software is available. Consequently, it is necessary to take a look at an interworking of SGML- and XML-based environments.

Since every XML document is, by definition, an SGML document, there is no need to actually transform XML documents to SGML, it is only necessary to remove the XML declaration. However, since XML is a subset of SGML, not all SGML documents are XML documents. Section 7.6.2.2 discusses what has to be done in order to convert an arbitrary SGML document into a valid XML document.

Section 7.6.2.3 takes the considerations one step further, by discussing how SGML declarations and DTDs can be converted to XML. This is important if an SGML-based environment should be converted to an XML-based environment, a process which may become important in the future.

7.6.2.1 Restrictions of XML

In section 7.2.1, the differences between XML and SGML are described. XML has been designed to avoid some of the complexity which is inherent to SGML, such as markup minimization. The overall goal of XML is to provide the versatility of SGML without the overhead of full SGML. As a consequence, many SGML applications (such as HTML) can not be used with XML without modifications. Depending on the original design of the application (SGML declaration and DTD), this may be more or less easy, and it is possible that some structural information will be lost when converting from SGML to XML.

7.6.2.2 Converting SGML documents to XML

If there is an SGML environment which should be conserved, the only requirement may be to export and import document from this environment. In this case, documents must be converted from SGML to XML and vice versa. Converting from XML to SGML is trivial, since every XML document also is an SGML document.

Converting from SGML to XML can be more difficult, depending on the SGML declarations and DTDs used in the SGML environment. It may be necessary to perform some conversions (such as creating full markup), and in general there should be a target XML DTD and a mapping should be defined between the SGML DTD and the XML DTD. If structural conversions are necessary (eg, because the SGML DTD uses exceptions which are not allowed in XML), there are different ways how a target XML DTD could be defined.

7.6.2.3 Converting SGML environments to XML

If XML proves to be successful, it is possible that SGML environments will be replaced by XML environments, in which case it is necessary to convert the complete processing environment to XML.

In general, the requirements are the same as for converting SGML documents to XML. However, if the complete processing environment is converted to XML, all structural information which is lost when converting SGML DTDs or documents to XML is irrecoverable. Therefore, the decision how to convert SGML DTDs to XML DTDs should be made very carefully, and the best solution is entirely application-dependent.

7.7 The future of XML

XML surely is the greatest innovation of content architectures for the web since its introduction. When XML with all its components is used on a large scale, the web will provide richer content and more structural information than it does today. Although there is still a long way to go for XML to be as widespread as HTML today, the advantages of XML should be sufficient to serve as a motivation, and to begin thinking about converting existing HTML or proprietary solutions towards XML.

Currently, only XML has the status of a W3C recommendation. XLink, XPointer, XSL, and XML namespaces are W3C working drafts, so they still can change substantially until the final approvement as a recommendation (and they first have to go through the intermediate state of a proposed recommendation).

XML namespaces specified in a W3C working draft [35], define a mechanism for uniquely qualifying names in XML documents by assigning prefixes to them. The problem addressed by XML namespaces is that a document could contain markup from different DTDs, in which case name clashes could occur. XML namespaces defines a mechanism how this can be avoided. XML namespaces are based on the use of qualified names, which contain a single colon, separating the name into a namespace prefix and the local name. The prefix, which is mapped to a URI, selects a namespace. The combination of the universally-managed URI namespace and the local schema namespace produces names that are guaranteed to be universally unique.

Since XML documents must also be identified when being sent to a client via HTTP or other data transfer mechanisms (such as email), new *XML media types* are defined in Internet informational RFC 2376 [274]. These types are used in the `Content-Type` header of an HTTP response if an XML entity is returned.

Many other activities are also supporting the introduction of XML. Important new trends, such as the *Resource Description Framework (RDF)* described in section 10.5.3, are built on top of XML, so XML is quickly becoming a general platform for structured data on the web. Application software supporting XML is already available, but only after the currently unstable specifications XLink, XPointer, XSL, and XML namespaces are finalized and implemented in a variety of platforms, XML will be usable as a replacement for HTML.

8. Scripting and Programming

The web is primarily focused on delivering content of various types using standardized transport mechanisms and data types. As a generalization of this architecture, there are also a number of technologies for defining active components, such as scripts and programs. The most widespread technology in this area is *Dynamic HTML (DHTML)*, which uses a scripting language to add active functionality to otherwise passive HTML pages. In most cases, these actions are used to trigger some actions (ie, script portions) upon certain user actions such as mouse movements and button clicks. Scripting languages are discussed in section 8.1.

A more general solution than a scripting language is a programming language, which is not interpreted upon execution, but compiled into an executable form which is then distributed. *Java*, originally designed as a programming language totally independent from the web, has been very successful by being marketed as the programming language for the web. Programming languages used for web-based applications are described in section 8.2. The embedding of programs into web resources raises the question how these programs can communicate with other programs, for example for implementing client/server-scenarios. This question is discussed in section 8.3.

8.1 Scripting languages

One of the most important additions to pure HTML documents was the introduction of a scripting language, which was first introduced by Netscape. Scripting makes it possible to achieve effects and a degree of interactivity which cannot be provided by a content-oriented language as HTML.

A study of web servers in the UK carried out by Beck [15] gives some figures which can be seen as representative for the web in general, although only web servers in the UK were used to collect the data. The way the data was collected is quite simple, all UK domains were searched for hosts named www, and if such a host was present, an HTTP request was sent to the host's standard HTTP port (80)[1]. The results of this survey are shown in table 8.1.

Table 8.1   Usage of scripting languages

	Scripting language	Count	Percentage
1.	JavaScript	2573	97.98%
2.	VBScript	42	1.60%
3.	LiveScript	11	0.42%

The results show that almost all pages using scripting use the same language. The reason for this result is that *JavaScript* is the only scripting language supported by the two major browsers, while *VBScript* support is only provided by Microsoft's Internet Explorer. The third language, *LiveScript*, is simply the older name of JavaScript.

Scripting in web pages is supported by the <SCRIPT> element usually containing function definitions, and by events, which are specific actions associated with elements. Depending on the element, HTML defines different events, each event being represented by an attribute. The event's attribute specifies a script to be executed, in many cases this is a call of a function which has been defined using the <SCRIPT> element.

- ONBLUR is triggered if a region loses focus.

- ONCHANGE is triggered if a control loses focus and its value has been modified since gaining focus.

- ONCLICK is triggered if the corresponding element is clicked.

- ONDBLCLICK is triggered if the corresponding element is double-clicked.

- ONFOCUS is triggered if a region receives focus.

- ONKEYDOWN is triggered if a key is pressed while the mouse pointer is over the element.

- ONKEYPRESS is triggered if a key is pressed and released while the mouse pointer is over the element.

- ONKEYUP is triggered if a key is released while the mouse pointer is over the element.

- ONLOAD is triggered when the document is loaded into the browser.

---

[1] Although the description of the survey is taken from the original paper, the survey's figures presented here are from a newer survey (carried out in August 1997) which is available at http://www.hensa.ac.uk/uksites/survey/.

- **ONMOUSEDOWN** is triggered if the mouse button is pressed over the element.

- **ONMOUSEMOVE** is triggered if the mouse is moved while the pointer is over the element.

- **ONMOUSEOUT** is triggered if the mouse pointer is moved away from the element.

- **ONMOUSEOVER** is triggered if the mouse pointer is moved over the element.

- **ONMOUSEUP** is triggered if the mouse button is released over the element.

- **ONRESET** is triggered if a form is reset.

- **ONSELECT** is triggered if text inside text boxes is selected.

- **ONSUBMIT** is triggered if a form is submitted.

- **ONUNLOAD** is triggered when the page is removed from the browser's window.

Scripting languages differ from programming languages in that they are interpreted rather than compiled. That means that a script is sent in source form to the client. The client interprets the script while executing it, which makes scripting much slower than programming languages. Furthermore, scripting languages often are less powerful than programming languages, because it is assumed that they will only be used for simple tasks, while complex problems will be handled using programming languages. The most common scripting languages for embedded scripting are *ECMAScript* as described in section 8.1.1, and *VBScript* as described in section 8.1.2.

8.1.1 ECMAScript

The *European Computer Manufacturers Association (ECMA)* has standardized the most common scripting language of the web as *ECMAScript* [74]. ECMAScript therefore is based on *JavaScript*, which was introduced by Netscape. At the time of writing, JavaScript is not fully ECMAScript compliant, because the standard, although based on JavaScript, includes a number of enhancements.

Originally named LiveScript, and then renamed after the programming language Java had become a huge success, JavaScript is by far the most popular scripting language on the web. Although they have quite similar names, Java and JavaScript have not much in common. Java is a complete programming language which can be used to implement large software projects, while JavaScript is a rather simple scripting language which is targeted at small tasks. The syntax of both languages looks somewhat similar, but this is a purely syntactical aspect which does not say much about the design of a language.

With the limited success of VBScript (shortly described in section 8.1.2), Microsoft now supports ECMAScript, with *JScript* being the first fully compliant ECMAScript implementation.

Although the term "JavaScript" originally named the language itself, it is now more appropriate to see "ECMAScript" as the language's name, with JavaScript and JScript being two products implementing this language.

The advantage of a scripting language is the relative simplicity in comparison with a full programming language, as well as its not relying on any development environment. By simply inserting the following HTML markup into a page, an author can use a script without any additional software:

```
<p>Last updated :
<script language="JavaScript">
document.write(document.lastModified);
</script>
```

This simple example inserts the date of the last modification of the document (as given by the HTTP `Last-Modified` header field in the response) into the document's text. Without a script, this information would not be available to an HTML author.

8.1.2 VBScript

Visual Basic Scripting Edition (VBScript) was Microsoft's attempt to define its own scripting language as a competitor to Netscape's JavaScript. Since VBScript is only supported by Internet Explorer, while JavaScript can be used with Internet Explorer and Navigator, VBScript never was widely accepted. After the standardization of JavaScript as ECMAScript, and Microsoft's decision to fully support ECMAScript with its JScript implementation, it seems likely that VBScript will not be very successful.

The idea behind VBScript was to define a scripting language which can easily be used by someone being familiar with *Visual Basic*, which is a very popular programming language for Windows. VBScript therefore is a subset of Visual Basic, designed for the needs of a simple scripting language.

8.2 Programming languages

Programming languages normally are of no special importance to the web, because the implementation of a particular component of the web infrastructure (such as a browser or a server) can be done in any programming language considered appropriate for the task. However, one exception is to see programs themselves as resources, which can be distributed over the web and executed locally. This introduces the problem of platform-dependency of resources into the web. Normally, a program is executable on a particular platform, and this platform is characterized by hardware (in particular, a processor) and software (in particular, the operating system).

The idea of platform-independence of executable programs is not very new, but only the *Java* programming language was successful as a language for platform-independent executable programs distributed over the web.

8.2.1 Java

Java as described by Campione and Walrath [40] is an object-oriented language with strong syntactical similarities to *C++*, but the ideas behind Java have more in common with *Ada* than they have with C++. The main difference between Java and most other programming languages is that Java programs are compiled into *Java bytecode* instead of an actual machine language. Java bytecode is the language of the *Java Virtual Machine (JVM)*. As much as normal programs (being compiled for a particular platform) are executed by that platform (eg, an Intel processor running the Windows operating system), Java bytecode is executed on the JVM.

Rather than being an actual machine[2], JVM is an execution environment that can be implemented on any platform. JVM implementations are available for virtually all platforms, so the same Java program can be executed on all these platforms without the need to be recompiled. This platform-independence of Java makes it a good candidate for distributing programs among heterogeneous platforms. Java programs come in two flavors:

- *Applications*
  A Java application is a normal application as other stand-alone programs. The only difference to applications written in other programming languages is that a Java application uses Java bytecode and therefore must be executed by a JVM implementation instead of the processor.

- *Applets*
  A Java applet is a special form of Java application. Applets are more restricted than applications, because they run in an environment (usually a web browser) that provides a limited window space and other restrictions. Technically, an applet is not a complete application but an implementation of a special Java class. Applets can be inserted into web pages by using HTML's <APPLET> or <OBJECT> elements.

---

[2] Processors using Java bytecode as native machine language have already been developed. In this case there is no need for a virtual machine because the bytecode can be executed by the processor.

Consequently, in the context of the web, Java is most important as the language to write applets. Because Java is also used for stand-alone applications, the support for Java includes a large variety of class libraries and development kits, which can be used to create applets. The most popular components for Java development are:

- *Java Foundation Classes (JFC)*
  The Java Foundation Classes extend the original Java windowing support by adding a comprehensive set of graphical user interface class libraries. JFC provides support for GUI functionality such as color handling, event delegation, different menus, clipboards, and mouse-less operation.

- *Java Naming and Directory Interface (JNDI)*
  This Java component defines a framework for integrating naming and directory services into Java applications. JNDI does not include components for accessing these services, but defines two interfaces for using and providing, respectively, naming and directory services:

  - *Application Programming Interface (API)*
    This interface is used by applications using naming and directory services through JNDI. The API defines procedures for accessing naming and directory services in an abstract way (ie, independent from a specific service).

  - *Service Provider Interface (SPI)*
    This interface is used by a service provider to integrate a service into JNDI. When using a naming service, a client calls JNDI through the API, which then calls a specific provider implementation through the SPI.

  JNDI's design makes it possible to integrate arbitrary naming and directory services with Java applications. An application using JNDI's API does not have to be modified if naming services are changed, it is only necessary to change the provider implementations.

  Typical naming and directory services used through JNDI are the *Domain Name System (DNS)* and directory services accessed by the *Lightweight Directory Access Protocol (LDAP)*. Proprietary naming and directory services can also be integrated, and JNDI allows different provider implementation to cooperate to complete client JNDI operations.

- *JDBC Database Access*
  A usual requirement for applets or applications providing access to data is to query databases. JDBC is an API for accessing databases, in particular it defines Java classes to represent database connections, SQL statements, result sets, database meta data, and other things. It allows a Java programmer to issue SQL statements and process the results. The actual

database access is performed using a *JDBC driver*, which is typically provided by the vendor of a database.

- *JavaBeans*
  This is an architecture to develop component-based software. Components are self-contained, reusable software units that can be visually composed into applets or applications using visual application builder tools. The key idea of JavaBeans is the definition of a number of conventions a component (called a *bean*) must adhere to.

- *Just In Time (JIT) Compiler*
  By using bytecode instead of machine language, Java programs are slower in execution than programs using native machine language, because the JVM has to interpret the bytecode before actually executing it. JIT compilers are part of the JVM and are used to translate bytecode to native machine language. JIT compilers are a performance optimization of the JVM and reduce the performance difference between Java programs and programs using machine language.

In addition to these components, Java programming can be facilitated by a number of other class libraries and interfaces. Comprehensive information about Java and Java development can be found on Sun's Java site at http://java.sun.com/.

8.3 Distributed programming

Programming as described in the previous section is restricted to code execution on a single platform. A more general approach to programming is *distributed programming*, which makes communications part of the programming model.

In the context of the web, distributed programming is mainly of importance for programs distributed over the web. The basic scenario is that a program (usually a Java applet) is executed locally after being downloaded from a web server, and that this program is communicating with other programs, for example acting as a client and requesting services from a server. Although the program itself has been downloaded using standard web mechanisms (most likely HTTP), the communication between the program and the server is part of a distributed programming architecture. There are several distributed programming architectures which can be used to implement such a client/server scenario between a locally executed applet and the remote server.

Java's native distributed programming architecture is *Remote Method Invocation (RMI)* and is described in section 8.3.1. A language-independent model for distributed programming using the client/server paradigm is the *Common Object Request Broker Architecture (CORBA)* as described in section 8.3.2. Microsoft's product for distributed programming is the *Distributed Component object Model (DCOM)* architecture explained in section 8.3.3. Finally, section 8.3.4 discusses interworking issues.

8.3.1 Remote Method Invocation (RMI)

At the most basic level, *Remote Method Invocation (RMI)* is Java's *Remote Procedure Call (RPC)* mechanism. While traditional RPC systems only allow the transport of call parameters via the network, RMI allows to pass objects as arguments and return values. The platform-independence of Java makes this extended mechanism possible.

RMI's ability to pass objects as parameters makes it possible to move behavior in a distributed application. Instead of implementing a server processing all data in a client/server-scenario, the server can store objects, which are transfered to clients upon requesting particular services. Clients execute these objects (which implement a certain behavior) locally. Such a design encourages the splitting of processing between clients and the server, but it still makes it possible for the server to control all behavior. If the behavior has to be changed, the clients can remain the same, only the object on the server has to be changed. When clients request the service again, they get the new object, implementing the modified behavior.

Behavior can also be transferred from a client to a server. The most popular example for an application is a compute server. With RMI, clients can submit arbitrary objects to the server for computation. The server executes the object submitted with the request and returns the results of the computation to the client.

Although RMI mainly focuses on a Java environment, it can also be used to integrate existing solutions using other programming languages. The *Java Native Method Interface (JNI)* can be used for this purpose, for example providing RMI access to a server which is implemented in another programming language.

8.3.2 Common Object Request Broker Architecture (CORBA)

The *Common Object Request Broker Architecture (CORBA)*[198] as specified by the *Object Management Group (OMG)* is a middleware platform for supporting applications in distributed and heterogeneous environments. The key component of CORBA is the *Object Request Broker (ORB)*. An ORB is responsible for transferring operations from clients to servers. The general design of a CORBA-based client/server-application is shown in figure 8.1.

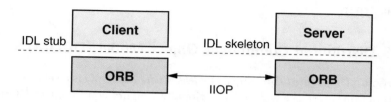

Fig. 8.1 CORBA building blocks

As the protocol for communications between ORBs, CORBA specifies the *General Inter-ORB Protocol (GIOP)*. GIOP is implemented in specialized mappings for one or more network transport layers. One of these mappings of GIOP is the *Internet Inter-ORB Protocol (IIOP)*, which passes requests or receives replies through the Internet's transport layer using the *Transmission Control Protocol (TCP)*.

CORBA interfaces are described using the *Interface Definition Language (IDL)*. IDL is a language which is only used for defining the interface for a CORBA application, the implementation is done using standard programming languages. An IDL compiler is used to generate language specific interfaces from IDL specifications. The CORBA standard defines language mappings from IDL to a number of common programming languages. Currently, mappings are defined for *C, C++, Smalltalk, COBOL, Java,* and *Ada*. Other language mappings are possible (such as the mapping from IDL to *ECMAScript* which is used for the *Document Object Model (DOM)* as described in section 10.5.5), but are currently not standardized. An IDL compiler can create language-specific code for the client- or for the server-side of a CORBA application.

- *Client-side (stub)*
  A stub is the caller side of a CORBA application. It contains virtual function definitions, which can be invoked by a program using the operations defined by the IDL specification, as if they were local. However, the stub contains code to execute the operations remotely.

- *Server-side (skeleton)*
  The server-side of a CORBA application implements the operations defined by the IDL specification. It does so by accepting operation calls, which are invoked through the skeleton, and returning the results through the skeleton.

CORBA therefore defines two different types of interfaces. It defines horizontal interfaces between the application and the ORB using IDL specifications, and it defines a vertical interface between ORBs using GIOP or, more specific, IIOP.

8.3.3 Distributed Component Object Model (DCOM)

Microsoft's *Distributed Component Object Model (DCOM)* is a set of concepts and program interfaces which is functionally roughly equivalent to CORBA, supporting client/server-applications in a distributed environment. DCOM is the extension of the *Component Object Model (COM)*, which provides support for client/server-applications on the same machine. DCOM is part of the *ActiveX* family of technologies.

CORBA and DCOM currently are the two competing technologies for heterogeneous distributed programming. In contrast to CORBA, which started as a specification now being implemented on a large number of platforms, DCOM mainly is a product. Implementations for platforms other than Windows and Macintosh are currently not available.

8.3.4 Interworking

RMI, CORBA, and DCOM are competing technologies for distributed programming. The basic functionality of these technologies is similar, but there are differences in specific features, as well as in supporting interworking in heterogeneous environments. A possible scenario for a heterogeneous environment is shown in figure 8.2, where a Java client (which may be an applet contained in a web page) contacts a server implemented in C++, using the CORBA platform.

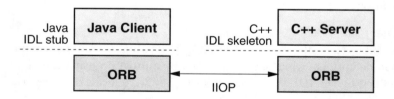

Fig. 8.2   CORBA in a heterogeneous environment

The interworking of Java applications and other programming languages in a CORBA based environment as described by Orfali and Harkey [200] is one of the most promising architectures, allowing interworking independent from the programming language. DCOM, based on the *Remote Procedure Call (RPC)* mechanism defined in the *Distributed Computing Environment (DCE)* standard [261][3], also allows language-independent interworking, but is more restricted in its support for programming languages and operating systems it is running on.

---

[3] DCE is a set of standards for distributed computing, a good overview is given by Rosenberry et al. [232] or can be found in a general introduction [199].

9. HTTP Servers

Although HTTP as a protocol describes the way an HTTP server should interpret and service HTTP requests, there are many possible ways how this could be implemented in a program. A very simple and intuitive way is described by Hethmon [96], who uses the implementation of a simple HTTP server to explain HTTP as a protocol. In fact, the first HTTP server was a very small program mapping the name of the requested resource onto a file name sending the contents of the file as reply (the very first version of HTTP used at that time was HTTP/0.9 as described in section 3.1.1). However, the success of the web and the appearance of web servers hosting a large number of documents, as well as the increasing complexity of HTTP (adding new methods and a multitude of header fields), made the proper configuration and efficient management of an HTTP server a rather complex task.

It is therefore appropriate to dedicate an entire chapter to HTTP servers, which are the most important programs for the web's infrastructure, but rarely experienced first-hand by web users. Instead, from the user perspective a server either works (returning a resource) or somehow does not work, responding with an error message. The internal workings of an HTTP server are something which is important for the web infrastructure, but seldom accessible to web users. This chapter on HTTP servers can therefore be regarded as additional material concerning HTTP as described in chapter 3. It is also helpful in understanding how web sites can be structured, and which aspects of web server behavior can be affected by configuring it in one way or the other.

In section 9.1 some standard tests are described which are commonly used to measure server performance, even though in many cases the primary reason for choosing a particular HTTP server will not be performance. But especially for large sites server performance is a critical issue which has to be taken seriously when a server receives tens of requests per second[1]. However, in many cases the main criterion will more probably be the versatility of the

---

[1] Popular web sites today are accessed in the magnitude of tens of millions accesses per month, resulting in an average of about ten accesses per second and much higher at peak times.

web server, and this aspect is discussed in section 9.2, describing possible server features and configurations. It should always be kept in mind that these are only examples of web server configurations.

As an example of a server, the Apache web server is described in section 9.3, being a free (ie, public domain) server implementation. Apache is consistently the most popular web server (the latest survey from September 1998 shows that 51.9% of all running web servers are Apache servers), and its market share is permanently increasing[2]. However, due to the complexity of Apache (and the large number of third-party modules available for it), only a small fraction of its functionality is described, which is merely intended to give an idea how a real web server can be installed and configured.

Finally, section 9.4 describes how servers can interact with other programs[3]. Although it could be entirely left to the web server implementation to define a way of interaction with external programs, the *Common Gateway Interface (CGI)* defines a standard way of interprocess communications which makes external programs independent from a particular web server implementation. Using CGI, external programs can be developed and used independently from any specific web server.

9.1 Server performance

Measuring the performance of web servers can be done in a number of different ways and using a number of different testing patterns. The two main performance tests for web servers differ significantly in their testing philosophy.

- The *WebStone* benchmark originally developed by *Silicon Graphics, Inc. (SGI)* is a highly configurable test, designed to be used by web site administrators testing web servers. A test pattern is defined which is repeatedly executed between a client machine and the web server running on a different machine. After a number of repetitions statistics are generated which can be used to compare the performance of different web servers. The configurability of the WebStone benchmark, which is useful for designing a test specific for a given access pattern, on the other hand makes it hard to compare results obtained from different test patterns, because web servers may handle individual test patterns very differently.

---

[2] The two web servers dominating the market today are Apache and Microsoft's Internet Information Server, both having increasing market shares over the last years, together a total of 74% of all running web servers.

[3] This functionality is useful if an external program has to be used to service requests. For example, this happens when a server receives a request containing form data. Another possible scenario is a request for a resource which has to be generated dynamically, for example by querying a database.

- The *SPECweb96* benchmark developed by the *Standard Performance Evaluation Corporation (SPEC)* uses a fixed set of test patterns which has been derived from usage patterns of large web servers. This test is mainly designed to be used in closed testing environments, using a server machine and a number of client machines on an isolated network. For this reason, SPECweb96 results can be compared more easily and can be evaluated and published by web server vendors. However, since the test pattern is fixed, the test results can be of limited usability if the web server will eventually be presented with very different usage patterns.

A paper by Hu et al. [104] describes the differences between the two benchmarks and why each of them has a different application area. When comparing benchmark results, it should always be kept in mind that they are both based on simplifications (fixed or limited test patterns, unloaded networks, unloaded machines). Furthermore the two tests described above currently do not take into account CGI interactions and some other issues which may be important for the performance of a web server in a realistic scenario.

9.2 Server configuration

A web server can be configured in a number of different ways. The first question is how a server is running on a machine, which can be either permanently, or only if a request has to be serviced. This question is discussed in section 9.2.1.

The second basic question of server configuration is the question of how many host names should be served by one web server. If more than one host name should be served, it is necessary to use *virtual hosts*, which are described in section 9.2.2.

The two basic modes how a web server may be configured while it is serving a particular host name is as an *origin server* as described in section 9.2.3, or as a *proxy server* as described in section 9.2.4.

9.2.1 Server start

By definition, a server is a program waiting for requests from clients which are then processed, resulting in a response being sent. A web server is expected to perform like this, but the exact mechanism of how incoming requests from clients are handled can vary. The older (and increasingly unpopular) method is to start the web server on request, this is described in section 9.2.1.1. The other method is to have the server running continuously, this configuration is described in section 9.2.1.2.

9.2.1.1 Started on request

This server configuration has its origins in times when memory was a precious resource on computer systems, and many services that were provided by a host were only used occasionally. The basic idea is to have one program running, called the *Internet superserver (inetd)*[4], which listens for requests on a number of ports which are associated with services. If a connection request is received, the Internet superserver starts the appropriate server (ie, the server which has been configured to handle connection requests on this port), which then processes the request.

The advantage is that the Internet superserver can be configured to listen to a large number of ports, thus representing a large number services, without the need to have all servers running constantly. On a system where the number of running processes is crucial to system performance, this is very useful. Furthermore, if services are used infrequently, it makes sense to only start the server if it is needed.

A possible configuration for a web server running in Internet superserver mode includes a configuration entry for the Internet superserver associating the web server's port (typically HTTP standard port 80) with the web server executable program. This program is started by the Internet superserver if a connection request is received on the configured port. The web server takes over the connection[5], processes it, generates and sends a response, and terminates.

However, there are some drawbacks to this approach. The most important drawback is that process creation on most operating systems is a rather costly operation, requiring a lot of system resources (because a lot of system data structures have to be modified to make the new process known to the system, and because the program code has to be loaded from the file system to system memory). If the number of requests for a particular service is high, the Internet superserver model results in a large number of process creations and terminations. This can create significantly more load than a constantly running server process. Furthermore, on modern systems main memory is abundant, so the requirement to keep the number of running processes as small as possible is not a critical issue anymore.

The Internet superserver still is useful for services which are only rarely used and require need a process consuming many system resources. However,

---

[4] The name "inetd" is a combination of the abbreviated word "Internet" and the Unix convention to suffix server programs (or "daemons" as they are frequently called in Unix) with the letter 'd'.

[5] This taking over of a connection is a built-in feature of Unix, where a process started by another process inherits the execution environment of the so-called parent process, including open files and network connections.

for a web server, typically receiving a large number of requests which can be serviced rather easily, the Internet superserver model is not really appropriate, and its use is discouraged by most web server installation guides[6]. Only for experimental reasons and systems with very limited system resources the Internet superserver model should be considered.

9.2.1.2 Permanently running

In almost all cases, a web server is installed as permanently running. In this case, it has to be made sure that the web server is started on system startup, which is typically done in a system startup file. It is not a very reliable configuration to start the web server manually, because it will not be running if the system reboots after a crash or power failure.

After being started, the web server listens on the port that has been configured, and accepts any incoming connections on that port. Thus, a permanently running web server will handle requests faster than a web server configured in Internet superserver mode, because it is already running and is therefore able to handle requests instantaneously, while the web server configured in Internet superserver mode first has to be started.

9.2.2 Virtual hosts

A very frequent requirement for web server configuration is the usage of so-called *virtual hosts*. A server configured this way is able to serve requests for different hosts, where a host is identified by a DNS name. There are several reasons why virtual hosts can be very useful for a server administrator:

- *Server software administration*
  If only one server is used, there is only one instance of the server software and the server administrator can upgrade the whole server (and not only a single host) by upgrading this instance of the server software.

- *Server configuration*
  Since a lot of a server's configuration is common for all hosts, it is much easier to have only one server configuration with all common definitions, and to use virtual host configurations only where they need to be different from each other.

- *Maintenance*
  Server maintenance is easier with only one server running on a machine. It is easier to monitor only one instance of a server than to monitor a

---

[6] For example, the Apache documentation contains the following warning: "Inetd mode is no longer recommended and does not always work properly. Avoid it if at all possible."

number of independently running servers for each host. It is also easier to create and analyze log files if there is only one set of them.

- *Performance*

  The load on a machine will be higher if there are multiple servers running for each host, in terms of CPU usage as well as in terms of memory requirements. Furthermore, optimizations like the dynamic allocation of server processes are more efficient if all hosts share the same pool of server processes.

So there are a number of good reasons to use virtual hosts on a server if it is necessary to have one machine serving multiple host names. There are two methods to implement virtual hosts. *IP-based virtual hosts* is the older method of implementing virtual hosts and is still in use in many cases, because it does not have to make any assumptions about the HTTP version being used. It is described in section 9.2.2.1. *Non-IP-based virtual hosts*, as described in section 9.2.2.2 are the newer method of implementing virtual hosts, but can only be used if the client and the server use at least HTTP/1.1.

9.2.2.1 IP-based virtual hosts

The basic idea of IP-based virtual hosts is to treat every virtual host as if it were a separate IP host, having an individual IP number. For the configuration of IP-based virtual hosts, it is necessary to reserve as many IP addresses as IP-based virtual hosts are required, and to create DNS entries for all host names of the IP-based virtual hosts which are resolved to the individual IP addresses. This basic setup is shown in figure 9.1, where the left box represents the DNS entries, and the right box shows the server which is configured for two IP-based virtual hosts.

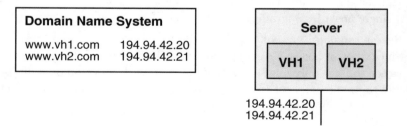

Fig. 9.1 IP-based virtual hosts

The next step in the configuration of IP-based virtual hosts is to assign all the IP addresses to the machine on which the server is running. In most cases, this will result in one interface having multiple IP addresses. The server has to be configured in a way that it listens to all IP addresses, so there must be a list in the server configuration which gives a mapping for all virtual hosts and their IP addresses.

If a connection request is received, the server knows for which IP address this request has been made, and therefore also knows for which virtual host this request has been made. The server can respond to the request according to the configuration for this virtual host.

This type of virtual hosts configuration is rather simple, but it has two disadvantages, which led to a demand for another way to configure virtual hosts. The first disadvantage is the need for one IP address for each virtual host. For large service providers, this means that one machine will have a large number of IP addresses. This obviously is a waste of IP addresses (which are a finite resource), and it would be desirable to have another way of configuring virtual hosts.

The other drawback of this type of virtual host configuration is that, although a machine having hundreds or thousands of IP address is not a theoretical problem, in practice it may cause serious problems. Operating systems and routers have not been designed to deal with hosts which are configured in this way, and therefore many implementations of networking software have problems dealing with it. Although this is only a problem of implementations, it would be better to avoid this type of configuration in the first place rather than changing the implementations of networking software.

However, although all these problems were well-known, there was no way to deal with them prior to HTTP/1.1, because the protocol specification did not contain a way to identify for which virtual host a request had been sent, so the only way to make this distinction was using different IP addresses for each virtual host.

9.2.2.2 Non IP-based virtual hosts

Since it was clear that there had to be some kind of protocol support to distinguish the requests for different virtual hosts on one server, HTTP/1.1 introduced the Host header field and made this header field mandatory. The Host header field contains the host name for which a request is sent. This protocol feature makes it possible to use non IP-based virtual hosts. The configuration of non IP-based virtual hosts is similar to that of IP-based virtual hosts, but instead of defining DNS entries which have different IP addresses, all DNS entries for the virtual hosts have the same IP address. Therefore, the network interface of the server only needs to have one IP address. This setup is shown in figure 9.2, which shows the same configuration

than the example in the previous section, but uses non IP-based virtual hosts
instead of IP-based virtual hosts

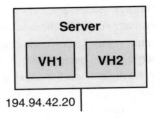

Fig. 9.2 Non IP-based virtual hosts

The server now only listens to one IP address, and since every incoming
request contains an identification for which virtual hosts it has been sent
(specified in the Host header field), the server can use this information to
reply to the request according to the virtual host's configuration. If the URL
in the request line is an absolute URL (ie, contains a host name as well as
path information), the server has to ignore the Host header field and has to
use the host name from the absolute URL.

An important advantage of non IP-based virtual hosts is that the creation
of a new virtual host is easier than with IP-based virtual hosts. For a new non
IP-based virtual host, it is necessary to create a new DNS entry which has
the server's address, and to configure the virtual host inside the server. With
IP-based virtual hosts, it is also necessary to change the network interface
configuration, because a new IP address had to be assigned to it.

The main drawback of non IP-based virtual hosts is that they are only
defined in HTTP/1.1 or newer[7]. However, since the problem of IP-based
virtual hosts has been around for a while, most clients which do not yet
implement HTTP/1.1 do send a Host header field in every request (although
not defined by the protocol specification) for compatibility with non IP-based
virtual hosts.

9.2.3 Origin servers

Most often a web server is configured as an origin server. An origin server
receives requests and handles them locally, in contrast to a proxy server which
has the ability to forward requests to other servers (either origin servers or
other proxies). Running an origin server involves mainly questions how to

---

[7] Because only HTTP/1.1 requires every request to contain the Host header field.

handle incoming requests, ranging from administrative issues to performance questions. In this section, only a selection of relevant issues is discussed.

The most basic question is how requests, including a URL path, should be handled in terms of locating resources. This question is discussed in section 9.2.3.1. An additional question is how to handle user-specific web pages on multi-user systems. The most popular approaches to this problem are described in section 9.2.3.2.

More generally, it has to be decided how incoming requests should be handled which do not refer to a resource. This question is discussed in section 9.2.3.3.

Finally, because of its implications with regard to security issues, the question of CGI scripts, their handling, authorization, and execution should be considered before running a web server. Section 9.2.3.4 briefly describes possible ways to deal with that problem.

9.2.3.1 General file system layout

Although a URL path closely resembles a file name (it uses the Unix file name conventions, separating hierarchical elements with a slash character '/'), it does not necessarily correspond to any given file system structure on the web server. It is entirely up to the server to define a mapping between URL paths and local resources (which do not even have to be organized in a file system). In many cases, however, this mapping will simply use the URL path as a suffix to a file system prefix pointing to the place inside the file system where web resources reside.

However, even though the mapping from the URL path to a local resource can be freely defined by the server (because the only semantics defined for a URL path is the use of an hierarchical structure), there are two fundamentally different resources which have to be handled differently by the server:

- *Static resources*
  Static resources are resources which reside inside the file system and can be simply accessed by the server by reading the corresponding file. Depending on the resource type, some processing may be necessary (such as scanning the file for server-side includes as described in section 9.3.2.5). However, in all cases the web server can generate the response without the help of any other process. Typically, static resources are defined by a rather simple mapping of URL paths onto file system paths.

- *Dynamic resources*
  Dynamic resources on the other side are dynamically generated by external programs. Consequently, the URL path does not refer to a resource

inside the file system, but to an external program, which has to be activated by the server in order to generate the response. The most common way to do this is CGI as described in section 9.4. Because dynamic resources have to be handled in a special way, in most cases servers have special URL path prefixes as described in section 9.2.3.4 to identify them.

The server has to handle these two types of resources differently because in one case it simply can read the static resource from the file system, while in the other case an external program has to be started or contacted which generates the resource.

9.2.3.2 User specific web pages

A frequent requirement in multi-user environments is that users are able to create their own web pages and can make them available via the web server without the help of the web server administrator (this is sometimes called the provision of *web space* to users). The usual approach is to provide users with a special location somewhere in the file system where they can put their web pages.

The web space of users on a server is usually referred to with a URL containing the tilde character '~' and the user's name. Using this convention, the URL http://www.company.com/~name refers to the web space of user name on the web server www.company.com[8]. Basically, there are two ways how a web server may organize the individual web space of users, and how it therefore may map such a request to an actual location in the file system:

- *Creating a central space for user pages*
  In this case, a file system or directory is created containing individual directories for all users. The access rights of these directories are set in a way that the server may read all of them, but only the users themselves are allowed to write to their directories.
  For example, a webhome/ directory may be created in a central file system, containing a webhome/name/ directory. Only user name is allowed to write to this directory, but the web server can read it. The web server maps all requests with a URL path of ~name to the file system location webhome/name/ and therefore looks in the user's personal web space for the requested resource.

- *Accessing special directories*
  The second alternative is to have special directories in the users' personal directories. In this case, each user has the web space directly in his per-

---

[8] In section 9.2.3.3 it is discussed how a server may handle this request, since it does not specify a document name (such as index.html).

sonal directory, so the access rights must be set in a way which allows the web server access to the user's web space.

An example for this setup is to have a WWW/ directory inside a user's home directory, so the user name would have a /home/name/WWW/ directory[9] as personal web space. The web server in this case maps all requests with a URL path of ~name to a location /home/name/WWW/ and therefore looks in the user's personal web space for the requested resource[10]

Which of these methods is chosen is to a large extent a matter of taste. The advantage of the first method is that all user web pages are in a central location and can more easily be managed. Furthermore, if a user's personal directory becomes unavailable (eg, because the user switches off the machine on which it is located), the web pages are still accessible, since they usually are in a separate file system.

The second approach is less centralized and has the advantage that the system administrator has one less centralized file system to manage. In addition, any disk quotas enforced for users will include the web pages without further configuration.

However, in both cases it is important to make clear to users that all data that they write to their personal web space is world wide accessible via the web server, so care should be taken not to accidentally copy sensitive data to the web space.

9.2.3.3 Handling requests

It is possible that an incoming request does not correctly refer to a resource on the system, neither a resource within the file system, nor a script to be executed. There are two popular reasons for this to happen. The first is an error in the URL, which can be caused by a typographic error, or an old URL which is no longer valid. In case of typographic errors, the server in most cases will simply report an error[11], while in case of old URLs the server

---

[9] This assumes that home directories start with /home/. The Unix file name convention is to denote user name's home directory as ~name, but this can easily be confused with the URL convention for personal web space. The Unix convention is where the URL convention for naming personal web space actually originated.

[10] As a consequence of URL and Unix conventions about user data, the web server actually maps the URL path ~name to the Unix directory path ~name/WWW/.

[11] It is possible that the server tries to guess the right resource name by assuming a maximum number of typographic errors and looking for resources with these names. Apache includes a module for spell checking which can be enabled to automatically search for resources with slightly different names. However, this spell checking involves a search of possibly many directories of the file system and can have a serious impact on the server's performance.

could reply with an error message specifically saying that the document is no longer available, using a 410 (gone) instead of a 404 (not found) status code. If the new location of the resource is known to the server, it could also reply with a redirection response using a 301 (moved permanently) or 302 (moved temporarily) status code.

The second reason for URLs not referring to resources is the use of directory names rather than file names. Strictly speaking, there is no concept of directories in URLs, since the components separated by slash characters simply form a hierarchical name. Omitting the last component of such a hierarchical does not necessarily refer to a resource, but in file system semantics this refers to a directory. For this reason, it is common practice that users request URLs which they assume to be directories of resources. It is up to the server to decide how to reply to these requests.

1. *Accepting directory names*

   As a first alternative, the server may reject requests using directory names in the URL path because they do not refer to resources, which are usually represented by files. However, this can be seen as a philosophical question, because from another point of view directories are also resources, containing a number of file names (thus leading to other resources). In the end, it is up to the administrator to decide whether directory information should be made available via the web.

2. *Using default file names*

   If the server accepts a directory as URL path, it can assume a number of default file names in the directory (index.html and welcome.html are popular default file names) and look for these file names. If such a file is found, the server sends as a response the content of the file.

3. *Sending directory listings as results*

   If a directory name as URL path is accepted, and the server does not find any files matching default file names, it may either reject the request (because it is not willing to make directory information available via the web), or send as response an HTML page containing the directory listing, including links to all files in the directory.

   The option of sending back directory listings is the most relaxed form of server security and is regarded as being too insecure by many server administrators, because it lets clients learn about file names (and directory structures) on the server without prior knowledge of any of them. It is easy to traverse and examine the server's file system using the generated directory listings.

   If this option is being used, care should be taken to exclude security sensitive files from directory listings and to somehow prevent users from saving any sensitive files in the file system part which can be accessed by the HTTP server.

Apart from these rather basic decisions when servicing requests, the server is free to interpret requests in any way as long as the response is a valid HTTP message and contains the information a client expects in a response (such as the media type and date information). A frequent requirement for servers is to write log files which can be analyzed to produce server usage statistics. Typically, a server writes one line per request, containing the most important information about the request as well as the generated response. The most common file format for log files is the *Common Log Format (CLF)*, which can be generated and analyzed by many applications.

9.2.3.4 CGI scripts

A special case of request is a request for a *CGI script* (as described in section 9.4) or any other resource which involves invoking an external program instead of simply reading a file from the file system. Syntactically, requests for scripts are not different from requests for files, but in many cases the URL path of such a request has the form /cgi-bin/scriptname. Generally, a server identifies external programs either by this special path prefix or by their file name extensions.

The reason for this special path prefix is that most server administrators prefer to have all external programs in one place, making it easier to manage them and to set special precautions for access to them. External programs have to be treated with special care because they are essentially programs on the server which can be invoked from anywhere (unless access restrictions are specified), often using parameters. Although in most cases it is not possible to extensively test external programs before making them available on the web, it should always be kept in mind that external programs are the biggest security problem for web servers.

In many cases, a web server is configured to only execute external programs if they are stored in a dedicated directory, such as the cgi-bin/ directory. Even if the server is configured to allow users to publish their own web pages as described in section 9.2.3.2, users are often not allowed to make external programs available in their individual web space. If a user needs to make an external program available, the server administrator copies the program to the cgi-bin/ directory after a security check to see whether the server's security guidelines are met by the program.

9.2.4 Proxies

As explained in section 3.2, apart from origin servers, proxies are the most important form of web server configuration. A proxy accepts requests for resources and either serves them from the local cache (containing resources which has been cached after servicing earlier requests), or forwards the request. This aspect of proxy behavior is described in section 9.2.4.1.

Apart from serving as a cache, a proxy also can be used primarily for security reasons. A proxy as an intermediary between a client and an origin server can be used for filtering requests, and for converting protocols between secure and insecure variants of HTTP. This usage of a proxy is discussed in section 9.2.4.2.

9.2.4.1 Caching

The configuration of a proxy as a cache highly depends on the particular server program. Generally, the cache must be configured specifying at least the following information:

- *Cache size*
  The cache size specifies the maximum amount of information that should be stored by the proxy. The bigger the cache is, the more likely it is that a request for a resource can be served from the cache.

- *Cache location*
  Although the cache in most cases is organized according to rules internal to the server, there must be a location inside the file system of the server where the server stores the cached files. Typically, the server creates its own directory hierarchy in that location.

- *Cache handling*
  Cache handling involves a strategy how the cache is to be managed, in particular according to which strategy cache entries should be removed from the cache. Furthermore, the caching strategy can include rules overriding the expiration dates specified by the resources themselves.
  In general, a proxy is entirely free to use its own caching policy, as long as it operates in accordance with the caching semantics as defined by HTTP, in particular semantic transparency. Caching policies can be based on resource sizes, content types, resource locations, preferred or ignored domains, and other criteria which are deemed useful by the cache administrator.

When configuring a proxy as a cache, it must always be kept in mind that clients must be explicitly configured to use the proxy cache instead of the origin server for sending requests. The most common scenario is to configure a proxy as a cache for an intranet, for example a company network. In this case, the proxy is located between the intranet and the Internet.

Another common scenario is the use of a proxy cache by an Internet service provider. In this case, the browser configuration distributed to the provider's customers involves a cache which is located between the access points of the customers (eg, the modems where the customers dial in), and the provider's connection to the Internet.

A properly placed and configured proxy cache is useful for all involved parties. It reduces the load on the origin servers by using cached copies instead of requesting the same resource from the origin server repeatedly, it reduces the amount of traffic on the Internet connection of the proxy operator by avoiding requests to origin servers, and it reduces the latency for users of the cache by delivering cached copies which are available much faster than accessing the origin server.

9.2.4.2 Security

Another reason for using a proxy can be security considerations. Secure servers, using the *HTTP over SSL (HTTPS)* protocol as described in section 3.3.1, often provide services which involve sensitive information, such as credit card numbers. A proxy can be used to access secure servers in two different ways.

HTTPS proxying

In the case of *HTTPS proxying*, the proxy is used as a gateway between HTTP and HTTPS. This configuration is shown in figure 9.3, where the proxy is connected to the client using HTTP, and connected to the origin server using HTTPS.

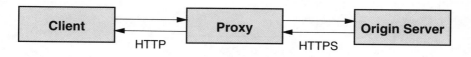

Fig. 9.3 HTTPS proxying

In this case, the client does not need to have an HTTPS implementation, because it uses normal HTTP to connect to the proxy. This configuration is based on the assumption that the intranet (ie, the connection between the client and the proxy), is secure, and that only the data exchanged between the proxy and the origin server needs to be protected.

In this case, the proxy can interpret data received from the origin server as usual and store it in its cache. However, there are some disadvantages to this approach:

- *Insecure client/proxy connection*
  Depending on the scenario, this may be an issue. TCP/IP is a rather insecure protocol, and as long as the entire network is not physically shielded from unauthorized access, it is very easy to perform eavesdropping on the insecure client/proxy connection.

- *Full SSL implementation on proxy required*
  Because only the proxy uses HTTPS, it must contain a full SSL implementation (which is the underlying protocol of HTTPS). If the proxy is heavily loaded, the additional overhead of SSL may become a performance problem.

- *No SSL client authentication is possible*
  Because the client uses normal HTTP, the server cannot perform SSL client authentication (an optional mechanism of SSL to determine the identity of the client by using cryptographic methods).

These disadvantages of HTTPS proxying motivated the invention of another scheme of using secure servers and proxies. The alternative approach is based on the goal to implement a secure connection between the client and the origin server.

SSL proxying

Luotonen [163] describes a method how a proxy may be used to directly connect a client to an origin server using HTTPS. Because this approach works with any application protocol based on SSL, this method is called *SSL proxying*. In figure 9.4 it is shown how SSL proxying connects a client to an origin server through a proxy.

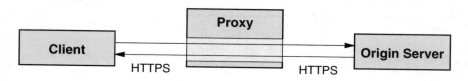

Fig. 9.4 SSL proxying

SSL proxying is based on a new HTTP method, which is called CONNECT. This method is used by a client to communicate to the proxy to which origin server a tunnel should be created. The proxy connects to the origin server and after that simply forwards all data from the client to the origin server and vice versa. With this approach, a secure connection between the client and the origin server can be implemented, so that SSL client authentication is possible. Furthermore, the proxy does not need to contain an SSL implementation, all it has to do is support the CONNECT method.

9.3 The Apache HTTP server

The Apache web server described by Laurie and Laurie [158] is a web server implementation which is available for a large number of operating systems free of charge. It can be downloaded and installed by anyone interested in running a web server, and the availability in combination with the extensive functionality have made Apache the most prevalent server on the web.

One key issue of Apache is its *Application Programming Interface (API)* as described by Thau [260], which is designed to make Apache easily extensible by additional *modules*. The modular approach of Apache makes it easy for anyone to develop additional functionality for the server, and many modules which are now part of the standard distribution have been contributed to the Apache project by third parties.

Based on the NCSA web server (which originally was the most frequently used web server), Apache now contains much more functionality than this older server. This section about Apache only describes a small fraction of the installation and configuration possibilities, intended to give a flavor of how a web server is managed. If the complexity of handling Apache seems to be overwhelming, one can choose from numerous companies offering commercial Apache support, so that the usage of a free product can be combined with the security of professional configuration, maintenance, and trouble-shooting.

Apache is configured using various configuration files, and it takes some time to get used to the configuration process. However, after this initial period, configuration can be done rather quickly. Basically, Apache is controlled by *Apache directives*, which are used to specify the behavior of the server in a number of ways.

In addition to the normal directives which can be used to set certain parameters, Apache defines a number of *block directives* limiting the effect of other directives. The block directives have the same syntax as HTML elements, the block starts with <name>, contains the directives which should be limited to the block, and ends with </name>.

The <VirtualHost> directive limits the directives inside it to a particular virtual host (described in detail in section 9.3.2.1). The <Directory> directive limits the directives inside it to a directory or a group of directories, thus acting on the file system level. The `<Files>` directive can be used to limit directives inside it to specific files, therefore also acting on the file system level. The `<Location>` directive is used to limit the directives inside it to a particular URL prefix, thus acting on the URL level instead of the file system[12]. Finally, the `<Limit>` block directive can be used to enclose a group of access control directives applying only to the specified HTTP methods.

Apache as a program can be downloaded from many sources on the Internet. After downloading, it must be installed on the designated web server machine. The installation process is described in section 9.3.1. The most complex part of Apache is its configuration, described in section 9.3.2.

9.3.1 Installation

Basically, the installation of Apache requires two steps. The first step is the installation of Apache as an executable program and is described in section 9.3.1.1. The second step involves the decision already described in section 9.2.1 when the server should be started. This step of Apache installation is described in section 9.3.1.2.

9.3.1.1 Program installation

Apache installation very much depends on the computer platform on which it should be installed. Basically, Apache can be downloaded as source code and compiled on the target platform, or it can be downloaded as pre-compiled binary[13] distribution for many popular platforms. Both methods have advantages and drawbacks.

- *Compiling the source code*
  Using this method, it is possible to compile a version of the server which is tailored to the specific server requirements (such as special modules and special configuration variables) and the computing environment. It is also possible to create a version which is optimized by a compiler in a way which is not possible for pre-compiled versions. Furthermore, it may be necessary to create a binary for a platform which is not supported with a pre-compiled binary version.

  The disadvantage of compiling the source code is that it is more complicated than simply downloading a pre-compiled binary version, and that

---

[12] Starting with Apache 1.3, it is furthermore possible to use `<DirectoryMatch>`, `<FilesMatch>`, and `<LocationMatch>` directives each accepting regular expressions in addition to text strings.

[13] A *binary* is an executable version of a program. In contrast to the program *source code*, which can be compiled on different platforms, a binary is specific to a. particular platform (ie, operating system and hardware).

it may be harder to find errors, because the self-compiled version may be very different from a standard setup.

- *Using a binary distribution*
  In most cases, it will be sufficient to use a pre-compiled binary version. These versions are available for a large number of popular platforms, and for the average user the configuration of the pre-compiled binary versions will be appropriate.

  However, a pre-compiled binary version may not be as optimized as a custom-built version can be, and it is also possible that many of the modules which are compiled into the binary are not required at all.

Seeing these alternatives, the best approach is to use a pre-compiled binary version as long as one is experimenting with the Apache Software, and as long as it is not necessary to achieve optimum performance. The two main reasons for compiling an own version of Apache will be the inclusion of modules which are not integrated in the pre-compiled binary versions, and the creation of an optimized version of Apache. The optimization will be mostly in terms of size (only including the modules which are required), and customization for a given platform.

9.3.1.2 Startup installation

After the Apache program is available as an executable file, it must be decided how and when the server should be started. This is done using the `ServerType` directive, which determines whether the server should be started on request, or should be permanently running. Both variants are described in section 9.2.1. In both cases, the operating system must be configured to actually start the server, either on request usually triggered by the *Internet superserver (inetd)*, or at system startup time if the server should be running permanently.

If the server is configured to run permanently (which is the normal configuration), some other directives can be used to determine the behavior of the server. The `MaxServers` directive configures the maximum number of servers running concurrently. Usually, when the server receives a request, it creates a copy of itself (a child process) which handles the request, while the server waits for new requests directly after creating the child. The `MaxRequestsPerChild` directive decides how many requests are to be handled by a child process after it terminates. This is a security mechanism avoiding the possibility of very old server processes. The `MinSpareServers` and `MaxSpareServers` directives are used to determine how many server processes

should be left idle at least and at most while waiting for incoming requests[14].
If less servers are idling than the configured minimum, child processes are
created, and if more servers are idling than the configured maximum, they
are terminated.

9.3.2 Configuration

Apache is configured by using configuration directives. The configuration
directives are interpreted by different modules, so the allowed configuration
directives depend on the modules which are compiled into one particular
version of Apache. A number of directives are *core* directives, meaning that
they are not implemented in an additional module. Core directives provide
basic functionality and can be used in any version of Apache, independently
from any specific modules.

9.3.2.1 Virtual hosts

Virtual hosts as described in section 9.2.2 can be configured using Apache's
`<VirtualHost>` block directive. If non-IP-based virtual hosts are configured, it is necessary to use the `NameVirtualHost` directive. Inside the
`<VirtualHost>` directive, the `ServerName` directive is used to specify the
name of the virtual host. This name has to be a DNS name resolving to the
IP address for which the virtual host is defined.

In addition to the `ServerName` directive, a number of other Apache directives can be used inside the `<VirtualHost>` directive. These directives can
be used to set the `DocumentRoot` for a virtual host (the file system location
where resources for the virtual host reside), error or log file names, or other
specifications only affecting a specific virtual host:

```
NameVirtualHost 18.23.0.22

<VirtualHost 18.23.0.22>
DocumentRoot /www/company1
ServerName www.company1.com
</VirtualHost>

<VirtualHost 18.23.0.22>
DocumentRoot /www/company2
ServerName www.company2.com
</VirtualHost>
```

---

[14] The `StartServers` directive can be used to determine the number of servers
started initially. Since after startup this number is dynamically controlled by the
`MinSpareServers` and `MaxSpareServers` directives, the initial setting is of minor
importance.

When configuring virtual hosts, it should be kept in mind that the `<VirtualHost>` directive does not affect what IP addresses or ports Apache listens on. It may be necessary to ensure that Apache is listening on the correct addresses using either the `BindAddress` or `Listen` directive.

9.3.2.2 Authentication

User authentication as described in section 3.2.6 can be used in two different ways. Both ways require different modules to be compiled into Apache.

- *Text files*
  In this case, standard text files are used for user authentication, having the same syntax as Unix *passwd* and *group* files. The `AuthUserFile` directive is used to specify the location of the user (ie, passwd) file, and the `AuthGroupFile` directive specifies the location of the group file.

- *Database files*
  Another way to store user and group information is in *Berkeley DB* files (usually available on BSD systems and derivatives), or *DBM* database files. Optional Apache modules support these file formats, providing directives to access either DB or DBM files containing user and group information.

The actual authentication requirements for resources are specified for directories or individual files using the `require` directive. The `AuthType` directive specifies the type of authentication to be used, it can specify either *basic authentication* as described in section 3.2.6.1, or *digest access authentication* as described in section 3.2.6.2. The `AuthName` directive is used to define the *realm* value, identifying a particular protection space of the server. The realm value is transmitted to the client so that the user knows which name and password to send.

```
<Directory /web/company1/securedocs>
AuthType       Basic
AuthName       secure
AuthUserFile   /web/admin/company1/users
AuthGroupFile  /web/admin/company1/groups
require        valid-user
</Directory>
```

This example sets authentication for a specific directory of the server. The authentication mechanism is basic authentication, the realm is named `secure` (this will be displayed to users requesting resources from that directory), the user and group files are normal text files, and it is required that a user is a valid user (ie, listed in the user file) in order to access the directory.

9.3.2.3 Content negotiation

Content negotiation as described in section 3.2.5 can be realized as a server mechanism, in which case it is called *server-driven* content negotiation. Apache supports content negotiation using two different mechanisms.

Variants files

Using the AddHandler directive, Apache can be instructed to interpret *variants files*. A variants file (typically having the file name extension .var) contains a list of all variants of a resource. The URL referring to the resource must specify the variants file, which is interpreted by Apache to find the closest matching resource. A sample variants file may look like this:

```
URI: english-intro.html
Content-Language: en

URI: german-intro.html
Content-Language: de
```

If Apache receives a request for intro.var (the name of the variants file shown above), it interprets the Accept-Language header of the request and returns either the english or the german version of the resource. The Accept-Language in the request usually has been set according to user preferences configured in the browser sending the request.

File extensions

The variants file approach has the disadvantage that existing links must be updated to refer to the variants file instead of the resources themselves. Apache supports a mechanism which makes it possible to provide content negotiation without the need to change existing links. This mechanism uses file extensions for the identification of resource variants and must be enabled by setting the MultiViews option for a number of resources using the Options directive.

Using the AddLanguage, AddEncoding, and AddType directives, a mapping between a file extension and resource variants can be defined. The following configuration file excerpt shows possible mapping:

```
AddLanguage en .en
AddLanguage de .de
```

Using this configuration, language-dependent resources can be named intro.en.html and intro.de.html, and Apache selects one of these documents if it receives a request for intro.html. Basically, this mechanism extends Apache's mapping from file extensions to MIME types, which normally is only used to conclude from a file extension what the content type of a resource is. The `MultiViews` option effectively causes Apache to interpret file extensions as if they were specifications in a variants file.

9.3.2.4 Proxies

To configure an Apache server as a proxy, the most important step is to use the `ProxyRequest` directive to enable proxy mode. This means that the server accepts requests for resources which are not local to the server, and forwards these requests to the appropriate origin server. If the configured server should also use proxies, these can be configured with `ProxyRemote` directives in a way similar to proxy configuration in a browser.

In most cases, a proxy is also configured as a cache. This can be done using the `CacheRoot` directive specifying a location in the file system where the cached files should be stored. The organization of this cache using several directories is done by Apache, but can be influenced by specifying the `CacheDirLevels` and `CacheDirLength` directives. These directives should be set according to the characteristics of the file system. Cache size is controlled by Apache, but an upper limit should be set using the `CacheSize` directive.

9.3.2.5 Server-Side Includes (SSI)

For some application areas, Server-Side Includes (SSI) are a simple alternative to CGI scripts. SSI provides a mechanism where the server parses an HTML file, in the process executing embedded commands, and sends the modified resource as response. A simple example for SSI is the inclusion of a file, which may be a standard header or footer to be displayed on each of a number of pages. The advantage of SSI over CGI is that it is simple to use, and that it faster than CGI, because no external program has to be executed.

In Apache, SSI is enabled setting the `Includes` option for a number of resources using the `Options` directive. There are two possible ways to identify resources as containing SSI instructions:

- *File names*
  In this case, a special file name extension (usually `.shtml`) is used to identify a resource as containing SSI instructions.

- *File modes*
  Using the `XBitHack` directive, Apache can be instructed to use the file mode for determining SSI files. If a file has the execute bit set, it is considered to be an SSI file.

It is important that SSI files can be identified using these parameters, because the parsing of HTML files is time-consuming and should only performed for files actually containing SSI commands.

A SSI command has the syntax of an SGML *comment*, which means it is started by a *markup declaration open* delimiter (MDO), represented by '<!', directly followed by a *start or end of comment* delimiter (COM), represented by '--', and it is ended by another *start or end of comment* delimiter (COM) directly followed by a *markup declaration close* delimiter (MDC), represented by '>'. SGML (and thus HTML) ignores everything inside SGML comments, but the server interprets the content as an SSI command if it adheres to the following syntax:

```
<!-- #element attribute=value attribute=value ... -->
```

The `element` specifies the SSI command, and the parameters of the SSI command are specified as attribute/value pairs. Apache defines a number of basic elements as well as some advanced features, which are known as *Extended Server-Side Includes (XSSI)*.

Basic elements

The following basic elements can be used as SSI commands in HTML pages:

- `config`
  This command controls aspects of the parsing, it does not produce any output. The `config` command controls error messages and the formatting of sizes and dates.

- `echo`
  The `echo` command is used to print a variable. All CGI variables described in section 9.4.1.1 as well as some additional variables can be used with this command.

- `exec`
  This command can be used to execute either a CGI script or a shell command. The output of the script or the command will be included into the document.

- `fsize`
  The `fsize` command prints the size of a specified file.

- `flastmod`
  This command prints the last modification date of a specified file.

- `include`
  The `include` command includes the text of another document or file into the parsed file. If the included file is an SSI file, it is also parsed by the server, thus included files can be nested.

- `printenv`

  This command prints a list of all existing variables and their values. It is mainly used for debugging purposes.

- `set`

  The `set` command is used to set a variable to a given value.

With these commands it is possible to create pages containing dynamic information such as modification dates and file sizes. Carefully designed web sites using SSI can define entire hierarchies of include files, providing document headers, footers, or other functional blocks to be used by many documents.

Flow control

In addition to the simple replacing mechanisms described in the previous section, Apache also defines *Extended Server-Side Includes (XSSI)*. XSSI provides flow control by introducing the four new commands `if`, `elif`, `else`, and `endif`. The following example of an XSSI file[15] uses a CGI variable for conditionally created text:

```
<!-- #if expr="\"$SERVER_PROTOCOL\" = \"HTTP/1.1\"" -->
<p>Your request was sent using the latest version of HTTP. Thank you.
<!-- #else -->
<p>Your browser uses an old version of HTTP (it uses
<!-- #echo var="SERVER_PROTOCOL" --> instead of HTTP/1.1).
<!-- #endif -->
```

All CGI variables can be accessed using this method, and XSSI defines a number of more powerful conditions than simply testing for equality. Although XSSI can be used to perform rather complex generation of web pages based on the request, it should be kept in mind that XSSI is specific to Apache, whereas a CGI script performing the same task can be used with any server.

9.4 Common Gateway Interface (CGI)

Normally, a web server receives requests for resources it can handle by itself, the most common case being a request for a web page with a particular path on the server. The web server has a set of rules to map the URI's path onto a path name of its local file system, reads the file, and sends it as a response. The web server may also decide to set some headers of the response message

---

[15] The syntax of the `if` command uses some escape sequences for quotes inside quotes and therefore looks a little bit confusing.

according to properties of the file, such as the `Last-Modified` header field according to the last modified date from the file system, and the `Content-Type` header field according to mapping rules which map file extensions onto MIME types.

However, in some cases this functionality (ie, reading passive pieces of data from the file system and returning them in responses) will not be sufficient, because the request needs some processing to be performed. The first approach to this problem is to include the processing in the server process, but this is sometimes undesirable[16] since it ties the processing to one particular server software and also may create considerable security problems. The next logical step therefore is to create a separate process and to use some mechanism to invoke this process (including input and output of data) from the server. However, this also ties the processing to one particular type of server software, because the interface to external processes may be entirely different for another type of server software[17]. The goal is to have a solution making external programs independent from a particular server software.

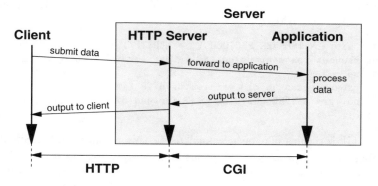

Fig. 9.5   Client/server interaction involving CGI

As a general solution to this problem, the *Common Gateway Interface (CGI)* has been defined, defining an interface between information servers (such as web servers) and external programs. The current version of the specification is CGI/1.1. A complete guide on how to use CGI on most platforms with a multitude of systems has been published by Gundavaram [91].

---

[16] An exception of this is the processing of rather simple and general tasks, which on some servers can be done using *Server-Side Includes (SSI)* as described in section 9.3.2.5.

[17] A new approach to this problem is the introduction of *Java servlets* as described in section 10.1.2, defining a Java execution environment on servers rather than clients (as is the case with the well-known applets).

Figure 9.5 shows the general idea of CGI and its placement in the web infrastructure.

In this figure, the term *server* refers to the server machine (ie, the computer the web server is running on), while the term *HTTP server* refers to the actual web server software. CGI is defined as a purely local interface. Consequently, it is not possible to have a configuration where the HTTP server is running on one machine and the CGI application on another (although it would be simple to create this type of configuration by implementing a small CGI application handling the communication between the server machine and the remote machine on which the application is running).

CGI is defined as a language-neutral interface, using standard ways of interprocess communications. It is therefore possible to implement CGI applications (often referred to as *CGI scripts*) in any language supporting interprocess communications. In many cases, scripting languages such as *Perl*, *Python*, or *Tcl* are used. Stein et al. [254] give an overview of using CGI with a variety of scripting languages.

CGI itself is defined as an interface between an information server and an external program. Information exchange between these to processes is using four different ways, which are described in section 9.4.1. A common application of CGI scripts is the processing of HTML form data, described in section 9.4.2. Finally, CGI can also be used as a means of implementing server-independent server-side includes. This usage of CGI is described in section 9.4.3.

9.4.1 Communication with the server

A CGI script communicates with the information server using four different mechanisms. The general scenario of CGI is based on the assumption that the server receives a request for a resource represented by a CGI script. The server first sets a number of environment variables, as described in section 9.4.1.1. Afterwards, the server starts the CGI script, possibly using command line parameters as described in section 9.4.1.2. The server writes data to the script using its standard input as described in section 9.4.1.3. Eventually, the script produces a result, sends this result to the server using its standard output as described in section 9.4.1.4, and terminates.

9.4.1.1 Environment variables

After receiving a request, and before starting the CGI script, the server sets a number of environment variables. These environment variables are inherited by the CGI script process (under Unix this is a feature of the operating system). In all cases and independently from the request, the following environment variables are set:

- SERVER_SOFTWARE
  This variable identifies the server software and the version of the server software. The format of this variable is "name/version".

- SERVER_NAME
  The SERVER_NAME variable specifies the host name or IP address of the server.

- GATEWAY_INTERFACE
  This variable specifies the version of CGI being used. The format of this variable is "CGI/version".

In addition to these request-independent variables, the server sets a number of other variables specific to the request:

- SERVER_PROTOCOL
  This environment variable is used to indicate the name and revision of the protocol this request came in with. The format of this field is "protocol/revision", so in case of HTTP in most cases it will be HTTP/1.1.

- SERVER_PORT
  Because in a TCP environment requests can be sent to a server on different ports, the SERVER_PORT environment variable contains the port number on which the request was received by the server.

- REQUEST_METHOD
  This environment variable specifies the request method with which the request was made. In case of HTTP, the request methods as described in section 3.2.3.1 will be used to set this environment variable.

- PATH_INFO
  Extra path information can be given by a client as part of the URL. In contrast to the query string, which in case of HTML forms (as described in section 5.2.7.2) contains the values of the form fields, the path information is contained in the CGI script's URL as given by the <FORM> element's ACTION attribute. The server places the extra path information[18] in the PATH_INFO environment variable.

- PATH_TRANSLATED
  Because there often is some kind of mapping between the extra path information as specified by the request URL, and the actual path as it

---

[18] The extra path information is the information of the request URL between the name of the CGI script and the query string (if present) as identified by a question mark '?' as described in section 2.2.

should be used on the server machine (usually a mapping between a virtual name space and the physical file system), the server also provides a CGI application with the translated extra path information.

- SCRIPT_NAME

  This environment variable contains the name of the CGI script being executed. It is given as a virtual name (as specified in the URL of the request) and can be helpful if a script can be executed using different URLs.

- QUERY_STRING

  According to the URL syntax as described in section 2.2, this environment variable contains the query string, which is the string following the question mark '?' in the request URL.

- REMOTE_HOST

  This environment variable contains the host name (as described in section 1.4.1.2) of the client making the request. If the server does not have this information, it should leave this environment variable unset and set the REMOTE_ADDR instead.

- REMOTE_ADDR

  The REMOTE_ADDR environment variable contains the IP address (as described in section 1.4.2.2) of the client making the request.

- AUTH_TYPE

  If the server supports user authentication (the authentication methods for HTTP are described in section 3.2.6), and the CGI script has been requested using an authentication method, this is indicated by setting the AUTH_TYPE environment variable to the authentication method which has been used. Currently, the two types of user authentication supported by HTTP are *basic authentication* and *digest access authentication*.

- REMOTE_USER

  If the CGI script has been requested using an authentication method, this variable contains the user name under which the requesting client has been authenticated.

- REMOTE_IDENT

  This environment variable contains the remote user name as received from the client machine by using the method described in Internet proposed standard RFC 1413 [250][19]. However, because the server may not support

---

[19] This RFC defines a method, called the *Identification Protocol*, how the identity of a user of a particular TCP connection can be determined. The server can use this protocol to query the client about the user of the TCP connection that the client opened to contact the server.

this operation at all, or because the client may not respond to the server's request honestly or at all, it is a very unreliable way of identifying a user.

- CONTENT_TYPE
  If the request sent to the server contains any information in addition to the query string, the CONTENT_TYPE environment variable identifies the content type of the data. The content type is specified using a MIME type identifier as described in section 1.4.3.2.

- CONTENT_LENGTH
  This environment variable specifies the length of the content passed to the CGI script through standard input as described in section 9.4.1.3. It is only set if the request contained any information in addition to the query string.

If HTTP is the request protocol, in addition to these environment variables the header lines received in the client's request are placed in environment variables with a prefix of HTTP_ followed by the header name[20]. Any hyphen characters in the header name are changed to underscore characters. The server (creating the environment variables) may choose to exclude any headers which it has already processed and used for other CGI environment variables, such as CONTENT_TYPE or CONTENT_LENGTH.

9.4.1.2 Command line

The command line should only be used for queries generated by using the deprecated <ISINDEX> element. The method for detecting this is for the server to search the query string of the request for a non-encoded '=' character. If such a character is found, it is assumed that the client coded the query as attribute/value pairs and the query string is placed in the QUERY_STRING environment variable. Otherwise, it is concluded that the query has been created by an <ISINDEX> element and the CGI script is called with the query string as command line parameter.

If for any reason the command line cannot be used (for example, because of internal limitations imposed by the operating system), the query string is placed in the QUERY_STRING environment variable.

9.4.1.3 Standard input

For requests which have additional information attached after the header, such as HTTP POST or PUT requests, this information is sent to the CGI

---

[20] An example for this is the environment variable HTTP_ACCEPT which was explicitly defined in CGI/1.0.

script over the standard input. The server sends as many bytes as specified in the CONTENT_LENGTH environment variable. If the request specified the data's content type, the server sets the CONTENT_TYPE environment variable with the MIME type of the data to be sent to the script over standard input.

9.4.1.4 Standard output

After getting its input data from environment variables, standard input, and maybe command line arguments, the CGI script processes the input and generates output to be sent to the client. The script writes its output to the standard output, and the server sends it back as a response to the client. The server either interprets the script's output to generate a valid response header, or simply forwards the script's output as response, in which case the script itself is responsible for generating a valid response header. The first variant is called *parsed headers*, the second *no parsed headers*.

- *Parsed headers*

  Normally, a CGI script does not want to be responsible for creating a valid response header, instead, it passes some information about the output to the server using CGI header fields, and relies on the server to generate a valid header in the response to the client. CGI defines three header fields, which are sent before the data separated by an empty line:

  - Content-Type

    This header specifies the MIME type of the script's output. Normally, the server uses this value to set the Content-Type header of the response.

  - Location

    In this case, the script generated a reference to a document rather than a document. If the CGI Location header specifies a complete URI, the server generates a response with a 3xx (redirection) response containing a Location header. If the CGI Location header specifies a local path, the server retrieves the document specified as if the client had requested that document originally.

  - Status

    If the script wants to set a certain status code in the server's response, it can specify this code using the CGI Status header.

  The server takes the CGI headers specified by the script and generates a response header, followed by the data which was following the CGI headers. The resulting response is sent to the client.

- *No parsed headers*

  Scripts that do not want to have their output parsed by the server are called *no parsed headers* scripts. CGI specifies that the name of these scripts must begin with "nph-", in order to distinguish these scripts from *parsed headers* scripts. It is the responsibility of *no parsed headers* scripts to generate valid responses, including a status line and all required header fields.

Generally, *parsed headers* scripts are used more often than *no parsed headers* scripts. Generating valid HTTP headers can be complicated, and in many cases the server includes information in the response which is not available to the CGI script.

9.4.2 Forms and CGI

One of the most frequent applications of CGI is the processing of form data. HTML forms are described in section 5.2.7.2. The ACTION attribute of the <FORM> element specifies a URI which is used for submitting the form. Depending on the METHOD attribute of the <FORM> element, the form is submitted using the GET or POST method. In both cases, the interaction between the user, the server and the application processing the form data can be depicted as shown in figure 9.6. It should be noted that the forms HTML document and the CGI script processing the form data are not necessarily located on the same server as shown in this figure.

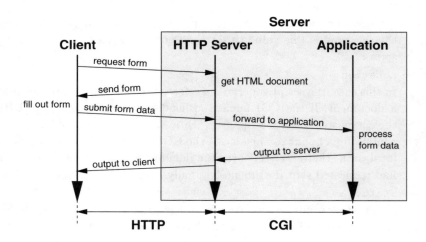

Fig. 9.6 Forms and CGI

However, the form data which is transmitted from the client to the server and then to the application is coded in different ways for both methods.

- GET

  In this case, the form data is appended to the URI specified in the ACTION attribute (using the query string URI notation), which is used in an HTTP GET request. The server identifies the CGI script by taking the URI part before the query string, and calls the CGI script. The query string is placed in the QUERY_STRING environment variable.

- POST

  In the second case, the original URI specified in the ACTION attribute is taken to create an HTTP POST request. The form data is included in the body of the request. The server identifies the CGI script by taking the URI from the POST request, and calls the CGI script. The body of the request is written to the standard input of the CGI script.

Although in many cases the CGI script will be designed to support the method which has been specified in the form, there are scenarios where it is necessary for the CGI script to find out which request method has been used by the client. An example for such a scenario is the creation of a general form handling CGI script, which can be used for both methods.

The CGI script can determine which request method has been used by the client by examining the REQUEST_METHOD environment variable. It is also possible to find out from which page a form has been submitted by looking at the HTTP_REFERER environment variable[21].

CGI scripts processing form data often need access to additional data about the client. The host name of the client can be accessed using the REMOTE_HOST environment variable, and the IP address is available using the REMOTE_ADDR environment variable. If the form required authentication, the AUTH_TYPE environment variable identifies the HTTP authentication scheme, and the REMOTE_USER environment variable identifies the name that has been used for authentication. Using all this information, CGI scripts processing forms can keep a very detailed record of accesses.

9.4.3 Server-Side Includes (SSI)

Server-Side Includes (SSI) as described for the Apache server in section 9.3.2.5 can also be implemented using CGI scripts. The advantages of providing SSI functionality using a CGI script are greater flexibility, because the commands

---

[21] This method can be used to prevent unauthorized usage of form-processing CGI scripts. The CGI script only accepts form data if the HTTP_REFERER environment variable is set to an authorized URI. However, because the HTTP Referer header field which is used to set the HTTP_REFERER environment variable is not mandatory, and can also easily be forged, this method is not very secure or reliable.

can be designed specifically for the application, and portability, because CGI scripts can be used with any server, while SSI syntax and functionality is server-specific. The disadvantages of providing SSI functionality using a CGI script are greater complexity, since parsing and all kinds of required commands must be implemented in the CGI script, and slower execution times resulting in higher server load, because running a CGI script is much slower than SSI processing within the server.

10. Miscellaneous

In addition to the basic architectural concepts described in the main chapters of this book, many additional technologies and concepts for the web infrastructure have been defined and implemented. Due to the speed of development, many new technologies and concepts appear every month. This chapter describes some of the more important components and concepts.

The main components of the web infrastructure are servers and browsers. From a purely technical point of view, these are nothing but implementations of usually a number of standards, in most cases also implementing some non-standard extensions. However, since the standards are heavily influenced by these implementations, it is always interesting to have a look at the newest features of servers and browsers. Some of these features will disappear because of limited user acceptance or newer technical concepts being developed, other features set de-facto standards which are finally adopted as official standards (the *JavaScript* scripting language being a good example). Section 10.1 briefly describes new developments on the server side. Browsers are much more visible to users, and therefore subject to more attention and marketing efforts than servers. Some of the basic issues of browser implementations are described in section 10.2.

Search engines as described in section 10.3 are implementing both sides, acting as clients while collecting data and making this data accessible as a server. As the amount of data on the web continues to grow at an astounding rate, search engines and new ways of categorizing resource contents become increasingly important for locating information.

Independently from particular implementations, new concepts for the web are continuously developed. Section 10.4 describes some trends for new content types, while section 10.5 describes complete architectural concepts, often involving several content types as well as communication protocols.

10.1 Server-side technologies

A web server accepts HTTP requests and generates HTTP responses. The actions which the web server takes to generate a response are not part of

HTTP and entirely up to the server. It is therefore easy to think of many scenarios where the server in some way communicates with other processes or machines to generate a response.

Many web servers implement proprietary gateways to other processes. Examples for this kind of web servers are servers made available by database vendors, which are essentially HTTP front ends to their databases. A more general approach is the *Common Gateway Interface (CGI)* as described in section 9.4. CGI defines an interface between information servers and applications. A newer version of CGI providing additional features is *FastCGI (FCGI)* as described in section 10.1.1. CGI and FCGI are language independent. A Java-specific approach to linking web servers and applications are Java *servlets* as described in section 10.1.2.

10.1.1 FastCGI

There are two major disadvantages to CGI, which in some cases make it almost impossible to use CGI for communications between a web server and an application:

- *CGI scripts terminate after execution*
  CGI defines scripts to be started by the server if a request for a script is received. After sending the response to the server, the script terminates. If a script is called frequently, this behavior results in many process creations and terminations.

- *CGI defines a local interface*
  Through its use of environment variables, command line parameters, standard input, and standard output, CGI defines a local interface which can only be used between processes running on the same machine. Although it is possible to create a small CGI script running locally and acting as an interface to a remote application, this creates the overhead of this script being started and terminating after each request only for the purpose of forwarding data between the web server and the remote application.

FastCGI (FCGI) defines a variant of CGI avoiding these disadvantages. Essentially, FCGI multiplexes all the information of CGI (environment variables, command line parameters, standard input, and standard output) onto one TCP connection. This approach makes it very easy to convert CGI applications to using FCGI, since the structure of the information being received by the application is the same. The FCGI information has to be read from a TCP connection and can be de-multiplexed into its original CGI form. FCGI implementations are available as a free module for the Apache web server, and as commercial products for Netscape and Microsoft web servers.

10.1.2 Java servlets

CGI as described in section 9.4 has been defined to provide an interface between web servers and external programs being executed by web servers. CGI
therefore makes these programs independent from a particular web server,
but they are still depending on the platform (operating system and hardware) they were implemented and compiled for.

Java as described in section 8.2.1 can be used to solve this problem, resulting in external programs which can be moved from one server machine to
another without any modification. Java *servlets* are pieces of code which are
executed on the server when a client sends a request containing the servlet's
URL. This process is very similar to a server running a CGI script[1]. The
results of the servlet execution are sent with the response. To support such
a scheme, the web server must contain a *Java Virtual Machine (JVM)*.

10.2 Browsers

While most topics of this book are independent from actual implementations,
describing concepts, formats, or languages, for most web users the browser
is the most visible component of the web. Currently, the two browsers competing on the market are Netscape's Navigator and Microsoft's Internet Explorer. Recently, in an attempt to stop Microsoft's increase of market shares,
Netscape has made Navigator's source code made available free of charge
under the name of *Mozilla.* The idea is to make Navigator available on more
platforms, and to include new features in Navigator faster and more completely than it would have been possible if only Netscape itself was writing
the code.

However, it is still not clear which one of the two will win (if it is appropriate to use this term at all). Both browsers are implementing very similar
things, although there are always subtle differences in how perfectly a new
standard has been implemented. For example, the current versions of the
browsers (both using version 4) implement CSS1, but both implementations
are not complete. While Internet Explorer implements more features of CSS1
than Navigator does, on the other hand Navigator implements CSS-P, which,
although currently not being a standard, is part of the next version of CSS
(CSS2).

This section does not give an introduction or overview of particular
browsers, instead it discusses some aspects which are of interest from the
conceptual point of view. The idea of an integrated work environment, which

---

[1] Instead of passing the information to the CGI script using CGI mechanisms, the
server calls the servlet and provides the information through the *servlet API.*

today's browsers make available, is described in section 10.2.1. A more technical issue, the idea of prefetching, is described in section 10.2.2.

10.2.1 Integration

Although browsers today very often are referred to as "web browsers", they effectively are general-purpose programs for accessing resources on the Internet using a large variety of content types and communication protocols. The following functionality, which is not connected to the web in any direct way, is contained in most browsers:

- *Electronic mail*
  Electronic mail as described in section 11.1 is one of the most important uses of the Internet. Electronic mail uses rather simple protocols for sending and receiving emails:

  - *Sending electronic mail*
    For sending electronic mail, the *Simple Mail Transfer Protocol (SMTP)* as described in section 11.1.1 is used. Without implementing SMTP, a browser cannot support links which are mail addresses (using the "mailto:" prefix).
  - *Receiving electronic mail*
    Receiving electronic mail is a completely different issue from sending electronic mail. The *Post Office Protocol (POP)* and the *Internet Message Access Protocol (IMAP)* as described in section 11.1.2 are the most common protocols for receiving electronic mail.
    Receiving electronic mail not only requires the implementation of these protocols, but also the provision of some functionality for handling received emails, such as support for multiple email folders.

  Since electronic mail has become a ubiquitous way of communications in many communities and environments, the implementation of complete and comfortable email messaging functionality is essential for browsers.

- *Usenet news*
  Being much older than the web, Usenet news still is a useful source of information for many users. Although it is possible to use web servers implementing a gateway between the web and Usenet news, the most common and practical way to read Usenet news still is the *Network News Transfer Protocol (NNTP)* as described in section 11.3. Consequently, most browsers implement this protocol as well as the news reader functionality which is necessary to provide a comfortable user interface.

- *FTP*

  Many resources on the Internet are available in FTP archives, providing an easy way of accessing files on remote systems. Most browsers implement FTP and provide a way of navigating through FTP archives using a graphical user interface.

In addition to these rather basic services, many other services are also integrated into browsers. In many cases, a directory service as described in section 11.2 can be accessed. Browsers may also support the *gopher* and *WAIS* protocols. In the beginning of the web, when web servers were not so widespread and gopher and WAIS servers often provided information that could not be accessed using the web, this support was very useful. However, because gopher and WAIS servers are becoming less and less popular and will completely disappear in the future, it is also likely that browser support for gopher and WAIS will eventually be removed.

Browsers also very often contain a *Java Virtual Machine (JVM)* for executing Java applets, and an interpreter for a scripting language such as *ECMAScript*. Furthermore, extensible mechanisms for handling new content types are important. Most browsers support two models of how handling of new content types can be accomplished:

- *Plug-ins*

  A plug-in is an additional module of a browser that interprets a particular content type. After installation, the plug-in is an integral part of the browser program and consequently has access to the browser's resources, which makes it possible for the plug-in to use the browser's display.

  The advantage of plug-in is the seamless integration of their output into the normal browser display, a user does not notice whether a part of the page is displayed by the browser's standard mechanisms or by a plug-in. The disadvantage of plug-ins is that they are highly browser-specific.

- *External viewers*

  An external viewer is a program that is started by the browser. After starting the external viewer, the browser forwards the content for which the viewer has been started to it. The external viewer reads this content, and interprets and displays it.

  The advantage of this mechanism is the browser-independence. If a program for a particular platform is able to handle some content type, it can in almost all cases be used as external viewer. The disadvantage of this approach is the lack of integration, since an external viewer always displays the results in a separate window.

  Depending on the content type, the lack of integration is more or less disturbing. If images are displayed in separate windows, a document containing several images will be hard to read. If, on the other hand, the control panel for playing an audio clip appears in a separate window, this is acceptable.

Both plug-ins and external viewers must be installed in a browser. The installation mainly involves an association between a content type (or a set of content types) and the plug-in or external viewer. If the browser receives a response indicating this content type, it forwards the response's content to the plug-in or external viewer for presentation.

10.2.2 Prefetching

Prefetching is a technique which should be entirely transparent for the user, but which can help in reducing user-perceived latency, or in reducing network load. Basically, prefetching is based on the idea to fetch resources before they are actually requested by a user.

In today's browsers, a simple kind of prefetching is implemented for displaying images, which are embedded in an HTML document using the <IMG> element described in section 5.2.5. Most browsers can be configured to automatically load all images on an HTML page, or to load only the document and not the images[2]. Loading the images assumes that the user is interested in all images (which in most cases is not true), and that the user is willing to wait the additional time that it takes to download and display the page with all images. Typically, users with low bandwidth connections tend to turn off automatic image loading, thereby reducing the time it takes to download a document.

Images are only one special kind of link in HTML documents. Other links are used for the more general <OBJECT> element as described in section 5.2.8.2, hypertext links inside the document body specified with the <A> element as described in section 5.2.6, and links between documents using the document head's <LINK> element as described in section 5.2.3.1. For all these links, it is possible to define different prefetching strategies, which can be based on additional information derived from the respective element instance (such as the REL attribute of the <A> and <LINK> elements), or specified by user preferences.

However, whatever strategy is used for prefetching, there are always two conflicting goals, one being the reduction of user-perceived latency (suggesting to prefetch as much as possible) as described in section 10.2.2.1, the

---

[2] In case of *XLinks* as described in section 7.3, the actuate attribute could be used by the document author to specify whether links should be followed automatically or only on user request.

other being the reduction of network load (suggesting to prefetch only very selectively) as described in section 10.2.2.2.

10.2.2.1 Reducing user-perceived latency

A good overview over techniques for reducing user-perceived latency by using prefetching is given by Padmanabhan [202]. One interesting aspect of this work is that it suggests that decisions about prefetching should be made not only by the user agent, but also by the server. The motivation for this model is that a server can collect usage data of resources (naturally, this only works for links to resources on the same server), and use this data for making decisions which resources should be prefetched for a particular resource. However, this would require the transmission protocol HTTP to contain specific methods for requesting not only a resource, but also a number of linked resources which should be prefetched with it, according to the server's rating. Since there is no such method in the current version of HTTP[3], this variant of prefetching currently cannot be implemented.

However, a user agent still could make decisions about prefetching by using information from the resource, for example by preferably prefetching resources which are on the same server, or by choosing to always prefetch the table of contents of a resource, but not its individual chapters (this could be done by interpreting the <LINK> element's REL attribute). There are many strategies which could be employed for doing prefetching, but whenever a user agent is using prefetching, it should be kept in mind that, unless there is a 100% hit rate (ie, the user agent only prefetches resources that are requested by the user at a later stage), prefetching will always generate additional network traffic.

10.2.2.2 Reducing network load

There is an area where prefetching can be advantageous for the network load. An investigation of this has been published by Crovella and Barford [56]. In most cases, network traffic generated by a human user is very bursty, consisting of short bursts of downloading a resource, and much longer idle periods which occur when the resource is read. For the network, it would be advantageous to spread out these bursts over longer periods of time, resulting in a more constant data rate. This, however, can only be achieved if prefetching

---

[3] In his report, Padmanabhan suggests two new HTTP methods, GETALL and GETLIST, which could be used by a server to return a number of resources as response to a single request. The set of returned resources is based on the server's knowledge of which resources should be prefetched. However, it is not very likely that newer versions of HTTP will include these or similar methods.

is used (otherwise, it would always result in longer download times, which is not acceptable for users).

If prefetching is used, the transfer of a resource can be initiated before a user actually requests it, and can therefore be spread out over a longer period of time. Using prefetching for this application area always involves a careful investigation of the trade-off between the additional traffic volume created by prefetching resources which are not used by the user, and the reduction of traffic bursts by spreading out the data transfers over longer periods of time. Heuristics (such as first prefetching resources which are specified at the top of the document being displayed) could be used to achieve an optimal balance between the initiation of prefetching a resource, and the likelihood of it actually being requested by the user.

10.3 Search engines

The amount of data available on the web and its speed of change makes it almost impossible to find information on the web without the help of dedicated searching services[4]. One of the first search engines was the *World Wide Web Worm (WWWW)* described by McBryan [171]. In the meantime, many search engines have become available, and most of them operate on a commercial base, selling advertisements on their query and result pages. It is therefore in the interest of these services to be used by as many people as possible, and the most successful way to do this is by providing good services.

The basic mechanism how search engines work is the same for all of them. They collect information by recursively requesting web pages, following links found in these pages, and use the collected web pages to build an index, which is used to respond to queries. Since the number of web pages is very largest (the largest of the search engines currently holds an index of 140 million web pages), it is difficult to build an index that can be searched with acceptable speed, in particular when taking into account that many search engines receive several query requests per second. The exact procedure how web pages are compiled into an index and how this index is searched is a well-kept secret of all search engines, but the basic mechanisms used by the search engines are the following:

- *Robot Exclusion Protocol*
  Since not all web sites want to be visited by search engines, a simple way of excluding them has been defined in an expired Internet draft by Koster [150]. Basically, a web site provides a document (named the

---

[4] It is estimated that the number of web pages is in the magnitude of hundreds of millions of web pages, and the billion pages mark will soon be reached.

`robots.txt` file) specifying rules for search engines. Before a search engine starts to request resources from a site, it first requests and interprets this file.

Search engines can be excluded from parts of the site or the entire site, and these rules can be specified for specific or all search engines. Search engines cannot be forced to follow these rules[5], but all major search engines do so.

- **<META> element**
  Since currently there is no reliable mechanism of how web pages could be rated except than using their text, most of the indexing is based on the pages' text. However, the <META> element as described in section 5.2.3.1 can be used to provide additional information about a page to search engines, but not all search engines interpret this information.

  The NAME and CONTENT attributes of the <META> element are used to specify meta information. The most popular values of the NAME attribute for specifying meta information are the following values, but it should be kept in mind that they are not standardized and simply ignored by some search engines:

  - AUTHOR
    This value indicates that the CONTENT attribute of the <META> element contains the name of the page's author.

  - DESCRIPTION
    The text specified in this <META> element is displayed in the list that most search engines show as a result of a query. If no DESCRIPTION meta information is available, most often the first few words of the page itself are displayed in the result list.

  - KEYWORDS
    The keywords of a page should list all search terms which are relevant to the page, separated by commas.

  Although the proper use of <META> elements provides information which cannot be deduced from the page's text, some search engines have decided not to support this method due to possible misuses. Most search engines use this information, and therefore it should be included in a page to make it better accessible through these search engines.

Since <META> tags are not standardized and not used by many pages, search engines rely on indexing a page's text. The main criteria for indexing are *location* (a word appearing near the top is more relevant than a word further down) and *frequency*. HTML provides other possible methods of rating

---

[5] For a web server, a search engine is a normal client, and it is practically impossible to reliably detect and block requests from search engines.

text, such as context (a term appearing in a heading is more important than a term appearing in a paragraph). Most search engines publish instructions on how documents should be authored for reliable indexing, and which pages are not indexed at all. Following these instructions it is likely that the page will be easily accessible using the search engine.

10.4 New content types

HTML is the basic content type of the web, and it is assumed that a web browser can interpret and display HTML. Other content types usually supported by browsers are plain text and raster images using the *Graphics Interchange Format (GIF)* or *JPEG*. This can be regarded as the lowest common denominator, and all other content types which are used on the web are probably not accessible by all users.

For all other content types, only particular browsers (if any) support this type internally, and all other browser must either install plug-ins or external viewers, or are not capable of handling this format. Possible content types of information on the web includes all data which can be represented by a stream of bytes. The MIME types registered by the *Internet Assigned Numbers Authority (IANA)* represent only a fraction of the content types in use today. In this section, some content types are discussed, and only those with a special significance for the web.

10.4.1 Virtual Reality Modeling Language (VRML)

HTML is a language for describing two-dimensional documents in a way similar to traditional media (such as books and newspapers). A very different approach is taken by the *Virtual Reality Modeling Language (VRML)* as specified by ISO draft international standard 14772 [134]. An annotated reference manual of the standard has been published by Carey and Bell [41]. VRML is a description language for three-dimensional scenes. In the same way as a user can navigate through an HTML document by scrolling up and down, a user can navigate through a VRML scene by moving in three dimensions.

VRML documents describe 3D-scenes which can contain links to other web resources. In the same way as a user can select a link in an HTML document, a link in a VRML scene (for example represented by a graphical object such as a switch or a door) can be selected. The main concepts of VRML can be summarized as follows:

- *Scene graph*
  A VRML document describes objects and scenes using a hierarchical graph structure, called the *scene graph*. The scene graph describes the

composition of a VRML scene by combining different basic elements, called *nodes*, into more complex descriptions. Possible node types of VRML are geometry primitives, appearance properties, sound and sound properties, and various types of grouping nodes.

- *Events*
  Events may occur in documents, and nodes define which events they generate or receive, and to which other nodes events should be forwarded.

- *Sensors*
  Sensors are special nodes generating events, either triggered by timing instructions (making animation possible), or by user interactions. A sensor only generates events, it must be connected with other nodes (through events) in order to have any visible effect on the scene.

- *Scripts*
  Scripts are intermediary nodes between event generators and event receivers. Scripts can define arbitrary behaviors, defined in any supported scripting language. The current VRML specification defines language bindings for Java and JavaScript.

- *Prototyping*
  This mechanism can be used to define user-specific node types in terms of a combination of existing node types. Prototypes facilitate the construction of complex scenes and the reuse of scene graphs.

- *Scene distribution*
  VRML supports distributed scenes in two ways. Scenes can be be included by a special node type, or external prototypes can be used.

VRML supports a number of concepts for creating scenes, such as a *lighting model*, *texture mapping*, and a number of *viewing parameters*. Shapes created by scene graphs can be *positioned*, *scaled*, and *rotated*.

VRML's lighting model by default includes a *headlight* always pointing in the direction of the user's view of a VRML scene. In addition to the headlight, VRML supports three other types of light sources. *Directional light* has no location, only a direction, and the light rays are parallel. A *point light* is a light source which has a location, and light rays from this light source are going in all directions. A *spot light* is a light source with a location and a direction, creating a cone of light. For point and spot light sources, light *attenuation* can be defined, describing how the light looses its intensity as distance from the light source increases. Because of their prohibitive computational complexity, VRML does not support light reflection and shadows.

Texture mapping can be used to create shapes having images attached to them. Generally, mapped textures can be specified as a location on the shape, and it can be specified whether the texture should be repeated horizontally and/or vertically. Textures can be specified as pixel arrays, as links to external images (using GIF, JPEG, or PNG), or as links to MPEG files, in which case the texture is animated.

In addition to shapes, a VRML document can also specify a ground, a panoramic background, and a sky (which is modeled as a sphere around the scene). These concepts allow more realistic scenes.

VRML is a powerful language for creating 3D-scenes, possibly containing links to other web resources. Like documents of many complex content types, VRML scenes are more easily created by using authoring tools than coding them by hand.

10.4.2 Mathematical Markup Language (MathML)

Plans for integrating markup for mathematical expressions into HTML were made for very early HTML versions, but even the current version of HTML does not support mathematical expressions. The only method to reliably display mathematical expressions on web pages therefore is the generation of images of these expressions, with all the disadvantages of this approach, mostly the loss of content information and structure.

The *Mathematical Markup Language (MathML)* [142] specified by W3C as an XML DTD rectifies this situation by providing a framework for expressing mathematical semantics. The goal of MathML is to be flexible enough to provide for dynamic interaction with mathematical expressions, to substitute values, apply transformations, draw graphs, animate formulas and perform other actions for which expressions must be specified semantically. MathML therefore defines a DTD as well as semantics for all elements and attributes.

Since HTML will probably evolve from a fixed SGML DTD into a set of XML DTDs representing functional areas (such as a DTD for tables, or a DTD for forms), MathML can easily fit into this framework. An author who wants to include mathematical expressions in a document only has to make a reference to the MathML DTD.

MathML defines a top-level `math` element, and a set of elements which are either used for specifying mathematical presentation, or mathematical content. The following description explains the difference between these two types of elements using the simple mathematical expression $(a + b)^2$ as an example:

- *Presentation elements*
  Presentation elements capture *notational structure*. If the author of a mathematical expression is interested in the presentation, MathML's pre-

sentation elements can be used to mark up the notation of an expression. Presentation elements specify layout classes of their content:

```
<msup>
  <mfenced>
    <mrow>
      <mi>a</mi>
      <mo>+</mo>
      <mi>b</mi>
    </mrow>
  </mfenced>
  <mn>2</mn>
</msup>
```

In this example, the `mi` element marks up an identifier, and the `mo` element marks up an operator. The containing markup specifies parentheses and a superscript. MathML in this case only captures the information relevant for presentation, such as the spacing between identifiers and operators.

- *Content elements*
  Content elements capture *mathematical structure*. Using content elements, the author of a mathematical expression can specify the mathematical content of the expression. This is made possible by providing MathML elements representing mathematical concepts:

```
<apply>
  <power/>
  <apply>
    <plus/>
    <ci>a</ci>
    <ci>b</ci>
  </apply>
  <cn>2</cn>
</apply>
```

In this example, the markup specifies the expression as functions being applied to elements, for example the addition is represented by the `plus` operation being applied to the two identifiers represented by the `ci` elements.

As a very simple example for the fundamental difference between presentation and content elements, the respective element for specifying numbers can be examined. The presentation element for numbers `mn` has attributes for setting font attributes and the color. The content element for number `cn` has attributes for a number's type (eg, integer or floating point) and its base (eg, for binary or hexadecimal numbers, the default is 10).

From the semantic point of view, content elements are preferable. However, not all mathematical concepts can be captured using MathML content elements, and therefore in some cases the only possible way is to use presentation elements instead of content. Since in some cases it may be required to combine both types of elements, MathML allows mixed markup, where presentation elements are used inside content elements or vice versa.

The MathML DTD is a complex example of an XML DTD, and it is obvious that it is not suitable to produce anything but the most simple MathML expressions manually. If MathML is supported by the major browsers and accepted by the user community, it is expected that tools will emerge for the comfortable creation of MathML markup.

MathML is a new recommendation and it needs to be aligned with a number of other standards. An important issue is the *Document Object Model (DOM)* as described in section 10.5.5, which is necessary for making MathML content accessible to scripts. MathML also has to be aligned to the *Extensible Linking Language (XLL)* for linking into and out of mathematical parts of a web document. Traditionally, layout of mathematical expressions is considered the most difficult task for formatting, and MathML imposes new requirements on style sheet languages such as *Cascading Style Sheets (CSS)* and the *Extensible Style Language (XSL)*.

Furthermore, it should be possible to transform expressions from older languages such as TEX and ISO 12083 [119] to MathML. A subset of MathML is implemented in the current version of W3C's *Amaya* browser, which also contains an editor for MathML expressions.

10.4.3 Portable Network Graphics (PNG)

Apart from hypertext using the HTML language, images are the most prevalent content type on the web. Most web pages contain images, and the integration of image display with a page's text creates the impression that the complete document (including the images) is one resource. Images are individual resources, linked into pages with the <IMG> element, and the content type of these resources is not defined or restricted by any standard. The two formats currently supported by most browsers are the *Graphics Interchange Format (GIF)* and *JPEG*. A new content type for images, the *Portable Network Graphics (PNG)* [27] format as specified by W3C is expected to gain more support in the near future. The latest versions of the major browsers provide built-in support for PNG images. Webster [272] describes these three formats and their properties in detail. Table 10.1 summarizes the most important differences between these image formats.

GIF and JPEG are not competing formats, because GIF is designed for graphic images, while JPEG is optimized for photographic images. GIF has some serious technical shortcomings and uses a patented compression algorithm, and for these reasons PNG has been developed as a replacement for

Table 10.1 Comparison of graphics formats

Format	GIF	JPEG	PNG
Color depth	8-bit	24-bit	32-bit
Lossless?	lossless	lossy	lossless
Interlacing	4 passes	progressive display	7 passes

GIF. In addition to supporting all features of GIF, PNG provides the following functionality:

- *Increased color resolution*
  GIF is limited to 8-bit resolution of colors. This results in a maximum of 256 colors for a GIF image. If an image contains shading effects, the number of color required usually exceeds 256. PNG support 32-bit colors, resulting in a number of colors sufficient for coding photographic images.

- *Increased grayscale resolution*
  GIF's 8-bit limit applies to grayscale images as well, only allowing images with 256 levels of gray. PNG allows grayscale images to use 16-bit resolution, resulting in over 65'000 levels of gray.

- *Increased alpha channel resolution*
  GIF supports transparency by assigning one transparent color to an image. Thus, GIF pixels are either transparent or cover the background entirely. PNG defines an 8-bit *alpha channel*. The alpha channel specifies the opaqueness of pixels, enabling smooth transitions between the background and the image.

- *Gamma correction*
  Image gamma information supports automatic display of images with correct brightness and contrast regardless of the machines used to originate and display the image.

- *Error detection*
  GIF contains no information for error detection. This makes it impossible to detect a corrupted GIF file. PNG includes error detection mechanisms using a *Cyclic Redundancy Check (CRC)* algorithm as specified in ISO 3309 [117].

- *Improved progressive display*
  Progressive (or *interlaced*) display is used to better display images while downloading them. PNG's progressive display method defines more passes of image display than GIF's algorithm. Progressive display slightly expands the file size on average, but it gives the user a meaningful display much more rapidly.

The only functionality which is currently not provided by PNG is the use of animations. Animated GIFs are a simple and popular way of attracting attention on web pages, often used for advertisements. The *Multiple-image Network Graphics (MNG)* format, based on PNG, is under development to provide this functionality as well.

10.4.4 Vector graphics

The use of images (or raster graphics) as content type in web documents is very common, but there currently is no established format for vector graphics. Many graphics are created by applications that manipulate graphic objects (such as circles and boxes) rather than pixels. Saving these graphics in a format that retains this object-oriented information permits resizing for any display or printer density. Furthermore, vector graphics are often much smaller than raster graphics.

Based on XML, the *Precision Graphics Markup Language (PGML)* [4] and the *Vector Markup Language (VML)* [170] have been proposed to W3C. Both languages are proposals of newly designed languages (although PGML is based on the PostScript imaging model), and it is not clear which (if any) of these proposals will be successful.

The only vector graphics format which is very popular in a large user community, although in other application areas, is the *Computer Graphics Metafile (CGM)* specified in ISO international standard 8632 [115]. CGM defines a file format for vector graphics based on a rather small number of graphic primitives. CGM defines three types of encodings, optimized for different application areas. *WebCGM* [57] as proposed to W3C is a profile of CGM based on CGM binary encoding. Due to some properties of CGM, WebCGM does not fulfill all requirements for scalable graphics for the web as specified by W3C.

It is currently not possible to predict which of the proposed formats will be most successful. While WebCGM has the advantage of being based on a well-known and time-tested international standard, it lacks some of the required functionality and uses a binary file format. PGML and VML are new languages based on XML. Consequently, all architectural concepts defined for XML (especially XLL for linking into and out of XML documents) are applicable to PGML and VML, which is an important advantage over WebCGM.

10.4.5 RealMedia Architecture (RMA)

The *RealMedia Architecture (RMA)* is a proprietary architecture for streaming media defined by RealNetworks. However, RMA uses some standards for data transmission and presentation specifications. From the user's point of view, the most important part of RMA is the *RealPlayer* application (providing RealAudio and RealVideo functionality), which usually is installed as an external viewer. When selecting a link referencing a RMA file, RealPlayer is started as external viewer and interprets this file.

In earlier versions of the RealPlayer product, presentations were specified using the *Real Time Session Language (RTSL)*, an SGML-based proprietary language defined by RealNetworks. The newest version of RealPlayer, called *RealPlayer G2*, uses the standardized *Synchronized Multimedia Integration Language (SMIL)* as described in section 10.5.6 for specifying presentations. A SMIL presentation is a description how individual multimedia contents (such as audio or video clips) are combined for a synchronized overall presentation.

After being started, RealPlayer interprets the SMIL presentation description. This description contains references to individual multimedia presentations on a RealMedia server. RealPlayer requests these presentations from the RealMedia server in the way described by the SMIL presentation description. Individual multimedia contents use the *RealMedia File Format (RMFF)* on the RealMedia server. The transport protocol used between the RealPlayer and the RealMedia server is the *Real Time Protocol (RTP)*.

RealPlayer receives and synchronizes individual media streams, thereby providing a synchronized multimedia presentation. There is no restriction on the source of media streams, so one multimedia presentation can integrate media streams received from different RealMedia servers. The *Real Time Streaming Protocol (RTSP)* is used for controlling individual media streams, enabling the RealPlayer to send control commands to a RealMedia server.

10.5 New architectural components

Content types can easily be integrated into the web from a user perspective, because it is only necessary to install a plug-in or an external viewer on the client side to handle new types. New architectural components include a number of other issues, for example new ways how resources should be described, and frameworks for delivering this information.

10.5.1 Platform for Internet Content Selection (PICS)

With the growth of the web, the amount and the nature of information available on the web encompasses many different cultures and lifestyles. One frequent requirement from web users has been to be able to select resources based on content. One approach to this problem is the *Platform for Internet Content Selection (PICS)* as described by Resnick and Miller [224]. The basic idea is to create a platform for the definition of *labels* attached to resources.

Each label describes a *rating* of a resource based on a particular *rating service*. It is important to notice that PICS itself does not define any labels or rating services, it only defines a standard format for the exchange of information based on the model of labels and rating services. The most common uses of PICS labels is in filtering products that block access to certain resources based on labels associated with those resources. The following components are important in the PICS architecture:

- *Clients*
  Clients using PICS can be configured to handle resources based on the PICS labels associated with them. A common use is to inhibit the display of particular web pages based on labels from rating services.

- *Servers*
  A server supporting PICS understands requests containing the PICS-specific `Protocol-Request` header field and generates responses containing the labels associated with a resource, using the PICS-specific `Protocol` and `PICS-Label` header fields.

- *Proxies*
  A proxy can perform filtering based on PICS labels. The most common scenario involves a proxy used as a firewall between an intranet and the Internet and filtering out responses based on labels from particular rating services.

- *Label distribution*
  PICS defines three different ways of label distribution. A label can be embedded in a document, can be transmitted together with a document using PICS-specific HTTP extensions, or it can be separately requested (using a special protocol) from a different server (called *label bureau*) than the resource itself. PICS label distribution mechanisms are described in detail in section 10.5.1.2.

- *Rating*
  A *rating service* is an organization creating PICS labels based on a particular rating system. These labels may be distributed together with the resource, or they can be made available through a label bureau.

PICS defines the components of the architecture in three specifications. In the *PICS Rating Services and Rating Systems*, described in section 10.5.1.1, a language for the description of rating services is defined. Section 10.5.1.2 explains *PICS Label Syntax and Communication Protocols*, effectively describing how labels based on rating services are specified, and how these labels are distributed. Finally, in section 10.5.1.3 *PICSRules* are described, a language for writing profiles, being filtering rules that allow or block access to URLs based on PICS labels that describe those URLs.

10.5.1.1 Services and ratings

W3C's *PICS Rating Services and Rating Systems* [174] recommendation describes a language for the description of rating services. A rating service is described by some administrative information and as the most important information the *rating system*. A rating system specifies the dimensions used for labeling, the scale of allowable values on each dimension, and a description of the criteria used in assigning values.

10.5.1.2 Label distribution

The W3C recommendation specifying *PICS Label Syntax and Communication Protocols* [151] describes how labels according to a given rating system have to be coded for distribution. The most important part of a PICS label is the *rating*. The rating is a set of attribute-value pairs that describe a document along one or more dimensions.

Once a rating service creates a label for a document, the label has to be made available to clients interested in the rating. PICS defines three different ways of label distribution.

Embedded in the document

The easiest way to distribute PICS labels is to embed them into HTML documents. With this method no protocol mechanisms are necessary for label distribution. Labels are embedded in HTML documents using the <META> element. The HTTP-EQUIV attribute is used to designate the <META> element as specifying a PICS label, and the element's CONTENT attribute contains one or more PICS labels.

Together with a resource

If a label is not embedded in the document, but stored on the same server, it can be transferred with the documents. PICS defines HTTP extensions which have to be used by clients being interested in PICS labels. The following additional information is exchanged when a client requests PICS labels:

- *Request*
  A client that is interested to receive PICS labels of resources uses the `Protocol-Request` header field. The content of this header field specifies the PICS version being used, and the services for which PICS labels are requested.

- *Response*
  A server supporting PICS sends back the resource along with the associated PICS information. The `Protocol` header field specified the PICS version, and the `PICS-Label` header field contains all labels associated with the resource.

PICS labels are distributed selectively, a client requests labels for particular rating services, and the server only replies with the labels for these services. If many and potentially large labels are associated with documents, this is a significant advantage over embedded labels.

Using a separate HTTP request

It is possible to requests labels independently from the resource. In this case, a client sends a request for a resource's label to a *label bureau*. The label bureau responds with the PICS labels associated with the response. The *PICS label bureau query protocol* is used for label requests to label bureaus. This protocol defines a particular query syntax for HTTP requests, so basically a label bureau is a specialized HTTP server for this query syntax.

10.5.1.3 PICSRules

The rules interpreting PICS labels are entirely local to clients. A client receives a PICS label and decides the effect that this particular label should have, based on local rules. Although these rules can be specified in a product-specific way, W3C has defined a language for them. This language is *PICSRules* [215]. PICSRules has the following advantages over proprietary approaches:

- *Sharing and installation of profiles*
  The creation of profiles (a certain set of rules) can be complicated, and by using a common language, a profile can be created and installed on a large number of machines.

- *Communication to agents, search engines, proxies, or other servers*
  It is possible to transmit a profile to a server and to have only resources returned from the server matching the profile. For example, a search engine could use a PICSRules profile (among other things, such as search

strings) as a search criterion, only returning matches that also satisfy the PICSRules profile.

- *Portability between filtering products*
  By defining a common language for specifying filtering rules, the same set of rules will work with any product supporting PICSRules.

A PICSRules rule can specify one or more PICS rating services to use, one or more PICS label bureaus to query for labels, and criteria about the contents of labels that would be sufficient to make an accept or reject decision.

10.5.2 Digital Signature Initiative (DSig)

PICS specifies a framework for making statements about resources (by creating labels based on a particular rating system) and distributing the statements either with the resources or separately. A problem with this approach is that it is possible to manipulate labels or to modify resources described by labels without the possibility for PICS users to detect these manipulations. W3C's Digital Signature Initiative (DSig) approaches this problem by specifying a format for *PICS Signed Labels (DSig)* [105].

DSig defines two extensions to standard PICS labels, making it possible to use PICS labels in combination with cryptographic methods:

- *Resource information*
  This information is used to create a cryptographic link between the PICS label and the resource it is describing. Although PICS labels and resources are separate entities, this link can be used to make sure that the resource has not been changed since the label had been created. Hash functions such as the *Secure Hash Algorithm (SHA)* or *MD5* are used to create this cryptographic link.

- *Label signatures*
  Since a label contains an assertion about a resource, a rating service may want to sign a label prior to distribution to make sure that the assertions given in the label are not modified. A label can therefore contain one or more digital signatures, using cryptographic methods such as the *Digital Signature Algorithm (DSA)* or *RSA*.

It should be noted that the resource information is not meaningful with *generic* PICS labels. Generic PICS labels define a rating for a set of resources based on a URI prefix. There is no practical way how a set of resources (such as all resources residing on a particular server) can be cryptographically linked to a label.

10.5.3 Resource Description Framework (RDF)

Web meta data is the semantic description of web resource contents. Although there are some loosely followed conventions how meta data about a web page should be included in the page (using the <META> element and a number of keywords, described in more detail in section 10.3 about search engines), this is a very simple approach relying on the page author's success to choose the right keywords. A far more powerful approach is the application of standardized semantics. The *Resource Description Framework (RDF)* is the W3C's standard for a framework which can be used for the definition of meta data.

A small set of standardized meta data has been defined in the *Dublin Core* set of meta data keywords, defining keywords for the use with HTML's <META> element. Due to the lack of support by search engines, the Dublin Core keywords never were widely adopted. In general, the Dublin Core, and now in a much more flexible way RDF, are approaches to define an *ontology*. Ontology is, according to Webster's dictionary, "a branch of metaphysics concerned with the nature and relations of being". In the context of web meta data, an ontology describes the building blocks out of which models for the real world are made. While the Dublin Core is a very simple ontology, defining a few keywords for the description of a web document, RDF defines a framework for defining and exchanging ontologies.

RDF as a knowledge representation mechanism has been influenced by many existing approaches to knowledge representation. RDF is not as powerful as modern knowledge representation mechanisms such as the *Knowledge Interchange Format (KIF)*, the de-facto standard for exchanging machine-readable knowledge representations. RDF has been designed to be easily usable by web users, and to be powerful enough to facilitate the meta data for web resources in a way that was not possible before. RDF was influenced by Netscape's *Meta Content Framework (MCF)* and by Microsoft's *XML-Data* (loosely based on Microsoft's earlier *Web Collections* proposal).

RDF uses XML for its syntax, but the basic model of how meta data is structured using RDF is independent from XML. The RDF model and syntax definition [157] specifies RDF data to consist of nodes and attached name/value pairs. A simple example for this is an RDF model attaching the name "Author" and the value "John Smith" to a document written by that author.

The key idea of RDF is to provide a flexible mechanism for the representation of semantics, rather than defining fixed semantics. RDF therefore does not define any predefined vocabularies. These vocabularies, called *RDF schemas* [37], will be defined by user communities specifically designed for their needs (this can be regarded as the equivalent to specific PICS rating systems as described in section 10.5.1.1). RDF defines the root of a hierarchy of schemas (containing basic classes), and users are free to extend this or other user-defined schemas.

10.5.4 Dynamic fonts

Although HTML has been greatly improved to allow for better specification of layout, especially with the introduction of *Cascading Style Sheets (CSS)*, the usage of dynamic fonts on web pages is a rather new field. The latest versions of the major browsers both implement dynamic font technologies, using different formats.

Microsoft's Internet Explorer currently uses embedded *TrueType* (described in section 10.5.4.1), and Netscape's Navigator uses *TrueDoc* (described in section 10.5.4.2). In both cases, the idea is to allow web page authors to specify fonts for their web pages and to define a format which can be downloaded by a browser to display these fonts. Before the introduction of dynamic fonts, some non-standard HTML constructs allowed the specification of a font face, but the font had to be installed locally (at the client side) for this specification to be working. If the font was not installed locally, it was up to the browser to substitute a locally available font for it.

With dynamic fonts, the <LINK> element using the (non-standard) *Font-def* link type for the REL attribute can be used to link a definition of a dynamic font to a web page. The browser follows the URI given in the HREF attribute and loads and interprets the font.

One problem with dynamic fonts is that most fonts are not free. They must be purchased, and making them available on the web and linking them to documents makes it fairly easy to download and use a font outside of the browser. However, this is more a problem with Microsoft's embedded TrueType approach, since it uses a font format which is also used for installing fonts on the system level. TrueDoc, on the other side, uses a custom format making it harder to illegally install such a font on the system level.

10.5.4.1 Embedded TrueType

Microsoft currently uses *embedded TrueType* for its dynamic font format. This limits the available fonts to TrueType fonts, excluding the large number of Type 1 (PostScript) fonts which are used[6]. Microsoft has announced that it

---

[6] The *OpenType* font format, which is currently used locally but not for dynamic fonts, is the result of a combination of two existing font formats, the *TrueType* format and the *Type 1* format used by Adobe for the *PostScript* page description language and specified in ISO international standard 9541 [122]. OpenType allows users to use fonts out of both worlds, making a larger number of fonts available.

will support Type 1 fonts in a later version of embedded TrueType, which will become embedded OpenType.

The dynamic font handling proposed and implemented by Microsoft results in a font definition to be distributed to browsers. This definition can rather easily be installed on the system level and therefore illegally exploited to permanently use the fonts. This violates the intellectual property rights of font designers, who therefore seem to favor TrueDoc. Furthermore, an ActiveX control has been made available which makes it possible to use True-Doc in Internet Explorer. This makes TrueDoc technology for dynamic fonts available for both major browsers, while embedded TrueType is limited to Internet Explorer. For these reasons, it is likely that TrueDoc will be the more successful dynamic font format.

10.5.4.2 TrueDoc

Bitstream's *TrueDoc* is a format which has been specifically designed as a font format for on-line viewing and distribution. It is currently built into Netscape Navigator and and can be used with Internet Explorer through an ActiveX control. TrueDoc supports both TrueType and Type 1 fonts. It consists of three main components:

- *Character Shape Recorder (CSR)*
  The CSR is used to match the outlines of a given font (TrueType and Type 1) with special TrueDoc outlines. The CSR only codes the outlines which are actually used inside a document. This makes the TrueDoc font description more compact and also adds some security, because the TrueDoc font description may not contain all characters of a font.
  The CSR is only used during the publishing process and is therefore part of the authoring environment. Once all fonts and characters used are known, the CSR can create the TrueDoc outlines for them.

- *Portable Font Resource (PFR)*
  This is the format which is created by the CSR, containing the TrueDoc outlines. These outlines are scalable and can therefore be displayed on any output device. The PFR format has been optimized for compactness, so that it can be transferred over the network as fast as possible.

- *Character Shape Player (CSP)*
  This component is part of the display device, in most cases this will be the browser. The CSP takes a character, reads the appropriate TrueDoc outline from the PFR, and displays the character according to the font.

TrueDoc contains three security features. The first feature is that the original font definition is not made available, only the TrueDoc outlines are contained in the PFR. Furthermore, the CSR only includes the characters in the PFR which are actually used in the document. Consequently, if characters are not used in the document, they are missing in the PFR, thus making the font less useful for general usage. The third security feature is the *DocLock* technology, which makes it possible to limit PFRs to URI prefixes. Using DocLock, it is only possible to use a PFR for a document with the specified URI prefix, so other page designers cannot link to PFRs that they do not own.

10.5.5 Document Object Model (DOM)

The *Document Object Model (DOM)* defines the connection between documents on the web, and programs and scripts that want to access and modify these documents. DOM is one of the key components of *Dynamic HTML (DHTML)*. The specification of DOM [277] still is in its early stages, but first documents have been published, and others will soon follow.

Scripting and programming languages have their own ways of accessing objects, variables, attributes, properties, or whatever manageable units of data are called in an actual language. Furthermore, scripting and programming languages have different models of how operations are modeled inside the language, the two most popular flavors being procedural and object-oriented languages. DOM defines two aspects of how a language can access and modify a document.

- *Data structures and functions*
  For different types of documents (currently, the scope of DOM comprises HTML, XML, and CSS), DOM describes the data structures which are visible to languages accessing the document through DOM, and the functions (or operations) which can be used to modify the document. DOM describes these data structures and functions as an interface, using OMG's *Interface Definition Language (IDL)*. Using IDL, it is possible to define the interface to a document in a language-independent way.

- *Language binding*
  In addition to the language-independent interface defined by IDL definitions, DOM also specifies language bindings for different languages. Currently, the only language bindings which are part of the DOM specification are language bindings for the core functionality. While OMG has standardized some language mappings for IDL (such as C++ and Java), there are no standardized mappings for other languages (such as ECMAScript).

Although DOM is general with respect to the document type and the language, the most popular application for DOM is the combination of HTML documents (possibly using CSS style sheets) and ECMAScript scripts. DOM defines a *core* set of attributes and functions which is not specific to a particular document type. In addition to this core, document type specific attributes and functions are defined. In the future, the XML part of DOM will become more important, because it facilitates the structural analysis and modification of XML documents.

The current version of the DOM specification defines language bindings for Java and ECMAScript, but only for the core functionality of DOM. Java and ECMAScript language bindings for HTML will be included in the next version of the DOM specification (currently, only an IDL specification for HTML is available).

10.5.6 Synchronized Multimedia Integration Language (SMIL)

The combination of various resources for one integrated presentation is most visible on HTML pages, where inline images, loaded by the browser while formatting the page, are displayed to achieve an integrated overall presentation. This integration of images is realized using information specified in the <IMG> element, such as the placement of the image in the document flow.

Similar integrated presentations are the goal of the *Synchronized Multimedia Integration Language (SMIL)* [100], which is targeted at synchronizing the presentation of multiple time-variant resources. SMIL does not prescribe any particular content type for the resources it synchronizes. The application scenario of SMIL involves a program handling the SMIL specification, and possibly other programs (if not built into the SMIL interpreter) used to actually play the time-variant resources. A SMIL presentation can be published as a resource made available on a web server, and one of the first applications being able to handle SMIL is RealNetworks' RealPlayer.

SMIL presentations specify a multimedia presentation by defining an initial layout, and a description of how content should be displayed using this layout. This involves three issues:

- *What to play*
  The most basic question of a language for synchronized presentation of multimedia resources is how these resources are referenced. SMIL defines a number of *media object elements*, and each of these elements allows the inclusion of specific media objects. SMIL defines media object elements for animation, audio, image, video, text, and textstream media objects, as well as a general media object element for references to other media objects.

The media object elements make no assumptions about specific content types of the media objects, the content type can be specified by an additional attribute, or can be dynamically detected by the playback mechanism.

```
<switch>
  <audio src="german-intro" system-language="de"/>
  <audio src="english-intro" system-language="en"/>
</switch>
```

SMIL defines a number of *test attributes* for media object elements, which in combination with a selection mechanism allow for the conditional playback of media objects. In this example, the language is used to play one of two possible audio clips.

- *Where to play*
  SMIL defines a presentation to have a head and a body, and the head defines the layout of the presentation. If a SMIL presentation does not define a layout, the presentation is application-dependent, otherwise the layout describes how the elements in the document's body are positioned on an abstract rendering surface.

```
<smil>
  <head>
    <layout>
      <region id="r" top="20" left="20" />
    </layout>
  </head>
  <body>
    <seq>
      <img region="r" src="test.jpeg"/>
    </seq>
  </body>
</smil>
```

In this example, the layout defines one region. The region element controls the position, size and scaling of media object elements. The image in the body is assigned to the region through the use of the region's identifier.

- *When to play*
  One of the main issues for presentations of time-variant media types is the synchronization of individual resources. SMIL defines implicit and explicit synchronization. Implicit synchronization can only be used for time-variant media types. The two basic synchronization primitives supported by SMIL are sequential and parallel presentation.

```
<seq>
  <text src="title.html" dur="20s"/>
```

```
<par>
  <audio src="audio1.au"/>
  <animation src="image.ani"/>
</par>
<textstream src="trailer.rt"/>
</seq>
```

In this example, the title document, which is a time-invariant media type and therefore has a duration assigned to it, is displayed before a parallel presentation of an audio clip and an animation, which subsequently is followed by a trailer.

SMIL is defined as an XML DTD (listed in appendix C.2). It defines a flexible framework for synchronized multimedia presentations. Because SMIL only defines the synchronization and layout aspects of the presentation, it relies heavily on content types for media objects. When assessing SMIL players, one of the most important issues therefore is the list of supported content types.

11. Related Technology

The technologies described in this book are the most important ones for the web. However, they are only a subset of the technologies which are used for the web or in some web applications today. It is possible to divide these remaining technologies (which are not the main topic of this book) into two categories:

- *Underlying technologies*
  Although the web technologies described in this book are sufficient to describe how the web works on an abstract level, a lot of other technologies are necessary to be able to apply web technologies to built a working system. For example, computer and network technologies, ranging from CPUs to optical fiber networks, have to be used to provide the infrastructure which is used to implement web technologies.
  Because these technologies are on a lower level of abstraction than web technologies (which simply assume that for example data can be sent reliably from one computer to another), they are most often referred to as underlying technologies.

- *Complementary technologies*
  Although the web technologies described in this book are sufficient to implement a complete web browser, the trend goes towards integrated solutions. The leading browsers contain much more than just web technologies, they also incorporate a number of other access protocols for information resources (such as FTP and gopher), as well as support for using electronic mail and Usenet news.
  Because support for additional protocols and features is not essential for a program using web technologies (although it may increase the program's usefulness), these protocols and features can be called complementary technologies.

Technologies of the first category will not be discussed any further. A short introduction to the technology directly below the web, the Internet environment, is given in chapter 1. Any further information can be found in one of the many publications on communication protocols and networks.

Very comprehensive books about computer networks and communications have been published by Halsall [92], Peterson and Davie [204], Stallings [252], and Tanenbaum [259].

Technologies of the second category are found in most browser implementations (section 10.2.1 describes this integration in more detail). Access protocols to other information services (such as FTP for accessing file archives) can be supported almost transparently, but some other technologies are more visible to users. The most popular and most commonly implemented technology is email. It is described in section 11.1. Another technology which becomes increasingly important is access to directory services as described in section 11.2. Also very popular among users and a much older technology for the world-wide distribution of information than the web itself is Usenet news, shortly explained in section 11.3.

However, it should be kept in mind that these technologies are related to the web from the user's point of view, because the browsers incorporates functionality for all of them. Technically speaking, they are not part of the web's infrastructure and are therefore only discussed shortly.

11.1 Electronic mail

The most important network application before the advent of the web surely was electronic mail (email), and it still is a very important application of computer communications. Email has revolutionized communications in many areas, its first application area being the scientific community (because there computers with network access were first available), and in the last years also as a means of personal communications between people using it as a supplement to older forms of asynchronous communications such as letters, telephone answering machines, or fax machines.

The popularity of email has risen so high that in the last years the misuses of older forms of asynchronous communications also started to appear with email, in particular unsolicited advertisements (often called *junk email* or *spam*). However, this is an indicator showing that email is becoming more popular, and undoubtedly the percentage of the population using email will further increase in the future.

Being one of the first Internet applications, email is based on remarkably simple models. The *Internet Mail Consortium (IMC)* is a good source of information about email. It is a consortium of many companies developing products based on or using email. A complete overview over all relevant standards of today's Internet email infrastructure is given by Hughes [106].

Email seen as a number of protocols and used to exchange electronic mails can be divided into two major areas. The first area is the problem of sending

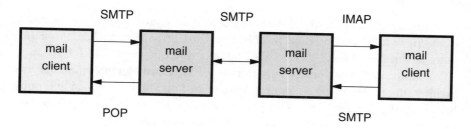

Fig. 11.1 Protocols for electronic mail transfer

mail through the Internet to its destination address[1]. This is handled by a protocol described in section 11.1.1. The second area concerning email is the question of how email messages can be retrieved from the mail server by users. The protocols used for this are described in section 11.1.2. An overall picture of protocols used for email is given in figure 11.1[2]. It should always be kept in mind that sending and receiving email uses entirely different protocols.

11.1.1 Sending electronic mail

Sending electronic mail can be considered to be more essential to a web browser than receiving mail. URLs can use a `mailto` scheme (explained in section 2.3.2), which should result in an email message to be sent upon selection of the link specifying the URL. Therefore, a web browser should at least contain a message composition facility and provide support for sending emails, otherwise `mailto` URLs can not be used.

The Internet protocol specifying the transfer of mails is the *Simple Mail Transfer Protocol (SMTP)*. Although SMTP can be implemented by following the protocol specification, the complexity of writing a reliable and complete SMTP implementation keeps many people and companies from doing it. Instead, the *sendmail* software[3] is by far the most popular software for SMTP servers, and it is included with many operating systems (although usually in an out of date version).

---

[1] At the destination address, which is the mail host specified in the email address, the message will be put into the electronic mailbox of the recipient also specified in the email address.

[2] Borrowing terminology from the ITU's X.400 series of recommendations, a mail client sometimes is referred to as *Mail User Agent (MUA)*, and a mail server is referred to as *Message Transfer Agent (MTA)*.

[3] The latest version of sendmail software is either available from the *Sendmail Consortium* (http://www.sendmail.org/) as free software, or from *Sendmail, Inc.* (http://www.sendmail.com/) as a complete product including support for installation and maintenance.

Although SMTP is the Internet protocol to transfer email, it actually exists in two flavors, original SMTP described in section 11.1.1.1, and the more recent *Extended SMTP (ESMTP)*, described in section 11.1.1.2.

A newer and functionally superior set of standards for an email system architecture is the *X.400* series of recommendations [141] developed and published by the *International Telecommunications Union (ITU)*. X.400 is the mail system to be used in environments based on ISO's *Open Systems Interconnection (OSI)* model of communications. A comprehensive overview of X.400 has been published by Plattner et al. [206]. However, although technically superior, X.400 did not succeed as a competitor of SMTP[4], and consequently the number of email systems using X.400 is decreasing.

11.1.1.1 Simple Mail Transfer Protocol (SMTP)

The *Simple Mail Transfer Protocol (SMTP)* is the Internet standard protocol for transferring email messages. It is defined in Internet standard RFC 821 [211]. SMTP's model of interaction is rather simple. A sender of an email message (usually an email program or a program containing this functionality such as a web browser) opens a connection to the receiver of the message[5] and sends the mail using a small number of SMTP commands. The basic SMTP standard only allows ASCII characters to be used.

11.1.1.2 Extended SMTP (ESMTP)

The basic SMTP protocol proved to be too simple in some application areas, so a framework for extensions was defined in Internet standard RFC 1869 [149]. This framework, which makes SMTP easily extensible (provided both sides support a specific extension), is called *Extended SMTP (ESMTP)*.

A large number of extensions have been defined in the meantime, and the definition of ESMTP as a framework for extensions makes it possible for ESMTP implementations to introduce new extensions without the need to change any of the existing standards. However, extensions only make sense if they are supported by both sides, so new extensions should be introduced with care and only if it seems likely that they are useful enough to be supported by a large number of ESMTP implementations.

Originally, ESMTP was defined to address some of SMTP's weaknesses, and the most popular and widely used extensions are described in the following list:

---

[4] An in-depth comparison of the competing email architectures X.400 and SMTP has been published by Rhoton [225].

[5] The receiver can either be the mail host of the message's recipient, or a relay system, which forwards the mail until it eventually is sent to the recipient's mail host.

- *Messages with 8-bit character sets*
  SMTP only recognizes ASCII characters, making it unsafe to use non-ASCII characters inside a mail. ESMTP defines a way how non-ASCII characters can be sent safely (it uses the mapping between non-ASCII and ASCII characters defined in Internet RFC 2047 [183]).

- *Message size declarations*
  Since mail messages can be rather large, it can be useful that the sender first informs the receiver of the size of a message. The receiver can decide whether it is willing to accept a message of the indicated size. The mechanism for this exchange of message size declarations is defined in Internet standard RFC 1870 [148].

- *Large and binary messages*
  When sending large mail messages, it may be useful to send a message as more than one part, and also to have a mechanism for check-pointing such a process, which allows to only repeat the sending of a message part if that transfer failed, instead of having to send all prior parts again. Internet experimental RFC 1830 [267] defines an extension for sending message chunks, and Internet experimental RFC 1845 [52] defines an extension for check-pointing and restarting the sending of messages.

Apart from these extensions, a number of additional extensions are defined in RFCs, and numerous other extensions have been defined for application-specific purposes. The *Internet Assigned Numbers Authority (IANA)* maintains a list of registered SMTP extensions with pointers to their specifications.

11.1.2 Receiving electronic mail

Although sending electronic mail is essential for successful mail transfer, the complementary problem is receiving electronic mail, which also has to be addressed. In the beginning, email was always read on the mail host (the machine which received the electronic mail via SMTP), so in most cases reading email was as simple as reading a file to which the SMTP program appended all incoming mail. However, this model only works if the user can access the same file system as the SMTP program.

A step further is the definition of network protocols for accessing email on the mail host (often called the mail server). Such a protocol can be used to access the mail server over a network, without the need for a shared file system. In such a model, the user is the client of the message access protocol, remotely accessing the mail server. Three different modes of access can be seen in such a scenario:

- *Offline*

  In offline operation, the client periodically connects to the mail server, retrieves new messages (which are deleted on the server), and disconnects. The mail is processed locally on the client machine.

- *Online*

  In online operation, the mail is left on the server and manipulated remotely by the client. The advantage of this model is that the user can use a different client and still has all the messages available, since they reside on the server[6].

- *Disconnected*

  Disconnected operation copies the mail from the server to the client, but does not delete them on the server. Therefore, the client can manipulate mail locally and later synchronize with the mail server. However, when a user accesses the server from another client, all messages are still accessible since they have been left on the server. For this type of operation, a client maintains a message cache, containing all messages which have been copied from the server. When connecting to the server, the message cache is synchronized with the messages stored on the server.

Two protocols are most popular, the *Post Office Protocol (POP)* described in section 11.1.2.1, and the functionally richer *Internet Message Access Protocol (IMAP)*, explained in section 11.1.2.2.

Other alternatives for message access protocols are the *P7* protocol of X.400 (specified in ITU recommendation X.419 [140]), and the *Distributed Mail System Protocol (DMSP)* specified in Internet informational RFC 1056 [156]. P7 presumes X.400 message formats and transport technology (which are not widely used), and DMSP is largely limited to a single application (PCMAIL). For these reasons, these two message access protocols are not further considered.

11.1.2.1 Post Office Protocol (POP)

After a mail has been transferred from the originator to the receiver's mail server, it is saved on the mail server to the receiver's mailbox, waiting for the receiver to read it. In most scenarios today, the receiver only occasionally contacts the mail server using a mail reading program and requesting new mail. Since this can be seen as the analogue of going to a post office and checking the mailbox, one of the most popular protocols for this purpose has

---

[6] In offline operation, emails are moved to the client and deleted on the server, so when using other clients the emails downloaded to the first client are not accessible.

been named the *Post Office Protocol (POP)*[7]. The protocol is specified in Internet draft standard RFC 1939 [187].

The basic interaction of POP is very simple. The POP server waits for incoming connections on a specific port (the default port for POP is 110), to which the client opens a TCP connection if a POP session is required. After sending a greeting, the client sends commands and the server generates responses, until the session is closed.

Authentication in POP can be done in different ways. The most basic way of authentication is using POP's USER and PASS commands. However, this sends the user name and the password unencrypted over a TCP connection, which is rather insecure. More secure ways of authentication have been defined in Internet proposed standard RFC 1734 [185], which are implemented using the optional AUTH command[8].

After successful authorization, the POP connection enters the transaction state and the client can issue a number of POP commands. Basically, the transaction state offers remote access to the user's mailbox. The number of POP commands is very small, so a POP server or client is rather easy to implement. The only commands for accessing the mailbox on the server are retrieving a message or deleting a message. Therefore, POP only supports the offline model of remote mailbox access.

11.1.2.2 Internet Message Access Protocol (IMAP)

Since POP is limited in its support for other modes of remote mailbox access than offline operation, a new protocol for accessing a remote mailbox is increasingly being used. This protocol is a superset (functionally, not syntactically) of POP. Originally named *Interactive Mail Access Protocol*, the name has been changed to *Internet Message Access Protocol (IMAP)*[9]. The protocol is specified in Internet proposed standard RFC 2060 [51]. The main advantages of IMAP over POP can be summarized as follows:

- *Multiple folder support*
  IMAP provides the ability to manipulate remote folders other than the folder with the incoming messages. This is supported by functions for listing, creating, deleting, and renaming remote folders. IMAP also supports folder hierarchies, so the remote folders on the IMAP server can be organized like local folders inside a file system.

---

[7] Since the current version of this protocol is version 3, it is also often referred to as *POP3*.

[8] The authorization procedures specified in RFC 1734 are the procedures which are used for IMAP.

[9] Since the current version of this protocol is version 4, it is also often referred to as *IMAP4*.

- *Remote folder manipulation*
  Messages can be moved from one folder to another, message flags can
  be set (to mark messages as read or answered), and shared folders (ie,
  folders which can be accessed by multiple users) can be updated with
  their update being notified to other users of that folder.

- *Online performance optimization*
  Since MIME messages can contain very large body parts (such as images
  or video clips), IMAP allows the individual fetching of MIME body parts.
  In order to do that, IMAP also provides support for determining the
  structure of a message (ie, its MIME body parts) without downloading
  the entire message. Furthermore, server-based searching and selection can
  be used to avoid the transfer of messages simply for searching.

Although IMAP is clearly functionally superior to POP, there are two
disadvantages to be mentioned. The protocol is considerably more complex
than POP and is thus harder to implement. Especially on systems with very
limited resources, this can be an important issue. Furthermore, being newer
than POP and providing functionality which is not required for all application scenarios, IMAP support currently is more limited than POP support.
However, in the last years IMAP has become more wide-spread, and it can
be expected that IMAP support will improve considerably in the future.

11.2 Directory services

In general, a directory contains information which is an alphabetical or otherwise classified list of resources of a specific domain. In the classical (ie,
printed) sense, a telephone directory contains an alphabetical list of all customers of the telephone service. It can be used to look up a name and find
the associated telephone number.

Electronic directories are very similar in nature, but due to their nature,
they allow for more flexible classification and querying. The most popular
directory service in use on the Internet is the *Domain Name System (DNS)*
described in section 1.4.1.2. DNS is used to map Internet host names to IP addresses. However, since DNS is most often used implicitly (eg, when a browser
resolves the host name of a web server to find out the associated IP address),
it is not recognized by most users. Furthermore, DNS is a highly specialized
directory service, which can not be used for user-specific information.

However, there are many application areas where a versatile electronic directory service could be very useful. Possible information to be made available
are names and corresponding email addresses, information on physical devices or services on a particular network, information for user authentication

or authorization, and many other things. The *X.500* series of recommendations [138] developed and published by the *International Telecommunications Union (ITU)* defines a directory service which can be used for all these application areas. X.500 is the directory system to be used in environments based on ISO's *Open Systems Interconnection (OSI)* model of communications. Among its main features is a sophisticated distribution and replication model as well as a security architecture.

Although X.500 is an ITU recommendation and belongs to the OSI set of applications, two reasons which are often attributed to the limited acceptance of X.400, it is more accepted than X.400. The main reason for this is that SMTP as a competitor of X.400 existed before X.400 appeared, while the Internet set of standards does not contain anything like X.500. Therefore, it is expected that X.500 will become the most important technology for directory services, and the *Internet Directory Consortium (IDC)* has been formed to coordinate the development and testing of directory products. Detailed descriptions of the X.500 directory and its applications have been published by Chadwick [43] and Steedman [253].

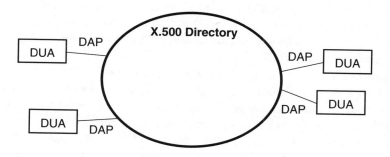

Fig. 11.2   X.500 directory access using DAP

The general model of X.500 from the user's point of view is shown in figure 11.2. The directory is a globally distributed database which can be accessed using a special protocol. In particular, the access protocol of X.500 is the *Directory Access Protocol (DAP)*, and a client using DAP to access X.500 is called a *Directory User Agent (DUA)*. Since distribution is transparent, it is not important where a DUA connects to, the directory handles distribution internally.

A closer view of X.500 is shown in figure 11.3. The X.500 directory is realized as a set of distributed cooperating agents using a communications protocol. The protocol used inside the X.500 directory is the *Directory System Protocol (DSP)*, and each component in the set of cooperating agents is called

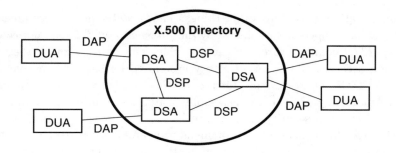

Fig. 11.3 X.500 data distribution using DSP

a *Directory System Agent (DSA)*. A DSA may or may not implement DAP support, in the latter case resulting in a DSA which communicates with other DSAs, but can not be directly contacted by a DUA.

The architecture shown in figure 11.3 is used to manage and provide access to hierarchically named information objects (which are called *entries*[10]) that users (by means of a DUA) can browse and search using arbitrary fields. Although the idea for X.500 originated from the requirement for a rather simple email address lookup service for X.400, it has evolved into a very general directory service supporting information objects using arbitrary data types and complexity.

In addition to the system architecture, the communication protocols, and the information being managed, X.500 also defines a hierarchical model for naming and organization of entries, an access control model together with an authentication framework, an administrative model for the global management of data, a replication model for the creation of copies of entries, and a multitude of other details to minimize the amount of non-standard agreements necessary to make the system work.

Since DSP is only important for the communication among DSPs, it is not explained any further. DAP, however, is the protocol to be implemented in user agents, and a web browser implementing DAP is one example of a DUA. DAP is therefore explained in section 11.2.1. Since DAP was considered too complex and too much focused on an OSI environment, a functional subset of DAP based on TCP/IP has been specified in the *Lightweight Directory Access Protocol (LDAP)*, which is explained in section 11.2.2.

---

[10] A minimalistic but still typical example is an entry consisting of the two fields "real life name" and "email address".

11.2.1 Directory Access Protocol (DAP)

The *Directory Access Protocol (DAP)* is specified in ITU recommendation X.519 [139]. It is a protocol for accessing X.500 directory servers (DSAs) and can be used by computer systems or human users (through a DUA implementing DAP and a user interface). The most important feature of DAP is its provision of powerful searching facilities which make it possible to construct arbitrarily complex queries.

The problem of DAP is that it is part of the OSI stack of protocols, which are rather complex and bulky in comparison to TCP/IP. Today's personal computers are capable of running an OSI protocol stack, but when X.500 first appeared in 1984, it was not possible to run a full DAP implementation on a personal computer. It was therefore decided to develop a lighter protocol not based on OSI but on TCP/IP, which could be used on systems with limited resources. This lighter protocol was called the *Lightweight Directory Access Protocol (LDAP)*.

11.2.2 Lightweight Directory Access Protocol (LDAP)

The *Lightweight Directory Access Protocol (LDAP)* is specified in Internet proposed standard RFC 2251 [270]. LDAP is designed to run directly on top of TCP/IP, and some of the DAP protocol functions which have been considered esoteric and non-essential have been removed.

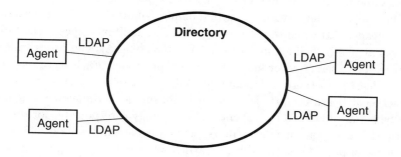

Fig. 11.4 Directory access using LDAP

In figure 11.4 it is shown how LDAP fits into the architecture defined by X.500. LDAP can either be built directly into DSAs, or it is possible to use protocol converters, which on the client side use LDAP (allowing a client to connect using LDAP), and on the server side use DAP. However, with the growing interest in LDAP, an increasing number of DSP implementations provides native LDAP support.

It is important to notice that LDAP merely defines an access protocol to a directory service, while X.500 specifies a complete directory system, including agents, internal communication protocols, and management issues. LDAP can also be used as access protocol for other directory services than X.500, but then many issues lying outside the scope of LDAP (such as management and replication of entries) must be specified elsewhere.

Since LDAP runs on top of TCP/IP, it can rather easily be integrated into Internet applications. One possibility is to implement LDAP in a web browser. In order to integrate directory services into the web, a URL format for LDAP queries has been defined in Internet proposed standard RFC 2255 [103].

11.3 Usenet news

Usenet news can be viewed as the oldest Internet application for global distribution of information. It originated in 1979 at the University of North Carolina. It is simply a set of machines (news servers) which cooperate to exchange articles tagged with one or more labels, which are called *newsgroups*. Newsgroups are organized hierarchically according to the subjects of the articles belonging to them.

In the beginning, the system was only used locally (on the campus), and the number of newsgroups was very small. Today, it is used on a world-wide scale, there are tens of thousands of newsgroups, and Usenet traffic is believed to consume between 20–40% of the Internet's bandwidth.

Basically, Usenet news consists of a number of articles which have a number of headers attached to them (very similar to mail messages). The format of news articles is defined in Internet RFC 1036 [99]. Articles are transferred from server to server according to a very simple policy. Each server is peered with at least one other server and offers all news articles to all servers except the server it heard the article from (or to all servers if the article originated locally, being submitted by a client). This strategy is responsible for the huge bandwidth overhead of Usenet news, since a server individually offers each article to all peered servers. With an article volume in the range of hundreds of thousands per day, this produces a lot of traffic only for advertising articles.

The protocol used for the transfer of Usenet news between servers is the *Network News Transfer Protocol (NNTP)* described in section 11.3.1. The *Network News Reading Protocol (NNRP)*, which is a subset of NNTP, is the protocol used between a client (such as a browser used for reading news) and a server. For a thorough discussion of many aspects of Usenet news (including the administration of news servers), the book by Spencer and Lawrence [247] provides a lot of interesting information.

11.3.1 Network News Transfer Protocol (NNTP)

The *Network News Transfer Protocol (NNTP)* is used between news servers[11] to exchange articles. It is specified in Internet standard RFC 977 [146]. Basically, a server periodically connects to other servers and advertises its new articles. The other server can decide whether it already has the article, does not want it for other reasons (eg, because the newsgroup is not necessary for this server), or accepts the article.

---

[11] The *Internet News Server (INN)* is by far the most popular software for NNTP servers. It is available as free software and runs on a variety of operating systems.

Part III

Appendices

A. HTTP/1.1 Definitions

In this appendix, some definitions from the revised HTTP/1.1 standard [76] are listed. The complete and most up to date version of these definitions should always be taken from the newest version of the standard, which is available from the W3C's web site or other information resources.

Section A.1 lists the message types of HTTP, showing their syntactic structure and which methods and header fields can be used. Section A.2 lists all status codes. Section A.3 lists all warning codes.

A.1 Messages

HTTP messages are either requests or responses. Both types of messages share a common structure, defined by a generic message type. Section A.1.1 lists this generic message type. In section A.1.2, the syntactic definition of a request is given. Section A.1.3 shows the syntactic definition of a response. This section contains only the most important elements of the definition of messages, for a complete listing the most recent version of the protocol specification should be consulted.

A.1.1 General definitions

The general definitions contain definitions for a generic HTTP message format, which is used for requests and responses. They also contain definitions for elements which are used in requests and responses, such as general and entity headers and the HTTP version number.

```
generic-message =
  start-line
  *message-header
  CRLF
  [ message-body ]

start-line =
  request-line | status-line
```

```
message-header =
  field-name ":" [ field-value ] CRLF

message-header =
  general-header | entity-header | request-header | response-header

message-body =
  entity-body | <entity-body encoded as per Transfer-Encoding>

general-header =
  Cache-Control | Connection | Date | Pragma |
  Trailer | Transfer-Encoding | Upgrade | Via

entity-header =
  Allow | Content-Base | Content-Encoding | Content-Language |
  Content-Length | Content-Location | Content-MD5 | Content-Range |
  Content-Type | ETag | Expires | Last-Modified

HTTP-version =
  "HTTP" "/" 1*DIGIT "." 1*DIGIT
```

A.1.2 Request

An HTTP request is a message consisting of the `request-line` specifying the `method` and other information, zero or more header lines, followed by an empty line and an optional message body.

```
request =
  request-line
  *( general-header | request-header | entity-header)
  CRLF
  [ message-body ]

request-line =
  method SP request-URI SP HTTP-version CRLF

method =
  "OPTIONS" | "GET" | "HEAD" | "POST" | "PUT" |
  "DELETE" | "TRACE" | "CONNECT" | extension-method

request-URI =
  "*" | absoluteURI | abs_path

request-header =
  Accept | Accept-Charset | Accept-Encoding | Accept-Language |
  Authorization | Expect | From | Host | If-Match |
  If-Modified-Since | If-None-Match | If-Range |
  If-Unmodified-Since | Max-Forwards | Proxy-Authorization |
```

Range | Referer | TE | User

A.1.3 Response

An HTTP response is a message consisting of the status-line specifying the status-code and other information, zero or more header lines, followed by an empty line and an optional message body.

```
response =
  status-line
  *( general-header | response-header | entity-header)
  CRLF
  [ message-body ]

status-line =
  HTTP-version SP status-code SP reason-phrase CRLF

response-header =
  Accept-Ranges | Age | Location | Proxy-Authenticate | Retry-After |
  Server | Vary | Warning | WWW-Authenticate
```

A.2 Status codes

The individual values of the numeric status codes defined for HTTP/1.1 and an example set of corresponding reason phrases (taken from the official standard document) are listed below. The status codes are three digit numbers, grouped according to the leading digit of the number. Each group represents status codes for a particular class of conditions. The reason phrases listed here are only recommended – they may be replaced by local equivalents without affecting the protocol.

A.2.1 Informational (1xx)

This class of status codes indicates that the request has been successfully received by the HTTP server, and that the server is processing the request. Thus, a response with a status code of this class is only provisional.

```
100 (continue)
101 (switching protocols)
```

A.2.2 Successful (2xx)

A status code of this class indicates that the processing of the request was successful.

```
200 (ok)
201 (created)
202 (accepted)
203 (non-authoritative information)
204 (no content)
205 (reset content)
206 (partial content)
207 (partial update ok)
```

A.2.3 Redirection (3xx)

If a response is received which carries a status code of this class, the client must take further action to complete the request, for example it must send a request to another server, which is specified in the response.

```
300 (multiple choices)
301 (moved permanently)
302 (moved temporarily)
303 (see other)
304 (not modified)
305 (use proxy)
307 (temporary redirect)
```

A.2.4 Client error (4xx)

If the HTTP request can not be processed because the client has made an error in its request (such as syntactical errors or sending unauthorized requests), the server responds with a status code of this class.

```
400 (bad request)
401 (unauthorized)
402 (payment required)
403 (forbidden)
404 (not found)
405 (method not allowed)
406 (not acceptable)
407 (proxy authentication required)
408 (request time-out)
409 (conflict)
410 (gone)
411 (length required)
412 (precondition failed)
```

```
413 (request entity too large)
414 (request-uri too large)
415 (unsupported media type)
416 (requested range not satisfiable)
417 (expectation failed)
418 (reauthentication required)
419 (proxy reauthentication required)
```

A.2.5 Server error (5xx)

In some cases the client's request may have been correct, but the server is incapable of performing the request. It then responds with a status code of this class. The server should specify whether the error situation is a temporary or permanent condition.

```
500 (internal server error)
501 (not implemented)
502 (bad gateway)
503 (service unavailable)
504 (gateway time-out)
505 (http version not supported)
506 (partial update not implemented)
```

A.3 Warn codes

The individual values of the numeric warn codes defined for HTTP/1.1, and an example set of corresponding warn texts (taken from the official standard document) are presented below. The warn codes are three digit numbers which are grouped according to the leading digit of the number. Each group represents warn codes for a particular class of conditions. The warn texts listed here are only recommended – they may be replaced by local equivalents without affecting the protocol.

A.3.1 Temporary warnings (1xx)

These warnings describe the freshness or revalidation status of the response and therefore must be deleted from a cache's entry after a successful revalidation.

```
110 (response is stale)
111 (revalidation failed)
112 (disconnected operation)
113 (heuristic expiration)
199 (miscellaneous warning)
```

A.3.2 Persistent warnings (2xx)

These warnings describe something which is not rectified by a revalidation and therefore must not be deleted from a cache's entry after a successful revalidation.

```
214 (transformation applied)
299 (miscellaneous persistent warning)
```

B. HTML 4.0 Definitions

This appendix gives a number of useful definitions for the *Hypertext Markup Language (HTML)* as described in chapter 5. In section B.1, the SGML declaration for HTML is listed. A number of entities which are used throughout the HTML DTD are listed and explained in section B.2.

The two most complex areas of HTML, tables and forms, are most easily used by looking at the DTD for content models and attributes. Sections B.3 and B.4 therefore contain the relevant excerpts from the HTML DTD.

B.1 SGML declaration

The purpose of an SGML declaration is to declare a concrete syntax, processing limits, character sets, and features to be used when processing SGML DTDs or documents. A more detailed explanation of SGML declarations and their syntax can be found in section 4.2.1. The following text is the SGML declaration for HTML 4.0.

```
<!SGML  "ISO 8879:1986"
        --

        SGML Declaration for HyperText Markup Language version 4.0

        With support for the first 17 planes of ISO 10646 [118]
        and increased limits for tag and literal lengths etc.
        --

    CHARSET
        BASESET  "ISO Registration Number 177//CHARSET
                  ISO/IEC 10646-1:1993 UCS-4 with
                  implementation level 3//ESC 2/5 2/15 4/6"
        DESCSET 0       9       UNUSED
                9       2       9
                11      2       UNUSED
                13      1       13
                14      18      UNUSED
                32      95      32
                127     1       UNUSED
```

```
                128      32        UNUSED
                160      55136     160
                55296    2048      UNUSED   -- surrogates --
                57344    1056768   57344


CAPACITY       SGMLREF
               TOTALCAP          150000
               GRPCAP            150000
               ENTCAP            150000


SCOPE DOCUMENT
SYNTAX
        SHUNCHAR CONTROLS 0 1 2 3 4 5 6 7 8 9 10 11 12 13 14 15 16
                 17 18 19 20 21 22 23 24 25 26 27 28 29 30 31 127
        BASESET  "ISO 646IRV:1991//CHARSET
                 International Reference Version
                 (IRV)//ESC 2/8 4/2"
        DESCSET  0 128 0


        FUNCTION
                 RE            13
                 RS            10
                 SPACE         32
                 TAB SEPCHAR    9


        NAMING   LCNMSTRT  ""
                 UCNMSTRT  ""
                 LCNMCHAR  ".-_:"
                 UCNMCHAR  ".-_:"
                 NAMECASE GENERAL YES
                          ENTITY  NO
        DELIM    GENERAL  SGMLREF
                 SHORTREF SGMLREF
        NAMES    SGMLREF
        QUANTITY SGMLREF
                 ATTCNT   60        -- increased --
                 ATTSPLEN 65536     -- These are the largest values --
                 LITLEN   65536     -- permitted in the declaration --
                 NAMELEN  65536     -- Avoid fixed limits in actual --
                 PILEN    65536     -- implementations of HTML UA's --
                 TAGLVL   100
                 TAGLEN   65536
                 GRPGTCNT 150
                 GRPCNT   64


FEATURES
   MINIMIZE
      DATATAG  NO
      OMITTAG  YES
```

```
      RANK      NO
      SHORTTAG  YES
   LINK
      SIMPLE    NO
      IMPLICIT  NO
      EXPLICIT  NO
   OTHER
      CONCUR    NO
      SUBDOC    NO
      FORMAL    YES
   APPINFO NONE


>
```

B.2 DTD Entities

In the detailed description of HTML 4.0, which is given in section 5.2, many DTD constructs use SGML entities as abbreviations for attributes or attribute values. The definitions for these entities are included in this section, which is intended to be used as a reference when reading section 5.2. Each entity's definition is accompanied by a short description of how and where it is used in the HTML 4.0 DTD.

Table B.1 can be used as a reference to find an entity's definition. While most entities are described in this section, the most important ones are explained in section 5.2.

- ```
  <!ENTITY % CELLHALIGN
     "ALIGN    (LEFT|CENTER|RIGHT|JUSTIFY|CHAR)  #IMPLIED
      CHAR     %CHARACTER;                       #IMPLIED
      CHAROFF  %LENGTH;                          #IMPLIED" >
  ```
  This entity is used to specify attributes for horizontal alignment of cells in tables. It is used in the <COLGROUP>, <COL>, <THEAD>, <TBODY>, <TFOOT>, <TR>, <TH>, and <TD> elements. HTML defines rules how these attributes are inherited or overridden. The ALIGN attribute specifies the horizontal alignment of table cells.

  – LEFT

  Using this value, cell content is flushed left. If the cell contains text, the text is left-justified. This is the default horizontal alignment for <TD> cells.

  – CENTER

  When the CENTER value is specified, cell content is centered. If the cell contains text, the text is center-justified. This is the default horizontal alignment for <TH> cells.
  ```

Table B.1 Overview of HTML 4.0 DTD entities

Entity name	Entity content	Page
ATTRS	attributes	184
BLOCK	content model	196
CELLHALIGN	attributes	473
CELLVALIGN	attributes	475
CHARACTER	attribute value	476
CHARSET	attribute value	476
CONTENTTYPE	attribute value	476
CONTENTTYPES	attribute value	476
COORDS	attribute value	476
COREATTRS	attributes	180
EVENTS	attributes	182
FLOW	content model	477
FONTSTYLE	content model	477
FORMCTRL	content model	477
FRAMETARGET	attribute value	477
HEAD.CONTENT	content model	478
HEAD.MISC	content model	478
HEADING	content model	479
HTML.CONTENT	content model	479
I18N	attributes	181
INLINE	content model	196
INPUTTYPE	attribute value	238
LANGUAGECODE	attribute value	479
LENGTH	attribute value	480
LINKTYPES	attribute value	480
LIST	content model	481
MEDIADESC	attribute value	481
MULTILENGTH	attribute value	482
MULTILENGTHS	attribute value	482
PHRASE	content model	482
PIXELS	attribute value	483
PREFORMATTED	content model	483
SCRIPT	attribute value	483
SHAPE	attribute value	483
SPECIAL	content model	484
STYLESHEET	attribute value	484
TEXT	attribute value	484
URI	attribute value	485

- RIGHT

  Using this value, cell content is flushed right. If the cell contains text, the text is right-justified.

- JUSTIFY

  This attribute value is used to justify text between the margins of a cell. This is done by adjusting the spacing between words, so that all lines have the same length.

- CHAR

  If the horizontal alignment is set to CHAR, the CHAR attribute must be used to specify a character which is then used to align table cells at that character. This is useful for aligning numbers at their decimal point. In addition to that, the CHAROFF attribute specifies the offset to the first occurrence of the alignment character on each line. If a line does not include the alignment character, it should be horizontally shifted to end at the alignment position.

The CHAR and CHAROFF attributes are only used if the ALIGN attribute is set to CHAR, otherwise they will be ignored.

- `<!ENTITY % CELLVALIGN`
  `"VALIGN (TOP|MIDDLE|BOTTOM|BASELINE) #IMPLIED" >`

  This entity is used for the same elements as the %CELLHALIGN; entity (which are the <COLGROUP>, <COL>, <THEAD>, <TBODY>, <TFOOT>, <TR>, <TH>, and <TD> elements). It specifies the VALIGN attribute, which is used to define the vertical alignment of table cells.

  - TOP

    This value specifies that cell content should be flushed to the top of the cell.

  - MIDDLE

    The MIDDLE value specifies that data should be centered between the top and the bottom of the cell. This is the default value.

  - BOTTOM

    This value specifies that cell content should be flushed to the bottom of the cell.

  - BASELINE

    All cells in the same row as a cell whose VALIGN attribute has this value should have their textual data positioned so that the first text line occurs on a baseline common to all cells in the row. This constraint does not apply to subsequent text lines in these cells.

Since the VALIGN attribute can be specified for a number of table elements, HTML defines rules how these attributes are inherited or overridden.

- `<!ENTITY % CHARACTER`
  `"CDATA" -- a single character from ISO 10646 [118] -- >`
  This entity is used for the ACCESSKEY attribute for a number of elements (<A>, <AREA>, <LABEL>, <INPUT>, <TEXTAREA>, <LEGEND>, and <BUTTON>) as well as for the CHAR attribute used in the %CELLHALIGN; entity. The %CHARACTER; entity defines a single character from the *Universal Multiple-Octet Coded Character Set (UCS)* standardized in ISO 10646 [118]. This character set includes all Unicode characters, therefore the %CHARACTER; entity accepts all characters from the Unicode character set as well.

- `<!ENTITY % CHARSET`
  `"CDATA" -- a character encoding, as per RFC 2045 [80] -- >`
  The %CHARSET; entity defines a character encoding for a linked resource. It is used for the CHARSET attribute of the <LINK>, <SCRIPT>, and <A> elements. A character encoding is a method of converting a sequence of bytes into a sequence of characters. A character encoding must be specified using a name registered in the official registry maintained by the *Internet Assigned Numbers Authority (IANA)*.

- `<!ENTITY % CONTENTTYPE`
  `"CDATA" -- media type, as per RFC 2045 [80] -- >`
  The %CONTENTTYPE; entity specifies a MIME type as described in section 1.4.3.2. It is used for attributes of a number of elements (<LINK>, <SCRIPT>, <STYLE>, <FORM>, <A>, <OBJECT>, and <PARAM>). The actual MIME types being used depend on the element, for example for the <STYLE> element's TYPE attribute the attribute value will identify a type of scripting language. A MIME type must be specified using a name registered in the official registry maintained by the *Internet Assigned Numbers Authority (IANA)*.

- `<!ENTITY % CONTENTTYPES`
  `"CDATA" -- comma-separated list of media types,`
  `            as per RFC 2045 [80] -- >`
  This entity specifies a list of MIME types. It is used for the <INPUT> element's file upload capability (using the FILE value for its TYPE attribute), where the ACCEPT attribute allows the specification of allowed file types for file upload.

- `<!ENTITY % COORDS`
  `"CDATA" -- comma separated list of lengths -- >`
  The %COORDS; entity is used to specify coordinates for regions inside image maps. It is used by the COORDS attribute of the <AREA> and <A> elements (which are used for defining client-side image maps using the <MAP> element). The number of lengths used with the COORDS attribute as well as their interpretation depends on the SHAPE attribute,

which always accompanies the COORDS attribute. The possible values of the SHAPE attribute as well as their implications for the format of the COORDS attribute are defined by the %SHAPE; entity.

- <!ENTITY % FLOW
    "%BLOCK; | %INLINE;" >

  As described in section 5.2.3.2, HTML groups elements into two categories, block-level elements and inline elements. There are, however, some elements which accepts as content both block-level and inline elements. These elements use the %FLOW; entity, which simply is a combination of the %BLOCK; and %INLINE; entities.

- <!ENTITY % FONTSTYLE
    "TT | I | B | BIG | SMALL" >

  A number of elements can be used to change the style of text, these element are grouped in the %FONTSTYLE; entity[1].

- <!ENTITY % FORMCTRL
    "INPUT | SELECT | TEXTAREA | LABEL | BUTTON" >

  A number of elements which normally are used within forms (as described in section 5.2.7.2) can also be used without being included in a <FORM> element. These elements are grouped in the %FORMCTRL; entity which is used inside the %INLINE; entity, which in turn generally defines inline elements. The %FORMCTRL; entity is also used for exclusion in the <BUTTON> element's definition.

- <!ENTITY % FRAMETARGET
    "CDATA" -- render in this frame -- >

  The %FRAMETARGET; entity is used to specify a target frame for a link. It is used for the TARGET attribute of an <A>, <AREA>, <BASE>, <FORM>, and <LINK> elements. A number of special target names are defined by the HTML 4.0 specification.

  - _blank

    This defines a new window into which the document should be loaded. This window lies outside any frame hierarchy, it is an entirely new, unnamed window.

  - _self

    The user agent should load the document in the same frame as the element that refers to this target. Although this is the default behavior, this is useful if the document contains a <BASE> element with its TARGET attribute set.

---

[1] In the transitional DTD, the deprecated <STRIKE>, <S> and <U> elements are also part of the %FONTSTYLE; entity.

— _parent

This instructs the user agent to load the document into the immediate frameset parent of the current frame. If the current frame has no parent, the document is loaded the current frame.

— _top

Using this value, the document is loaded into the original window, which will cancel all frames inside the window.

In addition to these special names, frames can be named using the **NAME** attribute of the <FRAME> element, and these names can also be used as targets. This is described in detail in section 5.2.7.1. The process how a browser determines which frame it should use is defined by four steps.

1. If the target name is one of the reserved words described above, it is interpreted accordingly and the document is loaded into the resulting frame or window.

2. The frame hierarchy in the current window is searched for a frame with the given name. If such a frame is found, the document is loaded into it.

3. All other windows and their frame hierarchies are searched for a frame with the given name. If such a frame is found, the document is loaded into it.

4. If no matching name has been found, a new window is created, assigned the target name, and the document is loaded into it.

It should be noticed that the %FRAMETARGET; entity respectively the **TARGET** attribute can be used to windows, and not only frames. However, the creation of new windows (using the _blank reserved word or a target name which has not been assigned to any frame) should be handled with great care, since it may irritate users.

- <!ENTITY % HEAD.CONTENT
  "TITLE & BASE?" >

This is the content model for the <HEAD> element, it contains a mandatory <TITLE> element and an optional <BASE> element[2].

- <!ENTITY % HEAD.MISC
  "SCRIPT | STYLE | META | LINK | OBJECT" >

The %HEAD.MISC; entity is defined to be included by the <HEAD> element. It allows zero or more inclusions of the <SCRIPT>, <STYLE>, <META>, <LINK>, and <OBJECT> elements.

---

[2] In the transitional DTD, the <ISINDEX> element is also allowed as optional content of the <HEAD> element. The <ISINDEX> element was used to mark an HTML document as a searchable index, allowing the user to input one line of text which was sent back to the server.

- `<!ENTITY % HEADING`
  `"H1 | H2 | H3 | H4 | H5 | H6" >`

  The %HEADING; entity simply is a short cut for all heading elements which are defined in HTML. These are the hierarchically ordered headings from <H1>, the highest level heading, through <H6>, the lowest level heading.

- `<!ENTITY % HTML.CONTENT`
  `"HEAD, BODY" >`

  This is the content model for the <HTML> element, defining that an HTML document is defined as a sequence of a <HEAD> element and a <BODY> element.

- `<!ENTITY % IALIGN`
  `"(TOP|MIDDLE|BOTTOM|LEFT|RIGHT)" -- >`

  This entity is used with the ALIGN attribute of the <IFRAME> element[3]. This attribute specifies the horizontal alignment the element with respect to the surrounding context.

  - TOP
    This value aligns the top of the element with the surrounding content.
  - MIDDLE
    The MIDDLE value aligns the middle of the element with the surrounding content, thereby centering it vertically.
  - BOTTOM
    This value aligns the bottom of the element with the surrounding content.
  - LEFT
    This value floats the element to the current left margin. Subsequent text flows along the image's right side.
  - RIGHT
    The RIGHT value floats the object to the current right margin. Subsequent text flows along the image's left side.

  These attributes values make it possible to use the element as either inline (using the TOP, MIDDLE, or BOTTOM value) or floating (using the LEFT or RIGHT value) element.

- `<!ENTITY % LANGUAGECODE`
  `"NAME" -- a language code, as per RFC 1766 [7] -- >`

  This entity is used for language codes as specified by Internet proposed standard RFC 1766 [7]. It is in the internationalization attributes defined by the %I18N; entity, and in the <A> and <LINK> elements to specify the language of a resource.

---

[3] The %IALIGN; entity is also used for the deprecated ALIGN attribute of the <INPUT>, <IMG>, <OBJECT>, and <APPLET> elements.

- `<!ENTITY % LENGTH`
  `"CDATA" -- nn for pixels or nn% for percentage length -- >`
  This entity specifies either a `%PIXEL;` value or a percentage of the available horizontal or vertical space. It is used for the WIDTH and HEIGHT attributes of the `<IMG>`, `<OBJECT>`, and `<IFRAME>` elements.

- `<!ENTITY % LINKTYPES`
  `"CDATA" -- space-separated list of link types -- >`
  The `%LINKTYPES;` entity specifies the semantics of a link, which is established using the REL or `<REV>` attribute of the `<LINK>` element. The HTML 4.0 standard defines a number of possible link types:

  - *Alternate*
    This value designates substitute versions for the document in which the link occurs. When used together with the LANG attribute, it implies a translated version of the document. When used together with the MEDIA attribute, it implies a version designed for a different medium.

  - *Stylesheet*
    If this value is used, the link refers to an external style sheet. This is used together with the link type *Alternate* for user-selectable alternate style sheets.

  - *Start*
    A link of this type refers to the first document in a collection of documents. This link type tells search engines which document is considered by the author to be the starting point of the collection.

  - *Next*
    If this value is used, the link refers to the next document in an linear sequence of documents. User agents may choose to preload the "next" document to reduce the perceived load time.

  - *Prev*
    This type of link refers to the previous document in an ordered series of documents.

  - *Contents*
    If there is a table of contents for the current documents, the *Contents* value can be used to refer to a document containing this table of contents.

  - *Index*
    If there is an index for the current documents, the *Index* value can be used to refer to a document containing this index.

  - *Glossary*
    If there is a glossary for the current documents, the *Glossary* value can be used to refer to a document containing this glossary.

– *Copyright*

This type of links refers to a document which contains the copyright notes for a document.

– *Chapter*

This type of link refers to a document serving as a chapter in a collection of documents.

– *Section*

This type of link refers to a document serving as a section in a collection of documents.

– *Subsection*

This type of link refers to a document serving as a sub-section in a collection of documents.

– *Appendix*

This type of link refers to a document serving as an appendix in a collection of documents.

– *Help*

If there is an document which offers help for using a document, such as links to other resources, information how to use the document, or similar things, the *Help* value for a link can be used to refer to such a document.

– *Bookmark*

This type of link refers to a bookmark. A bookmark is a link to a key entry point within an extended document. The title attribute may be used, for example, to label the bookmark. Note that several bookmarks may be defined in each document.

It should be noted that this list only describes the semantics for the forward direction of a link. Using the REV attribute of the <LINK> element results in the specification of a reverse link, which uses the reversed semantics.

- ```
<!ENTITY % LIST
   "UL | OL" >
```

This entity is a short cut for the two simpler list types of HTML, unordered lists defined by the <UL> element, and ordered lists defined by the <OL> element. Both types of lists are described in section 5.2.4.2.

- ```
<!ENTITY % MEDIADESC
    "CDATA" -- single or comma-separated list
             of media descriptors -- >
```

The %MEDIA; entity is used to specify a media type. It is used with the <LINK> element to specify for which media type a document to which a link points is intended. It is also used with the <STYLE> element to specify the media type for which a style sheet is intended. The HTML 4.0 standard defines a number of possible media types:

− *screen*
This is the default value, it specifies non-paged computer screens.
− *tty*
This value is used for fixed-pitch character grid displays.
− *tv*
This specifies television-type devices with low resolution and limited scroll-ability.
− *projection*
This specifies projection devices such as beamers.
− *handheld*
This value is used for hand-held devices (characterized by a small, monochrome display and limited bandwidth).
− *print*
This value specifies output to a printer.
− *braille*
This value is used for braille tactile feedback devices.
− *aural*
This value is used for speech synthesizers.
− *all*
This value specifies that the resource is intended for all media types.

Other attribute values could be used, but they will not be recognized by all HTML 4.0 applications.

- `<!ENTITY % MULTILENGTH`
  `"CDATA" -- pixel, percentage, or relative -- >`
  A %MULTILENGTH; value is either a %LENGTH; value (ie, a pixel length or a percentage) or a relative length specifying the length of an element in relation to the other elements also using relative lengths. This type of value is used for the WIDTH attribute of the <COLGROUP> and <COL> elements.

- `<!ENTITY % MULTILENGTHS`
  `"CDATA" -- comma-separated list of MultiLength -- >`
  This entity specifies a comma-separated list of %MULTILENGTH; values. It is used for the ROWS and COLS attributes of the <FRAMESET> element.

- `<!ENTITY % PHRASE`
  `"EM | STRONG | DFN | CODE | SAMP | KBD | VAR | CITE |`
  `ABBR | ACRONYM" >`
  HTML defines a number of elements which can be used for marking phrases. These elements are used for emphasis (<EM> and <STRONG>)

or special semantics of phrases (<DFN>, <CODE>, <SAMP>, <KBD>, <VAR>, and <CITE>) as well as for abbreviations (<ABBR>) and acronyms (<ACRONYM>). The %PHRASE; entity groups all these elements together.

- `<!ENTITY % PIXELS`
  `"CDATA" -- integer representing length in pixels -- >`
  This entity is used to specify a length which can only be defined using pixels. It is used for the BORDER attribute of the <TABLE> element, and for the MARGINWIDTH and MARGINHEIGHT attributes of the <FRAME> and <IFRAME> elements[4].

- `<!ENTITY % PREFORMATTED`
  `"PRE" >`
  Currently, there is only one element in HTML which is used for preformatted content, which is the <PRE> element. Therefore, the %PREFORMATTED; entity contains only this single element.

- `<!ENTITY % SCRIPT`
  `"CDATA" -- script expression -- >`
  Script data can be the content of the <SCRIPT> element and the value of intrinsic event attributes. User agents must not evaluate script data as HTML markup but instead must pass it on as data to a script engine. The case-sensitivity of script data depends on the scripting language. Script data may occur in all attributes defined in the %EVENTS; entity. It is also usable for the intrinsic event attributes ONLOAD and ONUNLOAD defined for the <BODY> and <FRAMESET> elements, the ONFOCUS and ONBLUR attributes defined for the <A>, <AREA>, and <INPUT> elements, the ONSUBMIT and ONRESET attributes defined for the <FORM> element, and the ONSELECT and ONCHANGE attributes defined for the <INPUT> element.

- `<!ENTITY % SHAPE`
  `"( RECT | CIRCLE | POLY | DEFAULT )" >`
  The %SHAPE; entity defines the possible shapes for the SHAPE attribute of the <AREA> and <A> elements (which are used for defining client-side image maps using the <MAP> element). In both cases, the SHAPE attribute specifies geometric regions of an image which are used for defining client-side image maps. All coordinates (which are specified in the COORDS attribute accompanying the SHAPE attribute) of area shapes are measured in pixels or percentages from the top-left corner of the image.

---

[4] In the transitional DTD, the %PIXELS; entity is also used for the HSPACE and VSPACE attributes of the <IMG>, <OBJECT>, and <APPLET> elements, for the SIZE attribute of the <HR> element, and for the WIDTH and HEIGHT attributes of the <TH> and <TD> elements.

- RECT

  Rectangles are specified using four coordinates, giving the left, top, right, and bottom boundaries of the rectangle.
- CIRCLE

  A circular region is specified using three values, the first two specifying the x- and y-coordinates of the center, the third one defining the circle's radius. A percentage radius value for circular regions is calculated relative to the smaller of the image's width and height.
- POLY

  A polygonal region is defined by a sequence of pairs of values, each pair specifying the coordinates of one point of the polygon.
- DEFAULT

  The default area of an image is the area which does not have any other area assigned to it. It is therefore implicitly defined and does nor require the specification of coordinates.

If two or more regions overlap when specifying areas using the <AREA> or <A> elements inside an image map, the earliest specified region takes precedence

- `<!ENTITY % SPECIAL`
  `"A | IMG | OBJECT | BR | SCRIPT | MAP | Q | SUB | SUP |`
  `SPAN | BDO" >`

  This entity groups together a number of elements which are used in the definition of the %INLINE; entity.

- `<!ENTITY % STYLESHEET`
  `"CDATA" -- style sheet data -- >`

  This entity is used for the <STYLE> element, as well as for the STYLE attribute, which is part of the %COREATTRS; entity as described in section 5.2.2. The %STYLESHEET; entity specifies style sheet data. The exact format of the data depends on the style sheet language being used.

- `<!ENTITY % TEXT`
  `"CDATA" >`

  This entity is used if text used as attribute value is meant to be "human readable", specifying short notes or hints. The %TEXT; entity is used for the TITLE attribute of the %COREATTRS; entity and the <STYLE> element, the ALT attribute of the <IMG> and <AREA> elements, the STANDBY attribute of the <OBJECT> element, the LABEL attribute of the <OPTGROUP> and <OPTION> elements, the SUMMARY attribute of the <TABLE> element, and the ABBR attribute of the <TH> and <TD> elements[5].

---

[5] The %TEXT; entity is also used for the PROMPT attribute of the deprecated <ISINDEX> element.

- `<!ENTITY % URI`
    `"CDATA" -- a Uniform Resource Identifier [19] -- >`
    The %URI; entity is used in places where URIs [19] can be specified (the new URI RFC will introduce some changes to Internet proposed standards RFC 1737 and 1808 [21, 77]). The entity is used for PROFILE attribute of the <HEAD> element, the HREF attribute of the <A>, <AREA>, <LINK>, and <BASE> elements, the SRC attribute of the <IMG>, <SCRIPT>, <FRAME>, <IFRAME>, and <INPUT> elements, the LONGDESC attribute of the <IMG>, <FRAME>, and <IFRAME> elements, the USEMAP attribute of the <IMG>, <INPUT>, and <OBJECT> elements, the ACTION attribute of the <FORM> element, the FOR attribute of the <SCRIPT> element, the CITE attribute of the <BLOCKQUOTE>, <Q>, <INS>, and <DEL> elements, the PROFILE attribute of the <HEAD> element, and the CLASSID, CODEBASE, DATA, and ARCHIVE attributes of the <OBJECT> element[6].

B.3 HTML 4.0 table DTD

This is the DTD for tables, which originally appeared in Internet experimental RFC 1942 [216], but now is part of HTML 4.0. It lists all elements and attributes which can be used for tables, thus providing a complete reference to HTML tables (which are described in section 5.2.4.3). In particular, HTML tables contain many layout-oriented attributes, due to the fact that table layout is not supported in CSS1.

```
<!ENTITY % TFRAME
 "(VOID|ABOVE|BELOW|HSIDES|LHS|RHS|VSIDES|BOX|BORDER)" >
<!ENTITY % TRULES "(NONE|GROUPS|ROWS|COLS|ALL)" >
<!ENTITY % TALIGN "(LEFT|CENTER|RIGHT)" >
<!ENTITY % CALIGN "(TOP|BOTTOM|LEFT|RIGHT)" >
<!ENTITY % SCOPE "(ROW|COL|ROWGROUP|COLGROUP)" >

<!ELEMENT TABLE     - - (CAPTION?,(COL*|COLGROUP*),
                        THEAD?,TFOOT?,TBODY+) >
<!ELEMENT CAPTION   - - (%INLINE;)*
<!ELEMENT THEAD     - O (TR)+
<!ELEMENT TFOOT     - O (TR)+
<!ELEMENT TBODY     O O (TR)+
<!ELEMENT COLGROUP  - O (COL)*
<!ELEMENT COL       - O EMPTY
<!ELEMENT TR        - O (TH|TD)+
<!ELEMENT (TH|TD)   - O (%FLOW;)* >
```

---

[6] The %URI; entity is also used for the deprecated BACKGROUND attribute of the <BODY> element, and the CODEBASE attribute of the deprecated <APPLET> element.

```
<!ATTLIST TABLE
  %ATTRS;
  SUMMARY      %TEXT;   #IMPLIED
  WIDTH        %LENGTH; #IMPLIED
  BORDER       %PIXELS; #IMPLIED
  FRAME        %TFRAME; #IMPLIED
  RULES        %TRULES; #IMPLIED
  CELLSPACING  %LENGTH; #IMPLIED
  CELLPADDING  %LENGTH; #IMPLIED
  DATAPAGESIZE CDATA    #IMPLIED >

<!ATTLIST CAPTION
  %ATTRS; >

<!ATTLIST COLGROUP
  %ATTRS;
  SPAN         NUMBER        1
  WIDTH        %MULTILENGTH; #IMPLIED
  %CELLHALIGN;
  %CELLVALIGN; >

<!ATTLIST COL
  %ATTRS;
  SPAN         NUMBER        1
  WIDTH        %MULTILENGTH; #IMPLIED
  %CELLHALIGN;
  %CELLVALIGN; >

<!ATTLIST (THEAD|TBODY|TFOOT)
  %ATTRS;
  %CELLHALIGN;
  %CELLVALIGN; >

<!ATTLIST TR
  %ATTRS;
  %CELLHALIGN;
  %CELLVALIGN; >

<!ATTLIST (TH|TD)
  %ATTRS;
  ABBR         %TEXT;  #IMPLIED
  AXIS         CDATA   #IMPLIED
  HEADERS      IDREFS  #IMPLIED
  SCOPE        %SCOPE; #IMPLIED
  ROWSPAN      NUMBER  1
  COLSPAN      NUMBER  1
  %CELLHALIGN;
  %CELLVALIGN; >
```

B.4 HTML 4.0 form DTD

This is the part of the HTML 4.0 DTD which specifies forms and form elements. It is listed as a reference, because the description of form elements in section 5.2.7.2 does not contain all DTD specifications.

```
<!ELEMENT FORM - - (%BLOCK;|SCRIPT)+ -(FORM) >
<!ATTLIST FORM
  %ATTRS;
  ACTION          %URI;             #REQUIRED
  METHOD          (GET|POST)        GET
  ENCTYPE         %CONTENTTYPE;     "application/x-www-form-urlencoded"
  ONSUBMIT        %SCRIPT;          #IMPLIED
  ONRESET         %SCRIPT;          #IMPLIED
  ACCEPT-CHARSET  %CHARSETS;        #IMPLIED >

<!ELEMENT LABEL - - (%INLINE;)* -(LABEL) >
<!ATTLIST LABEL
  %ATTRS;
  FOR             IDREF             #IMPLIED
  ACCESSKEY       %CHARACTER;       #IMPLIED
  ONFOCUS         %SCRIPT;          #IMPLIED
  ONBLUR          %SCRIPT;          #IMPLIED >

<!ELEMENT INPUT - 0 EMPTY >
<!ATTLIST INPUT
  %ATTRS;
  TYPE            %INPUTTYPE;       TEXT
  NAME            CDATA             #IMPLIED
  VALUE           CDATA             #IMPLIED
  CHECKED         (CHECKED)         #IMPLIED
  DISABLED        (DISABLED)        #IMPLIED
  READONLY        (READONLY)        #IMPLIED
  SIZE            CDATA             #IMPLIED
  MAXLENGTH       NUMBER            #IMPLIED
  SRC             %URI;             #IMPLIED
  ALT             CDATA             #IMPLIED
  USEMAP          %URI;             #IMPLIED
  TABINDEX        NUMBER            #IMPLIED
  ACCESSKEY       %CHARACTER;       #IMPLIED
  ONFOCUS         %SCRIPT;          #IMPLIED
  ONBLUR          %SCRIPT;          #IMPLIED
  ONSELECT        %SCRIPT;          #IMPLIED
  ONCHANGE        %SCRIPT;          #IMPLIED
  ACCEPT          %CONTENTTYPES;    #IMPLIED >

<!ELEMENT SELECT - - (OPTGROUP|OPTION)+ >
<!ATTLIST SELECT
  %ATTRS;
```

```
    NAME          CDATA             #IMPLIED
    SIZE          NUMBER            #IMPLIED
    MULTIPLE      (MULTIPLE)        #IMPLIED
    DISABLED      (DISABLED)        #IMPLIED
    TABINDEX      NUMBER            #IMPLIED
    ONFOCUS       %SCRIPT;          #IMPLIED
    ONBLUR        %SCRIPT;          #IMPLIED
    ONCHANGE      %SCRIPT;          #IMPLIED >

<!ELEMENT OPTGROUP - - (OPTION)+ >
<!ATTLIST OPTGROUP
   %ATTRS;
   DISABLED      (DISABLED)        #IMPLIED
   LABEL         %TEXT;            #REQUIRED >

<!ELEMENT OPTION - O (#PCDATA) >
<!ATTLIST OPTION
   %ATTRS;
   SELECTED      (SELECTED)        #IMPLIED
   DISABLED      (DISABLED)        #IMPLIED
   LABEL         %TEXT;            #IMPLIED
   VALUE         CDATA             #IMPLIED >

<!ELEMENT TEXTAREA - - (#PCDATA) >
<!ATTLIST TEXTAREA
   %ATTRS;
   NAME          CDATA             #IMPLIED
   ROWS          NUMBER            #REQUIRED
   COLS          NUMBER            #REQUIRED
   DISABLED      (DISABLED)        #IMPLIED
   READONLY      (READONLY)        #IMPLIED
   TABINDEX      NUMBER            #IMPLIED
   ACCESSKEY     %CHARACTER;       #IMPLIED
   ONFOCUS       %SCRIPT;          #IMPLIED
   ONBLUR        %SCRIPT;          #IMPLIED
   ONSELECT      %SCRIPT;          #IMPLIED
   ONCHANGE      %SCRIPT;          #IMPLIED >

<!ELEMENT FIELDSET - - (#PCDATA,LEGEND,(%FLOW;)*) >
<!ATTLIST FIELDSET
   %ATTRS; >

<!ELEMENT LEGEND - - (%INLINE;)* >
<!ATTLIST LEGEND
   %ATTRS;
   ACCESSKEY    %CHARACTER;       #IMPLIED >

<!ELEMENT BUTTON - - (%FLOW;)* -(A|%FORMCTRL;|FORM|FIELDSET) >
<!ATTLIST BUTTON
```

```
%ATTRS;
NAME        CDATA                       #IMPLIED
VALUE       CDATA                       #IMPLIED
TYPE        (BUTTON|SUBMIT|RESET)       SUBMIT
DISABLED    (DISABLED)                  #IMPLIED
TABINDEX    NUMBER                      #IMPLIED
ACCESSKEY   %CHARACTER;                 #IMPLIED
ONFOCUS     %SCRIPT;                    #IMPLIED
ONBLUR      %SCRIPT;                    #IMPLIED >
```

C. XML 1.0 Definitions

This appendix contains definitions for the *Extensible Markup Language (XML)* as described in chapter 7. section C.1 lists the SGML declaration of XML. As an example of an XML DTD, section C.2 lists the DTD of the *Synchronized Multimedia Integration Language (SMIL)*.

C.1 SGML declaration

The general purpose of an SGML declaration is described in section 4.2.1. It should be kept in mind that the SGML declaration for XML does not completely define XML. XML also specifies some modifications of SGML which can not be expressed in the SGML declaration.

```
<!SGML  "ISO 8879:1986 (ENR)"
    --

        SGML Declaration for XML

    --

  CHARSET
      BASESET "ISO Registration Number 176//CHARSET
               ISO/IEC 10646-1:1993 UCS-4 with implementation
               level 3//ESC 2/5 2/15 4/6"
      DESCSET 0        9        UNUSED
              9        2        9
              11       2        UNUSED
              13       1        13
              14       18       UNUSED
              32       95       32
              127      1        UNUSED
              128      32       UNUSED
              160      55136    160
              55296    2048     UNUSED  -- surrogates --
              57344    8190     57344
              65534    2        UNUSED  -- FFFE and FFFF --
              65536    1048576  65536

  CAPACITY     SGMLREF
```

```
                    -- Capacities are not restricted in XML --
               TOTALCAP 99999999
               ENTCAP   99999999
               ENTCHCAP 99999999
               ELEMCAP  99999999
               GRPCAP   99999999
               EXGRPCAP 99999999
               EXNMCAP  99999999
               ATTCAP   99999999
               ATTCHCAP 99999999
               AVGRPCAP 99999999
               NOTCAP   99999999
               NOTCHCAP 99999999
               IDCAP    99999999
               IDREFCAP 99999999
               MAPCAP   99999999
               LKSETCAP 99999999
               LKNMCAP  99999999

     SCOPE DOCUMENT
     SYNTAX
          SHUNCHAR NONE
          BASESET  "ISO Registration Number 176//CHARSET
                    ISO/IEC 10646-1:1993 UCS-4 with implementation
                    level 3//ESC 2/5 2/15 4/6"
          DESCSET  0 1114112 0

          FUNCTION
                    RE            13
                    RS            10
                    SPACE         32
                    TAB SEPCHAR    9
          NAMING    LCNMSTRT ""
                    UCNMSTRT ""
                    NAMESTRT
                      58 95 192-214 216-246 248-305 308-318 321-328
                      330-382 384-451 461-496 500-501 506-535 592-680
                      699-705 902 904-906 908 910-929 931-974 976-982
                      986 988 990 992 994-1011 1025-1036 1038-1103
                      1105-1116 1118-1153 1168-1220 1223-1224
                      1227-1228 1232-1259 1262-1269 1272-1273
                      1329-1366 1369 1377-1414 1488-1514 1520-1522
                      1569-1594 1601-1610 1649-1719 1722-1726
                      1728-1742 1744-1747 1749 1765-1766 2309-2361
                      2365 2392-2401 2437-2444 2447-2448 2451-2472
                      2474-2480 2482 2486-2489 2524-2525 2527-2529
                      2544-2545 2565-2570 2575-2576 2579-2600
                      2602-2608 2610-2611 2613-2614 2616-2617
                      2649-2652 2654 2674-2676 2693-2699 2701
```

```
                  2703-2705 2707-2728 2730-2736 2738-2739
                  2741-2745 2749 2784 2821-2828 2831-2832
                  2835-2856 2858-2864 2866-2867 2870-2873 2877
                  2908-2909 2911-2913 2949-2954 2958-2960
                  2962-2965 2969-2970 2972 2974-2975 2979-2980
                  2984-2986 2990-2997 2999-3001 3077-3084
                  3086-3088 3090-3112 3114-3123 3125-3129
                  3168-3169 3205-3212 3214-3216 3218-3240
                  3242-3251 3253-3257 3294 3296-3297 3333-3340
                  3342-3344 3346-3368 3370-3385 3424-3425
                  3585-3630 3632 3634-3635 3648-3653 3713-3714
                  3716 3719-3720 3722 3725 3732-3735 3737-3743
                  3745-3747 3749 3751 3754-3755 3757-3758 3760
                  3762-3763 3773 3776-3780 3904-3911 3913-3945
                  4256-4293 4304-4342 4352 4354-4355 4357-4359
                  4361 4363-4364 4366-4370 4412 4414 4416 4428
                  4430 4432 4436-4437 4441 4447-4449 4451 4453
                  4455 4457 4461-4462 4466-4467 4469 4510 4520
                  4523 4526-4527 4535-4536 4538 4540-4546 4587
                  4592 4601 7680-7835 7840-7929 7936-7957
                  7960-7965 7968-8005 8008-8013 8016-8023 8025
                  8027 8029 8031-8061 8064-8116 8118-8124 8126
                  8130-8132 8134-8140 8144-8147 8150-8155
                  8160-8172 8178-8180 8182-8188 8486 8490-8491
                  8494 8576-8578 12295 12321-12329 12353-12436
                  12449-12538 12549-12588 19968-40869 44032-55203
LCNMCHAR ""

                  UCNMCHAR ""
                  NAMECHAR
                  45-46 183 720-721 768-837 864-865 903 1155-1158
                  1425-1441 1443-1465 1467-1469 1471 1473-1474
                  1476 1600 1611-1618 1632-1641 1648 1750-1764
                  1767-1768 1770-1773 1776-1785 2305-2307 2364
                  2366-2381 2385-2388 2402-2403 2406-2415
                  2433-2435 2492 2494-2500 2503-2504 2507-2509
                  2519 2530-2531 2534-2543 2562 2620 2622-2626
                  2631-2632 2635-2637 2662-2673 2689-2691 2748
                  2750-2757 2759-2761 2763-2765 2790-2799
                  2817-2819 2876 2878-2883 2887-2888 2891-2893
                  2902-2903 2918-2927 2946-2947 3006-3010
                  3014-3016 3018-3021 3031 3047-3055 3073-3075
                  3134-3140 3142-3144 3146-3149 3157-3158
                  3174-3183 3202-3203 3262-3268 3270-3272
                  3274-3277 3285-3286 3302-3311 3330-3331
                  3390-3395 3398-3400 3402-3405 3415 3430-3439
                  3633 3636-3642 3654-3662 3664-3673 3761
                  3764-3769 3771-3772 3782 3784-3789 3792-3801
                  3864-3865 3872-3881 3893 3895 3897 3902-3903
                  3953-3972 3974-3979 3984-3989 3991 3993-4013
```

```
                     4017-4023 4025 8400-8412 8417 12293 12330-12335
                     12337-12341 12441-12442 12445-12446 12540-12542
            NAMECASE GENERAL NO
                     ENTITY  NO

            DELIM    GENERAL SGMLREF
                     NET "/>"
                     PIC "?>"
                     SHORTREF NONE
            NAMES    SGMLREF
            QUANTITY SGMLREF
               -- Quantities are not restricted in XML --
               ATTCNT     99999999
               ATTSPLEN   99999999
               -- BSEQLEN  not used --
               -- DTAGLEN  not used --
               -- DTEMPLEN not used --
               ENTLVL     99999999
               GRPCNT     99999999
               GRPGTCNT   99999999
               GRPLVL     99999999
               LITLEN     99999999
               NAMELEN    99999999
               -- no need to change NORMSEP --
               PILEN      99999999
               TAGLEN     99999999
               TAGLVL     99999999

FEATURES
  MINIMIZE
    DATATAG  NO
    OMITTAG  NO
    RANK     NO
    SHORTTAG YES    -- SHORTTAG is needed for NET --
  LINK
    SIMPLE   NO
    IMPLICIT NO
    EXPLICIT NO
  OTHER
    CONCUR   NO
    SUBDOC   NO
    FORMAL   NO
    APPINFO  NONE

>
```

C.2 XML DTD for SMIL

The DTD for the *Synchronized Multimedia Integration Language (SMIL)* as described in section 10.5.6 is one example for an XML DTD. The following DTD defines SMIL as an XML document type as specified in W3C's SMIL specification [100].

```
<!-- This is the XML document type definition (DTD) for SMIL 1.0 -->

<!-- Generally useful entities -->
<!ENTITY % id-attr "id ID #IMPLIED" >
<!ENTITY % title-attr "title CDATA #IMPLIED" >
<!ENTITY % skip-attr "skip-content (true|false) 'true'" >
<!ENTITY % desc-attr "
  %title-attr;
  abstract        CDATA    #IMPLIED
  author          CDATA    #IMPLIED
  copyright       CDATA    #IMPLIED " >

<!--=========== SMIL Document ==============================-->
<!-- The root element SMIL contains all other elements. -->
<!ELEMENT smil (head?,body?) >
<!ATTLIST smil
  %id-attr; >

<!--=========== The Document Head ===========================-->
<!ENTITY % layout-section "layout|switch" >
<!ENTITY % head-element "(meta*,((%layout-section;), meta*))?" >

<!ELEMENT head %head-element; >
<!ATTLIST head %id-attr; >

<!--=========== Layout Element ==============================-->
<!-- Layout contains the region and root-layout elements defined by
     smil-basic-layout or other elements defined an external layout
     mechanism. -->
<!ELEMENT layout ANY >
<!ATTLIST layout
  %id-attr;
  type CDATA       "text/smil-basic-layout" >

<!--=========== Region Element ==============================-->
<!ENTITY % viewport-attrs "
  height               CDATA    #IMPLIED
  width                CDATA    #IMPLIED
  background-color     CDATA    #IMPLIED " >

<!ELEMENT region EMPTY >
<!ATTLIST region
```

```
  %id-attr;
  %title-attr;
  %viewport-attrs;
  left                 CDATA     "0"
  top                  CDATA     "0"
  z-index              CDATA     "0"
  fit                  (hidden|fill|meet|scroll|slice)    "hidden"
  %skip-attr; >


<!--=========== Root-layout Element =========================-->
<!ELEMENT root-layout EMPTY >
<!ATTLIST root-layout
  %id-attr;
  %title-attr;
  %viewport-attrs;
  %skip-attr; >


<!--=========== Meta Element===============================-->
<!ELEMENT meta EMPTY >
<!ATTLIST meta
  name    NMTOKEN #REQUIRED
  content CDATA   #REQUIRED
  %skip-attr; >


<!--=========== The Document Body ==========================-->
<!ENTITY % media-object
          "audio|video|text|img|animation|textstream|ref" >
<!ENTITY % schedule "par|seq|(%media-object;)" >
<!ENTITY % inline-link "a" >
<!ENTITY % assoc-link "anchor" >
<!ENTITY % link "%inline-link;" >
<!ENTITY % container-content "(%schedule;)|switch|(%link;)" >
<!ENTITY % body-content "(%container-content;)" >

<!ELEMENT body (%body-content;)* >
<!ATTLIST body %id-attr; >


<!--=========== Synchronization Attributes =================-->
<!ENTITY % sync-attributes "
  begin   CDATA   #IMPLIED
  end     CDATA   #IMPLIED " >


<!--=========== Switch Parameter Attributes ================-->
<!ENTITY % system-attribute "
  system-bitrate              CDATA            #IMPLIED
  system-language             CDATA            #IMPLIED
  system-required             NMTOKEN          #IMPLIED
  system-screen-size          CDATA            #IMPLIED
  system-screen-depth         CDATA            #IMPLIED
```

```
      system-captions              (on|off)              #IMPLIED
      system-overdub-or-caption    (caption|overdub)     #IMPLIED " >

<!--=========== Fill Attribute =============================-->
<!ENTITY % fill-attribute "
  fill    (remove|freeze)      'remove' " >


<!--=========== The Parallel Element ======================-->
<!ENTITY % par-content "%container-content;" >
<!ELEMENT par     (%par-content;)* >
<!ATTLIST par
  %id-attr;
  %desc-attr;
  endsync CDATA             "last"
  dur     CDATA             #IMPLIED
  repeat  CDATA             "1"
  region  IDREF             #IMPLIED
  %sync-attributes;
  %system-attribute; >

<!--=========== The Sequential Element ====================-->
<!ENTITY % seq-content "%container-content;" >
<!ELEMENT seq     (%seq-content;)* >
<!ATTLIST seq
  %id-attr;
  %desc-attr;
  dur     CDATA             #IMPLIED
  repeat  CDATA             "1"
  region  IDREF             #IMPLIED
  %sync-attributes;
  %system-attribute; >


<!--=========== The Switch Element =========================-->
<!-- In the head, a switch may contain only layout elements,
     in the body, only container elements. However, this
     constraint cannot be expressed in the DTD (?), so
     we allow both. -->
<!ENTITY % switch-content "layout|(%container-content;)" >
<!ELEMENT switch (%switch-content;)* >
<!ATTLIST switch
  %id-attr;
  %title-attr; >


<!--=========== Media Object Elements ======================-->
<!-- SMIL only defines the structure. The real media data is
     referenced by the src attribute of the media objects.  -->
<!-- Furthermore, they have the following attributes as defined
     in the SMIL specification. -->
```

```
<!ENTITY % mo-attributes "
  %id-attr;
  %desc-attr;
  region      IDREF             #IMPLIED
  alt         CDATA             #IMPLIED
  longdesc    CDATA             #IMPLIED
  src         CDATA             #IMPLIED
  type        CDATA             #IMPLIED
  dur         CDATA             #IMPLIED
  repeat      CDATA             '1'
  %fill-attribute;
  %sync-attributes;
  %system-attribute; " >

<!-- Most info is in the attributes, media objects are empty or
     contain associated link elements. -->
<!ENTITY % mo-content "(%assoc-link;)*" >
<!ENTITY % clip-attrs "
  clip-begin    CDATA   #IMPLIED
  clip-end      CDATA   #IMPLIED " >

<!ELEMENT ref            %mo-content; >
<!ELEMENT audio          %mo-content; >
<!ELEMENT img            %mo-content; >
<!ELEMENT video          %mo-content; >
<!ELEMENT text           %mo-content; >
<!ELEMENT textstream     %mo-content; >
<!ELEMENT animation      %mo-content; >

<!ATTLIST ref            %mo-attributes; %clip-attrs; >
<!ATTLIST audio          %mo-attributes; %clip-attrs; >
<!ATTLIST video          %mo-attributes; %clip-attrs; >
<!ATTLIST animation      %mo-attributes; %clip-attrs; >
<!ATTLIST textstream     %mo-attributes; %clip-attrs; >
<!ATTLIST text           %mo-attributes; >
<!ATTLIST img            %mo-attributes; >

<!--=========== Link Elements ===============================-->

<!ENTITY % smil-link-attributes "
  %id-attr;
  %title-attr;
  href            CDATA                    #REQUIRED
  show            (replace|new|pause)      'replace' " >

<!--=========== Inline Link Element ========================-->
<!ELEMENT a (%schedule;|switch)* >
<!ATTLIST a
  %smil-link-attributes; >
```

```
<!--=========== Associated Link Element ====================-->
<!ELEMENT anchor EMPTY >
<!ATTLIST anchor
  %skip-attr;
  %smil-link-attributes;
  %sync-attributes;
  coords          CDATA                   #IMPLIED >
```

References

1. Marc Abrams, Charles R. Standridge, Ghaleb Abdulla, Stephen Williams, and Edward A. Fox. Caching Proxies: Limitations and Potentials. In *Proceedings of the Fourth International World Wide Web Conference*, pages 119–133, Boston, Massachusetts, December 1995.
2. Adobe Systems Inc. *Postscript Language Reference Manual*. Addison-Wesley, Reading, Massachusetts, 2nd edition, December 1990.
3. Adobe Systems Inc. *Postscript Language Reference Manual*. Addison-Wesley, Reading, Massachusetts, 3nd edition, January 1999.
4. Nabeel Al-Shamma, Robert Ayers, Richard Cohn, Jon Ferraiolo, Martin Newell, Roger K. de Bry, Kevin McCluskey, and Jerry Evans. Precision Graphics Markup Language (PGML). World Wide Web Consortium, Note NOTE-PGML-19980410, April 1998.
5. Paul Albitz and Cricket Liu. *DNS and BIND*. O'Reilly & Associates, Inc., Sebastopol, California, January 1992.
6. Aldus Corporation. TIFF – Revision 6.0. Seattle, Washington, June 1992.
7. Harald Tveit Alvestrand. Tags for the Identification of Languages. Internet proposed standard RFC 1766, March 1995.
8. American National Standards Institute. Coded Character Set – 7-Bit American National Standard Code for Information Interchange. ANSI X3.4, 1992.
9. American National Standards Institute. Information Retrieval (Z39.50): Application Service Definition and Protocol Specification. ANSI/NISO Z39.50-1995, July 1995.
10. Mark Andrews. Negative Caching of DNS Queries (DNS NCACHE). Internet proposed standard RFC 2308, March 1998.
11. Farhad Anklesaria, Mark McCahill, Paul Lindner, David Johnson, Daniel Torrey, and Bob Alberti. The Internet Gopher Protocol. Internet informational RFC 1436, March 1993.
12. Apple Computer, Inc., Cupertino, California. *The TrueType Reference Manual*, October 1996.
13. Helen Ashman and Paul Thistlewaite, editors. *Proceedings of the Seventh International World Wide Web Conference*, Brisbane, Australia, April 1998.
14. Michael Baumgardt. *Creative Web Design*. Springer-Verlag, Berlin, Germany, April 1998.
15. Dave Beckett. 30% Accessible – A Survey of The UK Wide Web. In Imbach [108].
16. Tim Berners-Lee. The World Wide Web. In *Proceedings of the 3rd Joint European Networking Conference*, Innsbruck, Austria, May 1992.

17. Tim Berners-Lee. Universal Resource Identifiers in WWW. Internet informational RFC 1630, June 1994.
18. Tim Berners-Lee and David Connolly. Hypertext Markup Language – 2.0. Internet proposed standard RFC 1866, November 1995.
19. Tim Berners-Lee, Roy Fielding, and Larry Masinter. Uniform Resource Identifiers (URI): Generic Syntax and Semantics. Work in progress, June 1998.
20. Tim Berners-Lee, Roy T. Fielding, and Henrik Frystyk. Hypertext Transfer Protocol – HTTP/1.0. Internet informational RFC 1945, May 1996.
21. Tim Berners-Lee, Larry Masinter, and Mark McCahill. Uniform Resource Locators (URL). Internet proposed standard RFC 1738, December 1994.
22. Tim Bienz and Richard Cohn. *Portable Document Format Reference Manual*. Addison-Wesley, Reading, Massachusetts, July 1993.
23. Tim Bienz, Richard Cohn, and James R. Meehan. Portable Document Format Reference Manual – Version 1.2. Technical report, Adobe Systems Inc., San Jose, California, November 1996.
24. N. Borenstein. A User Agent Configuration Mechanism For Multimedia Mail Format Information. Internet informational RFC 1524, September 1993.
25. Bert Bos, Håkon Wium Lie, Chris Lilley, and Ian Jacobs. CSS2 Specification. World Wide Web Consortium, Recommendation REC-CSS2-19980512, May 1998.
26. Thomas Boutell. PNG (Portable Network Graphics) Specification – Version 1.0. Internet informational RFC 2083, March 1997.
27. Thomas Boutell and Tom Lane. PNG (Portable Network Graphics) Specification. World Wide Web Consortium, Recommendation REC-png, October 1996.
28. Robert Braden. Towards a Transport Service for Transaction Processing Applications. Internet RFC 955, September 1985.
29. Robert Braden. Requirements for Internet Hosts – Application and Support. Internet standard RFC 1123, October 1989.
30. Robert Braden. Requirements for Internet Hosts – Communication Layer. Internet standard RFC 1122, October 1989.
31. Robert Braden. Extending TCP for Transactions – Concepts. Internet informational RFC 1379, November 1992.
32. Robert Braden. T/TCP – TCP Extensions for Transactions Functional Specification. Internet experimental RFC 1644, July 1994.
33. Scott Bradner and Allison Mankin. The Recommendation for the IP Next Generation Protocol. Internet proposed standard RFC 1752, January 1995.
34. Tim Bray. Measuring the Web. In Eligh and Kastelein [72].
35. Tim Bray, Dave Hollander, and Andrew Layman. Namespaces in XML. World Wide Web Consortium, Working Draft WD-xml-names-19980802, August 1998.
36. Tim Bray, Jean Paoli, and C. M. Sperberg-McQueen. Extensible Markup Language (XML). World Wide Web Consortium, Recommendation REC-xml-19980210, February 1998.
37. Dan Brickley, R. V. Guha, and Andrew Layman. Resource Description Framework (RDF) Schemas. World Wide Web Consortium, Working Draft WD-rdf-schema-19980409, April 1998.
38. Nat Brown and Charlie Kindel. Distributed Component Object Model Protocol – DCOM/1.0. Internet draft, Network working group, January 1998.

39. Martin Bryan. *SGML and HTML Explained.* Addison-Wesley, Reading, Massachusetts, 2nd edition, May 1997.

40. Mary Campione and Kathy Walrath. *The Java Tutorial.* Addison-Wesley, Reading, Massachusetts, 1996.

41. Rikk Carey and Gavin Bell. *The Annotated VRML 2.0 Reference Manual.* Addison-Wesley, Reading, Massachusetts, June 1997.

42. Brian E. Carpenter and Yakov Rekhter. Renumbering Needs Work. Internet informational RFC 1900, February 1996.

43. D. Chadwick. *Understanding X.500 – The Directory.* Chapman & Hall, London, UK, 1995.

44. Lyman Chapin. The Internet Standards Process. Internet informational RFC 1310, March 1992.

45. Abhijit K. Choudhury, editor. *Proceedings of the IEEE INFOCOM '98 Conference on Computer Communications,* San Francisco, California, March 1998. IEEE Computer Society Press.

46. James Clark. Comparison of SGML and XML. World Wide Web Consortium, Note NOTE-sgml-xml-97121, December 1997.

47. James Clark and Stephen Deach. Extensible Stylesheet Language (XSL). World Wide Web Consortium, Working Draft WD-xsl-19980818, August 1998.

48. Douglas E. Comer. *The Internet Book.* Prentice-Hall, Englewood Cliffs, New Jersey, 2nd edition, August 1997.

49. CompuServe, Incorporated. GIF – Graphics Interchange Format. Columbus, Ohio, June 1987.

50. CompuServe, Incorporated. Graphics Interchange Format – Version 89a. Columbus, Ohio, July 1990.

51. Mark R. Crispin. Internet Message Access Protocol – Version 4rev1. Internet proposed standard RFC 2060, December 1996.

52. Dave Crocker and Ned Freed. SMTP Service Extension for Checkpoint/Restart. Internet experimental RFC 1845, September 1995.

53. David H. Crocker. Standard for the Format of ARPA Internet Text Messages. Internet standard RFC 822, August 1982.

54. David H. Crocker and Paul Overell. Augmented BNF for Syntax Specifications: ABNF. Internet proposed standard RFC 2234, November 1997.

55. Steve Crocker, Ned Freed, Jim Galvin, and Sandy Murphy. MIME Object Security Services. Internet proposed standard RFC 1848, October 1995.

56. Mark Crovella and Paul Barford. The Network Effects of Prefetching. In Choudhury [45], pages 1232–1239.

57. David Cruikshank, John Gebhardt, Lofton Henderson, Roy Platon, and Dieter Weidenbrück. WebCGM Profile. World Wide Web Consortium, Note NOTE-WebCGM-19980819, August 1998.

58. Leslie L. Daigle, Dirk-Willem van Gulik, Renato Iannella, and Patrik Faltstrom. URN Namespace Definition Mechanisms. Internet draft, Uniform resource names working group, March 1998.

59. Ron Daniel. A Trivial Convention for using HTTP in URN Resolution. Internet experimental RFC 2169, June 1997.

60. Ron Daniel and Michael Mealling. Resolution of Uniform Resource Identifiers using the Domain Name System. Internet experimental RFC 2168, June 1997.

61. Stephen E. Deering and Robert M. Hinden. Internet Protocol, Version 6 (IPv6) Specification. Internet proposed standard RFC 1883, December 1995.

62. Steven J. DeRose. *The SGML FAQ Book: Understanding the Foundation of HTML and XML.* Kluwer Academic Publishers, Boston, Massachusetts, July 1997.

63. L. Peter Deutsch. GZIP file format specification version 4.3. Internet informational RFC 1952, May 1996.

64. Tim Dierks and Christopher Allen. The TLS Protocol Version 1.0. Internet draft, TLS working group, November 1997.

65. W. Diffie and M. E. Hellman. New Directions in Cryptography. *IEEE Transactions on Information Theory,* 22(6):74–84, June 1977.

66. Adam Dingle and Tomas Partl. Web Cache Coherence. In Eligh and Kastelein [72], pages 907–920.

67. Nikos Drakos. From Text to Hypertext: A Post-Hoc Rationalisation of La-TeX2HTML. In Nierstrasz [197].

68. Steve Dusse, Paul Hoffman, Blake Ramsdell, Laurence Lundblade, and Lisa Repka. S/MIME Version 2 Message Specification. Internet draft, November 1997.

69. Steve Dusse, Paul Hoffman, Blake Ramsdell, and Jeff Weinstein. S/MIME Version 2 Certificate Handling. Internet draft, November 1997.

70. Donald E. Eastlake. Secure Domain Name System Dynamic Update. Internet proposed standard RFC 2137, April 1997.

71. Donald E. Eastlake and Charles W. Kaufman. Domain Name System Security Extensions. Internet proposed standard RFC 2065, January 1997.

72. Mark Eligh and Jan Kastelein, editors. *Proceedings of the Fifth International World Wide Web Conference,* Paris, France, May 1996.

73. Castedo Ellerman. Channel Definition Format (CDF) – Version 1.01. Technical report, Microsoft Corporation, Redmond, Virginia, April 1998.

74. European Computer Manufacturers Association. ECMAScript, A general purpose, cross-platform programming language. Standard ECMA-262, June 1997.

75. R. Fielding, J. Gettys, J. Mogul, H. Frystyk, and T. Berners-Lee. Hypertext Transfer Protocol – HTTP/1.1. Internet proposed standard RFC 2068, January 1997.

76. R. Fielding, J. Gettys, J. C. Mogul, L. Masinter, P. Leach, H. Frystyk, and T. Berners-Lee. Hypertext Transfer Protocol – HTTP/1.1. Internet draft, HTTP Working Group, March 1998.

77. Roy T. Fielding. Relative Uniform Resource Locators. Internet proposed standard RFC 1808, June 1995.

78. J. Franks, P. Hallam-Baker, J. Hostetler, P. Leach, A. Luotonen, E. Sink, and L. Stewart. An Extension to HTTP: Digest Access Authentication. Internet proposed standard RFC 2069, January 1997.

79. Ned Freed and Nathaniel Borenstein. Multipurpose Internet Mail Extensions (MIME) – Part Five: Conformance Criteria and Examples. Internet draft standard RFC 2049, November 1996.

80. Ned Freed and Nathaniel Borenstein. Multipurpose Internet Mail Extensions (MIME) – Part One: Format of Internet Message Bodies. Internet draft standard RFC 2045, November 1996.

81. Ned Freed and Nathaniel Borenstein. Multipurpose Internet Mail Extensions (MIME) – Part Two: Media Types. Internet draft standard RFC 2046, November 1996.

82. Ned Freed, John Klensin, and Jon B. Postel. Multipurpose Internet Mail Extensions (MIME) – Part Four: Registration Procedures. Internet best current practice RFC 2048, November 1996.

83. Alan O. Freier, Philip Karlton, and Paul C. Kocher. The SSL Protocol – Version 3.0. Internet draft, Transport Layer Security Working Group, November 1996.

84. Henrik Frystyk Nielsen, Dan Connolly, Rohit Khare, and Eric Prud'hommeaux. PEP – an Extension Mechanism for HTTP. Internet draft, HTTP Working Group, December 1997.

85. Jim Galvin, Sandy Murphy, Steve Crocker, and Ned Freed. Security Multiparts for MIME: Multipart/Signed and Multipart/Encrypted. Internet proposed standard RFC 1847, October 1995.

86. Jim Gettys and Henrik Frystyk Nielsen. SMUX Protocol Specification. Working Draft WD-mux-19980708, July 1998.

87. Andreas Girgensohn and Alison Lee. Seamless Integration of interactive forms into the Web. In Imbach [108], pages 1531–1542.

88. Charles F. Goldfarb. *The SGML Handbook*. Oxford University Press, Oxford, UK, February 1991.

89. David Goldsmith and Mark Davis. UTF-7: A Mail-Safe Transformation Format of Unicode. Internet informational RFC 2152, May 1997.

90. Ian S. Graham. *HTML Stylesheet Sourcebook*. John Wiley & Sons Ltd, New York, October 1997.

91. Shishir Gundavaram. *CGI Programming on the World Wide Web*. O'Reilly & Associates, Inc., Sebastopol, California, April 1996.

92. Fred Halsall. *Data Communications, Computer Networks and Open Systems*. Addison-Wesley, Wokingham, England, 4th edition, January 1996.

93. Eric Hamilton. JPEG File Interchange Format (Version 1.02). Technical report, C-Cube Microsystems, Milpitas, California, September 1992.

94. John Heidemann. Performance Interactions Between P-HTTP and TCP Implementations. *ACM Computer Communications Review*, 27(2):65–73, April 1997.

95. John Heidemann, Katia Obraczka, and Joe Touch. Modeling the Performance of HTTP Over Several Transport Protocols. *IEEE/ACM Transactions on Networking*, 5(5), 1997.

96. Paul S. Hethmon. *Illustrated Guide to HTTP*. Manning, Greenwich, Connecticut, March 1997.

97. Koen Holtman and Andrew H. Mutz. HTTP Remote Variant Selection Algorithm – RVSA/1.0. Internet experimental RFC 2296, March 1998.

98. Koen Holtman and Andrew H. Mutz. Transparent Content Negotiation in HTTP. Internet experimental RFC 2295, March 1998.

99. M. Horton and R. Adams. Standard for Interchange of USENET Messages. Internet RFC 1036, December 1987.

100. Philipp Hoschka. Synchronized Multimedia Integration Language. World Wide Web Consortium, Recommendation REC-smil-19980615, June 1998.

101. Russell Housley. Cryptographic Message Syntax. Internet draft, March 1998.

102. Tim Howes and Mark Smith. An LDAP URL Format. Internet proposed standard RFC 1959, June 1996.

103. Tim Howes and Mark Smith. The LDAP URL Format. Internet proposed standard RFC 2255, December 1997.

104. James C. Hu, Sumedh Mungee, and Douglas C. Schmidt. Techniques for Developing and Measuring High-Performance Web Servers over High Speed Networks. In Choudhury [45], pages 1222–1231.

105. Yang hua Chu, Philip DesAutels, Brian LaMacchia, and Peter Lipp. PICS Signed Labels (DSig) 1.0 Specification. World Wide Web Consortium, Recommendation REC-DSig-label-19980527, May 1998.

106. Lawrence E. Hughes. *Internet E-Mail: Protocols, Standards, and Implementation.* Artech House, Norwood, Massachusetts, July 1998.

107. Christian Huitema. The H Ratio for Address Assignment Efficiency. Internet informational RFC 1715, November 1994.

108. Sarah Imbach, editor. *Proceedings of the Sixth International World Wide Web Conference,* Santa Clara, California, April 1997.

109. International Electrotechnical Commission. Colour measurement and management in multimedia systems and equipment - Part 2: Colour Management in Multimedia Systems. IEC 61966-2, August 1998.

110. International Organization for Standardization. Information Processing – Text and Office Systems – Standard Generalized Markup Language (SGML). ISO/IS 8879, 1986.

111. International Organization for Standardization. Information technology – 8-bit single-byte coded graphic character sets – Part 1: Latin alphabet No. 1. ISO/DIS 8859-1, 1987.

112. International Organization for Standardization. Code for the representation of names of languages. ISO/IS 639, 1988.

113. International Organization for Standardization. Information technology – ISO 7-bit coded character set for information interchange. ISO/IS 646, 1991.

114. International Organization for Standardization. Information technology – SGML support facilities – Registration procedures for public text owner identifiers. ISO/IS 9070, 1991.

115. International Organization for Standardization. Information technology – Computer graphics – Metafile for the storage and transfer of picture description information. ISO/IS 8632, 1992.

116. International Organization for Standardization. Information technology – Coding of moving pictures and associated audio for digital storage media at up to about 1.5 Mbit/s. ISO/IS 11172, 1993.

117. International Organization for Standardization. Information technology – Telecommunications and information exchange between systems – High-level data link control (HDLC) procedures – Frame structure. ISO/IS 3309, 1993.

118. International Organization for Standardization. Information technology – Universal Multiple-Octet Coded Character Set (UCS). ISO/IS 10646, 1993.

119. International Organization for Standardization. Information and documentation – Electronic manuscript preparation and markup. ISO/IS 12083, 1994.

120. International Organization for Standardization. Information processing systems – Open Systems Interconnection (OSI) – Basic reference model. ISO/IS 7498 (Second Edition), 1994.

121. International Organization for Standardization. Information technology –
Digital compression and coding of continuous-tone still images: Requirements
and guidelines. ISO/IS 10918-1, 1994.

122. International Organization for Standardization. Information technology –
Font information interchange. ISO/IS 9541, 1994.

123. International Organization for Standardization. Information technology –
Digital compression and coding of continuous-tone still images: Compliance
testing. ISO/IS 10918-2, 1995.

124. International Organization for Standardization. Information technology –
Processing languages – Standard Page Description Language (SPDL). ISO/IS
10180, 1995.

125. International Organization for Standardization. Information technology –
Generic coding of moving pictures and associated audio information. ISO/IS
13818, 1996.

126. International Organization for Standardization. Information technology –
Open systems interconnection – Transport service definition. ISO/IS 8072,
1996.

127. International Organization for Standardization. Information technology –
Processing languages – Document Style Semantics and Specification Language (DSSSL). ISO/IS 10179, 1996.

128. International Organization for Standardization. Codes for the representation
of names of countries and their subdivisions. ISO/IS 3166, 1997.

129. International Organization for Standardization. Graphic technology – Pre-
press digital data exchange – Tag image file format for image technology
(TIFF/IT). ISO/DIS 12639, 1997.

130. International Organization for Standardization. Information technology –
Digital compression and coding of continuous-tone still images: Extensions.
ISO/IS 10918-3, 1997.

131. International Organization for Standardization. Information technology –
Digital compression and coding of continuous-tone still images: Registration
of JPEG profiles, SPIFF profiles, SPIFF tags, SPIFF colour spaces, APPN
markers, SPIFF compression types and Registration Authorities (REGAUT).
ISO/DIS 10918-4, 1997.

132. International Organization for Standardization. Information technology –
Hypermedia/Time-based Structuring Language (HyTime). ISO/IS 10744,
1997.

133. International Organization for Standardization. Information technology –
Open Distributed Processing – Interface Definition Language. ISO/DIS
14750, 1997.

134. International Organization for Standardization. Information technology –
Virtual Reality Modeling Language (VRML). ISO/DIS 14772, 1997.

135. International Organization for Standardization. Information Technology –
Document Description and Processing Languages – Hypertext Markup Language (HTML). ISO/CD 15445, April 1998.

136. International Organization for Standardization. Very-low bitrate audio-visual
coding. ISO/DIS 14496, 1998.

137. International Telecommunication Union. The Directory – Authentication
framework. ITU-T Recommendation X.509, November 1993.

138. International Telecommunication Union. The Directory – Overview of concepts, models and services. ITU-T Recommendation X.500, November 1993.
139. International Telecommunication Union. The Directory – Protocol specifications. ITU-T Recommendation X.519, November 1993.
140. International Telecommunication Union. Information technology - Message Handling Systems (MHS) - Protocol specifications. ITU-T Recommendation X.419, November 1995.
141. International Telecommunication Union. Message Handling System and Service Overview. ITU-T Recommendation X.400, July 1996.
142. Patrick Ion and Robert Miner. Mathematical Markup Language (MathML) 1.0 Specification. World Wide Web Consortium, Recommendation REC-MathML-19980407, April 1998.
143. Van Jacobson and Michael J. Karels. Congestion Avoidance and Control. *ACM Computer Communications Review*, 18(4):314–329, August 1988.
144. Bill Janssen, Henrik Frystyk Nielsen, and Mike Spreitzer. HTTP-ng Architectural Model. Working Draft WD-HTTP-NG-architecture-19980710, July 1998.
145. Burton S. Kaliski. The MD2 Message-Digest Algorithm. Internet informational RFC 1319, April 1992.
146. Brian Kantor and Phil Lapsley. Network News Transfer Protocol. Internet proposed standard RFC 977, February 1986.
147. Richard M. Keller, Shawn R. Wolfe, James R. Chen, Joshua L. Rabinowitz, and Nathalie Mathe. A Bookmarking Service for Organizing and Sharing URLs. In Imbach [108], pages 1103–1114.
148. John Klensin, Ned Freed, and Keith Moore. SMTP Service Extension for Message Size Declaration. Internet standard RFC 1870, November 1995.
149. John Klensin, Ned Freed, Marshall T. Rose, Einar A. Stefferud, and Dave Crocker. SMTP Service Extensions. Internet standard RFC 1869, November 1995.
150. Martijn Koster. A Method for Web Robots Control. Internet draft, Network working group, December 1996.
151. Tim Krauskopf, Jim Miller, Paul Resnick, and Win Treese. PICS Label Distribution – Label Syntax and Communication Protocols. World Wide Web Consortium, Recommendation REC-PICS-labels-961031, October 1996.
152. David M. Kristol and Lou Montulli. HTTP State Management Mechanism. Internet proposed standard RFC 2109, February 1997.
153. David M. Kristol and Lou Montulli. HTTP State Management Mechanism. Internet draft, HTTP working group, February 1998.
154. Xuejia Lai and James L. Massey. Markov ciphers and differential cryptanalysis. In D. W. Davies, editor, *Proceedings of EUROCRYPT '91 – Advances in cryptology*, volume 547 of *Lecture Notes in Computer Science*, pages 17–38, Brighton, UK, April 1991. Springer-Verlag.
155. Xuejia Lai and James L. Massey. A proposal for a new block encryption standard. In I. B. Damgard, editor, *Proceedings of EUROCRYPT '90 – Advances in cryptology*, volume 473 of *Lecture Notes in Computer Science*, pages 389–404, Aarhus, Denmark, May 1991. Springer-Verlag.
156. M. Lambert. PCMAIL: A Distributed Mail System for Personal Computers. Internet informational RFC 1056, June 1988.

157. Ora Lassila and Ralph R. Swick. Resource Description Framework (RDF) – Model and Syntax. World Wide Web Consortium, Working Draft WD-rdf-syntax-19980216, February 1998.

158. Ben Laurie and Peter Laurie. *Apache: The Definitive Guide.* O'Reilly & Associates, Inc., Sebastopol, California, March 1997.

159. Håkon Wium Lie and Bert Bos. Cascading Style Sheets, level 1. World Wide Web Consortium, Recommendation REC-CSS1-961217, December 1996.

160. Håkon Wium Lie and Bert Bos. *Cascading Style Sheets.* Addison-Wesley, Harlow, England, April 1997.

161. J. Linn. Privacy Enhancement for Internet Electronic Mail – Part I: Message Encryption and Authentication Procedures. Internet proposed standard RFC 1421, February 1993.

162. Brian Lloyd and William Allen Simpson. PPP Authentication Protocols. Internet proposed standard RFC 1321, October 1992.

163. Ari Luotonen. Tunneling TCP based protocols through Web proxy servers. Internet draft, August 1998.

164. Mark Lutz. *Programming Python.* O'Reilly & Associates, Inc., Sebastopol, California, October 1996.

165. Eve Maler and Steve DeRose. XML Linking Language (XLink). World Wide Web Consortium, Working Draft WD-xlink-19980303, March 1998.

166. Eve Maler and Steve DeRose. XML Pointer Language (XPointer). World Wide Web Consortium, Working Draft WD-xptr-19980303, March 1998.

167. Massimo Marchiori and Dan Jaye. Platform for Privacy Preferences (P3P) – Syntax Specification. World Wide Web Consortium, Working Draft WD-P3P-Syntax-19980519, May 1998.

168. April N. Marine, Joyce K. Reynolds, and Gary Scott Malkin. FYI on Questions and Answers – Answers to Commonly asked "New Internet User" Questions. Internet informational RFC 1594, March 1994.

169. Evangelos P. Markatos. Main Memory Caching of Web Documents. In Eligh and Kastelein [72], pages 893–905.

170. Brian Mathews, Daniel Lee, Brian Dister, John Bowler, Howard Cooperstein, Ajay Jindal, Tuan Nguyen, Peter Wu, and Troy Sandal. Vector Markup Language (VML). World Wide Web Consortium, Note NOTE-VML-19980513, May 1998.

171. Oliver A. McBryan. GENVL and WWWW: Tools for Taming the Web. In Nierstrasz [197].

172. Michael Mealling and Ron Daniel. URI Resolution Services Necessary for URN Resolution. Internet draft, Uniform resource names working group, March 1998.

173. MIDI Manufacturers Association. Complete MIDI 1.0 Detailed Specification, March 1996.

174. Jim Miller, Paul Resnick, and David Singer. Rating Services and Rating Systems (and their Machine Readable Descriptions). World Wide Web Consortium, Recommendation REC-PICS-services-961031, October 1996.

175. David L. Mills. Network Time Protocol (Version 3) – Specification, Implementation and Analysis. Internet draft standard RFC 1305, March 1992.

176. Ryan Moats. URN Syntax. Internet proposed standard RFC 2141, May 1997.

177. P. Mockapetris. Domain Names – Concepts and Facilities. Internet standard RFC 1034, November 1987.

178. P. Mockapetris. Domain Names – Implementation and Specification. Internet standard RFC 1035, November 1987.

179. Jeffrey Mogul and Paul Leach. Simple Hit-Metering for HTTP. Internet draft, HTTP Working Group, January 1997.

180. Jeffrey C. Mogul. The Case for Persistent-Connection HTTP. *ACM Computer Communications Review*, 25(4), October 1995.

181. Jeffrey C. Mogul, Fred Douglis, Anja Feldmann, and Balachander Krishnamurthy. Potential benefits of delta-encoding and data compression for HTTP. *ACM Computer Communications Review*, 27(4), October 1997.

182. Jeffrey C. Mogul, Roy T. Fielding, Jim Gettys, and Henrik Frystyk. Use and Interpretation of HTTP Version Numbers. Internet informational RFC 2145, May 1997.

183. Keith Moore. Multipurpose Internet Mail Extensions (MIME) – Part Three: Message Header Extensions for Non-ASCII Text. Internet draft standard RFC 2047, November 1996.

184. Keith Moore, Shirley Browne, Jason Cox, and Jonathan Gettler. Resource Cataloging and Distribution System. Technical Report UT-CS-97-346, University of Tennessee, Knoxville, Tennessee, January 1997.

185. John G. Myers. POP3 AUTHentication command. Internet proposed standard RFC 1734, December 1994.

186. John G. Myers and Marshall T. Rose. The Content-MD5 Header Field. Internet draft standard RFC 1864, October 1995.

187. John G. Myers and Marshall T. Rose. Post Office Protocol – Version 3. Internet draft standard RFC 1939, May 1996.

188. National Institute of Standards and Technology. The Digital Signature Standard, proposal and discussion. *Communications of the ACM*, 35(7):36–54, July 1992.

189. National Institute of Standards and Technology. Data Encryption Standard. FIPS Publication 46-2, December 1993.

190. National Institute of Standards and Technology. Secure Hash Standard (SHS). FIPS Publication 180, May 1993.

191. National Institute of Standards and Technology. Announcement of Weakness in the Secure Hash Standard, May 1994.

192. National Institute of Standards and Technology. Digital Signature Standard (DSS). FIPS Publication 186, May 1994.

193. Peter Naur. Report on the Algorithmic Language ALGOL 60. *Communications of the ACM*, 3(5):299–314, May 1960.

194. Ernesto Nebel and Larry Masinter. Form-based File Upload in HTML. Internet experimental RFC 1867, November 1995.

195. Ted Nelson. *Computer Lib/Dream Machines*. Microsoft Press, Austin, Texas, 1987.

196. Henrik Frystyk Nielsen, Jim Gettys, Anselm Baird-Smith, Eric Prud'hommeaux, Håkon Wium Lie, and Chris Lilley. Network Performance Effects of HTTP/1.1, CSS1, and PNG. *ACM Computer Communications Review*, 27(4), October 1997.

197. Oscar Nierstrasz, editor. *Proceedings of the First International World Wide Web Conference*, Geneva, Switzerland, May 1994.

198. Object Management Group, Framingham, Massachusetts. *The Common Object Request Broker: Architecture and Specification – Version 2.2*, July 1998.

199. Open Software Foundation. *Introduction to OSF DCE*. Prentice-Hall, Englewood Cliffs, New Jersey, July 1992.

200. Robert Orfali and Dan Harkey. *Client/Server Programming with Java and CORBA*. John Wiley & Sons Ltd, New York, 2nd edition, February 1998.

201. John K. Ousterhout. *Tcl and the Tk Toolkit*. Addison-Wesley, Reading, Massachusetts, May 1994.

202. Venkata N. Padmanabhan. Improving World Wide Web Latency. Technical Report CSD-95-875, University of California, Berkeley, May 1995.

203. Andrew Pam. Where World Wide Web Went Wrong. In *Proceedings of the Asia-Pacific World Wide Web '95 Conference*, Sydney, Australia, September 1995.

204. Larry L. Peterson and Bruce S. Davie. *Computer Networks*. Morgan Kaufmann Publishers, San Francisco, California, April 1996.

205. James Pitkow. In Search of Reliable Usage Data on the WWW. In Imbach [108].

206. Bernhard Plattner, Cuno Lanz, Hannes Lubich, Markus Müller, and Thomas Walter. *X.400 Message Handling: Standards, Interworking, Applications*. Addison-Wesley, Reading, Massachusetts, November 1992.

207. J. Postel and J. Reynolds. File Transfer Protocol (FTP). Internet standard RFC 959, October 1985.

208. Jon B. Postel. User Datagram Protocol. Internet standard RFC 768, August 1980.

209. Jon B. Postel. Internet Protocol. Internet standard RFC 791, September 1981.

210. Jon B. Postel. Transmission Control Protocol. Internet standard RFC 793, September 1981.

211. Jon B. Postel. Simple Mail Transfer Protocol. Internet standard RFC 821, August 1982.

212. Jon B. Postel. Telnet Protocol Specification. Internet standard RFC 854, May 1983.

213. Jon B. Postel. Domain Name System Structure and Delegation. Internet informational RFC 1591, March 1994.

214. Jon B. Postel. Internet Official Protocol Standards. Internet historic RFC 2300, May 1998.

215. Martin Presler-Marshall, Christopher Evans, Clive D.W. Feather, Alex Hopmann, Martin Presler-Marshall, and Paul Resnick. PICSRules 1.1. World Wide Web Consortium, Recommendation REC-PICSRules-971229, December 1997.

216. Dave Raggett. HTML Tables. Internet experimental RFC 1942, May 1996.

217. Dave Raggett. HTML 3.2 Reference Specification. World Wide Web Consortium, Recommendation REC-html32, January 1997.

218. Dave Raggett. Clean up your Web pages with HP's HTML Tidy. In Ashman and Thistlewaite [13].

219. Dave Raggett, Arnaud Le Hors, and Ian Jacobs. HTML 4.0 Specification. World Wide Web Consortium, Recommendation REC-html40-19980424, April 1998.

220. Dave Raggett, Jenny Lam, Ian Alexander, and Michael Kmiec. *Raggett on HTML 4*. Addison-Wesley, Harlow, England, 2nd edition, January 1998.

221. T. V. Raman. Cascaded Speech Style Sheets. In Imbach [108].

222. Eric Rescorla. HTTP over TLS. Internet draft, TLS working group, March 1998.

223. Eric Rescorla and Allan M. Schiffman. The Secure HyperText Transfer Protocol. Internet draft, November 1997.

224. P. Resnick and J. Miller. PICS: Internet Access Controls without Censorship. *Communications of the ACM*, 39:87–93, 1996.

225. John Rhoton. *X.400 and SMTP: Battle of the E-Mail Protocols.* Digital Press, Oxford, UK, September 1997.

226. Ronald L. Rivest. The MD4 Message-Digest Algorithm. Internet informational RFC 1320, April 1992.

227. Ronald L. Rivest. The MD5 Message-Digest Algorithm. Internet informational RFC 1321, April 1992.

228. Ronald L. Rivest. The RC5 Encryption Algorithm. Technical report, MIT Laboratory for Computer Science, Cambridge, Massachusetts, March 1997.

229. Ronald L. Rivest, Adi Shamir, and Leonard M. Adleman. A Method for Obtaining Digital Signatures and Public-Key Cryptosystems. *Communications of the ACM*, 21(2):120–126, February 1978.

230. J. Romkey. A Nonstandard for Transmission of IP Datagrams over Serial Lines: SLIP. Internet standard RFC 1055, June 1988.

231. Marshall T. Rose and Dwight E. Cass. ISO Transport Service on top of the TCP. Internet standard RFC 1006, May 1987.

232. Ward Rosenberry, David Kenney, and Gerry Fisher. *Understanding DCE.* O'Reilly & Associates, Inc., Sebastopol, California, September 1992.

233. RSA Laboratories. *PKCS-1: RSA Encryption Standard.* Redwood City, California, November 1993.

234. RSA Laboratories. *PKCS-3: Diffie-Hellman Key-Agreement Standard.* Redwood City, California, November 1993.

235. RSA Laboratories. *PKCS-7: Cryptographic Message Syntax Standard.* Redwood City, California, May 1997.

236. Peter Scheuermann, Junho Shim, and Radek Vingralek. A Case for Delay-Conscious Caching of Web Documents. In Imbach [108], pages 997–1005.

237. Henning Schulzrinne, Stephen L. Casner, Ron Frederick, and Van Jacobson. RTP: A Transport Protocol for Real-Time Applications. Internet proposed standard RFC 1889, January 1996.

238. Henning Schulzrinne, Anup Rao, and Robert Lanphier. Real Time Streaming Protocol (RTSP). Internet proposed standard RFC 2326, April 1998.

239. Secure Electronic Transaction LLC. SET Secure Electronic Transaction Specification – Version 1.0, May 1997.

240. James L. Seidman. A Proposed Extension to HTML: Client-Side Image Maps. Internet informational RFC 1980, August 1996.

241. Keith Shafer, Stuart Weibel, Erik Jul, and Jon Fausey. Introduction to Persistent Uniform Resource Locators. In *Proceedings of International Networking Conference INET'96*, pages BFC-1–BFC-9, Montreal, Canada, June 1996.

242. John F. Shoch. Inter-Network Naming, Addressing, and Routing. In *Proceedings of the Seventeenth IEEE Conference on Computer Communication Networks*, pages 72–79, Washington, D.C., 1978.

243. William Allen Simpson. The Point-to-Point Protocol (PPP). Internet standard RFC 1661, July 1994.

244. William Allen Simpson. PPP Challenge Handshake Authentication Protocol (CHAP). Internet draft standard RFC 1994, August 1996.

245. Karen Sollins. Architectural Principles of Uniform Resource Name Resolution. Internet informational RFC 2276, January 1998.

246. Karen Sollins and Larry Masinter. Functional Requirements for Uniform Resource Names. Internet informational RFC 1737, December 1994.

247. Henry Spencer and David Lawrence. *Managing Usenet*. O'Reilly & Associates, Inc., Sebastopol, California, January 1998.

248. C. M. Sperberg-McQueen and Lou Burnard. Guidelines for Electronic Text Encoding and Interchange (TEI P3). Technical report, Text Encoding Initiative, Chicago, Illinois, April 1994.

249. Simon E. Spero. Analysis of HTTP Performance problems. http://www.w3.org/Protocols/HTTP/1.0/HTTPPerformance.html, July 1994.

250. Michael St. Johns. Identification Protocol. Internet proposed standard RFC 1413, February 1993.

251. Margaret St. Pierre, Jim Fullton, Kevin Gamiel, Jonathan Goldman, Brewster Kahle, John A. Kunze, Harry Morris, and François Schiettecatte. WAIS over Z39.50-1988. Internet informational RFC 1625, June 1994.

252. William Stallings. *Data and Computer Communications*. Prentice-Hall, Englewood Cliffs, New Jersey, 5th edition, August 1996.

253. Douglas Steedman. *The Directory Standard and its Application*. Technology Appraisals, Twickenham, UK, 1993.

254. Lincoln Stein, Clint Wong, and Shishir Gundavaram. *Scripting Languages: Automating the Web*. O'Reilly & Associates, Inc., Sebastopol, California, May 1997.

255. Robert Stevahn, Scott Furman, and Scott Isaacs. Positioning HTML Elements with Cascading Style Sheets. World Wide Web Consortium, Working Draft WD-positioning-19970819, August 1997.

256. W. Richard Stevens. *Unix Network Programming*. Prentice-Hall, Englewood Cliffs, New Jersey, April 1990.

257. W. Richard Stevens. TCP Slow Start, Congestion Avoidance, Fast Retransmit, and Fast Recovery Algorithms. Internet proposed standard RFC 2001, January 1997.

258. Sam X. Sun. Handle System: A Persistent Global Naming Service – Overview and Syntax. Internet draft, Network Working Group, November 1997.

259. Andrew S. Tanenbaum. *Computer Networks*. Prentice-Hall, Englewood Cliffs, New Jersey, 3rd edition, March 1996.

260. Robert Thau. Design Considerations for the Apache Server API. In Eligh and Kastelein [72], pages 1113–1122.

261. The Open Group, Cambridge, Massachusetts. *DCE 1.2.2 Documentation*, November 1997.

262. Stephen A. Thomas. *IPng and the TCP/IP Protocols*. John Wiley & Sons Ltd, New York, January 1996.

263. Brian Travis and Dale Waldt. *The SGML Implementation Guide*. Springer-Verlag, Berlin, Germany, December 1995.

264. Gene Trent and Mark Sake. WebSTONE: The First Generation in HTTP Server Benchmarking. Technical report, Silicon Graphics, Inc., Mountain View, California, February 1995.

265. Unicode Consortium. *The Unicode Standard: Version 2.0.* Addison-Wesley, Reading, Massachusetts, September 1996.

266. Gregg Vanderheiden, Wendy Chisholm, and Ian Jacobs. WAI Accessibility Guidelines: Page Authoring. World Wide Web Consortium, Working Draft WD-WAI-PAGEAUTH-0203, February 1998.

267. Gregory M. Vaudreuil. SMTP Service Extensions for Transmission of Large and Binary MIME Messages. Internet experimental RFC 1830, August 1995.

268. Paul Vixie. A Mechanism for Prompt Notification of Zone Changes (DNS NOTIFY). Internet proposed standard RFC 1996, August 1996.

269. Paul Vixie, Susan Thomson, Yakov Rekhter, and Jim Bound. Dynamic Updates in the Domain Name System (DNS UPDATE). Internet proposed standard RFC 2136, April 1997.

270. Mark Wahl, Tim Howes, and Steve Kille. Lightweight Directory Access Protocol (v3). Internet proposed standard RFC 2251, December 1997.

271. Larry Wall, Tom Christiansen, and Randal L. Schwartz. *Programming Perl.* O'Reilly & Associates, Inc., Sebastopol, California, September 1996.

272. Timothy Webster. *Web Designer's Guide to Graphics: PNG, GIF & JPEG.* Hayden Books, Indianapolis, Indiana, June 1997.

273. Terry A. Welch. A Technique for High Performance Data Compression. *IEEE Computer*, 17(6):8–19, June 1984.

274. E. James Whitehead and Murata Makoto. XML Media Types. Internet informational RFC 2376, July 1998.

275. Allison Woodruff, Paul M. Aoki, Eric Brewer, Paul Gauthier, and Lawrence A. Rowe. An Investigation of Documents from the World Wide Web. In Eligh and Kastelein [72], pages 963–979.

276. Roland P. Wooster and Marc Abrams. Proxy Caching That Estimates Page Load Delays. In Imbach [108], pages 977–986.

277. World Wide Web Consortium. Document Object Model Specification. Working Draft WD-DOM-19980416, April 1998.

278. François Yergeau. UTF-8, a transformation format of ISO 10646. Internet proposed standard informational RFC 2279, January 1998.

279. François Yergeau, Gavin Thomas Nicol, Glenn Adams, and Martin J. Duerst. Internationalization of the Hypertext Markup Language. Internet proposed standard RFC 2070, January 1997.

280. Robert H. Zakon. Hobbes' Internet Timeline. Internet informational RFC 2235, November 1997.

281. Jacob Ziv and Abraham Lempel. A Universal Algorithm for Sequential Data Compression. *IEEE Transactions on Information Theory*, 23(3):337–343, May 1977.

Glossary

The glossary contains short explanations of many terms which are relevant for the subject of this book. If possible, references in forms of URIs as well as bibliographic references are given. The goal is to only include authoritative and long-term URIs, but it may happen that a URI is no longer valid. In this case, please send a message to dret@tik.ee.ethz.ch, as well as for any other suggestions or updates concerning the glossary.

When searching for information about something, the index (starting on page 577) should be used to find occurrences of a term within the book's text. Furthermore, in many cases it is also rather simple to find a good information on the web by using one of the many search engines.

ABNF – AUGMENTED BACKUS-NAUR FORM
Reference: [54]
Internet technical specifications often need to define a format syntax and are free to employ whatever notation their authors deem useful. Over the years, a modified version of *Backus-Naur Form (BNF)*, called Augmented BNF (ABNF), has been popular among many Internet specifications. It balances compactness and simplicity with reasonable representational power.

ActiveX
URI: http://www.microsoft.com/com/activex.htm
ActiveX is the name Microsoft has given to a set of object-oriented concepts, technologies, and tools. The main technology is the *Component Object Model (COM)*. Used in a network with a directory and additional support, COM becomes the *Distributed Component Object Model (DCOM)*. The main object that is created when writing a program to run in the ActiveX environment is a component, a self-sufficient program that can be run anywhere in the ActiveX network (currently a network consisting of Windows and Macintosh systems). This component is known as an *ActiveX control*. An ActiveX control is roughly equivalent to a Java applet.

One important difference is that an ActiveX control must be compiled for a specific platform, while an applet is platform-independent.

AIFF – AUDIO INTERCHANGE FILE FORMAT

The Audio Interchange File Format (AIFF) is a proprietary standard for audio files developed by Apple. The format can store monaural or multi-channel sampled sounds in a range of sample rates and sample resolutions. Although originally AIFF did not support compressed audio data, a new version of the format called *AIFF compressed (AIFF-C)* has been defined which allows compression.

ANSI – AMERICAN NATIONAL STANDARDS INSTITUTE

URI: http://www.ansi.org/

The American National Standards Institute (ANSI), founded in 1918, does not itself develop American National Standards; rather it facilitates development by establishing consensus among qualified groups. The Institute ensures that its guiding principles – consensus, due process, and openness – are followed by the more than 175 distinct entities currently accredited. ANSI promotes the use of US standards internationally, advocates US policy and technical positions in international and regional standards organizations, and encourages the adoption of international standards as national standards where these meet the needs of the user community.

Apache

URI: http://www.apache.org/, http://www.apacheweek.com/

The Apache project is a collaborative software development effort aimed at creating a robust, commercial-grade, feature-full, and freely-available source code implementation of an HTTP server. The project is jointly managed by a group of volunteers located around the world, using the Internet and the web to communicate, plan, and develop the server and its related documentation. These volunteers are known as the Apache Group. In addition, hundreds of users have contributed ideas, code, and documentation to the project.

applet

URI: http://java.sun.com/applets/

A Java applet is a special type of Java program that can be included in an HTML page, much as an image can be included. When using a Java-compatible browser to view a page that contains a Java applet, the applet's code is transferred to and executed by the browser. Since an applet is platform-independent, the same applet can be executed on all types of platforms, as long as they support Java.

ARPA $\longrightarrow$ DARPA

ASCII – AMERICAN NATIONAL STANDARD CODE FOR INFORMATION IN-
TERCHANGE

Reference: [8]

ASCII specifies the coding of space and a set of 94 characters (letters,
digits and punctuation or mathematical symbols) suitable for the interchange of english language documents. ASCII forms the basis for most
computer code sets and is the american national version of ISO 646 [113].

ASF – ADVANCED STREAMING FORMAT

URI: http://www.microsoft.com/asf/

Microsoft's Advanced Streaming Format (ASF) is an extensible file format designed to store synchronized multimedia data. It supports data
delivery over a wide variety of networks and protocols while still proving
suitable for local playback. The explicit goal of ASF is to provide a basis
for industry-wide multimedia interoperability. Each ASF file is composed
of one or more media streams. The file header specifies the properties
of the entire file, along with stream-specific properties. Multimedia data,
stored after the file header, references a particular media stream number
to indicate its type and purpose. The delivery and presentation of all media stream data is synchronized to a common time-line. The intent is that
in the long run ASF will replace the *Audio Video Interleave (AVI)* format.
ASF's functionality is similar to the one provided by W3C's standardized
Synchronized Multimedia Integration Language (SMIL).

AVI – AUDIO VIDEO INTERLEAVE

Microsoft's Audio Video Interleave (AVI) file format is used for storing
audio and video information. It is the most common format for audio and
video files within PC environments. Being a proprietary technology, AVI
can be functionally compared to Apple's *QuickTime* and the *MPEG* video
standards.

Base64

Reference: [80]

The Base64 encoding is designed to represent arbitrary sequences of octets
in a form that need not be humanly readable. The encoding and decoding
algorithms are simple, but the encoded data are consistently only about
33 percent larger than the unencoded data. This encoding is virtually
identical to the one used in *Privacy Enhanced Mail (PEM)* applications,
as defined in RFC 1421 [161].

BIND – BERKELEY INTERNET NAME DOMAIN
URI: http://www.isc.org/bind.html
The Berkeley Internet Name Domain (BIND) implements an Internet name server for BSD-derived operating systems. BIND consists of a server called *named* and a *resolver* library. BIND is an implementation of the *Domain Name System (DNS)*, both server and client. Development of BIND is funded by the *Internet Software Consortium (ISC)*. BIND has been ported to Windows NT and VMS, but is most often found on Unix. BIND source code is freely available and very complex; most of the development on the DNS protocols is based on this code; and most Unix vendors ship BIND-derived DNS implementations. As a result, the BIND name server is the most widely used name server on the Internet. The newest version of BIND includes features which implement the latest DNS developments defined in Internet proposed standards RFC 1996 [268] and RFC 2136 [269].

BNF – BACKUS-NAUR FORM
Reference: [193]
The Backus-Naur Form (BNF) is a formal meta-syntax used to express context-free grammars. BNF is one of the most commonly used meta-syntactic notations for specifying the syntax of programming languages, command sets, protocol data units, and similar things. However, pure BNF is rather limited, so the two variations *Extended BNF (EBNF)* and *Augmented BNF (ABNF)* have become more popular.

browser – A browser is a program which is used to view web pages. The most popular browsers today are Netscape's *Navigator* and Microsoft's *Internet Explorer*. The first browser which led the way to today's easily usable *Graphical User Interface (GUI)* applications was NCSA's *Mosaic*, which is not supported anymore. A typical browser has to understand HTTP, HTML, a few graphics formats (at least GIF and JPEG), and should also be extensible using a model of external viewers or plug-ins. Navigator and Internet Explorer are also usable for email and Usenet news (implementing the SMTP, POP, IMAP, and NNTP protocols), which is independent from their web functionality. Both browsers implement a number of additional protocols (eg, protocols for accessing FTP or HTTPS servers as well as proprietary protocols).

CCITT – COMITÉ CONSULTATIF INTERNATIONALE DE TÉLÉPHONES ET TÉLÉGRAPHES
Former name of the *International Telecommunications Union (ITU)* before it was renamed in 1993.

ccTLD – COUNTRY-CODE TOP-LEVEL DOMAIN
Reference: [213]
A country-code Top-Level Domain (ccTLD) is a DNS top-level domain identifying domain names for a given country. The country-codes being used are the two letter codes defined by ISO 3166 [128]. The *Internet Assigned Numbers Authority (IANA)* is not in the business of deciding what is and what is not a country. The selection of the ISO 3166 list as a basis for ccTLDs was made with the knowledge that ISO has a procedure for determining which entities should be and should not be on that list.

CDF – CHANNEL DEFINITION FORMAT
URI: `http://www.microsoft.com/standards/cdf/`
Reference: [73]
The Channel Definition Format (CDF) provides publishers with the ability to author content a single time for publishing via different ways – web browsers, web crawlers, push clients, or direct streaming push. A channel is defined as a set of documents or a grouping of content that can be pushed, pulled, or operated on as a unit. In today's applications, the types of operations on a channel primarily involve automatic scheduled download for offline use ("smart pull"), or multicast delivery for later use. However, the emergence of a standard in this space will also enable the next generation of applications and technology in content publishing – searching, indexing, profiling, filtering, and personalizing content independent of the publishing mechanism.

CERN – EUROPEAN LABORATORY FOR PARTICLE PHYSICS
URI: `http://www.cern.ch/`
The European Laboratory for Particle Physics (CERN) is the birthplace of the web. The first proposal and first prototype applications were written at CERN by Tim Berners-Lee. CERN continued to lead web development until late 1994, when budget reasons caused CERN to stop its web activities. Since then, the main responsibility for developing standards and recommendations for the web lies in the hands of the *World Wide Web Consortium (W3C)*.

certificate – Certificates are digital documents attesting to the binding of a public key to an individual or other entity. They allow verification of the claim that a given public key does in fact belong to a given individual. Certificates help prevent someone from using a phony key to impersonate someone else. In their simplest form, certificates contain a public key and a name. As commonly used, a certificate also contains an expiration date, the name of the certifying authority that issued the certificate, a serial number, and perhaps other information. Most importantly, it contains the digital signature of the certificate issuer. The most widely accepted format for certificates is defined by ITU recommendation X.509 [137], thus, certificates can be read or written by any application complying with X.509.

CGI – COMMON GATEWAY INTERFACE

URI: http://hoohoo.ncsa.uiuc.edu/cgi/

The Common Gateway Interface (CGI) is a standard for interfacing external applications with information servers, such as HTTP servers. A plain HTML document that the web server retrieves upon a request is static, which means it exists in a constant state, for example as a text file that does not change. A CGI program, on the other hand, is executed in real-time, so that it can generate dynamic information.

CGM – COMPUTER GRAPHICS METAFILE

URI: http://www.cgmopen.org/

Reference: [115]

The Computer Graphics Metafile (CGM) is a machine and operating system independent interchange format that provides elements to represent geometric graphics (eg, polygons or circles) and raster graphics (eg, pixel arrays). It consists of a functional specification and multiple encodings for different purposes. There are three standardized encodings for CGM, clear-text, character and binary. Clear-text is human-readable. Character encoding is more compact, but still uses ASCII characters, so that it can be interchanged without protocol problems. The binary encoding is more compact still, and quick to encode and decode, but completely unreadable.

chunked encoding – With the introduction of persistent connections in HTTP/1.1, the length of a resource which is sent in a response can no longer be implicitly signaled by closing the connection. However, for the majority of resources, the length is known in advance and be given in the Content-Length header field. For all other resources (such as dynamically created content), chunked encoding can be used. Chunked encoding transfers the message body as a sequence of chunks of known length.

CLF – COMMON LOG FORMAT

The Common Log Format (CLF) is a log file format for HTTP servers including information about the host, identification of the user (if available), authorized user-name (if available), date, the request line itself, and the returned status and number of bytes. Although most servers can be configured to produce other formats of log files, many tools exist to analyze CLF files, so custom log file formats should only be used if absolutely necessary.

client – A client is one side of a client/server relationship. The client side requests services from the server, which processes the request and generates a response. In case of the web, a client is defined by the client side of HTTP, sending requests to a web server. Usually, a client will be a browser such as Netscape's *Navigator* or Microsoft's *Internet Explorer*, but in general a client can be any program which implements HTTP. The second very popular example for a client is therefore a search engine, which systematically gathers information from web servers by sending requests and collecting the responses in a large database.

CMS – CRYPTOGRAPHIC MESSAGE SYNTAX
Reference: [101, 235]
The Cryptographic Message Syntax (CMS) is used to digitally sign or encrypt arbitrary messages. CMS describes an encapsulation syntax for data protection. It supports digital signatures and encryption. The syntax allows multiple encapsulation, so one encapsulation envelope can be nested inside another. Likewise, one party can digitally sign some previously encapsulated data. It also allows arbitrary attributes, such as signing time, to be authenticated along with the message content, and provides for other attributes such as counter-signatures to be associated with a signature.

COM – COMPONENT OBJECT MODEL
URI: http://www.microsoft.com/com/
Microsoft's Component Object Model (COM) is a software architecture that allows applications to be built from binary software components. COM is the underlying architecture that forms the foundation for higher-level software services, like those provided by *Object Linking and Embedding (OLE)*. COM defines a binary standard for function calling between components, a way for components to dynamically discover the interfaces implemented by other components, and a mechanism to identify components and their interfaces uniquely.

content negotiation – Content negotiation is an HTTP mechanism which is used to make a selection between different representations for a resource. Different representations can be characterized by language, quality, encoding, or other parameters which do not affect the content of a resource. HTTP defines two types of content negotiation, server-driven and agent-driven. In server-driven content negotiation, the server makes the selection and sends a response with the representation of a requested resource which it thinks matches the user's needs, based on the request, available representations, and other information. In agent-driven content negotiation, the server responds with a list of all representations and the client (or the user) makes the selection and requests the selected representation.

cookie

Reference: [152]

Originally introduced by Netscape, cookies are a general mechanism which server side applications, such as *Common Gateway Interface (CGI)* scripts, can use to both store and retrieve information on the client side of the connection. The addition of a simple, persistent, client-side state significantly extends the capabilities of web-based client/server applications.

CORBA – COMMON OBJECT REQUEST BROKER ARCHITECTURE

URI: http://www.omg.org/corba/

Reference: [198]

The Common Object Request Broker Architecture (CORBA) describes the architecture of a middleware platform that supports the implementation of applications in distributed and heterogeneous environments. The CORBA standard is issued by the *Object Management Group (OMG)*. In contrast to other middleware platforms such as Microsoft's *Distributed Component Object Model (DCOM)*, CORBA is a specification that does not prescribe any specific technology.

CORE – INTERNET COUNCIL OF REGISTRARS

URI: http://www.corenic.org/

The Internet Council of Registrars (CORE) is a non-profit organization founded as result of a plan initiated by the *Internet Society (ISOC)* and the *Internet Assigned Numbers Authority (IANA)* in 1996 to add new structure, free enterprise, and competition to the Internet *Domain Name System (DNS)* when the old monopoly on the com, org, and net domains ends in 1998. CORE operates according to well-defined standards, global constitution and ethics documented in the *generic Top Level Domain Memorandum of Understanding (gTLD-MoU)*.

crawler $\longrightarrow$ search engine

CSP – CHARACTER SHAPE PLAYER

TrueDoc's Character Shape Player (CSP) uses the *Portable Font Resource (PFR)* to render characters at the receiving system, usually a browser supporting dynamic fonts. It scales the characters to the desired size and rasterizes them at the required output resolution. The CSP includes built-in hinting, anti-aliasing, digital edge filtering, and sub-pixel positioning to achieve superior quality on all kinds of output devices.

CSR – CHARACTER SHAPE RECORDER

TrueDoc's Character Shape Recorder (CSR) is incorporated into authoring tools for creating documents containing dynamic fonts. When an author publishes a document, the CSR analyzes the fonts used and creates a *Portable Font Resource (PFR)* containing the glyphs (character shapes) necessary to display the document later.

CSS – CASCADING STYLE SHEETS

URI: http://www.w3.org/Style/

Reference: CSS1 [159], CSS2 [25]

Cascading Style Sheets (CSS) is the style sheet language which has been designed for HTML. While HTML should be used to define the contents of a web page, CSS is the language for specifying the presentation aspects of it. The two main advantages of HTML with CSS over HTML without CSS are the clear separation of content and presentation (which makes the automated processing of web pages much easier and also enables users to apply their own style sheets instead of the defaults provided by their browser or a web page's designer), and the greatly enhanced formatting capabilities with CSS. The first version of CSS (CSS1) has a number of shortcomings (such as the impossibility to specify the formatting of tables) which have been resolved in CSS2.

CSS-P – CASCADING STYLE SHEETS POSITIONING

Reference: [255]

In the first implementation of *Cascading Style Sheets (CSS)* in Netscape's Navigator additional functionality was included which added absolute positioning and layering to the initial CSS1 specification. Netscape submitted the proposal for this version of CSS to W3C, which decided to incorporate the functionality of CSS-P into the next version of CSS (which is CSS2). Consequently, CSS2 contains absolute positioning and layering, and (apart from the intermediate draft of Netscape's original submission) there is no official CSS-P recommendation.

DAP – DIRECTORY ACCESS PROTOCOL

Reference: [139]

The Directory Access Protocol (DAP) is the original protocol for accessing X.500 directory services. Since DAP is OSI-based and rather complex, a TCP-based and simplified variant of DAP, the *Lightweight Directory Access Protocol (LDAP)*, has been designed, which today is more popular than DAP itself.

DARPA – DEFENSE ADVANCED RESEARCH PROJECTS AGENCY
URI: http://www.darpa.mil/
The Defense Advanced Research Projects Agency (DARPA), until 1973 known as *Advanced Research Projects Agency (ARPA)*, is the main source for research funds in the US. In particular, the Internet (its first infrastructure as well as the protocol suite) originated from the ARPANET, a network which was first designed for US military purposes with the primary design goal to be robust.

DCE – DISTRIBUTED COMPUTING ENVIRONMENT
URI: http://www.opengroup.org/dce/
Reference: [261]
The Distributed Computing Environment (DCE) is an industry-standard, vendor-neutral set of distributed computing technologies. It provides security services to protect and control access to data, name services that make it easy to find distributed resources, and a highly scalable model for organizing widely scattered users, services, and data. DCE runs on all major computing platforms and is designed to support distributed applications in heterogeneous hardware and software environments.

DCOM – DISTRIBUTED COMPONENT OBJECT MODEL
URI: http://www.microsoft.com/com/dcom.htm
Reference: [38]
The Distributed Component Object Model (DCOM) is a protocol that enables software components to communicate directly over a network in a reliable, secure, and efficient manner. Previously called "Network OLE", DCOM is designed for use across multiple network transports, including Internet protocols such as HTTP. DCOM is based on the Open Group's DCE *Remote Procedure Call (RPC)* specification and works with both Java applets and *ActiveX* components through its use of the *Component Object Model (COM)*.

DES – DATA ENCRYPTION STANDARD
Reference: [189]
The Data Encryption Standard (DES) was originally developed at IBM. DES has been extensively studied since its publication and is the most well-known and widely used cryptosystem in the world. DES is a symmetric cryptosystem, when used for communications, both sender and receiver must know the same secret key, which is used both to encrypt and decrypt the message. DES can also be used for single-user encryption, such as to store files on a hard disk in encrypted form. In a multi-user environment, secure key distribution may be difficult. Public key cryptography provides an ideal solution to this problem.

DHTML – Dynamic HTML

Dynamic HTML (DHTML) does not refer to a specific version or a specific feature of HTML. It is an expression which is commonly used to refer to all features of HTML or specific HTML variants which go beyond the presentation of static documents. The most popular mechanisms which are encompassed by the term DHTML are *Cascading Style Sheets (CSS)*, scripts (embedded with the <SCRIPT> element), and objects (embedded with the <OBJECT> element). DHTML also often refers to browser-specific enhancements of particular mechanisms, such as extensions to the basic scripting methods, or the ability to dynamically download fonts. The "glue" between the different components which make up DHTML (mainly HTML, CSS, and a scripting language) is provided by the *Document Object Model (DOM)*.

Diffie-Hellman

Reference: [65, 234]

Diffie-Hellman key agreement describes a method whereby two parties, without any prior arrangements, can agree upon a secret key that is known only to them (and, in particular, is not known to an eavesdropper listening to the dialogue by which the parties agree on the key). This secret key can be used, for example, to encrypt further communications between the parties. The intended application of this standard is in protocols for establishing secure connections. Details on the interpretation of the agreed-upon secret key are outside the scope of Diffie-Hellman key agreement, as are details on sources of the pseudo-random bits required by this method. The Diffie-Hellman key exchange is vulnerable to a middleperson attack. This vulnerability is due to the fact that Diffie-Hellman key exchange does not authenticate the participants.

DNS – Domain Name System

Reference: [177, 178]

The Domain Name System (DNS) is a distributed, replicated, data query service mainly used on the Internet for translating host names to IP addresses. The three main components of DNS are: the *domain name space* and *resource records*, which are specifications for a tree structured name space and data associated with the names; *name servers*, which are server programs which hold information about the domain tree's structure and set information; and *resolvers*, being programs that extract information from name servers in response to client requests.

DOI – Digital Object Identifier
URI: http://www.doi.org/
The Digital Object Identifier (DOI) system is a mechanism for marking digital objects in order to facilitate electronic commerce and enable copyright management in a digital environment. DOI not only provides a unique identification for digital content, but also a way to link users of the materials to the rights holders themselves to facilitate automated digital commerce. The underlying technology of DOI is the *Handle System*, which associates each DOI name with one or more locations where the object may be found.

DOM – Document Object Model
URI: http://www.w3.org/DOM/
Reference: [277]
The Document Object Model (DOM) is a platform- and language-neutral interface that allows programs and scripts to dynamically access and update the content, structure and style of web documents (currently, definitions for HTML and XML documents are part of the specification). The document can be further processed and the results of that processing can be incorporated back into the presented page.

DRP – Distribution and Replication Protocol
The Distribution and Replication Protocol (DRP) was designed to efficiently replicate a hierarchical set of files to a large number of clients. No assumption is made about the content or type of the files, they are simply files in some hierarchical organization. After the initial download a client can keep the data up-to-date. Using DRP the client can download only the data that has changed since the last time it checked. DRP uses content identifiers to automatically share resources that are requested more than once. This eliminates redundant transfers of commonly used resources. The content identifiers used in DRP are based on widely accepted checksum technology.

DSA – Digital Signature Algorithm $\longrightarrow$ DSS

DSig – Digital Signature Initiative
URI: http://www.w3.org/DSig/
The Digital Signature Initiative (DSig) proposes a standard format for making digitally-signed, machine-readable assertions about a particular information resource. PICS 1.1 labels are an example of such machine-readable assertions. The DSig specification describes a method of adding extensions to PICS 1.1 labels for purposes of signing them. More generally, it is the goal of the DSig project to provide a mechanism to make the

statement: *signer* believes *statement* about *information resource*. In DSig 1.0, *statement* is any statement that can be expressed with PICS 1.1.

DSS – DIGITAL SIGNATURE STANDARD
Reference: [188, 192]
The *Digital Signature Algorithm (DSA)* was published by the National Institute of Standards and Technology in the Digital Signature Standard (DSS). DSA is for authentication only. In DSA, signature generation is faster than signature verification, whereas in *RSA*, signature verification is faster than signature generation (if the public and private exponents, respectively, are chosen for this property, which is the usual case). NIST claims that it is an advantage of DSA that signing is faster, but many people in cryptography think that it is better for verification to be the faster operation.

DSSSL – DOCUMENT STYLE SEMANTICS AND SPECIFICATION LANGUAGE
URI: http://www.jclark.com/dsssl/
Reference: [127]
The Document Style Semantics and Specification Language (DSSSL) is an international standard for specifying document transformation and formatting in a platform- and vendor-neutral manner. DSSSL can be used with any document format for which a property set can be defined according to the *Property Set Definition Requirements* of the *HyTime* standard. In particular, DSSSL can be used to specify the presentation of documents marked up according to the *Standard Generalized Markup Language (SGML)* standard. DSSSL consists of two main components, a transformation language and a style language. The transformation language is used to specify structural transformations on SGML source files. For example, a telephone directory structured as a series of entries ordered by last name could, by applying a transformation spec, be rendered as a series of entries sorted by first name instead. The transformation language can also be used to specify the merging of two or more documents, the generation of indexes and tables of contents, and other operations. While the transformation language is a powerful tool for gaining the maximum use from document databases, the focus in early DSSSL implementations will be on the style language component.

DSSSL-Lite – DSSSL-Lite was an early approach to define a profile (ie, a functional subset) of DSSSL in an attempt to create a version of DSSSL which is less complex and still powerful enough to be sufficient for a large number of applications. DSSSL-Lite never became an actual standard, but the work on it was used as input for the *DSSSL-Online (DSSSL-O)* activity.

DSSSL-O – – DSSSL-ONLINE
Based on results from the *DSSSL-Lite* activity, DSSSL-Online (DSSSL-O) was an attempt to define a profile (ie, a functional subset) of DSSSL. This profile should be less complex than full DSSSL and particularly suited to the needs of on-line publishing. DSSSL-O never became an actual standard, but it was used as the base for the *Extensible Style Language (XSL)*, which is used as the style sheet language for documents using the *Extensible Markup Language (XML)*.

DTD – DOCUMENT TYPE DEFINITION
Reference: [110]
A Document Type Definition (DTD) is one component inside an SGML environment. It defines the syntactic rules according to which a document can be composed. There are no semantics associated with the elements and attributes defined in a DTD, although normally the names chosen for elements and attributes will have some meaning to them. Using a DTD and an SGML parser, an SGML document can be validated against the DTD, which means it can be tested whether it conforms to a given DTD. HTML is one example of a DTD.

EBNF – EXTENDED BACKUS-NAUR FORM
An Extended Backus-Naur Form (EBNF) is any variation on the basic *Backus-Naur Form (BNF)* meta-syntax notation with (some of) the following additional constructs: square brackets surrounding optional items, suffix '*' for a sequence of zero or more of an item, suffix '+' for one or more of an item, curly brackets enclosing a list of alternatives, and super- and subscripts indicating the number of possible occurrences. All these constructs can be expressed in plain BNF using extra productions and have been added for readability and succinctness.

ECMA – EUROPEAN COMPUTER MANUFACTURERS ASSOCIATION
URI: http://www.ecma.ch/
ECMA is an international, europe-based industry association founded in 1961 and dedicated to the standardization of information and communication systems. Many ECMA standards have been accepted as a base for international and european standards. To ensure close cooperation ECMA has established formal liaisons with all european and international standardization bodies. ECMA standards are developed by highly qualified experts from information technology and telecommunication industry with the commitment to provide in a consensus mode technical solutions ready for implementation in product development and conformity testing.

ECMAScript

Reference: [74]

ECMAScript is the standardized version of the scripting language originally known as *JavaScript*. After the standardization of the language by the *European Computer Manufacturers Association, (ECMA)*, references to the language itself should use the term "ECMAScript", while *JavaScript* and *JScript* are two implementations of this language.

EFF – ELECTRONIC FRONTIER FOUNDATION

URI: http://www.eff.org/

The Electronic Frontier Foundation (EFF) is a non-profit organization working in the public interest to protect fundamental civil liberties, including privacy and freedom of expression, in the arena of computers and the Internet. EFF works to make sure that common carriage principles are upheld in the information age. Common carriage principles require that network providers carry all speech, regardless of its controversial content. EFF supports a new common carriage system in which system operators are shielded from liability for the actions of users, but without the regulatory burden presently associated with common carriage.

ESMTP – EXTENDED SIMPLE MAIL TRANSFER PROTOCOL

Reference: [149]

The Extended Simple Mail Transfer Protocol (ESMTP) describes a framework for extensions of the *Simple Mail Transfer Protocol (SMTP)*. SMTP still provides the base mechanism for exchanging email messages, but it has become apparent that it lacks some important functionality. Instead of defining a revised but static new version of SMTP, ESMTP defines a mechanism how extensions can be integrated into the basic protocol, and how these extensions can be used in an interoperable way.

expiration – The cache mechanisms of HTTP are based on an expiration

model, assigning expiration times to responses which are stored in caches. Expiration times may either be server-specified or heuristic, depending on whether the origin server specified an expiration time for the response. If a response is expired, usually it should be validated by the cache before it is used in a response.

FCGI – FASTCGI

URI: http://www.fastcgi.com/

FastCGI (FCGI) is an extension of the *Common Gateway Interface (CGI)* which eliminates CGI drawbacks and provides high performance, while remaining highly compatible with existing CGI applications. FCGI is conceptually very similar to CGI, with two major differences. As the first difference, FCGI processes are persistent, after finishing a request, they wait for a new request instead of exiting. The second difference is that, instead of using operating system environment variables and pipes, the FCGI protocol multiplexes the environment information, standard input, output and error over a single full-duplex connection. This allows FCGI programs to run on remote machines, using TCP connections between the web server and the FCGI application.

FQDN – FULLY-QUALIFIED DOMAIN NAME
A Fully-Qualified Domain Name (FQDN) is a domain name that includes all higher level domains relevant to the entity named.

FQHN – FULLY-QUALIFIED HOST NAME
A Fully-Qualified Host Name (FQHN) means either the *Fully-Qualified Domain Name (FQDN)* of a host (ie, a completely specified domain name ending in a top-level domain), or the numeric *IP address* of a host.

freshness – The freshness lifetime of an HTTP response is the length of time between the generation of a response and its expiration time. The HTTP caching model is heavily based on a model of expiration times and thus the freshness of responses stored in caches. If the freshness lifetime of a response has expired, it is said to be *stale*, otherwise it is *fresh*.

FTP – FILE TRANSFER PROTOCOL
Reference: [207]
The File Transfer Protocol (FTP) is a protocol for file transfer between hosts on the Internet. The primary function of FTP is to transfer files efficiently and reliably among hosts and to allow the convenient use of remote file storage capabilities. The objectives of FTP are to promote sharing of files (computer programs and/or data), to encourage indirect or implicit (via programs) use of remote computers, to shield users from variations in file storage systems among hosts, and to transfer data reliably and efficiently. FTP, though usable directly by a user at a terminal, is designed mainly for use by programs.

gateway – In general, a gateway is a system which forwards requests from one communication domain to another (generally on the transport layer of a communications architecture). In the context of HTTP, a gateway is a program which acts as an intermediary for some other server, therefore it is similar to a proxy. However, an HTTP client sending a request to a gateway does not know that it is not communicating with the origin server, while a client communicating with an HTTP proxy does so explicitly.

GIF – GRAPHICS INTERCHANGE FORMAT
  Reference: GIF87 [49], GIF89a [50]
  GIF is a data stream-oriented file format used to define the transmission
  protocol of LZW-encoded bitmap data. GIF images may be up to eight
  bits (256 colors) in depth and are always compressed. Despite the fact that
  GIF supports only 8-bits worth of colors, and the multimedia extensions
  introduced in the GIF89a release have not been widely utilized, GIF still
  remains a popular choice for storing lower resolution image data. Any
  software created or modified after 1994 that supports the capability of
  reading and/or writing GIF files must obtain a patent license agreement
  from Unisys Corporation. For publishing on the web, *JPEG* is a good
  companion format for photo-realistic images, while the *Portable Network
  Graphics (PNG)* format has been designed to replace GIF in the long run.

gopher
  Reference: [11]
  The Internet gopher protocol is designed primarily to act as a distributed
  document delivery system. While documents (and services) reside on
  many servers, gopher client software presents users with a hierarchy of
  items and directories much like a file system. In fact, the gopher interface is designed to resemble a file system since a file system is a good
  model for locating documents and services. The user sees what amounts
  to one big networked information system containing primarily document
  items, directory items, and search items (the latter allowing searches for
  documents across subsets of the information base). Since the web allows
  greater flexibility in the structure and presentation of distributed information, the usage of gopher services and the number of gopher servers is
  getting smaller.

grammar – A grammar is a set of rules defining how the words of a language
  may be used to form sentences. In a formal context, a grammar can be
  defined by rules which use different ways to combine words, for example
  sequences or optional occurrences. Examples of grammars in the context
  of the web are SGML and XML DTDs. For example, the HTML DTD can
  be seen as a grammar which defines how the various elements of HTML
  may be combined to create a valid HTML page. A program which checks
  an input for compliance to a grammar usually is called a *parser*.

gTLD – GENERIC TOP-LEVEL DOMAIN
  Reference: [213]
  A generic Top-Level Domain (gTLD) is a TLD which is not specific to
  a country. Each of the gTLDs was created for a general category of organizations. Generally, under the gTLDs the structure is very flat. That

is, many organizations are registered directly under the gTLD, and any further structure is up to the individual organizations. The gTLDs which are currently defined are the old gTLDs `edu`, `com`, `net`, `org`, `gov`, `mil`, and `int`, as well as the new gTLDs `firm`, `shop`, `web`, `arts`, `rec`, `info`, and `nom` as defined by the *Generic Top Level Domain Memorandum of Understanding (gTLD-MoU)*.

gTLD-MoU – GENERIC TOP LEVEL DOMAIN MEMORANDUM OF UNDER-STANDING

URI: `http://www.gtld-mou.org/`

The Generic Top Level Domain Memorandum of Understanding (gTLD-MoU) is an international framework in which policies for the administration and enhancement of the Internet's generic *Domain Name System (DNS)* are developed and deployed. These policies are developed in cooperation with the *Internet Assigned Numbers Authority (IANA)*, who manages the DNS root to promote stability and robustness. The *Internet Council of Registrars (CORE)* will administer the registration of new domain names.

Handle System

URI: `http://www.handle.net/`

Reference: [258]

The Handle System is a comprehensive system for assigning, managing, and resolving persistent identifiers, known as "handles", for digital objects and other resources on the Internet. Handles can be used as *Uniform Resource Names (URNs)*. The Handle System includes an open set of protocols, a name space, and an implementation of the protocols. The protocols enable a distributed computer system to store handles of digital resources and resolve those handles into the information necessary to locate and access the resources. This associated information can be changed as needed to reflect the current state of the identified resource without changing the handle, thus allowing the name of the item to persist over changes of location and other state information. Combined with a centrally administered naming authority registration service, the Handle System provides a general purpose, distributed global naming service for the reliable management of information on networks over long periods of time.

HTML – HYPERTEXT MARKUP LANGUAGE

URI: `http://www.w3.org/MarkUp/`

Reference: HTML 2.0 [18], HTML 3.2 [217], HTML 4.0 [219]

The Hypertext Markup Language (HTML) is a simple markup language used to create hypertext documents that are platform independent.

HTML documents are *Standard Generalized Markup Language (SGML)* documents with generic semantics that are appropriate for representing information from a wide range of domains. HTML markup can represent hypertext news, mail, documentation, and hypermedia, menus of options, database query results, simple structured documents with in-lined graphics, and hypertext views of existing bodies of information.

HTTP – HYPERTEXT TRANSFER PROTOCOL
URI: `http://www.w3.org/Protocols/`
Reference: HTTP/1.0 [20], HTTP/1.1 [75]
The Hypertext Transfer Protocol (HTTP) is the protocol used for information exchange on the web. HTTP defines how messages are formatted and transmitted, and what actions web servers and browsers should take in response to various messages. HTTP uses a reliable, connection-oriented transport service such as the *Transmission Control Protocol (TCP)*. HTTP is a stateless protocol, where each message is interpreted independently, without any knowledge of the commands that came before it. The latest version of HTTP implements *persistent connections* and *pipelining* in order to use one transport connection for multiple request/response interactions.

HTTP-ng – HYPERTEXT TRANSFER PROTOCOL – NEXT GENERATION
URI: `http://www.w3.org/Protocols/HTTP-NG/`
As HTTP has developed, many requests and proposals for extensions and new features have been made. The purpose of HTTP-ng is to design and prototype a new generation of the HTTP protocol using sound engineering practices: modularity, simplicity, and layering. The project will design, implement, and test a new architecture for the new HTTP protocol based on a simple, extensible, distributed, object-oriented model. A key part of development work is the characterization of the web, involving measurement and analysis of the system in real life; work that will help in designing the new protocol and an understanding of how to manage a smooth transition.

HTTPS – HYPERTEXT TRANSFER PROTOCOL OVER SSL
URI: `http://home.netscape.com/newsref/std/SSL.html`
Reference: [222]
The Hypertext Transfer Protocol over SSL (HTTPS) is a secure way of using HTTP. HTTP provides almost no security features, it contains only basic authentication mechanisms, and no support for privacy. HTTPS solves this problem by replacing HTTP's transport layer, the insecure *Transmission Control Protocol (TCP)*, with the *Secure Sockets Layer (SSL)*, a secure transport layer. In the near future, SSL will probably

be replaced by the more general *Transport Layer Security (TLS)* protocol, but it is unlikely that the already established name of HTTPS will
be changed to reflect this change.

HyTime – HYPERMEDIA/TIME-BASED STRUCTURING LANGUAGE
Reference: [132]
The Hypermedia/Time-based Structuring Language (HyTime) is an application of the *Standard Generalized Markup Language (SGML)* that
provides facilities for describing the relationships between different types
of data. It provides standardized methods for describing hypertext links,
time scheduling, event synchronization, and projection in multimedia and
hypermedia documents. In keeping with the character of the SGML standard, HyTime does not seek to provide a standardized way of coding
hypermedia presentations but instead provides a language that can be
used to describe how any set of hypermedia objects has been interconnected, and how users are meant to access them. User communities will
define their own application specifications, which will be interchanged in
the form of an SGML document type definition. The emphasis in HyTime
is on identifying specific types of hypermedia objects, such as links and
other locatable events, and on providing addressing mechanisms that will
identify any segment of data that may need to be accessed or presented
to users in a special way, irrespective of how the source data has been
coded.

IAB – INTERNET ARCHITECTURE BOARD
URI: http://www.iab.org/iab/
The Internet Architecture Board (IAB) is the technical body that oversees
the development of the Internet suite of protocols. It has two task forces:
the *Internet Engineering Task Force (IETF)* and the *Internet Research
Task Force (IRTF)*.

IANA – INTERNET ASSIGNED NUMBERS AUTHORITY
URI: http://www.iana.org/
The Internet Assigned Numbers Authority (IANA) is the central coordi-
nator for the assignment of unique parameter values for Internet protocols.
The Internet protocol suite, as defined by the *Internet Engineering Task
Force (IETF)* and the *Internet Engineering Steering Group (IESG)*, contains numerous parameters, such as Internet addresses, domain names,
autonomous system numbers (used in some routing protocols), protocol
numbers, port numbers, management information base object identifiers,
including private enterprise numbers, and many others. The common use
of the Internet protocols by the Internet community requires that the
particular values used in these parameter fields be assigned uniquely. It

is the task of the IANA to make those unique assignments as requested and to maintain a registry of the currently assigned values.

ICC – INTERNATIONAL COLOR CONSORTIUM
URI: http://www.color.org/
The International Color Consortium (ICC) was established in 1993 by eight industry vendors for the purpose of creating, promoting and encouraging the standardization and evolution of an open, vendor-neutral, cross-platform color management system architecture and its components.

IDEA – INTERNATIONAL DATA ENCRYPTION ALGORITHM
Reference: [154]
IDEA (International Data Encryption Algorithm) is the second version of a block cipher designed and presented by Lai and Massey [155]. The speed of IDEA in software is similar to that of the *Data Encryption Standard (DES)*. One of the principles during the design of IDEA was to facilitate analysis of its strength against differential cryptanalysis. IDEA is considered to be immune from differential cryptanalysis. In addition, no linear cryptanalytic attacks on IDEA have been reported and there is no known algebraic weakness in IDEA.

IDL – INTERFACE DEFINITION LANGUAGE
URI: http://www.omg.org/library/idlindx.htm
Reference: [133]
The Interface Definition Language (IDL) is a language and environment neutral notation to describe computational operation interface signatures. The IDL grammar is a subset of C++ with additional constructs to support an operation invocation mechanism. IDL obeys the same lexical rules as C++, but introduces new keywords to support distribution concepts. IDL is used for the *Common Object Request Broker Architecture (CORBA)* and for ISO's *Open Distributed Processing (ODP)* framework.

IEC – INTERNATIONAL ELECTROTECHNICAL COMMISSION
URI: http://www.iec.ch/
Founded in 1906, the International Electrotechnical Commission (IEC) is the world organization that prepares and publishes international standards for all electrical, electronic, and related technologies. The membership consists of more than 50 participating countries, including all the world's major trading nations and a growing number of industrializing countries. The IEC's mission is to promote, through its members, international cooperation on all questions of electrotechnical standardization and related matters, such as the assessment of conformity to standards, in the fields of electricity, electronics, and related technologies. The IEC

charter embraces all electro-technologies including electronics, magnetics and electro-magnetics, electro-acoustics, telecommunication, and energy production and distribution, as well as associated general disciplines such as terminology and symbols, measurement and performance, dependability, design and development, and safety and the environment.

IESG – INTERNET ENGINEERING STEERING GROUP
URI: http://www.ietf.org/iesg.html
The IESG is responsible for technical management of *Internet Engineering Task Force (IETF)* activities and the Internet standards process. As part of the *Internet Society (ISOC)*, it administers the process according to the rules and procedures which have been ratified by the ISOC trustees. The IESG is directly responsible for the actions associated with entry into and movement along the Internet "standards track", including final approval of specifications as Internet standards.

IETF – INTERNET ENGINEERING TASK FORCE
URI: http://www.ietf.org/
The Internet Engineering Task Force (IETF) is a large open international community of network designers, operators, vendors, and researchers concerned with the evolution of the Internet architecture and the smooth operation of the Internet. It is open to any interested individual. The actual technical work of the IETF is done in its working groups, which are organized by topic into several areas (eg, routing, transport, security, etc.).

IIOP – INTERNET INTER-ORB PROTOCOL
URI: http://www.omg.org/corba/corbiiop.htm
Reference: [198]
The Internet Inter-ORB Protocol (IIOP) is the most commonly used protocol for communications in the *Common Object Request Broker Architecture (CORBA)*. IIOP is a protocol for the client/server scenario between two CORBA implementations. In a similar way to HTTP, which uses URIs to locate servers and in requests from clients to servers, CORBA uses an *Interoperable Object Reference (IOR)* for identifying remote objects. IORs can be used to invoke operations on remote CORBA systems, using IIOP for communications.

IMAP – INTERNET MESSAGE ACCESS PROTOCOL
URI: http://www.imap.org/
Reference: [51]
The Internet Message Access Protocol (IMAP) is a protocol allowing a client to access and manipulate electronic mail messages on a server. It

permits manipulation of remote message folders (mailboxes) in a way that is functionally equivalent to local mailboxes. IMAP includes operations for creating, deleting, and renaming mailboxes; checking for new messages; permanently removing messages; searching; and selective fetching of message attributes, texts, and portions thereof. It does not specify a means of posting mail; this function is handled by a mail transfer protocol such as the *Simple Mail Transfer Protocol (SMTP)*. IMAP is newer and more powerful than the *Post Office Protocol (POP)*, which is used for the same application area.

IMC – INTERNET MAIL CONSORTIUM
URI: `http://www.imc.org/`
The Internet Mail Consortium (IMC) is an international organization focused on cooperatively managing and promoting the rapidly-expanding world of electronic mail on the Internet. The goals of the IMC include expanding the role of mail on the Internet into areas such as commerce and entertainment, advancing new Internet mail technologies, and making it easier for all Internet users to get the most out of this growing communications medium. The IMC is an industry organization, not an end-user group. Its members are primarily Internet mail software vendors in many parts of the market. Other members include hardware vendors who sell Internet mail servers, companies and online services who have Internet mail gateways, and other similar companies in the Internet mail market.

InterNIC – INTERNET NETWORK INFORMATION CENTER
URI: `http://www.internic.net/`
Formed in January 1993, the Internet Network Information Center (InterNIC) is a collaborative project for management of the Internet domain name data base and registration process. The InterNIC provides domain name registration services for the generic top-level domains `com`, `net`, `org`, and `edu`.

IP – INTERNET PROTOCOL
Reference: [209]
The Internet Protocol (IP) is specifically limited in scope to provide the functions necessary to deliver a package of bits (an Internet datagram) from a source to a destination over an interconnected system of networks. There are no mechanisms to augment end-to-end data reliability, flow control, sequencing, or other services commonly found in host-to-host protocols. In most cases, the *Transmission Control Protocol (TCP)* is used on top of IP.

IPng – INTERNET PROTOCOL NEXT GENERATION
URI: http://playground.sun.com/pub/ipng/html/
Reference: [33]
Although the Internet Protocol (IP) is the most visible protocol of the
Internet, there are many other protocols which are also part of the Internet architecture and which also have to be changed when making the
transition from IPv4 to IPv6. In the context of IPv6, there are also a number of protocols which are new to the Internet architecture. The common
practice is to use the term IPng to refer to all protocols which have to be
changed or added when switching to IPv6.

IPv6 – INTERNET PROTOCOL VERSION 6
Reference: [61]
The Internet Protocol version 6 (IPv6) is a new version of IP which is
designed to be an evolutionary step from IPv4 (commonly referred to
simply as IP). It can be installed as a normal software upgrade in Internet devices and is interoperable with the current IPv4. Its deployment
strategy was designed to not have any "flag" days. IPv6 is designed to
run well on high performance networks (eg, ATM) and at the same time
is still efficient for low bandwidth networks (eg, wireless). In addition, it
provides a platform for new Internet functionality that will be required
in the near future.

IRTF – INTERNET RESEARCH TASK FORCE
URI: http://www.irtf.org/
The Internet Research Task Force (IRTF) is composed of a number of
focused, long-term and small research groups. These groups work on topics
related to Internet protocols, applications, architecture and technology.
The IRTF focuses on longer term research issues related to the Internet
while the parallel organization, while the *Internet Engineering Task Force
(IETF)* focuses on the shorter term issues of engineering and standards
making.

ISC – INTERNET SOFTWARE CONSORTIUM
URI: http://www.isc.org/
The Internet Software Consortium (ISC) is a nonprofit corporation dedicated to production-quality software engineering for key Internet standards. Reference implementations of Internet standards often have the
weight of "de-facto standards" and ISC wants to make sure that those
reference implementations are properly supported. ISC is also committed
to keeping these reference implementations freely available to the Internet
community. ISC funds these efforts by selling support for the software and
by donations.

ISO – INTERNATIONAL ORGANIZATION FOR STANDARDIZATION
URI: http://www.iso.ch/
The International Organization for Standardization (ISO) is a worldwide federation of national standards bodies from some 100 countries, one from each country. ISO is a non-governmental organization established in 1947. The mission of ISO is to promote the development of standardization and related activities in the world with a view to facilitating the international exchange of goods and services, and to developing cooperation in the spheres of intellectual, scientific, technological and economic activity. ISO's work results in international agreements which are published as International Standards.

ISOC – INTERNET SOCIETY
URI: http://www.isoc.org/
The Internet Society (ISOC) is a professional membership society with more than 100 organizational and many individual members in over 100 countries. It provides leadership in addressing issues that confront the future of the Internet, and is the organization home for the groups responsible for Internet infrastructure standards, including the *Internet Engineering Task Force (IETF)* and the *Internet Architecture Board (IAB)*.

ITU – INTERNATIONAL TELECOMMUNICATIONS UNION
URI: http://www.itu.int/
The International Telecommunications Union (ITU) is an intergovernmental organization, within which the public and private sectors cooperate for the development of telecommunications. The ITU adopts international regulations and treaties governing all terrestrial and space uses of the frequency spectrum as well as the use of the geostationary-satellite orbit, within which countries adopt their national legislation. It also develops standards to facilitate the interconnection of telecommunication systems on a worldwide scale regardless of the type of technology used. The ITU fosters the development of telecommunications in developing countries, by establishing medium-term development policies and strategies in consultation with other partners in the sector and by providing specialized technical assistance in the areas of telecommunication policies, the choice and transfer of technologies, management, financing of investment projects and mobilization of resources, the installation and maintenance of networks, the management of human resources as well as research and development.

JAR – JAVA ARCHIVE
The Java Archive (JAR) is a platform-independent file format that aggregates many files into one. Multiple Java applets and their requisite

components (class files, images, and sounds) can be bundled in a JAR file and subsequently downloaded to a browser in a single HTTP transaction, improving the download speed. The JAR format also supports compression, which reduces the file size, further improving the download time. In addition, the applet author can digitally sign individual entries in a JAR file to authenticate their origin.

Java

URI: `http://java.sun.com/`

Java is a general-purpose object-oriented programming language. Java is interesting in the context of the web because it is compiled into *Java bytecode*, which is executed on the *Java Virtual Machine (JVM)*. This design makes Java programs platform-independent, and Java *applets*, a special form of Java programs, can be integrated into web documents. Most browsers today contain a JVM and a run-time environment for applets.

JavaScript – JavaScript is a scripting language designed to be used for web pages. Scripts are embedded within web pages, and browsers interpret these scripts after loading the page. JavaScript has a syntax similar to Java, but it is an entirely different and much less powerful language. JavaScript has been the source for the standardization of *ECMAScript*.

JEPI – JOINT ELECTRONIC PAYMENTS INITIATIVE

URI: `http://www.w3.org/ECommerce/`

The Joint Electronic Payments Initiative (JEPI) is a project with a number of industry partners to explore the process that takes place, typically, after shopping and before actual payment begins. This is the point in time where the exact payment instrument (credit card, debit card, electronic check, electronic cash, etc.) must be agreed upon between the browsing client and the merchant server, and then the transaction can take place. With the development of appropriate HTTP extensions like the *Protocol Extension Protocol (PEP)* and the *Universal Payment Preamble (UPP)*, JEPI offers an automatable payment selection process, which allows the coexistence of multiple payment systems.

JFIF – JPEG FILE INTERCHANGE FORMAT

Reference: [93]

JPEG File Interchange Format (JFIF) is the technical name for the file format better known as JPEG. This term is used only when the difference between the JPEG file format and the JPEG image compression algorithm is crucial. Strictly speaking, however, JPEG does not define a file format, and therefore in most cases it would be more precise to speak of JFIF rather than JPEG. Another file format for JPEG is the *Still Picture Interchange File Format (SPIFF)* defined by the JPEG standard itself, but JFIF is much more widespread than SPIFF.

JPEG – JOINT PHOTOGRAPHIC EXPERTS GROUP
Reference: [121, 123, 130]
Joint Photographic Experts Group (JPEG) is the original name of the committee that designed this image compression algorithm. JPEG is designed for compressing either full-color or grayscale digital images of "natural", real-world scenes. It does not work very well on non-realistic images, such as cartoons or line drawings. JPEG does not handle compression of black and white (1 bit per pixel) images or moving pictures. JPEG itself does not describe a file format, it only specifies the compression algorithm. File formats for exchanging images compressed with the JPEG algorithm are the *JPEG File Interchange Format (JFIF)* and the *Still Picture Interchange File Format (SPIFF)*.

JScript
URI: http://microsoft.com/jscript/
Microsoft's JScript scripting language is a superset of the standardized *ECMAScript* scripting language. It is mainly intended to be used as a scripting language on HTML pages.

LDAP – LIGHTWEIGHT DIRECTORY ACCESS PROTOCOL
Reference: [270]
The Lightweight Directory Access Protocol (LDAP) was defined in order to encourage adoption of X.500 directories. The *Directory Access Protocol (DAP)* [139] was regarded as being too complex for simple Internet clients to use. LDAP defines a relatively simple protocol for updating and searching directories running over TCP/IP.

LiveScript – LiveScript is the name Netscape used for the proprietary scripting language built into Navigator 2.0 before it was renamed to *JavaScript* in Navigator 3.0 and later.

LZW – LEMPEL-ZIV-WELCH
Reference: [273]
The Lempel-Ziv-Welch algorithm (LZW) is a data compression algorithm that builds a dictionary of frequently repeated groups of bit patterns on a per-file basis and represents these frequent patterns as shorter bit patterns (using the dictionary). It is a refinement of an algorithm originally developed by Lempel and Ziv [281]. The LZW algorithm is patented by Unisys Corporation and used by the *Graphics Interchange Format (GIF)*.

MAC – MESSAGE AUTHENTICATION CODE

A Message Authentication Code (MAC) is an authentication tag (also called a checksum) derived by application of an authentication scheme, together with a secret key, to a message. MACs are computed and verified with the same key so they can only be verified by the intended receiver, unlike digital signatures. MACs can be derived from various cryptographic techniques and algorithms, such as *SHA*, *MD5*, or *DES*.

MathML – MATHEMATICAL MARKUP LANGUAGE

URI: http://www.w3.org/Math/

Reference: [142]

MathML is an XML application for describing mathematical notation and capturing both its structure and content. The goal of MathML is to enable mathematics to be served, received, and processed on the web, just as HTML has enabled this functionality for text. MathML is not intended for direct use by authors. While MathML is human-readable, in all but the simplest cases, it is too verbose and error-prone for hand generation. Instead, it is anticipated that authors will use equation editors, conversion programs, and other specialized software tools to generate MathML.

MCF – META CONTENT FRAMEWORK

The XML Meta Content Framework (MCF) is a proposal authored by Netscape for the definition of web meta data. The proposal has been used as input for W3C's work on the *Resource Description Framework (RDF)*, which is currently under development by W3C.

MD2, MD4, MD5 – MESSAGE DIGEST 2/4/5

Reference: MD2 [145], MD4 [226], MD5 [227]

The MD algorithms take as input a message of arbitrary length and produces as output a 128-bit "fingerprint" or "message digest" of the input. It is conjectured that it is computationally infeasible to produce two messages having the same message digest, or to produce any message having a given pre-specified target message digest. The MD algorithms are intended for digital signature applications, where a large file must be "compressed" in a secure manner before being encrypted with a private (secret) key under a public key cryptosystem such as RSA. While the structures of the MD algorithms are somewhat similar, the design of MD2 is quite different from that of MD4 and MD5, and MD2 is optimized for 8-bit machines, whereas MD4 and MD5 are aimed at 32-bit machines. It has been shown how collisions for the full version of MD4 can be found in under a minute on a typical PC. Therefore, MD4 should now be considered broken.

meta data – Meta data simply is data about data. Since the term "data" is general in the sense that it may also be meta data, there is no such thing as meta meta data. The *Resource Description Framework (RDF)*, which is currently under development by W3C is an attempt to define a general and machine understandable format for web meta data. The benefits of machine understandable meta data are more powerful ways of information search and retrieval.

MIDI – MUSICAL INSTRUMENT DIGITAL INTERFACE
URI: http://www.midi.org/
Reference: [173]
The Musical Instrument Digital Interface (MIDI) enables people to use multimedia computers and electronic musical instruments. There are actually three components to MIDI, which are the communications *Protocol* (language), the *Connector* (hardware interface) and a distribution format called *Standard MIDI Files*. In the context of the web, the most interesting component is the file format. In principle, MIDI files contain sequences of MIDI protocol messages. However, when MIDI protocol messages are stored in MIDI files, the events are also time-stamped for playback in the proper sequence. Music delivered by MIDI files is the most common use of MIDI today.

MIME – MULTIPURPOSE INTERNET MAIL EXTENSIONS
Reference: [79, 80, 81, 82, 183]
The Multipurpose Internet Mail Extensions (MIME) provide facilities to allow multiple objects in a single Internet mail message, to represent body text in character sets other than ASCII, to represent formatted multi-font text messages, to represent non-textual material such as images and audio fragments, and generally to facilitate later extensions defining new types of Internet mail for use by cooperating mail agents.

MNG – MULTIPLE-IMAGE NETWORK GRAPHICS
The Multiple-image Network Graphics (MNG) format is a proposed addition to the *Portable Network Graphics (PNG)* format for storing and transmitting multiple-image animations and composite frames. This would make it possible to create animations based on PNG, which are designed to replace *Graphics Interchange Format (GIF)* animations.

MOSS – MIME OBJECT SECURITY SERVICES
Reference: [55]
MIME Object Security Services (MOSS) is a protocol that uses the multipart/signed and multipart/encrypted framework defined in Internet proposed standard RFC 1847 [85] to apply digital signature and encryption

services to MIME objects. The services are offered through the use of end-to-end cryptography between an originator and a recipient at the application layer. Asymmetric (public key) cryptography is used in support of the digital signature service and encryption key management. Symmetric (secret key) cryptography is used in support of the encryption service. The procedures are intended to be compatible with a wide range of public key management approaches, including both ad hoc and certificate-based schemes. Mechanisms are provided to support many public key management approaches.

Mozilla

URI: http://www.mozilla.org/

In March 1998, Netscape decided that the Communicator product (including the Navigator web browser) would be available free of charge, and that the source code would also be available free of charge. The idea behind this decision is to encourage the public to take part in the development of Navigator (which has the nickname of Mozilla). Hopefully, this will result in more functionality and availability for more platforms than could be provided by Netscape alone. The Mozilla organization is hosted by Netscape and tries to coordinate the efforts by managing the source code and maintaining a list of what should be implemented in the future.

MPEG – MOVING PICTURES EXPERTS GROUP

URI: http://drogo.cselt.stet.it/mpeg/

Reference: MPEG-1 [116], MPEG-2 [125], MPEG-4 [136]

The Moving Picture Experts Group (MPEG) is a working group of ISO/IEC in charge of the development of international standards for compression, decompression, processing, and coded representation of moving pictures, audio, and their combination. So far, MPEG has produced MPEG-1 (the standard for storage and retrieval of moving pictures and audio on storage media), MPEG-2 (the standard for digital television), and is now developing MPEG-4 (the standard for multimedia applications). Although the term MPEG-3 is in frequent use, there is no MPEG-3 standard, the term refers to the audio coding layer 3 of the MPEG-1 and MPEG-2 standards.

NIST – NATIONAL INSTITUTE OF STANDARDS AND TECHNOLOGY

URI: http://www.nist.gov/

The National Institute of Standards and Technology (NIST) is a division of the US Department of Commerce, it was formerly known as the *National Bureau of Standards (NBS)*. Through its *Computer Systems Laboratory* it aims to promote open systems and interoperability that will spur development of computer-based economic activity. NIST issues standards and guidelines that it hopes will be adopted by all computer systems in the US, and also sponsors workshops and seminars. Official standards are published as *Federal Information Processing Standards (FIPS)*.

NNTP – Network News Transfer Protocol
Reference: [146]
The Network News Transfer Protocol (NNTP) specifies a protocol for the distribution, inquiry, retrieval, and posting of Usenet news articles using a reliable stream-based transmission of news among the Internet community. NNTP is designed so that news articles are stored in a central database allowing a subscriber to select only those items he wishes to read. Indexing, cross-referencing, and expiration of aged messages are also provided.

nonce – A randomly generated value used to defeat "playback" attacks in communication protocols. One party randomly generates a nonce and sends it to the other party. The receiver encrypts it using the agreed upon secret key and returns it to the sender. Since the nonce was randomly generated by the sender, this defeats playback attacks because the replayer can not know in advance the nonce the sender will generate. The receiver denies connections that do not have the correctly encrypted nonce.

NTP – Network Time Protocol
Reference: [175]
The Network Time Protocol (NTP) provides the mechanisms to synchronize time and coordinate time distribution in a large, diverse internet operating at rates from mundane to light-wave. It uses a returnable-time design in which a distributed subnet of time servers operating in a self- organizing, hierarchical-master-slave configuration synchronizes local clocks within the subnet and to national time standards via wire or radio. The servers can also redistribute reference time via local routing algorithms and time servers.

OLE – Object Linking and Embedding
Object Linking and Embedding (OLE) is a compound document standard developed by Microsoft. OLE makes it possible to create objects with one application and link or embed them in a second application. Embedded objects retain their original format and links to the application that created them. Support for OLE is built into the Windows and Macintosh operating systems. A competing compound document standard developed mainly by IBM and Apple is called *OpenDoc*.

OMG – OBJECT MANAGEMENT GROUP

URI: `http://www.omg.org/`

Established in 1989, the Object Management Group (OMG) promotes the theory and practice of object technology for the development of distributed computing systems. The goal is to provide a common architectural framework for object oriented applications based on widely available interface specifications. OMG has a membership of over 800 software vendors, software developers, and end users. The *Common Object Request Broker Architecture (CORBA)* is standardized by the OMG.

OpenDoc

URI: `http://www.opendoc.apple.com/`

OpenDoc is an open, multi-platform architecture for component software developed mainly by Apple and IBM. It is a standard as well as an application programming interface that makes it possible to design independent programs (components) that can work together on a single document. In favor of Java technology, Apple recently announced its plans to reduce its investment in OpenDoc technologies. The competing product to OpenDoc is *Object Linking and Embedding (OLE)* created by Microsoft.

OpenType

URI: `http://www.microsoft.com/typography/OTSPEC/`

The OpenType font format is an extension of the *TrueType* font format, adding support for *Type 1* font data. The OpenType font format was developed jointly by Microsoft and Adobe. As with TrueType fonts, OpenType fonts allow the handling of large glyph sets using *Unicode* encoding. Such encoding allows broad international support, as well as support for typographic glyph variants. Additionally, OpenType fonts may contain digital signatures, allowing operating systems and browsing applications to identify the source and integrity of font files, including embedded font files obtained in web documents, before using them. Also, font developers can encode embedding restrictions in OpenType fonts, and these restrictions cannot be altered in a font signed by the developer.

ORB – OBJECT REQUEST BROKER

The Object Request Broker (ORB) is the key component of the *Common Object Request Broker Architecture (CORBA)* programming model. An ORB is responsible for transferring operations from clients to servers. This requires the ORB to locate a server implementation (and possibly activate it), transmit the operation and its parameters, and finally return the results back to the client.

OSD – OPEN SOFTWARE DESCRIPTION

Microsoft's Open Software Description (OSD) format provides a standard way for describing software packages and dependencies. OSD gives vendors a format for listing the packages which make up a software component. OSD is based on the *Extensible Markup Language (XML)* and is best suited for vendors whose components are used as enabling technologies for other software products.

OSI – OPEN SYSTEMS INTERCONNECTION

Reference: [120]

Open Systems Interconnection (OSI) data communication standards belong to the *Application Layer (Layer 7)* of the ISO OSI *Basic Reference Model*. The application layer is specified in terms of *application contexts* and using building blocks called *Application Service Elements (ASEs)*. It resides above the *Presentation Layer (Layer 6)*, which identifies alternative encodings, and the *Session Layer (Layer 5)*, providing dialogue control. Collectively, the three layers provide application services, and are commonly referred to as the *upper layers*. The lower layers of the OSI stack are *Transport (Layer 4)*, *Network (Layer 3)*, *Link (Layer 2)* and *Physical (Layer 1)*.

P3P – PLATFORM FOR PRIVACY PREFERENCES PROJECT

URI: http://www.w3.org/P3P/

Reference: [167]

The goal of the Platform for Privacy Preferences Project (P3P) is to deal with the constant struggle between the need for web content providers to gain information about their readership and the need for these individuals to control the release of this information to others. P3 addresses the twin goals of meeting the data privacy expectations of consumers on the web while assuring that the medium remains available and productive for electronic commerce. Following the principle of providing consumers notice of site privacy polices, and allowing users to express and act upon their privacy preferences in a flexible manner, one goal enhances the success of the other.

PDF – PORTABLE DOCUMENT FORMAT

Reference: PDF 1.0 [22], PDF 1.2 [23]

The Portable Document Format (PDF) is a file format for representing documents in a manner that is independent of the original application software, hardware, and operating system used to create those documents. A PDF file can describe documents containing any combination of text, graphics, and images in a device-independent and resolution independent format. The advantage of PDF over *PostScript* is the better accessibility of text within PDF files, which can still be searched for text and can also contain structural information like a table of contents.

PEM – PRIVACY ENHANCED MAIL
Reference: [161]
Privacy Enhanced Mail (PEM) is a standard to provide secure electronic mail over the Internet. PEM includes encryption, authentication, and key management, and allows use of both public key and secret key cryptosystems. Multiple cryptographic tools are supported. For each mail message, the specific encryption algorithm, digital signature algorithm, hash function, and so on are specified in the header. PEM explicitly supports only a few cryptographic algorithms, others may be added later. DES in CBC mode is currently the only message encryption algorithm supported, and both RSA and DES are supported for key management.

PEP – PROTOCOL EXTENSION PROTOCOL
URI: http://www.w3.org/Protocols/PEP/
Reference: [84]
HTTP is being used for an increasing number of applications involving distributed authoring, collaboration, printing, and various *Remote Procedure Call (RPC)* like protocols. The Protocol Extension Protocol (PEP) is an extension mechanism for HTTP designed to address the tension between private agreement and public specification, and to accommodate extension of HTTP clients and servers by software components.

Perl – PRACTICAL EXTRACTION AND REPORT LANGUAGE
URI: http://www.perl.com/, http://www.perl.org/
Reference: [271]
The Practical Extraction and Report Language (Perl) is a general purpose interpreted language, often used for scanning text and printing formatted reports. It provides extensive support for regular expression matching, dynamically scoped variables and functions, extensible run-time libraries, exception handling, and packages. Perl is frequently used for programming *Common Gateway Interface (CGI)* applications.

persistent connections – Persistent connections are a mechanism to make HTTP work more efficiently. Rather than using a connection only for one request/response interaction between a client and a server, the model of persistent connections makes it possible to send many requests over one connection. This significantly reduces the overhead of opening and closing an individual connection for each request/response interaction. It is especially useful because in many cases clients retrieve multiple resources (such as all embedded images in a web page) from one server when loading a web page.

PFR – PORTABLE FONT RESOURCE

TrueDoc's Portable Font Resource (PFR) is a compact, platform independent representation of the glyphs necessary to render one or more documents. The outlines in the PFR are fully scalable, and can be played back at any size, and on any resolution device. It is created by the *Character Shape Recorder (CSR)* and displayed using the *Character Shape Player (CSP)*.

PGML – PRECISION GRAPHICS MARKUP LANGUAGE

Reference: [4]

The Precision Graphics Markup Language (PGML) is a 2D graphics language meant to satisfy both the web's scalable lightweight vector graphics needs and the precision needs of graphic artists who want to ensure that their graphic designs appear on end user systems with precisely the correct fonts, color, layout and compositing that they desire. PGML uses the imaging model of to the *PostScript* language.

PGP – PRETTY GOOD PRIVACY

URI: http://www.pgp.com/

Pretty Good Privacy (PGP) is a software package originally developed by Phil Zimmerman, providing cryptographic routines for email and file storage applications. Zimmerman took existing cryptosystems and cryptographic protocols and developed a freeware program that can run on multiple platforms. It provides message encryption, digital signatures, data compression, and email compatibility. The algorithms used for message encryption are *RSA* for key transport and the *International Data Encryption Algorithm (IDEA)* for bulk encryption of messages. Digital signatures are achieved by the use of *RSA* for signing and *MD5* for computing the message digest. The freeware program *zip* is used to compress messages for transmission and storage. Email compatibility is achieved by the use of Radix-64 conversion.

PHP – HYPERTEXT PREPROCESSOR

URI: http://php.net/

PHP is an HTML-embedded scripting language. Much of its syntax is borrowed from C, Java, and Perl, with the addition of a couple of unique PHP-specific features. The goal of the language is to allow web developers to write dynamically generated pages quickly. PHP is either executed as a *Common Gateway Interface (CGI)* script, or it is integrated into web server software, for example as an *Apache* module.

P-HTTP – PERSISTENT HTTP

   Reference: [180]

   Persistent HTTP (P-HTTP) refers to a variant of HTTP which does not
   close the connection between the client and the server after a single re-
   quest/response interaction. This saves the overhead of multiple open and
   close connection operations when issuing multiple requests to the same
   server. HTTP/1.1 implements persistent connections, it therefore is one
   way to implement P-HTTP. The term P-HTTP was mainly used during
   the discussion phase which turned up after the performance problems of
   HTTP/1.0 became so apparent that it became clear that something had
   to be done in the next version of HTTP.

PICS – PLATFORM FOR INTERNET CONTENT SELECTION

   URI: http://www.w3.org/PICS/

   Reference: [151, 174, 215]

   The Platform for Internet Content Selection (PICS) is a pair of protocols, allowing labels to be applied to Internet content. These protocols
   empower any individual or organization to design and distribute labels
   reflecting their views about the content. PICS was pioneered by W3C as
   a practical alternative to global governmental censorship of the Internet.
   In addition, the same technology facilitates searching the web and provides a foundation for establishing trust in information on the web. PICS
   label are rather limited in their expressiveness. A new version of PICS
   will be based on the *Resource Description Framework (RDF)*, facilitating
   more complex labeling of resources.

pipelining – Pipelining is an HTTP mechanism which further enhances the
   efficiency of persistent connections. Pipelining is used to eliminate the
   need for a client to wait for a server's response. Without pipelining, a
   client has to wait for the response to a request before it can send the next
   request over a persistent connection. With pipelining, a client simply sends
   all or a number of requests and waits for the responses from the server.

PKCS – PUBLIC KEY CRYPTOGRAPHY STANDARDS

   URI: http://www.rsa.com/rsalabs/pubs/PKCS/

   RSA Laboratories' Public Key Cryptography Standards (PKCS), the in-
   formal inter-vendor standards, were developed in 1991 by RSA Laboratories with representatives of Apple, Digital, Lotus, Microsoft, MIT, North-
   ern Telecom, Novell and Sun. Since its publication in June 1991, PKCS has
   become a part of several standards and products. These standards cover
   RSA encryption, *Diffie-Hellman* key agreement, password-based encryption, extended-certificate syntax, cryptographic message syntax, private

key information syntax, and certification request syntax, as well as selected attributes.

PNG – PORTABLE NETWORK GRAPHICS
URI: `ftp://ftp.uu.net/graphics/png/`
Reference: [26, 27]
Portable Network Graphics (PNG) is an extensible file format for the lossless, portable, well-compressed storage of raster images. PNG provides a patent-free replacement for the *Graphics Interchange Format (GIF)* and can also replace many common uses of the *Tag Image File Format (TIFF)*. Indexed-color, grayscale, and truecolor images are supported, plus an optional alpha channel. Sample depths range from 1 to 16 bits. PNG is designed to work well in online viewing applications, such as the web, and so it is fully streamable with a progressive display option. PNG is robust, providing both full file integrity checking and simple detection of common transmission errors. Also, PNG can store gamma and chromaticity data for improved color matching on heterogeneous platforms.

POP – POST OFFICE PROTOCOL
Reference: [187]
The Post Office Protocol (POP) allows a client computer to retrieve electronic mail from a POP server. It does not provide for sending mail, which is assumed to be done via the *Simple Mail Transfer Protocol (SMTP)* or some other method. POP is useful for computers without a permanent network connection which therefore require a "post office" (the POP server) to hold their mail until they can retrieve it. POP is older and less powerful than the *Internet Message Access Protocol (IMAP)*, which is used for the same application area.

PostScript
Reference: PostScript 2 [2], PostScript 3 [3]
PostScript is an interpreted, stack-based language. Its primary application is to describe the appearance of text, graphical shapes and sampled images on printed or displayed pages. A program in PostScript can communicate a document description from a composition system to a printing system in a device-independent way. PostScript is an unusually powerful printer language because it is a full programming language, rather than a series of low-level escape sequences. The latest version of PostScript, version 3, fully integrates the *Portable Document Format (PDF)*.

PPP – Point to Point Protocol

Reference: [243]

The Point-to-Point Protocol is designed for simple links which transport packets between two peers. These links provide full-duplex simultaneous bi-directional operation, and are assumed to deliver packets in order. Although PPP is not tied to a particular type of packets it transports, its most common use is the encapsulation of IP packages over modem lines. Basically, PPP is similar to the *Serial Line Internet Protocol (SLIP)*, but it has the advantages of not being limited to one type of protocol it can transport, a configuration negotiation phase at the start of a connection (for determining connection configuration parameters automatically), and the possibility to use standardized authentication procedures for automated login. The two authentication schemes supported by PPP are the *Password Authentication Protocol (PAP)* defined in Internet proposed standard RFC 1334 [162], and the *Challenge Handshake Authentication Protocol (CHAP)*, defined in Internet draft standard RFC 1994 [244].

proxy – In the context of HTTP, a proxy is an intermediary program which acts as both a server and a client, receiving a request and then acting as a client and making requests on behalf of other clients. However, requests to a proxy can also be serviced internally, for example if the proxy uses its cache instead of sending a request to the origin server. The client's request is explicitly addressed to the proxy, which then sends a request to the origin server.

public key encryption – Public key encryption is a technique that leverages asymmetric ciphers. A public key system consists of two keys: a public key and a private key. Messages encrypted with the public key can only be decrypted with the associated private key. Conversely, messages encrypted with the private key can only be decrypted with the public key. Public key encryption tends to be extremely compute intensive and so is not suitable as a bulk cipher.

PURL – Persistent URL

URI: http://purl.oclc.org/

Reference: [241]

A Persistent Uniform Resource Locator (PURL) is a special form of URL which is intended to have a longer lifetime than a normal URL. Functionally, a PURL is a URL. However, instead of pointing directly to the location of an Internet resource, a PURL points to an intermediate resolution service. The PURL resolution service associates the PURL with the actual URL and returns that URL to the client. The client can complete the URL transaction in the normal fashion. This is done by using a standard HTTP redirect response.

Python
URI: http://www.python.org/
Reference: [164]
Python is an interpreted, interactive, object-oriented programming language. The language has a concise syntax; a small number of powerful high-level data types are built in. Python can be extended in a systematic fashion by adding new modules implemented in a compiled language such as C or C++. Such extension modules can define new functions and variables as well as new object types. Python is frequently used for programming *Common Gateway Interface (CGI)* applications.

QuickTime
URI: http://www.apple.com/quicktime/
QuickTime is Apple's architecture for handling multimedia data. First versions of QuickTime were basically a file format for audio and video, newer version integrate more media types, including support for 3D and virtual reality. Being a proprietary technology, QuickTime can be compared to Microsoft's *Audio Video Interleave (AVI)* format and the *MPEG* video standards.

RC2, RC4, RC5 – RIVEST'S CIPHER 2/4/5
URI: http://www.rsa.com/
The RC2 and RC4 algorithms are confidential and proprietary to RSA Data Security. RC2 is a variable key-size block cipher, it can be made more secure or less secure than DES against exhaustive key search by using appropriate key sizes. It has a block size of 64 bits and is about two to three times faster than the *Data Encryption Standard (DES)* in software. RC4 is a variable key-size stream cipher, it can be expected to run very quickly in software. RC5, a fast block cipher, has been published by Rivest [228] (it will be patented by RSA Laboratories), it is a parameterized algorithm with a variable block size, a variable key size, and a variable number of rounds.

RDF – RESOURCE DESCRIPTION FRAMEWORK
URI: http://www.w3.org/RDF/
Reference: [37, 157]
The Resource Description Framework (RDF) is a specification currently under development within the W3C metadata activity. RDF is designed to provide an infrastructure supporting meta data across many web-based activities. RDF is the result of a number of meta data communities bring-

ing together their needs to provide a robust and flexible architecture for supporting meta data on the Internet and the web. Example applications include site maps, content ratings, stream channel definitions, search engine data collection (web crawling), digital library collections, and distributed authoring. RDF allows different application communities to define the meta data property set that best serves the needs of each community. RDF provides a uniform and interoperable means to exchange the meta data between programs and across the web. Furthermore, RDF provides a means for publishing both a human-readable and a machine-understandable definition of the property set itself. RDF uses the *Extensible Markup Language (XML)* as the transfer syntax in order to leverage other tools and code bases being built around XML.

RDS – RESOLVER DISCOVERY SERVICE
Reference: [60, 245]
A Resolver Discovery Service (RDS) is a service to help in the learning about *Uniform Resource Name (URN)* resolvers. An RDS helps in finding a resolver to contact for further resolution of URNs. Some RDS designs may also incorporate resolver functionality.

revalidation $\longrightarrow$ validation

RFC – REQUEST FOR COMMENT
Reference: [44]
RFCs form a series of publications of networking technical documents, started in 1969 as part of the original DARPA wide-area networking (ARPANET) project. RFCs cover a wide range of topics, from early discussion of new research concepts to status memos about the Internet. The *Internet Architecture Board (IAB)* views the RFC publication process to be sufficiently important to warrant including the RFC editor in the IAB membership. The status of specifications on the Internet standards track is summarized periodically in a summary RFC entitled "Internet Official Protocol Standards" (the most recent version is Internet historic RFC 2300 [214]). This RFC shows the level of maturity and other helpful information for each Internet protocol or service specification. The "Internet Official Protocol Standards" RFC is the authoritative statement of the status of any particular Internet specification, and it is the "Publication of Record" with respect to Internet standardization.

RMA – REALMEDIA ARCHITECTURE
URI: http://www.real.com/
The RealMedia Architecture (RMA) defined by RealNetworks is the de-facto standard for streaming media on the web. RMA defines a

client/server architecture, where a client connects to a media server for receiving a continuous stream of data. *RealAudio*, *RealVideo*, and *RealPlayer* (combining audio and video) are products using RMA. RMA is based the *Real Time Streaming Protocol (RTSP)* as the control protocol, and a proprietary protocol (RDP) or the *Real Time Protocol (RTP)* as packet protocol. The newest version of RealPlayer supports the *Synchronized Multimedia Integration Language (SMIL)*.

RMI – REMOTE METHOD INVOCATION
URI: http://java.sun.com/products/jdk/rmi/
Remote Method Invocation (RMI) enables the programmer to create distributed Java-to-Java applications, in which the methods of remote Java objects can be invoked from another *Java Virtual machine (JVM)*, possibly on a different host. A Java program can make a call on a remote object once it obtains a reference to the remote object, either by looking up the remote object in the bootstrap naming service provided by RMI, or by receiving the reference as an argument or a return value. A client can call a remote object in a server, and that server can also be a client of other remote objects. RMI uses object serialization to marshal and unmarshal parameters and does not truncate types, supporting true object-oriented polymorphism.

robot $\longrightarrow$ search engine

RSA – RIVEST, SHAMIR, AND ADLEMAN
URI: http://www.rsa.com/
Reference: [229, 233]
RSA is a public key cryptosystem for both encryption and authentication (its name is derived from the surnames of the three inventors, Rivest, Shamir, and Adleman). For encryption, RSA is combined with a secret key cryptosystem, such as the *Data Encryption Standard (DES)*, to encrypt a message by means of an RSA digital envelope. For authentication, RSA is usually combined with a hash function, such as *MD5*, to sign a message.

RTCP – REAL TIME CONTROL PROTOCOL
Reference: [237]
The Real Time Control Protocol (RTCP) is the control protocol that works in conjunction with RTP. RTCP control packets are periodically transmitted by each participant in an RTP session to all other participants. Feedback of information to the application can be used to control performance and for diagnostic purposes.

RTP – REAL TIME PROTOCOL
Reference: [237]
The Real Time Protocol (RTP) provides end-to-end network transport functions suitable for applications transmitting real-time data, such as audio, video, or simulation data, over multicast or unicast network services. RTP does not address resource reservation and does not guarantee quality-of-service for real-time services. The data transport is augmented by a control protocol (RTCP) to allow monitoring of the data delivery in a manner scalable to large multicast networks, and to provide minimal control and identification functionality. RTP and RTCP are designed to be independent of the underlying transport and network layers.

RTSP – REAL TIME STREAMING PROTOCOL
Reference: [238]
The Real Time Streaming Protocol (RTSP) is an application-level protocol for control over the delivery of data with real-time properties. RTSP provides an extensible framework to enable controlled, on-demand delivery of real-time data, such as audio and video. Sources of data can include both live data feeds and stored clips. This protocol is intended to control multiple data delivery sessions, provide a means for choosing delivery channels such as UDP, multicast UDP and TCP, and use delivery mechanisms based upon RTP.

SDQL – STANDARD DOCUMENT QUERY LANGUAGE
Reference: [127]
The Standard Document Query Language (SDQL) is part of the *Document Style Semantics and Specification Language (DSSSL)* standard. SDQL allows queries and navigation in a document's tree representation.

search engine
URI: http://searchenginewatch.com/
A search engine is a program that automatically traverses the web's hypermedia structure by recursively retrieving documents based on hyperlinks that are found within these documents. It is important to notice that this does not limit the definition to any specific traversal algorithm. Even if a search engine applies some heuristic to the selection and order of documents to visit and spaces out requests over a long space of time, it still is a search engine. Normal web browsers are not search engines, because the are operated by a human, and do not automatically retrieve referenced documents (other than inline images). Web search engines are sometimes referred to as robots, wanderers, crawlers, or spiders. These names are a bit misleading as they give the impression the software itself moves bet-

ween sites like a virus. This not the case, a search engine simply visits sites by requesting documents from them.

semantic transparency – A cache is said to behave semantically transparent if the use of the cache does nothing but improve performance when a request for an entity which is stored by the cache is served by the cache rather than the origin server. Neither the requesting server nor the origin server should notice any difference in the overall behavior of the system, except for connection dependent data of the request, such as header fields which are used to trace the request. Semantic transparency can only be achieved efficiently if the origin server is capable to communicate certain attributes of a resource (for example its expected duration of validity) to a cache.

semantics – While the syntax of a language defines how sentences of a language can be put together, the semantics define the meaning of the sentences. This is much harder to define formally than the syntax, so normally, the syntax of a specific data format (for example the messages of a protocol such as HTTP) is defined formally, while the semantics are defined in plain text. This often introduces problems of ambiguity and interpretation, but it still is the most widely adopted technique of specifying semantics.

server – Generally speaking, a server as understood in the client/server paradigm is a program waiting for requests from a client. The server provides a service which can be used by calling the server using the appropriate access protocol. In case of the web, a web server provides the service of accepting HTTP requests and generating responses, usually including information resources maintained or cached by the server.

servlet – Java servlets are modules that extend request/response-oriented servers, such as Java-enabled web servers. Servlets are to servers what applets are to browsers. Unlike applets, however, servlets have no graphical user interface. Servlets can be embedded in many different servers because the servlet API, which is used to write servlets, assumes nothing about the server's environment or protocol.

SET – SECURE ELECTRONIC TRANSACTIONS
Reference: [239]
URI: http://www.setco.org/
The Secure Electronic Transactions (SET) standard is an industry-wide protocol designed to safely transmit sensitive personal and financial information over public networks. The SET protocol contains state-of-the-art cryptographic technology that provides on-line transaction security that

is equivalent or superior to the safeguards in present physical, mail and telephone card transactions. The *RSA Public Key Cryptography Standards (PKCS)* is the set of public-key algorithms used in SET. The symmetric key algorithm is *Data Encryption Standard (DES)*.

SGML – Standard Generalized Markup Language
Reference: [88, 110]
SGML provides an object-oriented method for describing documents (and other information objects with appropriate characteristics). The standard defines a set of semantics for describing document structures, and an abstract syntax of formally coding document type definitions. Apart from defining a default (concrete) syntax (based on the ISO 646 [113] code set) that can be used for text and markup identification when no alternative is specified, SGML does not suggest any particular way in which documents should be structured but allows users to define the structure they require for document capture or presentation. Each SGML document starts with a *Document Type Definition (DTD)* or a pointer to an externally stored DTD. Externally stored files, which can contain either SGML coded data or non-SGML data (coded in a declared notation) can be referenced using public identifiers conforming to the rules for *Public Text Object Identifiers* specified in ISO 9070 [114].

SHA – Secure Hash Algorithm $\longrightarrow$ SHS

SHS – Secure Hash Standard
Reference: [190, 191]
The Secure Hash Standard (SHA), the standard that specifies the *Secure Hash Algorithm (SHA)*, was published by NIST. SHA takes a message of less than 2^{64} bits in length and produces a 160-bit message digest. The algorithm is slightly slower than *MD5*, but the larger message digest makes it more secure against brute-force collision and inversion attacks.

S-HTTP – Secure Hypertext Transfer Protocol
Reference: [223]
Secure HTTP (S-HTTP) is an extension of HTTP providing independently applicable security services for transaction confidentiality, authenticity/integrity and non-repudiability of origin. The protocol emphasizes maximum flexibility in choice of key management mechanisms, security policies and cryptographic algorithms by supporting option negotiation between parties for each transaction. Message protection can be provided on three orthogonal axes: signature, authentication, and encryption. Any message may be signed, authenticated, encrypted, or any combination of these (including no protection). Several cryptographic message format

standards may be incorporated into S-HTTP clients and servers, particularly, but in principle not limited to, *PKCS-7* and *Privacy Enhanced Mail (PEM)*. S-HTTP aware clients can communicate with S-HTTP oblivious servers and vice-versa. Cryptographic algorithms supported by S-HTTP include DES, two-key and three-key triple-DES, DESX, IDEA, RC2, and CDMF.

SLIP – SERIAL LINE INTERNET PROTOCOL
Reference: [230]
The Serial Line Internet Protocol (SLIP) is a packet framing protocol, it defines a sequence of characters that frame IP packets on a serial line. It provides no addressing, packet type identification, error detection/correction or compression mechanisms. It is used for the same purpose as the *Point to Point Protocol (PPP)*, which is the encapsulation of IP packages over modem lines. SLIP does not have PPP's configuration negotiation or authentication schemes, which can make the configuration of SLIP connections more complicated.

SMIL – SYNCHRONIZED MULTIMEDIA INTEGRATION LANGUAGE
URI: http://www.w3.org/AudioVideo/
Reference: [100]
The Synchronized Multimedia Integration Language (SMIL) allows a set of independent multimedia objects to be integrated to form a synchronized multimedia presentation. Using SMIL, presentations such as a slide show synchronized with audio commentary, or a video synchronized with a text stream, can be described. SMIL has been designed so that it is possible to author simple presentations with a text editor. The key to success for HTML was that attractive hypertext content could be created without requiring sophisticated authoring tools. SMIL achieves the same for synchronized hypermedia. SMIL documents are well-formed *Extensible Markup Language (XML)* documents.

S/MIME – SECURE MIME
URI: http://www.rsa.com/smime/
Reference: [69, 68]
S/MIME is a specification for secure electronic mail and was designed to add security to email messages in *Multipurpose Internet Mail Extensions (MIME)* format. The security services offered are authentication (using digital signatures) and privacy (using encryption). S/MIME uses a hybrid approach to providing security, often referred to as a "digital envelope". The bulk message encryption is done with a symmetric cipher, and a public key algorithm is used for key exchange. A public key algorithm is also used for digital signatures. S/MIME recommends three symmetric en-

cryption algorithms: DES, Triple-DES, and RC2. The adjustable key-size of the RC2 algorithm makes it especially useful for applications intended for export outside the US. RSA is the required public key algorithm.

SMTP – SIMPLE MAIL TRANSFER PROTOCOL
Reference: [211]
The Simple Mail Transfer Protocol (SMTP) is used to pass electronic mail messages between Internet servers. Each message has a standardized header that is used to identify email address(es) of the person(s) the message is to be sent to, the email address and name of the sender (to whom responses can be sent automatically), and details of those nodes on the network through which the message passed. A number of extensions to SMTP have been defined using the *Extended Simple Mail Transfer Protocol (ESMTP)*, which is mostly in use today.

SMUX – SESSION MULTIPLEXING PROTOCOL
URI: `http://www.w3.org/Protocols/MUX/`
The Session Multiplexing Protocol (SMUX, formerly called MUX) is a session management protocol separating the underlying transport from the upper level application protocols. It provides a lightweight communication channel to the application layer by multiplexing data streams on top of a reliable stream oriented transport. By supporting coexistence of multiple application level protocols (eg, HTTP and HTTP-ng), SMUX will ease transitions to future web protocols, and communications of client applets using private protocols with servers over the same transport connection as the HTTP conversation.

SPDL – STANDARD PAGE DESCRIPTION LANGUAGE
Reference: [124]
The Standard Page Description Language (SPDL) has its origins in the goal to provide a complete set of standard interchange languages for all stages of the traditional publishing process. The *Standard Generalized Markup Language (SGML)* provides the language used in interchange at the authoring and editorial stages. The *Document Style Semantics and Specification Language (DSSSL)* provides the language for specifying to the typesetter (formatter) how the document is to be composed and presented. SPDL provides the language that enables the style and layout decisions of the formatter to be realized on a variety of imaging surfaces (screen, paper, film, etc.). The SPDL standard is effectively an international reference version of *PostScript*.

SPEC – STANDARD PERFORMANCE EVALUATION CORPORATION
URI: http://www.specbench.org/
The Standard Performance Evaluation Corporation (SPEC) was founded in 1988 by a small number of workstation vendors. SPEC has grown to become one of the more successful performance standardization bodies with more than 40 member companies. SPEC publishes several hundred different performance results each quarter spanning across a variety of system performance disciplines. The goal of SPEC is to ensure that the marketplace has a fair and useful set of metrics to differentiate candidate systems. The path chosen is an attempt to balance between requiring strict compliance and allowing vendors to demonstrate their advantages.

SPECweb96 – SPEC PERFORMANCE TEST FOR HTTP SERVERS
URI: http://www.specbench.org/osg/web96/
SPECweb96 a standardized benchmark for comparing web server performance. The benchmark is designed to provide comparable measures of how well systems can handle HTTP GET requests. SPEC based the workload upon analysis of server logs from web sites ranging from a small personal server up through some of the web's most popular servers.

spider $\longrightarrow$ search engine

SPIFF – STILL PICTURE INTERCHANGE FILE FORMAT
Reference: [131]
The Still Picture Interchange File Format (SPIFF) is the "official" file format for images using the *Joint Photographic Experts Group (JPEG)* image compression algorithm. Part 3 of the JPEG standard includes a fully defined file format for storing JPEG data. When the JPEG format was first standardized, disagreements among ISO committees prevented a standard JPEG file format from being created. The de-facto format that appeared was the *JPEG File Interchange Format (JFIF)* from C-cube Microsystems. The JFIF format, although now widespread, is very limited in capability as file formats go. SPIFF is intended to replace the JFIF file format, adding features (more color spaces, a recognized way of including text blocks, and so forth), and providing a backwards-compatibility allowing SPIFF files to be read by most JPEG/JFIF decoders. JFIF, however, has a five-year head start on SPIFF, so the likelihood of it being completely replaced anytime soon is not good.

sRGB – STANDARD RGB
Reference: [109]
The aim of the Standard RGB (sRGB) color space is to complement the current color management strategies by enabling a third method of

handling color in operating systems, device drivers and the Internet that utilizes a simple and robust device independent color definition. This will provide good quality and backward compatibility with minimum transmission and system overhead. Based on a calibrated colorimetric RGB color space well suited to cathode ray tube (CRT) monitors, television, scanners, digital cameras, and printing systems, such a space can be supported with minimum cost to software and hardware vendors.

SSI – SERVER-SIDE INCLUDES
Server-Side Includes (SSI) make it possible to include information into web pages before delivering them to a client. A web page using SSI contains special instructions which are interpreted by the server whenever the web page is requested. These instructions may specify to include other documents (eg, document headers or footers) or to insert dynamic information, such as the current date or an access count. There is no standard for SSI, so each server implementation uses its own syntax and functionality.

SSL – SECURE SOCKETS LAYER
URI: http://home.netscape.com/newsref/std/SSL.html
Reference: [83]
The primary goal of the Secure Sockets Layer (SSL) protocol is to provide privacy and reliability between two communicating applications. The protocol is composed of two layers. At the lower level, layered on top of some reliable transport protocol, for example the *Transmission Control Protocol (TCP)*, is the *SSL Record Protocol*. The SSL Record Protocol is used for encapsulation of various higher level protocols. One such encapsulated protocol, the *SSL Handshake Protocol*, allows the server and client to authenticate each other and to negotiate an encryption algorithm and cryptographic keys before the application protocol transmits or receives its first byte of data. One advantage of SSL is that it is application protocol independent. A higher level protocol can layer on top of SSL transparently. For Internet applications, a variant of SSL called *Transport Layer Security (TLS)* is currently being developed.

syntax – A syntax is a definition of how to create valid sentences of a language. Usually, a syntax is defined by a set of symbols (the legal words of a language) and a set of rules how these symbols can be combined to form legal sentences. This set of rules is called the grammar of the language (in natural languages, the grammar defines how to combine different classes of words, such as nouns and adjectives). A syntax does not define any meaning of the sentences (which is defined by the semantics), so generally speaking, sentences which are syntactically correct may have no meaning at all (no meaningful semantics associated with them).

Tcl – TOOL COMMAND LANGUAGE
URI: http://www.tclconsortium.org/
Reference: [201]
The Tool Command Language (Tcl) is a general-purpose, robust command language that can easily be integrated into new applications. One of Tcl's most useful features is its extensibility. If an application requires some functionality not offered by standard Tcl, new Tcl commands can be implemented using the C language, and integrated fairly easily. Since Tcl is so easy to extend, many people have written extension packages for common tasks, and made these freely available. Tcl is frequently used for programming *Common Gateway Interface (CGI)* applications.

TCP – TRANSMISSION CONTROL PROTOCOL
Reference: [210]
The Transmission Control Protocol (TCP) is intended for use as a highly reliable host-to-host protocol between hosts in packet-switched computer communication networks, and in interconnected systems of such networks. TCP is a flow-controlled, connection-oriented, end-to-end reliable protocol designed to fit into a layered hierarchy of protocols supporting multinetwork applications. TCP provides for reliable interprocess communications between pairs of processes in host computers attached to distinct but interconnected computer communication networks. Very few assumptions are made as to the reliability of the communication protocols below the TCP layer. TCP assumes it can obtain a simple, potentially unreliable, datagram service from the lower level protocols, usually the *Internet Protocol (IP)*. TCP is able to operate above a wide spectrum of communication systems, ranging from hard-wired connections to packet-switched or circuit-switched networks.

TEI – TEXT ENCODING INITIATIVE
URI: http://www.uic.edu/orgs/tei/
The Text Encoding Initiative (TEI) is an international project to develop guidelines for the preparation and interchange of electronic texts for scholarly research, and to satisfy a broad range of uses by the language industries more generally. The growing diversity of applications for electronic texts includes natural language processing, scholarly editions, information retrieval, hypertext, electronic publishing, various forms of literary and historical analysis, and lexicography. The central objective of the TEI is to ensure that any text that is created can be used for any

number of these applications and for more, as yet not fully understood, purposes.

Telnet

Reference: [212]

The purpose of the Telnet protocol is to provide a fairly general, bi-directional, 8-bit byte oriented communications facility. Its primary goal is to allow a standard method of interfacing terminal devices and terminal-oriented processes to each other. The most popular usage of the Telnet protocol is for logging in into remote systems. In this scenario, the Telnet client is the remote terminal (usually running some kind of terminal emulation) which is connected to a terminal driver program using the Telnet protocol.

THTTP – TRIVIAL HTTP

Reference: [59]

The Trivial HTTP (THTTP) resolution protocol is a trivial convention for encoding *Uniform Resource Name (URN)* resolution service requests and responses as HTTP 1.0 or 1.1 requests and responses. The primary goal of THTTP is to be simple to implement so that existing HTTP servers may easily add support for URN resolution. Over time, it is expected that HTTP itself will be extended with new methods for URN resolution services.

TIFF – TAG IMAGE FILE FORMAT

Reference: [6]

TIFF defines a tag-based file descriptor that can characterize almost any form of 2D raster data using either ASCII or binary (byte, short, long or rational) coding. "Private" tags may be used to allow additional parameters to be added to the descriptor. "Standard" TIFF allows the use of PackBits, LZW, Group 3 or 4 fax, and JPEG compression schemes within transmitted images. Four photometric classes are supported: TIFF-B for monochrome, TIFF-G for grayscale, TIFF-P for palette-based coding, and TIFF-R for RGB coding.

TIFF/IT – TAG IMAGE FILE FORMAT FOR IMAGE TECHNOLOGY

Reference: [129]

TIFF/IT is a standard which provides a format for the subset of TIFF which is appropriate for pre-press applications. TIFF/IT is specifically designed so that any fields additional to TIFF 6.0 take default values equivalent to TIFF 6.0 practice, so that existing implementations should already be compatible with it.

TLD – TOP-LEVEL DOMAIN
> Reference: [213]
> A Top-Level Domain (TLD) is that part of an Internet DNS fully qual-
> ified domain name which stands right of the rightmost full stop. Two
> letter top-level domain names designate *country-code Top-Level Domains
> (ccTLD)*, three letter top-level domain names designate *generic Top-Level
> Domains (gTLD)*, and four letter top-level domain names will be used in
> the near future for new gTLDs as specified in the *Generic Top Level
> Domain Memorandum of Understanding (gTLD-MoU)*.

TLS – TRANSPORT LAYER SECURITY
> Reference: [64]
> The Transport Layer Security (TLS) protocol is currently being developed
> by the IETF TLS working group. It is based on the *Secure Sockets Layer
> (SSL)* protocol proposed by Netscape. The structure of the start of a
> TLS session allows negotiation of the level of the protocol to be used – in
> this way, a client or server can simultaneously support TLS and SSL and
> negotiate the most appropriate protocol for the connection.

TrueDoc
> URI: http://www.truedoc.com/
> TrueDoc is a flexible font portability, scaling, and rasterizing system ca-
> pable of filling a wide variety of font needs. It has been implemented
> as the core font system in laser printers, digital set-top boxes, and net-
> work computers. It is the underlying technology for dynamic fonts in
> Netscape's Navigator. TrueDoc lets users view pages with the author's
> font formatting intact and helps solve the font fidelity problem by mak-
> ing fonts portable. TrueDoc supports all font formats and encodings (such
> as *TrueType*, *Type 1*, and *Unicode*), as well as non-Latin typefaces such
> as Arabic, Chinese, Japanese (Kanji) and Korean.

TrueType
> URI: http://fonts.apple.com/
> Reference: [12]
> TrueType is a font format developed by Apple and licensed to Microsoft.
> TrueType is the native operating system font format for Windows and
> Macintosh. TrueType contains a hierarchical set of tables and glyph rep-
> resentations. Characters can be hinted on a per character and point size
> basis yielding excellent quality at screen resolutions. TrueType fonts for
> Windows and Macintosh have few differences, though they can be different
> enough to prevent cross platform usage. Font foundries provide TrueType
> fonts for each platform and usually include a license preventing electronic

manipulation to achieve cross platform transparency. TrueType is one of the foundations for the *OpenType* font format.

TSAP – TRANSPORT SERVICE ACCESS POINT
  Reference: [231]
  A Transport Service Access Point (TSAP) is the abstraction for an transport service as defined by ISO's *Open Systems Interconnection (OSI)* model of communications. The Internet community has a well-developed, mature set of transport and internetwork protocols (TCP/IP), which are quite successful in offering network and transport services to end-users. Both the Internet protocol suite and the ISO OSI protocol suite are layered systems. Internet RFC 1006 uses the layer-independence of these protocol suites to define a TSAP which appears to be identical to the services and interfaces offered by the ISO TSAP (as defined in ISO 8072 [126]), but it will in fact be implemented on top of TCP/IP, not on top of an ISO network protocol. This allows ISO higher level layers (all session, presentation, and application entities) to operate fully without knowledge of the fact that they are running on a TCP/IP network.

T/TCP – TRANSACTION TCP
  Reference: [31, 32]
  Transaction TCP (T/TCP) extends the *Transmission Control Protocol (TCP)* to implement the transaction service model, while continuing to support the virtual circuit model. Distributed applications, which are becoming increasingly numerous and sophisticated in the Internet, tend to use a transaction-oriented rather than a virtual circuit style of communication. Currently, a transaction-oriented Internet application must choose to suffer the overhead of opening and closing TCP connections or else build an application-specific transport mechanism on top of the connection-less *User Datagram Protocol (UDP)*.

tunnel – In the context of HTTP, a tunnel is a program which acts as a blind intermediary program for HTTP communication, which means it does not interpret or understand (and therefore also not modify) passing messages.

Type 1
  Reference: [122]
  Originally developed by Adobe for their *PostScript* page description language, the Type 1 font format has been accepted as an ISO international standard. Type 1 fonts use a specialized subset of the PostScript language which is optimized for better performance and a more compact representation. The Type 1 operator set includes hint information which

helps font rasterizers create more accurate bitmaps for smaller sizes and lower resolutions. Type 1 is one of the foundations for the *OpenType* font format.

UCS – UNIVERSAL MULTIPLE-OCTET CODED CHARACTER SET
Reference: [118]
The Universal Multiple-Octet Coded Character Set (UCS) standardized in ISO 10646 integrates all previous internationally/nationally agreed character sets into a single code set. UCS is based on 4-octet (32-bit) coding scheme known as the "canonical form" (UCS-4), but a 2-octet (16-bit) form (UCS-2) is used for the *Basic Multilingual Plane (BMP)*, where octets 1 and 2 are assumed to be 00 00. The code set is split into 128 "groups" of "planes" containing 256 "rows" with 256 "cells" for characters. Each character is addressed using multiple octets, the third (in UCS-2 the first) of which identifies the row containing the character and the fourth (in UCS-2 the second) its cell number. The first 127 characters of the BMP used for 16-bit code interchange are those of ISO 646 [113]. The characters forming the second half of the first row are those used in ISO 8859-1 [111], the Latin-1 character set.

UDP – USER DATAGRAM PROTOCOL
Reference: [208]
The User Datagram Protocol (UDP) provides a simple but unreliable datagram service. UDP neither guarantees delivery nor does it require a connection. As a result it is lightweight and efficient, but all error processing and retransmission must be taken care of by the application program. Like the *Transmission Control Protocol (TCP)*, UDP is layered on top of the *Internet Protocol (IP)*.

Unicode
URI: http://www.unicode.org/
Reference: [265]
The Unicode Standard is the international standard used to encode text for computer processing. It is a subset of ISO 10646 [118], also known as *Universal Multiple-Octet Coded Character Set (UCS)*. Unicode's design is based on the simplicity and consistency of ASCII, but goes far beyond ASCII's limited ability to encode only the Latin alphabet. The Unicode Standard provides the capacity to encode all of the characters used for the major written languages of the world. To accommodate the many thousands of characters used in international text, the Unicode Standard uses a 16-bit code-set that provides codes for more than 65'000 characters. To keep character coding simple and efficient, the Unicode Standard assigns

each character a unique 16-bit value, and does not use complex modes or escape codes.

UPP – Universal Payment Preamble
URI: http://www.w3.org/ECommerce/
The Universal Payment Preamble (UPP) provides two capabilities: payment service negotiation and initiation of the specific payment system. The payment service and initiation information are sufficient to smoothly bridge from shopping to payment and, if appropriate, from payment back to other customer/vendor interaction. It is the specific payment system invoked, and not UPP, that is responsible for the secure transmission of funds. UPP is built on top of the *Protocol Extension Protocol (PEP)*.

URC – Uniform Resource Characteristics
URI: http://www.w3.org/Addressing/
The Uniform Resource Characteristics (URC) of a resource is a set of attribute/value pairs describing the resource. Some of the values may be URIs of various kinds. Others may include, for example, authorship, publisher, data type, date, or copyright status. Usually, an object which is named by a *Uniform Resource Name (URN)* also has URC assigned to it, so even if the object itself is unavailable, a minimum of information can be obtained from the URC (which is stored by the naming system performing URN resolution).

URI – Universal Resource Identifier
URI: http://www.w3.org/Addressing/
Reference: [17]
The web is considered to include objects accessed using an extendable number of protocols, existing, invented for the web itself, or to be invented in the future. Access instructions for an individual object under a given protocol are encoded into forms of address string. Other protocols allow the use of object names of various forms. In order to abstract the idea of a generic object, the web needs the concepts of the universal set of objects, and of the universal set of names or addresses of objects. A Universal Resource Identifier (URI) is a member of this universal set of names in registered name spaces and addresses referring to registered protocols or name spaces. A *Uniform Resource Locator (URL)* is a form of URI which expresses an address mapping onto an access algorithm using network protocols. A *Uniform Resource Name (URN)* is a form of URI which uses a name space (and associated resolution protocols) for persistent object names.

URL – Uniform Resource Locator

URI: http://www.w3.org/Addressing/

Reference: [21, 77]

A Uniform Resource Locator (URL) basically is a physical address of an object which is retrievable using protocols already deployed on the Internet. A URL defines an access protocol, called a scheme, and a scheme-dependent part, which has to provide sufficient information to locate an object using the specified scheme. In case of HTTP URLs, the scheme is HTTP, and the scheme-dependent part specifies the name of the HTTP server as well as the path of the object on the server.

URN – Uniform Resource Name

URI: http://www.w3.org/Addressing/

Reference: [246, 176]

A Uniform Resource Name (URN) is a persistent, globally unique name assigned to an object. In contrast to a *Uniform Resource Locator (URL)* which changes whenever the location of an object changes, a URN has no location dependence and therefore a longer lifetime. This is realized by using a naming service which in most cases will provide a mapping from URNs to URLs. Thus, even if the URL of an object changes, its URN remains the same, since only the object's entry in the naming service has to be updated.

user – The user in the context of the web usually is a human user controlling a client (which therefore sometimes also is called a user agent). The usual scenario therefore involves a user, using a client through a user interface, which in most cases is a *Graphical User Interface (GUI)*. The client interacts with servers using access protocols on behalf of the user.

user agent ⟶ client

UTF – UCS Transformation Format

Reference: [278, 89]

A UCS Transformation Format (UTF) is used for coding UCS characters. Although UCS defines character codings (UCS-2 and UCS-4), they are hard to use in many current applications and protocols that assume 8- or even 7-bit characters.

validation – The caching model of HTTP relies on expiration times which are assigned to responses stored in caches. Once a response has reached its expiration time (ie, it is *stale*), it must be validated with the origin server before it can be used in a response from the cache. Validation is the process of sending an identification (a validator) to the origin server, getting as a result either the indication that the resource has not changed, or the changed resource.

VBScript – Visual Basic Scripting Edition
URI: `http://www.microsoft.com/vbscript/`
Microsoft's Visual Basic Scripting Edition (VBScript) is a subset of the Microsoft Visual Basic programming language. VBScript is a portable, lightweight interpreter for use in web browsers and other applications that use *ActiveX* controls.

virtual hosts – A frequent requirement for a web server is to serve documents for more than one server name. Especially in the case of Internet providers, usually operating web services for many companies, it is important that the provider's web servers are able to respond to all the host names which have been defined for the individual companies. This can be done by configuring virtual hosts on the web server, effectively assigning multiple host names to one web server.

VML – Vector Markup Language
Reference: [170]
The Vector Markup Language (VML) defines an XML-based format for the encoding of vector information together with additional markup to describe how that information may be displayed and edited. VML uses *Cascading Style Sheets, Level 2 (CSS2)* in the same way as HTML to determine the layout of the vector graphics which it contains.

VRML – Virtual Reality Modeling Language
URI: `http://www.vrml.org/`
Reference: [134]
The Virtual Reality Modeling Language (VRML) is the file format standard for 3D multimedia and shared virtual worlds on the Internet. In comparison to HTML, VRML adds the next level of interaction, structured graphics, and extra dimensions (z and time) to the presentation of documents. The applications of VRML are broad, ranging from simple business graphics to entertaining web page graphics, manufacturing, scientific, entertainment, and educational applications, and 3D shared virtual worlds and communities.

W3C – World Wide Web Consortium
URI: `http://www.w3.org/`
Founded in 1994 to develop common protocols for the evolution of the web, the World Wide Web Consortium (W3C) is an international association of industrial and service companies, research laboratories, educational institutions and organizations of all sizes. All of these organizations

share a compelling interest in the long term evolution and stability of the web. W3C is a non-profit organization funded partly by commercial members. Its activities remain vendor neutral, however. W3C also receives the support of governments who consider the web the platform of choice for a global information infrastructure. W3C was originally established in collaboration with CERN, birthplace of the web, with support from DARPA and the European Commission.

WAI – WEB ACCESSIBILITY INITIATIVE
URI: `http://www.w3.org/WAI/`
Reference: [266]
The Web Accessibility Initiative (WAI) is pursuing accessibility of the web through five primary areas of work: addressing accessibility issues in the technology of the web; creating guidelines for browsers, authoring tools, and content creation; developing evaluation and validation tools for accessibility; conducting education and outreach; and tracking research and development. Depending on an individual's disability (or the circumstances in which one is browsing the web, for instance on a device with no graphics display capability, or in a noisy environment), graphics, audio content, navigation options, or other aspects of web design can present barriers.

WAIS – WIDE AREA INFORMATION SERVERS
Reference: [251]
The Wide Area Information Servers (WAIS) system is designed to help users find information over a computer network. The WAIS software architecture has four main components: the client, the server, the database, and the protocol. The WAIS client is a user-interface program that sends requests for information to local or remote servers. The WAIS server is a program that services client requests. The server generally runs on a machine containing one or more information sources, or WAIS databases. The protocol, Z39.50-1988, is used to connect WAIS clients and servers and is based on the 1988 version of the NISO Z39.50 Information Retrieval Service and Protocol Standard [9]. Since the web allows greater flexibility in the structure and presentation of distributed information, the usage of WAIS services and the number of WAIS servers is getting smaller.

wanderer $\longrightarrow$ search engine

WAVE – WAVEFORM AUDIO FILE FORMAT
The Waveform Audio File Format (WAVE) is a proprietary standard for audio files developed by Microsoft. The format can store monaural or

multichannel sampled sounds in a range of sampling types, sample rates and sample resolutions.

WDG – WEB DESIGN GROUP
URI: http://www.htmlhelp.com/
The Web Design Group (WDG) was founded to promote the creation of non-browser specific, non-resolution specific, creative and informative sites that are accessible to all users worldwide. To this end, the WDG offers material on a wide range of HTML related topics, in particular good online references of HTML and CSS and links as well as additional information such as FAQs and articles.

Web Collections – XML Web Collections was an early proposal authored by Microsoft for the definition of web meta data. The proposal has been used as input for Microsoft's *XML-Data*, which has also been submitted to W3C.

WebCGM
Reference: [57]
WebCGM is a profile of the ISO *Computer Graphics Metafile (CGM)* standard, tailored to the requirements for scalable 2D vector graphics in electronic documents on the web. The WebCGM profile is a subset of the ISO standard, and a set of specifications targeted especially at the effective application of the ISO standard to representation of 2D graphical content within web documents.

WebDAV – WWW DISTRIBUTED AUTHORING AND VERSIONING
WWW Distributed Authoring and Versioning (WebDAV) will define HTTP extensions necessary to enable distributed web authoring tools to be broadly interoperable. The HTTP protocol already contains functionality which enables the editing of web content at a remote location, without direct access to the storage media via an operating system. This capability is exploited by several existing HTML distributed authoring tools, and by a growing number of mainstream applications (eg, word processors) which allow users to write (publish) their work to an HTTP server. To date, experience from the HTML authoring tools has shown they are unable to meet their user's needs using the facilities of the HTTP protocol. The consequence of this is either postponed introduction of distributed authoring capability, or the addition of nonstandard extensions to the HTTP protocol. These extensions, developed in isolation, are not interoperable.

WebSGML – Recently, the SGML standard [110] has been updated with two annexes which add some corrections as well as new features to SGML making some specifications possible which are desirable for using SGML as the basis for HTML and XML. Basically, the WebSGML extensions allow a number of additional features to be defined in an SGML declaration and DTD. However, when using these features in an SGML environment, it is necessary that both the generator and the interpreter of a document are capable of processing the WebSGML extensions, since a conforming SGML implementation does not have to implement the WebSGML extensions.

WebStone – PERFORMANCE TEST FOR HTTP SERVERS
URI: `http://www.mindcraft.com/webstone/`
Reference: [264]
WebStone is a benchmark developed by Silicon Graphics (SGI) for measuring the performance of web server platforms (software and hardware combined). It is designed to measure the performance of HTTP servers under multiple scenarios which reflect different web site profiles. The test uses workload parameters and clients to generate HTTP traffic that allows an HTTP server to be stressed in a number of different ways.

X.500 – THE DIRECTORY
Reference: [138]
X.500 is an open, distributed, on-line directory service which is intended to be global in scope. X.500 is a support service for data exchange which includes providing directory support for data communication services specified by other OSI application standards. The X.500 series of standards covers services available to users, the functional model and protocols connecting the component parts of the Directory, an information framework and a schema of the information held by the Directory, and a mechanism for allowing OSI components to authenticate each other.

X.509 – THE DIRECTORY – AUTHENTICATION FRAMEWORK
Reference: [137]
X.509 describes two levels of authentication, *simple authentication*, based on use of a password to verify user identity, and *strong authentication*, using credentials created by cryptographic methods. The standard recommends that only strong authentication should be used as the basis of providing secure services. Public key cryptography is used for strong authentication, but the authentication framework is not dependent on the use of a particular cryptographic algorithm, though two users wishing to authenticate must support the same algorithm. The *RSA* cryptosystem is defined as an informative annex to the standard.

Xanadu

URI: http://www.xanadu.net/

Reference: [195]

Xanadu is an overall paradigm – an ideal and general model for all computer use, based on sideways connections among documents and files. This paradigm is especially concerned with electronic publishing, but also extends to all forms of storing, presenting and working with information. It is a unifying system of order for all information, non-hierarchical and side-linking, including electronic publishing, personal work, organization of files, corporate work and groupware. All data (for instance, paragraphs of a text document) may be connected sideways and out of sequence to other data (for instance, paragraphs of another text document). This requires new forms of storage, and invites new forms of presentation to show these connections. On a small scale, the paradigm means a model of word processing where comments, outlines and other notes may be stored conceptually adjacent to a document, linked to it sideways. On a large scale, the paradigm means a model of publishing where anyone may quote from and publish links to any already-published document, and any reader may follow these links to and from the document.

XLink – XML LINKING LANGUAGE

Reference: [165]

The XML Linking Language (XLink) defines how to insert links in XML documents. It specifies a framework making it possible for XML applications to recognize XML elements as having link semantics. In addition to the simple, two-ended, unidirectional links which are well-known from HTML, XLink allows more general links, which must not be embedded in the document, can have any number of ends, and can be multidirectional.

XLL – EXTENSIBLE LINKING LANGUAGE

The Extensible Linking Language (XLL) is defined by the two components *XML Linking Language (XLink)* and *XML Pointer Language (XPointer)*. XLL defines how to use links in an XML environment, with XLink describing how to insert links into XML documents, and XPointer defining how to point into XML documents.

XML – EXTENSIBLE MARKUP LANGUAGE

URI: http://www.w3.org/XML/

Reference: [36]

The Extensible Markup Language (XML) is a subset of the *Standard Generalized Markup Language (SGML)* that is designed to make it easy to interchange structured documents over the Internet. XML files always clearly mark where the start and end of each of the component parts of an interchanged documents occur. XML restricts the use of SGML constructs to ensure that fall-back options are available when access to certain components of the document is not currently possible over the Internet. By defining the role of each element in a formal model, known as a *Document Type Definition (DTD)*, users of XML can check that each component of document occurs in a valid place within the interchanged data stream. However, unlike SGML, XML does not require the presence of a DTD. If no DTD is available, either because all or part of it is not accessible over the Internet or because the user failed to create it, an XML system can assign a default definition for undeclared components of the markup.

XML-Data – XML-Data is a proposal authored by Microsoft for the definition of web meta data. The proposal has been used as input for W3C's work on the *Resource Description Framework (RDF)*, which is currently under development by W3C.

XML namespaces
Reference: [35]
XML namespaces are used to qualify unique names in XML documents which use schemas from different sources. This can occur because schemas (such as DTDs) are reused. However, if schemas are combined, it is possible that name conflicts appear. XML namespaces defines a way how schema identification (through a URI) and names of a schema are combined to yield unique names.

XPointer – XML POINTER LANGUAGE
Reference: [166]
The XML Pointer Language (XPointer) supports addressing into the internal structures of XML documents. In particular, it provides for specific reference to elements, character strings, and other parts of XML documents, whether or not they bear an explicit ID attribute. XPointers can be used as fragment identifiers in conjunction with the URI structure to specify a more precise sub-resource. Any fragment identifier that points into an XML resource must be an XPointer.

XSL – EXTENSIBLE STYLE LANGUAGE
URI: http://www.w3.org/Style/XSL/
Reference: [47]
The Extensible Style Language (XSL) is used to specify the formatting of XML documents. Since XML elements and attributes are defined by applications, there are no standardized formatting semantics associated with them (as is the case with HTML elements and attributes). Without

additional information, XML documents therefore can not be formatted. XSL is a style sheet language based on the *Document Style Semantics and Specification Language (DSSSL)*. Each XSL style sheet describes rules for presenting a class of XML source documents. There are two parts to the presentation process. First, the result tree is constructed from the source tree. Second, the result tree is interpreted to produce formatted output on a display, on paper, in speech or onto other media.

Index

This index uses three different types of page numbers. Page numbers in the normal text font refer to an occurence of the term within the text, **boldface page numbers** refer to the main occurence of the term (most of the time a term's definition or most detailed description), and *italic page numbers* refer to the term's entry within the glossary (if there is one).

The index has been prepared with great care and effort, but it inevitably is less than perfect. Please send any suggestions to improve the index to dret@tik.ee.ethz.ch, helping that the next edition's index will be better than this one. Thank you very much.

Symbols

A

J

Z

Springer
and the
environment

At Springer we firmly believe that an international science publisher has a special obligation to the environment, and our corporate policies consistently reflect this conviction.
We also expect our business partners – paper mills, printers, packaging manufacturers, etc. – to commit themselves to using materials and production processes that do not harm the environment. The paper in this book is made from low- or no-chlorine pulp and is acid free, in conformance with international standards for paper permanency.

Springer